MÜNCHENER STUDIEN ZUR POLITIK

Herausgegeben vom
Geschwister-Scholl-Institut für Politische Wissenschaft
der Universität München
durch Gottfried-Karl Kindermann,
Nikolaus Lobkowicz, Hans Maier und Kurt Sontheimer

18. Band

Jean Bodin

Verhandlungen der internationalen Bodin Tagung in München
Proceedings of the International Conference on Bodin in Munich
Actes du colloque international Jean Bodin à Munich

Herausgegeben

von

Horst Denzer

VERLAG C. H. BECK MÜNCHEN

ISBN 3 406 02798 9

Umschlagentwurf: Wolfgang Taube, München
© C. H. Beck'sche Verlagsbuchhandlung (Oscar Beck) München 1973
Druck: Passavia Druckerei AG Passau
Printed in Germany

INHALT

TEIL III: BODIN-BIBLIOGRAPHIE

VORWORT

Über Jean Bodin, den großen politischen Denker des 16. Jahrhunderts in Frankreich, wird mehr gesprochen, als daß sein Werk gelesen wird. Sicher ist das das Los aller politischer Denker, und ein Großteil ihrer Wirkung verdanken sie auch nach der Verbreitung des Buchdrucks dem on-dit. Doch ist die Diskrepanz bei dem bedeutenden französischen Gelehrten besonders groß, größer als bei den Engländern Hobbes und Locke, mit denen zusammen er den Umbruch vom politischen Denken der Antike und des Mittelalters zu dem der Neuzeit markiert.

Man vergleiche einmal das Interesse, das die wissenschaftliche Forschung Bodin und den englischen Denkern zugewendet hat. Die Zahl der Abhandlungen und die Intensität der wissenschaftlichen Kontroversen sind ein beredtes Zeichen dafür, wie stiefmütterlich Bodin behandelt worden ist. Die letzte biographische Gesamtdeutung Bodins, Chauvirés Buch *Jean Bodin, auteur de la ‹République›*, liegt schon über ein halbes Jahrhundert zurück, und die größeren Abhandlungen, die sich seither mit Bodin befaßt haben, kann man an zehn Fingern abzählen.

Diese Tatsache hat das Geschwister Scholl Institut für politische Wissenschaft an der Universität München dazu angeregt, die bedeutenden Bodinkenner zu einer Tagung auf internationaler Ebene einzuladen, um einen Überblick über den gegenwärtigen Stand der Bodinforschung zu gewinnen und ihr durch diese Bestandsaufnahme, durch den Austausch von Wissen und Erfahrung unter den Teilnehmern und durch das Diskutieren verschiedener Positionen neue Impulse zu geben.

Noch eine andere Entwicklung hat diese Tagung nützlich und an der Zeit erscheinen lassen. Als Begründer der Souveränitätslehre, als derjenige, der in der Souveränität das zentrale Merkmal des Staates gesehen und dies systematisch dargestellt hat, ist Bodin immer schon gewürdigt worden, und seine Bedeutung für die Theorie des modernen Staates stand außer Frage. In neuerer Zeit hat sich die Forschung mehr und mehr damit befaßt, auch die philosophische Position Bodins, sein Weltbild und seine religiösen Anschauungen, seine Vorstellungen von Recht und Geschichte und seine Bedeutung für die Entwicklung der Jurisprudenz und Geschichtsschreibung zu untersuchen. Es hat sich gezeigt, wie wichtig dies alles für ein richtiges Verständnis seiner politischen Philosophie ist. Dadurch ist ein umfassenderes und differenzierteres Bild des Gelehrten Bodin entstanden. Außerdem wurde die Interdependenz von Bodins Werk einerseits und seiner persönlichen Entwicklung und seinem Engagement in der praktischen Politik im Wandel der geschichtlichen Entwicklung andererseits untersucht. Der politische Philosoph und der praktische Politiker wurde so aufeinander bezogen. Dies neue Bild Bodins aus den einzelnen Aspekten zusammenzufügen und abzurunden war eine weitere Aufgabe der Tagung.

Das vorliegende Buch ist die Frucht dieser internationalen Bodin Tagung, die vom 1. bis 3. April 1970 in München stattfand. Es enthält die von den Teilnehmern vorgelegten Arbeitspapiere, die der Diskussion während der Tagung zugrunde lagen, und eine Zusammenfassung dieser Diskussion, beides in der Folge der abgehandelten Themenbereiche: Philosophie und Religion bei Bodin, Bodins historisches Denken, Bodin und die Rechtstradition, Bodins politische Philosophie. Nachträglich hinzugefügt wurde eine Bibliographie der Ausgaben von Bodins Werken und der Sekundärliteratur über Bodin seit 1800; ohne den Anspruch auf Vollständigkeit zu erheben, ist es der erste Versuch, mit Hilfe des Wissens der Teilnehmer und der einschlägigen bibliographischen Hilfsmittel eine umfassende Bodin-Bibliographie zu erstellen.

Es kann nicht die Aufgabe dieses Vorworts sein, die Ergebnisse der Tagung zusammenzufassen. Die in diesem Band gesammelten Beiträge sollen in ihrer Pluralität für sich selber sprechen. Es sei hier nur auf einige immer wiederkehrende zentrale Themen hingewiesen, die den Facettenreichtum des Bodinbildes bestimmen. Es gibt eine Entwicklung in Bodins philosophischem und politischem Denken, die durch Bodins geistige Entwicklung, durch persönliche Erlebnisse (Dämonenerscheinung), durch seine berufliche Laufbahn, durch den Wechsel der Autoritäten und Quellen, auf die er sich beruft, und durch den Wandel der politischen Situation in Frankreich beeinflußt ist. Die Konstante in Bodins Denken ist seine Vorstellung von der Ordnung in Natur und Staat, die als Harmonie des Vielfältigen unter der Herrschaft des Einen gesehen wird. Bodin ist auf vielfältige Weise ein Mittler zwischen verschiedenen Positionen und spiegelt damit die Widersprüchlichkeit der Entwicklung seiner Zeit: er verbindet eine mittelalterliche Kosmologie mit dem modernen Verständnis von der Aufgabe des Fürsten, in der Methode die Vielfalt der empirischen Erfahrung mit synthetischen und universalen Konzepten, die Ausläufer des Feudalismus mit den Anfängen der bürgerlichen Gesellschaft, die absolute Souveränität des Herrschers mit der Mäßigung der Herrschaft und Wertschätzung der Stände.

Eine internationale Tagung, soll sie gelingen und erfolgreich sein, bedarf der Mithilfe vieler. Ich möchte an dieser Stelle allen danken, die daran ihren Anteil haben. Die Fritz Thyssen Stiftung und hier besonders Herr Dr. Coenen hat mit der schnellen und unbürokratischen Bereitstellung der finanziellen Mittel die Planung der Tagung erst ermöglicht; das Bundesministerium für Bildung und Wissenschaft und das Bayerische

Staatsministerium für Unterricht und Kultus haben durch ihre Zuschüsse die Finanzierung vervollständigt. Verpflichtet bin ich auch Herrn Prof. Dr. Roman Schnur, der die Tagung angeregt hat, und Herrn Prof. Dr. Hans Maier, der die Tagung leitete und mich bei den vielfältigen Schwierigkeiten der Vorbereitung vorbehaltlos unterstützt hat. Frau Hermine Fuhrmann danke ich die zuverlässige Erstellung der Manuskripte und ihrer Vervielfältigung, Herrn Emil Hübner, M. A. die Hilfsbereitschaft, mit der er mich bei den Engpässen der Organisation unterstützte. Für die mühevolle Arbeit, die Diskussion der Tagung vom Tonband zu schreiben und sie druckreif zusammenzufassen, bin ich Frau Edith Ziegler, Fräulein Helga Bröcker und Fräulein Lucie Maurey, sowie den Herren Dr. Roellenbleck, Prof. Freund, Prof. Kelley und Prof. Giesey verpflichtet. Die Bodin Bibliographie erstellte dankenswerterweise Herr Herbert Maier M. A.

Nicht zuletzt gilt mein Dank allen Teilnehmern der Tagung, die durch ihre ungewöhnlich sorgfältige Vorbereitung und intensive Mitarbeit eine ergebnisreiche und erfolgreiche Tagung ermöglichten und dem Kardinal Wendel Haus, das durch seine Gastfreundschaft den würdigen äußeren Rahmen bot. Dem C. H. Beck Verlag und seinem Lektor, Herrn Dr. Wieckenberg bin ich für die Bemühungen um die Drucklegung dieses Bandes dankbar.

München, im September 1971   Horst Denzer

ZITIERWEISE

Wenn nichts anderes vermerkt ist, werden Bodins *Six Livres de la Republique* grundsätzlich nach der Ausgabe Paris (Du Puys) 1583 (Bibliographie Nr. 7.11), die in einem Nachdruck Aalen 1961 vorliegt (7.26), der *Methodus ad facilem historiarum cognitionem* nach der von P. Mesnard edierten Ausgabe Paris 1951 (4.20 und 4.22) zitiert. Dabei werden die Abkürzungen *République* oder *Rép.* und *Methodus* oder *Meth.* benützt.

Bei in den Anmerkungen zitierten Bodin-Ausgaben und Werken der Sekundärliteratur weist eine Ziffer in eckigen Klammern (z. B. [7.14] oder [266]) auf den Fundort in der Bibliographie hin. Bei wiederholten Zitierungen erscheint nur der Autorenname, der Werktitel ist durch die Fundortziffer ersetzt.

Hans Maier

Begrüßung zur Eröffnung der Tagung

Mesdames, Messieurs, chers Collègues,

l'Université de Munich et l'Institut de Science Politique ont l'honneur d'accueillir cette semaine des savants connus dans le monde entier et qui se sont réunis ici à l'occasion de ce premier colloque international sur Jean Bodin. Au nom de mes collègues, au nom des professeurs et des assistants qui ont préparé ce congrès, je vous souhaite la bienvenue et espère que vous passerez d'agréables journées à Munich.

Notre lieu de réunion de cette semaine est l'Académie Catholique de Bavière, située en plein Schwabing, ce cadre pittoresque d'un vieux quartier, plus précisément d'un ancien village, aux portes du vieux Munich, aujourd'hui centre de la vie artistique. Tout près, vous trouverez «le Jardin Anglais», qui rappelle l'époque romantique, la rue Occam, qui porte le nom du grand penseur médiéval: Guillaume d'Occam, mort à Munich en 1346, et enfin, pour ne pas oublier l'histoire contemporaine, le petit château que vous apercevez peut-être et qui était la résidence du gouvernement révolutionnaire après la première guerre mondiale.

J'aimerais tout d'abord exprimer ma reconnaissance envers tous ceux qui ont bien voulu participer à la préparation de ce colloque: particulièrement à M. Schnur, qui eut l'idée de ce congrès et qui nous a fait profiter de son expérience acquise lors du congrès sur Thomas Hobbes; et à M. Horst Denzer, qui a permis par son travail infatigable l'élaboration et le fonctionnement de ce colloque. Je tiens également à remercier le gouvernement fédéral d'Allemagne, le gouvernement bavarois et la fondation Thyssen qui nous ont généreusement accordé une aide matérielle. J'adresserai, enfin, tous mes remerciements à l'Académie Catholique de Bavière et à son directeur, M. Franz Henrich, qui nous a offert l'hospitalité dans cette maison calme et attrayante.

Nous ne saurions inaugurer ce congrès sans rendre hommage à ceux qui ne peuvent plus y participer. Je rappelle deux noms: Jürgen Dennert, jeune politologue allemand de l'université de Hambourg, mort subitement il y a quelques semaines, et Pierre Mesnard, grand philosophe et humaniste français, mort en 1969.

Dennert, un élève du sociologue et philosophe Siegfried Landshut, s'était qualifié dans la recherche de l'histoire de la science politique. Dans sa thèse, qui n'a pas encore été publiée, il a examiné les origines de l'enseignement politique aux universités européennes du 17e et 18e siècle, spécialement du point de vue de la tradition qui découle de la source aristotélicienne de la théorie politique. Il avait préparé pour ce congrès une conférence portant sur la méthode de la pensée politique Bodin. Ce devait être sa dernière étude.

Non sans quelque hésitation j'ajouterai un mot sur Pierre Mesnard, cet esprit si riche, si complexe, et qui nous a laissé une œuvre incomparable. Bien des participants, parmi vous, seraient sans doute mieux qualifiés que moi à lui rendre hommage. Je me bornerai à quelques remarques biographiques:

Pierre Mesnard est né en 1900 à Surgères, dans la région de l'Aunis, d'une famille bourgeoise très ancienne. Après ses années de lycée à Poitiers, il entra à l'Ecole Normale Supérieure où il opta pour la section philosophie. C'était après la première guerre mondiale. L'agrégation passée, il fit plusieurs voyages et partit en mission d'études dans les pays de l'Est et de l'Europe centrale. Les étapes de sa carrière furent les suivantes: répétiteur à l'Ecole Normale Supérieure, maître de conférences à l'université de Jassy, en Roumanie, professeur aux lycées de Rochefort, Poitiers et Bône; et à partir de 1942, directeur de l'Institut d'études philosophiques à l'université d'Alger. En 1956, il fut chargé de créer, à Tours, le centre d'études supérieures de la Renaissance. Dès lors, il restera professeur de civilisation et philosophie de la Renaissance à la Faculté de Lettres de Poitiers d'abord, puis à la Faculté des Lettres de Tours jusqu'à sa mort, au printemps 1969.

Il serait difficile d'englober toute son œuvre, tellement riche, qui ne touche pas seulement à l'histoire de la philosophie, mais aussi à la critique d'art, à la critique de la littérature et à l'éthique. Depuis sa thèse magistrale sur «Essor de la philosophie politique au 16e siècle», il s'était attaché avant tout à l'étude de l'histoire de la Renaissance. Il y trouvait une philosophie qui était essentiellement sagesse et, pour lui, source d'un humanisme vivant. Je le cite: «retrouver au contact des grands esprits de la Renaissance cette allégresse féconde capable de nourrir la curiosité multiple de Léonard de Vinci ou de Rabelais et reprendre ainsi le sens d'une génialité authentique, capable de reamorcer l'Histoire au profit des vrais génereux. Ainsi doit se maintenir dans une atmosphère purifiée par l'Art et la Religion l'activité créatrice de la raison qui dans sa source jaillissante ignore la séparation entre science et lettres.»

TEIL I: BEITRÄGE

I. PHILOSOPHIE UND RELIGION BEI BODIN

Christopher R. Baxter

Jean Bodin's Daemon and his Conversion to Judaism

Introduction

In the *Démonomanie* Jean Bodin describes in vivid and circumstantial detail the apparition of a daemon to an unnamed acquaintance.[1] As long ago as 1910 von Bezold argued that the acquaintance was Bodin himself.[2] His extremely thorough article has had surprisingly little impact on the interpretation of Bodin's thought. Neither von Bezold himself, in his substantial article on the *Heptaplomeres*,[3] nor subsequent critics, have carried his arguments much further. Mesnard ignored the subject of Bodin's daemon completely.

In his book on Bodin's religious system, Roellenbleck is cautious.[4] He usefully underlines the Judaic atmosphere of the narrative, and concludes guardedly, from Bodin's treatment of the functions of daemons elsewhere, that it is «sehr wahrscheinlich, daß Bodin seine eigenen religiösen Erlebnisse in diesem Sinn verstand, und sich des Umgangs mit einem Engel gewürdigt fand». He remains uneasy about the details of the narrative: «Die wunderlichen spiritistischen Züge stechen befremdend heraus.»[5] This defensiveness is a long way removed from the traditional reaction to supposing that Bodin is describing his own daemon, as expressed with Enlightened impatience by Grosley.[6] Yet the continuing note of apologia,

---

[1] *La Démonomanie des Sorciers*, Paris 1580, Bk. I, ch. 2 (foll. 10–13). All references are to this edition [10.1].

[2] F. v. Bezold, Jean Bodin als Okkultist und seine Demonomanie, *Historische Zeitschrift* (105) 1910 [70].

[3] Das Colloquium Heptaplomeres und der Atheismus im 16. Jahrhundert, *Historische Zeitschrift*, 113/1914, 114/1915.

[4] G. Roellenbleck, Offenbarung, Natur und jüdische Überlieferung bei Jean Bodin, Kassel 1964 [239].

[5] Roellenbleck, [239], 120.

[6] «Grosley n'a pu se persuader que Bodin eût écrit sérieusement de telles rêveries.» Reported by L. Devisme in *Magazin Encyclopédique de Millin*, 40 (1801), 46 [18].

the urge to screen the disturbing potential of Bodin's demonology, remains insidiously pervasive of even the best interpretations of Bodin.

In a recent article Monter has countered some traditional attitudes to the *Démonomanie,* showing ways in which it is typical of Bodin's writing.[7] His rehabilitation is less concerned however with what Bodin says than with how he says it. Consequently we hear nothing of Bodin's daemon, and only some tentative suggestions about the role of daemons in Bodin's philosophical system. This is somewhat surprising in view of Monter's insistence on the interlocking relations between Bodin's works.

I shall argue in this paper that we can date fairly precisely the time when Bodin's daemon became part of his everyday consciousness, profoundly modifying his religious and philosophical development. I shall argue that Bodin's total vision owes its definitive structure to this daemonic experience, and that the daemon converted Bodin to the «simplified, archaic Judaism» succinctly described by Walker,[8] and which Roellenbleck's book systematically investigates.

The Daemonic Narrative

A useful place to start is at the beginning of the narrative itself.

«Je puis asseurer d'avoir entendu d'un personnage, qui est encores en vie, qu'il y avoit un esprit qui luy assistoit assiduellement, et commença à le cognaitre, ayant environ trente sept ans ... ce qui luy advint comme il dict, ayant un an au paravant continué de prier Dieu de tout son cueur soir et matin, à ce qu'il luy pleust envoyer son bon Ange pour le guider en toutes ses actions, et apres et devant la priere il employoit quelque temps à contempler les œuvres de Dieu ... et à lire la Bible, pour trouver laquelle de toutes les religions debatues de tous costez estoit la vraye, et disoit souvent ces vers (psaume 143)

<Enseigne moy comme il faut faire,
Pour bien ta volonté parfaire,
Car tu es mon vray Dieu entier,
Fais que ton esprit debonnaire
Me guide et meine au droict sentier.>

Blasmant ceux-là, qui prient Dieu qu'il les entretienne en leur opinions, et continuant cette priere, et lisant les sainctes escriptures, il trouva en Phi-

---

[7] E. W. MONTER, Inflation and Witchcraft: The Case of Jean Bodin, in Action and Conviction in Early Modern Europe, Princeton, 1969, 371–389 [268].

[8] D. P. WALKER, Spiritual and Demonic Magic from Ficino to Campanella, London 1958, [193], 171.

lon Hebrieu au livre des sacrifices, que le plus grand et plus agreable sacrifice, que l'homme de bien, et entier peut faire à Dieu, c'est de soy mesme, estant purifié par luy. Il suivit ce conseil, offrant à Dieu son ame. Depuis il commença comme il m'a dict, d'avoir des songes, et visions pleines d'instruction: et tantost pour corriger un vice, tantost un autre, tantost pour se garder d'un danger, tantost pour estre resolu d'une difficulté ... non seulement des choses divines, ains encores des choses humaines.»[9]

The daemonic narrative here describes religious attitudes strikingly like those expressed by Bodin in the *Methodus* of 1566,[10] and in his letter to Bautru des Matras, which is generally ascribed to the early sixties.[11] It seems to be the letter on an unorthodox Protestant, still wishing to describe himself as holding a version of Christianity (something he is nowhere else found doing), and able to conceive of changing his religious opinions by rational discussion.[12] He refers to previous correspondence in which he had written that «the true religion is none other but a sincere turning toward God of an cleansed spirit», an opinion he twice records in the *Methodus*.[13] In the *Methodus* Bodin is scrupulously neutral in describing his proposed book on comparative religion.[14] This neutrality derives in part from his own religious position – he was still genuinely searching to find which religion *was* true; in part from his persistent care never to appear offensively unorthodox, and thereby sow doubt in the minds of others; and in part from the generally secular frame of reference of the *Methodus*. On the other hand the *Methodus* has quite a strong Protestant flavour. Bodin refers very favourably to Calvin, Luther and

---

[9] *Dém.*, Bk. I, ch. 2, fol. 10–10v.

[10] *Methodus ad facilem historiarum cognitionem*, Paris 1566. All references are to the translation by Beatrice REYNOLDS, New York 1945 [4.23], followed in brackets by the page and column in MESNARD's French translation (see note 11).

[11] Printed in the *Appendix* to R. CHAUVIRÉ, Jean Bodin, auteur de la République, Paris 1914, 520–524 [76]. As a member of the Paris Parlement, Bodin took an oath of Catholicism in the summer of 1562. MESNARD makes this the *terminus ante quem* for dating the letter (e.g. in his introduction to the Œuvres Philosophiques de Jean Bodin, Paris 1951, XVI) [4.22]. But in previous correspondence with Bautru, written before December in an unspecified year, Bodin had already discussed the cause of the civil war. Mesnard's argument would make the dating of this improbably *precede* the war! Here as elsewhere Mesnard will not allow that Bodin could well be a Catholic, without necessarily being a Christian.

[12] «I beg and beseech you to make me of your opinion or to follow me in mine.»

[13] *Methodus*, 25, 33; (285 B, 290 A).

[14] *Meth.*, 25; (285 B).

Melanchthon. His historiography is inspired in part by Protestant historians,[15] and he always quotes the psalms in Protestant translations.[16]

The Bautru letter violently attacks what Bodin calls the worship of saints, of statues and of the Eucharist. His objection is the Calvinistic one – that to worship the «wafer-God» is to idolise bread, αρτολατρεια. Similarly, he sees the religious wars as involving «the murder and persecution of good men who are trying to overthrow the most shameful idolomania»: ειϑωλομανειαν – a coining significantly reminiscent of a later neologism which stuck, *Démonomanie*. He puts himself and Bautru amongst the persecuted; perhaps in this like the daemon informant with his singing of psalm 143, which in Marot's translation is headed: «C'est la prière qu'il fit (sc. David), quand par crainte de Saul il se cacha en une fosse, où il s'attendoit d'estre prins, dont il estoit en grande angoisse».

Already then, Bodin's position is intransigently monotheist. Christ is seen as one of a whole line of prophets, which includes most Greek philosophers with the notable exception of Aristotle, who have been sent from heaven to recall men to the worship of the one God. «And then Christ, seizing the sacred fires of the eternal Pallas, as with Prometheus' rod, came down from heaven to earth, so that he might cleanse the world, sullied by a host of debaucheries and crimes, and lead mankind, enslaved by execrable superstition, to the true worship of Almighty God». This reference to Christ is uniquely favourable in Bodin's writing, though even here he seems to be prophet rather than saviour.

Commentators on the *Methodus* often express surprise at the progressive intrusion into this mainly secular, empirical and analytical work of a moral even teleological dimension. Beatrice Reynolds put it this way: «As we read on into the last chapter, on the origin of races, we may well wonder if he (Bodin) had not become a convert to Judaism.»[17] For reasons which will be discussed below. I think this is unlikely, but Miss Reynolds' remark does point to the impending crisis.

Bodin's friend had his daemonic experience when thirty seven, after a year of prayer and contemplation along lines which correspond to Bodin's own religious preoccupations in the *Methodus,* notably his sense that the discovery of religious truths is essentially a private affair, to be sought less in the scientific, objective study of religious systems, than in «frequent prayers and the turning of a clean mind toward God».[18] Some

---

[15] See J. L. BROWN, The Methodus ad Facilem Historiarum Cognitionem of Jean Bodin, a critical study, Washington 1939 [140].

[16] Such clear indications of Protestant feeling are less obvious in the *République*.

[17] In the introduction to her translation of the *Methodus*, XXVI.

[18] *Methodus*, 25; (285 B).

twelve months or so after completing the *Methodus* Bodin himself was thirty seven. [19, 20]

Bodin's Daemon

In the year 1567 Bodin first seems to have become involved in the investigation of daemonic phenomena. A relevant passage occurs in a chapter of the *Démonomanie* which considers forms of protection against magic. Bodin thinks that the man who gives alms to the poor, for instance, is immune from *maleficia*.

«De faict j'ay sçeu estant à Poictiers aux Grands Jours parmi les substituts du Procureur general, qu'il y eust deux sorciers qui demanderent l'aumosne en une riche maison. On les refusa: ils jetterent là leur sort, et tous ceux de la maison furent enragés et moururent furieux … estans meschans et n'ayans pitié des pauvres, Dieu n'eut point pitié d'eux. Aussi l'Escripture Saincte appelle l'aumosne צידקת (shedakah), et au lieu que nous disons donnez l'aumosne, ils disent donnez la Justice, comme estant l'une des choses qui justifie plus le meschant.»

Several Old Testament instances of this usage follow. As Bodin already believed that Hebrew words expressed the ultimate meanings of the things they designated, this equivalence would have revelatory force for him. He now continues with a striking assertion.

«Brief toute l'Escriture saincte n'est pleine d'autre chose. Voila peut estre l'un des plus grands et des plus beaux secrets qu'on puisse remarquer pour oster à Satan, et a tous les Sorciers la puissance de nuire … Toutefois le plus asseuré moyen et qui passe tous les autres c'est de se fier en Dieu, et s'asseurer de luy comme d'une forteresse treshaute et inexpugnable (a reference to psalm 91): c'est dit Philon, le plus grand et le plus agreable sacrifice qu'on sçaurait faire à Dieu, et pour lequel Abraham receut tant de benedictions, et duquel l'Escriture dit qu'il se fia en Dieu, et qu'il luy fut imputé à justice.»[21]

In these lines, where Bodin is elucidating his own experiences at the age of thirty seven, with the help of the Old Testament, we meet in close proximity three similarities to the daemonic narrative. Firstly, there is the crucial sacrifice passage from Philo. Secondly, there is the Hebraic emphasis – for so Bodin considers it – on the beneficial value of almsgiving. His informant had told him that «il estoit souvent adverty de donner l'aumosne, et alors que plus il donnait l'aumosne, plus il sentoit que ses

---

[19] Bodin was born in 1529 or 1530.

[20] Bezold does not pursue this coincidence of age.

[21] *Dém.*, Bk. III, ch. 1, foll. 124v–125. Bodin's interest in *naement d'auguillette* while at Poitiers is described at length *Dém.*, Bk. II, ch. 1, foll. 57v–58.

affaires prosperoit.» And thirdly, there is the allusion to psalm 91, which the daemon had instructed the informant to recite. «Et apres avoir eschapé le danger, il dict qu'il ouyt en dormant une voix qui disoit: Il faut bien dire ‹Qui en la garde du haut Dieu pour jamais se retire.› » Later in this same chapter about the Poitiers witches Bodin again refers to the use of psalm 91 as an antidote to magic, quoting it at considerable length.

In fact all this chapter is very closely related to the daemonic narrative chapter. We read that Bodin's informant «employoit un jour de la sepmaine autre que le Dimenche (pour les debauches qu'il disoit qu'on faisoit ce jour là) pour lire en la Bible, et puis meditoit, et pensoit à ce qu'il avoit leu ... pui après il prenoit plaisir à louer Dieu, d'un Psalme de louange.»

Words like these are closely paralleled by Bodin's counsel that «Chacun doit instruire sa famille à prier Dieu matin et soir ... (et) donner pour le moins une ou deux heures en un iour de la sepmaine à faire lire la Bible par le chef de la famille»[22] and by his declaration that: «le Dimenche ... est souillé de toutes des desbauches et folies dont on se peut aviser au grand deshonneur de Dieu.»[23]

The heavily paternalistic tone of the first quotation is in turn matched in the daemonic narrative, where two of the informant's visions concern his father. In one instance the informant had asked God to bless him, and was rewarded with the vision of his human father giving his benediction, a vision which strikingly concludes the whole narrative.

These coincidences between the two chapters can hardly be merely coincidental. They are all the more noteworthy in view of the limited information given as to the exact form the daemon's religious teaching took. Roellenbleck goes so far as to say that we are not told of any theological information imparted by the daemon.[24] But this will hardly do. It is to overlook the rigorously simplified nature of Bodin's theology, the strongly ethical bias of his religion. Bodin insists that the daemon did explain difficulties «non seulement des choses divines, mais encores des choses humaines» and that the friend «avoit les songes veritables de ce qu'il devoit faire ou croire». The daemon's advice about almsgiving, psalm-singing, early morning prayer, is advice about «choses divines», and has theological implications. Thus in the *Heptaplomeres* the seven participants do have one form of worship in common, psalm-singing, because of its exclusively monotheistic orientation.

The main ground for Bodin's reticence – and anonymity – in the dae-monic narrative is probably his conviction that few people are granted

---

[22] *Dém.*, Bk. III, ch. 1, fol. 123.
[23] *Dém.*, fol. 127.
[24] *Dém.*, 118.

communication with a good daemon. The *Démonomanie* is dedicated to persuading its readers that large numbers of people invoke bad ones. For Bodin, white daemonic magic does not exist, nor for that matter does natural magic. He believes that the concept of good daemons is almost always used as a cover for Satan worship. «Satan a tousjours cherché de beaux mots comme d'Esprit familier, et blance Daemon, et Petitmaistre, parce que le mots de Satan et Diable sont odieux.»[25] Moreover, as the daemonic narrative tells us, the main and much-needed activity the daemon exercised was to save Bodin's friend from danger. Bodin would hardly want to increase the danger by revealing his friend's identity. All the more so in view of the highly dubious orthodoxy of the «friend's» religion, even before 1567.

The chapter in which the narrative occurs itself has radically anti-Christian implications. It starts off by describing man's intellectual soul as a mean between bad daemons and angels. This curious, neo-Platonising cosmology is given an apparently Christian gloss by maintaining that Adam's fall broke the continuity between God and Creation. The Christian gloss should continue to say that Christ restored the broken continuity. For Bodin the restoration is effected by prayer, and he explains later that «Les Hebrieux tiennent en leur Theologie secrete que l'Ange faict oblation à Dieu des âmes des esleus.»[26] Christ then seems to be replaced as mediator by the good daemon, who offers up souls in sacrifice. At the end of the daemonic narrative, Bodin goes on to make two observations of its significance, which show that the daemonic narrative is central to the origin and purpose of the whole book. Firstly, the circumstantially authenticated experience of a man communicating with a good daemon is a guarantee that communication with bad daemons is not some highly improbable conjecture.[27] And secondly, the physical phenomena

---

[25] *Dém.*, Bk. II, ch. 3, fol. 78v, and cf. Bk. II, ch. 1, fol. 52.

[26] *Dém.*, Bk. II, ch. 5, fol. 90.

[27] Johann WEYER's arguments against witchcraft persecution are largely based on the assertion that such communication with bad daemons is a case of melancholic delusion. Bodin's fury against Weyer, his certainty that Weyer was a Satanic double agent, was much intensified by this assertion that what Bodin experienced as fact was mere fancy. MONTAIGNE's too wellknown doubts about persecution (*Essais*, Bk. III, ch. 11) derive from humanitarian impulses, rather than, as MONTER asserts ([268], 389) from systematic scepticism. Montaigne did not, in fact, maintain his earlier disbelief in the reality of witchcraft, since such a denial would be to set limits to God's unknowable powers – a sceptical argument frequent in the *Démonomanie*. (*Essais*, Bk. I, ch. 27). There is a nicely ironic chassé-croisé here, for Montaigne, who much admired the *Methodus*, criticised Bodin for being too sceptical about prodigies in it. (*Essais*, Bk. II, ch. 10). This was a scepticism which Bodin was very soon to jettison.

reported by his informant match phenomena described in the Old Testament, and thus guarantee the daemon's reliability as a source of religious and moral enlightenment.

The *Démonomanie* is organised around this dual reference, empirical and scriptural. The scriptural reference is entirely to the Old Testament, which Bodin generally refers to as the «Loy de Dieu», particularly where the Pentateuch is concerned. Book One describes the «moyens divins naturels et humains de prévoir et de prévenir les choses futures». It exhaustively explores the nature of prophecy with the help of the Old Testament and confirms the prophetic status of the daemonic experience.[28] The second book described the unlawful practices of witches, which are proscribed by the Law of God. It is characterised by the fullness of Bodin's first hand researches into contemporary daemonic phenomena. Most of the third book, on means to combat magic, is taken up with the chapter in which, as we have seen, Bodin develops the religious implications of the daemonic narrative. The last book discusses means of exterminating witchcraft, using the rigorous legislation of Deuteronomy against idolatry, blasphemy and witchcraft (which involves the other two crimes). The devastating skill with which Bodin uses the double reference to Scripture and experience in the refutation of Johann Weyer, which follows as a lengthy appendix, has been well described by Monter.[29]

Bodin's conversion

From this point I shall refer to the daemon as Bodin's own.[30] I want to

---

[28] *Dém.*, Bk. I, ch. 4, foll. 23–24, especially where Bodin distinguishes different degrees of prophetic illumination, drawing heavily on Maimonides. He argues in the same chapter that the strictest monotheism is a sign of the true prophet, fol. 27, and that «les enfans d'Israel (sont) tous ceux qui se fient en Dieu», fol. 30v. Such views obviously facilitated his identification with the Hebraic outlook.

[29] MONTER is less convincing in comparing the organisation of the *Démonomanie* and the *Malleus Maleficarum* ([268], 386). There are closer comparisons to make with more recent Protestant writers on witchcraft, including WEYER. Thus PEUCER's *Commentarius de praecipuis divinationum generibus*, Wittenberg 1553, discusses witchcraft within the framework of divination, of which prophecy in one species, rather as the *Démonomanie* does. It begins by discussing lawful divination (fol. 9) then unlawful divination (fol. 13) then prophecy. Bodin had discussed lycanthropy with Peucer, and was interested in pursuing the question whether this was a natural or divine phenomenon (*Methodus*, 79).

[30] There is much additional justification for this in Bezold's article on the *Démonomanie*.

apply to his experience of the daemon seven characteristics which Nock refers to in his discussion of intellectual conversion.[31]

1. Conversion is generally preceded by a period of doubt and of searching. Thus we have seen Bodin seeking in his soul and in the Bible to find the true religion, whilst the avowed aim of his projected study of human, natural and divine affairs was to help men to «that intimate relationship which we have with God ... and again be united closely to him.»[32]

2. In many conversions a single phrase seems to alluminate the whole Bible or a mere image to bring peace and assurance to the soul. In Bodin's case the phrase from Philo about sacrifice seems to have played a crucial role in confirming Bodin's conviction of an impending resolution of his spiritual uncertainty. An uncertainty whose final resolution involves the intimate certainty of God as a tower of spiritual strength: thus the repeated use of psalm 91. A key to the whole Bible is provided for Bodin by the equivalence of the words charity and justice in Hebrew.[33]

3. Conversion comes to a person as something unforeseen, as a blinding revelation of something new. Even the notion of familiar spirits, of good daemons, is absent from Bodin's writings before 1567. The felt immediacy of the daemon's presence is abundantly clear in Bodin's conversion, especially in the miraculous escapes from danger which it facilitated. An observer can often trace the seeds and development of such revelation. Bodin himself writes of the daemonic voice that «luy sembla avoir ouy la voix de Dieu en dormant, qui luy dist, ‹Je sauveray ton ame: c'est moy qui t'ay apparu par cy devant›», a remark which suggests a previous history of spiritual intimations.

4. The sense of fresh understanding and of a new spiritual well being is often accompanied by psychosomatic disorders. The daemon would twitch Bodin's left and right ears, and even strike from his hands any «bad» book he might be reading. And the daemon also appeared to Bodin as a bright circle of light. In one case Bodin saw on his bed «un jeune enfant vestu d'une robe blanche changeant en couleur de pourpre, d'un visage de beauté esmerveillable.»

5. A conversion leads to a definite change in the conduct of one's daily

---

[31] A. D. NOCK, Conversion, London, 1933, esp. chapter I.

[32] *Methodus*, 16; (282 A).

[33] Bodin's discussion of justification in the *Heptaplomeres* is a re-working of this *Démonomanie* passage (*Dém.*, Bk. III, ch. 1, foll. 124v-125). Roughly speaking, Bodin replaces the doctrine of justification by a doctrine of *reward*. Compare the passage about political «justification» in the *République*, Bk. VI, ch. 1, referred to below, p. II, which is also based on the notion of reward and punishment.

life. It led Bodin to rise very early to pray. His feelings about the pollu-
tion of the Sabbath probably led him to keep the Sabbath. He certainly
put into practice in his own family the Judaic paternalism which he
advocates in the *Démonomanie*.[34]

6. Conversion frequently turns a man into a prophet, with a message
to deliver and a policy to pursue, and

7. Conversion means turning one's back on something.

The larger implications of the last two points are the subject of what
follows. In particular we shall be concerned with the policies advocated
in the *République,* and with Bodin's rejection of the basic Christian
mysteries, along with the Christian ethics of forgiveness.

The Law of God

References to the New Testament are as infrequent in the *République*
(1576) as in the *Methodus,* and when they occur are for purposes of
illustration. They never have prescriptive force. The normative use of
the Old Testament, the Law of God, on the other hand, has become all
pervasive, dominating the discussion at every important point. The conclusion to the chapter concerning sovereignty, the concept on which Bodin's fame is based, affirms with epigrammatic vigour that the Law of
God provides the pattern of all justice.

«For if iustice be the end of the law, and the law is the worke of the
prince, and the prince is the lively image of almightie God; it must needes
follow, that the law of the prince should be framed unto the modell of
the law of God.»[35]

Bodin specifically identifies the natural and divine law, which he
normally couples in the one phrase. Interestingly, in the final chapter of
the first book, concerning the attributes of sovereignty (which are most
easily exercised in a monarchy), Bodin refers only to the Law of God.
And in chapters six and seven of the following book, concerning the
characteristics of aristocraties and democracies, he refers to neither natural

---

[34] In his partial edition and translation of the *Heptaplomeres*, Berlin, 1841,
GUHRAUER prints a letter of Bodin about the education of his children: «Je leur
ai dressé trois cent sentences morales ... et pour leur apprendre les principales
congruités et concordances je leur ai appris ces mots: Ego cupio vehementer
laudare opificem mundi optimum et potentissimum omnium.» [23], 254.

[35] *The Six Books of a Commonweale*, ed. K. D. McRae, Harvard 1962, Bk. I,
ch. 10, p. 113 [7.44]. All references are to his edition, followed by the page in
the 1583 edition. Sometimes this is less full than the Knolles translation edited
by McRae, which uses the later Latin version.

nor divine law. For his concern in the *République* is almost exclusively with kings.

Time and again, Bodin insists that sovereign power can only be exercised within the constraining limits of the Law of God. On the other hand, as far as civil law goes, the sovereign has complete liberty of action. He cannot be bound by any charge or condition «except that such charge or condition ... be directly comprehended within the lawes of God and nature.»[36] In this sense a king is absolute, and for this reason Bodin roundly attacks whose who would «subject him to the generall estates, or to the councell ... (or) to his lawes ... Under this colour they make a mixture and confusion of civill lawes with the lawes of nature, and of both joyntly with the lawes of God.»[37] These assertions are flat contrary to a phrase like the following from the *Methodus*: «The more you can take from the power of the prince (and on this point one cannot go wrong) the more just will be the rule and the more stable for the future.»[38]

Discussions of the reasons for this change usually refer to the deterioration of the political situation in France between the appearance of the two works, and growth of the *politique* attempts at bolstering up Valois power. And it is quite true that, unlike the *Methodus*, the *République* comments directly about the French situation, and recommends remedies. But what sort of comments, and what sort of remedies?

Bodin ascribes the weakness of France at the beginning of the religious wars to Henry II's failure to punish the wicked and protect the poor, thereby breaking the Law of God.[39] Describing the lamentable state of the royal finances under Charles IX, Bodin refers to «the calamitie of those times when as children and women ruled», a punishment, he later explains, which is threatened in the Old Testament.[40] These calamities would have continued «if God had not sent our King Henrie 3 from heaven to restore it to the first beautie.»[41] Moreover Henry's rule, providentially thus established, against numerological law, is maintained by special divine favour.[42]

It will be obvious from these examples that it is not sufficient to point only to the contemporary situation to explain the concept of sovereignty

---

[36] *République*, Bk. I, ch. 8, p. 89; (128).

[37] *Rép.*, Bk. VI, ch. 4, p. 717; (965).

[38] *Methodus*, 256; (405 B).

[39] *République*, Bk. II, ch. 4, p. 217; (295); Bk. VI, ch. 2, pp. 677; (898), 681; (901).

[40] *Rép.*, Bk. VI, ch. 2, p. 679; (ef. 901); Bk. VI, ch. 4, p. 714; (960).

[41] *Rép.*, Bk. VI, ch. 2, p. 654; (863).

[42] *Rép.*, Bk. IV, ch. 2, p. 463; (567), and McRae's note.

in the *République*, but also to take into full account the moral and religious nature of its recommendations for restoring political stability. The naturalistic analysis of the *Methodus* has largely gone. Praise of Machiavelli has turned into vituperation, for having «laid down as the twin foundations of Commonweals impiety and injustice, and (having) condemned religion as hostile to the state ... as for justice, if Machiavelli had cast his eye ever so lightly over good authors, he would have found that Plato calls his *Republic* the books of justice, this being one of the firmest supports of all Commonweals.»[43]

In the *Methodus* Bodin confesses that he is so far relatively ignorant of Hebraic legal literature,[44] and nowhere does he suggest that Hebraic law is universally normative. We have moved a long way from this in the discussion of justice which climaxes the *République*. Here Bodin defines justice as essentially a strict system of rewards and punishments.

«(This justice) the Hebrewes by a strange word call *Credata*: for the difference betwixt this and the other Iustice given unto men by God, whereby we are justified, which they call *Tsedaca*. For that by these, as by most certain guides, wee must enter into this most religious and stately temple of Iustice.»[45]

Bodin argues at some length that justice should be implemented harmonically. He believes that this harmonic justice is exemplified only in the Law of God,[46] and in Hebraic legislation. The *lex talionis*, for example, is to be understood as describing this harmonic justice, rather than as demanding, with some naive arithmetic, one eye for one eye, one tooth for one tooth. «And so the auntient Hebrewes, the best interpreters of God his law, have understood it, expounded it, and also practised it: as is in their Pandects to be seene in the *Title of Penalties*.»[47]

A moral universe

Is it possible to see a development towards these ideas in the *Methodus*? There is no mention of divine law in the epistolary dedication, and in the discussion of the *Form of Monarchy*[48] neither natural or divine law are mentioned. In the section curiously headed *Form of Government in*

---

[43] *Rép.*, Preface of 1576, A 70.
[44] *Methodus*, 3; (274 A).
[45] *République*, Bk. VI, ch. 6, p. 755; (1014).
[46] *Rép.*, 784; (1049).
[47] *Rép.*, 781; (1045).
[48] *Methodus*, 201–206; (375 A–378 B)

Marseilles Bodin mentions the «loftiest knowledge of heavenly and natural things» possessed by the Druids, only to add tersely: «I discuss only the state», meaning that his investigation of political systems is solely concerned with *res humanae*.[49] A new pages later however he does criticise the gynocratic rule of Mary and Elisabeth I for contravening divine and natural laws.[50]

Only in the closing pages of this extremely long chapter on different types of political system, when Bodin discusses the Hebrews, does the notion of divine law become important.[51] Moses ordered that the Hebrews should be ruled by divine law. The history of his people is said to show that royal power was pleasing to God. And it is, significantly, immediately following this discussion that Bodin affirms monarchy to be the best political system.[52] The whole chapter concludes with a brief discussion on religion as the *fundamentum regni*, which seems extraordinarily slight after the massive weight of empirical political analysis which has come before.[53] Nevertheless it is indicative of a tension in Bodin's mind.

The rigid distinctions which Bodin's methodology sets up between human, natural and divine history in the *Methodus*, his attempt to construct a secularised *summa*, is under great strain at many points. The *Methodus* derives its fascination – and its unsatisfactoriness – from the sense it gives of a powerful mind gripped by enormous visions of intellectual investigation, but as yet unsure of the direction in which it will ultimately move. The observer can see that this direction is in fact towards a Hebraically inspired, morally organised universe. Bodin will abandon his triple concept of history and substitute for it a triple concept of Law – human, natural and divine. The Hebraic aspect of this development has its seeds in the notion of Moses as the first, divinely inspired lawgiver and supreme philosopher,[54] of the Hebrews as the best interpreters of natural and divine things[55] and as the fountainhead of all existing religions.[56] The moral emphasis is present in Bodin's assertion that to reject the tes-

---

[49] *Meth.*, 250; (402 AB). The assertion that he is studying only *res humanae* is repeated throughout the first half of the work (cf. pp. 1, 8, 14, 16, 42, 44, 153).

[50] *Meth.*, 253; (404 A).

[51] *Meth.*, 279–282; (418 B–420 A).

[52] *Meth.*, 282; (420 A).

[53] «Argomentazioni che appaiono come l'appendice posticcia di un rigoroso discorso politico» says Cotroneo, Bodin teoretico della storia Napoli 1966, [246], 169.

[54] *Methodus*, 201, 303, 340; (375 B, 431 B, 451 B). This view of Moses coexists with the argument that the *least* reliable witnesses are those closest to the events they describe.

[55] *Meth.*, 111, 130, 317; (327 A, 337 A, 438 B).

[56] *Meth.*, (463 B).

timony of Moses is eroneous, impious and immoral.[57] It is especially
apparent in the penultimate chapter, where Bodin argues that all the
peoples of the world are fundamentally one, and that the historical
process demands «that the peoples should unite their possessions and
ideas in mutual commerce».[58] The crucial notion – crucial for Bodin's
later development – occurs here. Divine vengeance is invoked to describe
the process by which «the Greeks were subject for a time to the Latins ...
and in turn the Latins ... to the Goths». The chapter concludes – and it
is followed only by the bibliography – that the only Jewish tribe which
had preserved a separate identity disappeared from history «not without
marked evidence of divine vengeance».[59] Yet these indications of a moral
universe, it is clear, go against, they do not constitute, the main purpose
of the *Methodus*.

Divine Retribution

If, as the *République* maintains, the king is bound by the Law of God,
it follows that he cannot allow his subjects to break it with impunity.
One of the fiercest notes in the *République* is the ringing denunciation
of pardon, especially for those who have transgressed God's laws:

«The wilfull murderer ‹You shall take him (saith the law) from my
sacred altar, neither shalt thou have pitie on him, but cause him to dye
the death: and afterwards I will stretch forth my great mercies upon
you›. Nevertheless the Christian kings on that day which they commaund
to bee most holy kept, as on Good Friday, use for the most part to pardon
some one man or other, condemned of most horrible and notorious
crime.»[60]

Or again: «the law of God expressly forbiddeth to have any pitie of
the poore in judgement.»[61] Rewards and punishments are essential for
maintaining the state, its two principal foundations,[62] and the fatal
weakness of democratic systems is the unwillingness of men to condemn
and punish their peers.[63] The corresponding advantage of monarchy is

---

[57] *Meth.*, (448 B).

[58] *Meth.*, (449 A).

[59] It is curious that Bodin does not apply the idea of retribution in discussing
the history of the Hebrews.

[60] *République*, Bk. I, ch. 10, p. 174; (240), with marginal reference to *Deuteronomy*, 19 and 21.

[61] *Rép.*, Bk. III ch. 5, p. 341; (449), Bk. IV, ch. 6, p. 509; (622). See also
Bk. V, ch. 3, 582; (725) and Bk. V, ch. 4, pp. 593, 595; (729, 742).

[62] *Rép.*, 584; (729).

[63] *Rép.*, 592; (742), also Bk. VI, ch. 4, p. 704; (943).

that rewards can be administered by the king and punishments by his ministers.[64]

Supposing the king does grant impunity to criminals, what sort of sanction can there be? The checks on sovereign power in the *Methodus* were constitutional, immanent ones. As a consequence (or is it a cause?) of the removal of these political safeguards in the *République*, the checks on the sovereign are necessarily religious, transcendental.[65] Thus, «pardons granted to such villaines (e.g. murderers) drawe after them plagues, famine, warres, and ruines of Commonweales: and that is it for which the law of God saith. That in punishing them that have deserved to dye, they shall take away the cause from among the people».[66]

All this is exactly the theory of the *Démonomanie*, which the critical tradition has unnecessarily separated from the *République*.

It is not the function of the *République* to describe in detail the mechanism of divine retribution. This fact is explained with lucid brevity in the chapter dealing with the *conversiones rerumpublicarum*. «The chaunges and ruines of Commonweales are human (e), or naturall, or divine.» «Politicians and astrologers» study the first two types of causation, and «divines» the third. Nevertheless, Bodin does sketch in the outlines of the mechanism of retribution. «The Divine constantly affirmeth all plagues, wars, dearth, destructions of cities and nations, to proceed from the contempt of God.»[67]

Now, just as with the monarch, who should not himself punish, but delegate the task to others, so with God, who acts «by meane causes and the ministerie and power of angels».

«In this all divines ... wholly agree, none of all these things to bee done by almightie God, as by an efficient cause: but by permission onely, and to bee from him divided, but as from a not letting cause: which cause the manner of the Hebrew phrase everie where signifieth by the word Hiphil, ordinarily used, when it speaketh of the vengeance of God.»[68]

Bodin reserves a full treatment of such «divine causes» to the *Démonomanie*, which explains the daemonic mechanism of the *conversiones rerumpublicarum*, a mechanism set in motion by the willed impiety of witches.

---

[64] *Rép.*, Bk. IV, ch. 6; (625). Bk. V, ch. 4, p. 593; (730).

[65] God may act through foreign rulers or a specially appointed subject. Otherwise tyrannicide is forbidden; see the 1578 Preface (A 70) and Bk. II, ch. 5.

[66] *Rép.*, Bk. I, ch. 10, p. 174; (240) and see Bk. IV, ch. 2., p. 438; (542). Bk. IV, ch. 6, p. 512; (625).

[67] *Rép.*, Bk. IV, ch. 2, pp. 437, 438; (542).

[68] *Rép.*, Bk. IV, ch. 6, p. 512; (625).

The Daemonic Machinery

We saw above that the *Methodus* moves only fitfully towards a providential doctrine of history. At one point, in defining «natural» history, Bodin even slips into a form of words which seems to deny the existence of a continually active providence. «Natural history presents an inevitable and steadfast sequence of cause and effect unless it is checked by divine will or for a brief moment abandoned by it.»[69] In later works, Bodin will assert that all non-regular or violent natural phenomena are under providential control, being produced by daemonic agents. The *Methodus* on the other hand is virtually innocent of demonology. But not quite. In two places Bodin refers in passing to «animi immortales».[70] And in refuting the doctrine of the eternity of the world, Bodin counters the argument of Proclus that, in creating the world, God must have been «carried from rest to action (which) involves a change... which is very far from that everlasting mind» by referring to Christ's assertion that «He might have, if He wished, twelve legions of angels for a guard. From this He wished to imply that this world is full of immortal souls (animorum immortalium) whose service God uses like that of servants».[71] These incidental references do not begin to constitute a theory of daemonic activity, and in any case, Bodin's later demonology almost totally ignores the rich material in the New Testament. The *Methodus* is not a «superstitious» book. Bodin is often sarcastically critical of stories of miracle and prodigy,[72] an attitude noticeably absent from works written after his daemonic experience.

In the *Theatrum Naturae*[73] Bodin does indeed insist that scientific truth is to be sought by reason and experiment – «experience«. But since Hebrew is the language of truth, and since the Hebrews are obviously best qualified to interpret their own books, a more certain – and a corroborative – method is to rely on Hebraic exegesis of the Law of God. So Bodin's science turns out to be the revealed science of the Book of Genesis and the Psalms. The main speaker in the *Theatrum* is called *Mystagogus*, a word which Bodin uses when explicating his daemonic experience in the *Démonomanie*, by quoting an anonymous Greek verse (actually Menander) which says: «To every man there is given a guide of his life, a mystagogue». Probably Bodin conceives of his daemon as having initiated him into the secrets of the universe.

---

[69] *Methodus*, 17; (282 A).

[70] *Rép.*, 11, 30; (279 A, 288 A).

[71] *Rép.*, 310, 311; (435 AB).

[72] *Rép.*, 57, 77; (301 A, 310 B).

[73] *Universae Naturae Theatrum*, Lyon 1596 [13.1].

At all events, Bodin is utterly persuaded of the omnipresence of the daemonic machinery in the physical world, and deeply concerned, in the *Démonomanie* and *Heptaplomeres*, to warn against adoration, or fear, of these spirits. In the first three books of the *Heptaplomeres* Bodin rejects the Aristotelean, mechanistic universe in favour of a moral universe (i.e. a rewarding and punishing one) operated by daemons on behalf of a totally transcendent deity. But these daemons, as mere creatures, must not be worshipped. To worship them, as witches, do, is an impious threat to strict Hebraic monotheism. The last three books of the *Heptaplomeres* are written to show that all versions of Christianity contain the same idolatrous threat. The doctrines of the incarnation, of atonement, of the forgiveness of sins, are absurdities: how can a finite creature have any contact with an infinite creator; how can one creature atone for the sins of others? The forgiveness of sins is incompatible with Bodin's Hebraic system of rewards and punishments, which he bases on an uncompromising voluntarism. There is no eternal damnation, merely annihilation for the very wicked. However, in spite of the idolatrous nature of Christianity, no blasphemy is involved in the worship and belief of most Christians, who, unlike witches, are merely mistaken in their religion. Witches, by rejecting the Christianity which they believe to be true, are not rejecting the true God, but they *are* rejecting God. And, since any sincere religion, even the most superstitious, is welcome to God, it is the duty of all princes to maintain the traditional religion, even Christianity, and to punish backsliders. If they do not do it, God will.[74]

Bodin conceives of divine rewards and punishments operating, in Hebraic fashion, in this world, though he does believe that the very best men turn into stars when they die. Now God, who punishes through the daemonic machinery, also rewards through it. In the *Paradoxon*[75] a treatise on the *summum bonum*, Bodin describes the highest reward of virtue as the gift of prophecy: prophets are those men «qui ont la communication du bon ange, que les autres appellent l'intellect actuel, de la splendeur duquel les gens de bien sont instruits par songes et visions de

---

[74] *Colloquium Heptaplomeres*, ed. L. Noack, Schwerin, 1857 [16.2] Bodin has a very acute insight into the historically conditioned interrelations of social and religious institutions, and is acutely apprehensive about the moral and religious confusion attendant on violent cultural change. Without the belief in a rewarding and punishing God, society will collapse. Any religion maintains this belief to some extent. Hence Bodin's resolute religious conformism.

[75] *Paradoxon, quod nec virtus ulla in mediocritate, nec summum hominis bonum in virtutis actione consistere possit*, Paris 1596 [14.1]. I quote from Bodin's French translation, *Le Paradoxe de Jean Bodin*, Paris 1598 [14.2].

tout ce qu'il faut suivre et fuir, et d'advertir les princes et les peuples de la volonté de Dieu.»[76]

Revelation

Bodin's own prophetic activity – his revealing to others of God's will – was partly a matter of foretelling the political future. This he did frequently, and with some success[77]. More interestingly, there is evidence to suggest that Bodin intervened personally to try to ensure the success of prophecies in which he had a vested interest. Some of the murkier parts of his career may conceal activities of this sort[78]. His most important prophetic activity was literary, notably the *Démonomanie,* and the *République.* The *Démonomanie,* which more than any other work was responsible for the European witch scare of the late sixteenth century[79], was extremely effective in securing the implementation of the Law of God, though by magistrates acting on their own initiative, rather than under royal guidance, as Bodin had intended. The *République* had a curious fate. It was an enormous publishing success, and became a landmark in intellectual history. But as far as Bodin's specific, Biblically-derived proposals were concerned, the voice of the prophet cried in a wilderness of unconcern. His proposals on alms-giving[80], on Sabbath observance[81], on the powers of the father, and husband[82], on the instituting of moral «censors»[83], on the abolition of usury[84], for all the vehemence with which they were uttered, fell on deaf ears, and have played little part in subsequent appreciation of his work.

---

[76] *Paradoxe,* [14.2] 31. Bodin's daemonic machinery has high ergonomic efficiency. Daemons reward individuals by the gift of prophecy, and prophets by their teaching ensure political stability. Daemons punish those who worship them, and by causing wars, plagues, etc., ensure political chaos. In either case society is recalled to that fear of God on which political prosperity is based. (Witches are in fact deluded in believing that they *control* their daemon. This delusion is an Satanic double-cross to gain their allegiance.)

[77] See Bezold [70].

[78] See J. MOREAU-REIBEL, Bodin et la Ligue d'après des lettres inédites, Humanisme et Renaissance 2 (1935), 422–440 [124], and S. BALDWIN, Jean Bodin and the League, *Catholic Historical Review,* 23 (1937/38), 160–184 [136].

[79] Cf. R. MANDROU, Magistrats et Sorciers en France au XVIIe siècle, Paris 1968, ch. 2.

[80] *République,* Bk. VI, ch. 2, p. 676; (897).

[81] *Rép.,* Bk. I, ch. 1, p. 7; (69); Bk. IV, ch. 2, pp. 461, 462; (566).

[82] *Rép.,* Bk. I, ch. 4, pp. 20, 22, 27; (30, 32, 38).

[83] *Rép.,* Bk. VI, ch. 1, p. 644; (835); Bk. VI, ch. 6, p. 771; (1030).

[84] *Rép.,* Bk. V, ch. 2, p. 572; (707).

In the 1572 edition of the *Methodus* Bodin refers to several works, *De Decretis, De Jure Imperio, De Imperio*, which have not survived[85]. As they are not mentioned in the 1566 edition, it is possible they could have helped us reconstruct the shift from the secular *Methodus* to the religious *République*.[86] In another 1572 addition, Bodin prefaces the discussion of the Hebrew monarchy by asserting that «Philo the Jew, in the book about the creation of a prince, taught that the rule of one prince had been established by the command of God.[87]» Now, Philo consistently interprets the Jewish history of political instability, breakdown, and exile as the result of divine retribution. Turnebus had published a Greek edition of Philo in 1552 and Gelenius a Latin edition in 1554 – the one Bodin used. In 1575, Pierre Bellier published a French translation of most of Philo's works[88]. The dedication of this translation contains what is almost a summary (minus the daemons) of the Hebraic political system of the *République* and the *Démonomanie* as I have described it in this paper. For this reason it is worth quoting at some length, since it illustrates how Philo is, almost certainly, a major new intellectual influence at work in the development of Bodin's political thought after the *Methodus*[89].

---

[85] *Methodus*, 355, 357, 360, 361. Cf. PIERRE BAYLE's article on Bodin (MESNARD, Œuvres Philosophiques de Jean Bodin, vol. I, p. XXXVI) [4.20]. The *De Decretis* and the *De Imperio* are specifically mentioned as having been burnt, at Bodin's death bed request. Mesnard thinks they were written in the fifties.

[86] In this connection it is interesting that Bodin begins to introduce the notions of justice and charity into his notion of legitimate political authority in the *Réponse aux paradoxe de M. de Malestroit*, Paris 1568. (Cf. HAUSER's edition, Paris 1932, 33.) [5.9]. It is even more significant that Bodin introduces comments on the contemporary political situation into the 1572 edition of the *Methodus*, and that after 1567 he was to involve himself very actively in political affairs. The crisis of 1566/67 is psychological, moral and intellectual. We have seen its origins in the letter to Bautru des Matras on the causes of the civil wars. But when the wars draw to their close in the 1590's, and Bodin returns to the less immediately committed, encyclopaedic, academic atmosphere of the *Methodus*, his works remain «religious» in the sense used here, and are only indirectly the fulfilment of the philosophic summa envisaged in his first major work.

[87] *Methodus*, 279, (418 B).

[88] *Les Œuvres de Philon Juif*, Paris 1575.

[89] I said that Bellier's words omit the daemon here. Yet it is worth noting the inspired, almost lyrical tone of this passage in which Philo is made to come alive again, and address the privy councillor Philippe Hurault directly. The fear of blasphemy and the attraction of retributionist political theories in this period are quite common. I discuss some of these matters in my chapter on Problems of the Religious Wars in J. CRUICKSHANK, ed., *French Literature and its Background*, vol. I, London, 1968, 166–185. For the Protestant use of retributionist

«J'ai seulement sur la fin à vous dire un mot de sa part (sc. de Philon): c'est qu'il vous prie bien fort de faire votre rapport d'une petite requeste verbale au conseil du Roy: petite dis-je en paroles mais de fort grande consequence, estant question de la paix et repos de toute la pauvre France, affligee des maux envoiés d'en haut, pour les execrables blasphemes prononcés journellement contre l'honneur de Dieu. Elle tend à ce que, pour les moyens et raisons au long desduites en son traitté du second commandement du Decalogue, l'Edit du ... Roy Francois ... contre ceux qui preignent le nom de Dieu en vain, et le blasphement, soit renouvelé ... et qu'avec ce le Dimanche sacré et jour du repos fut deuement ... solenizé, il y auroit esperance que Dieu feroit la paix avec nous ... il nous bailleroit la tant desirée paix: au lieu de stérilité abondacne de biens: au lieu de maladie santé, au lieu de peste un bon et salubre aer ... et ne se commettroient journellement tant de meurtres, lesquels sans doute, suivant la parole de Dieu, ne proviennent que desdits blasphemes, comme dit Moyse.»

In the *Heptaplomeres,* Philo, together with Moses Maimonides, is the most important Jewish authority. Maimonides is used rather more, in detail. But it is Philo who appears to afford the general frame. Guttmann's erudite essay on Bodin's Judaism [90] contains little mention of Philo. Philo was essentially a Greek in culture, and represented an extremely liberal form of Judaism. Briefer histories of Judaism are rather disparaging about him, if only because he played a considerable part in the development of early Christian thought.

For Bodin, however, Philo's Judaism is not in doubt. We have seen that it was the reading of Philo which led Bodin to an awareness of his daemon. It was probably Philo who provided Bodin with the main outlines of his religious system – above all its strict monotheism and its doctrine of daemons who, by carrying out divine rewards and punishments in this world, safeguard the absoluteness of God. Bodin is heavily dependent on Philo's efforts to unite philosophy and revelation, the secular and the religious, through allegorical exegesis of the Bible. Ultimately, no doubt, all effort to unite reason and revelation is doomed to failure, and commentators will continue to comment on the inadequacy of Bodin's attempts to do so.

Yet in the continually fascinating *Heptaplomeres* Bodin seems aware of the hopelessness of the task. The gap between Senamy the naturalist, and the six other speakers, is not meant to be bridged. Senamy shares *some*

ideas see V. DE CAPRARIIS, Propaganda e Pensiero Politico in Francia durante le guerre di religione, Napoli 1959, 32 and passim [195].

[90] J. GUTTMANN, Jean Bodin in seinen Beziehungen zum Judentum, *Monatsschrift für Geschichte und Wissenschaft des Judentums,* 1905 [59].

assumptions with the other speakers. He believes, like the Bodin of the *Methodus*, in «piety to God, reverence to parents, charity to individuals, and justice to all».[91] It is a refrain, which, with some modifications, is found in most of Bodin's works. But Senamy, though he believes in one God, and possibly in a moral universe, does not believe it is run by daemons, nor does he believe in revelation. He is the pre-daemonic, neutral Bodin, who planned the almost entirely secular *Methodus*.

But shortly after the *Methodus* was written revelation, and the activity of daemons in the world, became facts of experience for Bodin. It was not a position Bodin argued himself into. It just happened. What the profoundly autobiographical *Heptaplomeres* communicates, above all else, is the awareness that rational debate is not the mode through which religious insight is achieved. Thus, after the end of the *Heptaplomeres*, the speakers continue to meet as friends. «Mais on ne parla jamais plus de religion.» For revelations are sacred.

---

[91] *Methodus*, 11; (279 A).

W. H. Greenleaf

Bodin and the Idea of Order

During a fairly long life, Bodin produced some half-dozen major books, many of them large folios dealing with a great range of subjects: religious principles and toleration of belief, historical method and philosophy, politics, what he called «demonomania» (in effect, a study of spiritual influences both good and evil), natural history, and law. This list shows an impressive scope of interest typical perhaps of the medieval scholastic and the renaissance polymath. With it is coupled a considerable depth of analysis and a vast wealth of data deployed in support of the themes pursued. As might be expected of someone writing during the latter part of the sixteenth century, the ethos of this body of work is both old and new, recognisably modern elements of thought being displayed side by side, intermeshed, with ideas manifestly of traditional or even ancient substance. Inevitably, questions arise about the unity of these ideas, indeed whether there is any substantial uniformity or single world-view pervading this variety of expression.

In my *Order, Empiricism and Politics* (London, 1964) I suggested that Bodin's political thought at least might most appropriately be seen in terms of the old metaphysic of order notwithstanding the heavy historical and legal emphasis of his major political works. I was not able, however, to exemplify the presence of this philosophy in his writings as fully as I should have wished, and the object of this paper is to make good this deficiency. Nor is this mere antiquarianism. Sympathetic historical reconstruction of past ideas has an intellectual value of its own and also helps to prevent misunderstandings and difficulties of the kind likely to arise when a merely critical inquiry is in view.[1]

It seems clear that the concept of a hierarchical order of nature was of importance to Bodin because, apart from any other references to it, he devoted a whole book to an analysis of its main expression, the scale of creation or (in the term made famous by Professor A. O. Lovejoy) the great chain of being. This is his *Le Theatre De La Nature Universelle*, a

---

[1] Such deficiencies may be observed, e.g., in the recent study of Professor J. PLAMENATZ (Man and Society, vol. I, ch. 3) [229], which, despite its many virtues, shows no awareness of the real nature and consistency of Bodin's systematic philosophy rooted in the concept of order.

complete popular survey of contemporary scientific knowledge.[2] This work takes the form of a dialogue between a questioner, «Le Théoricien», and his informant, «Le Mystagogue», who initiates him into the secrets of nature. The whole discussion is really a commentary on the plenitude of God's power and the distribution of all things in orderly sequence as an ascending scale of creation in which, as usual, man occupies the crucial middle position: «il n'y a rien au monde, qui soit plus plaisant à voir, ou qui recrée auec plus grãd volupté l'esprit de l'homme, ou qui soit plus commode que l'ordre.»[3] A summary is given at the outset of the different planes of being of which the chain consists[4] and there are, too, tables which give a detailed diagrammatic survey of each plane, of stones, plants, animals, and so on.[5] And each of the five «books» of which the work consists is an elaboration of a particular part of this general scheme. Thus book II surveys the plane of inanimate creation (elements, meteors, stones, metal and other minerals); book III has an account of plants and animals, that is, vegetable and brute being;[6] and book IV deals with the spiritual sphere: the vegetable, animal and rational (or human) souls are analysed in turn and a discussion of the psychological hierarchy of perception is included.[7] Similarly, in Bodin's *Six Books of the Republic* there are detailed descriptions of the chain and its various planes with an emphasis on its continuity and on the harmony which pervades (or should pervade) the whole world:

«If we should enter into the particular nature of worldly creatures ... we should find a perpetuall Harmonicall bond, which vniteth the extreames by indissoluble meanes, taking yet part both of the one and of the other ... So we see the earth and stones to be as it were ioyned together by clay and chaulke, as in meane betwixt both: and so betwixt the stones and mettals, the Marcasites, the Calamites, and other diuers kinds of minerall stones to grow: So stones and plants also to be ioyned together by diuers kinds of Corall, which are as it were stonie plants, yet hauing in them life, and growing vppon roots. Betwixt plants and liuing creatures, the Zoophytes, or plant beasts, which haue feeling and motion, but yet take by the roots whereby they grow. And again betwixt the creatures which liue by land only, and those which liue by water only,

---

[2] I have used Fougerolle's French translation published at Lyon in 1597 [13.5]; the Latin original, *Universae Naturae Theatrum*, had appeared the previous year [13.1].

[3] *Theatre* [13.5], sig. [†† 6] verso.

[4] *Theatre* [13.5], sigs. [†† 8] recto-verso. On man's position, see pp. 777–778.

[5] *Theatre* [13.5], esp. tables 4–11 ad fin.

[6] In this book, too, the human body is discussed: «la fabrique de l'Homme, qui est le lien commun des Anges et des Bestes», p. 588.

[7] Sections VIII and IX.

are those which they call *Amphibia,* or creatures liuing by land and water both, as doth the Beuer, the Otter, the Tortoise, and such like: as betwixt the fishes and the fouls are a certain kind of flying fishes: So betwixt man and beasts, are to bee seene Apes and Munkies; except we shall with Plato agree, who placed a woman in the middle betwixt a man and a beast. And so betwixt beasts and angels God hath placed man, who is in part mortall, and in part immortall: binding also this elementarie world, with the heauens or the celestiall world, by the aetheriall region.»[8]

The familiar scale of degrees in nature and man appears, too, in Bodin's study of historical method where he wrote that «in all ages and centuries we see dominion given to each best man to the great advantage of the lowly. Thus, God governs the angels; the angels men; men beasts; and in general the soul, the body; reason, lust; and the intellect, reason.»[9]

This concept is indeed the presupposition of all Bodin's thought and so the basis of his political and moral ideas. It suggests, for instance, that the same harmony and continuity of degree to be observed in nature should also prevail in a well-ordered political system: «. . . if so be that in all things wee desire and seeke after a conuenient and decent order, and deeme nothing to be more ougly or foule to looke vpon, than confusion and broyle: then how much more is it to be sort for in a Commonweale, so to place the Citisens or subiects in such apt and comely oder, as that the first may be ioyned with the last, and they of the middle sort with both; and so all with all, in a most true knot and bond among themselues, together with the Commonweale?»[10]

---

[8] *Six Books of a Commonweale* (tr. Knolles, London, 1606), 792–793. Cf. pp. 4–5. (Subsequently referred to as «KNOLLES». I have used this, the only complete English translation of the *République,* throughout) [7.43].

[9] *Method for the Easy Comprehension of History* (tr. Reynolds, New York, 1945) [4.23] 63. (Subsequently referred to as «Meth.»).

[10] KNOLLES, 386. This passage continues in terms exactly like those of *Le Theatre:* «For why, it is a most antient and receiued opinion of the wise, Almightie God himselfe the greate and supreme workemaster and creator of this great and wonderfull Fabrick of all things, in the creating thereof, to haue performed nothing either greater or better, than that hee diuided the mingled and confused parts of the rude *Chaos,* and so setled euerie thing in his due place and order. Neither can there be any thing fairer to behold, more delightfull to the mind, or more commodious for vse, than is order it selfe.» (KNOLLES, 386–387). (Cf., especially this last sentence with that quoted from *Le Theatre* at p. 24 above.) Bk. III, ch. VIII «Of the orders and degrees of Citisens», from which the above quotation is taken, does not occur either in the 1st or 4th French editions of the *République* (1576, 1579), but was added to the 1st Latin edition (1586). For his own part, Knolles praises Order and degree as the basis of social wellbeing: «Amongst many the great and deepe deuices of worldly wisdome,

The lowest degree of subjects is the slaves;[11] then come the «State-free men» in their various degrees; then the «Libertines, or ... manumised men», of whom there are also divers orders; the rest of the citizens are divided «according to the varietie of their conditions and estates, and diuersitie of their manners and customes», generally into nobility, gentry, and common people.[12] Bodin devotes several folio pages in his *Republic* to a discussion of the differences between these estates at different times and places, and he gives a specimen Order of society which he considers appropriate to a monarchy, going into some detail about the relative degrees of professions and trades.[13] There are, likewise, three degrees of magistrates in a well-ordered state,[14] but above and controlling these is the prince, the highest in degree of all men and next unto God himself.[15] Indeed the rule of the prince over men corresponds with that of God over the universe. This Bodin affirms discussing the possibility of conflicts in the magistracy. He thinks that these are inevitable in any government but less

---

for the maintenance and preseruing of humane societie (the ground and stay of mans earthly blisse) the fairest, firmest, and the best, was the framing and forming of Commonweales; wherein people of all estates, sort and callings, being comprehended, are by many orderly degrees so vnited and combined together, as that the great are therein onely honoured, and yet the meanest not neglected, and they are in the middest betwixt both, of both according to their places duly respected and regarded: whereof proceedeth the mutuall exchange of all kind and friendly offices, the surest bond of all good and well ordered Commonweales: euery man so finding that which vnto him in priuate belongeth, well vnto himself assured, together with the common good, wherein euery priuate mans estate is also comprehended and included.» (‹To the Reader› Sig. [Aiij] verso.) Bodin's purpose in writing, says Knolles, was to indicate the basis of social Order, and «to make the subiects obedient vnto the magistrates, the magistrates vnto the Princes, and the Princes vnto the lawes of God and Nature.» (Ibid., sig. [Aiiij] recto). Bodin, further, refers to degree in the ends of man and state (op. cit., p. 5), and the nine degress of subjection of inferior to superior princes (115).

[11] Slaves, he writes later, drawing a correspondence with the body, are citizens, although they constitute the lowest degree of subjects, just as some members of the body natural are base and yet still an integral part of it (KNOLLES, 387).

[12] KNOLLES, 386–389, cf. 257. On the unity of the three estates – church, army and common people – see 790.

[13] KNOLLES, 389 ff., 402–403. He advises that, which few exceptions, the different orders of citizens should be scattered about a city, so that they may thus better contribute to the general good, and, at the same time, be prevented from gathering together seditiously. He even discusses which seats each degree should be permitted to occupy in a theatre (Ibid.).

[14] KNOLLES, 343.

[15] KNOLLES, 309.

to be feared in a monarchic than in a democratic or aristocratic state, in that a single prince is likely to be able more easily to reduce such magisterial conflicts to Order and harmony:

«For that as almightie God the Father of the whole Fabrike of the world, and of nature, doth with an admirable concord and agreement gouerne this world, composed of the contrarie conuersions and motions of the celestiall orbes among themselues, as also of the different natures of the starres and elements, and of the contrarie force and power of planets and of other liuing creatures; euen so also a king (the liuing image of God himselfe the prince of all things) should of the dissimilitude of magistrats, in some sort, at variance among themselues, keepe and maintaine the welfare of his subjects and people. And as in instruments, and song it selfe, which altogether out of tune, or all in the selfe same tune, the skilfull and learned eare cannot in any sort endure, is yet made a certaine well tuned discord, and agreeing harmonie, of most vnlike voices and tunes *viz.* of Bases, Trebles, and Meanes, cunningly confused and mixt betwixt both: euen so also of the mightie, and of the weake, of the hie, and of the low, and others of the middle degree and sort betwixt both; yea euen of the verie discord of the magistrats among themselues ariseth an agreeing welfare of all, the straitest bond of safetie in euerie well ordered Commonweale.»[16]

This long correspondence argument between God and prince, cosmos and state, shows, that is, that variety both in nature and in the body politic, even if apparently discordant, is to be reduced to the proper Order and harmony by the operation of the principle of Unity, the rule of one.[17]

Bodin repeats both the method of argument and the conclusion in the *Methodus* when he undertakes to discuss the best type of state. One of the

---

[16] KNOLLES, 498. This quotation is in fact an embroidery by Knolles on a somewhat shorter exposition by Bodin in the original French. This was not contrary to current scholarship and practice in translation; and, in any event, Bodin's view is the same as that quoted, albeit more shortly expressed.

[17] Cf. the passage with which the book concludes: «... Who denieth that the immortall God would euer suffer any euill or wickednesse to bee done, but that hee most certainly knoweth a greater good to ensure thereof. Wherefore as of Treble and Base voyces is made a most sweet and melodious Harmonie, so also of vices and vertues, of the different qualities of the elements, of the contrarie motions of the celestiall Spheres, and of the Sympathies and Antipathies of things, by indissoluble meanes bound together, is composed the Harmonie of the whole world, and of all the parts thereof: So also a well ordered Commonweale is composed of good and bad, of the rich and of the poore, of wisemen and of fools, of the strong and of the weake, allied by them which are in the meane betwixt both: which so by wonderfull disagreeing concord, ioyne

reasons he has for rejecting the popular form of government is that it is against nature, i.e. contrary to God's order:

«For if we refer all things to nature, which is chief of all things, it becomes plain that this world, which is superior to anything ever joined together by immortal God, consists of unequal parts and mutually discordant elements and contrary motions of the spheres, so that if the harmony through dissimilarity is taken away, the whole will be ruined. In the same way, the best republic, if it imitates nature, which it must do, is held together stable and unshaken by those commanding and obeying, servants and lords, powerful and needy, good and wicked, strong and weak, as if by the mixed association of unlike minds. As on the lyre and in song itself the skilled ears cannot endure the sameness of harmony which is called unison; on the contrary, a pleasing harmony is produced by dissimilar notes, deep and high, combined in accordance with certain rules, so also no normal person could endure equality, or rather that democratic uniformity in the state. On the other hand, a state graduated from the highest to the lowest, with the middle orders scattered between in moderate proportion, fits together in a marvellous way through complementary action.»[18]

He goes on to show that where the people have ruled, as in Rome, Athens and Florence, disorder has been frequent. Aristocratic government is rejected, too, for various reasons connected with harmony and Order as expressed in means and proportions.[19] That only leaves monarchy; and he repeats the conclusion of the *Republic* that «... if there is any

---

the highest with the lowest and so to all, yet so as that the good are still stronger than the bad; so as hee the most wise workeman of all others, and gouernour of all the world hath by his eternall law decreed. And as he himselfe being of an infinit force and power ruleth ouer the angels, so also the angels ouer men, men ouer beasts, the soule ouer the bodie, the man ouer the woman, reason ouer affection: and so euery good thing commaunding over that which is worse, with a certaine combining of powers keepeth all things vnder most right and lawful commands. Wherefore what vnitie is in numbers, the vnderstanding in the powers of the soule, and the center in a circle so likewise in this world holy, exalted far aboue the Fabricke of the celestiall Spheres, ioyning this elementarie world with the celestiall and intelligible heauens; with a certaine that most mightie King, in vnitie simple, in nature indiuisable, in puritie most secure care preserueth from destruction this triple world, bound together with a most sweet and Harmonicall consent: vnto the imitation of whome, euerie good prince which wisheth his Kingdome and Commonweale not in safetie onely, but euen good and blessed also, is to frame and conforme himself.» (KNOLLES, 793–794).

[18] *Meth.*, 268.
[19] *Meth.*, 269–270.

excellence in numbers, I suppose that unity is most to be praised of all . . .»[20]

This idea of musical harmony and of numerical proportion was, of course, one that fascinated Bodin. A Platonic-Pythagorean number mysticism was one of his most characteristic intellectual foibles. It is clearly connected with the ideas of harmony and Order: it is to be found combined with them in one of its great source books, the *Timaeus,* and it lies at the basis of much «modern» scientific thought, as in the case of both Kepler and Copernicus. Bodin believed that of the three forms of proportion (arithmetical, geometrical, and harmonical) only the last was conductive to good Order. Its form should, therefore, be emphasised in the state.[21] Government ought to be by «harmonical proportion» if Order is to be maintained. This principle should be applied to justice, punishment, distribution of offices, inheritance and many other matters.[22] Naturally, the best form of government is royal monarchy, that is, monarchy according to law, and ordered harmonically.[23] The form of all well ordered state, he says, «shall so long be firme and sure, as it shall keepe right consent and tune, well agreeing vnto the sweete delite of the eare».[24]

But, if the proportion of things is wrong, then «the proportion of these numbers being not harmonicall, there followeth thereof an vnpleasant discord, which marreth the whole harmonie of a Commonweale».[25] In fact, if the harmony is broken, by, for instance, «the subjects or citisens erring or declyning from the sweet and naturall harmonie of well tuned lawes, and customes», and turning to «most wicked and pernitious lawes and fashions», then the state must a length come to ruin and decay.[26]

In the *Methodus* Bodin devotes several pages to correlating changes in states with numbers, emphasising, however, that the relation lies in the power not of the numbers themselves but of God who so ordains the course of events in accordance with a numerical law. Reviewing the same theme in the *Republic* he writes: «. . . I thinke almightie God who with wonderfull wisdome hath so couched together the nature of all things, and with certain numbers, meanes, measures, and consent bound together all things to come: to haue also within their certaine numbers so shut vp and enclosed Commonweales, as that after a certaine period of yeares

---

[20] *Meth.,* 270–271.
[21] See e.g. KNOLLES, 793.
[22] KNOLLES, 757 ff. Almost the whole of Book VI, ch. VI is devoted to this theme.
[23] KNOLLES, 789–790; see also *Meth.,* 286–288.
[24] KNOLLES, 455.
[25] KNOLLES, 455.
[26] KNOLLES, 456.

once past, yet must they needes then perish and take end, although they vse neuer so good lawes and customes . . .»

He again emphasises, however, that the relation lies in the power of God and not the numbers as such.[27] In the *Methodus*, after having given many examples to show the importance of this numerical analysis, and especially the magic properties of the numbers 7, 9, and 496, to which all changes in governments conform, he is very careful to affirm that «These things show that human affairs do not occur accidentally and haphazard . . . but by divine wisdom».[28] The whole of this theme is, in effect, an interesting elaboration of the idea of the «cosmic dance» which is essentially an attempt to reduce Order to number by analogy with the musical harmonies.

In support of the idea of Order, Bodin has recourse naturally to the various correspondences or parallels between the different planes of being. So far as space is concerned, these similitudes occupy, it is true, a relatively slight portion of the argument. For example, when he discusses monarchy in the *Republic*, he hardly refers to any at all. He simply defines monarchy and then exemplifies its virtue and characteristics with historical and scriptural illustrations.[29] But correspondences do exist, and it must be said at once that they are, for Bodin, more than mere analogy; and the relatively small number of passages devoted to them as compared with historical illustration is not necessarily a good indication of the significance of Order in the formation of Bodin's political ideas.

One, a correspondence between the macrocosm and the state, has already been quoted;[30] and in another place Bodin affirms that he regards «this fabrick of the world» as «the true image of a perfect and most absolute commonweale».[31] In the *Republic* he writes that the position of the king corresponds to that of God, «the soueraigne prince of the whole world.»[32] In the *Methodus*, too, he had argued that the royal power was in accord with universal empire by reference to a macrocosm-body politic parallel: «If we should inspect nature more closely», he says, «we should gaze upon monarchy everywhere. To make a beginning from small things, we see the king among the bees, the leader in the herd, the buck among the flocks . . . (as among the cranes themselves the many follow one), and in the separate natures of things some one object excels: thus, adamant

---

[27] *Meth.*, 223–236. Cf. KNOLLES, 455-467 and *Le Theatre*, 191–194. The quotation is from KNOLLES, 457.

[28] *Meth.*, 235–236.

[29] See especially Book II, ch. II, «Of a Lordly Monarchie, or of the sole gournment of one.»

[30] See above, 27–29.

[31] KNOLLES, 7.

[32] KNOLLES, 505–506.

among the gems, gold among the metals, the sun among the stars, and finally God alone, the prince and author of the world. Moreover, they say that among the evil spirits one alone is supreme».[33]

All of this is sufficient indication to Bodin, arguing in terms of Order, that to have more than one ruler is to «violate nature». He follows up this statement by the usual historical illustrations indicating the efficacy of rule by one man.[34] The justice of monarchy, that is, is proved by Order, its utility by history; royal power, he thinks, is natural because instituted by God, and expedient because sanctioned by experience.[35] The two arguments are complementary, but quite distinct. At the same time, there is little doubt that, in terms of the basic presuppositions of Bodin's political views, the metaphysical themes must be seen as more fundamental than the historical data.

The policy of the prince, too, should, like that of God in nature, be moderate and slow.[36] If a ruler wishes to put a policy into effect, with «an vnruly and headstrong people» he will best follow the example of the sun, which, although carried by the motion of the spheres, nonetheless performs «his own naturall course»; he will, that is, while following in part «the affections and desires of the troubled people, so much the more easily afterwards attaine vnto the full of his designes».[37] A prince will not use force to control a people if it is possible to avoid it, just as a physician does not use harsh measures when less severe cures will do.[38] Bodin

---

[33] *Meth.*, 271.

[34] *Meth.*, 271–277.

[35] *Meth.*, 282. For his approval of hereditary rather than elective monarchy, see 282–286.

[36] «We ought then in the gouernment of a well ordered estate and Common-weale to imitat and follow the great God of nature, who in all things proceedeth easily and by little and little, who of a little seed causeth to grow a tree for height and greatnesse right admirable, and yet for all that insensibly; and still by meanes conioyning the extremities of nature, as by putting the Spring be-twixt Winter and Sommer, and Autume betwixt Sommer and Winter, moderat-ing the extremities of the times and seasons, which the selfe same wisedome which he vseth in all other things also, and that in such sort, as that no violent force or course therein appeareth.» (KNOLLES, 475). Bodin also elicits this point by a common microcosm correspondence: «... to vse ... a violent letting of blood, before the corrupt humors purged or a strong medicine, before any pre-paratiue giuen, is not the way to cure ... diseases but to kill the diseased. Where-fore in the gouernments of Commonweales, and healing the diseases thereof, we must imitat not the Physitians onely, but euen nature it selfe, or rather the great God of nature whom we see to do all things by little and little, and almost insensibly.» (*Meth.*, 472).

[37] KNOLLES, 532.

[38] KNOLLES, 532.

illustrates the dangers inherent in social change, which is something a wise ruler will avoid if he can, by a body-body politic correspondence.[39] The prince must beware seditions and civil wars, which often begin from quite trivial matters, as in the natural world great storms and tempests «are caused of most light and insensible exhalations and vapours».[40]

In fact, if the prince does evil to none, sedition need not be feared for he will be loved by all, «which euen nature hath figured out vnto vs in the King of Bees, who neuer hath sting, least he should hurt any».[41] Nor, of course, does Bodin neglect to discuss the influence of the planets on the affairs of men, although he is somewhat sceptical of extreme claims.[42] All these are relatively minor matters; and while (as I have observed) Bodin does not point the virtues of monarchy so far as space is concerned so much from correspondences as from the lessons of historical experience, it is evident from these examples that he does not consider lightly the theoretical lessons of the natural world.[43]

[39] KNOLLES, 194–195.

[40] KNOLLES, 524.

[41] KNOLLES, 512. Such correspondences with the animal world were, of course, widely used by political writers during the early modern period.

[42] During the course of a long discussion in the *Republic* on the various causes of earthly events, human, natural, and divine (see Book IV, ch. II), Bodin goes into the question of stellar influences on the mutable sphere of earth. He thinks nothing certain can be said of this influence (KNOLLES, 438 ff.), but follows this with a lengthy astrological discursus on the date of the creation, the founding of Rome, the rise and fall of states, and the like. Thus, he discusses the influence on political events of the conjunction of the superior planets (KNOLLES, 448–450); and he thinks that a more detailed analysis of history and of eclipses would probably lead to a more precise understanding of the causes of political mutations (450). In the *Methodus,* the influence of the celestial bodies is one of the factors he analyses in his theory of climate. The southerners, for example, are under the influence of Saturn and Venus. The former stimulates the understanding, and so makes them of greater wit than the inhabitants of the two other regions; the influence of the latter gives them their propensity to sexual indulgence (*Meth.,* 111–112; cf. KNOLLES, 561–562). However, only the sensual man, he says, will be subject to the power of the heavens; the wise man may evade it (KNOLLES, 467). This he reaffirms in the *Methodus;* stating the belief that celestial influences are great, but may be overcome (*Meth.,* 86). In any case, no one, he thinks, has yet fully understood the nature of these influences (*Meth.,* 146–152). Argument of this kind only makes sense on the assumption of an inherent correspondence between different spheres of creation.

[43] KNOLLES for his part writes that some who are «better aduised than the rest» would give the sovereignty «vnto one most royall Monarch; which both by reason and experience being found the best, is not onely of the more ciuile nations, but euen of the most barbarous people of the world (taught as should seeme by the onely and mightie gouernour thereof) in their gouernments re-

There is, however, a more explicit use of two other orthodox correspondences – between the body politic on the one hand, and the microcosm
and the family on the other. Comparing the body of a man to the body
of the State, Bodin finds that the ends of comely Order are the same in
both [44] and issue in each case in the rule of Unity. As the members of the
one obey the head, so the people obey their sovereign,[45] who will be one
man, a prince, for: «If ... a commonweale be but one body, how is it
possible it should haue manie heads, but that it must produce a monster ...
a hideous monster with many heads.»[46]

Similarly, the family, which is none «other than the true image of a
state ... directed by the rule of one», must have «but one head, one maister,
and one Lord» if disturbance is to be avoided.[47] Bodin derives instruction
as to the proper form of government by comparing the command of the
head of the family to the rule of the sovereign of a state.[48] The father is
the «true picture of a king».[49]

The rule of one is in fact taught by all aspects of creation, for, in a
multiplane correspondence, Bodin argues that, although it is not necessary
to rest solely on this proof, a monarchy is obviously the best and most
natural form of government: «Seeing that a familie which is the true
image of a Commonweale can haue but one head, and that all the lawes
of nature guide vs vnto a Monarchie, whether that we behold this little
world which hath but one bodie, and but one head for all the members,
whereon depends the will, mouing and feeling: or if we looke to this
great world which hath but one soueraigne God: or if we erect our eyes
to heauen, we shall see but one sunne: and euen in sociable creatures, we
see they cannot admit many kings, nor many lords, how good so euer ...
We also see that all nations of the earth from all antiquitie, euen when
they were guided by natural interest, had no other forme of gouernement
than a Monarchie ...»[50]

---

ceiued.» (KNOLLES, «To the Reader», Sig. [Aiij] verso. Bodin uses the macrocosm-body politic correspondence again, when he says that the power of magistrates ceases in the presence of their prince, as streams lose their identity in the
sea, and stars in the light of the sun (KNOLLES, 344). Elsewhere he makes the
sun correspond to the human soul (7); the element of water to woman, and of
fire to man (460). See also *Le Theatre*, 589.

[44] KNOLLES, 7, where Bodin also deals with disorder by a microcosm-macro-
cosm correspondence between the soul and the sun.

[45] KNOLLES, 253.

[46] KNOLLES, 717.

[47] *Meth.*, 271; KNOLLES, 15.

[48] KNOLLES, 49–50.

[49] *Meth.*, 271; cf. 204.

[50] KNOLLES, 718.

As well, like Filmer afterwards, Bodin held that the right of fatherhood is the only natural source of power,[51] and naturally, therefore, he finds the origin of the state in the family and makes the family a model for the ideal commonwealth, it being, in fact, no more possible to separate the one from the other than to «pull the members from the bodie».[52] Certainly the absolute government of the family by the father's keeping each member in due Order corresponds to the sovereignty of the prince. This aspect of power has its parallel in the microcosm as well: «. . . as a familie well and wisely ordered, is the true image of a Citie, and the domesticall gouernment, in sort like vnto the soueraigntie in a Commonweale: so also is the manner of the gouernment of an house or familie, the true modell for the gouernment of a Commonweale. And as whilest euery particular member of the bodie doth his dutie, we liue in good and perfect health; so also where euery familie is kept in order, the whole citie shall be well and peaceably gouuerned.»[53]

This Order in society has its correspondence to the body and mind of man. The prince is a Unity which will suffer no division and is above all the other degrees of men. In this he is like the head of the body, and the understanding of the mind. This latter, «like vnto the vnitie in numbers indiusible, pure, and simple, is of it selfe free from all concretion, and from all the other faculties of the soule apart separated and diuided . . .»

Beneath the understanding and the prince are the other faculties of the soul and the main orders of society, each of which corresponds the one to the other. To the faculty of wisdom corresponds the ecclesiastical order of society, while «the angry power with desire of reuenge resting in the heart, representeth the souldiers and other martiall men: and sensuall lust and desire resting in the liuer . . . betokeneth the common people. And as from the liuer (the fountaine of blood) the other members are all nourished, so husbandmen, merchants, and artificers doe giue vnto the rest of the subiects nourishment».

Many societies, he admits, do not have a king. But these are like men without understanding. They exist, but they live like beasts «moued with that only which is present and before them, without mounting any higher vnto the contemplation of things intellectual and diuine . . .:

---

[51] KNOLLES, Book I, ch. IV, passim. This power extends not only to the children of the family, but to the wife and the whole family, including slaves (Book I, chs. III and V). Earlier, Bodin had described the power of the husband over the wife as deriving not only from superior physical strength, but from the nature of their relationship, which corresponds to that in which the soul has a superior power over the body and the reason over the passions (KNOLLES, 15).

[52] KNOLLES, 8.

[53] KNOLLES, 8.

euen so also the Aristocratique and popular Commonweales without
vnderstanding, that is to say, without a prince, are in some sort able to
maintaine and defend themselues, though not long . . .»

Societies so governed would live in much more harmonious Order, and
much more contentedly if they had a prince to rule them, a prince who,
«with his authoritie and power might (as doth the vnderstanding) reconcile all the parts, and so vnite and bind them fast in happinesse together:
for why no gouernment is more happie or blessed, than where the reasonable soule of man is gouerned by wisedome, anger and desire of reuenge
by true valour, lust by temperance; and that vnderstanding bearing the
rule, and as it were holding the reines, guideth the chariot, whereafter all
the rest follow whether sœuer he will lead them . . .»

Only thus, by the rule of the understanding in the mind, and by the
rule of a prince in the body politic can good Order be maintained and
all «honestie, all the lustre of vertue and dutie . . . euery where flourish.»
Therefore, concludes this lengthy correspondence, «nothing is more like
vnto a well gouerned Commonweale, than that most faire and fit comparison of the soule and the powers thereof, there being therein so established a most Harmonicall proportion of iustice, which giueth to euerie
part of the soule that which vnto it of right belongeth. The like whereof
we may say also of the three estates of a Commonweale, guided by Wisdome, Fortitude, and Temperance: which [three] morall vertues vnited
together, and with their king that is to say, the intellectual and contem-
platiue vertue, there is thereby established a most faire and Harmonicall
forme of a Commonweale.»

From this he is able to draw the main point quite explicitly: «For that
as of vnitie dependeth the vnion of all numbers, which haue no power
but from it: so also is one soueraigne prince in euery Commonweale
necessarie, from the power of whome all others orderly depend.»[54]

There are implied in all these correspondences, then, the ideas of
absolute monarchy as the best and most natural form of government, the
stratification of society, and the maintenance of Order by a harmonious
union of the different degrees and estates of the body politic. One point
remains: that of disorder and rebellion. Bodin mentions it in the course
of equating rebellion against the prince in the state with the overthrow
of reason by the passion in the mind: «. . . when the power and command
of vnderstanding beaten downe and quite ouerthrowne, anger as a muti-
nous and vnruly souldier, and intemperat lust, as a turbulent and seditious people, shall take vpon them the gouernment, and so inuading the
state, shake wisedome and vnderstanding, and thrust it out of place:
euery Commonweale must needs euen like the powers of the soule and

---

[54] This and the preceeding quotations are at KNOLLES, 791.

mind needs so fall into all manner of reproch and filthinesse of vices.»[55]

Disorder in the state, therefore, can be caused by members of one degree, whether noble or common, trying to rise above their station. A man of base degree «suddenly mounted vnto the highest degree of honour» thinks that he is a god on earth, and nothing is more «intollerable».[56]

Disorder can be caused similarly by those who subvert degree in the name of an equality that is, in fact, neither founded in nature nor possible of achievement in practice. Where every man would be a lord, there can be no accord at all.[57] The attempt, therefore, to attain a parity of all citizens is totally inexpedient and wrong: «. . . they which goe about to make all subiects or Citisens equall one vnto another in dignitie, order, and place, as that there shall be nothing in a Citie or Commonweale first, or in the middest, but will haue all degrees so mingled together and confounded . . . seeme to mee to do as they doe which thrust barly, wheat, rise, mill, and all other kind of pulse into one heape together; whereby they loose the vse of euerie kind of graine in particular, as also of the whole heape together. Wherefore there was neuer any lawgiuer, so vnskilfull, but that he thought that there ought still to bee some diuision, ordering and sorting of the Citisens or subiects in a citie, or Commonweale.»[58]

Another cause of disorder in a kingdom would be its division. A monarchy must not be divided, «the inuiolat nature of vnitie being such, as that it can abide no partition» without disorder.[59]

But one of the greatest causes of disorder in the body politic is dissension among the magistrates. Wise men have always thought that a well-ordered state ought to resemble a man's body, «wherein all the members are conioyned with a marvellous bond, euerie one of them doing their office and duty; and yet neuerthelesse when need is, one of them still aideth another, one of them releeueth another; and so all together strengthen themselues to maintaine the health, beautie, and welfare of the whole bodie . . .»

This is what ought to be the case. But what if the members do not so exist in concord, what if «it should happen them to enter into hatred of them one against another; and that the one hand should cut the other,

---

[55] KNOLLES, 791.
[56] KNOLLES, 725, cf. p. 481.
[57] KNOLLES, 571, 707–708, 725.
[58] KNOLLES, 387.
[59] KNOLLES, 741. This is the theme of «Gorboduc» and «King Lear» and was employed by many royalist writers.

or the right foot supplant the left, and that the fingers should scrape out the eyes, and so euerie member should draw vnto it selfe the nourishment of the other next vnto it; it must needs fall out, that the bodie in the end must become maimed, lame, and impotent, in all the actions thereof . . .»

The same applies to the body politic, the honour and welfare of which depends on «the mutuall loue and good will of the subiects among themselues, as also toward their soueraigne prince.» Now, this necessary «sweet vnitie and agreement» is not to be hoped for if the magistrates are «at variance and discord among themselues», for they are the most important of subjects and ought to bind the rest together by their example. If disorder exists in their ranks, it will lead to factions in society at large, and so at least to the sore troubling of the state and the hindrance of public actions, or at most to open enmity, civil discord, and, perhaps, even the destruction of the state. To sum up the matter, «most certaine it is, that dissentions and ciuill warres (the capitall plagues of Commonweales) take foot, root, encrease, and nourishment, of nothing more than of hatred and enmitie of the magistrats among themselues. Whereof it followeth the vnitie and concord of them among [themselves] to be vnto the subiects not only profitable, but euen necessarie also».[60]

Any such disorders and seditions are as dangerous and pernicious to all estates and commonwealths as vices and diseases are hurtful to the body and soul.[61] And Bodin warns princes that a tyrannical expropriation of the goods their subjects will procure a seditious populace and lead to their own ruin and decay of the whole state, for, in the terms of the usual correspondence, it is impossible «that spleene should fill it selfe, or that the ouergrowing of corrupt proud fleshe should fatten it selfe, but that the other members must drie, and so the whole bodie shortly after perish and consume also».[62] Nevertheless, it is not conformable to Order that every citizen should be a judge of this matter. Give every man a right to call his prince a tyrant and then what Order will be possible in a state?[63] The prince must be supreme and his sovereignty absolute.

---

[60] This and the preceeding quotations are at KNOLLES, 493–494. One short passage recalls Ulysses' speech in «Troilus and Cressida»: «. . . what good successe may a man expect of an armie, or what victorie is to bee hoped for ouer the enemie, where the captaines and commaunders are at discord among themselves» (KNOLLES, 494).

[61] KNOLLES, 519 – except insofar as, he adds, they act as purgatives, removing civil and corrupt humours and causing the banishment or death of wicked men (ibid.).

[62] KNOLLES, 520.

[63] KNOLLES, 225.

Bodin is, then, clearly enough concerned with the well-ordered state and its maintenance, and the avoidance of the disease of the body politic. He presents a view of Order and a series of correspondences which together provide a sufficient basis for the royalist development of the political theory of Order in all its aspects. That he prefers largely to develop his variation on the theme of the virtues of monarchy in terms of other forms of evidence is not to say he rejects the idea of Order. It is clear, he did not. His use of this theme, even to a relatively small extent in terms of the space he devoted to it, and the nature of his conclusions, obviously contradict this idea. All that he did was to prefer another procedure, to use the fashionable and persuasive method of supporting his proposition by reference to historical example. The political theory of Order is there in Bodin's thought, indeed is basic to it; but in the presentation of his political ideas it is overwhelmed – though only apparently – by a vast mass of erudition drawn from other sources. Nor is the distinction between the two sorts of evidence so great as might at first sight appear.[64]

---

[64] Thus, so far as his development of the idea of sovereignty is concerned, the Roman law *imperium* on the legal plane, and the idea of Order on the philosophical plane, probably gave him his basic insight. The very detailed «marks» of sovereignty, which he discusses, could only have been derived from historical sources and political practice.

Margherita Isnardi Parente

Le Volontarisme de Jean Bodin: Maïmonide ou Duns Scot?

I

Si, pour rechercher une définition précise de la conception bodinienne de l'ordre de l'univers, on se proposait de s'en tenir avec fidélité aux distinctions que Bodin lui-même a tracées dans sa *République*,[1] on pourrait dire tout d'abord que nous ne trouvons pas, chez Bodin, une conception du *droit* naturel, mais une conception de la *loi* naturelle: «il y a bien une différence entre le droit et la loy: l'un n'emporte rien que l'équité, la loy emporte commandement: car la loy n'est autre chose que le commandement du souverain, usant de sa puissance.»

La loi naturelle n'est en effet, pour Bodin, qu'une autre sorte de loi positive, établie au dessus de la loi positive du souverain de l'état. C'est une ordonnance qu'on peut trouver écrite dans les livres sacrés aussi bien qu'imprimée dans le rythme de la nature, l'ordonnance d'un roi absolument souverain qui peut changer ses lois ‹à son plaisir›. On connait bien la comparaison que Bodin trace souvent entre la *Torah* et la loi des XII tables, et, conséquemment, entre les livres rabbiniques, la *Mishnah* et le *Talmud*, et le *Digeste* («les Pandectes des Hébreux», c'est sa façon la plus habituelle de citer les livres rabbiniques). Comme toute loi positive, cette loi donnée par Dieu à la nature ne consiste pas en un ordre raisonnable, relativement indépendant de la volonté du legislateur, ou tel qu'il pourrait subsister (rappelons Grotius) «etsi daremus non esse Deum»; c'est, au contraire, un commandement qui a sa seule source et sa seule raison d'être dans la volonté du seigneur souverain de la nature. Il faut rappeler ici non seulement certaines pages de la *République* dans lesquelles on indique la limite du pouvoir du prince dans la reconnaissance de sa propre dépendance d'un pouvoir supérieur et suprême; mais aussi et surtout celles où les relations entre Dieu et l'univers sont evidemment modélées sur les relations entre le souverain et l'état. Qu'on regarde, par exemple, ce passage de l'*Universae Naturae Theatrum* où Dieu est censé être libre par rapport à la loi sans besoin d'aucune autorisation du sénat et du peuple: «at mundi princeps opti. max. non a senatu aut populo, sed a se ipso

---

[1] *Les Six Livres de la République* [7.11], Paris (Du Puys) 1583, 155.

legibus naturae, quas finxit ac iussit, semper solutus erit.»[2] Ici le parallèle
entre Dieu et le prince ne pourrait être tracé plus ouvertement: on pense
tout de suite à Auguste et à cet acte du sénat et du peuple dont nous parle
Dion Cassius, acte dans lequel Bodin croyait pouvoir reconnaître la ‹lex
regia› d'Ulpien.[3] Qu'on regarde, aussi, cet autre passage où, étant donné
que la condition du souverain est celle du ‹superiorem non recognoscens›,
on emploie pour définir la condition de souveraineté de Dieu les mêmes
argumentations de goût juridique: «si coacta, non est voluntas, sed a
superiore, aut ab aequabili, aut ab inferiore, aut a se ipsa cogi oportet:
non a superiore, quia principio nihil prius, supremo nihil superior, etc.»[4]

Plusieurs fois, dans le cours de son œuvre, Bodin revient sur le problème
de la liberté absolue de la volonté divine et sur l'essence éminemment
volontaire de la loi imposée par Dieu à la nature. On peut remarquer tout
de suite que, dans les différents ouvrages, d'autres problèmes et d'autres
argumentations théoriques s'ajoutent à celui qui est le problème fondamental. Ainsi, dans la *Methodus ad facilem historiarum cognitionem* et
dans le *Universae Naturae Theatrum* la question est directement liée à
celle de la genèse de l'univers et à la réfutation de la théorie de l'éternité
de celui-là; tandis que dans la *Démonomanie des sorciers* et dans le *Colloquium Heptaplomeres* on trouve le même problème traité à côté de l'affirmation de l'existence du merveilleux dans le domaine de la nature et de
la réfutation de toute immobilité et constance dans les ›lois naturelles‹.
Mais surtout, puisque Bodin retient de sa formation humaniste l'habitude
constante de s'appuyer sur des autorités et de les citer toujours avec com-
plaisance et avec ampleur, on peut remarquer dans les différents développements de ses théories une sorte de déplacement, pour ainsi dire, dans le
choix des sources. Si dans la *Methodus* le volontarisme de Jean Bodin
semple reposer sur la tradition patristique, sur la philosophie juive du
Moyen Age représentée surtout par Maïmonide, sur le platonisme de la
Renaissance, au contraire dans le *Universae Naturae Theatrum* le panorama des autorités est devenu en forte mesure scolastique, au même
temps que l'allure de la démonstration et de l'argumentation se revèle,
bien plus sensiblement que dans l'ouvrage de sa jeunesse, empruntée aux
méthodes scolastiques.

---

[2] *Universae Naturae Theatrum*, Lyon, Roussin 1596, 40 [13.1]; *Hepta-
plomers Colloquium de rerum sublimium arcanis abditis*, ed. Noack, Schwerin
(Mecklenburg) 1857, 22 [16.2].

[3] Cf. Dion Cassius, *Hist.* LIII, 28, 2; Ulpien dans *Dig.* I, 4 (de const. princ.),
1. Pour la question, je renvoie à mon commentaire à la traduction italienne des
deux premiers livres de la *République*: J. Bodin, *I Sei Libri dello Stato*, I, Torino
1964, 375 n. 58 [7.63].

[4] *Naturae Theatrum* [13.1], 34. Voir encore l'Introduction à la traduction
italienne cité, 31 et suiv., pour un traitement de cette question.

On va tacher de repondre à la question de savoir si ce changement est capable d'apporter à la pensée bodinienne une nouveauté substantielle, et si la marque du volontarisme des derniers ouvrages de Bodin peut vraiment se dire scolastique et scotiste; car c'est Duns Scot l'auteur qui detient, parmi les citations de cette période, la place la plus large. Dans la critique récente, on a souligné déjà quelques fois, mais assez en passant, ces sympathies scotistes des derniers ans d'activité de Bodin;[5] ça vaut peut-être la peine d'aller un peu au fond de la question.

Or, nous voyons avant tout que les argumentations spécifiques qui sont apportées par Bodin à soutien de la théorie de la liberté absolue de la volonté divine et du gouvernement absolu de Dieu sur la nature ne varient pas sensiblement dans les différents contextes. On se trouve toujours devant une polémique antiaristotelicienne très poussée: Aristote est présenté, soit dans la *Methodus* soit dans la *Démonomanie*, et encore dans le *Theatrum Naturae* et dans le *Heptaplomeres*, comme le porte-parole du nécessitarisme philosophique et théologique. On peut dégager de cette polémique deux différentes attaques: a) Aristote a conçu le rapport entre Dieu et le monde d'une façon naturaliste, d'une façon tout à fait semblable au rapport qui existe entre une cause physique et son effet, le feu et la chaleur, le soleil et la lumière; en faisant le monde coéternel à Dieu, il a montré qu'il concevait ce rapport d'un point de vue déterministe, comme l'action necessaire qui existe entre deux corps. b) Aristote, en affirmant que l'action de Dieu est dirigée par la necessité, a nié à Dieu toute liberté et l'a soumis à une loi servile, tandis qu'il a pourtant bien reconnu la liberté de la volonté dans l'être humain, en refusant ainsi à Dieu ce qu'il a concedé à l'homme, ce qui est au même temps une impiété et une absurdité manifeste. Bodin souligne à plusieurs reprises, contre Aristote, qu'il faut reconnaître la liberté absolue de la puissance et de l'action divine, ce qui implique en premier lieu le caractère temporaire de l'univers, sa dépendance totale de Dieu et la possibilité, de la part de Dieu, de l'annihiler à sa discrétion; en deuxième lieu, la présence du mystérieux, de l'extraordinaire, de l'inexplicable dans le domaine de la nature, qui est reglée par des lois auxquelles Dieu n'est pas tenu, qu'il peut, ainsi que tout prince souverain, suspendre ou changer ‹car tel est son plaisir›.

La première de ces deux argumentations apparait dans la *Methodus*: «sic enim Aristoteles philosophatur de mundo ac Deo, ut de calore et igne, de sole ac luce» etc.,[6] et revient dans le *Naturae Theatrum* et dans le

---

[5] Cf. P. Mesnard, Le platonisme de Jean Bodin, Congrès de Tours et Poitiers, Paris 1954 [185]; T. W. Tentler, The Meaning of Prudence in Bodin, *Traditio* 15 (1959), 365–384 [203].

[6] *Methodus ad facilem historiarum cognitionem*, ed. P. Mesnard d'après l'édition de 1572, Paris 1951, 232 B [4.22].

Heptaplomeres.[7] Dans le *Naturae Theatrum* on trouve un développement plus large de la question spécifique du rapport entre la cause infinie et l'effet fini: mais les termes de la question sont substantiellement partout les mêmes. Entre ce passage de la *Methodus* qu'on a cité et ceux correspondants des deux écrits de la vieillesse, il y a une différence, qui ne modifie pourtant pas l'aspect théorique de la question: dans la *Methodus* on accuse ensemble ‹Aristoteles et Abenreis› d'avoir conçu Dieu comme premier moteur des cieux, en lui attribuant ainsi le rôle d'un agent naturel, et on loue Avicenne pour avoir refusé cette conception et pour avoir rendu à l'Être divin sa spiritualité, en éloignant Dieu du ciel physique, tandis que dans le *Naturae Theatrum* et dans le *Heptaplomeres* Averroès a pris la place d'Avicenne: «hoc quidem Averroi tam ineptum et incongruum visum est, ut ab Aristotelis sententia discesserit, et primam causam... segregaverit a coeli motione.»[8] À remarquer aussi le curieux échange chronologique entre les deux philosophes arabes: la phrase «quae secutus est Avicennas»[9] ne semble admettre que cette interprétation.

Quant à l'autre argumentation antiaristotelicienne, celle fondée sur la théorie du libre arbitre, on peut voir encore la *Methodus*: «ut homini quidem arbitrium dare omni necessitate solutum, Deum vero ac naturam necessitate obligaret» etc.,[10] ainsi que le *Naturae Theatrum* et le *Heptaplomeres*.[11] Il n'existe aucune différence entre les trois textes si ce n'est qu'une variation dans les citations des textes aristotéliciens: dans la *Methodus,* Bodin croit pouvoir mieux lire le théorie du libre arbitre dans le *De interpretatione,* qui est substitué par le livre III du *De anima* et le livre II de la *Métaphysique* dans le *Naturae Theatrum,* par le livre IV de la *Métaphysique* dans le *Heptaplomeres.*

Dans la *Methodus,* ainsi qu'on l'a déjà dit, le problème de l'éternité du monde acquiert une importance particulière; et c'est bien naturel, du moment que Bodin se propose en cet ouvrage de tracer un tableau de la *universa historia.* Dans l'histoire des disputes philosophiques sur la genèse du monde et sa fin, il donne à Platon une place particulière: Platon a compris le premier que la conservation du monde repose dans la libre volonté de son créateur. Mais Platon s'est trompé lui aussi en supposant que le monde n'est pas destiné par Dieu à la destruction finale, et il a entrainé dans son erreur nombre de philosophes: Panétius, Posidonius, Boèce, Senèque, Philon, au Moyen Age, «inter theologos», aussi Thomas d'Aquin.[12] Bodin soutient qu'il faut progresser au delà de cette position,

---

[7] *Naturae Theatrum* [13.1], 33 et suiv.; *Heptaplomeres* [16.2], 23 et suiv.

[8] *Naturae Theatrum* [13.1], 33.

[9] *Naturae Theatrum* [13.1], 34.

[10] *Methodus,* 229 B.

[11] *Naturae Theatrum* [13.1] 31 et suiv.; *Heptaplomeres* [16.2], 20.

[12] *Methodus,* 232 A.

et reconnaître le caractère tout à fait périssable du monde: il donne à ce sujet dans la *Methodus* l'esquisse d'une argumentation philosophique qu'il conduira après plus longuement dans le *Naturae Theatrum*. La *creatio ex nihilo* du monde et sa *reductio ad nihilum* trouvent leur explication dans la necessité de supposer une cause efficiente pour toute la réalité dans son ensemble et particulièrement pour la forme des choses sensibles: la forme ne peut pas être engendrée par la matière, ni s'engendrer par elle-même: il faut donc admettre qu'elle soit engendrée du déhors, par l'action d'un artisan supérieur.[13] Dans le *Naturae Theatrum*, on voit ce thème développé avec prolixité: on démonstre la necessité de présupposer à toute forme la matière première, pas encore ordonnée, et Dieu à cette matière;[14] ce qui n'ajoute d'ailleurs rien de véritablement nouveau, si ce n'est qu'une série de subtilités de goût scolastique et de genre assez commun à propos du rapport entre la matière et la forme, la puissance et l'acte (à remarquer aussi la forme de dialogue didascalique de l'ouvrage, qui consiste en une série de reponses données par le savant Mystagogos aux questions du disciple Theoros; Bodin suit, en cela aussi, des exemples philosophiques du Moyen Age, ainsi qu'il fera analoguement dans le *Heptaplomeres*).

Pour sa démonstration de la destruction finale de l'univers, on pourrait dire que Bodin n'a pas su trouver d'efficaces soutiens en déhors de la considération très générale que ce qui a été produit du rien doit retourner au rien, et que la réalité sensible est de sa même nature périssable; dans le *Heptaplomeres*, où les sources bibliques acquièrent, soit dans la bouche du savant Toralba soit dans celle de l'interlocuteur juif Salomon, une importance particulière, on s'appuiera surtout sur la ‹voix de Dieu›: «amicus tamen Plato, amicus Philo, sed magis amica Dei vox».[15]

Le merveilleux joue un rôle très important, ainsi qu'on peut facilement supposer, dans la *Démonomanie des sorciers*. Ici Bodin affirme, dès la *Préface*, qu'il ne faut pas se donner la peine de chercher une raison aux événements là où il n'y en a aucune;[16] et il croit de pouvoir arracher à Aristote lui-même, en citant le livre IV et VII de la *Métaphysique*, une sorte de reconnaissance du fait que c'est impossible de vouloir donner une explication de tout ce qui arrive dans l'univers. Malgré cela, la polémique contre Aristote est dans la *Démonomanie* très violente: on accuse Aristote de ne rien avoir compris dans la réalité naturelle en supposant un univers reglé par des lois qui n'admettent pas de changement; on affirme que c'est pure impiété que de croire que les *monstra* se vérifient seulement à cause du défaut de la matière et non par la volonté mystérieuse du seigneur de

---

[13] *Meth.*, 230 B.
[14] *Naturae Theatrum* [13.1], 62 et suiv.
[15] *Heptaplomeres*, 26. [16.2].
[16] *Démonomanie des sorciers* [10.1], Paris (Du Puys) 1580, Prèface, 6 (n. num.).

la nature.[17] Dieu dispose de la nature à sa discrétion: les comètes aussi ce sont des signes évidents de sa colère;[18] on voit le merveilleux de l'action divine dans le fait même que les eaux se tiennent à leur place sans envahir les terres, ainsi qu'il a été commandé par Dieu, selon le *Liber Genesis*.[19] La thèse de la volonté divine et du caractère arbitraire de sa puissance est ici bien plus poussée que dans la *Methodus*. Il faut rappeler, et ça n'est pas sans importance, que c'est à un autre aspect du merveilleux que la *Methodus* fait confiance: aux découvertes, au progrès technique, aux merveilles qui se vérifient dans l'action de l'homme; cette page du chapitre VII de la *Methodus* qui fait pressentir déjà les thèmes de la querelle, où l'on exalte la superiorité des modernes sur les anciens, est témoignage d'un esprit que Bodin ne va jamais plus retrouver dans son œuvre ultérieure.[20] Le merveilleux qui est au centre du développement philosophique dans la *Démonomanie* et qui va jouer un rôle très important dans le *Heptaplomeres* se revèle, dans le cours de l'exposition, confié surtout à l'action des puissances intermédiaires, anges ou démons; dans le *Heptaplomeres* on trouve aussi une large comparaison entre les ministres de la volonté du prince, magistrats et officiers, avec les ministres de la volonté du Tout-puissant, ce qui revèle une fois de plus le fond pragmatique de la conception bodinienne du divin.[21] Ici, dans le *Colloquium*, là où Toralba et Salomon réfutent les argumentations d'Aristote en reduisant au silence l'interlocuteur Senamus qui soutient une conception nécessitariste, on trouve aussi les mots les plus incisifs pour souligner la toute-puissance divine: «hominum ac belluarum impetus cœrcere, naturas exanimes regere, ignes quominus ardeant prohibere, rerum universitatem nutu quatere ac rursus erigere, si velit, possit.»[22] L'univers est le royaume du miracle.

II

Après tout ça, on peut aborder le problème des sources. Qui, pour un auteur tel que Bodin, est d'une importance remarquable.

Les thèmes de la polémique antiaristotélicienne, dans la *Methodus* ainsi qu'ailleurs, sont clairement inspirés à la polémique médiévale contre une image d'Aristote empruntée à la tradition arabe, de Alfarabi à Averroès.

---

[17] *Dém.*, fol. 48v.

[18] *Dém.*, fol. 49r.

[19] *Dém.*, fol. 49r.

[20] *Methodus*, 227–228. Cf. là-dessus P. Rossi, I filosofi e le macchine, Milano 1962, 79 et suiv.

[21] *Heptaplomeres*, 23 et suiv., 34 et suiv., 50 et suiv.

[22] *Heptapl.*, 19.

On y avertit plutôt l'influence de la philosophie juive que celle de la philosophie chrétienne. Bodin peut sans doute puiser aux sources patristiques son interprétation de la necessité comme contrainte, ‹servile officium› ou ‹violenta necessitas›, pour s'en tenir aux expressions qu'il employera dans le *Heptaplomeres*: cet équivoque d'interprétation est déjà bien présent dans la philosophie des pères; il suffit de penser à Saint Augustin (cet Augustin que Bodin mentionne plusieurs fois dans la *Methodus*, comme l'autorité la plus haute parmi ceux qui ont soutenu la thèse de l'existence du monde dans le temps), à ces pages, par exemple, de l'*Enarratio in Psalmum* CXXXIV[23] où l'on trouve tracée l'opposition entre la ‹necessitas›, qui ‹cogit facere›, et la ‹bonitas› ou la ‹voluntas› qui a présidé à l'œuvre de la création. Mais la source de la polémique antiaristotélicienne dans la *Methodus* est surtout dans Maïmonide: c'est à cet auteur en premier lieu – et ce n'est pas par hazard qu'on le trouve si souvent cité – que Bodin emprunte ici les argumentations de sa polémique contre le nécessitarisme d'Aristote. Le nom de Maïmonide ne cesse de revenir dans la *Démonomanie* et dans le *Naturae Theatrum*; il faudra pourtant descendre jusqu'au *Heptaplomeres* pour le retrouver mis particulièrement en relief.

Cependant, l'intention polémique de Bodin semble dépasser en intensité celle de sa source, dont il est porté à en accentuer l'antiaristotélisme. Par exemple, lorsque Bodin affirme que Maïmonide a reconnu et souligné le manque de valeur scientifique et démonstratif des argumentations d'Aristote dans le *De caelo*,[24] il force véritablement la pensée de son auteur: Maïmonide en réalité affirme simplement qu'Aristote n'a point voulu donner, dans le *De caelo*, une démonstration de l'éternité du monde, ce qu'il eût pu et su bien faire si cela eût été son intention, mais qu'il n'a présenté que des opinions probables, et qu'Alfarabi et d'autres interprètes ont eu le tort de vouloir considérer ces opinions comme des démonstrations véritables.[25] Ainsi, lorsque Bodin remarque que ‹Moses Aegyptius› a accusé Aristote de contradiction pour avoir parlé d'une volonté divine et conçu au même temps cette volonté comme n'admettant que d'objets immuables,[26] il néglige d'ajouter que Maïmonide, dans le même lieu,[27] a tâché de pénétrer plus profondement dans la pensée d'Aristote, en remarquant que pour Aristote ôter à Dieu toute liberté, c'est à dire toute contingence, n'équivaut pas à le rendre impuissant, mais, au contraire, c'est un effort pour lui donner la perfection de l'immobilité; il ne mentionne pas non plus que Maïmonide s'est aussi empressé d'ajouter que, s'il est

---

[23] *Enarratio in Psalmum* CXXXIV, 10 (P. L. Aug. IV, col. 1745).
[24] *Methodus*, 229 A.
[25] *Guide des égarés*, ed. MUNK, II, 28 et 121–126.
[26] *Methodus*, 229 B.
[27] *Guide* II, 112, 178 et suiv.

difficile de suivre Aristote dans tout ce qu'il dit à propos des regions au
dessus de la sphère de la lune, on doit pourtant le suivre dans ses théories à
propos des regions sublunaires, ce que Bodin ne serait pas disposé à reconnaître. Il faut encore rappeler que, si Maïmonide a plusieurs fois manifesté
l'intention d'opposer une conception volontariste de Dieu à la conception
nécessitariste d'Aristote, il s'est pourtant bien gardé de tomber dans une
interprétation tout à fait naturaliste de la philosophie aristotélicienne, et
qu'il a, au contraire, blâmé les interprètes qui (ainsi que fera plus tard
Bodin) ont cru de pouvoir concevoir le rapport entre le Dieu d'Aristote
et son univers comme le rapport entre le feu et la chaleur, le soleil et la
lumière.[28] On peut donc affirmer que, malgré l'importance de Maïmonide
pour l'antiaristotélisme bodinien et pour la formation de la théorie
bodinienne de la contingence de l'action divine, la philosophie un peu
grossière de notre auteur ne lui permet pas de suivre exactement la pensée
de Maïmonide dans toutes ses nuances.

On trouve souvent, dans le VIII chapitre de la *Methodus*, le rapprochement entre un auteur de l'antiquité, ou plus souvent encore de la patristique, et un auteur de la Renaissance: Plotin est cité avec Jean François
Pico de la Mirandola, Lactance avec Léon l'Hébreu. La *Methodus* nous
revèle un Bodin vivement engagé dans le debat culturel de son époque et
dans le dialogue avec ses contemporains: les pôles de son horizon philosophique d'humaniste se trouvent dans l'antiquité classique et le platonisme du XVᵉ et XVIᵉ siècle, sans qu'il trouve nécessaire de faire appel à
des autorités scolastiques – dans la philosophie du Moyen Age, ce sont les
deux traditions juive et arabe qui intéressent le savant formé au Collège
des Quatre Langues plutôt que la scolastique chrétienne. Or, la pensée de
la Renaissance et surtout le platonisme de la Renaissance ont déjà pour-
suivi les thèmes antiaristotéliciens chers à Bodin, en denonçant largement
le nécessitarisme d'Aristote; ainsi a fait Bessarion, mais trop faiblement,
selon Bodin, qui range le Cardinal entre ceux qui ont essayé d'accorder
Aristote avec Platon (cela, du moins, dans la *Methodus*;[29] mais il faut
remarquer que dans la *Démonomanie* il n'aura pas de difficulté à ranger
Bessarion parmi les ennemis d'Aristote);[30] ainsi a fait Léon l'Hébreu, qui
a su trouver des argumentations décisives pas seulement contre l'erreur
d'Aristote mais aussi contre celle, plus excusable, de Platon et de Philon.[31]
Et, encore dans la *Préface* de la *Démonomanie*, Bodin citera aussi en
l'approuvant, Cusan, dont il rappelle peut-être la condamnation du
nécessitarisme d'Aristote dans le *De Beryllo*, dans le *De venatione sapien-*

---

[28] *Guide* II, 166.
[29] *Methodus*, 231 A.
[30] *Démonomanie*, Préf., 7 (n. num.).
[31] *Methodus*, 234 A.

tiae.[32] En effet, parmi les auteurs de la Renaissance, celui dont il dépend de plus près, du moins dans la *Methodus*, c'est sans doute Léon l'Hébreu: de Léon vraisemblablement, il emprunte l'argumentation selon laquelle la coéternité du monde à Dieu impliquerait une dépendance nécessaire «come de la luce del sole»,[33] et peut-être aussi l'exposition de la doctrine de Dieu premier moteur des cieux dans la forme qu'elle a dans la *Methodus*, forme sur laquelle, on l'a vu, Bodin va revenir plus tard pour y modifier le rôle d'Averoès. Il faut remarquer encore une fois qu'aussi l'antiaristotélisme de Léon est plus modéré que celui de Bodin: sur ce dernier point, à propos de la théorie du premier moteur, Léon manifeste la tendance à considérer la théorie plutôt une mauvaise interprétation d'Averroès qu'une véritable faute métaphysique et théologique d'Aristote,[34] et l'on doit reconnaître qu'ici aussi la source a été utilisée et forcée par Bodin au même temps.

C'est dans la *Démonomanie* qu'on voit paraître le nom de Duns Scot, dès la *Préface*, entre ceux d'autres ‹ennemis d'Aristote›: «l'Escot, des plus subtils philosophes qui furent oncques.»[35] Mais c'est surtout dans le *Universae Naturae Theatrum* que, malgré la présence des citations de Maïmonide, des Arabes, de Léon l'Hébreu, de Marsile Ficin, les auteurs de la Scolastique semblent désormais l'emporter sur les autres sources. Parmi ces auteurs, Duns Scot occupe sans doute la première place: on dirait que Bodin a découvert, dans la Scolastique, son nouveau Maïmonide. Il ne connait évidemment de Duns que le *Scriptum Oxoniense in quattuor Sententiarum libros*, paru à Lyon en 1520 d'après une édition venitienne précédante. Il cite cet écrit très fréquemment, en lui accordant une place toute particulière parmi nombre d'autorités du Moyen Age scolastique dont certaines il est bien difficile de supposer qu'il ait connu par lecture directe (tel, par exemple, ce Godefroi de Fontaines cité par lui à côté d'Henri de Gand, et dont les *Quodlibeta* sont mentionnés par Scot lui-même; ce qui fait supposer que ce soit là la source des connaissances de Bodin au sujet de cet auteur).[36] Parmi ces nombreuses autorités, on pourrait s'y attendre de rencontrer le nom de Guillaume de Ockham; mais Bodin ne semble pas connaître la pensée de celui-là, qui eût été pourtant si importante pour lui et pour sa conception du caractère arbitraire de la volonté de l'être divin. D'autre part, dans la *Démonomanie*, on trouve

---

[32] *Opera*, Basileae 1557, 275 et 304.

[33] *Dialoghi d'amore*, ed. CARAMELLA, Bari 1929, 240.

[34] *Dialoghi*, 159 et suiv.

[35] *Démonomanie*, Préf., 8 (n. num.). On cite ici les argumentations de Duns Scot contre les contradictions du *De anima*.

[36] Cf. par exemple *Naturae Theatrum*, 42; citation sans doute de deuxième main.

une citation de Pierre d'Ailly[37] qui dépend si étroitement de la pensée ock-
hamiste, et qui a pu etre intermédiaire de celle-là, de quelque façon, à Bodin.

Pour évaluer la portée de l'influence de Duns Scot sur Bodin on peut
tâcher d'examiner de près quelques unes des citations les plus significatives. Par exemple, on voit Duns cité comme autorité pour la doctrine
selon laquelle, si la cause première agissait d'une façon necessaire, elle ne
produirait que des effets infinis, ce qui s'oppose au caractère fini du
monde dans son essence;[38] or, on trouve sans doute une argumentation
de la sorte chez Duns;[39] mais il faut remarquer que la même argumentation a été déjà avancée dans la *Methodus*,[40] et que l'autorité visée
dans cet ouvrage c'était Avicenne. On cite Duns Scot avec Grégoire le
Grand, Albert le Grand, Avicenne lui-même pour la doctrine de l'absolue
liberté de Dieu dans sa toute-puissance;[41] mais on a déjà vu la constance
de la pensée de Bodin, d'ouvrage en ouvrage, sur ce point. Si quelques
fois l'on oppose Scot à Aristote,[42] ou à Thomas d'Aquin,[43] on souligne
aussi certaines concordances avec Aristote: le même Scot n'a-t-il pas
affirmé que la matière ne peut subsister sans forme, ou que la forme est
toujours «simul cum subjecto»?[44] Ce que Bodin refuse, en traduisant la
question du rapport entre matière et forme en termes chronologiques:
il y a bien une matière qu'il faut concevoir comme existant ‹avant la
forme›, car elle est encore depourvue de forme, une matière originaire
crée sans forme qui va recevoir ses formes aussi par un acte de «creatio
ex nihilo‹. On blâme aussi. Duns Scot pour avoir tenté une justification de
la théorie aristotélicienne de la dépendance necessaire et éternelle du monde
de Dieu en reconduisant cette théorie à celle de la causalité efficiente;[45]
mais en cela Bodin pourrait dépendre non pas tant d'une impression
reçue par la lecture directe de Scot que de l'exposition faite par Bessarion
de l'interprétation scotiste d'Aristote.[46] On néglige ici les citations de
Duns Scot qui sont très nombreuses surtout dans le livre I à propos de
questions plus particulières; on souligne seulement, tout en passant, que,
si elles ne touchent pas le problème central de la métaphysique volontariste de Bodin, elles témoignent quand-même de l'intérêt très large porté
par Bodin à la doctrine scotiste dans son ensemble.

---

[37] *Démonomanie*, Préf., 7 (n. num.) [10.1].
[38] *Naturae Theatrum*, 33 [13.1].
[39] *In I Sententiarum*, Dist. 2, quaestio 3, Lugduni 1520, fol. 66v et suiv.
[40] *Methodus*, 232 B.
[41] *Naturae Theatrum*, 40.
[42] *Naturae Theatrum*, 105; à propos de la théorie du mouvement.
[43] *Naturae Theatrum*, 133; et aussi dans le livre IV, p. 466 et suiv.
[44] *Naturae Theatrum*, 73 et 87.
[45] *Naturae Theatrum*, 65.
[46] *In calumniatorem Platonis*, III, 21, ed. MOHLER, Paderborn 1927, 352.

Naturellement, on peut chercher l'influence de Duns Scot là aussi où la citation de son nom ne revient pas ouvertement. Par exemple, on trouve dans le *Naturae Theatrum* des formulations qu'on pourrait dire scotistes même s'il n'y a pas de référence directe à Duns: il y a sans doute une analogie frappante entre Bodin: «voluntas autem et natura duo sunt agendi principia, quorum alterum vi ac impetu naturae fertur, alterum nulla necessitate cogitur»[47] et Duns Scot: «necessitas naturalis non stat cum libertate... quia natura et voluntas sunt principia activa habentia oppositum modum principiandi.»[48] Bodin semble ici simplement traduire en latin humaniste le latin médiéval et scolastique de Scot. Mais on pourrait bien dire que la doctrine de Duns n'a donné à Bodin qu'une exactitude nouvelle dans la formulation philosophique de la théorie. Ce que Bodin accepte de Duns Scot, si l'on regarde de près, c'est seulement l'aspect le plus général de son volontarisme, ou, si l'on veut, l'exegèse que Scot accomplit, à la lumière de sa propre conception, de textes doctrinaires consacrés par la tradition patristique. Par exemple, dans ce texte du commentaire de Duns au II livre des *Sentences* dont il fait mention déjà dans la *Démonomanie*[49] et sur lequel il revient après dans le *Naturae Theatrum,* Bodin ne trouve pas seulement une réfutation de la *Physique* d'Aristote qu'il devait accepter avec empressement, comme une confirmation de remarquable poids de ses propres opinions, mais aussi une exegèse de certaines doctrines patristiques. Scot déclare dans ce passage de se référer à l'autorité de Saint Ambroise pour la distinction entre ‹agens naturale et liberum›, entre ‹contingenter et naturaliter agere›; à cet Ambroise qui a enseigné, dans son *De incarnatione Verbi,* que «si Deus naturaliter causaret, necessario causaret».[50] Et, si Bodin sait bien saisir d'emblée, dans la doctrine de Duns Scot – pour parler avec les mots d'Etienne Gilson[51] – ce «ressort secret» qui est «sa décision sans cesse réaffirmée d'interdire au monde d'émaner de l'entendement divin comme la conséquence d'un principe», il est cependant trop médiocre métaphysicien pour pouvoir progresser au delà des principes généraux de la doctrine scotiste et en pénétrer plus exactement la subtilité.

Le ‹scotisme› du dernier Bodin ne signifie donc un enrichissement véritable de sa pensée philosophique. Il est plutot le fruit et le résultat d'une changement d'attitude philosophique et culturelle. Le volontarisme de Jean Bodin, on l'a vu, est déjà complètement formé dans la *Methodus* dans son cadre général, même si certains thèmes vont s'accentuer dans

---

[47] *Naturae Theatrum*, 37.
[48] *In I Sententiarum*, Dist. 1, qu. 4, fol. 43r, col. b.
[49] *Démonomanie*, Préf., 8 (n. num.).
[50] *In II Sententiarum* Dist. 1, qu. 3. fol. 11 r–v.
[51] *La Philosophie au Moyen Age*, Paris ²1944, réimpr. 1952, 605.

le développement de son œuvre. Mais le Jean Bodin qui écrit à Laon, dans la déception de sa triste retraite dans la vie de province, après 1590, est bien loin du Bodin humaniste de l'Université de Toulouse, dont les pages de la Methodus gardent encore le souvenir très proche.

Rien à surprendre qu'il cherche maintenant des autorités scolastiques, qu'il ait appris à aimer l'allure didactique de la summa et les disputes sur la substance et les accidents, la matière et la forme; qu'il aime de soutenir ses opinions concernant la liberté divine par un étalage de pièces d'appui traditionnelles. Rien aussi à surprendre que, parmi ces autorités, ce soit la doctrine de Duns Scot à l'attirer comme l'expression la plus prochaine de sa croyance profonde dans la contingence de l'action de Dieu sur le monde.

III

Mais, dans les dernières années de sa vie, Bodin n'écrit pas seulement le *Universae Naturae Theatrum*; il écrit aussi, avec toute la liberté qui est propre d'un ouvrage qui n'est pas destiné à voir la lumière pendant la vie de son auteur, cet admirable *Colloquium Heptaplomeres*, si important pour la naissante théorie de la religion naturelle; une religion naturelle qui d'ailleurs n'est qu'une forme pure, libérée de superfétations cultuelles, de la religion juive. On peut donc, en conclusion de ces considérations, se demander quels sont les témoignages dont Bodin, ici dans le *Heptaplomeres,* aime à se servir.

Or, dans le *Heptaplomeres* les auteurs du Moyen Age chrétien, et Duns Scot parmi eux, sont sans doute présents: dans le livre II, où l'on traite de nouveau, ainsi que dans la *Methodus*, les auteurs de la tradition arabe apparait comme ‹acutissimus theologus›;[52] et pourtant on voit Toralba, le personnage principal du dialogue, réfuter son opinion à propos de l'impossibilité de démontrer l'infinitude de l'essence divine. Mais ce sont de nouveau, ainsi que dans la *Methodus*, les auteurs de la tradition arabe et juive à tenir la première place; et on voit qu'il servent quelque fois de canon d'interprétation et de mesure pour l'évaluation des auteurs chrétiens («thomistae ac averroistae» sont parfois unifiés dans la meme catégorie de jugement).[53] On a déjà plus haut fait mention de la portée du biblicisme dans le *Heptaplomeres;* on devrait écrire bien de pages pour exposer quelle est aussi dans cet ouvrage l'importance et la fréquence du recours aux textes de la tradition religieuse juive, des livres talmudiques, de la paraphrase araméenne de la Bible ou *Targum,* à travers laquelle on voit souvent lu et interprété l'Ancien Testament (à voir, par

---

[52] *Heptaplomeres,* 38.
[53] *Hept.,* 45.

exemple, l'interprétation à l'aide du *Targum* que Bodin a fait des psaumes 46 (47) et 67 (68) à fin d'y lire la théorie des anges officiers et magistrats de Dieu).[54] Ainsi, la citation d'après la Scolastique se revèle ici pour ce qu'elle est véritablement: un document de l'aspiration toujours poursuivie par Bodin, et plus vive au fur et à mesure que la véritable source d'inspiration se tarit en lui, à donner un panorama d'autorités culturelles totalement exhaustif, à se soutenir par l'apport le plus large des différentes traditions philosophiques et théologiques.

Le *Colloquium Heptaplomeres* est sans doute bien loin de l'esprit de la *Methodus*, de cette confiance dans le progrès de l'homme qui inspire certaines pages de l'ouvrage de la jeunesse de Bodin, et de cette vivacité de dialogue avec les contemporains qui caractérise son attitude culturelle en 1566 ou encore en 1572. Mais, si une chose relie cet ouvrage, en particulier parmi les autres, à la *Methodus*, c'est l'intéret très vif, gardé par Bodin à travers trente ans de vicissitudes, pour la tradition juive et aussi, si l'on pense à la richesse des citations qu'il en tire, à la tradition arabe: le réverence pour Maïmonide, l'intéret pour Avicenne ou Averroès ou Algazel, ce sont des liens très significatifs entre le début et la conclusion de l'activité de notre auteur. On pourrait se demander si Bodin, après les amères vicissitudes, les soupçons, les accusations, les dangers de ses dernières années, ne peut avoir jugé opportun de forcer un peu l'importance et l' extension des citations scolastiques dans l'ouvrage qu'il se proposait de rendre publique, ce *Naturae Theatrum* qui parut en effet le même an de sa mort. Serait-il la première fois que certaines circonstances extérieures de la vie incident sur le cours d'une activité philosophique? Dans ce cas, cette incidence ne serait certainement pas une trahison, mais une sorte de nicodémisme bien modéré.

---

[54] *Hept.*, 49–50.

Georg Roellenbleck

Der Schluß des «Heptaplomeres» und die Begründung der Toleranz bei Bodin

Bodins nachgelassenes Religionsgespräch, das *Colloquium Heptaplomeres de rerum sublimium arcanis abditis,* wahrscheinlich 1593 abgeschlossen,[1] gilt allgemein als eine der gründlichsten und radikalsten Programmschriften für religiöse Toleranz, die das 16. Jahrhundert hervorgebracht hat.[2] Der Rezeptionsgeschichte des bis ins 19. Jahrhundert hinein Manuskript gebliebenen Werks ist öfter dargestellt worden[3] und braucht uns hier nicht zu beschäftigen. Der Umfang der kritischen Literatur ist allerdings nicht bedeutend, vor allem in den letzten Jahrzehnten.[4]

[1] Pierre Mesnard, Vers un Portrait de J. B., in J. B., Œuvres philosophiques, texte établi, traduit et publié par P. M., t. I *(Corpus général des philosophes français, t. V, 3),* Paris 1951 [4.20], S. XX. – Eine kritische Ausgabe des ganzen Dialogs ist bisher nicht erschienen; immerhin liegt die Schweriner Edition von L. Noack (1857) [16.2] seit 1966 in einem Nachdruck (Stuttgart-Bad Cannstatt, Frommann–Holzboog) vor.

[2] «... the completest statement of a philosophy of religious toleration that was given in the sixteenth century», nennt es z. B. George H. Sabine, The «Colloquium Heptaplomeres» of J. B., in: Persecution and Liberty. Essays in Honour of George Lincoln Burr, New York 1931, 308 [114].

[3] Z. B. von Roger Chauviré in der Einleitung zu seiner kommentierten Teilausgabe einer zeitgenössischen französischen Übersetzung des Dialogs: Colloque de J. B. des secretz cachez des choses sublimes..., Paris 1914 [16.4].

[4] Die mir bekannten neueren Titel sind in dem Literaturverzeichnis meiner 1964 in Gütersloh erschienenen Dissertation: Offenbarung, Natur und jüdische Überlieferung bei J. B. Eine Interpretation des Heptaplomeres, zusammengestellt. Diese Liste ist durch folgende Titel zu ergänzen: Henry Hornik, J. B. and the Beginnings of Voltaire's Struggle for Religious Tolerance, *Modern Language Notes* 76 (1961), 362–375 [213] (ein Satz aus dem Hept. ist möglicherweise die Quelle für eine frühe Formulierung Voltaires, die ihrerseits nach der Meinung von Bestermann den Beginn seines Toleranzdenkens und damit den Ausgangspunkt seines späteren Kampfs gegen religiöse Intoleranz bezeichnet). F. A. Kogan-Bernstein, J. B. et sa critique du christianisme, *Annuaire d'Etudes françaises,* Moskau 1961 (1962), 2–35 [214] (russisch, ist mir nur in einer französischen Zusammenfassung zugänglich gewesen). – Pierre Mesnard, der unermüdliche Erforscher von Bodins Leben und Werk, hat leider keine Studie zu dem Religionsgespräch mehr vorlegen können.

Gegenstand der folgenden Seiten ist der Toleranzbegriff des *Hepta-plomeres* sowie die dort gegebene Motivierung der Forderung nach Duldung Andersgläubiger; schließlich, im Blick auf das übrige Oeuvre, die Frage nach ihrer Genese in Bodins Denken. Ein näheres Studium des Dialogs und der einschlägigen Arbeiten zeigt nämlich, daß gerade diese Motivierung nicht durchaus eindeutig ist. Die Zeitgenossen und spätere Kritiker in einer Zeit, der das Problem noch kontrovers war, sahen begreiflicherweise nur die Forderung selbst und ihre theologischen Implikationen, ohne sich bei der Erwägung aufzuhalten, ob die politische Erfahrung seiner Epoche dem Autor vielleicht Konsequenzen unausweichlich erscheinen lassen mußte, gegen die er mannigfaltige Vorbehalte gehabt und behalten haben mochte.[5]

Eine historische Betrachtungsweise kann sich dagegen den Luxus genaueren Sondierens leisten und hoffen, auf diese Weise nicht nur das Denken eines bedeutenden Mannes und die Entwicklung dieses Denkens besser zu verstehen, sondern darüber hinaus den Beitrag einer der großen philosophischen Strömungen Europas, des Humanismus, zur Ausbildung eines der Grundsätze moderner Weltanschauung schärfer zu erfassen.

Bei der Beurteilung dieser Frage gibt es im wesentlichen zwei Meinungen. Die eine sieht in der Toleranz-Empfehlung, wie sie der Schluß des Dialogs ausspricht, die letzte logische Konsequenz von Bodins Theorien über Mensch, Staat, Gott.[6] Die andere glaubt, daß diese Theorien eine solche Konsequenz an sich nicht zulassen, daß Bodin aber unter dem Eindruck der politischen Veränderungen im Verlauf der Bürgerkriege resigniert Positionen aufgegeben und die Lösung akzeptiert habe, welche

---

[5] Wenn BOCCALINI an einer bekannten Stelle der *Ragguagli di Parnaso* (Centuria prima, 1612, Ragg. LXIV) schon den Verfasser der «Six Livres de la Republique» als Atheisten verurteilt und verbrannt werden läßt, weil er die Freiheit des Gewissens fordere, so ist klar, daß das Religionsgespräch mit seinem schrankenlosen Freimut der Erörterung nicht publiziert werden konnte. Soweit es bekannt wurde, ist es deshalb zunächst auch ausnahmslos scharf verurteilt worden, vgl. etwa die Stimmen, die BAYLE in der Remarque O des Bodin-Artikels seines *Dict. Hist. et Crit.* gesammelt hat.

[6] Das ist etwa GUHRAUERS [23] Ansicht, die er in der Einleitung zu seiner Teilausgabe des Dialogs (Berlin 1841) vertritt; die Tendenz des Werks beschreibt er S. LX folgendermaßen: «Das Heptaplomeres entwickelt eine theoretische und praktische Tendenz, welche gegenseitig, die eine von der anderen, postuliert wird. Bodin strebt durch die, theoretisch nicht zum Schluß kommende, Dialektik der Religionen zu zeigen, daß alle geschichtlich bestehenden Religionen und Sekten − so fern sie gegen Staat und Sittlichkeit und Gottesfurcht nicht streiten − auch ihr inneres objektives Recht des Bestehens haben, wonach sie sich gegen alle anderen erhalten: und daraus folgt, daß alle Religionen auf Duldung im Staate Anspruch und Recht haben ...»

er als einzige für das Dilemma des in zwei konfessionelle Lager gespaltenen Staats geblieben sah.[7]
Um hier ein zutreffendes Bild zu gewinnen, muß zunächst der Schluß des Dialogs in Erinnerung gerufen und skizziert werden, ob er den Gang der Auseinandersetzung der sieben Freunde sinnvoll zu Ende führt. – Das sechste Gespräch hatte die konzentrierteste Kritik an der christlichen Theologie gebracht, zuletzt an Transsubstantiation, Sündenvergebung, Ewigkeit der Höllenstrafen, Fürbitten für Verstorbene. Wie immer kommt man in der Diskussion nicht weiter; es charakterisiert ja ihren Ablauf von Anfang an, daß Angreifer und Verteidiger nie um Argumente verlegen sind, daß aber keiner je nachgibt und sich, sei es im kleinsten Punkt, für besiegt oder überzeugt erklärt. Wie sich diese Situation also zum x-ten Mal wiederholt, lenkt Toralba den Blick des Kreises erneut auf seine Grundthese: wenn alle Religionen und Sekten einander nur bekämpfen, wäre es nicht besser, alle bekennten sich zu der natürlichen Religion, deren Prinzipien doch den Kern eines jeden Glaubens bildeten?[8] Aber sofort erhebt im Gefolge des von Salomo gebrachten Einwands, daß eine Religion ohne Riten keine Aussicht auf Verwurzelung in der Masse der Ungebildeten habe, der alte Partikularismus wieder sein Haupt, und jeder empfiehlt seine Form als die reinste (S. 352). Auch der Gedanke, man müsse nicht nur für die anderen, sondern auch für sich selbst um Erleuchtung über den rechten Weg beten, findet bei dem seines Glaubens gewissen Lutheraner Fridericus Widerspruch (S. 352 f).
Da ist Senamus an der Reihe: wenn die beste Form also ganz offenbar nicht auszumachen sei, sei es wohl das Vernünftigste, alle gleichermaßen gelten zu lassen und sich, was die Praxis anlange, der jeweils ortsüblichen anzupassen (S. 353 f). Allein dagegen meldet sich ein doppeltes Bedenken: die Frömmigkeit des Einzelnen werde bei einer solchen Haltung leiden; und dann sei es schwer, in einem Staat die Ordnung aufrecht zu erhalten, in dem die religiösen Leidenschaften ungehindert aufeinanderprallen können. Der Rat des Coronaeus, die konfessionelle Einheit des Staats also mit allen Mitteln, einschließlich dem der Gewalt, zu bewahren oder wiederherzustellen, wird jedoch einhellig abgelehnt (S. 354–358).
An dieser Stelle erinnert der Franzose Curtius die Freunde an das

---

[7] Vgl. etwa G. Radetti, Il problema della religione nel pensiero di J. B., *Giornale critico della filosofia italiana* 19 (1938) [139] (Toleranz bei B. kein Ziel an sich, vielmehr Mittel zur Befriedung des Staats). P. Mesnard spricht in Le Platonisme de J. B. [185], (360) von einem «désastre profond», von dem Zusammenbruch des B.schen Willens zur Synthese auf religiösem Gebiet. In meiner erwähnten Dissertation habe ich den Schluß des Dialogs ebenfalls als Ausdruck völliger Resignation interpretiert (147 ff.).

[8] S. 351 ff. Ich zitiere nach der Ausgabe von Noack [16.2]. Die Kenntnis der Personen und der großen Züge der Debatte setze ich hier voraus.

Henotikon des Jovian, das allgemeine Duldung verkündet hatte mit der
Auflage, sich der Agitation zu enthalten, nach der Weise der eigenen
Religion fromm zu leben, und allen anderen mit Liebe zu begegnen
(S. 358). Und auf diese Sätze hin folgt ganz persönlich der Schluß (ebd.): «Quae cum omnibus probarentur, Coronaeus jussit me pueros arcessere,
quibus obtulit canticum: Ecce, quam bonum et quam jucundum, cohabitare fratres in unum, non diatonicis vulgaribus aut chromaticis, sed enharmonicis rationibus, diviniori quadam modulatione compositum, quo
suavissime omnes delectati ac seipsos mutua caritate amplexati discesserunt.
Deinceps mirabili concordia pietatem ac vitae integritatem communibus
studiis ac convictu coluerunt, sed nullam postea de religionibus disputationem habuerunt, tametsi suam quisque religionem summa vitae sanctitate
tueretur.»

Der Dialog als ganzer zerfällt in zwei Teile, deren erster (die Bücher
I–III) sich mit naturphilosophischen Fragen befaßt; erst der zweite wendet sich der Erörterung der wahren Religion zu, die auch sein alleiniges
Thema bildet. Diese Frage ist am Ende der Lösung nicht näher als zu
Beginn; Einigkeit wurde nur über das rechte Verhalten in einer heillos
zerfallenen Gesellschaft erzielt.

Man muß natürlich untersuchen, ob der Dialog Momente aufweist, die
auf eine agnostische Position seines Verfassers hindeuten, und gegebenenfalls fragen, warum dieser sie dann am Ende der Gespräche nicht deutlicher herausgestellt hat. Man darf so fragen, denn es kann kein Zweifel
sein, daß von den sieben Teilnehmern Salomo und Toralba in den meisten
Fällen Meinungen vertreten, die sich mit denen Bodins in seinen anderen
Büchern decken.[9] Warum ließ er seiner Sicht des Problems nicht das
letzte Wort? Aus Resignation, aus der Redlichkeit heraus, keine Illusion
nähren zu wollen? Oder hatte sich seine Überzeugung gewandelt?

Eine Beantwortung dieser Frage verfehlt ihr Ziel, wenn sie die *Form*
nicht ernst nimmt, in die Bodin die neuerliche Erörterung einer von ihm
schon oft berührten, aber noch nie systematisch durchgearbeiteten Materie kleidet, nämlich den Dialog unter gleichberechtigten Partnern und
ohne einen Arbiter oder Deus ex Machina, der am Ende einer der konkurrierenden Ansichten zu allgemeiner Billigung verhülfe, und wenn
man nicht sorgfältig die kleinen Szenen und die Gespräche beachtet, die
die letzten drei Bücher eröffnen, sowie den Psalm, den der Hausherr
am Schluß des Ganzen vom Chor singen läßt.

Um mit letzterem Punkt zu beginnen, so fassen diese Szenen nicht nur
die drei Grundpositionen des Gesprächs zusammen und zeichnen in dramatischer Verkürzung den Ablauf des Ganzen nach: Die Einheit des

---

[9] Diesem Aufweis und damit dem der Einheit des B.schen Werks ist meine
Dissertation im wesentlichen gewidmet.

Kosmos erwächst aus einer Harmonie von Gegensätzen (IV) – es gibt
wahre und falsche Glaubensformen (V[10]) – was dem einen heilig ist, ist
dem anderen profan, die einzelnen Formen heben sich also gegenseitig
auf (VI, Gespräch über das freitägliche Fischmahl); vielmehr gibt die
endliche Rückkehr zum Thema der Harmonie (VI, Psalm) einer solchen
Sicht des Problems – mit der Konsequenz der Toleranz – deutlich den
Vorzug.

Noch gewichtiger scheint mir aber das Argument zu sein, welches
das Verhältnis der sieben Partner zueinander dem Betrachter an die
Hand gibt. Das wird besonders deutlich, wenn man an die Personen in
den beiden anderen (gleichfalls späten) Dialogen Bodins denkt. In beiden
nämlich, im *Universae naturae theatrum* wie im *Paradoxon*, haben
wir einen Schüler und einen Meister, einen Fragenden und einen Lehren-
den vor uns, und in den Antworten des Mystagogus und des Vaters
kommt die Bewegung des Suchens immer wieder wie selbstverständlich
zur Ruhe (auch wenn Mystagogus manche Lösung nur als Möglichkeit
vorschlägt). Im *Heptaplomeres* dagegen ist die Perspektive eine andere. Die Personen sind nicht sozusagen vertikal angeordnet, sondern
horizontal, und es gibt keinen archimedischen Punkt außerhalb der
Ebene, auf der sich die Debattierenden bewegen, von dem aus der Wider-
streit der Kräfte in Wahr und Falsch sich auflösen ließe.[11]

---

[10] Daß es sich bei der Einleitung zu Buch V nicht um eine einfache Parallele
zur Ringparabel handelt, wie öfter gesagt wurde, sondern um die – freilich in
einem ähnlichen Bild ausgedrückte – gegenteilige Aussage, habe ich in meiner
Dissertation ausgeführt (136 ff.).

[11] Es ist vielleicht kein Zufall, daß schon im Titel die Siebenzahl der Dialog-
partner als das dominierende Wort erscheint, anstatt, wie sonst wohl allgemein
üblich, von Namen von Gesprächspartnern oder einer Bezeichnung des Inhalts.
Das Wort *Heptaplomeres* scheint Bodin verwandten, aber andersartige Eintei-
lungen des Stoffs visierenden Titeln wie *Heptaplus*, *Heptameron* nachgebildet zu
haben (an eine Abhängigkeit von Pico denkt SABINE [114], 285. Picos Schrift
kombiniert ja gleichfalls Sechs- und Siebenzahl, und das bereits im Titel: «De
septiformi sex dierum geneseos ennarratione»). Das Bodinische Wort selbst ist
in den Wörterbüchern des Alt- und des Mittelgriechischen nicht nachgewiesen;
Sophokles (Greek Lexikon of the Roman and Byzantine Periods) kennt immerhin ἑπταμερής, «consisting of seven parts». – Daß in Bodins Gedankengebäude
die Zahlenspekulation einen wichtigen Platz hat, ist bekannt. Die Bedeutung
der *Sieben* als einer Zahl heiliger Fülle wird im IV. Buch des *Heptaplomeres*
eingehend behandelt (153 ff.). Die *Sechs* erscheint gleich zu Beginn des Dialogs
in der Beschreibung der «Pantothek» des Coronaeus (2 f.), jenes großen Schau-
kastens, in dem in 6 × 6 × 6 durch die 6 einfachen Farben unterschiedenen
Fächern alle Bestandteile des Universums vom Stern bis zu den niedersten
Pflanzen und den Elementen durch Exemplare vertreten bzw. abgebildet bzw.
beschrieben waren. Die Sechszahl hatte der Hausherr gewählt, «quod is nume-

Bedenkt man dies, wird man trotz der erwähnten Übereinstimmungen Bedenken tragen, den Autor mit einer oder zwei seiner Personen derart zu identifizieren, daß damit behauptet wird, seine «eigentliche» Meinung entspreche nicht der dogmatischen Offenheit des Endes.[12] Vielmehr wird man in dem Umgreifen einer Pluralität divergierender Sehweisen das Wesentliche von Bodins Position sehen. Es fragt sich nur, ob es sich da um eine kapitulierende oder um eine zustimmende Hinnahme handelt. Für das erstere spräche etwa das plötzliche Abbrechen der Debatte, das den Eindruck erweckt, als seien die Teilnehmer der fruchtlosen Auseinandersetzung müde geworden, sowie deren durchgängige Ergebnislosigkeit überhaupt. Auf der anderen Seite wird man doch erwarten, Resignation so ausgedrückt zu finden, daß ein optimistisch begonnener Aufbruch zum Stillstand kommt, daß anfängliche Erfolge von Ratlosigkeit und Scheitern abgelöst werden. Die Debatten des *Heptaplomeres* stehen jedoch, wie bemerkt, von Anfang an unter dem Gesetz des Aufeinandertreffens unreduzierbarer Positionen, nie wird auch nur der geringste Fortschritt erzielt, es sei denn auf Gebieten, die nicht strittig, sondern als Grundpositionen des Denkens eines jeden der Sieben Gegenstand gemeinsamer Zustimmung sind. Von einem Umschlagen der Stimmung, von dem Erlahmen einer hoffnungsvoll entworfenen Bewegung kann keine Rede sein.

Wenn man also nicht annehmen will, daß Bodin den Dialog von allem Anfang an zu nichts anderem bestimmt hätte, als Demonstration der Absurdität von Diskussionen über die wahre Religion zu sein – und das verbietet schon der riesige Aufwand an Scharfsinn und Belegmaterial, der in einem solchen Fall für nichts vertan wäre –, so wird man den Realismus des unaufgelösten Nebeneinanders der Partikularismen[13] im

---

rus solus inter reliquos perfectus esset ac latissime in universa natura pateret . . .» (2). Man könnte also die Sechszahl der Bücher, kombiniert mit der Siebenzahl der Sprecher, als Symbol für Bodins Absicht verstehen, im Modell des Dialogs die harmonische Ordnung der Erscheinungsformen des Religiösen in Übereinstimmung mit der harmonischen Ordnung des Kosmos darzustellen bzw. entstehen zu lassen.

[12] Außer SABINE [114], 294 ff. hat besonders GUHRAUER [23], XLIX diesen Gesichtspunkt herausgearbeitet und darauf hingewiesen, daß eine jede der sieben Personen gelegentlich zum Sprecher Bodins wird und Ansichten vertritt, die an anderen Stellen des Œuvre wiederkehren.

[13] Dem gleichen Verdikt der Einzelkraft, die keine Chancen hat, das Ganze zu bestimmen, unterwirft Bodin neben den fünf Vertretern der Offenbarungsreligionen auch den Vertreter des Versuchs, die religiöse Einheit durch eine Reduktion der historisch gewachsenen Formen auf ihre gemeinsame Grundlage zu retten, sowie den Propagandisten einer Bindungslosigkeit, die glaubt, sich je nach den Umständen aller Formen bedienen zu können; zwei Entwürfe also,

Licht des Gedankens sehen, der Bodins Werk wie ein Leitwort durchzieht und hier die Bücher IV–VI, das eigentliche Religionsgespräch, zu einer Einheit verklammert: des Gedankens der *Harmonie*. Die Schlußworte des *Heptaplomeres* sind in ihrem vollen Sinn nur verständlich, wenn man sie auf die Erörterung bezieht, die das IV. Buch eröffnet hatte. Unter dem Eindruck eines gerade gehörten Chors unterhalten sich die Freunde, die sich in der Geringschätzung des einstimmigen Gesangs einig sind, über die Bedingungen für das Zustandekommen von Harmonie. Verschiedene Theorien werden vorgetragen, und die Erklärung findet Beifall, welche sie aus dem Zusammenklang von gegensätzlichen Größen ableiten will, welche ihrerseits durch Mittelwerte vermittelt sind. Dieser Satz findet auch auf die Natur Anwendung, heißt es weiter; und was diese Harmonie zu trüben scheint, Krankheit, Schmerz, Unruhe usw., erweist sich geradezu als notwendig, weil es sie überhaupt erst wahrnehmbar macht wie das Dunkel das Licht. Der Calvinist Curtius faßt das in einem Gedicht in Distichen zusammen, dessen Schlußverse lauten:

«...Haec hujus orbis maxima *concordia*
discors salutem continet» (S. 115).

Die Nutzanwendung aus diesem Text zu ziehen, überläßt Bodin nicht dem Leser. Toralba wendet die gewonnene Erkenntnis gleich auf die Debatten des Kreises an, und gemeinsam bespricht man, ob sie auch für die Vielfalt der Religionen in einem Staat Gültigkeit habe. An dieser Stelle wird freilich noch keine Übereinstimmung erzielt; der Einwand, was denn bei einer solchen Betrachtungsweise aus der Frage nach der wahren Religion werde, mobilisiert im Gegenteil alle Kräfte und treibt den Kreis nach einer Kontroverse über die grundsätzliche Zulässigkeit derartiger Erörterungen (S. 125–133) zu den Gesprächen, die die Bücher IV–VI ausmachen. Wenn also am Schluß dieser Gespräche die Harmonik des Chorsatzes beschrieben wird, den Coronaeus zum Zeichen der erreichten Einigung singen läßt, so bedeutet das, daß jetzt endlich auch für die Beziehungen der Religionen untereinander die Harmonie gefunden ist, und daß es die Einsicht in diese Harmonie ist, die dem Leser durch das Werk vermittelt werden soll.

Nach dieser vorläufigen Charakterisierung des *Heptaplomeres* ist zu fragen, ob bzw. in welcher Bedeutung «Toleranz» und «Harmonie» in den übrigen Schriften Bodins vorkommen. Wenn wir zunächst die – wie

---

von denen der erste wohl eine «Durchgangsphase» des Bodinischen Denkens bezeichnet, während der zweite zwar an die Bodinsche Praxis der äußeren Anpassung an den herrschenden Kult erinnert, ihm zugleich aber fremd sein mußte, weil hier die Anpassung nicht als Tarnung gemeint, sondern bereits die Sache selbst war.

bemerkt zahlreichen – Stellen, an denen von Harmonie die Rede ist, ansehen, fällt auf, daß diese Vorstellung stets im Zusammenhang mit einer anderen, umgreifenden erscheint, mit der der *Einheit,* und zwar der Einheit nicht nur des gerade behandelten Teilstücks oder Teilaspekts der Welt, wie Staat, historisch-geographisch begründeter Anthropologie, Natur, sondern darüber hinaus der Einheit der Schöpfung als Ganzem.

Das beginnt in der *Methodus,* die den Kosmos unter dem Bild des Organismus *(animal)* beschreibt [14] und die monarchische Verfassung als ideal für die Staaten bezeichnet, weil sie auf der harmonischen Proportion beruhe;[15] das ganze V. Buch ist der Erklärung der Verschiedenartigkeit der Völker aus ihrer Lage auf der Erde und relativ zu den Zonen des Himmels gewidmet, womit ihre Einheit durch den Bezug auf verschiedene Punkte desselben Systems bzw. mehrerer Systeme behauptet ist.

Die *Demonomanie* entwirft in gleicher Weise eine harmonische Hierarchie der Geistwesen und gliedert sie ausdrücklich der Weltharmonie ein.[16] Auch in dem nach dem *Heptaplomeres* entstandenen *Universae naturae theatrum* finden dieselben Gedanken, oft ganz ähnlich formuliert, Anwendung.[17]

Der Erörterung unseres Dialogs stehen jedoch gewisse Stellen der *Six Livres de la Republique* am nächsten, weil da bereits von der Eingliederung unterschiedlicher Religionsformen in den *einen* Staat die Rede ist. Es handelt sich vor allem um das 7. Kapitel des IV. Buchs,[18] wobei die Frage im Zusammenhang der Haltung des Souveräns bei Parteiungen erscheint. Die *Methodus* von 1566 hatte das Problem noch nicht aufgegriffen und lediglich vermerkt (VI, S. 223 A), es sei von größter Wich-

---

[14] *Meth.* V, 153 f., VIII, 233 B (ich zitiere nach der Neuausgabe von MESNARD [4.20]).

[15] *Meth.* VI, 222: «Est igitur regia potestas ... omnium, ut quidem mihi videtur, praestantissima, civitatibusque maxime salutaris, ac velut harmonia suavi moderata concentu. (...) hanc (sc. die harmonica ratio) tamen velut omnium pulcherrimam, ad imperii optimi statum pertinere puto.»

[16] *Dém.* [10.17] I 2, S. 55: «Deum enim Opt. Max. videmus res omneis à natura constrinxisse mediis, quae suis extremitatibus respondeant, & in rebus intelligentibus, coelestib. atque elementaribus harmoniam mundi certis medii & adamantinis vinculis compegisse. Quemadmodum autem, si contrarias voces mediis non temperaueris, concidit harmonia: sic etiam fit mundo, & illius partibus.»

[17] Vgl. *Theatrum* [13.1] I, 32, II, 143 f., III, 310 f.

[18] *Rép.,* 652 ff. = Rép. [7.35], 752 ff. – Von der Harmonie im allgemeinen und in Anwendung auf den Staat handelt Bodin auch an anderen Stellen, z. B. in den Kapiteln IV 1 und VI 6 (Schluß des Werks!); in V 1 nimmt er die Diskussion der *Methodus* über die geographische Bedingtheit der menschlichen Denkweisen und Temperamente wieder auf.

tigkeit für den Staat, wenn der Fürst in der wahren Religion erzogen werde und sich seiner Verpflichtung ihr gegenüber immer bewußt bleibe, denn sie sei nicht zuletzt die beste Stütze seiner Macht. Die *Republique* von 1576 setzt sich nun ausführlich mit den Situationen auseinander, die durch das Auftreten einer Mehrzahl von Religionen im Staat für den Fürsten und für den Staat entstehen können.

Die Forderung, der Herrscher müsse sich zum wahren Glauben bekennen, tritt hier zurück (Bodin mochte diesen wohl nicht mehr mit dem Christentum gleichsetzen, und sein etwa auf der Linie der Salomo-Toralba des Religionsgesprächs liegendes Ideal durfte er nicht zu deutlich machen), und die Frage nach der Einheit rückt an ihre Stelle. Dabei ist zu beachten, daß es einer von Bodins Grundgedanken war, der Staat, d. h. die Macht des Herrschers und der Gesetze, bedürften der Frömmigkeit des Volks, ohne die sie keinen Bestand haben könnten;[19] alle eventuellen Maßnahmen zur Verteidigung der Einheit oder aber zur Sicherung eines friedlichen Nebeneinanderlebens der Konfessionen müssen deswegen so beschaffen sein, daß sie diese Frömmigkeit nicht antasten.

Die erste Empfehlung, die Bodin in IV 7 ausspricht, ist nun die, unter keinen Umständen Debatten über Religionsformen zuzulassen (S. 652). Desgleichen ist jede Gewalt zu verwerfen. Hat eine neue Glaubensform im Staat soviel Boden gewonnen, daß ein Kampf gegen sie die Gefahr eines Bürgerkrieges bedeutete, so soll man sie dulden, denn Gewalt erzeugt entweder Fanatisierung, oder das schlimmste aller Übel, Gleichgültigkeit, d. h. Gottlosigkeit. Im Vergleich mit ihr ist sogar jeder Aberglaube vorzuziehen.

Diese Toleranzforderung ist ganz von den Erfordernissen des Staats her bestimmt. Sie verlangt Religionsfreiheit, weil man die Gewissen nicht zwingen kann und Glauben nur auf freier Zustimmung beruht. Sie zieht ein Nebeneinander von mehreren Glaubensformen dem von nur zweien, vor, weil sich zwei zu zerfleischen die Tendenz haben, mehrere sich aber gegenseitig neutralisieren (eine «negative» Anwendung des Harmoniebegriffs von der Vermittlung der Gegensätze durch Zwischenwerte). Und vor allem verliert Bodin dabei nie die Wiederherstellung der Einheit völlig aus dem Auge. Da Gewalt als Mittel ausscheidet, wird dem Souverän ein vorbildliches Leben empfohlen, das zur Nachfolge anspornt. An einer früheren Stelle (III 498, lat. 538) drückt sich der Autor jedoch weit weniger zurückhaltend aus: fürstliche Mißbilligung vermöge auf die Dauer eine Menge: «Mais il est certain que le Prince portant faueur à vne secte, & mesprisant l'autre, l'aneantira sans force ny contrainte ny vio-

---

[19] Vgl. die erwähnte Stelle *Meth.* VI 223 A und *De la Rép.* IV 7, 653 (Die bekanntlich von Bodin selbst stammende lateinische Fassung ist gelegentlich ausführlicher und deutlicher als das französische Original).

lence quelconque, si Dieu ne la maintient . . .» – Man brauche etwa nur die Anhänger der anderen Richtung von Ehrenstellen auszuschließen, und man entziehe ihr damit auf die Dauer den Boden.

Die Einheit und Funktionsfähigkeit des Staatsgebildes zu bewahren, ist ein Ziel, dem Bodin also im Notfall auch die Reinheit der religiösen Gestalt unterordnet, nicht aus Zynismus, sondern in der Überzeugung, der Staat stelle die primäre irdische Ordnung dar.[20] Allein die letzte Konsequenz aus diesem Gedanken zieht er, wie man sieht, nicht im *Staat*, sondern erst im *Heptaplomeres*. Erst hier findet sich der Harmoniegedanke auf die gegensätzlichen Religionsformen ausgedehnt. Die Wurzel dieser Konzeption ist zwar schon in der *Methodus* zu finden, in der die Vielfalt der menschlichen Lebensformen theoretisch begründet und jeder von ihnen – ohne ausdrücklichen Bezug auf die Religion – als Teil des Weltganzen prinzipiell das gleiche Recht zuerkannt wurde. Der Unterschied liegt jedoch darin, daß im Geschichtstraktat an die ursprüngliche Verteilung über die einzelnen Zonen der Erde gedacht ist, während der *Staat* und noch mehr das *Heptaplomeres* sich dem Problem ihres gleichzeitigen Vorhandenseins am selben Ort gegenüber sehen.

Das *Heptaplomeres* erörtert seiner Fragestellung entsprechend die Toleranz in erster Linie unter dem Gesichtspunkt der Wahrheit, der Möglichkeit der Wahrheitsfindung, des Verhältnisses von Wahrheit und Geschichte. Die politischen Argumente fehlen nicht, kehren vielmehr sämtlich wieder, aber als Argumente unter anderen. Erst am Schluß des Dialogs wird die Suche nach dem Modus vivendi thematisch, um dann das letzte Wort zu behalten.

Man kann also sagen, daß im Religionsgespräch Bodins Position noch liberaler ist als in den *Six Livres de la Republique*. Nicht nur ist die Forderung nach der Wiederherstellung der Glaubenseinheit verschwunden; auch die Frage nach der wahren Religion ist aufgehoben in der Erkenntnis von dem unreduzierbaren Pluralismus der Erscheinungsformen der einen allen zu Grunde liegenden *religio naturalis*.

Es ist dies die Erkenntnis von der *Geschichtlichkeit* dieser Formen und damit von der Geschichtlichkeit als einer psychologischen Realität, über die man sich in der Politik nicht unter Berufung auf den gemeinsamen Kern hinwegsetzen kann in der Absicht, die eine Erscheinungsform in die andere zu überführen, oder gar mit dem Ziel, sie aufzulösen, um nur den puren Kern bestehen zu lassen.

---

[20] Bereits in der *Methodus* wendet er das geläufige Wort von der Kirche, der wir nach Gott alles verdanken, auf den Staat an: «. . . ut tempus omne vacuum à forensibus negotiis in legitima studia conferrem, ac reipublicae, cui post Deum immortalem omnia debemus, . . . gratias referrem» (107 A, Widmungsepistel). – Die Sache ist bekannt und muß hier nicht weiter belegt werden.

Mit dieser Hinnahme der Geschichtlichkeit vollzieht Bodin endlich auch die uneingeschränkte Übertragung seines Grundgedankens von der Harmonie auf den Bereich des Religiösen, in welchem er ihn bis dahin noch wesentlich im Sinn einer strengeren Einheit der Form verstanden hatte oder gehofft hatte, verstehen zu dürfen.

Diese Entwicklung in Bodins Toleranzlehre muß natürlich auch im Zusammenhang mit der gleichzeitigen politischen Geschichte Frankreichs gesehen werden, die der *politique* Bodin als Beobachter genauestens verfolgte, und die er als Berater und Akteur nach Kräften mitzugestalten suchte. Es wird nicht nötig sein, an dieser Stelle den Verlauf der Bürgerkriege, das Wirken der *politiques* zwischen den Fronten der Orthodoxien und die Schicksale des Versuchs nachzuzeichnen, das Land durch Toleranzedikte und Religionsgespräche zu befrieden. Ebensowenig wird es einer Erinnerung an Bodins Biographie bedürfen und an sein furchtloses Eintreten in Blois und in Laon für die konkrete Anwendung seiner Ideen.

Das Scheitern der Politik der *colloques* bezeichnete ohne Zweifel eine Niederlage des humanistischen Vertrauens in die Macht der Vernunft, die historisch gewachsenen Differenzen und Leidenschaften überwinden und in Dienst nehmen zu können. Ob Bodin zeitweilig geglaubt hat, die Reinigung oder gar Ablösung der Religionen durch eine «Zurückführung» in eine stark vom Judentum her gesehene Form natürlicher Religion sei wirklich realisierbar, mindestens bei einer Elite der Gelehrten, oder ob ihm ein solcher, zahlreichen Stellen seiner Schriften zu Grunde liegender, Gedanke nie mehr als ein idealer Maßstab für die Kritik an einzelnen Erscheinungsformen kirchlicher Frömmigkeit gewesen ist, wüßte ich nicht mit Sicherheit zu entscheiden. Fest steht jedenfalls, daß der Schluß des *Heptaplomeres* die erstere Lösung als schiere Utopie erweisen will.

Wenn auch der humanistische Wille zur Synthese und die Hoffnung auf einen Sieg der Vernunft in Gesprächen in diesen Jahrzehnten eine bittere Niederlage erlitten hat, so bedeutet die Lösung, zu der Bodin zuletzt vorgestoßen ist, doch gerade den Triumph ursprünglicher Einsichten desselben Humanismus, in deren Geschichte die Träume und Entwürfe einer *concordia* bei Nikolaus von Cues, bei Pico, bei Postel nur Durchgangsstadien sind. Es sind das der bereits bei Petrarca ausgesprochene Vorrang des Guten vor dem Wahren und das Prinzip des Pluralismus, wie es sich etwa in der Weigerung des Landino der *Quaestiones Camaldulenses* ausdrückt, in dem Streit um die zwei Lebensformen der *vita activa* und der *vita contemplativa* die eine Seite der anderen unterzuordnen. Beide Beispiele zeigen eine Anschauung vom Menschen, die die Vielfalt und auch Widersprüchlichkeit seines Denkens und Handelns bejaht und nicht zugunsten einer, ihr wohl bewußten, tieferen Einheit in der Praxis leugnet, zu beseitigen oder auch nur zu hierarchisieren wünscht.[21] Diese Skizze von der Toleranzvorstellung des *Heptaplomeres* bliebe aber ungenau, wenn nicht auch deren *Grenzen* deutlich gemacht würden. Zu Beginn des IV. Buchs, nach dem Harmoniegespräch, erscheint die Frage nach der wahren Religion (S. 125); die Debatte darüber kommt, wie erwähnt, erst nach einer Voruntersuchung über die Frage ihrer prinzipiellen Zulässigkeit und dann gegen den Widerstand der Nichtchristen zustande. Deren Argumente sind schon die der *Six Livres de la Republique* und lassen sich in dem Satz zusammenfassen: Gespräche über die Religion sind schädlich und deshalb abzulehnen. (Daß sie auch nutzlos sind, zeigt der Gang des Dialogs und vermittelt damit dem Leser die Erkenntnis von der Machtlosigkeit des abstrakt kalkulierenden Verstandes gegenüber dem Denken aus einer Tradition. Das *colloques*-Denken hat sich hier gerade in sein Gegenteil verkehrt.) Ihre Gefahr besteht nach Salomos Formulierung darin, daß sie zum Zweifel führen können oder müssen, und dieser wieder zur Gottlosigkeit; es ist aber höchst leichtsinnig, die Grundlagen des eigenen oder des fremden Heils zu erschüttern.[22] Aus

---

[21] Das Verständnis von *Humanismus*, das ich hier in äußerster Verkürzung andeute, verdanke ich einigen Humanismus-Seminaren von Professor Grassi. – Mit der auf diesen Seiten vorgeschlagenen Deutung des *Heptaplomeres* korrigiere ich diejenige meiner oben erwähnten Dissertation, in der ich auch für den Bodin des Religionsgesprächs noch eine partikularistische Sicht des Nebeneinanders der Glaubensformen vindiziert und den Schluß des Dialogs als Ausdruck der Resignation angesichts einer Entwicklung erklärt habe, die seinen Ideen jede Chance einer Verwirklichung genommen zu haben schien. Diese Interpretation scheint mir jetzt nicht mehr aufrechtzuerhalten. – Wenn das zutrifft, ist natürlich auch die These von Bodins *Judaismus* dahingehend zu modifizieren, daß dieser im *Heptaplomeres* jedenfalls weit genug überwunden sein muß, um dem Autor die Hinnahme gleichberechtigter Formen, ja die Erkenntnis von ihrer «Concordia discors» zu gestatten. Wie weit er, der als Korrelat der Toleranz präzise persönliche Überzeugung gefordert hat, für sich selbst bei einem solchen Judaismus verblieb, oder wie die Frage nach dem Glauben seiner späten Jahre sonst zu beantworten sein mag, möchte ich hier nicht erneut untersuchen. Zweifel an Bodins Judaismus, den schon Guhrauer rundweg abgestritten hat (LV ff. u. ö.), [23] hat in letzter Zeit wieder ERICH HASSINGER angemeldet: Religiöse Toleranz im 16. Jh. Motive – Argumente – Formen der Verwirklichung. Basel–Stuttgart 1966, Vorträge der Aeneas-Silvius-Stiftung an der Universität Basel, VI, 33 [249].

[22] «Nam quaecunque disputantur, in opinionem cadunt; opinio autem verum inter et falsum ambigit, dubitatio rursus impietatis opinionem parit. (...) ... nihil perniciosius mihi videtur quam ea, quae omnibus demonstrationibus certiora esse debeant et quibus salutis fundamenta nitantur, dubia disputatione discutere conari.» *Heptaplomeres*, 127.

den gleichen Gründen, hatte Senamus eine Seite zuvor erklärt, sei sogar eine neugefundene Wahrheit nicht zu verbreiten, wenn das einen Religionswechsel nach sich ziehen müsse, denn der Schaden, der damit der Frömmigkeit zugefügt werde, sei zu groß.[23] Ob derartige Debatten auch unter Gelehrten zu meiden sind, bleibt im Kreis der Freunde zunächst strittig; der Schluß zeigt jedoch, wie auch sie in der Absicht auseinandergehen, nicht wieder auf das Thema zurückzukommen. Wenn aber schon der Ratio keine Durchschlagskraft in der Materie zugetraut wird, so darf dem unerleuchteten Meinen der Masse des Volkes auf gar keinen Fall hier ein Urteil überlassen werden.[24]

Also ein Gespräch gegen Religionsgespräche? Ohne Zweifel. Für die Toleranz bedeutet das, daß Bodin keine Gewissensfreiheit in dem Sinn propagiert, jeder möge jederzeit das glauben und bekennen, was ihm als Individuum gut scheint.[25] Es fällt auf, daß die Debatte, die unbekümmert um die Frage der Anwendbarkeit auf die Wahrheitsfindung konzentriert begann, die Wahrheit nicht außerhalb der sozialen Funktion des Religiösen findet. Die Toleranz findet nach wie vor da ihre Grenze, wo sie mit den Lebensgesetzen des Staats in Konflikt gerät.[26] Der Staat ruht auf der Religion seiner Bürger. Sind mehrere Formen im Staat vorhanden, wird ihnen gleichmäßige Duldung zugesichert unter der Bedingung, daß sie sich loyal zueinander und zum Staatsganzen verhalten. Im Prinzip besteht die Forderung, daß jeder sich zu einer der im Staat an-

---

[23] «Ut religio nova melior ac verior sit vetere, non tamen evulganda mihi videtur, quia non tantum utilitatis allatura videtur nova religio, quantum ex ipsius novitatis contemtu detrahitur de pietate veteri, aut certe de mortalibus necessario numinis metu.» (*Heptaplomeres*, 126). Man beachte, daß es *Senamus* ist, der hier spricht.

[24] Vgl. z. B. V 185 Octavius, der eine Entscheidung in religiösen Fragen den Geistlichen vorbehalten wissen will, und 186 Toralba, der sie auch den Gelehrten, besonders den Naturgelehrten, zubilligt.

[25] Einen vollkommenen religiösen Individualismus hielt nicht nur Rom für unerträglich, sondern ebenso Genf; vgl. JOSEPH LECLER [188], Histoire de la tolérance au siècle de la réforme, Paris 1955, Bd. II, 125; und neuerdings HEINRICH LUTZ, Zum Problem der Gleichberechtigung der Konfessionen im 16. und 17. Jht. (II): Die Konfessionsproblematik außerhalb des Reiches und in der Politik des Papsttums, *Archiv f. Religionsgeschichte* 56 (1965), 219 ff. – Demokratische Anschauungen waren Bodin auf allen Gebieten fremd, und wenn er als das Wesentliche an der Religion den Aufstieg der geläuterten Seele zu immer höherer Erkenntnis bezeichnet, schied er die Masse der Gläubigen von der Beurteilung theologischer Fragen bereits aus, bevor er die Ergebnislosigkeit solcher Auseinandersetzungen realisierte.

[26] Und damit die Durchsetzung der Wahrheit; Bodin beruft sich gern auf den Satz, die Verantwortlichen dürften zum Wohl des Staats auch lügen: *Meth.* V 157 A; *République* [7.35], IV 7, 748, im *Hept.* etwa IV 176, V 179.

erkannten Formen bekennen muß; wie Bodin neu auftretende Formen
behandelt sehen will, ist bekannt: den Anfängen sollte man wehren,
haben sie sich aber einmal etabliert, sind sie auf die genannten Grundsätze zu verpflichten und zu dulden. Unter keinen Umständen Anspruch
auf Duldung haben dagegen Gottesleugner, sowie Menschen, die sich
der Magie ergeben haben.[27]
Die vollkommene Freiheit der Diskussion endet also mit einer energi-
schen Beschränkung der Freiheit. Diese Feststellung macht nicht den
Fehler, von neuem Einzelpositionen des Gesprächs als Bodins Meinung
zu bezeichnen, sie ergibt sich vielmehr zwingend aus Gang und Ende der
Auseinandersetzung, aus dem Consensus der Sprecher und schon aus der
Auswahl der Sprecher selbst, unter denen sich keine Vertreter der inkri-
minierten Anschauungen befinden.

Die Kühnheit des Entwurfs, mag sie, von der Aufklärung des 18. Jahrhunderts her betrachtet, auch zu relativieren sein, wird dagegen niemand
übersehen. Bodin war zu sehr Realist, um sich nicht letztlich doch wieder
dem Möglichen zuzuwenden.[28] Das zeigt schon der Schauplatz, den er

---

[27] Ersteres ist nach dem Gesagten ohne weiteres einsichtig und war in seiner
Zeit unbestritten (HASSINGER [249], 24 ff.). Alle Gesprächsteilnehmer sind sich
darüber einig, daß es besser ist, einer falschen Religion treu ergeben zu sein, als
gar keine zu haben. – Die andere Verurteilung hängt mit Bodins philosophisch-
theologischem System zusammen, das einen Stufenkosmos in der Art des Neu-
platonismus mit absoluter Jenseitigkeit und Allverursachung Gottes zu verbinden sucht. Bei der Diskussion der Magie geraten beide Vorstellungen miteinander in Konflikt. Bodin leugnet die Möglichkeit, mit magischen Mitteln Einfluß
auf höhere Seinsstufen zu nehmen, verdammt den, der es will und versucht, aber
trotzdem, weil er sich einer teuflischen Illusion überlasse und Gottes Ehre an-
taste. (Stellen s. in meiner Dissertation, 126 ff.)
[28] Vgl. HASSINGER, [249], 19.
Es läßt sich natürlich der grundsätzliche Einwand machen, das *Heptaplomeres*
sei von vornherein nicht zur Veröffentlichung bestimmt gewesen und deshalb
als ein Gedankenexperiment anzusehen, das nicht in gleicher Weise wie die übrigen Schriften die Überzeugung seines Autors wiedergebe; und es ließe sich in
diesem Zusammenhang auf das *Theatrum* und das *Paradoxon* verweisen, die
gleichzeitig oder gar später entstanden sind und keine Spuren der Liberalität
des Religionsgesprächs zeigen. – Ein solcher Einwand ist weder zu widerlegen,
noch ist seine Tragweite genau zu bestimmen. Ich selbst würde meinen, daß
Bodin hier in großer Luzidität und sicher unter Kämpfen die letzten Konsequenzen seiner Gedanken gezogen hat, und daß er nicht der Mann war, eine solche
Problematik einmal gleichsam «durchzuspielen» und sich dann wieder weit
hinter die Frontlinie der Ergebnisse solchen Durchdenkens häuslich einzurichten.
Wie er über den Abstand von dem, was man denkt, zu dem, was man sagen
dürfe, dachte, ist ja bekannt. – Im übrigen berührt diese Erwägung die *Wirkung*
seiner Thesen in keiner Weise und bleibt ein rein biographisches Problem.

seinem «religiösen Testament»[29] gab, das Haus des *Katholiken* Coronaeus
in einem als vorbildlich beschriebenen, aber keinesfalls idealisierten Venedig. Die Geschichte ging über die Grenzen hinweg, die er seinen Gedanken gesetzt hatte; schon die ersten Leser erkannten ihre Stoßrichtung
nur allzu deutlich. Sowohl in dem Willen, an der Lösung brennender
Probleme des Frankreich seiner Tage mitzuarbeiten, ist er groß, als auch
in dem Mut und der Konsequenz, mit der er diese Probleme und die
möglichen Lösungen durchdachte und dabei auch frühere Vorstellungen
und Ziele opferte. Gerade der Kontext der mächtigen, sorgfältigen Gelehrsamkeit gibt seinem Wort Gewicht. Die Entwicklungen, denen er,
ohne Lohn zu erhalten, vorgearbeitet hat, haben seine Einsichten bestätigt und seine Forderungen – wenigstens zum Teil – erfüllt. Immer zu
bewundern bleibt sein Engagement als Gelehrter und Politiker.

---

[29] Der Ausdruck stammt von GUHRAUER [23], LXXIV, der darauf aufmerksam macht, daß es Bodin in dem von ihm selbst für den Menschen als hochbedeut-
sam beschriebenen 63. Lebensjahr abgefaßt oder zumindest vollendet habe.

Michel Villey

La Justice Harmonique selon Bodin

Bodin conclut *Les six Livres de la République*[1] par un chapitre intitulé «De la justice distributive commutative et *harmonique* et laquelle des trois est propre à chacune République». (p. 1013 et s.)[2] Ce chapitre est souvent négligé par les interprètes. Il mérite notre attention. Non seulement il est très curieux et poétique, mais loin de n'être qu'un épisode ou qu'une fioriture, l'idée de justice harmonique tient le rôle d'un *leit-motiv,* ou plutôt d'un fil conducteur, courant à travers tout l'ouvrage.[3] Elle n'est pas moins mise en relief dans la *Juris Distributio,* pour définir la «fin» du droit,[4] y servir aussi de conclusion, et dans la *Méthode de l'histoire,* où elle vient à peu près conclure le chapitre VII consacré à la Politique.[5]

Ce dernier chapitre de la *République* veut dévoiler la quintessence, la clé de l'ouvrage tout entier, du moins la clé philosophique. Le meilleur de Bodin n'est pas sa philosophie – Bodin peut nous intéresser plutôt comme homme politique, juriste, historien, érudit, écrivain, poète –. Il n'empêche que cette philosophie dite de la justice harmonique, logiquement, soit le sommet de la théorie bodinienne.

Et de ce point de vue l'on essayera:

I. de saisir les principes directeurs de la Politique de Bodin, la cohérence du système, pour autant que la matière s'y prête, et que Bodin soit systématique,

II. de porter ensuite sur cette œuvre un jugement de valeur. Peut être la philosophie autorise-t-elle à juger. Et la fortune de cette œuvre a été si grande que nous ne pouvons nous dispenser de prendre position à son

---

[1] Nos citations renvoient à l'édition de la *République* Paris 1583 reproduite en 1961 par Scientia Aalen [7.11].

[2] *Rép.,* 1013 «la plus belle conclusion qu'on peut faire à cest œuvre est de la Justice comme le fondement de toutes Républiques».

[3] En dehors du dernier chapitre, il est notamment fait appel au thème de la justice harmonique p. 15, 254, 272, 341, 608 etc. Le thème voisin de «l'accord» auquel la politique doit tendre et du «discord» à éviter, revient constamment.

[4] *Juris Universi Distributio* ed. MESNARD – Œuvres philosophiques de Jean Bodin I, 1951, 80 [4.20].

[5] *Methodus ad facilem historiarum cognitionem* [4.20], 222 (cf. 388, 412, 422 de la traduction française).

égard: (Car Bodin n'avançait pas seul; il fut un témoin de l'esprit juridique moderne et ses options philosophiques, celles d'un secteur considérable de la pensée juridique moderne.)

I. Exposé

Nous tenterons donc de résumer cette philosophie. Travail déplaisant: un chapitre de la *République* de Bodin, fût-ce celui là, ne se résume pas sans que s'en évanouisse la saveur, qui naît du détail et même du désordre. Mais nous tâchons d'en extraire la philosophie, cachée sous la couverture luxuriante des anecdotes et des images.

Nous poserons d'abord qu'il s'agit d'une philosophie du *Nombre*. On dirait presque que pour Bodin au commencement était le Nombre. Ou plutôt: «Dieu a disposé toutes choses par nombres».[6] S'il n'était ici retenu par des scrupules théologiques, Bodin serait tenté d'expliquer tout le cours de *l'histoire* par le nombre, d'abord l'histoire universelle, celle du *macrocosme*, les révolutions politiques auxquelles président les multiples de 7 et 9;[7] puis l'histoire individuelle gouvernée par le chiffre 6, s'il s'agit des femmes, 7 pour les mâles[8]; ainsi seraient réfutées l'hérésie des épicuriens, qui livrent le monde au hasard, et l'idolâtrie du Destin de la philosophie stoicienne.[9]

«Et je ne me laisserai pas troubler par la critique d'Aristote, lorsqu'il déclare... que les nombres n'ont absolument aucune importance. Pourquoi dans ce cas le septième garçon guérit-il des écrouelles? Pourquoi les enfants vivent-ils lorsqu'ils arrivent au septième ou au neuvième mois, et meurent-ils au huitième? Pourquoi y a t-il sept planètes et neuf mondes?»[10] etc. etc.

Cependant Bodin se défend contre la séduction de ce déterminisme des nombres, obligé qu'il est de préserver dans l'histoire la liberté de l'homme et celle surtout de la Providence: «Dieu n'est pas tenu à ses propres lois.»[11] Mais où le Nombre reconquiert son autorité souveraine, c'est dans la sphère de la Justice, de la philosophie du droit. Sur la justice, «fondement de toutes républiques»,[12] doivent régner le Nombre, *l'harmonie, les lois de la Musique*; Bodin conçoit la Musique à la mode antique comme fille de *l'arithmétique* (sœur de l'astrologie). Ceci n'empêche qu'il en parle avec dévotion, répète volontiers que les fautes contre l'harmonie

---

[6] *Rép.*, 564, cf. *Methodus* 195 et s. (texte français 389 et s.).

[7] *Rép.*, 566 et s., *Méthode de l'histoire* 390 et s.

[8] *Rép.*, 565, *Méthode*, 389 et s.

[9] *Méthode*, 389–394.

[10] *Méthode*, 394.

[11] *Méthode*, 395; cf. *Rép.*, 542 et s.

[12] *Rép.*, 595, 802, 1013 etc.

sont causes des révolutions, ou que la musique est en médecine la plus efficace psychothérapie. (Ce qui a fait des farouches gaulois décrits par Julien l'Apostat la merveille de civilisation qu'est devenu le peuple français, c'est la musique «car chacun sait qu'il n'y a peuple qui plus s'exerce à la musique et qui chante plus doucement.) *(sic)*[13]

On ne s'étonnera pas qu'il prenne soin de nous apporter les formules de la science musicale. C'est le fondement de son système. Je me dispense de reproduire toutes ces formules,[14] assez diverses, agrémentées de figures géométriques, plus compliquées qu'il ne faudrait, parfois même contradictoires.[15] Mais, pour comprendre la République, il se pourrait que la connaissance de ce langage musical ne soit pas inutile. Comment se construit l'harmonie?

1. De la note dominante

On risque aujourd'hui de s'y mal reconnaître dans les explications de Bodin, cette science n'étant plus familière comme elle l'était aux honnêtes gens de la Renaissance. Même supposé que le lecteur fût un mélomane, il reste ceci que nous autres depuis le triomphe des sciences modernes, sommes accoutumés à penser l'harmonie en *physiciens*. Nous expliquons l'harmonie par la résonance, à partir de la *fondamentale*, le *la* par exemple du diapason produisant par ondes succesives ses harmoniques vers l'aigu (le mi, le do dièze etc....).

La doctrine pythagoricienne (transmise notamment par Boèce au monde médiéval[16]) reliait l'harmonie directement aux *mathématiques*, en calculant les intervalles en fonction de la longueur de la corde qui, sur une lyre comme aujourd'hui un violoncelle ou un violon, sert à produire

---

[13] *Rép.*, 563, cf. *Rép.* 681, Apologie de R. Herpin, 31 verso.
[14] *Rép.*, 562, 1016, 1019, 1020, 1052, 1053, 1056, 1059; *Methodus* 388 et s. (texte latin 195).
Dans l'ouvrage de Dıès: Le nombre de Platon, 1936 sont étudiées les oscillations de Bodin à la recherche de la science des nombres.
[15] Aveu d'incompétence technique: Ap. de R. Herpin p. 31 recto.
[16] Cf. JACQUES CHAILLEY; Comprendre l'harmonie, M. EMMANUEL, Histoire de la langue musicale 1951, p. 66.

telle ou telle note; et, contrairement à notre usage, elle procédait en descendant de l'aigu au grave. Prenons une corde de longueur 1 : elle produit un *mi*, qui jouera le rôle de *dominante*, et sert dans la théorie des anciens de point de départ à l'harmonie. Doublons cette corde: nous obtenons le *mi* à l'octave inférieure. Donnons à la corde maintenant une longueur triple de la première, et nous avons une quinte plus bas, la note de *la*. Si nous multiplions par quatre, nous retrouverons un *mi*, deux octaves au dessous de la note initiale etc. . . .[17]

(en descendant)

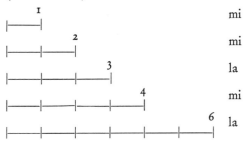

On voit que la théorie musicale ainsi donnée n'est que l'effet dans le monde des sons, des lois mathématiques des nombres. Considérons la figure tracée par Bodin, *République* p. 562. La série des nombres harmoniques est disposée sur les 3 côtés d'un triangle: au sommet le 1 – Sur le côté gauche 2, 4, 8, série obtenue par multiplications par 2. Sur le côté droit, 3, 9, 27, par multiplications par 3. Entre 4 et 9 Bodin insère, au centre du triangle, le 6, appelé «nombre nuptial», parce qu'il emprunte aux deux lignées, étant le produit du mariage de 2 × 3 ; plus bas, 12, multiple de 2 et 6; 18, de 3 et 6 etc. . . .[18]

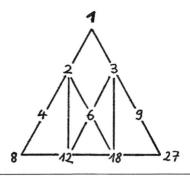

---

[17] Autre explication, dans «l'Apologie» de R. Herpin, p. 33, physique, par le rapport des poids qui servent à tendre la corde, qui prouve le désarroi de Bodin écartelé entre les musiques ancienne et moderne.

[18] *Rép.*, 562, cf. 1056.

Interprétation musicale: si 1 représente la dominante *mi*, le chiffre 2 qui est avec lui en «raison double» (multiplication par 2) désigne, comme nous l'avons vu, à une octave plus bas, le *mi* grave; *3* le *la* à la quinte inférieure; entre ces deux notes est une *quinte*, équivalente à la relation entre 2 et 3 c'est à dire multiplication du premier nombre par (1 +1/2) *(ratio sesquialtera)*. De même on aura des octaves entre 2, 4 et 8; des quintes entre 4 et 6, 8 et 12; des quartes, entre 3 et 4, 6 et 8 etc. . . .[19]. Et tous ces rapports sont chiffrés mathématiquement.

$$\left.\begin{array}{l} \text{1 mi} \\ \text{2 mi} \end{array}\right) \text{octave}$$

$$\left.\begin{array}{l} \text{3 la} \\ \text{4 mi} \end{array} \begin{array}{l}\text{) quinte} \\ \text{) quarte}\end{array}\right) \text{octave} \qquad \frac{2}{3} = \frac{4}{6} = \frac{8}{12} = \text{quinte}$$

$$\left.\begin{array}{l} \text{6 la} \\ \text{8 mi} \end{array} \begin{array}{l}\text{) quinte} \\ \text{) quarte}\end{array}\right) \text{octave} \qquad \frac{3}{4} = \frac{6}{8} = \text{quarte}$$

Mais que Bodin veut il prouver? Premièrement que toute harmonie procède d'une note souveraine, comme dans le royaume de l'Arithmétique, tout procède de l'Un, disposé, dans notre figure, au sommet, principe de la série des nombres – de *l'unité* qui est l'absolu et l'indivisible, la «Vierge inviolable»[20] – auquel encore correspond le point en géométrie. Il n'est de «symphonie», de consonance, d'échelle harmonique, que dérivée de la dominante.[21]

Je ne m'attarde pas à déduire la primauté de *l'Un*, qui ne fera doute pour aucun amoureux de la logique pure. Mais passons à ses conséquences, telles que nous les voyons fleurir dans la République:

a) D'abord la souveraineté de *Dieu*, l'Un qui règne sur l'univers. «Et tout ainsi que l'unité sur les trois premiers nombres . . . le poinct indivisible sur la ligne, superficie et le corps: ainsi peut on dire que ce grand Roy éternel, unique, fera reluire la splendeur de sa majesté et la douceur de l'harmonie.»[22] Donc autorité de la loi révélée de Dieu, ainsi que de sa «loi naturelle», qui seront le rempart des libertés et propriétés de bourgeois.

---

[19] Déjà remarquons sur ce schéma que pour avoir les intervalles de quinte ou de quarte, il faut passer d'un côté à l'autre du triangle, d'une série à l'autre. On doit sortir de la série géométrique des octaves (2.4.8), ce qui peut s'opérer également ment par voie d'addition (2 + 1) (cf. infra p. 75)

$$3 = \begin{cases} 2 \times (1 + 1/2) = \text{ratio sesquialtera} \\ 2 + 1 \qquad\quad = \text{emprunt à la serie arithmétique} \end{cases}$$

[20] *Rép.*, 561.

[21] Dans notre théorie moderne on pense l'harmonie au contraire à partir de la fondamentale (la), mais les effets pour notre propos reviennent au même, avec des formules inversées. Pour simplifier nous parlerons dans les pages suivantes à la moderne en fonction de la fondamentale.

[22] *Rép.*, 1060.

b) Le monde est construit tout entier, par proportions géométriques ou analogies, à l'image de son créateur. Le microcosme, ce «petit monde, n'a qu'*un* corps, et pour tous les membres *un* seul chef»[23] «parmi les pierres règne le diamant, parmi les astres le soleil»... quant à la famille aucun doute qu'elle ne «repose sur l'autorité d'*un* seul chef...»[24]

c) Ainsi sommes nous en Politique, contraints d'accepter le principe des *souverainetés* qui font le cœur de la théorie des *Etats:* souverainetés impartageables, indivisibles et semblables au «poinct en la géométrie»; mais cette même philosophie ne peut mener qu'à la *monarchie* en laquelle seule se parachève le règne de l'Un dans l'harmonie. Les deux «états» démocratique et aristocratique, impurs, engendrent le «discord».[25] Il faut arriver au monarque «eslevé par dessus tous les subjects, la majesté duquel ne souffre non plus division, que l'unité qui n'est point nombre, ni au rang des nombres, jaçoit que tous les autres n'ont force ny puissance que de l'unité».[26] Or l'absolutisme du monarque c'est l'absolutisme de sa *loi*, «playsir du prince», dont l'autorité sera souveraine pour autant que le prince n'enfreint pas les lois divines. S'il y eût bien sûr d'autres raisons pratiques à son éclosion, ce positivisme juridique, *philosophiquement*, est le fruit du culte logique de l'Un.

2. *Présence des harmoniques*

Mais chacun sait que la Politique de Bodin ne se réduit pas à l'invention prétendue de la souveraineté. «Entre les cordes de la lyre ou les diverses parties d'un chœur, une oreille experte supporte mal cet accord plat qu'on nomme l'unisson».[27] L'intervalle même de l'octave, auquel correspond le *carré* en géométrie, le rapport 1 à 2 (répétition à l'aigu de la fondamentale) laisse une impression de pauvreté.[28] Que dit la théorie musicale? On le rappelait tout à l'heure, que la fondamentale secrète naturellement ses harmoniques. C'est ici que Bodin nous propose une profusion de formules[29] dont je ne retiendrai qu'un exemple.

Au début de son dernier chapitre sur les justices distributive, commutative et harmonique[30] il montre la justice harmonique produite par «l'entremellement» des deux séries de chiffres constitués par progression *arithmétique et géométrique*. La progression *arithmétique* est celle formée par

[23] *Rép.*, 968.
[24] *Méthode*, 414
[25] *Rép.*, 608 , 950, Méthode 412, 413.
[26] *Rép.*, 1056.
[27] *Méthode*, 412.
[28] *Rép.*, 1020: «Entre 2, 4, 8 et 16 il ne se peut faire aucun accord».
[29] Supra p. 71 n. 14.
[30] *Rép.*, 1016.

l'addition du même nombre réitérée: 2 · 4 · 6 · 8. La différence est toujours 2 — comme dit Bodin les «raisons» des intervalles y sont *égales*. La progression *géométrique* opère par *multiplication:* 2 · 4 · 8 · 16. Entre chacun des intervalles, il n'y a plus égalité (au sens arithmétique du mot) mais «raisons semblables», (comme entre des triangles semblables), les rapports étant seuls égaux.

progression géométrique: 2 − 4 − 8 − 16

progression arithmétique: 2 − 3 − 4

ou: 4 − 6 − 8

ou: 8 − 12 − 16

progression harmonique: 2 − 3 − 4 − 6 − 8 − 12 − 16

Nous réaliserons l'harmonie en combinant les deux principes: entre les chiffres obtenus par multiplication par 2 (2 · 4 · 8 · 16), on intercale des intervalles «arithmétiquement» égaux: 3 par exemple entre 2 et 4, 6 entre 4 et 8. Nous obtenons la série: 2 · 3 · 4 · 6 · 8 · 12. Autrement dit dans les *octaves* (2 · 4 · 8 · 16) de la progression géométrique, nous insérons les harmoniques (3 · 6 · 12) (dans l'exemple choisi le sol). Nous obtenons l'accord de quinte (le rapport entre 2 et 3 · 4 et 6 · 8 et 12 — accords d'ut à sol) et par là même celui de quarte (le rapport entre 3 et 4 — égal au rapport entre 6 et 8, accord de sol à l'ut aigu).[31]

$$
\begin{array}{ll}
1 & \text{ut} \\
2 & \text{ut} \\
3 & \text{sol} \\
4 & \text{ut} \\
6 & \text{sol} \\
8 & \text{ut}
\end{array}
\left.
\begin{array}{l}
\text{) quinte} \\
\text{) quarte} \\
\text{) quinte} \\
\text{) quarte}
\end{array}
\right.
$$

$$\frac{2}{3} = \frac{4}{6} = \frac{8}{12} = \text{quarte}$$

$$\frac{3}{4} = \frac{6}{8} = \frac{12}{16} = \text{quinte}$$

Et ainsi aurons nous gagné l'accord merveilleux: nous avons uni les «extrêmes» par le «milieu» qui les «conjoint» — «comme la voix moyenne entre la basse et le dessus — pour faire un accord doux et mélodieux».[32] Fidèle aux traditions antiques, Bodin refuse de pousser la construction des harmoniques au delà de la quinte et de la quarte.[33]

---

[31] Cf. le schéma *Rép.*, 1059, que nous avons un peu simplifié à l'usage du lecteur moderne moins familier de ces matières.

[32] *Rép.*, 1018, 1019, 562.

[33] Cf. *Methodus*, 195 et 222, et la controverse avec Forestier l'allemand, reprise dans la *République* 562 et s. L'accord le plus suave est la quinte correspondant au rapport 1 + ½ qui se situe entre 2 et 3, ou 4 et 6: «itaque suavissimus ac primus omnium concentus, cum ab unitate discesseris, est ea quae ratione sesquialtera dicitur duorum ac trium, quae nullo interjecto medio copulentur». (*Methodus* 195). La quarte même semble ici proscrite, mais plutôt les autres intervalles: «quartum nullum efficit concentum, consequentia intervalla vehe-

Permettons nous une parenthèse. Quitte à faire de l'histoire de la musique, il est étonnant que Bodin n'ait pas tiré meilleur profit de l'exemple de la musique de son temps. A l'âge de la polyphonie; où se constitue le mode d'ut majeur, et avec lui l'accord «parfait», formé de la quinte et de la tierce naturelle majeure, quand l'harmonie devient enfin l'étude d'accords simultanés (non plus seulement des intervalles et de l'art de constituer la gamme)[34] et que les «consonances imparfaites» de tierce et de sixte,[35] considérées autrefois comme des dissonances, des «diaphonies», font leur entrée dans l'harmonie, Bodin ne sait que répéter les leçons de la musique antique, n'acceptant d'autres consonances que la quinte et la quarte. La *tierce* eût mieux tenu, du moins pour nos oreilles modernes, le rôle, de cet intermédiaire dont avait besoin son système. Ce n'est pas que Bodin soit absolument insensible à la polyphonie de son temps; il lui arrive de louer l'agrément des dissonances qui préparent la solution de l'accord parfait: les dissonances auront aussi leur fonction dans sa politique.[36] Mais pour l'essentiel il s'enferme dans l'harmonie de l'antiquité: les sources de Bodin sont livresques.

On estimera que ces minuties musicologiques sont superflues pour nous juristes et politologues d'aujourd'hui. Alors suivons plutôt Bodin dans ses déductions. Les harmoniques, procédant de la fondamentale, n'entrent pas moins dans son système politique que la fondamentale. Bodin en tire un art de vivre, art du «sage symposiaque» qui sait disposer les places des convives «entremellant» les hommes aux femmes, «le poure désireux au riche libéral»; le professeur et l'homme d'affaires;[37] art d'organiser les

---

menter discrepant» (*Meth.*, 222). Il n'est possible de relier harmonieusement deux notes distinctes d'un intervalle plus éloigné, qu'en les «conjoignant» au moyen de notes intermédiaires: entre 4, 9, qui discordent, il suffira de disposer 6, le nombre nuptial, obtenant une succession de quintes: 4.6.9. De la même manière, dans le *Methodus*, 195, Bodin irait jusqu'à admettre une *succession* de tierces. Mais le plus souvent il nous paraît interdire le rapport de tierce. Ainsi dans Rép. 1056 «Et qui voudra passer à 5, il fera un discord insupportable».

[34] Voir sur ces points en langue française M. EMMANUEL, Histoire de la langue musicale (1951), 63 et s., 169 et s., 335 et s.

[35] Maître Ange Ferrier reproche à Bodin d'avoir calomnié la tierce et la sixte entrelassée, qui «lient divinement bien les mélodies des instruments et des voix» ce que discute l'Apologie de R. Herpin, p. 33 recto et verso.

[36] *Rép.*, 1058: «Et tout ainsi qu'il ne se peut faire si bonne musique, où il n'y ait quelque discord, qu'il faut par nécessité entremesler pour donner plus de grâce aux bons accords: ce que fait le bon musicien pour rendre la consonance de la quarte, de la quinte et de l'octave plus agréable, coulant auparavant quelque discord ... aussi est il nécessaire qu'il y ait quelques fols entre les sages ...» cf. 603 ... 1060 etc.

[37] *Rép.*, 1018.

mariages;[38] puis toutes sortes de conséquences en droit privé, droit des biens[39] et droit contractuel,[40] droit des successions, [41] droit pénal pour la distribution des peines.[42] Mais de quoi s'agit il surtout, au point culminant de l'ouvrage? De fonder la *monarchie royale*: à la fois *«l'état* monarchique», comme il n'est pas de bonne harmonie sans que nous posions la souveraineté de la fondamentale – et le *«gouvernement* royal»[43] puisque la note fondamentale, libre d'entraves et parvenue à son parfait épanouissement, déployera toutes ses harmoniques. Le pouvoir souverain du monarque sous le respect des lois divines s'y répercutera par degrés, à travers la distribution, «par proportion harmonique»,[44] des commissions et des offices, «conjoignant» les forts et les faibles, les riches et les pauvres[45] par la médiation des états, clergé, noblesse, tiers état,[46] corporations et ménages. Sans que la puissance descende trop bas: car «la puissance du son décroit» à partir de la fondamentale; pour que nous comprenions que la nature abhorre le pouvoir de la multitude autant que l'accord qu'on obtiendrait en poursuivant jusqu'au bout la série des nombres.[47] L'harmonie s'arrête à la quarte, et à la quinte, lesquelles suffisent à «conjoindre» le peuple tout entier sous l'absolutisme du monarque: ce qui ne pouvait être obtenu dans l'état aristocratique, géométriquement distribué, ni dans l'état égalitaire ou arithmétique populaire – où sévit le «discord» – non plus que dans la monarchie seigneuriale ni tyrannique.

Et le fait est que Bodin en infère toute une *philosophie* du droit: partant de la souveraineté de la *loi* – non point cependant légaliste – le légalisme appartenait au système *démocratique*[48] qui veut l'égalité de tous

---

[38] *Rép.*, 1016 avec exemples de droit romain et de droit moderne.

[39] *Rép.*, 15, *Méthode*, 412.

[40] *Rép.*, 1047 – Le médecin fait plus payer le riche, que le malade pauvre, mais en proportion harmonique. Notons pourtant que Bodin dans la Méthode préfère appliquer aux contrats la proportion arithmétique plus conforme à son idéal juridique bourgeois (*Méthode*, 422); cf. *Juris Distributio* [4.20], 97.

[41] *Rép.*, 1016 – Voir aussi les exemples du Digeste allégués p. 1016, d'ailleurs assez peu concluants.

[42] *Rép.*, 1031, 1043. Tout meurtre sera puni de la mort, arithmétiquement, mais le noble aura le bénéfice de la décollation, par entremellement d'une proportion géométrique.

[43] *Rép.*, 254, 272, 280, 608, 1013, Méthode, 422.

[44] *Rép.*, 750.

[45] *Rép.*, 536.

[46] *Rép.*, 1057–1018. Toutes ces citations comportent la référence à l'harmonie.

[47] «Ut perspicuum sit tam abhorrere a natura ut imperium pluribus tribuatur quam concentus numerorum multitudini si perpetuam numerorum seriem sequamur.» (*Methodus*, 222.)

[48] *Rép.*, 1017 etc.; cf. 341.

devant la règle légale rigide, selon le principe arithmétique. Mais la justice démocratique légaliste est déficiente.[49] Il faut aussi de *l'équité*, qui est proportion géométrique, usage de la règle lesbienne pliant aux contours de chaque cas d'espèce.[50] Serait ce qu'il nous faudrait céder au principe géométrique de la justice «proportionnelle»? Non, c'est là l'excès de l'état *aristocratique* et sa faute est de refuser à la loi sa part nécessaire.[51] Dans le gouvernement royal, s'entremêlent les deux principes.

République p. 1020: La *loi*, représenté ici par *4*, sera suivie de ses harmoniques: la *quinte* qui est *l'équité* du prince; puis *l'octave*, le *legis actio* l'obéissance stricte à la loi par le magistrat, notons la par le chiffre 8; et finalement l'*office du juge* (quinte supérieure, exprimé par le chiffre 12).[52] Si l'on traduit en bon français: les officiers du Parlement, bien que subordonnés à la loi, possédent cette sphère d'autonomie qu'est l'*officium judicis*.

   4   lex
   6   equitas
   8   legis actio
 12   judicis officium

Ainsi s'accomplit la justice, elle atteint à sa fin suprême. Thémis, la Justice a trois filles dont les trois noms sont Eunomia, Eipieika, et Eirené, «c'est à dire loy droite, Equité et *Paix*»;[53] la Paix est le terme visé. La paix, l'amitié, le bon accord, qui rendent durables les Républiques et que manquent les autres régimes, sont le fruit de la «justice harmonique».

A la rigueur, logiquement, toute la politique de Bodin, le système dissimulé sous le foisonnement des exemples, peut s'expliquer à la lumière de sa philosophie du nombre. Je ne dis pas que nous ayons gagné à substituer au souverain la fondamentale, au conseil du Roi le nombre 6, et 12 à l'officier de justice, à mettre la politique en nombres. Mais que la progression harmonique était pour Bodin sa «raison», ou son chiffre cabalistique.

II. Commentaire

Nous nous bornerons à observer
1. le choix impliqué dans cette théorie parmi les sources traditionelles de la philosophie du droit; et
2. que cette option est contestable.

---

[49] *Rép.*, 331: «car ne n'est pas la loy qui fait le vrai gouvernement ains la vraye justice» etc. ... 943, 950 etc. ...

[50] *Rép.*, 1019.

[51] *Rép.*, 1021.

[52] Rép., 1020, cf. *Méthode*, 360; *Juris Distributio*, 84 et 93.

[53] *Rép.*, 1058; *Methodus*, 222; *Juris Distributio*, 97, qui usent d'une autre mythologie.

1. Sources de la philosophie de Bodin

Nous n'allons pas faire un relevé général des sources de la philosophie de Bodin. Il faudrait connaître ses rapports avec la *kabbale*, dans le sein de laquelle est entretenue la superstition du nombre;[54] et faire la part de l'influence de la pensée *juive*, de l'Ancien Testament lui même, où Bodin puise des nombres sacrés.[55] Cette philosophie de l'Un a derrière elle une tradition, pythagoricienne, gnostique, surtout *néoplatonicienne*; un immense passé. On ne sous-estimerait pas non plus l'apport de la *théologie* du moyen-âge finissant, nominaliste, volontariste, qui a mis l'accent sur la puissance «absolue» et l'unicité divines. S'y mêlent des sources stoïciennes. Fouillis d'influences.

Puisque nous n'envisageons ici que sa théorie de la *justice*, je voudrais seulement souligner que Bodin traitant ce chapitre, opte pour Platon contre Aristote.

a) Aristote

C'est d'Aristote (plus exactement d'Aristote *traduit* et traduit *inexactement* par les scolastiques) que vient la distinction célèbre des deux justices *distributive* et *commutative*.[56] Bodin s'est servi de ces deux mots; mais ne soyons pas dupes des termes: il est clair que chez Aristote (non plus que dans les commentaires excellents qu'en donne Saint Thomas) ils n'avaient aucunement le sens que Bodin leur prête.

Lorsqu'il expose la fonction de la première espèce de justice, qui «joue dans les distributions» et vise à donner à chacun sa part selon une certaine proportion *(égalité géométrique)* l'intention d'Aristote n'est pas, bien que Bodin veuille le lui faire dire,[57] d'exprimer la moindre préférence pour un ordre aristocratique; puisqu'Aristote laisse en suspens le critère de partage adopté, ayant soin même de préciser que le partage peut se faire également entre tous les citoyens libres en régime démocratique.[58] Pour la

---

[54] On pourrait aussi comparer la philosophie de Bodin à celle de Nicolas de Cues («per unum ergo fit omne numerus – numerus est post unum etc.»); la comparaison ferait ressortir la richesse de Nicolas de Cues.

[55] Par ex. dans *Méthode*, 394.

[56] *Eth. Nic.*, l. V, chap. III, IV et s.; cf. St. Thomas, In decem libros Aristotelis ad Nichomacum expositio ed. Marietti, 259 et s.; S. Theol. IIa, II ae, qu. 61.

[57] *Rép.*, 1015. D'après Bodin, le parti d'Aristote serait «de garder la justice géométrique ayant égard aux bienfaits et mérites et à la qualité d'un chacun» ... du moins «quand il serait question de partager des derniers publics ou les pays conquestés»; cf. 1034.

[58] *Ethique de Nicomaque* V 624 et s.; cf. Summa Theol., qu. 61, art. 2 «In aristocratica communitate attenditur secundum virtutem; in oligarchica, secundum divitias; in democratica, secundum libertatem, et, in aliis, aliter.»

seconde sorte de justice qu'Aristote appelle *corrective (diorthotiké)* et St. Thomas dans son commentaire de l'Ethique *directiva in commutationibus,* elle n'implique aucune préférence pour le système démocratique; puisque son objet n'était pas la distribution des honneurs, des biens et des charges; elle ne s'exerçait que dans les échanges *(sunallagmata, commutationes)*; il est bon que l'échange soit égal pour qu'il ne vienne pas perturber le partage effectué, quel qu'il soit.[59] Bodin n'a pas été chercher sa doctrine chez Aristote, ou bien il n'y a rien compris. L'érudition historique lui mangeait trop de temps.

Sans doute, Aristote, élève de Platon, instruit des thèses de Pythagore, n'avait pas manqué d'en nourrir sa philosophie juridique. Il professe que la justice *vise* à ce qu'elle peut atteindre d'harmonie; selon les cas de proportions dites géométriques, ou d'égalités dites arithmétiques. Telle est sa fin, et le «juste milieu», qui est la *mèse* des musiciens. La recherche de la bonne proportion *(suum cuique tribuere)* définit le domaine du droit. Mais pour lui les mathématiques ne peuvent apporter les *solutions:* il n'est pas question de soumettre l'invention du partage juste aux lois du nombre, à une quelconque formule musicale ou mathématique; à un *algorithme.* Le contenu du juste se cherche, prosaïquement, par l'observation de la nature, des cités et des groupes sociaux,[60] prenant modèle de préférence de la méthode biologique, avec l'aide de la dialectique et de la procédure tâtonnante de la controverse judiciaire.[61]

Bodin ignore outrageusement le texte de l'Ethique (livre V). Les attaques dont est parsemé le dernier chapitre,[62] comme d'ailleurs l'ouvrage tout entier de la *République*[63] contre Aristote, reposent sur de grossiers contresens.

Nous ne prétendons pas que Bodin n'ait, au fond, rien pris d'Aristote. Toute la modération de Bodin, sa fameuse douceur «angevine», ou sa modération «française» peut être aristotélicienne. Mais transposée à sa manière, qui est très différente. La philosophie de Bodin traitant des sources de la justice est incompatible à celle d'Aristote. Il ne comprend rien à la prudente démarche dialectique d'Aristote. «Ses paroles ne sont» –

---

[59] Cf. nos Seize Essais, Paris 1969, chap. XIII: Le contrat. Il est à noter que Bodin lui même, dans la *Méthode* (422) et la *Juris Distributio* (97) consent encore à ce que les échanges soient gouvernés par le principe de l'égalité arithmétique.

[60] Seize Essais, 49 et s.

[61] Seize Essais, 270 et s. Aristote, sur le fondement des exemples, et des opinions, cherche à constituer sa doctrine; Bodin applique à des exemples une doctrine constituée d'avance.

[62] *Rép.,* 1034, 1037, 1038, 1045, 1046 etc.

[63] *Rép.,* 8, 10, 70, 212, 216, 252, 264, 273, 281, 282, 508, 593, 750 etc.; cf. *Méthode,* 350, 357, 359, 373, 377, 413, 414 etc.

dit Bodin dans la *Méthode* – «ni d'un philosophe ni d'un géomètre; elles sentent le *dialecticien* hésitant devant une proposition, ainsi que le remarque finement le rabbin Maïmonide ... les démonstrations véritables ne laissent personne dans le doute».[64] Et puis Aristote attribue tous les effets aux causes secondes;[65] il offense la majesté de Dieu, qui est la cause première;[66] il profane l'Un, il s'enfonce dans le pluralisme, il n'a pas même le culte du Nombre.[67] D'ailleurs la mode est de rabaisser Aristote; à ce moment, on est fatigué de son «autorité»; on le rejette d'un seul bloc avec les plus dégénérés de ses commentateurs scolastiques; et c'est le tournant décisif pour la philosophie du droit; on part en quête de sources nouvelles, stoiciennes, épicuriennes, académiques.[68] En ce qui concerne la justice, Bodin se tourne vers Platon.

b) Platon – Pythagore
En fait, la doctrine bodinienne sur la justice se trouve préconstituée chez Platon – par excellence philosophe *mathématicien,* encore que les mathématiques ne soient pas pour lui la science suprême.[69] Platon lui, respectait le *nombre*: Aristote lui a reproché une théorie des idées-nombres.[70] Et lui aussi se trouvait tenté d'expliquer l'histoire par le nombre, et des chiffres cabalistiques;[71] cherchait précisément cet «ordre dont les nombres sont le principe»;[72] avait subi progressivement l'emprise du *pythagoricisme.*

Platon a la hantise de l'*Un* (et même de la Monarchie), Bodin reconnaît qu'il la lui doit: «si la série des nombres nous offre un objet digne de louange, c'est assurément l'unité, *ainsi que Platon* lui même l'a si magistralement exposé dans son Traité de l'Etre et l'Unité.»[73] Mais, pour Platon, dans ce monde de la multiplicité, on ne peut que participer à l'Un, rechercher une imitation de l'Un dans le multiple, et c'est l'harmonie.[74] D'où l'omniprésence de la *musique* à travers son œuvre. Tout le monde

---

[64] *Méthode,* 431; cf. *Rép.* 77, 329, 337 etc.

[65] *Méthode,* 387.

[66] *Méthode,* 432.

[67] *Méthode,* 394.

[68] Cf. notre Formation de la Pensée juridique moderne (1969) 410 et s.

[69] *Rép. de Platon,* VII 522 a, livre VI etc. Cf. Dıès, Le nombre de Platon. J. Adam, The number of Platon. L. Robın, La théorie Platonicienne des idées et des nombres selon Aristote. Ch. Mügler, Platon et la recherche mathématique etc.

[70] Arıstote, *Métaphysique* 1, M et N.

[71] Notamment, le thème bodinien que la corruption des régimes commencerait par la corruption de la musique est pris à Platon, cf. *Rép. de Pl.,* (VIII 546 et s.), Lois, 700, 702.

[72] *Lois,* 747a.

[73] *Méthode,* 413; cf. Lois, 965b, Parménide etc.

[74] Cf. *Lois,* 965 b.

sait la place éminente que Platon donne à la musique dans la *République* et les *Lois* et combien d'espace il consacre à la culture de la musique, enseignée, non à la manière empirique de certains esthètes, mais à l'école de *Pythagore,* c'est à dire comme gouvernée par le nombre et non par les sens.[75]

Or la *justice* est harmonie: l'accord interne entre la raison, le cœur et les instincts; proportionnelle, géométrique «comme entre la nète, l'hypate et la mèse».[76] Dans le macrocosme de la cité la *proportion* harmonieuse entre les honneurs distribués entre les personnes. L'idée de justice *distributive,* même en ce qui concerne les biens, substantiellement est de Platon,[77] et cette fois ci dans le sens même où l'entend Bodin.

Et même, celle de «justice *harmonique».* Qu'il y ait «deux sortes d'égalités», l'une stricte, légaliste, pratiquée dans le régime «democratique», l'autre proportionnelle, «monarchique», qu'il faille entre les deux chercher *un mélange,* toutes ces idées se trouvaient présentes en toutes lettres dans les *Lois* de Platon – livre VI.[78] La formule même de la progression harmonique – milieu entre la géométrique et l'arithmétique est inscrite dans le *Timée.*[79]

Bien sûr, Bodin n'a pas suivi l'enseignement de Platon à la lettre. Il avait trop de vanité pour ne pas prétendre faire du neuf, et affectait de critiquer Platon presque autant qu'Aristote, allant jusqu'à faire grief à Platon sur la foi de quelques passages de *Lois,*[80] d'être démocrate et égalitaire.[81] Quant à sa théorie des nombres, il la pille mais il la déclare incompréhensible.[82]

---

[75] *Rép. de Pl.,* VII., 531 c; cf. VII., 522 a etc.

[76] *Rép. de Pl.* 443 d, *Lois* III, 689 d etc. (c'est à dire les trois voix du choeur).

[77] *Rép. de Pl.* 297 b, *Lois,* 632, 738, 746, 747, 847, 848 (où la distribution des biens est faite selon l'égalité dans la similitude).

[78] *Lois,* 756, 757, 758 a – «Il y a en effet deux espèces d'égalité». La seconde, «la vraie, la meilleure» «attribue aux uns et aux autres proportionnellement sa part» ... «On doit recourir à l'une et à l'autre» et «le choix fait de cette manière tiendrait le milieu entre un régime monarchique et un régime démocratique» cf. *Lois,* 744 b et c – distributions des biens, des charges et magistratures «avec toute l'égalité possible quoique dans une proportion inégale».

[79] *Timée* 31 c, 32. Voir la note de l'ed. de la Pleiade p. 1488 mêmes proportions de 3/2, 4/3,2, quintes, quartes et octaves mais formule un peu différente de celles de Bodin, cf. *Rép.* 561. «Mais voyons l'opinion de Platon qui dit que les Républiques viennent à se ruiner quand l'harmonie défaut: et l'harmonie défaut quand on se despart de la quarte et la quinte au nombre nuptial; lequel commence par l'unité qui demeure vierge inviolable», etc.

[80] Sans doute *Lois,* livre VI, 753 b, 759 b, 768 b etc.

[81] *Rép.,* 1014, 1015, *Méthode* 412.

[82] *Rép.,* 562 et s.; *Méthode,* 388: «Rien n'est plus difficile ni obscur que les nombres de Platon».

Il y a bien de la différence entre la richesse et la hauteur des vues de Platon et le systématisme de Bodin. Bodin durcit la doctrine platonicienne; il a beaucoup plus que Platon privilégié l'*Un* et la *loi*.[83] (Ici a dû jouer le néoplatonisme et l'influence de la pensée religieuse judéochrétienne, du volontarisme occamien, ainsi que des juristes défenseurs du roi). N'empêche que Bodin a choisi le platonisme contre Aristote, contre la modestie, la prudence et le réalisme, il enfourche l'idéalisme, le culte des idées, l'hégémonie des mathématiques. Et cette option fut aussi celle de beaucoup de ses contemporains.

2. *Critique*

Là dessus, je me permets pour finir quelques réflexions. Puisque nous envisageons Bodin du point de vue de la philosophie, que nous discutons les principes *philosophiques* de son système, on n'a pas à traiter ici de l'*opportunité* pratique qu'il eut en son temps, à court terme: je ne vais pas nier que la *République* de Bodin n'ait répondu aux exigences de la situation: renouveau d'ordre, mesure bourgeoise. Nous ne contestons pas non plus la *beauté* de l'œuvre de Bodin: quand on construit la Politique à l'image de la musique et quand on s'inspire de Platon, on peut faire une œuvre charmante de philosophie politique. Laissons lui ce mérite rarissime. Mais la vraie science n'accepte pas d'être immolée au pragmatisme ou à l'esthétique.

a) Nous pouvons en juger d'abord par ses *résultats à long terme*, puisque la doctrine de Bodin sévit encore parmi nous, mais que se révèle aujourd'hui sa nocivité.

La *souveraineté*, primat de l'*Un*, nous vivons encore dominés par cette thèse sortie de Bodin; mais aujourd'hui elle nous encombre, gêne la constitution de l'Europe, interdit le fédéralisme et l'autonomie des régions. Combien plus vraie, plus réaliste, la description par Aristote du *régime mixte*, et du partage naturellement opéré des pouvoirs publics, combien plus juste la mesure que fait Aristote du degré d'«autarchie» nécessaire à chaque cité! Quant aux harmoniques, aux quintes et aux quartes, à la doctrine bodinienne du *gouvernement*, l'image est plus jolie que féconde. Elle ne me paraît apporter aux sujets contre l'absolutisme que des garanties illusoires, plutôt verbales que substantielles. – Ou bien la monarchie

---

[83] La vraie justice pour Platon est proportionnelle, égalité géométrique, qu'il faudra seulement tempérer par quelque chose de l'arithmétique (*Lois*, 756 à 758 cit.) – Au contraire Bodin place en tête l'unité, la fondamentale, le souverain, la loi: et c'est l'équité qui tient le rôle de la quinte, de l'harmonique (supra p. 76-77).

«royale» est, d'après Bodin, celle où le prince observait les «lois divines»; mais que diront les lois divines? Bodin déduit du Décalogue la garantie des libertés et propriétés des bourgeois, d'après une exégèse alors communément acceptée par la bourgeoisie.[84] Malheureusement le Décalogue ni l'Evangile ne disent rien de tel; ils disent très peu de choses sur le droit. Il ne faut pas abuser de l'Unité divine: nous ne savons pas ce qu'est Dieu, ni le contenu de la loi éternelle, comme Bodin aurait pu l'apprendre de la *Somme* de Saint Thomas.

Alors – seconde définition du gouvernement modéré – reste à se fier aux *harmoniques* de la volonté souveraine. Au lieu de bâtir comme Aristote une procédure de découverte du juste par l'observation et la discussion dialectique, et de maintenir la loi positive à sa place subsidiaire, nous en remettre aux conséquences de la loi positive du monarque du soin d'engendrer l'équité, la répartition des offices, honneurs, biens et charges. On compte que la loi produira ses quintes et ses quartes. Le moins qu'on puisse dire de ces garanties est qu'elles manquent de certitude! La suite des temps l'a montré.

b) Remontons aux *principes*. Dans le système d'idées générales qui préside à la *République* – tout est contestable et fragile.

A commencer par la théorie de la *musique*. Elle tient plus des mathématiques que de l'analyse musicale. Pour nous, contrairement à Platon, nous ne voyons pas la musique procédant des lois de Pythagore; la beauté procède du génie de chaque compositeur; les lois de l'harmonie viennent ensuite et ne disent peut être pas l'essentiel ou ne le disent qu'avec retard. Déjà la musique de la Renaissance avait dépassé la quinte et la quarte et l'harmonie des anciens. Les traités d'harmonie ne sont pas le compendium de la musique.

Ensuite la *théorie du droit*. Malheureusement les comparaisons musicales conviennent mal à la science du droit. Il se trouve encore moins de régularité harmonique (et mathématiquement chiffrable) dans la justice que dans la musique. On pourrait rêver d'harmonie (du règne retrouvé de l'Un et de ses harmoniques) dans certaines *familles* idéales, ou des communautés religieuses: moins dans le *justum politicum*, comme le remarquait Aristote. Il n'est guère de parallélisme entre le droit et la musique. Rien ne prouve que les français d'aujourd'hui aient la pire des constitutions parce que maintenant ils chantent faux.[85]

---

[84] Ce qui reviendrait, contre toute justice, au nom de «tu ne voleras pas» à consacrer l'état actuel des *possessions* quel qu'il soit. Bodin ne parle plus d'attribuer à chacun la part qui lui revient, mais de *«rendre* à chacun le sien» (*Rép.*, 948); Cf. nos Seize Essais, 117 et s.

[85] Supra n. 13.

Or la source du mal se situe au niveau de la *philosophie*: dans le rejet de la tradition du Lycée à laquelle vient se substituer le déferlement des trompeuses mystiques néoplatoniciennes, et la vogue de Platon. Dans l'abandon du réalisme pour l'attitude *idéaliste*.

Moment où la philosophie cesse de se fonder sur l'expérience, l'observation du monde sensible, pour s'accrocher aux idées pures, sacrifiant au simple, au logique. C'est dans ce climat retrouvé de l'idéalisme platonicien qu'a pu s'opérer chez Bodin la réduction du juste au beau, et du beau au mathématique; et de là sous les formes diverses qu'elle revêt à l'époque moderne, l'emprise croissante des mathématiques sur le droit. Il n'en est pas de forme plus extrême que la religion de *l'Un*, qui est suprême valeur *logique*, la suprême valeur pour l'esprit laissant le réel pour l'idée. La plus grande part de la théorie juridique moderne a vécu fascinée par *l'Un*: qu'il s'agisse de l'Un du *cosmos* ou de la cité utopique – harmonieuse et communautaire – ou que l'on entreprenne de reconstruire des «sociétés» artificielles à partir de l'*Un* de l'individu: – nominalisme,[86] refondant toute la science du droit comme système de droits subjectifs[87] – doctrines de Hobbes ou de Locke. Une solution intermédiaire (et c'est surtout dans cette voie que travaille Bodin) est d'axer l'ordre politique sur l'Un de la personne du prince: Bodin fut aussi le successeur des jurisconsultes royaux, dressant la liste des droits subjectifs de leurs maîtres, *jura regalia*, devenus chez lui les sept marques de la souveraineté.

Pour ma part, je me méfierais de l'*Un*, se présentât-il accompagné de ses «harmoniques» naturelles, ou plus tard chez Fichte ou Hegel de ses suites prétendues «dialectiques». Aux *systèmes* qui sortent de l'*Un*, procédant par voie descendante, s'opposent les sciences qui partent de l'observation du *multiple*, de là s'élevant à ce qu'elles peuvent d'ordre et d'intelligibilité. Les systèmes sont illusoires. Et c'est pourquoi nous préférons la théorie du régime *mixte*, de la pluralité des pouvoirs, et le pluralisme des sources du droit (nature-loi-opinions diverses discordantes des jurisconsultes).

Mais voici l'heure où l'on construit, à partir de l'Un; où l'on «progresse», on produit des *systèmes* de droit, par voie de déduction logique, ou plus joliment, comme Bodin, par quintes et quartes. Systèmes de normes coupées des faits,[88] châteaux de cartes théoriques. A commencer par les systèmes dits du droit naturel moderne, que préfigurait le projet

---

[86] De l'*Un* peut sortir l'anarchisme, aussi bien que l'ordre, selon que l'on part de l'individu ou de la collectivité.

[87] Cf. nos Seize Essais, 140 et s.

[88] Isolement du droit chez Bodin dans la théorie des *Etats*, qui est théorie pure; cf. chez Kelsen l'obsession de «l'unité de l'ordre juridique», et de la formation progressive du droit par degrés.

bodinien de «droit universel».[89] Viendra plus tard la réaction du sociologisme, la réalité se vengera.

L'idéalisme se recommande par ses ambitions. Bodin se figurait que la justice ne fait «pas doute», ni ne prête à la «controverse», que «la vraye justice naturelle est plus luisante que la splendeur du soleil»;[90] et il se vantait d'en avoir trouvé l'algorithme, la formule de «l'harmonie». Les systèmes politiques modernes construits comme celui de Bodin sous l'emprise de l'idéalisme, visent communément très haut dans leur effort pour astreindre le monde à l'idée; en fin de compte ils retombent bas, et à côté de la question.

---

[89] *Juris Universi Distributio* etc., *Méthode*, 275: Bodin glorifie les juristes formés dans la philosophie qui auraient l'avantage de comprendre que «la nature de la justice n'est pas de changer» et savent «déduire les origines du droit d'un premier principe» etc.

[90] *Rép.*, 419.

II. BODINS HISTORISCHES DENKEN

Girolamo Cotroneo

Le Quatrième Chapitre de la Methodus
Nouvelles Analyses et Perspectives Historiographiques

I. Critère pour un jugement de valeur sur l'œuvre historiographique

Parmi les nombreux problèmes historiographiques posés par Jean Bodin dans sa *Methodus ad facilem historiarum cognitionem,* on remarque, pour leur originalité, ceux qu'il aborde dans le quatrième chapitre de l'œuvre où, sous le titre de «De historicorum delectu», sont indiqués les critères qui permettent de porter un jugement de valeur sur les œuvres historiographiques, et où est faite pour la première fois une tentative d'histoire de l'historiographie. On a plusieurs fois observé combien cette partie de l'œuvre bodinienne s'est directement inspirée du premier livre du *De institutione historiae* de François Baudouin, qui aurait servi de modèle à Bodin, ajoutant même que Baudouin aurait sur lui l'avantage de n'avoir pas puisé à des sources exclusivement littéraires, mais d'avoir senti la nécessité de lire aussi l'histoire ancienne sur les monnaies, les pierres tombales, dans les chants et dans les symboles des peuples primitifs. Mais, en fait, les préoccupations qui animent les deux auteurs sont différentes: d'un côté Baudouin est engagé dans une leçon de caractère exclusivement méthodologique et didactique; son exposé veut démontrer à travers quelles sources l'histoire universelle peut être reconstruite de façon cohérente, et c'est pour cela qu'il fait appel aux symboles et aux chants des anciens qui peuvent être traduits en histoire, pour passer ensuite aux sources historiographiques traditionnelles, dont la première est la Bible, puis aux autres sources possibles, revendiquant en termes passionnés la légitimité de cette méthode de reconstruction. Son exposé est donc purement indicatif: la valeur et la portée des auteurs et des œuvres historiographiques qu'il cite l'intéressent relativement; il ne fait pas une enquête critique mais il indique seulement quels sont, à son avis, les meilleurs historiens. Bodin se place au contraire sur un plan différent: tout d'abord, il a déjà passé en revue, même s'il l'a fait d'un point de vue général et sans les divisions par périodes de Baudouin, les instruments utilisables pour la reconstruction du récit historique: le problème est donc clos désormais pour lui; d'autre part, plus qu'une recherche de sources historiques, son ouvrage est un examen critique de la littérature historique, une série d'idées-jugements sur les figures les plus représentatives de l'historiographie ancienne et moderne: le fait d'accepter ou de refuser les auteurs qu'il considère, lui est dicté non par des exigences didactiques mais par des exigences critiques; et ses jugements, souvent tranchants, sont restés célèbres et ont influencé considérablement la littérature historique qui a suivi (La Popelinière, par exemple, s'inspira de ce chapitre pour son *Histoire des histoires*) et ont contraint d'éminents lettrés comme Montaigne, nous le verrons, à intervenir dans le débat suscité par Bodin dans cet ouvrage.

Le critère général, selon lequel sont établis ces jugements de valeur, se ressent du changement radical, opéré dès le siècle précédent, dans la conception de l'œuvre historiographique, qui était devenue surtout une œuvre littéraire et politique et devait être jugée comme telle: Bodin ne manque pas de relever combien peuvent être déterminantes, dans la rédaction du traité historique, la personalité de l'auteur, sa formation culturelle, sa capacité littéraire, son expérience politique, sa conception du monde. Or, ces éléments ne pouvaient être exigés que de l'historien moderne, dont la manière de composer était tout à fait différente de celle des chroniqueurs du moyen âge, qui n'avaient certes pas besoin de formation politique et littéraire pour rédiger leurs chronologies. C'est pourquoi le critère de jugement devait être tout à fait nouveau et par conséquent la critique ne pouvait être faite aux historiens que par ceux qui posséderaient eux-mêmes des dons d'historien: Bodin suit donc une démarche pratiquement inconnue à toute la critique historique de l'époque, démarche que nous pourrions dire de «personnalisation» du travail historique, car il introduit, parmi les critères de choix, un élément psychologique concernant la personne même de l'auteur, dont le comportement humain – sérieux, engagement politique, culture – doit être nécessairement pris en considération, du moment que l'on prétend juger son œuvre. Que ces pétitions de principe se soient avérées par la suite contradictoires par rapport à certains «choix» postérieurs, c'est ce que nous verrons lorsque nous avancerons dans la lecture du chapitre: mais nous pouvons dès maintenant anticiper, et l'occasion ne nous manquera pas de le répéter, en disant que l'opposition fondamentale réside dans le fait que Bodin était sollicité, d'un côté par des impératifs classificatoires avec les formes schématiques qu'ils comportent et de l'autre par des impératifs politiques et littéraires qui devaient s'exprimer sous la forme de traités: son hésitation entre ces tendances constitue le motif commun d'une grande partie des principes posés dans la *Methodus*.

Avant d'examiner individuellement les historiens les plus représentatifs, Bodin essaie de mettre au point d'autres problèmes concernant encore les critères qui doivent guider dans le choix des auteurs. Tout d'abord il y a deux sortes d'écrivains dont les œuvres ne peuvent en aucun cas, être considérées: ce sont les panégyristes et les écrivains gagés. On ne peut, en aucun cas, tenir compte, écrit Bodin, de ces auteurs qui chantent la gloire et les vertus d'un individu, sans jamais mentionner ses défauts: c'est ainsi que ne méritent aucune considération les écrits d'Eginhard sur Charlemagne, ceux d'Eusèbe sur Constantin, ceux de Paul Jove sur Côme de Médicis, etc. On peut remarquer dans ces passages le début d'une âpre polémique, qui atteindra son paroxysme dans les pages consacrées à l'analyse de l'œuvre de Paul Jove, contre les historiens de cour, les historiens officiels, qui ne pourront jamais, à cause de ce défaut originel, s'élever au niveau de l'objectivité, n'auront jamais l'esprit libéré des passions, et qui, en outre, n'ayant pas habituellement assumé de charges politiques puisqu'ils ont toujours vécu à l'ombre de leurs seigneurs, manquent de cet «usus», c'est-à-dire de cette expérience, qui, avec les «literae» (c'est-à-dire la culture) et la «natura» (c'est-à-dire le talent personnel), constitue l'élément indispensable à la formation du véritable historien.

Le problème de l'objectivité de l'historien et donc de la véracité de son récit même, conséquence directe des précédentes assertions de Bodin, constitue un des problèmes centraux de cette partie de la *Methodus*: Bodin se rend compte de l'énorme difficulté du problème, contre lequel il se débattra longtemps avant de pouvoir donner une solution cohérente. Quand il a placé l'historien au centre des événements qu'il raconte, il a admis implicitement sa participation directe au récit historique même avec tous les dangers, au détriment de l'objectivité, que cette participation comporte. Il lui faut maintenant, d'une part concilier ses précédentes assertions sur la participation de l'historien, et de l'autre insister sur la nécessité de l'entière objectivité du récit. Que l'historien doive être absolument objectif, c'est un axiome pour Bodin, mais «quoniam difficile est admodum omni perturbatione carere», il faudra prendre quelques précautions pour permettre à celui qui veut traiter des sujets historiques, d'exprimer en toute sérénité ses propres opinions. La seule manière de pouvoir écrire tranquillement l'histoire, affirme Bodin, est de ne jamais s'occuper de l'histoire de son époque: en effet peu nombreux sont ceux, dit-il, qui osent écrire sur les événements et les problèmes contemporains, par crainte de porter préjudice à quelque personnage vivant ou de l'irriter, et de courir ensuite le risque de subir quelques représailles; il est donc beaucoup plus opportun de laisser aux successeurs le soin de reconstruire historiquement les événements du présent; quant à ceux, conclut Bodin, qui chercheraient pendant leur vie la gloire d'écrire des œuvres historiques, la seule voie ne peut être que celle de la reconstruction du passé, grâce à l'étude des sources publiques et privées. La solution est naïve, même si au fond elle ne manque pas d'élégance: certes la situation politique des années au cours desquelles Bodin écrivait la *Methodus*, n'était pas des plus heureuses et la lutte entre les factions qui devenait plus dure de jour en jour, justifiait amplement les craintes de Bodin. Mais ce qui nous intéresse davantage et que nous pouvons découvrir dans l'œuvre bodinienne, si nous allons au-delà de la forme naïve de l'expression, c'est la conviction que l'œuvre historique doit toujours se présenter comme une œuvre politique et impliquer, en tant que telle, l'opinion de l'historien sur les faits qu'il raconte.

Si Bodin révèle ici d'un côté, sous une banale expression de prudence, sa manière de comprendre l'histoire, dans son rapport avec la politique, d'un autre côté il se montre très éloigné des conceptions historiographiques modernes: et nous le remarquons dans la conclusion de son dernier discours, quand il invitait à écrire l'histoire du passé, puisque là seulement l'objectivité de l'historien pouvait s'exercer entièrement. Le lien entre passé et présent, l'impossibilité d'écrire sur le passé si ce n'est sous l'impulsion de la situation présente, l'inutilité d'une recherche historique qui n'ait pas pour but d'éclairer des problèmes contemporains, ce sont là des concepts dont Bodin est encore bien loin. Si, en défendant, comme il l'a fait précédemment, l'étude désintéressée de l'histoire, il s'est éloigné de certaines de ces intuitions modernes, qui caractérisent au contraire une grande partie de ses pages, l'intuition centrale du lien entre historiographie et politique demeure néanmoins toujours en lui et ses choix ultérieurs, ses préférences pour les écrivains de traités politiques, confirmeront de plus en plus sa position d'historien engagé.

Voici, étroitement liée au problème de la vérité et de l'objectivité de l'historien, une question qui, d'un côté, semble de caractère exclusivement méthodologique, puisqu'elle concerne la forme du récit historique, et de l'autre, à cause des conséquences qui en découlent, se révèle d'une portée bien plus vaste: «Sed magna dubitatio me angit – écrit maintenant Bodin – utrum historici laudare, vituperare, ac de re proposita sententiam ferre; an vero legentibus judicium integrum relinquere debeant.» Le problème, on le voit, ne concerne plus désormais l'objectivité de l'historien, donnée ici pour certaine, mais bien au contraire la plus vaste question de l'intervention subjective de l'écrivain sans sa narration: les deux alternatives définies ici – la pure et simple narration des faits ou le jugement de valeur porté sur ces mêmes faits – révèlent une fois encore les deux pôles opposés entre lesquels Bodin oscille, en matière de composition du récit historique. Dans le «Proemium» par lequel débute son œuvre, Bodin semble avoir déjà pris une position claire à cet égard: «Ut ii qui se flagitiis penitus dedidissent – écrivait alors Bodin – iustissimis maledictis proeinderentur: qui autem ulla virtute claruissent, suo merito laudarentur.» La position de Bodin semble ici très claire; il est facile de déduire, d'après ces lignes, que le devoir de l'historien est d'intervenir, de servir de juge entre le bien et le mal, de décider entre le tort et la raison. Mais cette position originelle, dictée par l'enthousiasme avec lequel il abordait son œuvre, devient plus prudente lorsque Bodin pénètre davantage dans les problèmes qu'il envisage. Donner à l'historien le rôle de juge implique immédiatement un gros problème: l'historien sera-t-il en mesure de juger? A cette question Bodin répond par une argumentation qui semble avoir été calquée sur l'argumentation platonicienne du *Ione*: «Cum autem nihil difficilius sit quam recte iudicare, quis non graviter ferat historicum qui nullam publici muneris aut consilii partem attigerit, de summis Rerumpublicarum moderatoribus sententiam ferre? Quid autem ineptius quam eos qui numquam acies viderunt, imperatorum offensiones inter ipsos et victorias disceptare?» L'argument est suggestif, mais contradictoire, au moins dans sa première formulation, par rapport aux prémisses. En effet, après avoir tant insisté sur l'«usus», sur la compétence de l'historien, sur l'incidence que peut avoir son expérience sur son travail historiographique, au moment de donner une application cohérente à l'intuition centrale de sa doctrine, Bodin semble reculer, se rabattant sur les formes historiographiques sèches et dépouillées, comme celles de Xénophon, de Thucydide et surtout de César ou de Guichardin, «qui raro admodum, nec nisi oblique ac prudenter judicium ferunt», à l'opposé desquelles on trouve, au contraire, la forme historiographique adoptée par Paul Jove, «qui Selemi et Ismaëlis Sophi, tum etiam Caroli quinti et Pauli Pontificis max., atque aliorum principum odiosas comparationes suo judicio metitur». La polémique de Bodin a ici une signification plus profonde qu'il ne semblerait à première vue: si, comme nous le disions, il existe dans la *Methodus* une question sans équivoque, c'est bien celle de la signification politique de l'histoire à laquelle Bodin ne renonce jamais, même lorsqu'il semble en être très loin: en interdisant ici à l'historien de donner son opinion personnelle sur les faits qu'il raconte, Bodin en fait une simple question de forme et non pas de contenu: c'est ce que l'on voit d'après le choix de ses auteurs préférés, mentionnés plus haut, parmi lesquels figure un Guichardin, qui est l'écrivain politique par excellence.

Une question de forme, donc, disions-nous: dans ces passages, et on le verra mieux quand Bodin commencera sa célèbre polémique contre Paul Jove, la position que prend Bodin contre ce type d'historiographie ornée, où l'ornement littéraire préoccupe l'écrivain beaucoup plus que le contenu de l'œuvre, est implicite. Quand Bodin oppose la prudence de jugement qu'il a eu l'occasion d'admirer dans les œuvres de Thucydide ou de Guichardin, à l'exposé oratoire et aux comparaisons téméraires de Paul Jove, il sous-entend une polémique contre le ton rhétorique d'une certaine littérature historique humaniste, dans la mesure où les récentes conceptions de l'historiographie politique qu'il avait reçues des historiens italiens, subsistaient dans son esprit en même temps que les formes chronologiques,

que la tradition historiographique protestante lui inspirait; et il avait vu
que l'historiographie savante pouvait facilement dégénérer en forme oratoire, comme celle de Paul Jove et de Pietro Bembo précisement, faisant
perdre ainsi au récit historique ces caractères d' «essenzialità» dont les
œuvres de César offrent un exemple admirable. Mais c'est justement pour
cette raison que l'on se tromperait si l'on croyait que Bodin souhaite purement et simplement un retour à l'historiographie pré-humaniste ou du
moins à la tradition germanique: nous avons vu, du reste, que ses préférences vont à des écrivains tout à fait étrangers aux formes de la chronique. Le plus gros effort de Bodin est ici d'adapter entre elles ces deux
exigences, de les unifier dans une nouvelle forme historiographique, où la
beauté du style consisterait dans sa simplicité, suivant ainsi les grands
exemples de Xénophon, Thucydide et surtout César. La polémique qui
semblait nous éloigner des conceptions historiographiques fondamentales
de Bodin, ne fait que toucher, au contraire, le problème de la forme mais
non celui, bien plus important, du contenu ethico-politique de l'histoire.

Le rapport continu qui existe entre le monde de l'histoire et celui de la
politique, le lien entre le réel et l'idéal, sont des concepts que Bodin entre-
voit confusément, même s'il ne parvient pas à les développer de manière
cohérente: il arrive à certaines solutions, poussé par un certain goût et par
certains exemples d'historiographie politique, qui le séduisaient profond-
dément, mais il ne réussit pas à les théoriser de façon systématique. En
outre sa mentalité portée à la classification, sa tendance, même tempérée
par les nouvelles expériences historiographiques, à adopter des formes
schématiques, l'empêchent de formuler un discours rigoureusement logique sur ces problèmes que pourtant il sentait. La fonction didactique de
l'histoire était fortement ressentie dans son esprit et sa formation philosophique néo-platonicienne le portait à placer les vérités morales hors du
temps et de l'espace, catégories éternelles, auxquelles le bien et le mal
pouvaient facilement être réduits. Cependant sa polémique contre la
rhétorique et les préciosités stylistiques révèle clairement son effort pour
théoriser un concept pragmatique de l'histoire, alors que le rationnalisme
et le réalisme d'un Machiavel, par exemple, même si parfois il les repoussait avec indignation, influaient profondément sur ses conceptions.

Mais si, avant de conclure sur ce sujet, nous revenons sur le problème
de fond de ces pages, il n'est pas difficile de s'apercevoir que la position
de Bodin à l'égard de l'historiographie critique, n'est pas, en fin de
compte, aussi radicale qu'elle peut le sembler à première vue: il est vrai
qu'il a exalté la «nuda historia», qu'il a insisté sur la valeur de ces auteurs
qui ne participent pas avec passion aux événements qu'ils racontent, mais
on peut dire que tout cela a été écrit davantage sous l'impulsion de sa
fougue polémique contre les «lettrés», que dicté par de précises exigences
théoriques. Nous disions précédemment que Bodin, bien que séduit encore

par les formes de la chronique, n'en souhaite pas le retour, car il est
fasciné par les histoires politiques: ce qui explique la position tempérée et
cohérente qui ressort à la dernière analyse. Juger un événement historique, dit Bodin, est une entreprise difficile, et elle le devient d'autant plus
si l'historien n'a pas la compétence et les connaissances suffisantes: on
voit réapparaître ici cet «usus», que Bodin semblait avoir oublié et qui
au contraire, dans la dernière formulation qu'il s'apprête maintenant à
donner, devient l'instrument qui permet à l'historien d'entrer dans le
cœur du récit. Le jugement de l'historien, conclut Bodin, doit toujours
cependant être inspiré par la prudence («prestabilius sit historico narra-
tione proposita timide judicare»), mais quand la valeur de l'historien le
permet, le jugement sur les événements devient alors légitime: «Neque
enim magnorum virorum de rebus gestis judicia reprehendo, si modo
tales sunt qui recte judicium ferre possint.»

Par ces dernières précisions, nécessaires pour une définitive mise au
point de la question, Bodin a conclu la première partie de son discours.
Il s'agit, comme on l'a vu, d'une théorisation des critères de valeur sur
l'œuvre historiographique, travail indispensable pour celui qui se prépare,
comme c'est son cas, à examiner toute la littérature historique présente
et passée. Ces précisions données, Bodin est maintenant prêt à faire des
choix concrets; son immense érudition lui offrait un nombre incalculable
d'œuvres à juger; en établissant dans cette phase préparatoire des canons
de jugements, il a fixé clairement les limites entre lesquelles il s'apprête à
faire l'analyse des auteurs et des œuvres.

II. Histoire de l'historiographie

Il n'est pas du tout facile de suivre Bodin dans cet «excursus» parmi les
historiens, en raison du manque d'ordre de son exposé, à cause des omis-
sions, des retours en arrière et des interférences qui caractérisent ces pages:
en dernière analyse, parmi tous les jugements exprimés par Bodin sur un
nombre considérable d'historiens, n'ont d'importance que les plus originaux, qui révèlent une certaine tendance personnelle de l'auteur, et non
pas ceux qui reflètent un jugement conforme aux goûts de l'époque et que
l'on retrouve donc, de façon plus ou moins identique, dans les pages des
différents historiens de l'époque, comme par exemple ceux sur Cicéron,
sur Polybe, sur Salluste, sur César, sur Denys d'Halicarnasse, sur Dion
Cassius, etc. Fondamentaux au contraire sont certains jugements auda-
cieux de Bodin, tels que ceux qu'il exprime sur Plutarque, sur Guichardin,
sur Bembo, sur Tacite, sur Tite-Live. Il s'agit des jugements les plus polémiques, soit positifs, soit négatifs, formulés par Bodin, et qui s'opposaient
à une tradition, qu'elle fût ancienne ou récente: la défense de l'«impie»

Tacite ou la condamnation de Jove, le plus illustre représentant de l'histoire humaniste pure, sont les exemples les plus éclatants de la rupture de Bodin avec une tradition historiographique. Or, cette conception provenait de la différente perspective sous laquelle le problème de l'histoire se présentait ces années-là: l'élément politique tendait maintenant à supplanter, dans le récit historique, la dimension littéraire, et, comme nous l'avons déjà mentionné, le caractère «désintéressé» de l'étude historique avait perdu, après Machiavel et Guichardin, après l'introduction de l'étude historique du droit, après la dimension scientifico-naturaliste de l'histoire que Bodin lui-même s'apprêtait à introduire, avait perdu, disions-nous, toute sa vigueur, pour être remplacé, au moins dans l'esprit des écrivains les plus éclairés et les plus rationnels de l'époque, par une historiographie engagée, dont la valeur résidât non pas dans la forme mais dans le fond, dans l'utilité immédiate, dans les avantages qu'elle pouvait apporter pour définir les termes du débat enflammé qui avait lieu ces années-là.

C'est sous ce jour qu'il faut considérer la polémique déclenchée contre l'un des plus illustres historiens de Rome, contre l'ardent et poétique Tite-Live, auquel Bodin n'hésite pas, en contradiction évidente avec l'historiographie humaniste qui l'avait considéré comme modèle, à donner le qualificatif du plus superstitieux des historiens, le reconnaissant incapable d'expliquer de manière rationnelle ou du moins plausible les phénomènes historiques, et toujours prêt à se tirer d'embarras en recourant à un «Deus ex machina». Les pages que Bodin consacre à Tite-Live, auxquelles font «pendant», à notre avis, celles qu'il dédie à Guichardin, sont parmi les plus significatives, à cause de l'intelligence de sa conception historique mais aussi de toute sa philosophie. Il faut, avant tout, relever que Tite-Live était considéré comme un auteur tout à fait digne de foi, si l'on considère que même Machiavel, le rationaliste Machiavel, avait utilisé dans ses célèbres *Discours sur la première décade*, l'œuvre de l'écrivain romain, y cherchant des exemples à suivre pour l'exercice de l'art politique: et les mythes du passionné historien de Rome n'avaient pas le moins du monde troublé le plus réaliste des écrivains politiques de l'époque. Il convient cependant d'examiner l'attitude de Bodin surtout dans les résultats qu'il se proposait d'atteindre, dans la difficile doctrine de l'art historique: alors que Machiavel pouvait en toute tranquillité faire un usage libre et subjectif du texte de Tite-live, ne s'intéressant nullement aux faits historiques – qui, et cela est bien connu des lecteurs de l'œuvre de Machiavel, sont extraits non seulement de Tite-Live mais aussi d'autres historiens de l'époque –, mais aux théories politiques qu'il pouvait tirer de ces mêmes faits, indépendamment des explications fabuleuses de Tite-Live, Bodin, au contraire, abordait dans ces pages un tout autre genre de problèmes: il menait là sa bataille contre une certaine historiographie à caractère théiste, ou du moins quelque peu métaphysique, incapable de donner une explication purement humaine des faits historiques; et Tite-Live lui semblait être un représentant tellement illustre de cette tendance qu'il fallait le démolir rapidement. Machiavel réfléchissait, par l'intermédiaire de Tite-Live, sur l'histoire romaine pour en tirer des conséquences politiques actuelles: Bodin est, au contraire, occupé en ce moment à formuler une conception exclusivement pragmatique de l'histoire, à instaurer une méthode de recherche rationnelle d'où devaient être bannis tous les éléments mythiques dont étaient remplies à ses yeux les pages des écrivains anciens.

Il n'était certes pas facile pour Bodin, formé aux écoles philosophiques néo-platoniciennes et tourmenté par des problèmes de métaphysique, d'admettre une réalité qui ne fût qu'humaine et d'où était exclue une participation ou l'interférence de Dieu. Cependant la tentative qu'il fait pour trouver une solution, grâce à laquelle il essayait confusément de séparer les deux domaines de la raison et de la foi, même si elle apparaît timide et contradictoire sous bien des aspects, constitue un des motifs les plus originaux de la *Methodus*: et c'est sous cet angle qu'il faut voir la polémique contre Tite-Live, polémique qui va au-delà de la personne et de l'œuvre de l'historien de Rome et qui concerne le concept d'une histoire théiste, dans le sens le plus général du terme: Tite-Live représente ici toutes les tendances historiographiques à caractère vaguement métaphysique, qui entravaient le chemin d'une historiographie rationaliste et pragmatique, dont l'instauration est actuellement le problème fondamental de Bodin: les pages écrites contre Tite-Live ne font en somme qu'illustrer ce qui est une tendance diffuse dans toute la *Methodus,* et sont une étape du chemin que Bodin est en train de parcourir, pour créer un nouveau concept de l'histoire et une nouvelle historiographie.

Etroitement liée à l'interprétation de Tite-Live, est l'opinion que Bodin exprime sur Guichardin, laquelle, nous l'avons dit, fait «pendant» à la précédente: il faudra tout de suite observer que Guichardin, aussitôt défini «parens historiae» du moment que «omnium judicio verissime scripsisse putatur convinci potest», n'est pas cité à propos de Tite-Live, mais, étant présenté comme un exemple tout à fait digne de foi, opposé au mensonger Paul Jove. Toutefois, pour nous qui nous occupons surtout de tirer de ce traité bodinien la nouvelle méthode historique que le penseur angevin essaie de théoriser ici, l'allusion à Tite-Live est inévitable, puisqu'ils représentent les pôles opposés de deux tendances historiographiques: si Jove raconte dans ses histoires des choses fausses et peut être donc confronté avec le véridique Guichardin, à Tite-Live aussi, qui est incapable d'expliquer les événements historiques dans recourir au mythe et à l'imagination, peut être opposé le plus rationnel de tous les historiens: c'est pourquoi Guichardin, exalté non seulement pour sa veracité et son objectivité, mais aussi pour la finesse qu'il montre dans l'explication des faits historiques, représente donc l'opposé de Tite-Live et c'est pour cette raison que l'exaltation de l'historien italien, rationnel investigateur des causes, accentue, même si Bodin ne s'y réfère pas explicitement, le refus de la méthodologie de l'historien de Rome. La méthode rationaliste de l'auteur de l'*Histoire d'Italie*, son effort pour comprendre les motifs et les raisons politiques des faits, sans jamais céder à des motifs qui dépassent l'histoire ou sont en dehors d'elle, est, en effet, le thème commun de toute l'apologie bodinienne de Guichardin: «Nam ubi quid in deliberationem cadit quod inexplicabile videatur, illic admirabilem in disserendo subtilitatem ostentat, et graves ubique sententias veluti sal accommodate perspergit.» Nous avons ici dans un texte pourtant très synthétique, une nouvelle preuve de la méthode historique souhaitée par Bodin, pour qui n'importe quel fait historique, même le plus mystérieux et le plus complexe, peut s'expliquer rationnellement; les événements sont liés entre eux par une logique que l'historien attentif peut toujours retrouver. Si, dans la critique qu'il adresse à Tite-Live, ces propositions étaient sous-entendues, dans l'apologie de Guichardin elles sont clairement exprimées. L'étude scientifique des causes et l'enquête rationnelle sur les événements sont le fondement sur lequel la nouvelle méthode historique devra s'appuyer pour la recherche de la vérité; et Guichardin lui offrait précisément l'exemple le plus lumineux de cette méthode: «Est autem mirum in eo studium veritatis inquirendae. Nihil enim temere sed omnia necessariis argumentis confirmat.» Nous sommes arrivés ici au point de rupture avec toute la tradition historiographique: l'histoire ne se présente plus comme chronique, comme narration pure et simple des faits; au contraire, son rôle essentiel est de pénétrer les causes, de comprendre les liens rationnels des événements historiques. La méthode utilisée dans la chronique, qui, sous de nombreux aspects séduisait encore Bodin à cause de son caractère systématique, et qui le portait vers la «nuda historia», est maintenant définitivement désavouée: l'ouverture bodinienne vers les formes de l'historiographie politique constitue le fait nouveau de toute cette partie de la *Methodus*.

Mais à côté des raisons de caractère programmatique qui poussaient Bodin à écrire des pages enthousiastes sur l'auteur de l'*Histoire d'Italie*, nous pouvons en trouver une autre d'un caractère tout à fait particulier: nous avons vu les raisons fondamentales pour lesquelles Bodin admirait Guichardin, mais il y en a d'autres que nous dirions plus personnelles et qui lui étaient dictées par la sympathie que l'historien italien montrait envers les Français et le sens de la mesure avec lequel il parle d'eux: «Aliud argumentum est ejus integritatis et animi aegritudine vacui, quod cum Gallis vehementer infensus esse debuisset.» A l'opposé de cette attitude de Guichardin se place, en revanche, celle de Pietro Bembo, «quod vero Gallos ubique verborum contumelia insectatur; quod nihil sanctum ab illis aut tutum fuisse», qui en signe de mépris, «fugam appellat» le retour en France de Charles VIII après la bataille de Fornoue, et qui montre en toutes occasions son aversion pour le peuple français. Tout de suite, dès les premières lignes des pages que Bodin consacre à l'examen de l'œuvre historique de Pietro Bembo, on voit transparaître les raisons de sa profonde aversion envers l'auteur des *Rerum Venetarum*, dont les écrits le touchent au vif de son orgueil national. Mais son aversion à l'égard de Bembo n'a pas seulement son fondement dans l'offense qui est faite au sentiment national de Bodin: à côté de cette raison subjective demeure toujours l'impératif méthodologique: «Cavendum imprimis erit – avait-il écrit au début de son traité – ne scriptori de se suisque civibus et amicis quae laudibilia sunt, aut de hostibus turpia scribenti facile assentiamur.» Bembo a donc enfreint une des règles essentielles de la doctrine historiographique, en montrant qu'il ne possédait pas cette sérénité de jugement et cette objectivité qui doivent aller au-delà des passions partisanes. Mais, en dehors de cet aspect, il y en a un autre dans la critique adressée a Bembo, qui mérite d'être considéré plus attentivement: les questions de fond qui préoccupaient Bodin au moment de la rédaction de ce chapitre de la *Methodus*, c'est-à-dire la recherche et la réhabilitation de ces historiens qui se rapprochaient le plus de ses idéaux historiographiques, sont toujours présentes en lui, même lorsqu'il semble s'en être éloigné, comme c'est le cas ici. Ainsi, une fois passée l'impulsion disons émotionnelle, Bodin réexamine froidement la méthodologie historique de l'écrivain vénitien: ses critiques n'en sont pas pour autant moins acérées, mais elles prennent un caractère, plus conforme au texte de la *Methodus*: Bembo est ainsi assimilé à la foule des représentants de l'histoire humaniste pure, à ceux qui, se préoccupant peu des événements historiques, réduisent l'histoire même à un fait littéraire, à ceux pour qui une belle page est plus importante que le problème de la vérité historique. Bembo lui-même, écrit Bodin, qui commença à s'occuper d'histoire après soixante ans, et par conséquent avec un goût littéraire bien précis et dominant, admettait qu'il s'ennuyait lorsqu'il reconstruisait les événements détaillés, et, prévoyant le même ennui chez les lecteurs, il les embellissait grâce à un style fleuri et à une langue des plus pures, même si cela devait être au détriment de la vérité de la narration: «Puritatem enim dictionis ita consectatur, ut verbis quidem parum latinis, sed tamen ad significandum necessariis uti nolit»: c'est pourquoi Bodin conclut ironiquement que; «id quidem Latine, sed non satis, opinor, ad id quod decuit accomodate».

La polémique contre Bembo représente seulement une partie de l'attaque violente que Bodin lance contre la littérature humaniste pure: le moment le plus vif de toute la polémique, nous le trouvons en revanche dans les pages, plusieurs fois mentionnées, que Bodin consacre à Paul Jove et qui sont certainement parmi les plus significatives de la *Methodus*, si l'on veut chercher les raisons qui poussaient l'écrivain angevin à exprimer un jugement si éclatant et qui était destiné à avoir un tel retentissement sur le cours de l'histoire de l'historiographie qui suivra.

Les raisons de la polémique bodinienne y sont désormais en grande partie connues: toute une série d'impératifs poussait Bodin à théoriser une nouvelle conception méthodologique de l'histoire, plus adaptée à l'époque, où se rencontraient l'exigence d'ordre et de systématisation qui avait inspiré les historiens protestants, auteurs de chronologies et de généalogies, et l'exigence politique des écrivains italiens. Paul Jove, et plus que la personne de l'historien italien, la tendance qu'il représentait, n'entrait nullement dans les schémas historiographiques préconisés par Bodin: d'où les raisons de son hostilité à l'égard de l'historien italien, dont la manière de conduire la narration historique contrastait avec toutes les idées que s'était faites Bodin en matière historiographique. Si pour lui le «parens historiae» est maintenant Guichardin («cuius scripta si cum Jovio conferantur, non magis congruent quam rotunda quadratis»), il est évident que Jove précisément, qui en représentait l'antithèse, ne doit pas être considéré comme un historien, du moins dans le sens que Bodin donne à ce terme.

Le jugement sur Jove est mené en parallèle avec celui sur Polybe, du moment que l'écrivain italien aurait eu l'intention de procéder pour les *Historiarum sui temporis* tout à fait à la manière de Polybe, c'est-à-dire de faire une sorte d'étude historico-politique, ce qu'est justement l'œuvre du plus grand des historiens grecs qui se soient occupés de Rome pendant l'époque républicaine. Mais les résultats sont très différents à cause de la différence non seulement de valeur mais aussi de vie et de doctrine qui existe entre les deux: «Sed hoc inter utrumque interest, quod ille vel rebus gestis interfuit, vel praefuit, vel publica ubique monumenta vidit; hic audita et inaudita plerumque scripsit: ille in militari ac domestica disciplina diu se exercuit; hic neutram attigit: ille in sua Republica princeps; hic privatus; ille imperator; hic medicus: ille magnam Europae partem, oram Africae et Asiam Minorem, ut populorum mores intelligeret peragravit; hic annos septem et triginta, ut ipse gloriatur, in Vaticano consedit: ille Scipionis Africani moderator ac bellorum ubique socius; hic Pontificum perpetuus comes.»

Les arguments avancés ici par Bodin, à part les inexactitudes historiques qui y sont contenues, concernent surtout, comme on le voit, la personnalité humaine de l'historien davantage que son œuvre et avant elle encore: ceci confirme que dans l'esprit de Bodin le rapport auteur-œuvre se présente de manière tellement organique qu'il est inséparable: et il introduit cette nouveauté parce que sa conception de l'histoire est désormais tout à fait différente de la conception traditionnelle; de ces lignes ressort l'image de l'historien tel qu'il l'imagine, c'est-à-dire de l'historien engagé, dirions-

nous aujourd'hui, de l'historien qui participe de façon responsable aux
événements de son temps, qui ne se contente pas de participer activement
au débat idéologique, mais qui s'engage personnellement dans la réalité
politique: l'«usus» dont Bodin a parlé d'abord, et qui représente son refus
d'accepter des sentences et des conseils venant de quelqu'un qui ne peut
parler à la première personne, réapparaît ici dans sa forme la plus vigoureuse et dans son application intégrale. On sent dans ces passages l'esprit
moderne de Bodin, qui refuse pour la dernière fois la conception de cette
historiographie désintéressée et objectiviste (qui avait ensuite engendré la
chronique), qui avait ses canons dans la *Poetica* aristotélicienne, refusant
en même temps la forme littéraire que l'histoire avait prise chez certains
écrivains humanistes: ses expressions représentent le refus de cette culture
historique qui vivait comme dans une tour d'ivoire à cause de ces lettrés,
étrangers à la réalité politique de leur temps et sourds aux exigences
qu'elle offrait. Il est difficile de dire jusqu'à quel point Bodin était conscient alors de la révolution méthodologique qu'il était en train d'accomplir: certainement la théorisation qu'il fait était déjà réalisée dans la
pratique historiographique: c'étaient Machiavel et Guichardin qui la lui
avaient inspirée, mais ce n'est pas pour cela que son mérite en est diminué:
il était certainement conscient, parce que justement il y participait activement, que le débat politique ne peut être séparé du débat sur l'histoire: et
c'était cette conviction intime qui le portait à repousser avec dédain tous
ceux qui ne l'avaient pas compris. Il est peut-être injuste que dût faire les
frais de cette courageuse prise de position, un des plus illustres représentants de l'historiographie humaniste pure, qui n'a pas été certainement cet
exécrable historien que Bodin nous a dépeint: toutefois, si l'on va au-delà
de la simple donnée philologique du texte bodinien, on voit apparaître
dans toute leur importance les problèmes méthodologiques qui y sont
posés, même s'ils le sont par opposition: aux yeux de l'auteur de la *Methodus* l'histoire est une catégorie politique et elle doit être considérée comme
telle: ce que ne peut faire que celui qui possède à cet égard une expérience
intensément et dramatiquement vecue.

Parmi les jugements «extremely provocative», comme les appelle
Brown, exprimés par Bodin, il faut encore considérer, pour compléter la
grande fresque qui nous est présentée par l'auteur de la *Methodus*, deux
des plus importants historiens anciens: Plutarque et Tacite. Ce qu'il y a de
plus significatif dans les pages de Bodin c'est le revirement d'opinion qu'il
opère par rapport à la tendance commune de son temps qui acceptait et
louait Plutarque, et repoussait catégoriquement Tacite. Bodin, au contraire, se montre très méfiant à l'égard de l'auteur des *Vies parallèles*, dont
la méthode historique à caractère biographique ne le convainc pas tellement, car Plutarque est souvent amené, en raison de son excessive liberté
de jugement, à se transformer d'historien en moraliste: «Est autem quod

in eo miremur liberum de re quaque judicium, ut non tam historicum
quam principum censor esse videatur.» Ni même le système des vies
parallèles tel que l'a établi Plutarque, ne convainc beaucoup Bodin: et ceci
pourrait sembler étrange de la part d'un fervent partisan, comme Bodin
justement, de la méthode comparatiste, dont Plutarque semble avoir été,
parmi les historiens anciens, celui qui, même dans un sens large, s'en était
le plus rapproché. Mais ce n'est pas tant contre la méthode que Bodin se
prononce ici, mais bien au contraire contre les rapprochements inopportuns faits par Plutarque: «Idque facili intelligi potest in comparatione
Demosthenis ac Ciceronis: Catonis et Aristidis: Syllae ac Lysandri: Marcelli ac Pelopidae. Quid autem aliud est Agesilaum Pompeio, quam muscam elephanto conferre?». Les critiques qu'il adresse à Plutarque, même
si elles sont moins acérées que celles qu'il fait à Tite-Live, à Jove et à
Bembo, sont cependant très profondes: Bodin l'accuse d'avoir écrit sur des
sujets romains sans bien connaître le latin; de confondre les lois romaines
entre elles, et même les personnages historiques de l'ancienne Rome entre
eux; il lui reproche d'avoir fait beaucoup d'autres erreurs sur les coutumes
et sur les lois romaines, et pour conclure il affirme que «saepe incredibilia
et plane fabulosa narrat», même s'il emploie dans ces cas-là, la forme
dubitative. Certains thèmes fondamentaux de toute la problématique
historique de Bodin sont évoqués ici: Plutarque n'est pas un de ces historiens que Bodin rejette totalement; il lui reconnaît même, à côté des
erreurs qu'il relève en lui, tout autant de dons et de capacités: Plutarque
est un des rares historiens anciens qui se soient occupés des coutumes des
peuples et des lois des états et il possédait, en outre, une solide culture
philosophique et scientifique, ce qui augmentait ses capacités de jugement,
qui étaient déjà remarquables. Cependant, ce qui frappe davantage Bodin,
c'est la présence des fables incroyables qui sont mêlées au récit historique.
Nous voyons réapparaître ici, dans un certain sens, les critiques adressées
à Tite-Live et par conséquent la conception bodinienne d'une histoire
pragmatique qui entend ne rien concéder à l'imagination et au mythe.
Mais, en ce qui concerne Plutarque, peut-être l'accusation était-elle injuste.
Même si chez l'auteur des *Vies des Césars* perdues, beaucoup de personnages répondent à des exigences plus artistiques qu'historiques, il est difficile
de penser que certains épisodes relatifs aux coutumes, racontés par Plutarque, sont entièrement faux ou inventés. La sévérité de Bodin à son égard
est apparue excessive même à Montaigne qui, dans sa célèbre *Défense de
Sénèque et Plutarque,* tout en reconnaissant que «Bodin est un bon auteur
de notre temps et accompagné de beaucoup plus de jugement que la tourbe
des escrivailleurs de son siècle», le trouvait trop hardi dans ce passage de
la *Methodus*, où il taxait Plutarque d'ignorance et l'accusait d'être un
écrivain de fables.

Un des passages les plus importants de cette partie de la *Methodus* nous est donné sans aucun doute par la vaste défense de Tacite, qui représente le couronnement de toute la polémique anti-humaniste, qui, nous l'avons vu, sert de fond à une grande partie de ce chapitre.

La réhabilitation de Tacite par Bodin s'insère dans ce vaste mouvement intellectuel qui, au seizième siècle, remplaça dans la sympathie des historiens européens et en premier lieu italiens, Tite-Live, si cher aux humanistes (qu'on se rappelle Jove par exemple) par l'auteur de la *Germania*, même si, comme l'a démontré Toffanin, ces historiens interprètent le Tibère de Tacite comme une incarnation des systèmes de César Borgia. Cette réhabilitation qui peu à peu se dessinait timidement et qui éclatera ici dans la *Methodus*, se heurtait naturellement à l'historiographie traditionnelle, qui continuait à voir en Tacite, à la suite des jugements exprimés par Tertullien et Orose, l'écrivain anti-chrétien par excellence, et d'un autre côté, comme on reconnaissait en lui le promoteur de la doctrine politique de la «raison d'état», le maître idéal de l'exécré Machiavel. Cette prise de position de Bodin doit être considérée dans un contexte plus large que celui des seuls problèmes historiographiques qui lui servent de prétexte pour revendiquer la grandeur de Tacite: le problème de fond de ces pages est donc beaucoup plus vaste, et on y voit abordé pour la première fois un problème très important qui se présente dès maintenant de manière impérieuse dans l'esprit du jeune Bodin et qui se manifestera ensuite dans toute sa force au cours des dernières années de sa vie. Il s'agit du problème de la tolérance religieuse, à peine voilé maintenant dans la défense de Tacite, mais qui prendra force et consistance une trentaine d'années plus tard environ dans les vigoureuses pages de l'*Heptaplomeres*.

Naturellement Bodin ne perd pas de vue ici son problème fondamental, c'est-à-dire celui de l'historiographie: sauver Tacite de l'accusation d'impiété lui sert non seulement pour satisfaire son exigence personnelle de tolérance et de liberté de conscience, mais aussi pour pouvoir utiliser ensuite d'un point de vue méthodologique, les enseignements et les exemples de l'«historien» Tacite. Les objectifs que se fixe Bodin ici sont donc deux: l'un que nous appellerions intérieur, en tant que légitime revendication de ses idéaux en matière religieuse, et l'autre que nous dirions extérieur et qui s'insère dans le vaste programme de renouvellement des études historiques, qu'il est en train de tracer dans la *Methodus*. Pour ce dernier but, Tacite lui offrait un des plus grands exemples d'historiographie politique, engagée, responsable: l'écrivain romain avait tous les attributs requis pour être un grand historien puisqu'il avait voyagé, assumé des charges publiques, participé à la vie politique active: sa conception positive de l'histoire et de la réalité le rapprochaient donc de Bodin et de son temps, beaucoup plus que ne pouvait le faire un esprit poétique et religieux comme celui de Tite-Live. D'où la nécessité de revaloriser une œuvre «mirum in modo arguta et prudentiae plena» comme celle de Tacite précisément, dans laquelle on retrouve les sources les plus riches en ce qui concerne l'étude, si chère à Bodin, de l'organisation politique et des institutions législatives des peuples anciens: «Si forenses ac senatorias artes, si antiquitatem non Romanorum modo, sed aliorum quoque populorum quaerimus, nusquam uberior seges.» Or, pour un Bodin qui ne cherche pas tellement dans l'histoire les événements et les belles entreprises mais bien au contraire les lois, les institutions des peuples, en un mot la politique, et pour qui l'histoire naît de l'exigence de s'insérer dans le débat politique de l'heure, Tacite est le plus grand maître de l'antiquité en la matière, plus encore même que Polybe qui, à cause de sa situation de prisonnier de guerre grec, ne put jamais participer activement à la vie publique de Rome, mais parvenait seulement intellectuellement à formuler des jugements politiques.

Pour toutes ces raisons, disions-nous, à l'exigence idéale de sauver Tacite, qui lui était dictée par son esprit libre, s'ajoutait une exigence pratique due au caractère intrinsèque de l'historiographie tacitienne, dans laquelle Bodin voyait un modèle digne de la plus grande considération. Les mots avec lesquels il se prépare à défendre Tacite de l'accusation d'impiété sont parmi les plus chaleureux et passionnés qu'il ait écrits, et contrastent fortement avec le ton habituellement froid et détaché de la *Methodus*: «Ita quoque impie fecit Tacitus quod non fuerit Christianus: sed non impie adversus nos scripsit, cum gentili superstitione obligaretur. Ego vero impium judicarem nisi quancunque religionem veram judicaret, non eam quoque tueri et contrarias evertere conaretur.» On sent ici en Bodin un esprit libre qui, s'élevant au-dessus des idéaux communs de son temps, revendique pour chaque homme le droit de défendre ses propres idéaux religieux, pourvu qu'il s'agisse d'idéaux purs, désintéressés et défendus avec la plus pure bonne foi. N'est pécheur pour Bodin que le sceptique, celui qui n'a pas de religion et non celui qui en professe une différente. Si Bodin est très loin d'une quelconque solution athée, qui répugnait fort à son esprit religieux, il est néanmoins tout aussi loin du sectarisme et de l'intolérance. La défense passionnée de Tacite anticipe le thème de cette grande œuvre que sera l'*Heptaplomeres*, où la liberté de conscience est revendiquée résolument, non par l'affirmation sceptique que toutes les religions sont bonnes, mais en réaffirmant la validité de la formule de la liberté de pensée religieuse, lorsque celle-ci s'accompagne de la conviction profonde d'être dans le vrai. Ici dans la *Methodus*, cependant, Bodin n'en est pas encore là: la solution de ce problème est ici différente et dans un certain sens même ambiguë, dans la mesure où l'on justifie ici, comme est justifié Tacite, celui qui au nom de sa propre foi, combat les autres. Ce n'est que vers la fin de sa vie que Bodin concevra clairement le problème de la tolérance religieuse, qui dès maintenant pourtant, commence déjà à occuper l'esprit de l'écrivain qui n'a encore que trente-cinq ans.

Tacite n'avait pas respecté la religion des autres, mais avait de toute manière défendu la sienne: pour l'instant cela suffit à Bodin pour rejeter l'accusation d'impiété qu'on lui adressait: ainsi, en accord avec ses idéaux, Bodin redonne à Tacite la place qui lui revient, revendiquant pour lui, en s'opposant à un siècle qui au nom d'un exclusivisme religieux exacerbé le repoussait, une place prééminente parmi les maîtres de l'historiographie.

A ce point on peut considérer comme terminé le discours de Bodin, et complètement décrite la nouvelle dimension historiographique qu'il a recherchée. Certes, il n'est pas parvenu à formuler une perspective historiographique entièrement originale: au fond il n'apparaît que comme le codificateur d'une orientation méthodologique que les grands florentins avaient déjà réalisée. Et l'histoire même de l'historiographie qu'il a tracée dans ce quatrième chapitre de la *Methodus*, est dépourvue de cette considération dialectique qui permet de relever les développements et les progrès de l'historiographie même. En effet, les auteurs étudiés ne sont pas analysés sur la base de leur authentique contribution au progrès historiographique, mais examinés selon certains canons que Bodin avait construits «a priori». Cependant, en dépit de ces limites, il bouleversait toutes les conceptions traditionnelles, en opérant une révolution méthodologique qui ne passerait pas certainement sans laisser de traces. La conception de l'histoire comme histoire éthico-politique, la sensibilisation du récit historique aussi bien contre les schématismes des historiens réformés que contre les pages littéraires des humanistes sont les éléments qui le rapprochent définitivement des modernes. Et c'est pour cette raison que nous l'avons vu refuser le latin élégant de Pietro Bembo, le beau style de Paul Jove, les récits fantaisistes de Tite-Live et le moralisme de Plutarque, tandis que l'enthousiasmaient Polybe, Tacite, Guichardin, qui avaient compris qu'écrire l'histoire signifie exposer l'organisation militaire et administrative d'un état, ou pénétrer par le jugement dans les causes et dans les effets des événements: «Voilà – écrit Roger Chauviré – qui fait comprendre sa prédilection pour une certaine catégorie d'écrivains. Si l'histoire doit avant tout enseigner les hommes, il est évident que ni les contes d'Hérodote ni la chronique de Froissart ne peuvent remplir un tel rôle.»

Julien Freund

Quelques aperçus sur la conception de l'histoire de Jean Bodin

L'interprétation globale du *Methodus ad facilem historiarum cognitionem* peut donner lieu à des contre-sens suivant la manière dont on traduit certains concepts. Bodin se targue d'avoir été le premier à étudier l'histoire d'une certaine façon: analyser l'art qu'elle est ainsi que sa méthode. «Qui tamen historiae artem ac methodus tradidisset, fuisse neminem», écrit-il dans l'Avant-Propos de son ouvrage.[1] P. Mesnard traduit *artem* par *contenu*, ce qui revient à faire croire que l'intention de Bodin aurait été d'exposer ce qu'en langage moderne on appelle l'objet et la méthode de l'histoire, ou encore de faire de la philosophie de l'histoire, évidemment non pas au sens que Hegel a donné à cette expression, mais à celui par exemple de Rickert qui consiste à faire une analyse théorique ou épistémologique de la démarche de l'historien. Il est incontestable que le texte contient des éléments pour élaborer une telle théorie de l'histoire, mais ils ne définissent pas la véritable intention de Bodin. En effet, il déclare explicitement qu'il renonce à faire un travail sur l'historiographie, c'est-à-dire sur la manière de faire les recherches historiques et de composer un ouvrage d'histoire: «de instituenda» ou «de scribenda historia».[2] Cette voie d'autres l'ont suivie, elle n'est pas la sienne. Pour bien comprendre son projet, il faut donc d'abord saisir clairement ce qu'il entend par *ars* et *methodus*. Du moment que Mesnard a traduit *methodus* par méthode pourquoi n'a-t-il pas rendu tout aussi uniformément *ars* par art? Ce procédé permettrait d'éviter les équivoques et les malentendus. Au lieu de cela il donne presque chaque fois une autre traduction: art, genre, habileté, objet de la science, contenu, etc.[3] Il n'y a pas de doute que ce terme peut prendre ces diverses significations, mais, du moment que Bodin en a fait avec la méthode le thème essentiel de sa réflexion et l'objet privilégié de son entreprise, il est indispensable que la traduction respecte, à part quelques cas exceptionnels,

---

[1] *Meth.* Avant-Propos, 114, 23–24. Nous citons cet ouvrage d'après l'édition faite par P. Mesnard dans le Corpus général des Philosophes français, Auteurs modernes, V, 3, Paris 1951. Les chiffres qui suivent l'indication de la page renvoient aux lignes numérotées de cette édition [4.20].

[2] *Meth.* Avant-Propos, 114, 27 et 36.

[3] Il suffit de prendre la traduction de l'Epître dédicatoire à la page 107 de la ligne 35 (première colonne) à la ligne 7 (deuxième colonne). Le mot *ars* y revient au moins 6 fois et Mesnard en a donné chaque fois une traduction différente.

une certaine univocité, dans l'esprit même du projet bodinien. C'est ce projet qu'il importe de déterminer au départ pour comprendre en quoi Bodin croyait faire œuvre originale.

Le point de vue auquel il se place n'est pas celui d'une étude du métier d'historien – il ne le fait tout au plus qu'accessoirement – mais celui de *lecteur* d'ouvrages historiques qui peut être dérouté par le désordre qui règne dans cette discipline ou déconcerté par la dispersion et la multitude des écrits ainsi que par leur contenu disparate. Le *Methodus* traduit la perplexité du jeune humaniste (Bodin n'avait pas encore trente ans quand il rédigea ce livre) qui, comme le signale l'Epître dédicatoire, consacrait les loisirs que lui laissait le barreau à la lecture des historiens et qui a finalement réussi à surmonter son désarroi en se forgeant une vision d'ensemble sur l'histoire, dont il voudrait faire profiter ses contemporains. Aussi s'en prend-il à tous les glossateurs et grammairiens qui n'ont cessé d'accumuler les commentaires sans jamais chercher un lien entre la multitude des histoires et sans jamais s'interroger sur une possible cohérence de la discipline. C'est à trouver cette cohérence que Bodin a passé son temps et c'est en cela que consiste son originalité: «qui tamen arte concluserit ea quae dispersa, dissectaque leguntur, video fuisse neminem».[4] L'intention de Bodin fut donc de fournir à ceux qui s'intéressent à l'histoire une vue d'ensemble, synthétique et ordonnée, pour les aider à mieux connaître cette discipline *(ad facilem cognitionem).*[5] C'est ce qu'il appelle «doctrine»,[6] c'est-à-dire un traité pratique à l'usage des lecteurs.

Ce n'est qu'à la lumière de cette intention que le plan et les nombreuses classifications qui émaillent le texte deviennent intelligibles. En effet, Bodin n'hésite pas à procéder de façon didactique, voire scolaire, suivant en cela le précepte de Platon qui voyait dans les justes divisions l'art le plus difficile et le plus divin.[7] La cohérence est une question d'ordre, c'est-à-dire de divisions. Sur cette base on peut établir les postulats qui orientent une étude historique quelconque, préparer de bonnes définitions qui à leur tour conditionnent l'analyse et enfin dégager les préceptes ou règles,[8] étant donné que pour Bodin l'histoire n'est pas simplement un objet de pure curiosité, mais également un recueil d'enseignements pratiques. Aussi commence-t-il par distinguer les diverses sortes d'histoires et les définir, fixer ensuite les lieux communs ou rubriques de classement à

---

[4] *Meth.*, Epître dédicatoire, 107, 42–1.

[5] *Meth.*, 109, 15–17.

[6] *Meth.*, Avant-Propos, 114, 41.

[7] *Meth.* Epître dédicatoire, 107, 35–36. Voir également la *Juris universi distributio* publiée par Mesnard dans cette même édition des Œuvres de Bodin, 71, 25–28 et 6–12.

[8] *Meth.*, 107, 36–41.

partir d'une chronologie solide, faire un tri entre les nombreux historiens
afin de déterminer ceux qui sont les plus dignes de foi, etc. C'est dans ce
contexte que les notions d'*ars* et de *methodus* prennent une signification
précise. Elle n'est pas la même que celle que la notion de méthode a de nos
jours. Quant à celle d'art, elle lui est tout aussi spécifique.

Chaque fois qu'il utilise le terme d'*ars* pour définir son projet il déclare
vouloir réunir *(colligare)* des éléments épars dans les diverses histoires des
historiens, trouver un lien et une cohésion entre elles en vue d'établir une
vue synthétique de caractère universel: «sunt enim artes ac scientiae, id
quod tu minime ignoras, non singulorum sed universorum».[9] Prenant
l'exemple de l'histoire du droit il reproche aux glossateurs de nous transmettre pêle-mêle et de façon disparate les lois, sans se donner la peine d'en
présenter une vue d'ensemble et il précise: «nihil tamen artis dignitate ac
praestantia potuit alienus cogitari».[10] Il déclare même explicitement que
l'art en tant que cohésion capable de nous donner une unité de vue sur ce
qui se trouve dispersé dans les ouvrages constitue justement l'histoire: «Sed
iis omissis, qui sua se voluntate ex albo doctorum hominum exemerunt, ad
historiam, unde nostra fluxit oratio, relabor. Ex hac igitur veterum leges
huc illuc dispersas colligimus, ut huic quoque operi conjungamus.»[11] Dans
ces conditions on pourrait à la rigueur traduire *ars* par théorie, au sens
général d'une construction intellectuelle organisée, mais non pas par
contenu ou objet de l'histoire. Ces dernières notions, propres à l'épistémologie moderne, ne rendent pas compte de l'esprit qui oriente l'ouvrage de
Bodin. En concordance avec cette acquisition d'une vue d'ensemble cohérente, la *méthode* doit ensuite introduire les divisions et les classifications
utiles, afin de dissiper les confusions qui pourraient naître de cette vision
synthétique. Ainsi comprise la méthode consiste essentiellement en l'analyse – qu'il appelle justement *magistra artium*; elle consiste à décomposer
le tout en parties et celles-ci en éléments plus petits encore, tout en sauve-
gardant la cohésion entre le tout et les parties.[12] Il semble donc qu'il ne
faille pas entendre la notion de méthode au sens actuellement courant
d'un ensemble de moyens ou de démarches raisonnées pour parvenir à un
but défini, mais au sens aujourd'hui vieilli de mode de classement des
thèmes essentiels sous des rubriques déterminées. C'est ainsi en tout cas
qu'il expose à maintes reprises sa conception de la méthode, en particulier

---

[9] *Meth.*, 107, 5–7.
[10] *Meth.*, 107, 9–11.
[11] *Meth.*, 109, 15–17.
[12] «Principio adhibeatur praestans illa docendarum artium magistra, quae
dicitur analysis: quae universum in partes secare, et partis cujus que particulas
rursus dividere, totiusque ac partium cohaerentiam quasi concentum inter ipsa
mira facilitate docet.» Ch. II, 116, 44–49.

à la fin de l'Avant-Propos quand il déclare que pour écrire sur la méthode en histoire *(de historica methodo scribere)* il faut procéder par définitions et divisions *(historiam partiemur ac definiemus)*[13] et qu'il annonce les diverses rubriques de son ouvrage.

Il y revient au début du chapitre II quand il précise à nouveau comment il faut envisager la méthode en histoire et qu'il expose avec plus de détails une nouvelle fois les thèmes de son travail;[14] enfin il le répète à la fin de ce même chapitre: «non aliter historiam universam partiemur ac definiemus».[15] Ces textes suffisent, me semble-t-il, à nous faire entendre le sens qu'il donnait aux notions d'*ars* et de *methodus*, encore qu'il ne serait pas difficile d'en citer d'autres éparpillés tout au long de son œuvre.

On aurait cependant tort d'en conclure que Bodin négligerait la question de l'objectivité ou de la vérité historique. Il fait au contraire une distinction très nette entre la fable et l'histoire, celle-ci n'ayant de valeur qu'à la condition que le récit soit véridique.[16] Nous aurons encore l'occasion de revenir sur ce point. Ce qu'il importe de retenir, c'est que le problème de la vérité historique, essentiel du point de vue de l'historiographie *(de historia instituenda)*, c'est-à-dire celui de la démarche et du métier de l'historien, reste subordonné dans la perspective de Bodin, pour autant qu'il se place au point de vue du lecteur. Ce qui l'intéresse, ce sont avant tout les questions suivantes: Comment lire l'histoire? Comment pratiquer cette multitude d'histoires que nous possédons? Et cela pour tirer du récit des enseignements pratiques aussi bien pour l'organisation de la vie en général que pour l'orientation de l'activité politique ou juridique. Les différents paragraphes qui suivent n'ont d'autre but que d'illustrer cette interprétation de l'intention de Bodin par le commentaire de quelques passages remarquables de son œuvre, éventuellement par opposition aux analyses ou aux suggestions de Mesnard.

I. L'histoire à la portée de tous

Si Bodin a éprouvé le besoin de communiquer ses réflexions aux lecteurs, c'est parce que l'histoire jouit d'un avantage particulier: elle n'exige pas une initiation spéciale, de sorte qu'elle est accessible à tout le monde. C'est ce que Bodin note dans l'Avant-Propos, quand il fait l'apologie de l'histoire, pour souligner sa facilité et son agrément. A son avis elle est facile

---

[13] *Meth.*, Avant-Propos, 114, 42–44.

[14] *Meth.*, Ch. II, 116, 39–44 et 117–118.

[15] *Meth.*, Ch. II, 118, 28–29.

[16] *Meth.*, Avant-Propos, 114, 6–8: «Sed ea reprehensio fabularum sit non historarum, quae nisi vera sint ne historia quidem appelari debent.»

pour deux raisons: d'une part elle est intelligible par elle-même sans autre concours,[17] de l'autre elle est à la portée de tous.[18] Ces observations, en apparence anodines, expliquent pourquoi elle jouit d'une audience extrêmement large dans tous les milieux en même temps qu'elles déterminent son statut particulier par rapport aux autres sciences.

En premier lieu elle est une discipline pour ainsi dire démocratique, ou du moins la plus démocratique, car elle est à la base de la culture populaire avec la poésie et la chanson. Pour saisir pleinement la portée des observations de Bodin songeons aux jeux radiophoniques de nos jours où de simples ouvriers ou paysans, sans autre formation que celle reçue à l'école primaire, dament parfois le pion à ceux qui ont par ailleurs une instruction supérieure, même en ce qui concerne la culture historique. Il n'est pas nécessaire de savoir lire et écrire car, remarque Bodin, elle peut se transmettre par tradition orale,[19] si bien qu'elle peut captiver des êtres frustes et sans autre compétence intellectuelle.[20] Certes, la rédation d'ouvrages historiques suppose la connaissance du métier d'historien, mais une fois élaborés ils n'exigent aucune initiation particulière de la part des lecteurs. Il s'agit d'une discipline ouverte au plus grand nombre. En second lieu, pour être intelligibles les faits historiques n'exigent pas de connaissances spéciales en d'autres matières, à la différence des sciences proprement dites qui dépendent les unes des autres, si bien que l'on ne peut vraiment aborder l'une sans également posséder des connaissances dans les autres.[21] Ainsi pour être à même de lire sérieusement un ouvrage de physique il faut non seulement être courant de cette science, mais être quelque peu versé dans les mathématiques. De plus il existe un tel enchaînement des propositions dans ces dernières disciplines qu'il faut commencer par une information élémentaire et s'élever progressivement aux choses plus difficiles. Or, tout le monde n'en est pas capable au même titre, du fait qu'elles supposent des dons spéciaux. Rien de tel en histoire. On peut lire sans peine et avec profit une étude sur César ou sur Charlemagne et y trouver de l'intérêt et du plaisir sans être informé autrement de la période qui fut la leur. L'histoire ne connaît aucun enchaînement des idées ni de progression, si bien qu'on peut un jour se plonger dans la guerre du Péloponnèse, un autre dans l'histoire des Mérovingiens et revenir ensuite aux pharaons d'Egypte, sans posséder de formation spéciale. Aussi l'histoire semble-t-elle avoir un statut particulier, elle est une science à part et peut-être même occupe-t-elle une place privilégiée et prépondérante par rapport aux autres

---

[17] «Nullius eget ope ac ne literis quidem ipsis.» *Meth.*, 113, 17.
[18] «Ipsa per sese ab omnibus intelligatur.» *Meth.*, 113, 12.
[19] *Meth.*, 113, 17–18.
[20] *Meth.*, 113, 31–33 et 8–10.
[21] *Meth.*, 113, 13–15.

sciences.[22] Bodin la considère même comme une discipline éternellement jeune, qui restera sans doute toujours en vogue,[23] même lorsque les villes et Etats dont elle relate les événements ont disparu. Les faits historiques s'accumulent sans pouvoir être dépassés au sens où une théorie scientifique peut être dépassée par une autre.

II. Le récit véridique

La définition que Bodin donne de l'histoire, pour être commune, est analogue à celle que reprendront la plupart des historiens ultérieurs: elle est un récit véridique, *vera narratio*.[24] Cela ne soulèverait guère de difficultés s'il n'appliquait pas également cette définition à d'autres discours pour distinguer trois sortes d'histoires qui finalement seront quatre. En effet, au début du premier chapitre il fait une distinction entre l'histoire humaine, au sens ordinaire de l'étude des actions humaines au sein des sociétés, l'histoire naturelle entendue comme la science de la nature fondée sur la recherche de lois qu'il estime réductibles à un premier principe et l'histoire sacrée ou la manifestation de Dieu et des esprits dans le monde,[25] mais à la fin du même chapitre il ajoute une quatrième espèce, l'*historia mathematica*, qu'il n'expose pas autrement, sinon qu'il la considère comme la plus certaine, du fait qu'elle échappe à tout mélange de matière.[26] On peut cependant lever la difficulté si l'on prend en considération que Bodin prend le terme d'histoire dans le sens traditionnel des Grecs, repris par certains humanistes de la Renaissance. D'une part la notion a le sens large de toute connaissance discursive ayant pour base une recherche, à la différence de la fiction et de la poésie purement imaginatives,[27] et dans ce cas les mathématiques, la science et même la contemplation[28] peuvent tomber sous cette rubrique, d'autre part le sens étroit de l'histoire proprement dite ou étude des événements passés de l'humanité. Cependant, malgré la

---

[22] *Meth.*, 113, 15–16.

[23] «Historia nihilominus aeternum viget.» *Meth.*, 113, 22–23.

[24] *Meth.*, Ch. I, 114, 6.

[25] *Meth.*, 114, 5–14.

[26] *Meth.*, 116, 19–20. P. Mesnard suggère [4.20], 102, que le paragraphe du Ch. VI relatif aux Révolutions des Etats rapportées aux nombres serait le meilleur échantillon de cette histoire mathématique. Cette observation ne me semble pas pertinente du fait que Bodin conteste la validité d'une telle démonstration (voir en particulier, Ch. VI, 195, 38–53) et la présente même comme absurde (Ch. VI, 195, 21).

[27] A propos de cette distinction, voir la référence de Bodin à Platon: *Meth.*, Avant-Propos, 114, 10.

[28] Ce terme désigne évidemment chez Bodin la philosophie.

haute estime qu'il témoigne à l'histoire naturelle et à l'histoire sacrée – il appelle même cette dernière la véritable histoire, *vera historia*,[29] parce qu'elle nous conduit à la béatitude – il n'en considère pas moins qu'il vaut mieux aborder la lecture historique par l'histoire humaine, la plus accessible, pour s'élever ensuite progressivement à l'histoire naturelle et enfin à l'histoire sacrée.

Si l'histoire en général est récit véridique, l'histoire humaine se définit d'une façon encore plus précise comme le récit véridique des actions du passé, *rerum ante gestarum vera narratio*.[30] Qu'est-ce qu'un action? On pourrait dire que, à la différence du discours qui laisse derrière lui des traces matérielles, par exemple un livre, elle s'épuise et se consomme dans son présent sans laisser d'œuvre matérielle. Mais Bodin estime qu'il n'y a pas lieu de s'arrêter à cette distinction subtile de grammairiens[31] et qu'il vaut mieux entendre le terme dans son acception courante, plus large, comme embrassant tous les desseins, dits et faits qui procèdent de la volonté humaine.[32] Entrent à son avis dans ces catégories aussi bien les actes du sage que ceux qu'on accomplit sous l'empire des passions ou de la violence, mais non ceux du fou, qui appartiennent plutôt à la rubrique des phénomènes sacrés, parce qu'ils ne sont pas accomplis de volonté délibérée et avec conscience.[33] Les actions au sens véritable du terme sont donc celles qui se développent avec une volonté consciente, celles qui sont liées à notre instinct de conservation et qui donnent naissance aux divers arts qui concernent la protection de la vie comme la chasse, l'élevage, la gymnastique et la médecine, celles qui ont pour objet l'organisation de la vie sociale, telles que le commerce, les diverses industries ainsi que la direction et la gestion politiques, enfin celles qui conditionnent le développement de la civilisation et déterminent une culture brillante, grâce à l'enrichissement des hommes et aux corollaires que sont le luxe et les fastes, mais qui peuvent également se dégrader en ignobles prétextes à flatter la volupté.[34]

Cette insistance à définir l'action comme procédant d'une volonté libre devrait logiquement conduire Bodin à une conception plutôt volontariste de l'histoire, en harmonie avec la pensée développée dans les *Six Livres de la République*, et non pas à une conception déterministe. Or, certains textes semblent indiquer que c'est la deuxième orientation, qu'il faudrait retenir. Par exemple au début du chapitre V, cherchant un fondement

---

[29] *Meth.*, Ch. I, 114, 53–54.

[30] *Meth.*, Ch, III, 119, 15–16.

[31] *Meth.*, Ch. III, 119, 54–55.

[32] «Latius actionis verbum definiendum nobis est, ut consilia, dicta facta, quae prodeunt ab hominis voluntate.» *Meth.*, Ch. III. 119, 58–1 ainsi que 24–27.

[33] *Meth.*, Ch. III, 119, 12–16.

[34] *Meth.*, Ch. III, 120, 23–53.

assuré pour l'interprétation de la diversité des lois et des religions, il renonce à le trouver dans les institutions et propose de prendre pour base les faits de la nature en raison de leur stabilité.[35] L'importance qu'il attribue aux déterminations géographiques[36] et à l'explication des moeurs et des lois par le sol et le climat[37] semblent confirmer ce point de vue, de sorte que Mesnard aurait raison de lui attribuer un «déterminisme» qui permettrait d'en «tirer des lois générales applicables à tout fait social».[38] Une telle interprétation est évidemment difficilement conciliable avec la définition de l'action comme expression d'une libre volonté. Y aurait-il donc une contradiction fondamentale dans la conception de Bodin? En réalité, l'interprétation déterministe est absolument étrangère à Bodin, comme à la plupart des auteurs de son époque, et l'on ne peut la soutenir qu'en isolant certaines phrases du contexte général. Il faut lire Bodin avec ses propres catégories et non avec celles de l'épistémologie moderne.

L'importance qu'il accorde à la décision d'un homme seul qui peut par son action sauver un Etat[39] ne s'accomode guère d'une vision déterministe. Quand il parle des «lois éternelles de la nature» il ne les envisage nullement sous leur aspect strictement causal, mais, à la manière de l'aristotélisme de son époque, il fait intervenir la catégorie de la finalité.[40] Plus déterminant encore est sa manière de comprendre l'activité de la volonté dans l'histoire: elle n'est jamais semblable à elle-même *(semper sui dissimilis est)* et elle n'a pas de terme,[41] de sorte qu'elle produira sans cesse de nouvelles lois et coutumes, de nouveaux rites, mais aussi de nouvelles erreurs, qu'il faudra sans cesse corriger par la droite raison ou, à défaut, par la prudence.[42] Dans ces conditions on comprend aisément pourquoi, à son avis, le meilleur historien n'est pas celui qui, isolé de l'activité des hommes, cherche abstraitement et spéculativement à établir des causes entre les phenomènes ou à découvrir de prétendues lois invariables, mais celui qui a une connaissance directe des affaires pour y avoir participé.[43] Cela ne veut pas dire que le bon historien serait le mémorialiste qui rapporte les événements auxquels il fut mêlé;[44] au contraire, selon Bodin, il faut une certaine distance dans le temps pour être à même de comprendre les actions humaines. Cela signifie qu'à son avis, seul celui qui est instruit

---

[35] *Meth.*, Ch. V, 140, 35–42.
[36] *Meth.*, Ch. II, 118, 27–34.
[37] *Meth.*, Ch. V, 140, 46–50.
[38] MESNARD [4.20], 102.
[39] *Meth.*, Ch. III, 119, 40–42.
[40] *Meth.*, Ch. I, 115, 33–35.
[41] *Meth.*, Ch. I, 115, 48–49.
[42] *Meth.*, Ch. I, 115, 50–55.
[43] *Meth.*, Ch. IV, 125, 59–3 ainsi que 127–128, 59–2.
[44] *Meth.*, Ch. IV, 126, 24–26.

par sa propre pratique, est en même temps le plus apte à démêler les activités des hommes des périodes révolues, à découvrir des liens insoupçonnés, à mieux pénétrer le sens des actes et par conséquent à porter un jugement plus correct. Bodin est d'ailleurs trop convaincu de la relativité des choses pour se livrer au jeu qui consiste à décrire l'historien idéal.[45] Heureux si l'auteur d'un ouvrage parvient à faire taire ses passions, ses rancunes, mais il ne faut pas s'attendre à ce que, malgré son intégrité et ses intentions d'objectivité, il puisse s'abstenir de tout jugement de valeur, de toute louange ou blâme. Aussi convient-il de suivre le sage conseil d'Aristote: en lisant un récit il ne faut se montrer ni trop crédule ni totalement incrédule.[46] D'où précisément la peine que Bodin se donne pour conseiller les lecteurs et les rendre capable de mieux apprécier les historiens. Il est clair qu'une telle attitude n'est guère compatible avec les certitudes du prétendu déterminisme.

Comment évaluer dans ces conditions ses remarques sur l'importance du sol, du climat, etc.? Il faut porter à son crédit d'avoir attiré l'attention sur ces aspects bien avant Montesquieu et de ce point de vue il fit vraiment œuvre originale. Cependant il faut préciser que sa conception des éléments explicatifs de l'histoire est beaucoup plus variée et plus large qu'on ne l'indique en général. En effet il a insisté encore plus longuement sur d'autres phénomènes tout aussi essentiels, qui échappent au strict déterminisme, par exemple les apports de la linguistique: tout le chapitre IX est pratiquement consacré à cette question. Il a été un précurseur sous les formes les plus diverses. A propos des causes ou influences climatiques ou géographiques, sa position est très catégorique: il ne peut s'agir d'une nécessité absolue. Il ajoute même qu'il faut proscrire un tel langage,[47] non pas pour des raisons scientifiques, mais religieuses. Toutefois il suggère que bien loin qu'elles déterminent nécessairement les institutions, l'homme établit celles-ci pour lutter contre ces influences et corriger leurs effets. Sur ce point, la pensée de Bodin est fort claire: il est indispensable de tenir compte de toutes les influences naturelles si l'on veut instituer une science historique aussi accomplie que possible et porter un jugement exact et fondé.[48] Par conséquent elles constituent à ses yeux des éléments de l'explication, mais elles ne sont pas conditionnantes au sens du déterminisme.

Pour importantes que soient au regard de la méthode de l'histoire les considérations de Bodin sur les influences naturelles, elles n'ont pas chez lui de valeur pour elles-mêmes, comme si l'histoire devait se contenter de les dévoiler pour satisfaire aux besoins de l'explication, mais elles ne

---

[45] *Meth.*, Ch. IV, 129, 19–24.
[46] *Meth.*, Ch. IV, 124, 10–16.
[47] *Meth.*, Ch. V, 140, 1–3.
[48] *Meth.*, Ch. V, 167, 5–11.

prennent leur signification qu'intégrées dans une méthode plus vaste et plus souple, la méthode comparative dont il fut l'un des premiers théoriciens. Celle-ci est d'ailleurs liée directement à son projet de constitution d'une histoire universelle dont nous parlerons plus loin. La méthode comparative a pour objet d'analyser les diverses histoires des différents peuples sous le double aspect de la mise à jour de certaines constantes qu'on retrouve à peu près partout et de la détermination des particularités propres à chacun d'eux ou pour reprendre son langage faire la distinction entre ce qui répond à la nature et ce qui dépend de la loi et des conventions.[49] Autrement dit, l'étude des causes climatiques, géographiques et autres a pour objet d'établir, d'une part la constante générale suivant laquelle tous les peuples subissent ces influences, d'autre part le naturel propre à chaque population, compte tenu des influences auxquelles elles sont soumises.[50] Cette méthode comparative loin d'être déterministe est selon Bodin essentiellement probabiliste. En effet, au moment d'examiner les diverses sortes d'assentiment propres à chaque des trois espèces d'histoire, il remarque explicitement que si l'histoire sacrée a pour base la foi et l'histoire naturelle ou science de la nature la nécessité, l'histoire humaine ne donne lieu qu'à une probabilité.[51] Ainsi Bodin a eu l'intuition de la problématique propre à la méthodologie historique que la philosophie moderne a redécouverte après avoir été égarée par les mirages de la pure explication déterministe.

III. Le singulier et le pluriel.

Le titre de l'ouvrage que nous discutons parle de l'histoire au pluriel *(historiarum)* et non au singulier. Cela ne saurait étonner un connaisseur de cette époque, car le pluriel était d'un usage courant comme en témoignent le titre de l'ouvrage de Machiavel *Istorie fiorentine*, ainsi que celui d'ouvrages de ses compatriotes comme les *Historiarum florentini populi libri XII* de L. Bruni ou les *Storie fiorentine dal 1378 al 1509* de F. Guichardin. De même F. de la Noue dans ses *Discours Politiques et Militaires*, Montaigne dans ses *Essais* et même Descartes dans son *Discours de la Méthode*, ainsi que de nombreux autres auteurs qu'il serait trop long d'énumérer utilisent également le concept d'histoire au pluriel. On pourrait donc dire de Bodin qu'il ne fait que se conformer à l'usage de son temps. Cela n'est vrai qu'en partie, car à la différence des écrivains que nous venons de citer, sa réflexion porte justement sur la signification de la

---

[49] *Meth.*, Ch. V, 140, 35–44, ainsi que 167, 5–11.
[50] *Meth.*, Ch. V, 140, 24–28.
[51] *Meth.*, Ch. I, 114, 15.

distinction entre le singulier et le pluriel, entre *historia* et *historiae*. De ce point de vue aussi il inaugure un nouveau mode de pensée.

Nous avons vu que Bodin faisait une distinction entre l'histoire sacrée, l'histoire naturelle et l'histoire humaine. Cette dernière il la divise à son tour en *historia communis* et *historia propria*, celle-ci se limitant à rassembler les actions d'un seul homme ou tout au plus d'un seul peuple, l'autre faissant le récit de plusieurs hommes ou plusieurs peuples.[52] Quelques pages plus loin il définit l'*universa historia* comme celle qui rassemble les actions mémorables depuis l'origine, aussi bien celles accomplies en temps de guerre que celles accomplies en temps de paix par tous les peuples ou du moins les principaux d'entre eux, pour autant que nous les connaissons.[53] Il se pose à propos de cette distinction deux séries de questions, l'une de caractère philologique, l'autre de caractère philosophique.

Première série. Pour désigner l'un de ces types d'histoire Bodin utilise tantôt l'expression d'*historia propria*, tantôt celle d'*historiae singulae* et pour désigner l'autre, tantôt celle d'*universa historia*, tantôt celle d'*historia communis* et de même *historiae singulae* et *universa historia*.[54] On peut donc se demander si vraiment il entend les deux concepts d'*historia communis* et d'*universa historia* comme équivalents, tout comme ceux d'*historia propria* et d'*historiae singulae*, ou bien s'il faut introduire des nuances, en ce sens que par exemple l'*historia communis* traduirait un autre type d'histoire que l'*universa historia*. Se fondant sans doute sur le fait que Bodin utilise le concept d'*historia* de façon neutre et générale pour désigner aussi bien l'un que l'autre de ces deux types, P. Mesnard ne voit aucune difficulté et il rend indifféremment en français l'*historia communis* et l'*universa historia* par la même expression d'histoire universelle. En apparence il semble que le contexte pourrait justifier cette traduction, mais à y regarder de plus près elle n'est nullement évidente. C'est dans le chapitre I qu'apparaît la notion d'*historia communis*, quand après avoir fait la distinction entre les trois genres d'histoires, humaine, naturelle et sacrée, il subdivise l'histoire humaine en *historia propria* et *historia communis*.[55] On pourrait d'abord croire qu'il s'agit d'une distinction qui serait uniquement interne à l'histoire humaine, mais il note un peu plus loin qu'elle est également applicable aux deux autres genres, à l'histoire sacrée suivant qu'on étudie une seule religion ou toutes ou plusieurs religions et à l'histoire naturelle suivant qu'on étudie une plante ou toutes des plantes ou encore un élément physique ou la nature entière.[56] Si l'on traduit *historia*

---

[52] *Meth.*, Ch. I, 115, 24–30.
[53] *Meth.*, Ch. II, 116, 18–21.
[54] *Meth.*, par exemple Ch. I, 115, 24, Ch. II, 118, 33–34 et 50–51.
[55] *Meth.*, Ch. I, 115, 24.
[56] *Meth.*, Ch. I, 115, 24 à p. 116, 1–14.

communis par histoire universelle il faut admettre qu'il pourrait y avoir selon Bodin trois sortes d'histoire universelle, humaine, naturelle et sacrée, ce qui n'est peut-être pas contradictoire, mais confus. On peut donc se demander s'il ne faut pas faire une distinction entre *historia communis* et *universa historia* – cette dernière dénomination n'intervient d'ailleurs que dans le chapitre II, après que Bodin eut fait la classification des divers genres,[57] si bien qu'il faudrait peut-être entendre par l'*universa historia* une forme qui transcenderait toutes les sortes d'histoires, qu'elles soient communes ou singulières, et que par conséquent la *cognitio historiarum* du titre de l'ouvrage serait l'histoire universelle qui permettrait de mieux comprendre la diversité des études historiques.

On peut corroborer cette interprétation par le fait que, si l'*historia communis* et l'*universa historia* étaient identiques, on ne voit pas pourquoi Bodin aurait éprouvé le besoin de les définir séparément[58] dans deux chapitres différents ayant chacun son objet propre, alors qu'il aurait pu se contenter d'une définition unique. En outre, à propos de la définition de l'*historia communis* il parle seulement de plusieurs *(plurium)* hommes ou Etats,[59] ce qui laisse supposer qu'une telle histoire est purement comparative, tandis qu'il emploie le terme de tous *(omnium)* les peuples à propos de l'*universa historia* ou à la rigueur des plus illustres qui nous sont connus,[60] ce qui laisse supposer qu'il s'agit de quelque chose de plus que d'une comparaison, mais d'une condition permettant la compréhension de toutes les autres sortes d'histoire, qu'elles soient singulières ou communes.[61] Enfin, il se réfère à propos de l'*historia communis* aux historiens de l'Antiquité qui ont comparé le développement de divers peuples ou qui ont utilisé le procédé des éphémérides ou des Annales, par exemple Valerius Flaccus et Cicéron,[62] laissant entendre qu'une telle histoire doit être aussi complète que possible, tandis qu'à propos de l'*universa historia* il se réfère à des historiens contemporains qui ont pratiqué ce genre nouveau, en particulier J. Funck et Melanchton,[63] en même temps qu'il précise d'une part qu'elle doit remonter jusqu'aux origines des peuples,[64] d'autre part que, à la différence des Annales, elle peut omettre certaines choses, l'essentiel étant qu'elle soit cohérente et non pas complète.[65] Il faut toutefois convenir que la pensée de Bodin présente sur ce point quelques équi-

---

[57] *Meth.*, Ch. II, 116, 18.
[58] Voir les deux notes pécédentes, 56 et 57.
[59] *Meth.*, Ch. I, 115, 29–30.
[60] *Meth.*, Ch. II, 116, 18.
[61] *Meth.*, Ch. II, 118, 29–37.
[62] *Meth.*, Ch. I, 115, 30–59.
[63] *Meth.*, Ch. II, 116, 48–59.
[64] *Meth.*, Ch. II, 116, 20.
[65] *Meth.*, Ch. II, 116, 15 et 22–25.

voques, en dépit de sa volonté d'introduire pour des raisons de clarté le plus de divisions et de subdivisions possibles, car son vocabulaire est loin d'être toujours uniforme. Ainsi il lui arrive d'utiliser les termes d'*omnium* et de *totius* à propos de l'*historia communis* appliquée à l'histoire naturelle et sacrée[66] et d'autre part il confond au moins une fois les deux types d'histoire quand, parlant de l'*universa Rerum publicarum historia*[67], il désigne des faits qui relèvent plutôt de l'*historia communis*. Aussi présentons-nous cette interprétation uniquement à titre d'hypothèse.

Deuxième série. Comment Bodin entendait-il l'*universa historia*? Il s'agit de dresser un tableau panoramique et général de toute l'histoire connue pour permettre de saisir d'un coup, de façon simple et dépouillée,[68] l'évolution de l'humanité, c'est-à-dire la suite des peuples qui se sont succédes dans le temps depuis l'origine. Ce tableau doit d'abord reposer sur une chronologie éprouvée qu'il appelle *dux historiarum*,[69] pour que le lecteur ne se perde pas dans le labyrinthe des événements.[70] Aussi faut-il soigner tout particulièrement la détermination de l'origine de l'humanité et celle de chaque peuple – ce dont s'occupent les chapitres VIII et IX – et les dates essentielles du devenir humain,[71] l'important n'étant pas la synthèse mais l'analyse qui introduit, grâce aux divisions et aux subdivisions, un ordre qu'ont négligé les commentaires imparfaits et décousus de la plupart des historiens.[72] Evidemment cette méthode suppose un tri, une sélection entre ce qui est essentiel et secondaire, car il s'agit non de tout dire, mais de rendre intelligibles les actions humaines, en particulier l'activité politique, dont s'occupe le long chapitre VI, consacré à une analyse de la naissance et de la décadence des régimes et des diverses formes de gouvernement. La méthode employée doit enfin être critique et c'est pourquoi Bodin consacre tout le chapitre VII à réfuter la conception plutôt fantaisiste de l'histoire universelle de ses prédécesseurs, Melanchton, Sleidan, Funck et autres qui ont pris à leur compte la théorie des Quatre monarchies et des Quatre siècles d'or. Opposé à toute histoire partisane, il estime que la critique doit trouver les normes de ses jugements en elle-même. Aussi s'élève-t-il contre les conceptions de Melanchton qui, sur la base de la théorie des Quatre Monarchies, considère que la monarchie allemande est la plus puissante et le plus digne successeur de l'Empire romain.[73] D'une façon générale l'histoire universelle doit, à son avis, rester

---

[66] *Meth.*, Ch. I, 116, 5, ainsi que 9 et 12.
[67] *Meth.*, Ch. VI, 167, 24–25.
[68] *Meth.*, Ch. II, 116, 27.
[69] *Meth.*, Ch. VIII, 228, 17.
[70] *Meth.*, Ch. VIII, 228, 11.
[71] *Meth.*, Ch. VIII, 228, 20–25.
[72] *Meth.*, Ch. II, 116, 44–7.
[73] *Meth.*, Ch. VII, 241, 3–6.

neutre. Tout en reconnaissant qu'il est difficile à un historien de rester insensible au destin de sa patrie, il conseille néanmoins la prudence à l'égard de ceux qui acquiescent trop facilement à ce qu'on dit de louable de leurs compatriotes, en même temps qu'ils s'acharnent sur leurs ennemis,[74] et il regrette la maladie ou manie qui consiste à vouloir défendre l'honneur de ses amis au prix de mensonges.[75]

S'agit-il d'une philosophie de l'histoire? Oui, si nous entendons par cette notion toute réflexion qu'un historien ou philosophe peut faire à propos de la méthode, la nature ou le sens de l'histoire. Non, si on la comprend à la manière des modernes comme une discipline qui prétend pénétrer les secrets du devenir et la signification ultime des choses et se croit capable de déterminer les stades futurs de l'évolution qui conduiraient à une prétendue phase finale de l'humanité. Tout au plus peut-on trouver chez Bodin l'un ou l'autre rudiment d'une telle philosophie, car comme beaucoup d'autres historiens de son temps il penche pour l'idée du retour éternel. A ses yeux, en effet, l'histoire n'a point de terme – *nullum exitum habet*[76] – et par conséquent elle ne saurait connaître un stade ultime définitif.[77] Cela tient au fait qu'elle est l'œuvre de la volonté qui n'est jamais semblable à elle-même et qui comme telle n'a pas non plus de terme,[78] mais suscite sans cesse de nouvelles actions. Si l'histoire n'a pas de fin, c'est à la manière des révolution célestes,[79] suivant lesquelles les astres reviennent toujours à chaque point de leur orbite pour inaugurer une nouvelle révolution. Bodin revient à plusieurs reprises sur cette conception cyclique, car elle explique les constantes que nous découvrons dans l'histoire,[80] ainsi que la succession ininterrompue des vices aux vertus, de l'ignorance à la science, des ténèbres à la lumière et ainsi de suite.[81] Il est tout aussi faux de croire que le monde va sans cesse en s'améliorant qu'il est absurde de penser qu'il ne cesse de se dégrader, car la nature contient un trésor non dénombrable de sciences qu'aucune époque ne parviendra jamais à épuiser.[82] Il n'existe pas plus de siècle que d'état privilégié de l'humanité qui pouraient se prévaloir d'une supériorité définitive sur les autres. C'est une pensée de vieillard que de croire que nos temps seraient plus mauvais que les précédents, que l'amitié, la justice

---

[74] *Meth.*, Ch. IV, 125, 8–11. Voir également Ch. IX, 242, 47–58.
[75] *Meth.*, Ch. IV, 127, 24–26.
[76] *Meth.*, Epître dédicatoire, 109, 30.
[77] *Meth.*, Ch. VIII, 241, 19–22 et 39–42.
[78] *Meth.*, Ch. VIII, 241, 19–22 et 39–42.
[79] *Meth.*, Ch. VIII, 240, 13–16.
[80] *Meth.*, Ch. I, 115, 14–16.
[81] *Meth.*, VII, 228, 41–46.
[82] *Meth.*, Ch. VII, 228, 40–41.

et l'honnêteté disparaîtraient progressivement.[83] Après avoir atteint l'apogée d'une civilisation merveilleuse il s'est produit en Grèce une telle révolution qu'on peut se demander si ce pays a vraiment existé là où nous croyons. Les Romains ont acquis dans de nombreux domaines un prestige presque éternel et ils ont pourtant sombré dans la barbarie.[84] Les Anciens ont été admirables par leur science, leur art et nous le sommes aussi. Ils ont étalé leurs vices, leur dépravation et des forfaits exécrables, nous le faisons aussi.[85] La civilisation succède à la barbarie et la barbarie à la civilisation, peut-être même chaque civisilation renferme-t-elle sa propre barbarie. Si l'on souligne nos turpitudes et les vertus des Anciens pourquoi ne pas également souligner leurs déchéances et nos gloires? Les Anciens ont eu leur héros, mais ils n'étaient pas faits d'une meilleure argile que les nôtres.[86] «Cum aeterna quadam lege naturae conversio rerum omnium velut in orbem redire videatur.»[87]

IV. Le guide de la vie

Fondée uniquement sur des probabilités et non sur des certitudes l'histoire est un réservoir d'expériences et d'enseignements qui en font le guide de la vie, *humanae vitae moderatrix*.[88] Comme telle elle nous invite à la prudence,[89] vertu que doit acquérir le lecteur de l'histoire universelle. Elle nous aide non seulement à établir les préceptes nécessaires à la conduite de notre existence, mais encore à comprendre ce que nous pouvons espérer et ce que nous devons fuir, à faire la discrimination entre l'honnête et le honteux, à reconnaître les meilleures lois et le meilleur gouvernement et enfin à parvenir à la béatitude.[90]

C'est dire que pour Bodin l'histoire peut être profitable à de multiples égards et pour de nombreuses raisons. Il pousse parfois sa démonstration jusqu'à signaler des détails plutôt futiles et pleins d'ingénuité comme le récit d'Antiochus brûlant d'amour pour Stratonice et sauvé par le médecin Eristrate. Il voit dans ce fait toute une série de leçons, aussi bien une histoire d'amour qu'un exemple de guérison, de prodigalité et d'éloquence.[91] Autrement dit, on n'en finit pas de s'instruire grâce à cette

---

83 *Meth.*, Ch. VII, 228, 48-4.
84 *Meth.*, Ch. VII, 227, 20–25.
85 *Meth.*, Ch. VII, 227, 55–9.
86 *Meth.*, Ch. VII, 227, 38–55.
87 *Meth.*, Ch. VII, 228, 42–44.
88 *Meth.*, Ch. I, 114, 20.
89 *Meth.*, Ch. I, 114, 16 et 115, 12–13.
90 *Meth.*, Avant-Propos, 114, 15–18.
91 *Meth.*, Ch. III, 122, 37 à 123, 4.

discipline. Parmi tous les services qu'elle peut rendre, trois apparaissent comme plus essentiels.

Tout d'abord elle remplit une fonction morale, en ce qu'elle nous apprend à aimer la vertu et à détester les vices. Ce point de vue est même primordial, car il est à l'origine même de l'histoire, puisque les hommes ont voulu par son entremise louer les actions mémorables et belles et flétrir la méchanceté, même si la louange comportait parfois de pieux mensonges.[92] L'histoire est donc une sorte de tribunal qui condamne les scélérats et exalte les vertueux et les vaillants. Certes, il faut autant que possible présenter un récit véridique. Néamoins la distinction entre le vrai et le faux n'incombe pas à l'histoire, mais à l'histoire naturelle ou science, car son objet est la discrimination entre l'honnête et le honteux;[93] d'autre part elle peut remplir son office même si le récit n'est pas tout à fait authentique, pourvu qu'il laisse paraître un soupçon ou une étincelle de vérité,[94] car la présentation d'une action d'un homme juste et vaillant vaut parfois mieux que le souci de la vérité historique.[95]

En second lieu elle est un trésor d'expériences politiques qui sont profitables aux gouvernants. Comme telle, elle est le fondement de la science politique. En effet, c'est chez les historiens comme Polybe, Denys d'Halicarnasse, Plutarque et Tacite – Bodin ne cite pas à ce propos Thucydide – qu'on trouve les remarques les plus profondes sur le gouvernement des Etats. Il cite également Machiavel, le grand initiateur de la science politique moderne après plus d'un millénaire de barbarie en ce domaine, bien qu'il lui reproche de n'avoir pas su unir suffisamment la connaissance des philosophes et des historiens et l'expérience.[96] D'une part l'histoire enseigne la nécessité de constituer des sociétés, comment elles se forment par l'union de plusieurs familles,[97] la logique de chaque régime, etc. Ce rôle de l'histoire se comprend aisément puisqu'elle est presque entièrement consacrée à l'explication des diverses constitutions et des révolutions ou changements de régime. Aussi n'y a-t-il d'exercise plus fécond pour s'initier à la politique que la pratique de l'histoire.[98] D'autre part, du fait qu'elle ne parvient à établir que des probabilités qui nous apprennent la prudence, elle est aussi par certains aspects une école d'indulgence. En effet, quand les situations changent, les avis peuvent changer également, d'où une souplesse

---

[92] *Meth.*, Ch. IV, 125, 20–22.

[93] *Meth.*, Ch. I, 114, 18.

[94] *Meth.*, Avant-Propos, 113, 18–20.

[95] *Meth.*, Avant-Propos, 113, 38–40.

[96] *Meth.*, Ch. VI, 167, 44–57.

[97] *Meth.*, Ch. III, 120, 21–22. C'est là un des points essentiels de l'opposition de Bodin à la philosophie politique d'Aristote.

[98] *Meth.*, Ch. VI, 167, 16–31.

nécessaire dans le jugement politique. Il est par conséquent absurde de reprocher aux hommes politiques d'avoir modifié leur point de vue quand les circonstances l'exigeaient, s'ils ont agi avec la constance qui est aussi éloignée de la légèreté que de l'obstination. On a raison de se méfier de ceux qui préfèrent renoncer à la vie, plutôt que de modifier leurs principes, car ils font beaucoup de mal aux autres et risquent de perdre l'Etat.[99] En dernier lieu l'histoire est une école de philosophie, ce qui équivaut chez Bodin à une initiation raisonnée des choses religieuses. En effet, une fois que le lecteur se sera familiarisé avec l'histoire humaine et l'histoire naturelle il pourra mieux comprendre les diverses religions et, grâce aux connaissances morales, s'élever à la philosophie qui lui permettra de saisir la vraie religion.[100] De même la connaissance de l'histoire du droit, qui comporte en elle-même sa philosophie, facilitera la compréhension de la notion de justice qui consiste non pas à se conformer à la loi changeante des hommes, mais à la loi éternelle.[101] Bodin est, en effet, convaincu que l'histoire ne peut pas tout expliquer, même pas tout ce qui est historique; d'où la nécessité, soit de s'en remettre à Providence, soit de recourir à la bonté divine pour comprendre certains événements.[102] Sa théorie volontariste de l'histoire ne peut pas s'accomoder d'un monde qui serait uniquement soumis à la loi de la nécessité et qui ne serait pas lui aussi l'œuvre d'une volonté supérieure. Aussi s'en prend-il à Aristote et traite-t-il de téméraire et d'impie son argument qui établit l'éternité du monde, car il ruine aussi bien les décrets de la philosophie naturelle que la majesté divine.[103]

Ainsi que Bodin l'affirme à plusieurs reprises,[104] sa méthode comporte une ascension par degrés qui correspondent aux trois genres d'histoire qu'il a distingués. Il faut commencer par l'histoire humaine pour connaître l'origine du monde, la diversité des peuples, la vie domestique et politique, la guerre et la paix, l'agriculture, le commerce, l'industrie, mais aussi les arts et les préceptes de la morale. Muni de ces connaissances on s'initiera progressivement à l'histoire naturelle ou sciences pour se mettre au courant des principes de la physique, de la chimie, de la biologie, de l'astronomie et en général des principes de la nature. Enfin au dernier degré, celui de l'histoire sacrée, on s'informera des choses divines, de la distinction entre la religion et l'impiété, de l'action de Dieu qui se manifeste par des oracles et des miracles. Certes, la compilation n'est pas absente d'un pareil pro-

---

[99] *Meth.*, Ch. V, 157, 10–31.
[100] *Meth.*, Ch. II, 118, 1–12.
[101] *Meth.*, Epître dédicatoire, 108, 30–33.
[102] *Meth.*, Ch. VII, 227, 2–4.
[103] *Meth.*, Ch. VIII, 229, 2–6.
[104] *Meth.*, en particulier ch. I, 115, 15–26 et ch. III. 121, 22 à 122, 25.

gramme, mais l'essentiel est de pouvoir y puiser comme dans un trésor[105] pour parvenir graduellement à la contemplation de Dieu ou suprême félicité: ἱστορῆσαι τὸ θεᾶσθαι.[106] Cette ascension a pour but de purifier l'esprit de l'homme et le rendre plus sensible à la manifestation de Dieu.[107] Evidemment, cette contemplation sera celle d'un cœur solitaire:[108] elle conduit à la béatitude qui est sans commune mesure avec le bonheur de la cité.[109]

---

[105] *Meth.*, Ch. II, 119, 1.
[106] *Meth.*, Ch. I, 114, 54.
[107] *Meth.*, Ch. III, 121, 1.
[108] *Meth.*, Ch. III, 121, 2–3.
[109] *Meth.*, Ch. III, 121, 8–10.

Donald R. Kelley

The Development and Context of Bodin's Method

I. Bodin: Quid et Quotuplex

Jean Bodin is a many-sided figure who has been in recent years the subject of proliferating and increasingly specialized studies. The one persistent habit of Bodin scholars, it seems to me, has been to restrict themselves to one of two of these sides, which moreover are defined in terms of rather formal categories of political thought, historical method, law, geography, and the like. This habit is well illustrated by the agenda (though perhaps not the purpose) of the present conference, and I must confess that it has affected my own work. But I have for a long time been uncomfortably aware that Bodin's «method», like his «republic», is like no other, and that approaching him through modern compartments of knowledge is not only anachronistic but also somewhat distorting. In any case it is these convictions, which have proved stronger than my sense of scholarly caution, which have led to this experimental attempt to see Bodin in a somewhat broader perspective and more philosophic context.[1]

Bodin seems to present a historical paradox. On the one hand he was almost too typical of his age. «Humanist, jurist, astrologist», Etienne Fournol remarked, «here indeed is a man of the 16th century». On the other hand, and in a longer perspective, he was a man for many ages. «If he was one of the last of the legists», Fournol added, «he was also the first of the philosophes.»[2] Yet there is no real contradiction here, except to the extent that Bodin himself entertained extreme and conflicting views. For if he displayed the spirit, methods, and some of the substance of scholastic learning, he also rebelled against the restraints of conventional «authority» and set out quite deliberately to create a science of society that was, according to his lights, empirical as well as rational. Drawing

---

[1] In general this essay is a byproduct of my Foundations of Modern Historical Scholarship, New York 1970 and, in part, a justification for not including Bodin, except peripherally, in the constellation of érudits discussed there (though I confess that it was an interest in Bodin's work that provoked this book in the first place).

[2] FOURNOL [51] Bodin prédécesseur de Montesquieu, Paris 1896, 21, 27; cf. FOURNOL Sur quelques traités de droit public du XVI. siècle, Nouvelle revue historique de droit français et étranger 21 (1897), 298–325 [54].

upon the wisdom of the past, he tried to build a system for the future. «The republic never dies», ran the old maxim, and Bodin wanted to insure that his own *Republic* had a comparable longevity.

A man with a passion for the past and designs upon the future, Bodin does not seem to have been much at home in his own time; he might well have preferred to be a contemporary of St Thomas or of Descartes. For in an age of academic inhibition he was a boldly speculative thinker, in an age of doctrinal faction a philosophical syncretist, in an age of discriminating criticism a compulsive and rather credulous eclectic. Not satisfied merely with investigating the past, he sought to extract from it principles of universal and eternal import; not satisfied with determining rules of human behavior, he wanted to arrange them into a coherent system; not satisfied with analysing society in rational terms, he wanted to uncover the *arcana* of nature as well as of the imperium. These overreaching philosophical ambitions led him down strange and even forbidden paths and gave him an almost Faustian reputation. Small wonder that he inspired distrust among such careful scholars as Cujas and Scaliger. Several contemporaries suspected that Bodin literally did not quite belong to their world. According to François Pithou (who heard it from Claude Fauchet), «Bodin was a sorcerer».[3]

Bodin accepted no man as his master, though he learned from many; he belonged to no school of thought, though he attended several. His first intellectual allegiance was clearly to the legal profession, with all of its totems, taboos, and traditions. From the beginning, too, Bodin was attracted by the humanist movement and its concern for educational reform. Yet he submitted to the standards neither of the professional lawyer nor of the professional humanist. He shared neither the arrogance of the first, who insisted that his «science» was superior *(nobilior et dignior)* to all others, nor to the snobbery of the second, who seemed prize eloquence above doctrine.[4] On the contrary, to Bodin nothing human – or superhuman – was alien, and in effect he assumed the unity

---

[3] *Scaligerana, Pithoeana..*, Amsterdam 1740, I, 500. That Bodin shared some of Machiavelli's diabolical reputation is shown, e.g., by Antonio POSSEVINO's *Judicium de Nicola Machiavelli et Joannis Bodini scriptis* in his translation of the former's *Princeps*, Ursel 1600, 197. See also Mr. Baxter's paper on Bodin's «demon.» With all the books on Bodin there has been no satisfactory attempt to treat him as a philosopher.

[4] Two classic but seldom cited panegyrics of the «science» of law appear in CHASSENEUZ, *Catalogus gloriae mundi*, Paris 1529, pars X, passim, and JEAN CORRAS, *De Jure civili, in artem redigendo,* in the fundamental collection, *Tractatus universi juris,* Venice 1584, I, f. 62v. The various (sometimes «interdisciplinary») attempts of 16th century jurists to place law in the encyclopedia of arts and sciences deserve further investigation.

of all learning. If he preferred, in humanist fashion, to arrange this learning in a circular way *(encyclopaedia)* rather than according to a hierarchy, he did not hesitate to open this classical preserve to «barbarian» ideas. His attitude was at once inter-disciplinary and inter-cultural.

In general the pattern of Bodin's intellectual growth was one of exploring and charting large and distant fields of thought, but seldom of settling and cultivating them carefully. In particular his route led from a wide-ranging study of history, law, and philosophy to a system that embraced, while at the same time it transcended, all three. But Bodin rarely adopted other mens' views without transmuting them to suit his own goals, and so some of the most interesting features of his thought are not fully accessible through simple exegesis, conventional biography, or piecemeal *Quellenforschung*.[5] What I propose here is to supplement such studies (of which we have an abundance) by means of two related lines of inquiry: first to suggest, by comparison with views of contemporaries, certain features of his intellectual environment and certain scholarly traditions which helped to shape his historical and political philosophy; and second to reveal, by a kind of structural analysis, some of the changing configurations of his thought leading up to the *Republic*. What ever the merits of this approach, it seems to be in keeping with and perhaps even invited by Bodin's own «method», which likewise depended upon comparisons to locate essential, underlying principles, which likewise used logical rather than literal analysis to show these relationships, and which in general exhibited an *esprit de système* that seems to soar uncomfortably high above its alleged sources.

II. Bodin: Grammaticus

If Bodin had any single point of departure, it was the «new learning» of the Renaissance, for which his Toulouse oration of 1559 was an advertisement.[6] Here he rehearsed the story of the «translation of studies» from Italy to France, sponsored by that «father of letters», Francis I, with the help of Guillaume Budé, and given institutional embodiment in the royal

---

[5] So it would not be appropriate, even if it were possible, to cite here the vast and growing quantity of Bodiniana bearing upon such questions, though I should record my special debts to the work of MOREAU-REIBEL, BROWN, REYNOLDS, MESNARD, and CHURCH.

[6] *Oratio de instituenda in repub. juventute ad senatum populumque Tolosatem*, in *Œuvres philosophiques*, ed. PIERRE MESNARD, Paris 1951 [4.20], 9 ff; cf. LE ROY, G. *Budaei vita*, Paris 1540, 46 ff. The later parallels between the thought of these two is well known, having been discussed by J. B. BURY, ROGER CHAUVIRÉ, and others.

«College of Three Languages» established during the 1530's. This often told tale was sanctioned by Budé himself and by his first biographer, Louis Le Roy (who like Bodin was a graduate of the Toulouse law school and later a professor in this same royal college), and by the time Bodin gave his oration it had become quasi-official doctrine. But for Bodin and Le Roy and indeed most scholars of their generation the «studies» thus celebrated were exclusively neither ancient nor Italian; they were perforce joined to and colored by the whole glorious tradition of the French monarchy, barbarous and vernacular as it was. As a result the humanist «encyclopedia» was expanded to include the entire cultural past of Europe and came to resemble the usage of D'Alembert more closely than that of Budé.[7] Being heir to such eclecticism, Bodin could hardly help breaking out of the humanist mold.

Within the new learning Bodin attached special importance to the «new jurisprudence», which was one of its byproducts and which had flourished especially in France. This so-called *mos gallicus* had been pioneered by Budé, had been introduced into the universities by Andrea Alciato, and had been developed further by such «Alciatei» as François Connan, to mention the three jurists specifically named by Bodin at this time. The story of this phase of the humanist movement, a sort of companionpiece to the Budé legend just referred to, was also told by Le Roy, this time in his biography (again the first) of Connan.[8] Toulouse was not particularly cordial to «legal humanism», but it was here nonetheless that Bodin, like Cujas and Le Roy, became a devotee of this new school which, as he now thought, had enriched the study of law with philosophy as well as with classical learning. It is perhaps significant that already Bodin emphasized the philosophical rather than the philological aspect of the «reformed jurisprudence», that he gave no credit to the real founders of the school (Lorenzo Valla and Angelo Poliziano), and that of all the distinguished disciples of Alciato he singled out not one of the university jurists but a practicing advocate interested in legal reform. Connan did repeat certain humanist commonplaces, including strictures against a servile imitation of Aristotle and the neglect of history and philology, but of all the pro-

---

[7] BUDÉ himself, who helped to promote the Italianate «encyclopaedia», notably in his *Annotationes in Pandectas* of 1508 and his *De Philologia* of 1532, spoke of a «Minerva Franciae» in the preface to his *De Asse* of 1515, where he also celebrated the «translation of studies». Such naturalization of the classical idea of culture is even more conspicuous in such vernacular works as LE ROY's *De la vicissitude ou varieté des choses,* Paris 1575, and ETIENNE PASQUIER's *Recherches de la France,* Paris 1621, esp. book IX.

[8] *De Francisco Connano* ... (1553) in CONNAN's *Commentariorum juris civilis libri X,* Naples 1724; cf. BODIN, *Oratio* [4.20], 17. One of the earliest full versions of this story appears in PASQUIER, *Recherches,* X, 39.

ducts of the *mos gallicus* he was possibly the least typical excepting Bodin himself.[9] There has been much discussion of «legal humanism» in recent years, but the subject is still in some confusion. The trouble is that we continue to see the movement less in terms of its accomplishments than of its public image, whether through the panegyrics of its friends, such as Cujas, or through the invectives of its enemies, such as Alberico Gentili.[10] By Bodin's time, in fact, the contrast between the *mores gallicus* and *italicus* was not nearly so sharp as contemporary polemic suggests. On the one hand there were many conventional jurists (*Bartolisti, doctores scholastici, doctores italici* as they were variously, and almost always invidiously, called) who not only possessed elegant literary tastes but who, like Charles Dumoulin, «the glory of our profession», as Bodin referred to him, also had impressive philological skills and interests in textual emendation. On the other hand there were humanists (*grammatici, encyclopedei, Vallenses, Alciatei, Cujacii, docteurs humanistes,* and other epithets) who, like François Hotman and indeed Alciato himself, did not hesitate to revert to a basically scholastic method (and indeed for pedagogical purposes even Cujas recommended a conservative approach).[11] What is more significant, methodology was becoming a less divisive issue than ideology, especially as expressed in the conflict between the Italians (also called *doctores italici,* or *ultramontani,* here in a political, though still often derogatory, sense) and the Gallicans *(doctores citamontani).*[12] This distinction cer-

---

[9] CONNAN, *Commentarii,* Praefatio: «Nec hujus causa mali sunt fuit doctorum penuria (qua enim in scientia plures) sed ignoratio docendi, cum hi nullam artem scirent, neque Latinae linguae essent et historiae periti, quod utrumque fuerat necessarium.»

[10] *De Juris interpretibus dialogi sex,* London 1582, attacking not only the «encyclopedia» and Latin and Greek eloquence but dialectic and especially history («Pomponius. Historia non est cur legat Juris interpretes»). One famous reference to this conflict was made by a man who, like Bodin, rose above it: FRANÇOIS HOTMAN, *Antibribonian,* Paris 1603, ch. 15 (p. 120). distinguishing between «chauffoureurs, Bartholistes et barbares» and «Humanistes purifiez et grammariens desquels aucuns [referring to Bodin?] mettent le docte François Connan», for whose works Hotman himself had written a preface. The best and most relevant recent survey is JULIAN H. FRANKLIN [226], Jean Bodin and the Sixteenth Century Revolution in the Methodology of Law and History, New York 1963, though there are some further qualifications to be made.

[11] JACQUES FLACH, Cujas, les glossateurs et les bartolistes, *Nouvelle revue historique de droit français et étranger* 7 (1883), 205–32. These qualifications have been well brought out by GUIDO KISCH, Humanismus und Jurisprudenz, Basel 1955, 18 ff.

[12] A good example, again, is CHASSENEUZ, *Catalogus gloriae mundi,* V, 28, referring to an imperialist view held by «canonistae . . ., Bart. et omnes Itali, et

tainly meant more to Bodin himself, who was interested less in the language than in the concepts – less in making *restitutiones* than in discussing the *opiniones* – of civil law.

Nor was «legal humanism» itself a simple and coherent school of thought. Certain difficulties may be avoided by setting aside particular ideological overtones (such as the incidence and significance of «civic humanism» in legal scholarship, though this is indeed an interesting and almost totally neglected subject worth pursuing) and by regarding this movement in a more neutral fashion; that is, as a combination, in one way or another, of legal scholarship with the *studia humanitatis*, or better with the whole «encyclopedia» of subjects necessary for a proper, which is to say a historical, understanding of law.[13] It is also true that by the latter half of the 16th century there were few amateurs like Valla or Budé who had the temerity to interpret legal texts, and so there was a growing professional uniformity of standards. Nevertheless, within this professionalized tradition of legal humanism there were a number of distinguishable – and increasingly divergent – trends. Three of these were inherent in the civil law itself and were so described by François Baudouin just a year before Bodin's Toulouse oration. Just as the Digest title «de verborum significatione» required the jurist to know some philology, Baudouin wrote, so the title «de origine juris» demanded history and the title «de justitia et jure» demanded philosophy.[14] Each of these tendencies left a certain imprint on Bodin's thought.

In the first place there were the «pure grammarians» like Cujas and Antonio Agustín, whose principal interest was in separating Roman law from the jumbled Byzantine mosaic assembled by Tribonian and

---

ultramontani...,» in contrast to the «opinio contraria, quam doctores citramontani tenuerunt...,»

[13] Following here, in other words, the view of humanism taken by P. O. KRISTELLER in his various studies. It may be noticed that a major omission in the many discussions of «civic humanism» made and inspired by HANS BARON is the significance of civil law. As for the formal relations between jurisprudence and the «studia humanitatis», the most direct approach is through the various treatises on the best method of teaching law (see note 21), including those of LE DOUAREN, BARON, BAUDOUIN, HOTMAN, which are all in N. REUSNER, *Cynosura juris*, Spires 1588; also CORRAS (note 4), CUJAS (note 11), and MARIN LIBERGE, *De Artibus et disciplinis, quibus studiorum instructum et ornatum esse oportet*, Anjou 1592, among others; and through such counterattacks as those of GENTILI and GRIBALDI (the latter in Reusner). A study of this topic would be very useful.

[14] *Commentarius de Jurisprudentia Muciana* (1559), Halle 1729, «Epistola auctoris ad lectorem»; cf. LIBERGE, *De Artibus*, 4, attacking «perniciossimae eorum opinioni, qui sine philologia, philosophia, et antiquitatis cognitione juris scientiam et artem intelligi et doceri posse contendunt....»

Justinian's other editors, or at least in establishing a correct text of the Digest.[15] Their virtues included an often heroic erudition and an acute, indeed an unprecedented, sense of anachronism which permitted them to uncover many «Tribonianisms». Their conspicuous faults were a «trivial» concern with legal and literary vocabulary and a «juristic classicism», as a modern critic (Fritz Schulz) has called it, which not only deprived their work of some relevance but in its own way blocked a clear view of the development of, or changes in, civil law. Now Bodin was properly shocked by «Tribonian's crime» and the corruption of the texts of civil law, and he often relied upon the scholarship of modern critics. Yet he found it increasingly difficult to take seriously «those who would rather be called grammarians than jurists», a description which indeed fits his rival Cujas.[16] Toward the literary and antiquarian excesses of the «Cujacians», as Gentili called them, Bodin took precisely the same critical position as Alciato had taken toward Valla, the «emperor» of the grammarians.[17] Theirs was a game that Bodin would never play, though his understanding of Roman law certainly presupposed their work.

Secondly, there were the legal historians, and in fact it was to this circle – the fifth in Gentili's juridical Hades – that Bodin has often been consigned. More typical of this group were scholars like Baudouin and

---

[15] The symbol and relic as well as chief target of this school was the famous Florentine manuscript of the Digest, whose legendary provenance was repeated by many humanists, including BAUDOUIN, *Praefata de jure civili* (1545), in HEINECCIUS, col. 10; HOTMAN, *Antitribonian*, 124, and *Ex Indice universae historiae* in *Operum*, Geneva 1599, I, col. 1086; LIBERGE, *Universae juris historiae descriptio*, Poitou 1567, 95, as well as PASQUIER, *Recherches*, X, 33. The utility of this manuscript was also attacked by GENTILI, *De Juris interpretibus*, f. 92, who rejected it as an object of a kind of philological idolatry.

[16] *Oratio*, 9; cf. *Methodus ad facilem historiarum cognitionem*, prefatory letter to Jean Tessier [4.20], 108, 109, complaining again of the ineptitude of Justinian's editors and, at the same time, of the «pestis grammaticalis, in intimos omnium disciplinarum aditus usque coepit, ut pro philosophis, oratoribus, mathematicis, theologis: minutos de schola grammaticos fere cogamur.» Contrast this with the remark of FRANCOIS PITHOU about his mentor (*Scaligerana*, II 285): «Quand on vouloit mespriser Monsieur Cujas, on l'appeloit Grammarien, mais il s'en riot, et disait que telles gens estoient marris de ne l'estre pas.»

[17] ALCIATO, *Dispunctiones* (1518), III, 13, in *Opera omnia*, Frankfurt 1617, IV, 201. Even BAUDOUIN disassociated himself from the philological school; so in his *Commentarii de Pignoribus et hypothecis*, Basel 1563, 3, on the general usages of these terms, «Sed id grammaticis relinquo». Indeed, the question had been discussed at some length by VALLA, in his *Elegantiarum latinae linguae libri sex*, VI, 57 (on Digest, 20, 5, 1), and had been answered by ALCIATO, among others; the whole controversy has been assembled in C. A. DUKER, *Opuscula varia de Latinitate jurisconsultorum veterum*, Leiden 1711.

his disciple Marin Liberge, who came to regard civil law primarily as source material for the reconstruction of universal history. Baudouin had made important contributions to the study of early Roman law, especially that of the Republic, and to the search for «Tribonianisms»; and by 1559 these researches had led him to his grand design for an alliance between law and history. Moreover, when he published his *Method of History and its Conjunction with Jurisprudence* two years later, it was clear that history was to be the senior member of the partnership.[18] This was even more clearly the case with one of the later «methods» of history, that by Pierre Droit de Gaillard, who likewise proposed an alliance of law and history *(historiae et jurisprudentiae collatio)*. «All the law of the Romans and of other nations», he declared, «is nothing more than that part of history which describes the customs ... of each nation.»[19] It might be assumed that Bodin's own *Method of History*, which falls formally in this same genre *(artes historicae)*, would be in accord with this program, and indeed there are obvious similarities that have not gone unnoticed. And yet in certain more fundamental ways Bodin's work was irreconcilable with the others. Baudouin and his followers assumed, to take the most conspicuous example, that both law and history had to be understood in strictly chronological order. «Since later law abrogates earlier law», as Liberge explained, «we will commit many errors ... if we do not study history according to the sequence of times and keep the chronology of laws.»[20] To such scholarly scruples Bodin could not have been more indifferent; he quite deliberately sought a more rational and supra-temporal (which is to say super-human) arrangement in which, on the contrary, the substance of history would be subsumed under the categories of law.

---

[18] One may follow this shift in emphasis from the *Scaevola* of 1558, where, attempting to recover the legal contributions of this family, he remarked («Lectori»), that «Jurisprudentia cum Romana historia, et historia cum Jurisprudentia Romana perpetuam conjunctionem, ut duas unius veluti corporis partes indivisas esse sentirem», to the *De Institutione historiae universae et ejus cum jurispurdentia conjunctione* of 1561, where he remarks (Strasbourg 1608, 189): «Ego quidem nondum satis statuere potui, plusne lucis historia ex Jurisprudentiae libris, an Jurisprudentia ex historicis monumentis accipiat.» I focus more directly on this school in: The Rise of Legal History, *History and Theory* X (1970).

[19] *De Utilitate et ordine historiarum praefatio*, to BAP. FULGOSIAS, *Factorum dictorumque memorabilem libri IX*, Paris 1578, a little essay «deprompta ex suis institutionibus historicis», that is, from his *Methode qu'on doit tenir en la lecture de l'histoire*, Paris 1579 – from which circumstance I have taken the liberty of translating BAUDOUIN's own *Institutio* as «method».

[20] *De Artibus*, 85, citing and practically paraphrasing BAUDOUIN, *De Institutione*, 227.

This brings us to the third group, which included such philosophical jurists as Connan, Hugues Doneau, and to some extent François le Douaren, who wanted to establish a rational system of jurisprudence on the basis of Roman law as reconstructed by philology. There was much talk about refashioning law into an art *(jus civile in artem redigendo)* or restoring it to the status of a science which it properly enjoyed; almost every jurist devised his own particular «method» in order to make civil law more intelligible; and almost all of the legal humanists of Bodin's generation wrote at least one essay «de ratione docendi juris civilis» (a genre which which may be traced back to Justinian's often cited edicts prefacing the Digest).[21] Such reforming efforts had philosophical as well as pedagogical motives, and nothing was more common for these jurists than to make analogies with such better organized arts as geometry and to introduce Aristotelian terminology. But in general civil law had its own rationale, and most jurists before the time of Domat and Vico contented themselves with adjusting the schemes established by Justinian. In his «methodical interpretation» of the Digest Le Douaren followed roughly the usual sequence of topics but elaborated on and changed the particular rubrics, introducing his own precepts and theory of textual criticism, while his young protégé Doneau did not hesitate to depart from the order of titles in the Digest as well.[22] So, even more radically perhaps,

---

[21] «Discussion about method was in the air» is the appropriately unspecific remark of J. L. BROWN in his fundamental study of Bodin's *Methodus*, which is still the best discussion of the subject. It seems to me that the role of Ramus has been much exaggerated in this connection, though it is difficult to disagree with the spezific link with the *Juris universi distributio*, if not the *Methodus*, argued by KENNETH MC RAE [189, 228] in *Journal of the History of Ideas* 16 (1955), 306–23, and 24 (1963), 569–71. Useful for background is NEAL GILBERT, Renaissance Concepts of Method, New York 1956, 137 ff., but the subject of legal method needs to be investigated more thoroughly. Not quite to the point is F. EBRARD, Über Methode, Systeme, Dogmen in der Geschichte des Privatrechts, *Zeitschrift für Schweizerische Geschichte* 57 (1948), 95–136. There do seem to be some generally agreed-upon requirements for a proper «method». In one of the most extensive discussions CORAS (*De Jure civili*, f 59r) argues, among other things, that it must aim at «praecepta universalia», that it begin with «definitiones et divisiones», that it be in accord with «natura», and he goes on to make a very conventional analogy with geometry; see esp. ch. VIII, «De triplici methodo, resolutiva, compositiva, et definitiva», as well as the other works cited in note 13.

[22] *In Primam partem Pandectarum methodica enarratio*, in *Opera omnia*, Lucca 1765, I, 1; cf. *De Pandectarum compositione, ordine as methodo*, in *Opera*, IV, 47. An excellent discussion of these topics may be found ii EYSSELL, Doneau, Dijon 1860 and now in CHRISTOPH BERGFELD, Franciscus Connanus 1508–1551, Cologne 1968, the first useful treatment of this jurist so admired by Bodin.

did Connan, whose influential commentaries, published in 1557, included, among other things, comparative discussions of law and feudal institutions. Bodin shared the compulsion, common among jurists of his generation, to find a method which, through its mnemonic and logical virtues, would permit the construction of a system of universal law. And as usual Bodin would be satisfied with no one's handiwork but his own.

III. Bodin: Pragmaticus

In the seven years between his Toulouse oration and his *Methodus* Bodin was increasingly impressed by another tradition that was ultimately more significant than any variety of humanist jurisprudence. This was the practice of law and, inescapably, the Bartolist school on which it relied. At first Bodin had had the usual intellectual's contempt for the *pragmatici*, «those whom Cicero called mean and mercenary», as Hotman dismissed them at just this time. But in the course of his own legal career and especially the experiences of the wars of religion Bodin, like Hotman, came to prize the work of «those who have spent their lives serving the republic» above the «frivolities of the grammarians». He would agree with Baudouin's lofty ideal of «homo politicus, hoc est jurisconsultus».[23] Consequently, like Tiraqueau and others, he came to realize that the development of civil law had to be understood in terms of the later commentators as well as of the original sources. This was particularly necessary for public law, which classical jurists tended to avoid on principle. What is more, Bodin took very much the same attitude toward civil law as had the medieval commentators, regarding it as a treasury of accumulated wisdom (*rerum humanarum et divinarum notitia*, as Ulpian had defined it, if not *ratio scripta*) to be applied to contemporary problems. It was not without reason that Pasquier placed Bodin in «la chambre de Bartole italien».[24]

Yet it will not do simply to call Bodin a «neo-Bartolist». Although he had apparently graduated from academic to practical jurisprudence, he had not in fact merely substituted one tradition for another; as usual he tried to combine the best of both. In methodological terms, however, the Bartolists were hardly better off than the humanists. The crucial point

---

[23] BAUDOUIN, *Commentarius*, 20, and HOTMAN, *Jurisconsultus*, Basel 1559, 34. Cf. Bodin, *Methodus*, 134, attacking those «qui leviores Grammaticorum nugas malunt, quam gravissimas corum narrationes qui totum vitae suae tempus in Repub. gerenda consumpserunt». Here is the theme of «civic humanism», which may be traced back to Budé and especially to Valla (and perhaps earlier).

[24] PASQUIER, *Recherches*, 902.

Bodin made, and not for the last time, in his *Distribution of Universal Law*: unlike all other arts and sciences civil law dealt not with a general subject but with the creation of a particular society, and neither the humanist nor the scholastic jurists had escaped this narrow Romanism.[25] If legal humanism was unacceptable because it dealt with trivial (that is, historical) questions and scorned contemporary legal practice, Bartolism was unacceptable because it failed to notice the limitations and mutability of civil law. Bodin valued the work of the humanists for giving a clear picture of Roman law and that of the Bartolists for insights into the nature of society and politics, but neither offered an adequate basis for constructing a system of jurisprudence or even for drawing general conclusions about institutions. In general, he assumed, it was a fallacy to think that the experience of any single national group was sufficient for political philosophy. This was one of the unspoken axioms of Bodin's method – that the universal was never adequately represented in the particular.

Underlying this assumption, however, was a particular bias as well as a general methodological insight; and here Bodin was indebted to another legal tradition, namely, that of the royal legists in France. Beholden as they were to civil and canon law, these French *avocats du roi* had, over some three centuries, fashioned their own ideology and acquired their own scholarly habits. Most significant for Bodin was their practically unanimous rejection of the «authority» of Roman law. While «ultramontane» jurists, including Alciato as well as Bartolus, had to believe that their emperor was lord of the world *(dominus mundi)* and that «his» law was universal, their French critics, including humanists like Cujas as well as Bartolists like Chasseneuz, were bound by the contradictory rule that «the king of France has no superior in temporal things».[26] Although the

---

[25] *Juris universi distributio* [4.20], 71, remarking, «cum artes ac scientiae sint universorum: jus autem civile proprium sit unius civitatis», and (p. 73), «Jus civile, quod unius aut alterius civitatis est proprium, nec in arte cadit». He makes the point still more clearly in the *Methodus*, 107: «At illi juris civilis, id est, singularis cuiusdam civitatis artem tradere sunt conati, quam sapienter, non disputo: nihil tamen artis dignitate ac praestantia potuit alienus cogitari. omitto quam sit absurdum, ex Romanis legibus, quae paulo momento mutabiles fuerunt, de universo jure statuere velle».

[26] CHASSENEUZ, *Catalogus gloriae mundi*, V, 28–29 (see note 4). «Habet multa jura et singularia privilegia, quae non habet alii principes» (f. 141r): the 208 *jura* listed, adding to the well known set compiled by JEAN FERRAULT, constitute a kind of empirical definition of sovereignty that anticipates Bodin's in many ways. (See the discussion in Mr. Franklin's paper.) His key *opiniones*, that «Imperator non est dominus mundi», and that «Rex Franciae [est] Princeps neminens recognoscens, et non subditus Imperatori», were intended directly to

doctrinal basis for this principle was canon law, much historical evidence could also be adduced to show that «the king of France was not subject to the emperor», as Chasseneuz argued, and that consequently «the emperor was not lord of the world». Bodin was in agreement both with this and with his further declaration that the French king «has many unique privileges that other princes do not have», and presumably the reverse held as well. It was for precisely this reason that, in order to discuss a topic like «sovereignty» in general and philosophic terms, it was necessary to resort to a comparative method.

In more general terms, too, French legists had rejected the idea that the Roman tradition was universal. «There are many nations that have never been subject to the empire», declared Charles de Grassaille, «whence the most correct conclusion that the emperor was never in possession of the world».[27] This was a position that had been taken not only by generations of commentators but also, as Cosmo Guymier pointed out a century earlier, by many historians. And if Roman law could not claim universal jurisdiction, how much more circumscribed was that feudal law (the *Consuetudines feudorum*) sanctioned by the medieval German emperors? Not only were these customs without authority in civil (as well as French) law, charged Dumoulin, but the empire itself was merely a local institution.[28] This was quite in accord with Bodin's pluralistic views. What he did in his *Methodus*, in effect, was to transform this legal attitude into a methodological principle, that no national tradition could claim to represent humanity as a whole. It was essentially this Gallican view of the empire (*illa monarchia non fuit universalis* was the phrase of Chasseneuz and Grassaille) that inspired Bodin to his attack upon the political and cultural imperialism of Rome, notably in his famous refutation of the theory of Four World Monarchies, though

---

contradict those expressed by such Italian jurists as ALCIATO (*In aliquot primae Digestorum ... titulos commentaria*, in *Opera*, I), who held that «Imperator est dominus torius orbis», and that «Rex Francorum recognoscat Imperatorem de jure in superiorem». For the medieval background (centering on Innocent III's *Per venerabilem*) see SERGIO MOCHI ONORY, *Fonti canonistiche dell' idea moderno dello stato*, Milan 1951, 96 ff.; F. CALASSO, *I Glossatori et la teoria della Sovranità*, Milan 1951; and GAINES POST, *Studies in Medieval Legal Thought*, Princeton 1964, 453 ff.

[27] *Regalium Franciae libri duo*, Paris 1545, 82, citing and repeating Chasseneuz as well as Ferrault; cf. *Pragmatica sanctio glossata per Cosmam Guymier*, Lyon 1488, f. 1r: «Franci nulli umquam fuerunt subjecti in temporalibus, ut probatur ex antiquis historiis ...»

[28] *Commentarii in parisienses ... consuetudines*, in *Opera omnia*, Paris 1681, I, 22; cf. GRASSAILLE, *Regalium*, 106, «Leges seu consuetudines feudorum non habent locum in Francia.»

as always he provided his own perspective and supported his thesis with evidence of his own choosing.[29]

A most interesting corollary of this anti-universalist (and anti-imperialist) orientation of Gallicans was the common tendency among French jurists to make comparisons between civil law and institutions, ancient and modern, and those of French society. There were several obvious reasons for this: first because French lawyers were in fact trained in one law in the universities (or two, but the distinction between civil and canon laws was increasingly blurred) and obliged to practice another in many courts; second because civil law was the only feasible model for, and alternative or corrective to, French customary law (for which indeed it was *jus commune* in the so-called provinces of written law); third because customary law logically fit into the civilian category of *jus non scriptum* or *consuetudo* and was often discussed in that context; and fourth because of the growing need (and market) for polemic urging the independence and even the superiority of the French monarchy and its traditions. French historiographers had long argued that the «fortune and virtue» of their kings were not inferior to those of the Roman emperors, but this was little more than literary convention; in the 16th century this contrast was given substance through the study of legal institutional history.[30] It was just during Bodin's lifetime, in fact, that there arose a new kind of work devoted to the comparison of particular French offices, institutions, and laws with their Roman counterparts, real or supposed. It may be useful to offer a few examples of this literature, which merits further investigation in its own right as well as background for Bodin's thought.

On the one hand, and perhaps on the lowest level, was the work of the French feudists, who naturally had recourse to civil law as a standard of judgment and as a source of terminology and perhaps supplementary illustrations. This was most conspicuously true of that «prince of legists» Dumoulin, who was a master of every sort of law and who interlaced

---

[29] *Methodus*, ch. VII. Another casualty of Bodin's argument was the old medieval notion of the «translation of empire». With regard to Germany this has been treated extensively by W. GOEZ, Translatio Imperii, Tübingen 1958, but the interesting fortunes of the idea in Renaissance France await investigation.

[30] A striking example of this is the work of DU HAILLAN, who continued the conventional themes of Gaguin and Paolo Emilio, most conspicuously in his *De la Fortune et vertu de la France*, Paris 1570, which was a kind of advance announcement for his history of France – and whose *De l'Estat et succez des affaires de France*, Paris 1570, the first comprehensive history of French institutions, carried the somewhat invidious comparison of France and Rome into this area.

his commentaries with references to contemporary practice *(hodie, apud nos ...)*.[31] It was true as well of such lesser lights as Chasseneuz and Tiraqueau, who were among the first to bring something of humanist culture (though little of the philological method) to the study of customary law. Tiraqueau showed a particularly broad interest in the customs and institutions of other societies, and his biographer has suggested that, despite his indifference to any kind of system, his attitude not only resembled but even heralded that of Bodin. Still more impressive, it seems to me, is the work of Chasseneuz, who brought to bear upon the Burgundian custom a veritable encyclopedia of learning, philosophical and Biblical as well as historical and literary. His purpose was to enrich, perhaps to inflate, this vernacular text through comparisons with alien but logically similar concepts *(droits de justice* with the *jura meri imperii,* for example, and coutume itself with Roman conceptions of unwritten law).[32] He also tried to bring some order into customary law by the introduction (in Bartolist fashion) of Aristotelian categories such as genus and species for purposes of classification and the notion of final cause to explain the prooemium of this customal. Like Bodin, in short. Chasseneuz took an «unhistorical» approach, and like Bodin, too, he could claim a certain philosophical justification.

A similar pattern may be seen still more clearly in another, less traditional, kind of legal literature that emerged in the 16th century which may best be described as handbooks of administration. Among the most interesting of these are Vincent de la Loupe's *Origin of Dignities,* Bernard du Haillan's *State and Success of Affairs in France,* Lancelot de la Popelinière's *Admiral of France,* René Choppin's *Treatise on the Domain of France,* and Jean Duret's *Comparison of Roman Magistrates with French Officers,* which may all be located somewhere between the genre of technical legal monographes (like Jean de Montaigne's work on the parliament of Paris) and conventional historiography (like Du Haillan's history of France).[33] For these works reference to the Roman experience was both

---

[31] This point, which also deserves further investigation, was made by RALPH GIESEY [211], The Juristic Basis of Dynastic Right to the French Throne, Philadelphia 1961, a book which itself offers a useful study of comparative law (though this is not its main purpose) with respect to one major topic. On Tiraqueau see the remarks of JACQUES BREJON, André Tiraqueau (1488–1558), Paris 1937, introduction and p. 345.

[32] *Consuetudines ducatus Burgundiae,* Frankfurt 1572, especially the prooemium. Chasseneuz' work, too, would repay further investigation.

[33] The most striking, though by no means most significant, example is JEAN DURET, *L'Harmonie et conference des magistrats Romains avec les offices Français, tant laiz, que Ecclesiastiques. Ou succinctement est traicté de l'origine, progrez et iurisdiction d'un chacun, selon que les loix Civiles, Romaines, et Fran-*

a literary convention and a professional necessity, if not a conditioned reflex. Use of a «comparative method» ranged from such far-fetched analogies as that of the «Salic law» with the Roman *lex regia* to the most sophisticated discussions of judicial organizations or of fiscal resources or of the influence of foreign institutions.

Finally, there were the works of French civilians, especially the humanists, who strayed from the texts of Roman law into digressions or obiter dicta on French institutions. This tendency, which is already obvious in Budé's seminal *Annotations on the Digest*, is illustrated most clearly in Eguinaire Baron's little known «bipartite commentary» on Justinian's Institutes (1550), which contains parallel discussions of Roman and French laws and offices.[34] «To the Roman *princeps* we compare the king of France, who follows the same general pattern of establishing and promulgating laws», he wrote, going on to compare the imperium with *haute justice*, for example, as well as to point out certain unique institutions, such as the Roman *patria potestas* and French laws of succession. Similar in intention, but considerably more schematic, were the various attempts to shape French law directly into a Roman mold, as in Pasquier's *Interpretation of the Institutes of Justinian* and in Louis le Caron's *Pandects of French Law*, which originated as a plan to translate the Digest but which ended as a treatise on comparative law. The same impulse may be seen in Le Caron's pioneering edition of the *Grand Customal of France*. Perhaps the best illustration of all is Hotman's notorious *Anti-Tribonian*, which revealed at length the fundamental differences between Roman and French society and, in its own invidious fashion, brilliantly applied a comparative method to a set of problems involving both legal reform and the interpretation of history.[35]

Many of the intellectual habits underlying such works were shared by Bodin, but as usual they were transformed and adapted to his more

---

çoises l'ont permis, sans obmission de l'histoire aux lieux propres ..., Lyons 1574, which, despite its patriotic tone does not hesitate to reject the theory of Trojan origins (f. 9v); among the authorities cited are included not only Grassaille and Gaguin, but also Budé, Le Douaren, and (f. 6v) «Cujacius et Hotomanus, duo amplissimo veteris ac novae jurisprudentia lumina».

[34] *Institutionum civilium ab Justiniano Caesare editarum libri IIII*, Poitou 1550, in tit. and IX. (p. 6, 32). Most interesting of all is the work of Louis Le Caron, who was at once a student of Baudouin and, with respect to customary law, of Dumoulin; I am publishing a fuller investigation of this scholar.

[35] It should be remarked that the «comparatist» point of view was inherent in the century old search for «Tribonianisms», which assumed a fundamental disagreement between classical Roman and Byzantine law (and society as well); indispensable for this subject is LUIGI PALAZZINI FINETTI, Storia della ricerca della interpolazioni nel corpus iuris giustinianeo, Milan 1953.

transcendent purposes. What he wanted was not simply to make comparisons between French and Roman institutions but to inquire into those
of a multitude of societies and eventually to construct a legal system that
would encompass them all. Just as one obtained a knowledge of a species
through the investigation of individual specimens, so one could attain a
knowledge of universal law through positive law – that is, of the *jus
naturale* through the *jus gentium*.[36] In other words, just as Pico assumed
that every philosophical or religious tradition reflected one aspect of a
general and transcendent truth, so Bodin seemed to assume that the
customs and laws of particular societies reflected, however imperfectly,
one aspect of an ideal jurisprudence. The ultimate aim of Bodin's comparative method, it may be inferred, was likewise to achieve a kind of
«perennial philosophy».

This may suggest something of the breadth of Bodin's vision, the profusion of his ideas, and perhaps the flexibility of his standards. Bodin had
moved entirely beyond, and evidently lost interest in, the conventional
dichotomy of the *mores gallicus* and *italicus* and indeed that between the
grammatici and the *pragmatici*; and he admired scholars of both humanist and Bartolist persuasion. As examples of the first he commended
Baron and Connan, of the second Tiraqueau, Chasseneuz, and Dumoulin.
In one way or another they all combined formal knowledge with practical experience. But Bodin, needless to say, demanded still more, and no
wonder Gentili threw up his hands. According to the composite portrait
presented in the *Methodus*, the perfect jurist was a living encyclopedia
possessing at once a knowledge of history and philosophy, an understanding of natural law and equity, a familiarity with the commentators, a
competence in both Latin and Greek philology, and above all a proper
«method» to organize this refractory mass of material.[37] Given such an
intellectual appetite and given a special interest in public law, it was
obvious that legal sources alone were insufficient and that only an intense
investigation of the past would supply information about the *jus gentium*
in Bodin's sense of the term. *In historia juris universi pars optima latet:*
it was this axiom that, the essence of universal law would be found in
history, that led Bodin to formulate his iconoclastic and yet curiously
dogmatic *Method of History.*

---

[36] Bodin's statement of the method he wanted to follow in order to rise from
the particular to the universal, that is, from history to political science, appears
at the beginning of *Methodus,* ch. VI, which is essentially an early draft of the
Republic: «utile visum mihi est, ad eam quam instituto methodum, philosopho-
rum et historicorum de Republica disputationes inter se et majorum imperia, cum
nostris comparare, ut omnibus inter se collatis, universa Rerum publicarum
historia planius intelligatur».

[37] *Methodus,* 108–9.

IV. Bodin: Philosophistoricus

In this pivotal work, which looked at once back to his humanist sources of inspiration and forward to his system of political and social philosophy, Bodin set out to redefine the traditional «art of history». Unlike Baudouin he was not much interested in historical method in a modern sense, in *Quellenforschung* and *Quellenkritik*, and he never even distinguished very consistently between history as object *(actio)* and history as subject *(narratio)*. The main reason for this is that he was concerned not with the writing but with the reading of history: how to «pluck the flowers of history» and then arrange them in the best pattern, or in another image, how to extract from history its medicinal value. Although history was itself a form of memory, it could not in Bodin's view be grasped and retained by individuals in chronological order, that is, in its temporal disorder; it had to be arranged not according to the form of human experience *(ordo temporum* or *naturalis* in the conventional medieval formula)* but rather according to the form of human reason *(ordo artificialis)*.[38] Although history in a sense already held a position «above all sciences» *(supra scientias omnes),* it had itself to be converted into a science by the imposition of a rigidly logical «method». Although history retained its connection with the trivium in Bodin's view, its partner was not grammar or rhetoric (as for Baudouin and most other humanists) but rather dialectic.

It was inevitable that the form taken by Bodin's method should be pedagogical, or rather, since the principal aim was «to assist the memory», mnemonic. More specifically, he adopted the model of humanist logic, with its emphasis on topical distribution for handy reference for the resolution of particular problems; and his purpose was literally to define historical commonplaces *(loci communes)* and, without much regard for context, to relocate historical evidence in a rational or at least utilitarian way. The almost obsessively analytical character of Bodin's thought may be suggested by one of those diagrams to popular in dialectical, legal, and even historical works of Bodin's age.[39] Although

---

[38] *Methodus,* 116: «Principio adhibeatur praestans illa docendarum artium magistra, quae dicitur analysis: quae universum in partes secare, et partis cujusque particulas rursus dividere, totiusque ac partium cohaerentiam quasi concentum inter ipsa mira facultate docet.» Cf. BAUDOUIN, *De Institutione,* 38; and in general, MARIE SCHULZ, Die Lehre von der historischen Methode, Berlin 1909, 98 ff.

[39] The accompanying diagrams (see p. 148-149) are somewhat simplified analyses of the basic argument of the three principal works discussed here (and of the *Methodus* by itself). The pattern is particularly clear in chapter III («De Locis

Bodin did not here follow the rigidly bifurcating pattern of Ramus in the *Methodus,* he did move from large to small categories by making distinctions and sub-distinctions, with the expectation, at least in theory, of arriving eventually at the smallest units of historical discourse, that is, the plans, works, and deeds of individual men. For Bodin, then, history was to be methodized by rearrangement into parallel and proliferating sets of categories, or rather topics, which would ultimately accomodate not merely arguments (as in humanist logic) but the phenomena of history itself. The result may not have been a «philosophy of history», but it was a very impressive looking conceptual aid.

Like Baudouin, Bodin made a fundamental distriction between universal and particular history. In this he was following not only the Polybian and Eusebian pattern but also the current conviction of Protestant historians that «history was to encompass all ages», as Melanchthon put it, that it should provide a« portrait of the human race».[40] This fashion was introduced into the «arts of history» by Christophe Milieu, who offered what was perhaps the most comprehensive of all descriptions of the *universitas* of history during that century, making room for social, political, and cultural history *(prudentia, principatus,* and *sapientia,* including *historia literaturae)* as well as natural history. Bodin made a similar analysis, but he related these stages of development to various levels of the human will *(voluntas),* which related first to the problem of sustinence *(necessitas),* then to comfort *(commoditas),* and finally to the products of leisure *(splendor* and *voluptas).*[41] These motives, taken together with the social and political devices for accomplishing them, constituted the general rubrics under which the stories of particular nations could all be fitted.

One of Bodin's principal disciples complained that he «should have thrown more light upon particular history rather than digressing so upon universal history».[42] Yet in a sense the Bodin of the *Methodus* was interested more in the species than in the genera of the historical world, more in the variety than in the uniformity of human nature, and perhaps

---

historiarum recte instituendis»). What follows here is largely a commentary on this teaching aid which I have extraced from Bodin's writings. It may be added that this sort of diagram was very common in Bodin's age, not only in the works of logicians like RAMUS, but of jurists like HOTMAN *(Tabulae de criminibus* of 1543) and of authors of *artes historicae,* notably that of G. J. VOSSIUS, *Ars historica,* Leiden 1623 (diagram C).

[40] Preface to *Chronicon Carionis,* in his *Opera (Corpus Reformatorum,* XII, col. 705 ff.). In general, see ADALBERT KLEMPT, Die Säkularisierung der universalhistorischen Auffassung, Göttingen 1960 [205].

[41] MYLAEUS, *De Scribenda universita rerum historia,* Basel 1551.

[42] LA POPELINIÈRE, *Idee de l'histoire,* Paris 1599, 29.

more in the texture than in the structure of history. For his intelligible unit of study was not humanity but the national group. This was one reason why he was determined to demolish that myth of imperial historians, the theory of Four World Monarchies, which had established both a false universalism and a false uniformity of perspective. At the same time Bodin distrusted the particular national perspectives which arose from pride and ignorance. It was the question of national origins that furnished perhaps the most fertile field for the cultivation of legend and violation of chronology – and also for the exercise of historical criticism. In theory, that is, for in practice Bodin was still under the influence of the Celtic enthusiasm of the mid-16th century, which had touched scholars like Pasquier and moved Connan to suggest that even feudal institutions were by origin Gallic rather than German.[43] But the significant thing about Bodin's work was the continuing plea for a concentrated and controlled reading of the best historians.

Perhaps the most crucial, and certainly the most characteristic, aspect of Bodin's theory of history was his view of causation. Like Baudouin, Milieu, and others, he made a basic distinction between human and natural (leaving aside divine) history, corresponding of course to the three kinds of law. Unlike them he did not mind letting the human and natural spheres overlap, nor did he hesitate to introduce occult factors. There were three ways of accounting for the variety of human nature, Chasseneuz declared: that of the orthodox theologians (especially the Sorbonists), who attributed them simply to inherent qualities of the soul; that of the philosopheres and physiologists, who referred them to particular «complexions» which in turn were functions of the humors; and that of the astrologists – which Chasseneuz rejected – who traced them to the influence of the climata and location under the celestial sphere.[44] There was of course nothing revolutionary in bringing «natural» explanations into the field of human behavior. On the contrary, as Chasseneuz

---

[43] *Methodus*, 247. Cf. Pasquier, *Recherches de la France*, I, 3; and Connan, *Commentarii*, II, 9. There is need for a study of this Celtic movement of the 1550's, noted briefly by Mesnard [4.20], 37, n. 10; there are some remarks in R. E. Asher [186], The Attitude of French Writers of the Renaissance to Early French History (University of London, unpubl. Ph. D. thesis, 1955).

[44] *Catalogus gloriae mundi*, X; «Prima opinio est philosophantium et medicorum, quo complexioni attribuunt excellentiam ingenii ... Secunda ergo opinio, dicentium complexiones insequi climata et diversitatem coeli ... Omissa ergo opinione astrologorum, quae somnia et phantasmata recitat, ad tertiam opinionem veram, quae est theologorum, maxime Parisiensem, qui determinaverunt unam animam in naturalibus esse alia perfectiorem et excellentiorem, cui determinatione standum est.» And X, 18: «Scire est per causas cognoscere ... Legistae et canonistae cognoscunt per causas et rationes.»

and Coras stipulated, one of the basic characteristics of legal science was that it interpreted its subject in such terms, that is, *scire per causas*, which was a standard definition for science. But Bodin's conception of cause took him further and led him indeed into forbidden territory. Using the deterministic concepts of ancient (and medieval) medicine and astrology, Bodin sketched out a «geohistorical» science, which contained elements of anthropology and ethnography as well as sociology, and which seemed to fulfill the demand, made five years earlier by Baudouin, for an alliance between geography and history.[45]

In general Bodin's *Methodus* constituted an attempt to reduce the field of history to a hierarchical and branching set of topics in which historical information could be stored for use. The pattern may be quite simply diagrammed and the ingeniousness as well as the ambiguities this displayed. «History» itself he defined in three ways, or rather on three levels, though neither entirely explicitly nor entirely unequivocally. Most generally it was a true narrative *(vera narratio)*, and it could be pursued, as far as humanity is concerned, either on a universal plane or on a particular plane, that is, the history of nations, *(maximae respublicae)*, of cities *(minimae respublicae)*, or biography *(res gestae virorum)*. Secondly, history had to be understood from the point of view of the reader of the narration *(as cognitio)*, and this of course, as the principle subject of the book, required its own peculiar distribution. This included first the choosing *(delectus)* and classifying *(ordo et collectio)* of historical works in order to establish a basic reading list; and second the criticism *(judicium)* of these authors in terms of the auxiliary sciences of geography and chronology and in the light of what modern scholarship had to say about such problems as the theory of Four World Monarchies and myths of national origins. In these two ways Bodin discussed what may be called the subjective side of «history».

But the problem of historical knowledge was not one which Bodin was interested in pursuing further; and it was history in its third sense, history as «action» not thought *(res non verba*, in the conventional classical topos), that was to preoccupy him. The main thrust of his interest was clearly in the sphere of human action *(res humanae)*;[46] and the train of thought leading to the *Republic* appears unmistakeably in the third and sixth chapters The mechanism of history is explained here as the drive of human will toward increasingly civilized goals: that of indivi-

---

[45] *De Institutione*, 181. In general, M. J. Tooley [183], Bodin and the Mediaeval Theory of Climate, *Speculum* 28 (1953), 64–83; and A. Meuten, Bodins Theorie von der Beeinflussung des politischen Lebens der Staaten durch ihre geographische Lage, Bonn 1904 [58].

[46] Cf. Baudouin, *De Institutione*, opening and closing paragraphs.

dual man toward the necessities of life and that of man in communities toward the comforts and pleasures of life, hence toward a political organization *(respublica)* that can insure these. Thence Bodin moved to the question of political power (the *imperium*), its distribution and administration (through *concilium* and *executio*), and the complex social and cultural pattern underlying it. Such were the categories of human action (including *consilia* and *dicta* as well as *acta*) in which historical knowledge, after being analysed, was to be deposited. For Bodin, in short, history was to be transformed into an applied science.

Whatever the source of inspiration for his logical analysis, it seems clear that jurisprudence remained the principal model for Bodin's codification of history. Both history and law were conventionally equated with wisdom («the knowledge of things human and divine»),[47] and it was natural that Bodin, like Baudouin, should want to bring the two into closer alignment. The difference was that Bodin set out to impose his own almost totalitarian format on both. In both cases he began with a general definition and then distinguished its parts *(jus quit sit, ejus divisio; quid historia sit et quotuplex);* in both cases he recognized three principle types (human, natural, and divine) and a particular as well as universal form (corresponding to national and universal history was *jus civile* and *jus gentium*); in both cases he made a fundamental distinction between private and public (in history between man in community and man as citizen); and in both cases he wanted to find a scheme that would exhaust the substance of his subject (individual *leges* and, in a broad sense, individual *actiones*).[48] In general it is hard to disagree with the conclusion of one of Bodin's most devoted disciples that he was a «theoretical historian» *(historien contemplatif)* and that his book was in fact not a method of history at all but rather «method of law».[49]

---

[47] ULPIAN in Digest, 1, 1, 10: «Iuris prudentia est divinarum atque humanarum rerum notitia.» The Ciceronian formula was «sapientia est rerum humanarum divinarumque scientia» – on which see EUGENE RICE, The Renaissance Idea of Wisdom, Cambridge, Mass. 1958; it was applied to history, e.g., by BAUDOUIN, *De Institutione*, 9.

[48] Cf. *Juris universi distributio* [4.20], 72–73.

[49] LA POPELINIÈRE, *Histoire des histoires*, Paris 1599, 28, and see note 42. It may be noted that La Popelinière carried on, in several works, Bodin's concern with geo-history.

V. Bodin: Politicus

A «philosophistorian», according to Bodin, was one who combined the narration of facts with precepts of wisdom.»[50] If we add that Bodin ultimately hoped to dissolve narrative history altogether in his philosophic concoction, this prescription more than fits his work. Given his hyper-rationalizing tendencies and his overriding interest in public law (already evident in the *Methodus*), it is not surprising that he should have left behind the earth-bound concerns of historical scholarship (marginal as they were for him in any case) and moved into the higher sphere of political science *(civilis disciplina)*. And so to his collection of models Bodin added that of political philosophy, and especially Aristotle's. He proceeded with his usual idiosyncrasy, refusing either to be bound by Aristotle's conclusions or to discard any of the material he had accumulated previously; as before he simply moved on to a larger set of categories to accomodate his sources. At the same time, needless to say, the events of the 1560's and the early 1570's tended to sharpen his interest in, while modifying his views about, some of the more explosive issues of politics. Such was the path by which Bodin approached his *Republic*, the first comprehensive study of political science, as Bodin saw it, of modern times.

Among modern authors Bodin found few worthy of consideration and only Machiavelli deserving of praise – and even then rather for his pioneering effects that for his actual accomplishments. The similarities between these men have often been pointed out, but as Bodin himself suggested, the divergences may be more fundamental, especially by the time the *Republic* appeared (1576), when Machiavelli's name had become a synonym for hypocrisy, tyranny, and atheism. Yet there was more to Bodin's charge that Machiavelli identified political science with tyrannical and irreligion ruses than simply the fashionable anti-Machiavellianism of the aftermath of St Bartholomew.[51] For Bodin was also, at least implicitly, objecting to the narrowness of Machiavelli's intellectual horizons and to the superficiality of his conception of politics. Although

[50] *Methodus*, 138: «Ut autem Geographistorici regiones cum historia: sic Philosophistorici rerum gestarum narrationem cum sapientiae praeceptis cumularent.»

[51] *Methodus*, 167; cf. preface to the first edition of the *Republic*, translated by KENNETH D. McRAE in the introduction (A 70) to his edition, Cambridge, Mass., 1962 [7.44]. The view that Bodin was a «disciple» of Machiavelli was taken by CHAUVIRÉ [76], 207, among others. The contrast between the two I have elaborated upon in: Murd'rous Machiavel in France, *Political Science Quarterly* 85 (1970), 545–559.

Bodin and Machiavelli agreed upon some of the grand themes of political philosophy, such as the Polybian *anacyclosis,* and certainly shared the goal of constructing an intelligible science of politics, their modes of perceiving political reality were basically different and their respective methods in some ways irreconcilable.

The reasons for this go deeper than Bodin's obsession with system. To begin with there is an obvious contrast between their life situations. While Machiavelli was a political activist always concerned, directly or indirectly, with policy-making questions, Bodin never held comparable responsible office near the center of power, which seemed not only distant but, in keeping with official ideology, almost sacramental in character. While Machiavelli looked instinctively to the psychology of his fellow citizens, Bodin looked to the inherited traditions and the complex of institutions that circumscribed the actions of Frenchmen. It may be suspected, too, that whereas Machiavelli never lost his faith in the efficacy of individual action, Bodin naturally took a more pessimistic view – if not because of the political inertia of a structure as large and complex as the French monarchy, then surely because of the traumatic experiences of the religious wars. Most important of all, while Machiavelli had enjoyed military as well as diplomatic and administrative experience (and never distinguished too sharply between the arts of politics and of war), Bodin was a professional jurist little interested in diplomatic maneuvering and warfare (one of the few subjects, indeed, in which he was content to follow Machiavelli). In general Bodin worked in a much richer – and more inhibiting – context of legal, historical, and philosophical erudition, and he was by training and nature, if not by nationality, unable to separate politics from its legal and social environment.

In terms of method, then, Bodin and Machiavelli were literally worlds apart. As Bodin's most perceptive commentator summed it up. «The *Republic* is the work not so much of a great *politique* as of a great *legist,* the work of a successor not of Machiavelli but of Beaumanoir and Bartolus.»[52] Machiavelli's tendency was to concentrate upon individual motives and strategies, on discrete and even interchangeable factors, and on linear causal sequences. He viewed institutions, constitutional as well as religious, in a functional manner. He sought and usually found simple answers to simple questions; if not he could always take refuge in the old notion of fortune. And in applying the lessons of history he was normally content with easy analogies and accepted Roman experience as a sufficient model. By contrast Bodin could not discuss political change

---

[52] Moreau-Reibel [116], Jean Bodin et le droit public comparé, Paris 1933, 135.

without becoming involved in questions of social structure and relationships. Like Machiavelli he was concerned with questions of power, but for him this entailed private as well as public law, which meant the whole web of society from the family through the various corporate groups, social classes, and administrative hierarchy up to the central government. Between the citizen and the prince, in short, there were many gradations which obscured the lines of force and which greatly complicated the analysis of political transformation. Moreover, he assumed that any political situation or institution had to be understood in terms of a total social structure, a specific geographic milieu, a variety of customs, and a particular national tradition, if not (as in the case of France) a multiplicity of traditions.

As Walter Ullmann remarked about the medieval civilians, «By viewing law as a social phenomenon, medieval jurisprudence was forced to elucidate some basic principles about society, and thus was led to consider topics which, under modern conditions, would be dealt with, not by the lawyer, but by the sociologist.»[53] It was this school of thought above all that distinguished Bodin from Machiavelli – and established him as one of the founders of modern social science.

VI. Bodin: Dominus Factotum

In sum, to judge from the three works discussed here, it was Bodin's intention to do for the *jus gentium* in a general sense what medieval commentators had tried to do for the *jus civile*, that is, to rationalize it, to resolve conflicts and inequities, and to adapt it to contemporary problems; and ultimately he hoped thereby to formulate a social ideal that would approximate the *jus naturale*. Clearly, it was such an ideal, rather than any deep sympathy for humanist or legal erudition, that led him to his total attack upon history, to his search for underlying physical and especially geographical, principles underlying history, to his reassessment of Aristotelian political philosophy, and to his renowned «comparative method», if such indeed it was. In fact his method, to judge from the *Republic*, seems designed mainly to keep all restrictions off the riot of learning which he had gathered. Accepting no «law of citations», he was able to combine legal and philosophical «authorities» with historical and geographical evidence and so to disregard any distinction between historical inference and political generalization, which often

---

[53] The Medieval Idea of Law as Represented by Lucas of Penna, London 1946, 163.

meant between descriptive and normative statements.[54] A curious and confused sort of «empiricism», reminiscent rather of a scholastic than a comparative approach. To this extent, indeed, it may be suggested that Bodin did not altogether escape the utopian impulse.

So we return, again and finally, to the somewhat unearthly quality of Bodin's thought. He ignored the standards of established «disciplines». He rejected, too, the temporal limitations of human history and tried to fix the accumulated experience of humanity into a transcendent system. These characteristics may help to explain how, to one trying to assess the historical significance of Bodin's thought, he seems to be a man belonging to several ages. On the one hand he appears to have the scholastic philosopher's unhistorical and indiscriminate attitude toward his authorities and his faith that an ideal system may be assembled merely by the proper arrangement and criticism of these. On the other hand he sometimes seems, as in his discussion of feudal institutions, to be attempting to find the «spirit of the laws» (*mens legum* was a civilian expression which in fact did imply an ideal, since it referred to the intention or spirit as distinct from the letter of the law)[55] through the comparison of the customs of various societies. In this sense Bodin may be regarded as a significant member of that as yet untraced tradition of social thought leading from the legists of the middle ages to the philosophes of the 18th century – a prime mover in that shifting of the Heavenly City (according to Carl Becker's notorious thesis) to its «earthly foundations». The author of a veritable «Summa of political philosophy», as Henri Baudrillart declared over a century ago, Bodin was nevertheless a «Montesquieu of the 16th century».[56]

This has been only a provisional discussion, but perhaps it may suggest ways of bringing together some of the disparate features of Bodin's thought and of resolving some of the contradictions which many commentators (though not Bodin himself) have found in his work. As the papers of this conference (especially those of Messrs. Giesey and Reulos and Mme Isnardi Parente) have made abundantly clear, Bodin had access to a practically unlimited range of sources as well as to the

---

[54] More specifically, I doubt that Bodin's use of legal citations in the *Republic* is any more orthodox than his discussion of the art of history (in the rhetorical tradition) is in the *Methodus*. This seems to me to be a fundamental and unanswered question: not what his sources were, but what he thought (or assumed) their function was in his system.

[55] See NICOLAS VALLA, *De Rebus dubiis* ... (in *Tractatus universi juris*, XVIII, f. 317v): «Mens ergo legis nihil aliud est, quam sententia et ratio ejus manifesta, ex qua vel obscura, vel ambigua ipsius legis dispositio declaratur, aut generalis et indefinitiva expenditur, aut restringitur.»

[56] BAUDRILLART [27], J. Bodin et son temps, Paris 1853, 109.

Diagram A.

Bodin's Method of History

```
                                    ┌ origines      [II.
                    ┌ universa      ┤ eluviones
                    │ (communis)    └ initia rerumpub. & religionum
         humana ────┤               ┌ maximae respublicae: Caldaei ..., Graeci,
                    └ singularis    ┤    Romani, Germani ..., Americani
  I.                  geographia      minimae respublicae: Rhodes ...,
  narratio            chorographia      Venetia, Florentia
         naturalis    topographia    res gestae virorum
         mathe-       geometria
           matica
         divina
                                                        ┌ ad tuendam vitam:
                      homo singu- ┤ necessitas          │ agricultura, aedificatio, etc
                         laris      ┌ commoditas ┤ istitoria, fabriles artes, etc
                                    └ splendor            ad cultum et victum splendi-
                      societas                              diorem ...
         res                       └ voluptas        pictura, statuaria, etc
         humanae                                                  ┌ ars imperatoria
         (voluntas)                               ┌ magistrati ┤ jurisprudentia
         Civilis                     imperium     │ leges        ars oratoria
         disciplina                               │ bellum       religio
  III.                                            └ poena
  actiones            Respublica                   de vectigalibus        [VI.
         res naturales              concilium       de exercitu cogendo
         (per                                       de legationibus
         causas)                                    de propugnaculis
         res divinae                                necessitas ...
                                                   ┌ commoditas ...
                      executio      ┤ splendor ...
                                                    munera civiles (7):
                                    ┌ a natura        militia ..., magistrati
                      informatus    ┤ a doctrina
                                    │ a natura &
                                    └ doctrina     ┌ laudatio
                                      oratores     ┤ vituperatio
  IV.                                              ┌ de aliena recuspub.
  histori-            veritas                      └ de sua rebus pub.
  corum                                            ┌ historici             [X.
  delectus                            historici    └ geographistorici
                                                   ┌ paganae
                                      ecclesiastica┤ Christianae
                      ordo                         └ secta Arabica
                                      particularis  Caldaei, Graeci, Galli, etc
                                      coloni
                                      vires singu-                      ┌ Africani
                                        lares      ┌ loci (& cael.) ┤ media regio
                                                   │ corporis forma └ Scythae
                                      populi       │ humores
                                                   └ mores
                                                   ┌ terrae
                                      loci          res sub sensum ┌ humanitas
  V.                  natura                        calor            militaris
  judicium                                          pestes             disciplina
                                      disciplina   ┌ divina            religio
                               VII.               └ humana            philosophia
                                      refutatio IV                    geometria
                               VIII.  monarchia                       arithmetica
                      tempus    ┌ origo, finis                        astrologia
                               IX.  series         ┌ argumenta
                                    origo popu-    │ historia
                                      lorum        │ lingua
                                                   └ geographia
```

(vertical at left: H I S T O R I A)

cognitio

Diagram B

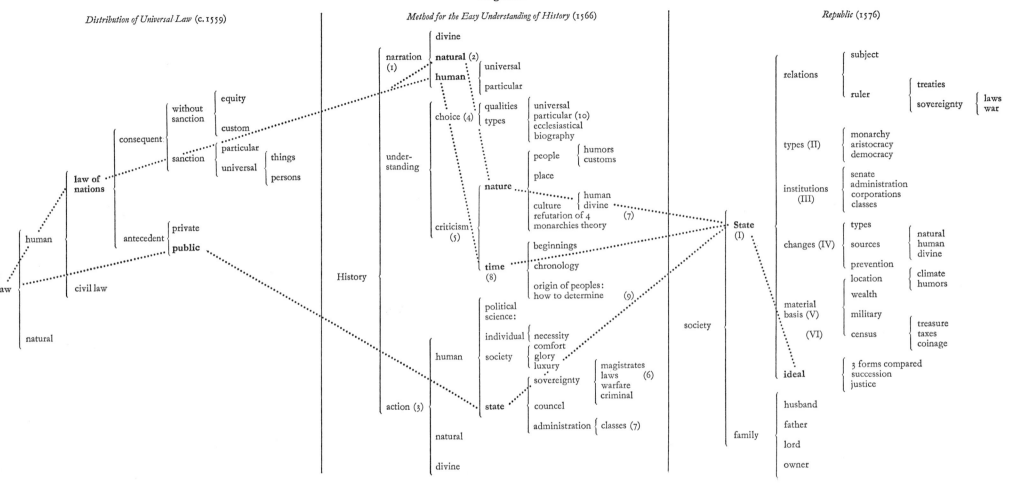

Distribution of Universal Law (c. 1559)　　　*Method for the Easy Understanding of History* (1566)　　　*Republic* (1576)

law

human
natural

law of
nations
civil law

consequent
antecedent

without
sanction
sanction

private
public

equity
custom
particular
universal

things
persons

History

narration
(1)

under-
standing

action (3)

divine
natural (2)
human

choice (4)

criticism
(5)

human

natural

divine

universal
particular

qualities
types

people
place

nature

time
(8)

political
science:

individual

society

state

universal
particular (10)
ecclesiastical
biography

humors
customs

human
divine
culture
refutation of 4
monarchies theory   (7)

beginnings
chronology

origin of peoples:
how to determine   (9)

necessity
comfort
glory
luxury

sovereignty
councel
administration

magistrates
laws   (6)
warfare
criminal

classes (7)

State
(I)

society

family

relations

types (II)

institutions
(III)

changes (IV)

material
basis (V)

(VI)

ideal

subject
ruler

treaties
sovereignty

laws
war

monarchy
aristocracy
democracy

senate
administration
corporations
classes

types
sources
prevention
location
wealth
military
census

natural
human
divine

climate
humors

treasure
taxes
coinage

3 forms compared
succession
justice

husband
father
lord
owner

Diagram C

Vossius: SYNOPSIS

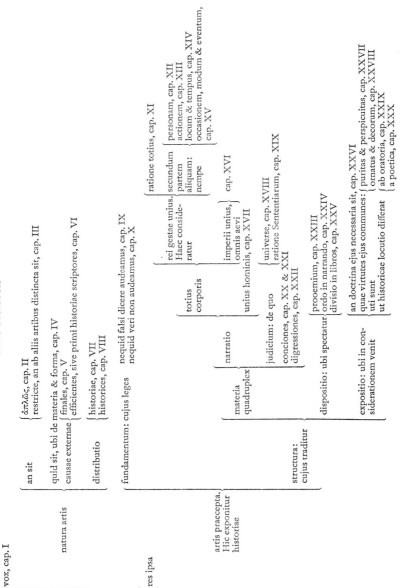

Historiae &
historices

vox, cap. I

natura artis

an sit ⎰ ἁπλῶς, cap. II
　　　 ⎱ restricte, an ab aliis artibus distincta sit, cap. III

quid sit, ubi de materia & forma, cap. IV
causae externae ⎰ finales, cap. V
　　　　　　　 ⎱ efficientes, sive primi historiae scriptores, cap. VI

distributio ⎰ historiae, cap. VII
　　　　　 ⎱ historices, cap. VIII

res ipsa

fundamentum: cujus leges　nequid falsi dicere audeamus, cap. IX
　　　　　　　　　　　　 nequid veri non audeamus, cap. X

artis praecepta.
Hic exponitur
historiae

structura:
cujus traditur

materia
quadruplex

narratio

totius
corporis

rei gestae unius. ⎰ ratione totius, cap. XI
Haec conside- ⎱ secundum ⎰ personam, cap. XII
ratur　　　　　　 partem　　 ⎪ actionem, cap. XIII
　　　　　　　　 aliquam: 　 ⎨ locum & tempus, cap. XIV
　　　　　　　　 nempe　　 ⎪ occasionem, modum & eventum,
　　　　　　　　　　　　　 ⎩ cap. XV

unius hominis

⎰ imperii unius, ⎰ cap. XVI
⎱ omnis aevi　 ⎱

universe, cap. XVIII
ratione Sententiarum, cap. XIX

judicium: de quo
conciones, cap. XX & XXI
digressiones, cap. XXII

dispositio: ubi spectatur ⎰ prooemium, cap. XXIII
　　　　　　　　　　　 ⎪ ordo in narrando, cap. XXIV
　　　　　　　　　　　 ⎩ divisio in libros, cap. XXV

expositio: ubi in con-
siderationem venit

an doctrina ejus necessaria sit, cap. XXVI
quae virtutes ejus communes: ⎰ puritas & perspicuitas, cap. XXVII
uti sunt　　　　　　　　　 ⎱ ornatus & decorum, cap. XXVIII
ut historicae locutio differat ⎰ ab oratoria, cap. XXIX
　　　　　　　　　　　　　 ⎱ a poetica, cap. XXX

Corollarium, de virtutibus in historico requisitis, cap. XXXI

most challenging political and social paradoxes of modern times. Yet it is no less obvious that Bodin entertained an almost compulsive monism that drove him to accommodate this personal and vicarious experience in a single and coherent system.

This has been reflected in part by Bodin's fascination with the «old metaphysics of order» (as Mr. Greenleaf put it) and in the new logic of Ramus (as Mr. McRae has shown), with ancient notions of harmony (as Mr. Villey has explained) and with modern notions of tolerance through the reconciliation of opposites (as Mr. Roellenbleck has argued). Above all it has been exemplified by Bodin's struggles to reconcile old ideas of corporate and «constitutional» order with with a new view of absolute sovereignty (as has been indicated in different ways by Messrs. Salmon, Franklin, Polin, Scheuner, and others). To what extent particular works may be reconciled with Bodin's general though changing system may be debated, but (as I myself believe) his last and most neglected work, the *Theater of Universal Nature,* shows that his systematizing urge never deserted him. To set for himself such transcendent goals Bodin must indeed have cast himself in the role of prophet (as Mr. Baxter has suggested) if not of sorcerer. Nor can I think of any more plausible way of accounting for the wonder, suspicious as well as worshipful, which Bodin has inspired in generations of scholars down to the present day, present company included.

III. BODIN UND DIE RECHTSTRADITION

Julian H. Franklin

Jean Bodin and the End of Medieval Constitutionalism

I

The purpose of this paper is to show that the absolutism of Bodin's *Six Livres de la République* was a turning point in French political thought – that it was not only a break with the received constitutional tradition, but was an important shift in Bodin's own idea of sovereignty.

Absolutism in the sense here used is the idea that the ruler, however much he may be responsible to God for observation of the higher law, does not require the consent of any other human agent in making public policy. As a developed legal doctrine, this conception of royal power appears rather late in European thought, and considerably later than is frequently supposed. The decay of the old medieval tradition that consent was required for the enactments of a ruler to be valid is often attributed to the rise of centralized monarchies in the late middle ages and the Renaissance.[1] But this is to misconstrue important aspects of the centralizing process. The subjection of the feudal magnates to the king's officials undoubtedly weakened the historic restraints. But it also went hand in hand with the formation of new administrative and consultative institutions which, although nominally created by the king, also served as limits on his arbitrary power.[2] And since the principle of limitation was deeply rooted in the legal sense of the community, the old constitution-

---

[1] Thus, for example, J. W. ALLEN [97], Political Thought in the Sixteenth Century, London 1951, 280–285. PIERRE MESNARD [129], L'Essor de la philosophie politique au XVIe^me siècle, Paris 1952, 490.

[2] This phase in the development of the territorial monarchies is not accorded much importance by ROLAND MOUSNIER and FRITZ HARTUNG in their Quelques problèmes concernant la monarchie absolue, *Relazioni del X congresso internazionale di scienze storiche, IV, Storia moderna*, Florence 1955, 3–55. «This notion of absolutism oscillates, as it were, around o point of equilibrium between a less and more limited conception of power. Depending on the circumstances, the personality of the sovereign and his ministers, the international situation, the movement of social classes, and economic contingencies, one or the other of these nuances of absolutism assumes more importance, without

alist conception of monarchy continued in an altered form, and remained intellectually predominant through the middle of the 16th century.

The rhetoric of this period may sometimes seem to point the other way. Since the crown had so expanded as the center of legal initiative and the focus of political expectations, celebration of its power became a characteristic theme among contemporary jurists. The legists, who had always been the stalwarts of the king's administration, not only repeat the flattering maxims of the *Corpus Juris* as to princely status, but lovingly and fulsomely embroider them. The flavor of their rhetoric may be readily conveyed by listing some of the paragraph headings in the *Regalium Franciae libri duo* by Charles de Grassaille (1538):

The king of the French is a great lord an more glorious than any other king.

The king of France compared to all other kings and princes of this age is like the morning star amidst the northern cloud, and holds the crown of liberty and glory before all the other kings of this world.

The king of France is the vicar of Christ in his kingdom.

The king of France is called the king of kings.

The king of France is called a second sun on earth.

When the Pope and the king of France agree, they can do everything.

The kingdom of the French is held of God alone.

Although certain other kings are anointed, only the most Christian king is anointed by oil miraculously conveyed.

The king of France is called the delegated minister and vicar of God.

The king of France performs miracles in life and heals Scrofula.

The king of France is like a corporeal god.[3]

Language of this sort is routine in legal writings of the time, and this has often prompted the conclusion that, in legal theory at least, the early 16th century was the very pinnacle of absolutism.

Yet this conclusion turns out to be utterly misleading. Works like the *Regalium Franciae* of De Grassaille or, even more clearly, the *Catalogus gloriae mundi* of Barthelemy de Chasseneuz, are books of courtesy the

---

there being, overall, any serious changes in the notion itself.» There would seem, however, to be a very important change, especially in ideology, in the last quarter of the 16th century in France, and something of this is indicated. But for Mousnier and Hartung the difference between the consultative and absolutist phase of the French monarchy is absorbed by the distinction between absolutism in the sense of royal supremacy and despotism in the sense of unlimited rights over persons and property.

[3] CHARLES DE GRASSAILLE, *Regalium Franciae libri duo* (1538), Paris 1545, Index. (The index is simply a list of the paragraph captions that appear in the margins of the text.)

aim of which is to explain and magnify the title and status of all components of the social hierarchy, not the king alone. The extravagant statements about royal power, as may be seen from the list of headings in De Grassaille, are almost always embroidered repetitions of traditional theses of the legists, who had always maintained that the king of France was politically independent of the Emperor and Pope and the equal or superior of all territorial rulers.[4] What is being celebrated here, accordingly, is the entire French society of which the king is taken as the symbol and the head. The exaltation of the royal status is not intended to debase the other components of the hierarchy, who are constantly associated with the royal dignity and similarly praised. Nor is it intended to reject the medieval principle that the king is subject to the laws and must govern with general consent. The writers of this period very rarely speak of the *proprio motu* of the prince, of his right to make enactments at his mere discretion. And even when they do, their remarks must be very cautiously interpreted.[5]

The truth, indeed, is that respect for the established rights of the community in general, and above all the privileges of the several regions, was a basic political condition for the formation of the centralized regime. Royal policy could not have succeeded in the long run without the support, or at least neutrality, of the chartered towns, ecclesiastical corporations, and the lesser nobles. And the price of this support was the willingness and ability of the kings to guarantee existing privileges even more effectively than the great feudatories they attempted to replace. In other words, the privileged elements of a particular region did not lose established rights when they came into more direct relation to the crown. They exchanged the protection of the local overlord for the protection of the crown itself. This principle was often made explicit in contractual agreements between the king and the provincial estates when a province was newly annexed to the royal domain. And the terms of these agreements were generally reconfirmed on the accession of a new incumbent to the throne.[6]

---

[4] This point may perhaps be generalized. Claims of the absolute authority of the Pope against the Emperor, on the part of medieval canonists, or of the absolute independence of the Emperor in temporal matters, on the part of civilians favorable to his cause, are rarely intended as comments on the internal constitution of the Church or of the Empire.

[5] See also CHASSENEUZ, *Catalogus gloriae mundi* (1529). Geneva 1649.

[6] A survey of the elements of decentralization remaining in the Renaissance monarchy and of the effective limits on absolutism is provided by J. RUSSELL MAJOR, The Renaissance Monarchy: A Contribution to the Periodization of History, *The Emory University Quarterly* 13 (1957), 112–114; aid also in chapter I of his Representative Institutions in Renaissance France, Madison 1960.

The Renaissance monarchy was thus required to consult and to obtain consent, and it adhered to this policy in one form or another even though the risks were sometimes great. The fiscal burdens of the new administration, together with the social changes accompanying its growth, were a source of political tensions that could be crystallized in nationwide assemblies. Hence the Estates General, which had been a forum for agitation against royal policy during the crises of the wars with England, were looked on with suspicion by the monarchs of the Renaissance, and were not assembled from 1484–1560. Yet even then the policy of consultation was continued through less volatile devices – through provincial or regional assemblies of the three estates, through regional or national assemblies of town delegations, through church assemblies, and also through nationwide assemblies of notables, essentially in the form of an expanded meeting of the king's great council, which provided a smaller, less formal, and therefore more readily manageable substitute for a full Estates assembly. And the idea of the Estates as the most solemn and beneficial form of consultation retained its vitality as a deep, if latent, community tradition.

But communication between the king and the community was not restricted to direct assemblies alone. It was also sustained, on a more continuing basis, by the mediation of the king's administration, which was not only an agency for enforcement of the royal will but an independent check upon its arbitrary exercise. In the Renaissance monarchy the complex and decentralized network of territorial officials was coordinated at the center by the great sovereign courts which were technically offshoots of the royal coucil. The oldest of these was the Parlement of Paris which was the final instance both for civil and criminal cases and for cases involving the powers and conduct of officials. In view of its multiple responsibilities, ecclesiastical as well as lay, the Parlement of Paris was divided into several chambers some of which had become independent institutions except for certain form. In the 16th century, however it was still regarded as a single entity, and the Great Chamber of the Parlement was a final instance of appeal from the other central courts. The Parlement of Paris, finally, was empowered, in principle at least, to hear appeals from the provincial Parlements which had been created, under varying names, beginning with the first quarter of the 15th century. Even though this procedure was now regarded as abusive and exceptional, the Parlement of Paris was above the others in prestige and its legal precedents were generally followed.

The officials of this apparatus were not regarded, and did not behave, as mere servants or dependents of the king. The most important officers were recruited from privileged strata which had an aristocratic sense of independence toward the crown. The *baillis* and *seneschaux* were normally members of the fighting nobility, often chosen from the district they administered. And they carried out their duties with lieutenants and counsellors who were often chosen from the area and who represented local interests. The sovereign courts, on the other hand, were increasingly staffed by legally educated members of the upper bourgeoisie, who might seem, on that account, to be more indebted to the king for the enhancement of their social status. But the Parlement of Paris was not strictly an appointive body since it was well established, in principle at least, that it was not required to receive a member unless it had examined and approved his qualifications.

According to what was regarded as the right procedure, the Parlement was virtually self-coopting in that the king was expected to make any new appointment from a list of candidates selected by the existing membership. By this and other legal devices, high judicial offices tended to be passed on from generation to generation within a single family, so that we may already think of this elite as a highly privileged and quasi-hereditary *noblesse de robe*. This new noblesse, moreover almost insensibly acquired further status from its association with the old. The Parlement was still regarded as a component of the royal council. It was also still the Court of Peers, and might sometimes be attended by the peers of France when it sat in that capacity. And some of its counsellors were still recruited from the nobility and higher clergy.

This sense of independence was also promoted by the deeply rooted principle that crown officers were irremoveable except for cause. In the Renaissance, as in the middle ages, office was a quasi-feudal dignity, the loss of which was a violation of the holder's status, and it was therefore treated as a kind of permanent usufruct which could not be recovered by its owner without proof of its abuse before the courts.[7] By the middle of the 16th century, the sale of judicial offices, formerly an occasional practice, had begun to be fairly common, and from Montesquieu on this has been interpreted as a prime source of judicial independence. But its importance ought not to be exaggerated. The sale of offices (which was

---

[7] Thus CHARLES DUMOULIN, eager as he is to strengthen royal power in his interpretation of feudal customs, nonetheless insists that these offices are «not banausic and revocable at pleasure (as court sycophants and mercenary lawyers prate). The members depend upon the head which cannot subsist without them or suppress its members, and the supreme prince cannot alienate or abdicate completely or, as they say, accomplish an expropriation of territorial dignities or jurisdictions, and yet he may concede incomes and usufruct, reserving superiority, recognition, and fealty». *Commentarii in consuetudines Parisienses,* in *Omnia quae extant opera,* I, 78. And so also, and more generally, Bodin: «He (the prince) cannot remove an office given to his subject without just cause.» *Six Livres de la Republique* (1576), Paris 1579, 152 [7.6].

bitterly protested by the Parlement as a violation of its honor) may well have strengthened preexisting tendencies for office to become hereditary. But it was not required to establish the irremovability of a particular incumbent, since this was already admitted universally.

The king's administration, furthermore, was not only independent in its status and its attitude, but had always held an exalted conception of its constitutional prerogatives. By the 15th century it was well established that the Parlement of Paris had the right to remonstrate, or protest, against any enactment of the king found incompatible with common law or local custom, unless the alteration could be justified by very strong considerations of public utility or equity. This was understood as something much more solemn than mere apprisal of the king of consequences that he might have overlooked. The Parlement of Paris, together with the other Parlements, claimed the right to withhold registration of an act, and thus to prevent its promulgation as a binding law, until their remonstrations had been satisfied.[8] Reiterated commands to register, backed up by a variety of threats, might ultimately secure compliance. But registration by command was regarded as contrary to good practice and abusive, and enactments thus imposed were recorded with the phrase «de mandato expresso», by which the Parlement declared that registration was reluctant and provisional, and that the act thus stigmatized either would not be enforced or would be very narrowly construed. In any event it would have no validity beyond the lifetime of the incumbent who had ordered it.[9]

The new monarchy of the later middle ages and the Renaissance thus presents a double aspect. On side of it was the formation of a centralized administration which registered the triumph of the royal government over its older, feudal opposition. But the other side was the institutionalization, within that same administration, of the medieval principle that the king must govern with consent.[10] This second side, no doubt, was

---

[8] «And the kings have found it neither bad nor strange that the counsellors of the Parlement who judge and ought to judge according to their conscience, informed of the truth through law and reason, may have responded, in the verification of letters with which they were charged, that they were unable to proceed, and used these words: *Non possumus, non debemus* (we cannot, and we ought not)!» Declaration of the Parlement of Paris, 5 December, 1556, quoted EDOUARD MAUGIS, Histoire du Parlement de Paris de l'avènement des rois Valois à la mort d'Henri IV, Paris 1913, vol. I, IX.

[9] For the development of the right of remonstration and registration, and the practice of this period, see MAUGIS, Histoire du Parlement vol. I, 517–601.

[10] «When he [the king] pleases, he will take it [the sovereign functions of the Parlement] away, and he will place it elsewhere, but it will always be required to be vested somewhere.» MAUGIS, Histoire du Parlement, I, 517–601.

not always accepted by the kings themselves. In periods of conflict with their Parlements they, or their chancellors, often argued that the functions of the courts were purely ministerial. And strong princes like Francis I and Henry II could sometimes act in defiance of restraints.[11] But the interesting point for present purposes is that the constitutionalist aspect of the monarchy was clearly recognized by jurists of the time and all but universally approved.

The main source for the constitutionalist doctrine of this period are the commentaries of the jurists on the Parlements, to which are sometimes joined descriptions of the powers and status of the Great Council, the Chancellor, or the Peers. And the key to all this literature[12] is the assumption that the Parlement of Paris was formed on the model of the Roman Senate as Romulus was supposed to have created it.[13] Like the Roman Senate, the Parlement was believed to contain a normal complement of just 100 members when all of its separate components were included, and its councillors are also called «senatores» or «patres» because of their venerable authority. According to the humanist Guillaume Budé, the comparison was inexact on certain points, and the Athenian Council of the Areopagus seemed the more appropriate analogue, at least for certain purposes.[14] For the jurists, however, and for Budé himself most often, the Senatorial comparison was central because it immediately enabled them to use the familiar materials of Roman law as a means of working out their juridical analysis.

---

[11] The king could attempt to force registration by threats to suppress or remove the court as well as by threats against its members personally, and he could seek to avert judicial sabotage subsequent to registration by removing key cases to the royal council. The tactics of Francis I are described by ROGER DOUCET, Étude sur le gouvernement de Francois Ier dans ses rapports avec le Parlement of Paris, Paris 1921, Ch. III (on the reception of the Concordat of 1516).

[12] The proximate source of this tradition is the gloss on the Pragmatic Sanction of Bourges apparently by COSMO GUYMIER – *Pragmatica Santio una cum repertorio* (1486), Paris 1504, and also ROBERT GAGUIN's *Compendium super Francorum gestis* (1491), s. l. 1511.

[13] *Pragmatica Sanctio una cum repertorio*, fol. CCIIIIr–CCVv. The comparison is also implied in GAGUIN, *Compendium*, fol XLVIIr.

[14] BUDÉ, *Annotationes in quatuor et viginiti Pandectarum libros* (1507) Paris 1535, 97, 127–8. The debt of the more orthodox jurists to Budé's more sophisticated comparison is acknowledged by NICHOLAS BOHIER, in his comments on JEAN MONTAIGNE's *Tractatus de parlamentis et collatione parlamentorum*, in *Tractatus Universi Juris*, Venice 1584, Vol XVI, fol. 274v–274r. Bohier's work apparently dates from 1512 and provides the fullest treatment up to DE GRASSAILLE.

On part of their interpretation was designed to show the great dignity and splendor of the Parlement. For this the most suggestive text was C 9, 8, 5 *(ad legem Juliam majestatis)* which defined the crime of high treason as extending to all those conspiring not only against the person of the Emperor but also against «the illustrious men who are in our councils and consistory, and especially the Senators (for they are part of our body).» The Senate, or Parlement, of France, accordingly was likewise *pars corporis principis* or *regis,* a part of the prince's body politic.[15] Although created by the king, and after him in precedence, it was associated in his dignity and status and is sometimes referred to as his peer or equal.[16]

The proof and expression of this status were its high regalian prerogatives. The Parlament, acting as a court, was like the Roman Senate and the Pretorian Prefect in that its decrees were final and not subject to appeal.[17] As with the emperor himself, the only recourse from its verdict was supplication for rehearing.[18] Its decrees were called *arresta* in order to indicate this ultimacy,[19] and, in contrast with the decrees of lower magistrates, they were pronounced in its own name, not the king's.[20]

The Parlement, furthermore, also possessed what would today be called high executive prerogative to act against or without established form. It could remove cases from inferior courts at its discretion[21] and was not restricted to the specific questions raised in the petitions brought before it.[22] In rendering judgements it was not bound by the «solemnities and subtleties of law», but might judge according to its

---

[15] Jean Montaigne (with comments by Bohier), *Tractatus de auctoritate magni concilii et parlamentorum,* in *Tractatus Universi Juris,* Vol XVI, 264r. *Pragmativ Sanctio una cum reportorio,* fol. CCIIIr-CCVr. Chasseneuz, *Catalogus gloriae mundi,* 281. De Grassaille, *Regalium* 123.

[16] De Grassaille, *Regalium,* 112. Also, p. 116: «It is also to be pointed out, that the king must do them honors ... and that they ought to sit not at the feet of the prince but at his side ... For the Chancellor and Senators are the prince's soul and make it possible for kings to reign *(et regem faciunt regnare).*» See also Chasseneuz, n. 34 below.

[17] De Grassaille, *Regalium,* 116–7 as well as all the other sources mentioned, including Guillaume Benedictus (Benoist) in *Repetitio in Cap. Rynutius, extra de testamentis* (1522) Lyon 1583 who does little more than repeat Gaguin at fol. 84r ff.

[18] De Grassaille, *Regalium,* 117 as well as all other sources mentioned.

[19] De Grassaille, *Regalium,* who, like the others, is here following Gaguin verbatim.

[20] De Grassaille, *Regalium,* 117–118.

[21] De Grassaille, *Regalium,* 122.

[22] De Grassaille, *Regalium,* 120.

conscience.[23] In particular, it could commute or lower sentences, and could waive requirements for legal standing.[24] But it could not, like the Roman Senate, declare oblivion for any crime, nor did it have the discretionary power of increasing punishments since this was reserved entirely to the king.[25] Furthermore, this power to dispense with law is associated with considerable authority to alter it. The Senate of France, it is agreed, had the power to make law, as did the Roman Senate and the Pretorian Prefect, although, unlike these latter, the Parlement of Paris could only do so with the specific authorization of the king.[26] The Parlement, accordingly, was considered to be a great center of sovereign political authority alongside of and all but equal to the king. And this conception is all the more significant since it is always implicitly assumed that its counsellors are irremoveable.[27]

The other question, of even greater interest politically, was whether the Parlements, created by the king, also had authority to disallow his acts. The jurists universally agree that «the authority of this parlement was always so great among the French that even decisions of the king himself on the public welfare, law, and finances, do not proceed without the decree of this Senate.»[28] But they were also well aware that this arrangement was peculiarly French and they move with considerable caution in the articulation of the legal grounds.

For this purpose the most suggestive classic texts were C I, 14, 4 and I, 14, 8. The title in question is «On the laws, constitutions, and edicts of the prince», the fourth law of which is a declaration to the Senate by Theodosius and Valentinian that «the voice of decency *(digna vox)* in the majesty of him who rules is to profess that he is bound by law. Indeed, our own authority depends on the authority of laws, and it is the greater part of majesty to submit to the laws of our principate». But even more germane was the 8th law of the same title in which the emperor assures the Senate that there is no better way to assure the justice of his laws and rescripts than to submit them to the Senate for discussion and to withhold their promulgation until a majority of the Senate has approved. The delaration ends with the promise that «in the future no law is to be promulgated by our clemency in any other fashion.»

---

[23] DE GRASSAILLE, *Regalium*, 118, 124.

[24] DE GRASSAILLE, *Regalium*, 122, 120.

[25] DE GRASSAILLE, *Regalium*, 122, 127. See also BUDÉ, *Annotationes*, 127.

[26] DE GRASSAILLE, *Regalium*, 117. He is here indebted to BOHIER, *Tractatus,* fol. 274v who is following BUDÉ, *Annotationes* ...

[27] Thus BOHIER, *Tractatus,* fol. 276r, and DE GRASSAILLE *Regalium,* 24.

[28] GAGUIN, *Compendium,* Fol. XLVIIIv. Gaguin's phrase is usually repeated verbatim in the subsequent writers.

And the gloss compiled around the middle of the 13th century interpreted this to mean that the Emperor had formally bound himself to
make no further legislation and to leave the *Corpus Juris* as it was.

The jurists of the late 15th and early 16th century were aware, however, that such interpretations were in error. Bartolus had already stated
that the procedure mentioned in C 1, 14, 8 was «not of necessity but
will, so that is omission does not vitiate (a law)»;[29] and he is confirmed
on this by Baldus, whose interpretation is the same.[30] The remarkable
point, however, is that French jurists of the Renaissance, fully agreeing
with this interpretation, explicitly reject it for the case of France. «The
(Roman) *princeps*», says Bohier, «can establish law without the council
of his notables, the Pope can make decretals without his Cardinals, by
the formula *non obstante*». And this is because the procedure of C 1, 14,
8 is «of decency more than of necessity, (and applies) mostly to ordinary
matters*(materia non ardua)*». «But this dictum», Bohier then points out,
«does not apply to my supreme, and most illustrious and sacred lord, the
king of France and the lord of Italy, who does nothing without his
great council.»[31]

This position of Bohier's is shared with varying degrees of caution by

---

[29] BARTOLUS, *Commentarii*, Venice 1590, fol. 28v. And also on Dig. I, 9
(omnes populi): «And if high judges or lords should do this (make statutes), it
is the part of humanity that they do it with the advice of the wise, as is
indicated by C, I, 14, 4. But if they wish, they can do this on their own *(proprio
motu)* and promulgate it to their subjects.»

[30] *Baldi di Perusio iurisconsulti clarissimi super primo, secundo et tertio
Codices commentaria*, Lyon 1529, fol. 66v.

[31] BOHIER *Tractatus*, 274r. «Thus the form described by the emperor in C I,
14, 4 is observed in the kingdom of France. When anything must be decided,
my supreme and most Christian lord convokes a number of prelates, governors,
and also counsellors of the parlements of his kingdom to meet with him and
his great council ... In this assemblage, acting through the most illustrious and
distinguished chancellor of France, he makes, establishes, and promulgates the
propositions, laws, and constitutions, which we call royal ordinances. This was
the procedure used in this very year of 1510 for the ordinances issued by him
at Lyon, and it has been observed by the other kings of France, his predecessors,
in all the ordinances formerly established by them, as is proven in the proemium
of the Pragmatic Sanction» 274r. Bohier here is thinking of an expanded version
of the Great Council. But for Budé, as well as the writers after Bohier, the
Senate is equated with the Parlement of Paris preeminently, which was regarded
as the stationary part of the council. Moreover, when they speak of the «Senate»
they normally mean the Parlement of Paris, which is not, however, sharply
distinguished from the Parlements collectively. The Parlement of Paris itself, it
might be noted did not regard itself as necessarily bound by other forms of
royal consultation, including even the consent of the Estates.

almost all the other commentators. The king of France, no doubt, is «absolute». But he has restrained his power «of his own accord», [32], and the principle of consultation and consent has been so continuously respected over so long a strech of time that it has become a part of fundamental law. This is not to say, of course, that enactments *non obstante*, omitting this procedure, do not in fact occur, or to hold that they are simply illegal (although at one point Chasseneuz comes very close to this).[33] But enactements of this sort are rare, improper, and defective in their legal force. Either they will not be enforced, or else they will be narrowly construed and rapidly forgotten. As Budé puts it, the approval of the Parlement, like the approval by the Roman Senate of legislation by the people, is an act of authorization which serves to corroborate and ratify a law, and thus to «make it firm».[34] The Senate, as the repository of the nation's wisdom, makes itself the «sponsor» *(auctor)* of the law, and by thus guaranteeing its utility or equity, gives it a respect and force that otherwise it would not have. «By its (the Parlement's) authority the acts of princes», says Budé, «are confirmed

---

[32] «Thirdly, adherence to justice by the kings of France is shown by this: Although Pope, king, and emperor have the power to judge in their own cause ... the kings of France submit themselves, of their own accord, to the judgment not only of their Parlements but even of their *baillis* and *seneschaux*. The kings invariably obey the judgments of these officers. And they wish and order that their [royal] letters be sent to them for execution, just as Valerian ... writes of Theompompus, king of the Spartans, who created those magistrates known as ephors similar to the tribunes of the people at Rome, for the purpose of restraining *(moderandam)* his royal will ... Since the wills of kings are impulsive, and often vacillate and contradict themselves ... the kings of France have ordered and declared through many constitutions and ordinances that letters or rescripts emanating from them can be publicly and juridically impugned in declared judgment for any nullity, inequity, or fraud.» DE GRASSAILLE, *Regalium*, 204–205.

[33] «And as to the power and preeminence of its [the Parlement's] jurisdiction, it is equal to the king's and the king, by his ordinary power, cannot abrogate anything enacted through his Parlements. Indeed, not even something ordained by his plenitude of power, according to my teacher Jason [de Mayno] in one of the opinions that he gave and which I once saw and read in his study but have not been able to obtain.» CHASSENEUZ, *Catalogus gloriae mundi*, 281. Chasseneuz might be taken to concede that some acts may be made (if not repealed) without the consent of the Parlements by invocation of plenary power. But this is less than clear since on this same page he repeats Gaguin to the effect that no royal decree proceeds «without the decree of this Senate.» The opinion attributed to Jason is cited on Chasseneuz's authority by DE GRASSAILLE, *Regalium*, 112.

[34] DE GRASSAILLE, *Regalium*, 99.

or disconfirmed in oder to forestall objections to them. This is the one court from which absolute princes take the law in a civil frame of mind, which they would like to have as sponsor to lend its sanction in the ratifying and promulgation of decrees. They would not wish to exempt their ordinances and edicts from the censure of this council, but would rather see their enactments sanctified for all eternity by its decrees».[35]

It thus appears that the jurists of this period, who are often taken as the «absolutists»,[36] are in rough agreement with Seyssel, who is rightly taken as a cautious constitutionalist. Like Seyssel, the jurists too believe that the «police», or basic legal order, of the kingdom is a limitation on the king who is checked in his ability to change it by the Parlements and other councils. And when they speak of absolute and plenary power in the king, they do not intend to undermine the force of these restraints, any more than does Seyssel, when he too says that the king of France is absolute or «almost» absolute.[37] Hence, despite occasional deviations, the constitutional conception of this period is fairly homogeneous. It is the idea of a limited or tempered monarchy in which the king is the center of political initiative but cannot properly exert it in matters of domestic law without the consent of established councillors and judges.

II

Bodin's earliest published work on politics seems at first sight to be a clearcut break with this tradition. In Chapter VI of the *Methodus*, which appeared in 1566, he already formulates the essential prerogatives of sovereignty and already asserts that all of these prerogatives, and each in its entirety, must be vested in a single individual or group. He seems to be saying, therefore, that the king of France, like every other sovereign, is absolute, that he has all the powers that a community can rightly exercise within the limits of the law of God and nature. The qualifications

---

[35] DE GRASSAILLE, *Regalium*, 128. Also, p. 127: «And so with the constitutions of princes as well as other enactments of this sort relating to the commonwealth; in order that they should have inviolable force *(ut vim sanctionum habeant)* it is necessary, under modern usage, that the *curia* should authorize them *(auctorem fieri)* and that they should be promulgated in the *curia*.»

[36] Thus J. W. ALLEN [97], Political Thought in the Sixteenth Century (1928), London 1951. WILLIAM FARR CHURCH [145], Constitutional Thought in Sixteenth-Century France, Cambridge, Mass. 1941, Ch. II gives a much more balanced opinion, but the line he draws between Seyssel and the legists is, in my judgment, too sharp.

[37] But despite these checks, says Seyssel, «... royal dignity and authority always remains intact, not totally absolute, and not too much restrained, but checked and regulated by good laws, ordinances, and customs, which are estab-

of absolutism still to be found in the *Methodus* would then seem best interpreted as minor hesitations and uncertainties that the *République* would soon remove.

Nevertheless, this early view of sovereignty neither intended nor implied a formula for absolutism and was basically in accord with the received tradition. In the middle of the 1560's there was a relative lull in the accumulating storm of civil war, which Bodin optimistically took to be a stable settlement.[38] Despite the beginnings of constitutional conflicts in the Estates of 1560 and 1561, both the Hugenot opposition and the court had tended to avoid extremes of principle, and in Bodin's work of 1566 the mood is, if anything, complacent and free of any sense of urgent choices. The *Methodus* was a scholarly and literary enterprise. And indeed the discussion of sovereignty in Chapter VI is almost surely the elaboration of academic interests that antedated the crisis of the early 60's and were essentially technical in nature. The theoretical core of *Methodus*, VI, goes back to an earlier, unpublished manuscript, probably begun in Bodin's law school days, on the *imperium* and jurisdiction of magistrates as defined by Roman law.[39] This was a popular and challenging topic for humanist jurists of the period, since the *Corpus Juris* was obscure and cryptic on the point, and the issue had been badly confused by the medieval commentators.[40] In order to resolve the problem, the humanists were naturally led to distinguish between *imperium* and *summum imperium*, between those prerogatives inherent in the office of a magistrate and those which had to be delegated specially since they were properly powers of the Emperor alone. This distinction had often been suggested and illustrated by the middle of the sixteenth century.[41] Bodin's

---

lished in such a way that they can hardly be broken or annulled (although sometimes and in some places an infraction and violation may occur). And now to speak of the aforementioned checks by which the absolute power of the king of France is regulated, I find three principal restraints: the first is religion, the second justice, the third, the basic legal order *(la Police)*.» CLAUDE DE SEYSSEL, La Monarchie de France (Jacques Poujol ed.) Paris 1961 (1519), 115.

[38] *Methodus ad facilem historiarum cognitionem*, ed. PIERRE MESNARD, [4.20], 210.

[39] See *Meth.*, 173, 175, 176 for Bodin's own references. According to Ménage these and other works, all of them apparently legal monographs, were burned at Bodin's request after he died. See ROGER CHAUVIRÉ, Jean Bodin, auteur de la République, La Flèche 1914, 95 [76].

[40] A survey of interpretation from the glossators to the beginning of the seventeenth century is provided by MYRON P. GILMORE, Argument from Roman Law in political thought 1200–1600, Cambridge (Mass.), 1941 [146].

[41] Thus ANDREA ALCIATO (1518), *Opera*, Basel 1582, Vol. IV, col. 39, and, more extensively, JEAN GILLOT (1538), *De jurisdictione et imperio*, in *Tractatus universi juris*, Venice 1584. III, fol. 7v, 15r–16v.

contribution was an effort to define precisely what others had passed over with allusions. He was launched upon his enterprise by an attempt to discover the most general legal prerogatives that a political authority might possess in order to be considered sovereign.

His conclusion furthermore, that these prerogatives are indivisible seems also to have been prompted by technical considerations. In the *Corpus Juris,* which deals primarily with private law, the rights of majesty are not defined, and Bodin, who was a humanist, was ultimately to find what he was looking for in hints afforded by classical commentators on the constitution of the Roman Republic. He tells us several times (although the significance of this has not been fully noted) that he came to his list of sovereign prerogatives from reading Aristotle, Polybius, and Dionysius of Halicarnassus.[42] And, indeed, his list of 1566 seems to have been directly suggested by Polybius' account of the powers of the Roman people.[43] Bodin, accordingly, was immediately confronted with an apparent contradiction in his sources. Polybius and other commentators had said that the Roman constitution was a mixture. But, juridically at least, the powers of the Roman people, on Polybius' own account, obviously amonted to supreme authority. From Bodin's legal standpoint, Polybius the commentator had to yield to Polybius the historian. The Roman constitution was unmixed, and so also were all the other city-state republics traditionally reputed mixed. From this observation Bodin then went on to his general conclusion that no mixed constitution had ever existed and that none could be imagined.[44]

The final point, however, is that this principle of indivisibility, as Bodin understood it, was free of absolutist implications because the meaning of a legislative act is very narrowly construed. One indication of this is Bodin's treatment of the legislative functions of the Roman Senate and of analogous councils in other city-state republics. In the classical period of the Roman Republic the people, in *comitia centuriata,* could not act upon a legislative proposal without the Senate's approval. Bodin is aware of this, and even approves it as a check on the license of the people, while yet maintaining that the Roman Republic was a pure democracy.[45] It seems clear enough, then, that the act of legislation for

---

[42] *Methodus,* 174. Bodin says that he compared them with each other and the jurisconsults.

[43] Compare POLYBIUS, *Histories,* VI, 14, with *Methodus,* 174–175.

[44] *Methodus,* 177.

[45] «But we are now discussing the democratic period [at Rome] when the tribunate was powerful. The Venetians have no tribunes, and so no shameless onators, who bent the people's will and boldly led them where they chose. The Senate is completely free, except on matters in which sovereignty inheres. But

Bodin was simply the decision to enact. The advice and authorization of the Senate are implicitly regarded not as a share of the legislative power but as an external condition for its valid exercise.

A second, and more revealing, indication is Bodin's treatment of the French Estates and the Estates of other monarchies whose institutions he believed were similar. The king of France is sovereign. But supreme authority need not be unlimited or absolute. The king of France is sworn by his oath of coronation to uphold the established customs of the provinces and realm.[46] He does not alter these in an important way without consulting the Estates.[47] The Parlements, presumably, are expected to enforce this limitation because they may ignore any edict that they have not approved.[48] Here again, accordingly, the king's exclusive legislative power is essentially the power to enact, which he may not exercise in many cases until certain procedures of consent have been completed.

This way of construing the legislative process may seem odd and strained to us, but is was quite natural in Bodin's time. The Estates were exceptional and extraordinary councils; they did not meet or separate at regular intervals or at their own initiative; and they had no resolutive power. In view of this restricted role, it was more convenient, as well as politically more tactful, to describe their participation not as a sharing of the legislative power but by some notion of external conditions. In any event, as late as 1672 this idea is explicitly used by Pufendorf to

---

this is common to all [three systems]. Nothing could be brought before the Athenian or Roman people unless the Senate had affirmed, as is indicated by the writings of Plutarch, and by Demonsthenes' speech against Andrioton. Demosthenes attacked him because he brought a law before the people without the approval of the Senate, and Andrioton replied by citing the established practice, under which it was the custom to do otherwise. Still worse, then, was the existence of a legal rule which permitted consultation of the Roman commons without approval of the Senate. The Venetians have very prudently arranged that no proposal on any matter whatsoever can be brought not only to the people but even to the Senate without the approval of the council of sixteen.» *Meth.*, 183.

[46] *Meth.*, 187.

[47] «He [the French king] may not subvert the laws special to the realm as a whole, nor in any way alter the institutions and ancient custom of the regions without the consent of the three estates.» *Meth.*, 187.

[48] *Meth.*, 208, and also the following: «But of all the laws of the realm, non is more sacred than that which denies any legal force to rescripts of the prince, unless they are in conformity with equity and truth. Hence many are rejected by the magistrates, and pardons procured from the prince are no avail for wicked men. For often, indeed, the voice of the magistrates is heard, that the king may not do anything against the law.»

account for instances of limited monarchy. A limited monarchy is sovereign, he holds, because it is the king alone who gives commands.[49]

Our conclusion, then, it that the absolutism of the *République* marks an important shift in Bodin's position and a break with the received tradition. The occasion for this shift was the Huguenot doctrine of resistance which developed after the St. Bartholomew's Day Massacre of 1572. In their justification of resistance to a tyrant-king, the Huguenots moved from the existence of limitations on the king to conclude that sovereign authority was ultimately located in the whole community. The king was but the people's delegate, and he could be kept within the limits of the law, and even be deposed if necessary, by the Estates or the lesser magistrates acting in behalf of the community. Bodin was thus confronted with a novel doctrine profoundly offensive to his feelings as a royalist. He was, moreover, sincerely convinced that the mere belief in justifiable resistance was a major, and perhaps the most important, cause of the political disorders of the time.[50] Repudiation of monarchomach doctrine thus appeared to him as the prime obligation of a loyal subject and he answered in the only way he could – by assuming that the ruler's authority was absolute with respect to ordinary law. The king of France was still subject to the law of God and nature for which he was responsible to God alone, and was also bound by certain rules attaching to the crown itself. But since he was legally free with respect to ordinary civil law, he had no responsibility to any human agent. And according to the established opinion of the time a king of this description could not be actively resisted even if he should become a tyrant.

This revised idea of sovereign authority was all but transparently incompatible with the powers, still admitted, of the Senate and inner councils of various city-state republics. And it could be maintained for France and other European monarchies only by ignoring or distorting considerable evidence pointing to a tradition of consent. But desire for an unquestioned focus of authority was deeply felt in France in reaction to the civil wars. Hence for all of its deficiencies, Bodin's principle of absolutism was to have a strong political appeal.

---

[49] *De jure naturae et gentium*, Oxford 1934, Bk. VII, Ch. VI, par. 10 (Vol. I, 733).

[50] *Six livres de la République*, Paris 1579, Preface, 5v.

Ralph E. Giesey

Medieval Jurisprudence in Bodin's Concept of Sovereignty

To the dictum that Jean Bodin's *République* is a work more read about than read, I would like to add the following codicil by way of a general theme for the present essay: those who have read the work have read only the text. Anyone who has perused a significant portion of the French or Latin versions of the *République* might recall vaguely the existence of some marginal apparatus, but surely he would be surprised to be told that in some chapters one-third of the margin is filled with notes. Readers of Knolles' English translation will be almost totally ignorant of the marginalia, since all but a handful of the marginal notes were suppressed there.

The margins of the chapters which people are most likely to read, the two «sovereignty» chapters (Book I, charpters 8 and 10) are forty per-cent filled with notes. The pages from *Répub.* I, 8 reproduced at the end of this essay (p. 184 f.) only mildly exaggerate the usual situation.

The marginal apparatus of *Répub.* I, 8 is prone to be neglected, I surmise, because four-fifths of its citations deal with the Two Laws and late medieval commentaries upon them. Even scholars who are capable of identifying stylized references to Roman law and canon law might scorn spending the time to chase them down, for it is the opinion of many that the heaping up of «allegations» – an old technical term which I shall use to designate citations of the Two Laws and commentators [1] – is pure pedantry, used either ostentatiously to support the obvious or deceptively to camouflage the untenable.

One should hesitate to entertain such derogatory notions about Jean Bodin. He was trained in the humanistic school of Roman law jurisprudence *(mos gallicus)* which stressed antique historical content and scorned medieval jurists' penchants to make Roman law suit contemporary needs *(mos italicus)*. This makes strange, indeed, Bodin's massive application of late medieval jurisprudence to the most famous piece of all his writings. Book I, chapters 8 and 10 of the *République* have altogether about six hundred separate marginal citations of the Two Laws and

---

[1] The Oxford English Dictionary calls obsolete the definition of «allegation» as «quoting or citing a document or author», but it remains in good usage in French according to Littré's Dictionnaire. Best of all, see DU CANGE, Gloss. lat. (s.v. allegare): «Allegationes partium rationes, quas reus et actor producunt.»

commentaries upon them. Most refer to Italian commentators of the
13th–15th centuries. The *République* as a whole has perhaps six thousand
legal citations, most of them in the style of and referring to medieval
jurisprudence. Had these allegations been inserted into the text in the
manner of a medieval commentary, portions of the *République* would
hardly be distinguishable from a medieval legist's *consilium*. Yet this
apparatus, the greatest in size of any genre of evidence adduced by Bodin
in the *République,* has been ignored by scholars.[2]

In the course of an investigation into the *République's* legal apparatus
which I undertook recently for pedagogical purposes, some interesting
hypotheses emerged concerning the role of medieval jurisprudence in
Bodin's concept of sovereignty.[3] In this paper I have limited myself to
Book I, chapter 8 – indeed, to just the latter part of it where, as Bodin
backs off from his earlier more rigorously «absolutist» stand in the text,
he swells the marginalia with the evidence of medieval jurisprudence.

I

Book I, chapter 8 of the *République* is famed because Bodin there defends
the principle that «the prince is freed from the laws.». The significance
of *princeps legibus solutus* (= *Dig.* 1, 3, 31) had been much contested
among medieval legists, and Bodin surely knew their texts.[4] He does

---

[2] M. REULOS' meritorious paper in this volume is the first attempt, to my
knowledge, to assess the entire legal apparatus of the *République*. Earlier
scholars, especially the admired JEAN MOREAU-REIBEL [116], Jean Bodin et le
droit public comparé, Paris 1933, have dealt with the revided classical tradition
of Roman law during the Renaissance, but are either ignorant of, or treat
slightingly, the great medieval legal inheritance in the *République*.

[3] The students of my seminar – Sally Madden, Lawrence Bryant, Edward
Deckert and Tom Prest – contributed much to the allegation-hunting and also
provided a forum for the discussion of ideas set forth in this paper; because of
them, potential drudgery became fun. Of the four dozen different works by
Italian jurists cited in *Répub.* I, 8, many are now bibliographical rarities difficult to procure; but a more frustrating problem is Bodin's persistently faulty
citation or poor proofreading. This chapter of the *République* is also especially
fraught with the work's two well-known linguistic problems: the notoriously
crabbed style of the original French and the freely executed alterations and
additions made in the Latin translation. It is usually true that scholarly work
on the *République* which is not based on careful examination of both the French
and the Latin versions is flawed. It is not always easy to decide whether the
Latin makes the meaning of the French clearer or simply alters it, but failure to
face up to this problem may lead swiftly to fanciful speculations.

[4] The old article by A. ESMEIN, La maxime Princeps legibus solutus dans

not, however, attempt to summarize the arguments of his juristic forbears. They were at best philosophically-minded legal commentators, while he was a legal-minded philosopher.

Bodin separates himself from earlier writers on sovereignty by declaring on two occasions that their main fault has been not to have defined the term. The first declaration of this comes in the second sentence of *Répub.* I, 8, as a preamble to his own famous definition: sovereignty is perpetual power and absolute power.[5] Bodin's treatment of perpetual power has never attracted much attention, and it need not detain us. When the ostentatious categorizing and exemplifying is stripped away, it is clear that Bodin really wanted only to show that in a true monarchy (the best kind of government in his mind) the prince's power must have no temporal limits, but rather must exist for his entire lifetime after accession.[6] More important than perpetual power, in Bodin's definition of sovereignty, is absolute power. This subject occupies by far most of the space in *Répub.* I, 8. Not long after taking it under consideration, he

---

l'ancien droit public français, in: Essays in Legal History ed. by P. Vinogra-doff, Oxford 1913, 201–214, has good material on application of the principle in edicts from the Middle Ages to the Revolution, but ignores the Italian legists' speculations which surely influenced French conceptions as much as anything else.

[5] «Il est icy besoin de former la définition de souveraineté, par ce qu'il n'y a ny jurisconsulte, ny philosophe politique, qui l'ayt definie»; *République*, 122. Bodin's own one-sentence definition has in fact already been given in the opening words of *Répub.* I, 8: «La souveraineté est la puissance absoluë et perpetuelle d'une République ... duquel mot ils [Latins, Grecs, Italiens] usent aussi envers les particuliers, & envers ceux-là qui manient toutes les affaires d'estat d'une Republique.» The paper of M. Derathé in the present volume covers this point, and those to be made by me in the next few paragraphs, in greater detail.

[6] In a general sense this is obvious from the root meaning of the word «monarchy», i.e., whenever power becomes collegial it is no longer monarchical. There remains, however, the ambiguity of whether monarchy means the rule of *some* one person or a *particular* person. Bodin was prepossessed by the latter. To Bodin, perpetual monarchical power meant the uninterrupted power of a given individual from the precise moment of accession of power until his natural death. (When matched up with the alternatives of royal succession, this notion turns out to be quintessentially dynastic.) The flaw lies in ignoring the natural infirmities of life, e.g., juvenility, senility, insanity, whereby physiology overthrows political needs. Never-failing perpetual power in a monarch would require belief in a *fictio juris* such as office or dignity, which never dies and needs no incumbent. This had been marvelously developed by medieval legists (cf. E. H. Kantorowicz, The King's Two Bodies, Princeton 1957), but Bodin was not well attuned to it. Further, see below, n. 24.

speaks for the second time about the inadequacies of his forerunners: «But no one has defined just what is meant by absolute power – or better, power freed from the law. For if we define it as freedom from all laws, no prince at all could be known for sure to have sovereignty, since divine law as well as natural law and even the law of nations – which is grounded on either (or both) divine and natural law – are binding upon all men.»[7] Only Bodin's Latin text, incidentally, brings out clearly the verbal and spiritual nexus of «absolutism» in medieval arguments about *princeps legibus solutus*.

That the prince must in principle be freed from obedience to civil law follows necessarily from what Bodin considers to be the most important aspect of sovereign power: the power to legislate. Civil legislation is the willful creation of the sovereign. So, while the good ruler should obey all laws – his own and his predecessors' – which are beneficial to the state, he must be free to disregard and annul any of them according to the needs of his country.[8] The passages driving home this point are the most cited parts of the *République*. Whenever they stand alone, they do indeed extol the «absolute» monarch.

What Bodin gives to the sovereign by way of absolute power, however, he takes back in large measure (to his own way of thinking, at least) by stating various exceptions. These are headed by the traditional medieval notion that all earthly powers must be beneath divine and natural law. This appears, for example, in the quotation just given and in the one to be given just below. Less clear, however, is the origin of another exception: that the prince is bound by contracts. Contracts, it would seem, are part of the civil law from which the prince is freed. This and a few similar matters were singled out by Bodin when he composed a new dedicatory letter for the third edition, in 1578. He laments that his critics have charged him with giving inordinate power to the rule of a single person: «For specifically in Book I, chapter 8 of my *République* and frequently elsewhere, I have been the very first, even in the most perilous times, to refute unhesitatingly the opinions of those who write

---

[7] «Quid autem sit absoluta, vel potius soluta lege potestas, nemo definit. Nam si *legibus omnibus solutam* [Bodin's italics] definiamus, nulles omnino princeps iura maiestatis habere comperiatur, cum omnes teneat lex divina, lex item naturae, tum etiam lex omnium gentium communis, quae a naturae legibus ac divinis divisas habet rationes.» *Répub.* [7.28], 132.

[8] Of the many appropriate passages that could be cited to illustrate this, the following is one of the best because Bodin calls it a maxim: «Et par ainsi nostre maxime demeure, que le Prince n'est point subiect à ses loix, ny aux loix de ses predecesseurs, mais bien à ses conventions [i.e., contracts] iustes & raisonnables, & en l'observation desquelles les subiects en general ou en particulier ont interest.» *Répub.*, 134.

of enlarging the rights of the treasury and the royal prerogative, on the ground that these men grant to kings an unlimited power, superior to divine and natural law. But what could be more in the interest of the people than what I have had the courage to write: that not even for kings is it lawful to levy taxes without the fullest consent of the citizens? Or of what importance is my other statement: that princes are more stringently bound by divine and natural law than those subject to their rule? Or that princes are bound by their contracts exactly as other citizens are? Yet nearly all the masters of legal science have taught the contrary.»[9]

Clearly Bodin did not consider himself an «absolutist» in the modern sense. The perusal of *Répub.* I, 8, bears out the contention that he did argue for limitations on royal power. More space is devoted to three such limitations than to any other matter: that the king is beneath divine and natural law, that he is forbidden to tax without consent, and that he is bound by his contracts *(pacta conventa)*.[10] In these sections, too, we find the greatest utilization of the texts of the Two Laws and of commentaries upon them. This conjunction of arguments for limited monarchy with intensive use of medieval legal allegations suggests that a spiritual bond exists between them.

---

[9] *République*, prefatory *Epistola*. I have followed the translation given by KENNETH MCRAE in his edition of Knolles' translation [7.44], p. A71.

[10] That the Prince is bound by contracts comes out less clearly in the French than in this Latin rendering: «Qui autem principes, legibus & pactis conventis solutos esse statuunt, nisi Dei praepotentis, ac naturae leges, tum etiam res ac rationes cum privatis justa conventione contractas excipiant, maximam immortali Deo, ac naturae injuriam inferunt»; *Répub.* [7.28], 153. Also, this passage: «nous pouvons tirer une autre reigle d'estat, c'est à sçavoir que le Prince souverain est tenu aux contracts par lui faicts, soit avec son subjeçt, soit avecques l'estranger; car puis qu'il est garant aux subiets des conventions & obligations mutuelles qu'ils ont les uns envers les autres, à plus forte raison est il debteur de justice en son faict»; ed. 1583, 152. See also above, note 8. MAX A. SHEPARD [110]. Sovereignty at the Crossroads: a Study of Bodin, Political Science Quarterly, 45 (1930), 590 ff., treats the problem of contracts well up to and including this summary sentence: «Contracts may not be laws in themselves, but the principle that contracts must be kept and that promises have binding force surely is a law and one derived directly from the law of nature» (591–592). But then Shepard wanders off into metaphysical speculations about contract as a kind of legal formalizing of the static social structure of the Middle Ages, which Bodin is supposed to imbibe still. Like many, Shepard understands too little about medieval jurisprudence.

II

Bodin's «anti-absolutism», such as it is, depends chiefly upon his feelings about the force of natural law in the world order, and upon the extension of natural law into temporal affairs. Natural law's force is something we must infer from Bodin's cosmology; it is largely taken for granted in *Répub*. I, 8.[11] The extension of natural law, however, is dealt with explicitly in a variety of instances in the text of that chapter. The corresponding marginal references refer most often to Roman, canon, and feudal law, along with the medieval commentaries upon them. We have, therefore, the apparently anomalous situation of natural law's being conflated with positive law. To understand how this happens is basic to the understanding of Bodin's concept of limited monarchy.

The opening chapters of the *Digest* define natural law in broad terms, and later chapters spell this out at length.[12] Several other places in the *Digest* and some in the *Code* give specific illustrations of the operation of natural law.[13] Likewise, the law of nations *(ius gentium)*, a category which Bodin did not differentiate from natural law in any meaningful way, is similarly defined and illustrated in the *Digest*.[14] These simple facts establish an important but easily overlooked consideration: Justinian's codification is not strictly a compilation of Roman civil law. Tribonian and his co-workers sought to locate what we would call the positive law of the Romans within the wider context of philosophy of law. The space devoted to this philosophical context is small, but its importance incalculable, for the dicta of the *Corpus Juris Civilis* con-

---

[11] See the papers in this volume of Mme. CHANTEUR, in general, and of Mr. BAXTER in relation to divine retribution in particular.

[12] *Digest* 1, 1, 1, 3: «Natural law is what nature teaches all animals ... not to the human species specially but all animals ... From it derives ... matrimony, ... child-bearing and education of children.» *Digest* 1, 1, 11: «There are many forms of the law. One form is the law of that which is equitable and good, as is natural law; another from, what is useful to all or to most in a given city, as is civil law.»

[13] E.g., *Digest* 12, 6, 14: «As it is only right, as a matter of natural law, that no one should become richer to the injury of another,» and *Digest* 2, 14, 1 (speaking of contracts): «The justice of this part of the Edict is founded on nature.»

[14] *Digest* 1, 1, 9 separates *ius gentium* from *ius civile* in much the same way that *Digest* 1, 1, 17 separates *ius naturale* from *ius civile*: i.e., that which befits a certain *civitas* is called *ius civile* whereas «what is established among all men by reason of nature, is observed by all and each and is called the law of nations as if it were the law observed by all people.» *Digest* 1, 1, 15 is very important for Bodin: «It was by this same *ius gentium* that war was introduced, nations were

cerning the confines of Roman civil law were taken to describe the limits of every nation's civil law. We should include also canon law and feudal law, which might be described as the civil law of the first and second estates of medieval society. Put another way, knowledge of Roman law in the totality of Justinian's compilation necessarily involved knowledge of the nature of natural law, because tiny but important fractions of the Corpus Juris Civilis dealt with that issue.

The commentaries of medieval legists abound in judgments about the borderlines between natural law, the law of nations, and civil law – as well, of course, as the superior category of divine law. Most of the argumentations drew upon *Corpus Juris Civilis* passages which make crucial distinctions. In time, the legists' interpretations far exceeded the primary passages in size, scope, and subtlety. This medieval apparatus began to develop a personality and character of its own. Statements about the extent of natural law were not gathered in one place, but remained scattered about in appropriate contexts. Some commentators, like Baldus, were more disposed than others to indulge in lofty philosophical observations. It took considerable experience, therefore, for a Renaissance lawyer like Bodin to assemble and impart order to the wide range of medieval juristic thought about natural law. Moreover, it might be difficult to recognize the result as a compendium of medieval thought, because Bodin's kind of philosophical synthesis was not the style of medieval jurists.

That Bodin quarried medieval arguments about the interpenetration of natural law and civil law does not mean that he slavishly followed or copied the medieval legists. He admired their works because they united actual legal practice with juristic theory in a way that his humanistic education had shunned. Bodin seems to have come to realize that some Bartolists possessed a strain of just that kind of philosophical humanism which the new school of Renaissance legal scholarship supposed they had lacked.

---

dinstinguished, kingdoms were established, rights of ownership were ascertained, boundaries were set to domains, buildings were erected, mutual traffic, purchase and sale, letting and hiring and obligations in general were set on foot, with the exception of a few of these last which were introduced by civil law»; translation of MONRO, I, 4. The final words of the last-quoted law touch upon the issue of «obligation», which Bodin argues vigorously (in *Répub.* I, 8) is a matter of natural law even thought the action in law with it is related is civil. From the law just cited, it is clear that obligation could be considered one of the «few of these last» introduced by civil law, although Bodin held the reverse.

III

By the count of separate citations in *Répub*. I, 8, Bartolus' student Baldus (d. 1400) is far ahead of all others with twenty-six. Bartolus himself is encountered fourteen times; the fifteenth-century civilian Alexander Tartagnus (d. 1477) and the canonist Panormitanus (Nicholaus de Tudeschis, d. 1445) twelve times each; and the canonist Felinus Sandaeus (d. 1503) fifteen times.

The last named, Felinus, is the most obscure member of this quintet of the *Répub*. I, 8's most cited authors. None, however, surpasses him in degree as a forerunner of the ideas in this chapter. Specifically, his long commentary on «Quae in ecclesiarum» *(Decretals, 1, 2, 7)* uses that law's concern with lay rulers' respect for the Church and its goods as a springboard to cover a score of major points concerning the sovereign's relations with his subjects' goods. These arguments fit perfectly Bodin's need to spell out the limits of the sovereign's *imperium* in public matters as against the subject's *dominium* over his own property. All three of the limits to princely power which Bodin in 1578 reminded his readers were involved in *Répub*. I, 8 are dealt with by Felinus: the prince bound by divine and natural law, by his own contracts, and by the need to have consent to taxation.[15]

Alexander Tartagnus' *Consilium 216* (in Book II of his collected *Consilia*) compares in importance with Felinus' commentary on «Quae in ecclesiarum». Alexander deals extensively with the question of the

---

[15] FELINUS SANDAEUS, *Commentaria in Lib. Decretalium*, on *Decretals* 1, 2, 7 («Quae in ecclesiarum»), ed. Basel 1567, 126 ff. The first and second conclusions show that secular princes and the Pope can both derogate divine law *ex causa* (the princes in cases of tolerating justifiable homicide, the Pope in dissolving marriage); the third conclusion begins by setting the general rule «Ex causa rationabili, & non aliter potest princeps statuere contra ea, quae sunt de iure naturali, vel gentium,» then gives more detailed applications: «etiam imperator non potest tollere ea, quae sunt de iure naturali, & sic non potest alicui auferre rem suam sine causa, quia licet habeat iurisdictionem in universo ...; etiam respectu bonorum infidelium nam sine causa nec Papa, nec imperator potest eis auferre bona ... ; nec princeps, nec civitas potest aliquem privare dominio rei suae sine causa» (§§ 25–27); «licet ex causa princeps possit uni auferre rem suam, & dare alteri, tamen illud est verum dummodo solvat pretium rei ille, cui eam aufert [lex «ita si verberatum» is alleged a few lines later – cf. below, n. 21] (§ 28); «princeps, vel habens iura principis, non potest etiam cum causa auferre rem suam non sibi subjecto» (§ 30); «(princeps) possit revocare suum privilegium ... sed si non est privilegium, sed conventio, tunc non potest revocare, nisi secundum ipsius rei naturam» (§ 51). I have examined less than a third of this very important commentary.

prince's power versus the subject's possession of private goods.[16] His arguments pro and con develop the same kind of tension which Bodin strives to create between freedom and restriction in the sphere of princely activity. So, the prince may not in general disturb proprietary rights or ignore his own contracts, but for the sake of public utility he may do both. The emphasis falls upon exceptional circumstances which allow the prince to do things normally prohibited him, but the unvoiced assumption holds that usually the prince is strictly limited in these matters.

Alexander and Felinus are masters of applied Roman and canon law. They build upon the work of Italian jurisprudence during the previous two centuries. They move easily between the Two Laws, and embrace readily feudal law as codified in the *Libri Feudorum*. They may lack the originality of their predecessors, but for someone like Bodin (himself a late-comer to the medieval Italian tradition of jurisprudence) they have the convenience of synthesizing the older learning under topical headings which are directly applicable to public law. Not only do they give general principles a lapidary form, but also they provide abundant examples.

Baldus, Bodin's seemingly favorite commentator, provides many examples of how *trecento* Italian jurisprudence put specific limits upon princely «absolutism». A typical instance occurs in Consilium 363 of Book I of Baldus' collected *Consilia*. At issue is the disposition by a Duke (who possesses full regalian rights by imperial concession) of certain goods to one person, while the former owner disposes of them to someone else. Public *imperium* and private *dominium* seem to lock horns. *Dominium* wins, because it stems from *ius gentium* which stems from natural law which binds the ruler: «Indeed, the Duke for his part does not seem to be able to take away the rights of ownership of another person, since those rights come from the law of nations, as said in the laws ‹quoties› and ‹rescripta› (*Code* 1, 19, 2 & 7), whence the prince is beneath the natural law, as in the law ‹digna vox.›» (*Code* 1, 14, 4.)[17] Other matters, such as the right of the fisc and the force of contract are also brought to

---

[16] ALEXANDER TARTAGNUS, *Consiliorum libri*, II, 216 (ed. Venice 1597, 181v ff., esp. 182v for these quotations): «licet princeps non possit auferre dominium acquisitum ex contractu iuris gentium, secundum magis communem sententiam, tamen ex causa illud tollere potest, & maxime si sit causa publicam utilitatem respiciens (§§ 18–19) «et dicunt Doctores quod decretum, quod transivit in contractum, potest revocari ex causa respiciente publicam utilitatem» (§ 20); «quando Imperator rescribit propter publicam utilitatem ... tunc potest res privatorum auferre, eodem modo civitas.» (§ 21).

[17] «Quinimo ipse dux non videtur posse auferre dominium alterius, cum dominia sint de iure gen. ut not. in l. quot. & in l. rescripta. C. de precib. Impera. unde princeps est sub l. naturali. ut C. de leg. l. digna vox.» BALDUS, *Consilia*, I, 363 (ed. Frankfurt 1589, fol. 108); in *Répub.* I, 8, p. 157.

bear on the question. In such well-reasoned and compact arguments as these by Baldus it is possible to appreciate how thoroughly the limits of public law were enunciated by the 14th century Italian legists.

The pages reproduced at the end of this essay contain a very complicated allegation which has a double lesson for the unwary: it reveals clearly Bodin's habit of slovenly writing or proofreading, and it illustrates the need always to consult the Latin as well as the French texts. Withal, when the problems are sorted out, we have a fine illustration of the process of alleging medieval legists. The critical phrases in each text have been underlined (the much greater length of the Latin, usually the more economical language, revealing at a glance the great changes wrought between 1576 and 1586), and the notes circled to faciliate locating them. The note I wish to deal with («2» in one text, «c» in the other) has had to be relocated in the Latin version. This can mislead the reader in itself, but the noteworthy difference really is in content of the marginalia: the French note, reversing the situation in the text, is twice as long as the Latin one. The Latin omits the latter part of the French, beginning with the words «Cum ansi. inco». Since these three words make no sense, they deprive the learned citations that follow of association with any author. When translating, Bodin may have been unable to unscramble the garbled reference and so have decided to eliminate the confusing parts. But the suppression only compounds the original blunder, as I shall show, because the part preserved – viz., everything up to «Cum ansi. inco». – consists of false or misleading allegations, while the part cut out contains a true one.

If one is not duped by the words «raison naturelle» in the text of the French version, one should expect the marginal allegations to provide evidence of «eminent domain», i.e., the right of the sovereign power to acquire the goods of a private person for reasons of the public good. Heading the note is a reference to the law «Item si verberatum» (*Digest* 6, 1 15), a law which states three instances of restitution owed by a defendant who has profited wrongfully from the use of another's goods: if he should have had to sell the goods out of necessity, if it were a question of land since given to soldiers, and if it concerned a slave or animal since deceased or destroyed. None of this random series clearly involves eminent domain, although the case of land given to soldiers seems to have the greatest possibility of doing so.

The citations of Felinus (commentary on *Decretals* 2, 26, 12), Corneaus (*Consilium* 100) and Alexander (*Consilium* 15) which precede «Cum ansi. inco.» are not relevant to eminent domain, so that the Latin note is virtually a phantom. Among the things suppressed, however, is a reference to «consil. 216», which rings a bell because of the unusual significance which a consilium of that number by Alexander Tartagnus turned out to have a few pages earlier in Bodin's argument. There, at last, one finds the mysterious Digest 6, 1, 15 («Item si verberatum») cited in relationship to eminent domain, specifically as proof of the statement that «when the Emperor issues a rescript for the sake of public utility ... he can in that case take the goods of private persons».[18] Alexander also hints that Bartolus is important for this doctrine. Going to Bartolus' commentary on *Digest* 6, 1, 15 (which it would have been wise to do in any event), one finds this declaration: «The prince, for cause, can take my right or my property and give it to another; the same, I believe, is true in the public affairs of any city.»[19] Finally, on the lookout for other legists who mention «Item si verberatum», one soon discovers it in Felinus' commentary «Quae in ecclesiarum», so often cited by Bodin. Felinus says that public goodwill is a legitimate cause for the emperor's taking a subject's goods, as is found in the Digest's «Item si verberatum», «where the land of a third party is given for the use of soldiers as a matter of public goodwill».[20]

There is no doubt, therefore, that Bodin was arguing from a strong medieval tradition when he invoked «Item si verberatum». He did indeed garble his references. A proper allegation would have read: «Bar. in l. item si verberatum, de rei vindic. Felin in c. quae in eccles. de constitut. Alexand. lib 2. cons. 216.»[21]

IV

The juristic apparatus in the margins of *Répub.* I, 8 takes us regularly into the world of 14th and 15th century Italian legal theory and practice. The example from Baldus shows this *in nuce*. In the *République's*

---

[18] Quoted above in note 16.

[19] BARTOLUS OF SAXOFERRATO, *Prima super digesto veteri*, on *Digest* 6, 1, 15 (ed. Lyon 1533, fol. 173): «Item si verberatum. Si quis rem [the law being commented upon]. Possessor qui dicit necessitate distraxit tenetur solum ad pretium quod recipit ... Ultimo not. quod princeps ex causa potest auferre ius meum seu rem meam et dare alteri; idem puto in republica alicuius civitatis.»

[20] § 27 of the source cited above, n. 15: «Causa autem legitima est favor publicus, per textum principalem in hac materia, in l. item si verberatum. ff. de rei ven. ubi fundus tertii datur ad usum militibus favore reipublicae.» (This is one answer to the riddle of which case of restitution mentioned in «Item si verberatum» is relevent to eminent domain.) For another citation of «Item si verberatum» by FELINUS, see next note.

[21] In FELINUS' passage quoted in the previous note the emphasis falls upon the right of eminent domain; but Felinus also cites «Item si verberatum» in a context stressing the recompense owed the deprived person (see above, n. 15). BARTOLUS' commentary, on the other hand, could serve different purposes for ALEXANDER and FELINUS; I suspect an earlier commentary known to all them but not to me.

text, however, Bodin relates not Italian but French juristic matters of the later Middle Ages. So, in the reproduced pages at the end of this essay, we find an incident from the reign of Louis XI used to illustrate a general legal-political issue raised in the underlined passages. This happens time and again, as Bodin strives to illustrate how French public law during recent centuries had carried out the principles of royal limitations which he was enunciating. Bodin's whole process of reasoning can be grasped, however, only by referring to the marginal apparatus. There one finds theory and practice intimately united by the genius of the Italian jurists, who argued about natural law and the law of nations in the course of applying Roman and Canon law to the ruling powers of their times. The limits which they set to princely absolutism can be found just as early in France (Bodin showed in his text) as in Italy, but French jurists were not as articulate about the theoretical side of the matter. Withal, the *République's* text and marginalia are meant to be equal representations of how natural law operated in two different late-medieval sovereign realms as a check upon arbitrary princely rule. The casual reader, who does not penetrate the evidence of the marginalia, will miss the Italian aspect altogether. A full knowledge of Bodin's allegations, on the other hand, reveals that the Italians were by far the more sophisticated thinkers, and that the applied *Corpus Juris Civilis* was the fundamental text. That compilation was not only a monument of a dead civilization, but was potentially a creative force in modern jurisprudence. Such a striking departure from Bodin's original view of the medieval legal tradition suggests some unusual experience in his life.

V

It has often been noted that Bodin moved steadily towards absolutism from the *Methodus* of 1566 to the *République* of 1576. The examples from the République which we have examined, however, show Bodin working for limited and not absolute monarchy. The quandary may be resolved, I believe, by reference to Bodin's *curriculum vitae* as revealed in this famous passage:

«When I was lecturing publicly on Roman Law at Toulouse [1550 to 1559] I deemed myself very wise to be one in company of young scholars, and I thought that princes of the legal science like Bartolus, Baldus, Alexander, Faber, Paulus, and Du Moulin – indeed, the entire corps of judges and order of advocates – knew little or nothing at all. But after I had been initiated into the mysteries of jurisprudence in the courts and had gained experience in the day-by-day workings of the law, I realized that a true and sound knowledge of it lay not in law-college debates but in courtroom battles, not in the quantities of syllables but in the scales of justice and equity. Those who know nothing about the art of pleading remain in the greatest ignorance of Roman law. Indeed, who ventures to use the formula *«Ex facto consultus respondi»* [«I answer by citing such-and-such decision»] when nobody asks his opinion on a point of law? or invokes the refrain of the jurisconsults, *«Hoc Iure Utimur»* [«We are following such-and-such law»] when he knows not by what laws he is proceeding?»[22]

He goes on then to declare that all teachers should have practical experience, so that they could show the students what is useful before overburdening their minds with the plethora of law and customs then extant.

Bodin seems to be telling us that after his scholastic years in Toulouse, 1550–1559, and during the ones at the bar in Paris, 1559–1566, he discovered the world of the *mos italicus*. He found it in French courts, especially in the Parlement de Paris. There one had to know Bartolus, Baldus, and company. Not only were they cited, but their arguments carried great meaning for the student of political philosophy. On this basis Bodin could have changed his mind concerning the concept of sovereignty which he had outlined in the *Methodus*.

Although Bodin's *Methodus* appeared only in 1566, actually at the end of his years of practicing in Paris, it has been soundly argued that the work was composed earlier during the years in Toulouse.[23] It is infused with humanistic learning. Roman law enters only as knowledge conditioned by education according to the *mos gallicus*. The *Methodus'* section on sovereignty is a good example: it lacks completely the medieval juristic apparatus with which the corresponding chapter of the *République* is so replete.

The passage quoted above extolling Bartolus and other medieval com-

---

[22] My translation differs in emphasis but not in substance from those of KENNETH MCRAE [7.44] – who explains the context of the writing of this second preface of the *République* – and of JULIAN FRANKLIN [226] Jean Bodin and the Sixteenth Century Revolution in Methodology, New York 1963, 64.

[23] Cf. PIERRE MESNARD [174], Jean Bodin à Toulouse, *Bibliothèque d'Humanisme et Renaissance* 12 (1950), 50, 54, relying upon John L. Brown [140], The Methodus ad facilem historiarum cognitionem of Jean Bodin, Washington 1939 for demonstration. Brown's valuable and useful dissertation errs somewhat in its account of the relationship of the *Methodus* to the *République*, at least in respect to the legal apparatus that concerns us here. Brown quotes the MAITLAND passage cited at the end of my text as evidence of medieval Italian influence on the *Methodus*, which otherwise his own arguments go against (cf. p. 30), as certainly do mine. He gives the impression that the *République* is more philosophical and classical (cf. p. 153 ff.) without accounting for the extensive medieval apparatus.

mentators is found in the same new prefatory letter of the 1578 edition of the *République* wherein we earlier saw Bodin harping upon the limits to princely power set forth in the first edition of 1576. The link between the medieval commentators and the limits of sovereignty, turns out usually to be the operation of natural law in living juridical practice. We may now speculate upon the broader implications of these facts for Bodin's doctrine of sovereignty.

VI

Most commentators who defend Bodin as a constitutionally minded political thinker rely heavily upon the few passages in the *République* which evoke *leges imperii*, or fundamental laws. For France this meant the Salic Law, for example. But Bodin himself makes no effort to delineate the proper nature of fundamental laws, and contradictions can be found in what he does say about them.[24] By contrast, he elaborates upon natural law's role in the actual operation of French public law at great length and with considerable subtlety. The trick, seen simply, is to discover that what appears often to be mere civil law actually is a manifestation of natural law. The category of laws which are «seemingly civil, actually natural» is, in my opinion, by far the most important element in whatever case can be made for Bodin the constitutionalist.

Bodin magnifies the scope of natural law by closely associating it with equity, and by stressing the difference between *lex* and *ius*. In a host of instances of *lex* (law as command) which operate in the world of jurisprudence, the discriminating and learned eye will see that the principle of *ius* (law as equity) is actually at stake.[25] If one were to imagine the spheres of natural law and civil law as hierarchically arranged, then

---

[24] In a brief note, J. H. Burns [194], Sovereignty and Constitutional Law in Bodin, *Political Studies* 7 (1959), 174–177, shows the complicated nature of the problem of fundamental law in Bodin. (It is a good example, inter alia, of the necessity of reading the Latin as well as the French texts.) Logically, things belonging to the office of the sovereign cannot be changed by the sovereign; the medieval distinction is crystal clear, and in effect Bodin is using it in the famous passage where he refers to the Salic Law and other *leges imperii* (the point of Burns' argument). But, on the whole, Bodin either does not understand or deliberately rejects the whole paraphernalia of the «two bodies» concepts of medieval political thought, (cf. Kantorowicz, as above n. 6). Bodin strives to root power in the living incumbent, not in the abstract office. I have touched upon these matters in The Juristic Basis of Dynastic Right to the French Throne (= Transactions of the American Philosophical Society, LI: 5; Philadelphia, 1961), 11, n. 29 and 30–31.

[25] The classic lines are these: «mais il y a bien différence entre le droit & la

natural law would appear to dip down into and overlap civil law to a very large extent. A given law may appear to be both civil and natural. This makes little difference to the ordinary subject, since he is normally bound to both. But it makes a great difference to the prince, since he is *legibus solutus* only in respect to civil law and *legibus alligatus* in respect to natural law. The latter aspect preempts the former whenever they appear together.[26]

In the years of his practice in Paris, Bodin discovered the juristic actuality of *princeps legibus alligatus* which had been created by courts and commentators from the 13th century until his own day. Italian legists of the 14th and 15th centuries were especially important. They had been concerned to establish a workable constitution for independent communes by establishing juridical limitations upon the *segnoria* (the word, by the way, given as the Italian equivalent of *souveraineté* in the opening sentence of *Répub.* I, 8). When an Italian jurist observes that the prince differs not from an ordinary private person in respect to the binding force of contracts, he probably had in mind a despot whose princely legitimacy bears no comparison with transalpine monarchs who ruled by the grace of God. Still, the Italian legists' evidence that princely obligations such as contract were part of natural law dovetailed with contemporaneous French historical examples found in the registers of Parlement and elsewhere.[27]

Bodin's experience in the courts brought the realization that the guarantee of subjects' proprietary rights within the French juristic tradition imposed clear limitations upon the sovereign's power. In the *République* he seems to see French history as the reverse of what François Hotman pictured it to be in the *Francogallia*. Hotman declared that

---

loy: l'un emporte rien que l'equité, la loy emporte commandement; car la loy n'est autre chose que le commandement du souverain, usant de sa puissance»; *Républ.* 155. This whole problem, nowadays, should be reviewed in the light of GUIDO KISCH's work on equity in Renaissance law, especially his Erasmus und die Jurisprudenz seiner Zeit, Basel 1960. See also Mme CHANTEUR's paper in this volume.

[26] Besides what Bodin himself claims (above, n. 9), I give this passage from SHEPARD [110], Sovereignty, 602–603, with which I concur exactly (but prefer *alligatus* to *tentus* as more idiomatic): «The general tone of his book, however, leads one to believe that he regarded the notion of a king *legibus tentus* as of at least as great significance as the idea of *legibus solutus*. Indeed, it seems correct to say that Bodin, in so far as he clearly faced the problem at all, reserved the force of the *legibus solutus* clause exclusively for those laws enacted inside the spere of the sovereign's restricted authority.»

[27] Besides the Registres du Parlement, Bodin's French historical examples are drawn from the *Olim* and JEAN LE COCQ's (Johannes Gallus') contemporary collection of royal edicts.

ancient constitutional limits upon kings had been abandoned, making it necessary to have a thoroughgoing reformation of institutions in order to recover the pristine virtuous state.[28] Bodin maintained that the existing juristic system imposed sufficient limitations upon the king. These are to be found *de facto* still argued in French courts; the *République,* one might say, aimed to render them *de jure* by revealing the underlying legal-philosophical principles.[29]

VII

Bodin's vision of legal restrictions upon the prince differs basically from the medieval idea of sovereignty, much as they would seem to have in common because of putting the king beneath the law in important respects. Medieval definitions of sovereignty proceeded by specific allocations of power to the ruler; he was given *certain* powers and no more. Bodin, contrariwise, granted the sovereign power *all* power except such and such. Bodin believed that he was a true adherent to limited monarchy, but by medieval standards this can be accepted only if one believes that the power which Bodin left to the king after imposing limitations upon him was not greater than the sum of specific powers typically allotted to the king by medieval political theory. On a theoretical level, this question must remain moot, but when considering the actualities of governance – where it is indisputable that Renaissance sovereigns had much greater potentiality to exert centralized authority than their predecessors had had, due to military and bureaucratic advances – it would seem much more risky to give all residual powers to the sovereign (even after having heeded natural law's domain) in the 16th century than at any earlier time.

---

[28] My views on Hotman's intent in the *Francogallia* are set forth in two articles in *Bibliothèque d'Humanisme et Renaissance* 29 (1967), 581–611, and 32 (1970), 41–56. J. H. M. Salmon's paper in the present volume goes much further, and still more on the Monarchomach influence on Bodin, and vice versa, appears in the introduction to *Francogallia* by François Hotman, edited by Salmon and me, Cambridge Univ. Press 1972.

[29] I do not mean to say that Bodin was correct in his estimate of judicial restraint upon the French monarch in the later middle ages or in his own. He knew recent French history no better than Hotman knew early Frankish history – which is not to condemn either, since they lived several centuries before anywhere nearly precise history of the Middle Ages was had. So, my efforts to delineate Bodin's potential constitutionalism in the *République* does not conflict necessarily with the estimate of Julian Franklin, in his paper in this volume, that Bodin was actually retreating from constitutionalism from the *Methodus* to the *République.*

If Bodin deemed himself an advocate of limited monarchy because of his extended application of natural law, then we may explain his later reputation as an absolutist in terms of the changing meaning of *ius naturale*. According to the millenia-old Aristotelian world system, which Bodin must have shared essentially with his contemporaries, the universe was rationally ordered as an hierarchy by the Creator. Natural law a first principle of that order, the very adhesive of the system. Violation of it had to bring anarchy, if not the wrath of God directly.[30] This applied as much to political and social matters as to physical ones. With the decline of this cosmology after the 16th century, however, natural law changed its character. In terms of the physical world it became more quantitatively defined, losing its character as a divine immanence, and in political terms it was ever increasingly equated with mere morality. If one reads Bodin's usage of *ius naturale* as meaning mere morality, then almost all meaningful checks upon the sovereign disappear, leaving him indeed *legibus solutus,* truly «absolute».[31]

There are, however, indications that Bodin's cosmology was not completely orthodox for his times. By embracing a voluntaristic philosophy, for example, Bodin did not have to consider God's creation of the world order as final and complete, but rather still amenable to change. If true that *ut deus, sic princeps,* then the innovative and generally creative role of the sovereign is vouchsafed. The king as judge is medieval; the king as legislator, modern. From judge to legislator denotes the shift from passive to active rulership, from a static to a dynamic state. In *Répub.* I, 8, we see this clearly manifested in passages where Bodin compares the king to God. The king is a creator, imitating God, not simply God's instrument to preserve God's own order.[32] The dilemma

---

[30] Cf. above, n. 11.

[31] SHEPARD [110], Sovereignty, 584 ff., sees the problem as one of whether *ius naturale* was «legal» (Bodin) or «moral» (Hobbes-Austin), with which many modern scholars agree; cf. e.g., SCHEUNER's paper in the present volume. This conforms with the view of W. H. GREENLEAF [238], Order, Empiricism and Politics, Oxford 1964 – expounded at greater length in his paper in the present volume – that Bodin's view was wholly that of the «political theory of order» (p. 134). For myself, I believe it necessary to stress that the sense of order, while certainly dominant, was beset by countervailing forces of the daemonic and the voluntaristic in Bodin's philosophy (as shown by the papers of BAXTER and ISNARDI-PARENTE in this volume).

[32] The classic passage constitutes the last sentence of *Répub.* I, 8: «Car si la justice est la fin de la loy, la loy œuvre du Prince, le Prince est image de Dieu, il faut par mesme suite de raison, que la loy du Prince soit faicte au modelle de la Loy de Dieu» (p. 161). Signora ISNARDI-PARENTE's paper in this volume cites other evidence of this kind of God-prince mimesis.

DE LA REPVBLIQVE.   157

foit iufte & raifonnable, foit par achet,ou efchange,ou
confifcation legitime, ou traittant paix auec l'ennemi, fi
autrement elle ne fe peut conclurre , qu'en prenant du
bien des particuliers pour la côferuation de l'eftat: quoy
que plufieurs①ne foyent pas de ceft.aduis : mais la rai-
fon naturelle②veut que le public foit preferé au particu
lier, & que les fubiects relafchent non feulement leurs
iniures & vengeances , ains auffi leurs biës pour le falut
de la Republique : comme il fe fait ordinairement, & du
public au public,& du particulier à l'autre. Ainfi voyons
nous au traicté de Peronne , faict pour la deliurance du
Roy Louys x 1.prifonnier du Comte du Charolois qu'il
fut dit que le feigneur de Torci pourroit faire executer fon arreft contre le fieur de Saueufes.C'eft pourquoy
on a loué Thrafybule,lequel apres auoir chaffé les x x x.
tyrans d Athenes , fit crier l'oubliance generale de toutes pertes & iniures entre les particuliers, qui fut auffi
depuis publiee en Romme par le traicté faict entre les
coniurés d'vne part,& les partifans de Cefar d'autre. Et
toutesfois on doit chercher tous les moyens de recom-
penfer la perte des vns,auec le proffit des autres : & s'il
ne fe peut faire fans trouble , on doit prendre les deniers
de l'efpargne,ou en emprüter:côme fit Aratus③ qui em-
prunta foixante mil efcus, pour aider à r'embourfer ceux
qui auoyent efté bannis & chaffés de leurs biens , qui
eftoyent poffedés & prefcrits par longues annees. Cef-
fant donc les caufes que i'ay dit , le Prince ne peut prendre ny donner le bien d'autruy, fans le confentement du
feigneur : & en tous les dons,graces, priuileges & actes
du Prince,toufiours la claufe, S A V F le droit d'autruy,
eft entendue,ores qu'elle ne fuft exprimee.Et de faict ce
fte claufe appofee en l'inueftiture du Duché de Milan,
que fit l'Empereur Maximilian au Roy Louys x 1 1.fut
occafion de nouuelle guerre , pour le droit,que les Sfor-
ces pretendoyent au Duché, que l'Empereur n'auoit
peu,ny voulu donner. Car de dire que les Princes font
feigneurs de tout,cela s'entend④de la droite feigneurie,
& iuftice fouueraine, demeurant à chacun la poffeffion
& propriété de fes biens. Ainfi difoit Seneque,⑥ *Ad reges*
poteftas omnium pertinet,ad fingulos proprietas : & peu apres:
Omnia Rix imperio pofsidet,finguli dominio. Et pour cefte
                                       caufe

Marginalia (right column):

① Hoftien. in c. quanto. de iure
② iurand. Butrio, ibi.col. 2. Innocent.& Panorm. in cap.in noftra. de iniur.
③ d.l. item fi ver beratum. Fel.in cap.cùm non liceat.col.5.de ref crip.Corne.côf. 100.li.j.Alex.c6 fil.15.li.col.2.Cû anfi.inco.l.53.& 158.col.j.& c6fi. 161.col.3.& confi.106.li.3. & latiff.confi. 216.& conf.65.li.j. nu. 3.& côf. 126. nu. j.lib. 2.
④ Poly.lib.2.

La force de la
claufe. Sauf le
droit d'autruy.
④ Felin. in cap. quæ in ecclefia rum. de conft. col.11.Bal.conf. 563. fine lib. j, Iaf.in authent. quas actiones. de facrof. c. 4.l. in re actio. de rei vindic.afflic. in conft.Neapol. lib.4.tit.10.
⑤ lib.7. c.4. & 5. de beneficiis.

De Repvblica, Lib. I.   161

fit:fic enim Pliniusiunior, ad Traianum Auguftum&. *Plin. in Pa-*
*Vt enim,*inquit,*felicitatis eft,poffe quantū velis,fic magnitudi-* *negyrico.*
*nis,velle quantum poßis.*hæc ille : quibus verbis efficitur,
nihil Prinsipes poffe,quod natura turpe fit,aut iniuflum. Iam
vero inepte loquatur,qui potentiæ fummæ tribuat,alie-
na diripere, aut prædari,aut vi ftuprum inferre ; quæ ab
animo fracto libidinis& cupiditatum impotentia profi-
cifcuntur.Quod fi Principi non licet mouere terminos,
quos Deus opt. max. cuius ipfe eft imago viuens ac
fpirans,fempiternis naturæ legibus pepigit;neque certe
licebit,alteri detrahere cp fuum eft , fiue iufta ratione,
fiue coemptione,fiue commutatione,fiue legitima præ-
fcriptione,fiue fœdere cum amicis feriendo,fiue pacis a-(b)*Hoftienfis in*
ctione cum hoftib.concipienda,fi aliter pax iniri neque- *c.quanto.de*
at, quam privatorum detrimento,quorum bona fæpe *iureiurando.*
hoftib.frueda permittunt Principes pro ciuium ac Rei- *Butrio ibid.*
pub.falute:tametfi quibufdam&placet,vt fuū quifq; te- *in c.in noftra,*
neat,nec de bonis privatorū publice diminutio fiat:aut *de iniuriu.*
fi vrget publica neceffitas,ab vniverfis farciendū effe; q̃ *(c) item fi ver*
fententia mihi probatur,fi tamen commode id fieri pof- *beratū,de rei*
fit.Sed cum falus privatorum,bona omnia civium , pa- *in c. cum non*
triæ falute contineantur, non folum privatas offenfio- *liceat.col.5.de*
nes,&acceptas ab hoftibus contumelias, fed etiam fua *refcript.Corn*
bona,privatos Reip.&non gravate concedere oportet : *conf.100.lib.1*
nam fere femper pax habet aliquid iniquum, quod pu- *Alexand.lib.*
blica vtilitate compenfatur;& eo quidem iure populi o- *5.conf. 15.*
mnes vtuntur,vt non modo publica publicis ac privata *in c.quāto,&*
privatis,fed etiam vtraq; vtrifq; in pacis actione,mutu- *ibi Butrio, de*
is vtilitatibus ac detrimentis farciantur. *iureiurando.*
Video plerofq;&uris vtriufq; magiftros,in ea fentē- *DD poft.In,o*
tia & effe,&fuiffe,vim eorum fœderum , quibus exce- *cent.in cap.in*
ptum eft,ne vlla detrimentorum hinc inde acceptorum *Bald.in l. ve-*
quæftio habeatur,inanem effe,nec priuatis præiudiciū *nia.de in ius*
afferre,alio tamen iure vtimur : nam in pace Peronen- *voc.Caftrei f,*
fi,vt Ludouicus x 1.Rex Francorum, carceribus Caro- *in l.2. de pact.*
li Burgundionum Comitis eriperetur, vno capite cau- *Mart. Laud.*
tum eft,*Ne Tortio fententiam curiæ Parifiorum,aduerfus Sa-* *in tract.de cō-*
     L   *nusium* *fœder.q.1.*

of Bodin, then, is to want to preserve an eternal and natural order guaranteed by natural law, so that the sovereign's domain is small in measure as natural law's is great, but at the same time to empower earthly sovereigns to act creatively on earth as does God in the macrocosm. The points of contact between the original Creator's legislation, *ius naturale,* and the new legislator's creations, *ius civile,* play a vital role in Bodin's definition of sovereignty in *Répub.* I, 8. How they can be reconciled, on the other hand, is perhaps better seen elsewhere in the *République,* above all in the final chapter on cosmic harmonics.[33]

Those who followed in Bodin's footsteps, starting a generation later, are notable for their greater clarity in rendering his ideas: Paurmeister, Arnisaeus, Bornitius, Reinking, Besold, Althusius, Grotius.[34] None of these, I would guess, knew anything but the text of the *République,* because I doubt that many legal writers after 1600 *could* have studied the marginal allegations. For one thing, hardly any of the late medieval legists' works were printed after 1600, when the manner of teaching the law in the humanistic fashion completely took over. Even more significantly, the edition of the *Corpus Juris Civilis* with Accursius' *glossa ordinaria,* which had served as the basic legal text for over three centuries, gave way after 1600 to the new humanistic edition edited by Denys Godefroy. Bodin, therefore, belongs to the last generation which had a thorough experience with the older medieval tradition. He himself learned it not in the classroom (although that still could have been done in some schools in his time) but in the courtroom. After him, however, it is doubtful that anyone could find the great tradition of Bartolus and his followers in either the universities or the courts.

Since the medieval legal tradition became moribund soon after Bodin's time, while the idea of sovereignty which he had propagated had a remarkably vigorous growth, the scholar today could be tempted to leave Bodin's marginalia resting in limbo. First, however, he might do well to ponder these words of Maitland's: «But Baldus and Bartolus, Innocentius and Johannes Andreae, them he [the modern reader] has never been taught to tackle, and they are not to be tackled by the untaught. And yet they are important people, for political philosophy in its youth is apt to look like sublimated jurisprudence, and, even when it has grown in vigor and stature, it is often compelled to work with tools – social contract, for example – which have been sharpened, if not forged, in a legal smithy.»[35]

---

[33] See the brillant exposition by M. VILLEY, elsewhere in the present volume.

[34] See E. HANCKE, Bodin, Breslau 1894, 5, n. 2 and *passim* [48]; also, now, the paper of M. HOKE in the present volume.

[35] FREDERIC W. MAITLAND, Introduction to O. GIERKE, Political Theories of the Middle Age, Cambridge 1900, VIII.

Michel Reulos

Les sources juridiques de Bodin: textes, auteurs, pratique

La plupart des auteurs qui se sont occupés de Jean Bodin ont souligné les caractères divers de cette œuvre et ont signalé la diversité de nature des sources utilisées par lui tant comme éléments de ses constructions doctrinales que pour appuyer d'exemples ses constatations de fait. Pierre Mesnard, dans l'Essor de la philosophie politique signale, en une brillante synthèse, les éléments de l'immense savoir juridique de Bodin «qui s'exprime parfois par d'interminables kyrielles de références. Bartole, Alciat, Balde, Connan, Cujas, Du Moulin chacun à son rang nous sont prodigués avec une libéralité excessive»; il note ensuite les sources en matière de droit constitutionnel, l'utilisation des arrêts des Parlements, des coutumes, du droit canonique (cf. éd. 1936, p. 478). Un auteur comme J. Basdevant étudiant la «Contribution de Jean Bodin à la formation du droit international moderne» (Rev. hist. de droit 1944, note p. 144 et s.) note aussi qu'à côté de ses connaissance en histoire, dans les sciences naturelles, en sociologie, Bodin est surtout un juriste, un avocat, c'est à dire un praticien du droit, qui a été mêlé à la vie publique et diplomatique et cet auteur rappelle le qualificatif de «légiste» parfois attaché à Bodin. Certains éléments de ces sources juridiques ont plus particulièrement attiré l'attention: Pierre Mesnard dans l'exposé qu'il présenta aux journées organisées en 1960 à Toulouse par la Société Jean Bodin sur la «monocratie» sur le thème «Jean Bodin a-t-il établi la théorie de la monocratie?»* relève qu'il convient, dans l'explication de la République de ne pas omettre, comme étrangers au droit public, la lecture des chapitres III à VII du premier livre; il note aussi que Bodin remonte systématiquement aux sources, et utilise sa rare érudition et notamment sa connaissance approfondie du droit romain, qu'il sollicite les textes les plus divers des Pandectes et des historiens classiques, notamment sur la patria potestas et la puissance maritale.

Ainsi, qu'il s'agisse de la partie proprement juridique des ouvrages de Bodin ou des parties où les textes et auteurs juridiques ne font que donner un témoignage d'un précédent, d'une pratique, l'étude des sources utilisées par Bodin parait utile: il ne s'agit aucunement pour Bodin d'un simple étalage d'érudition par une accumulation de références d'«auctori-

* Recueil de la Société Jean Bodin: La Monocratie, 1969, pp. 637–655.

tates», mais de la volonté d'appuyer des opinions ou des constatations de preuves certaines que le droit peut fournir, grâce aux textes des autorités publiques, aux décisions judiciaires d'autorités impartiales et non suspectes, aux textes des auteurs après éventuellement critique de leur témoignage.

Nous essayerons de présenter le résultat de nos recherches sur ces sources proprement juridiques et de dégager les idées directrices de Bodin dans leur mise en œuvre.

I. Textes à caractère législatif

Bodin cite de nombreux textes: tout d'abord les lois du Digeste et les constitutions du Code de Justinien; les citations sont faites de la façon courante à cette époque, c'est à dire par la loi, le titre et le livre, l'identification de la loi pouvant être faite grâce aux tables d'incipit qui furent publiées par Godefroy notamment. Les soucis critiques ne sont pas absents, p. ex. Livre I, chap. 6, (p. 91, note 8) on voit la remarque suivante «ubi inepta est lectio Florentini libri...»; on voit aussi des observations sur les textes dans les controverses avec Cujas: Liv. III, chap. 5, p. 463, note 3 à propos d'une correction de Cujas; discussion sur l'ignominie et l'infamie (Liv. III, chap. 3, p. 403); discussion notée comme postérieure à la première édition Liv. III, chap. 6, pp. 468–469 et Liv. IV, chap. I, p. 545.

Bodin note bien aussi le caractère technique du vocabulaire juridique: il note à propos d'une expression «en termes de droit» (cf. Liv. I, chap. 8, p. 125, note 4 ou Liv. I, chap. 9, p. 185, note 4).

La valeur normative des lois romaines, comme telles, est fort bien caractérisée dans le contexte du droit français, par rapport au droit coutumier et aux édits des rois (Liv. I, chap. 8, p. 155): les lois romaines sont donc bien des précédents, des éléments de solution.

Les édits des rois, et ici nous nous limitons aux édits des rois de France qui sont directement allégués, sans intermédiaires d'auteurs, d'historiens ou de jurisconsultes, sont cités par leur date et l'indication du souverain dont ils émanent. On peut se demander comment Bodin a constitué ses dossiers dans ce domaine:

Bodin a certainement eu accès aux archives du Parlement, c'est ainsi qu'il peut citer les textes enrégistrés. On peut remarquer qu'à son époque les édits royaux sont souvent publiés sous des formes variées et que même des recueils d'ordonnances ont déjà paru, mais nous ne trouvons aucune citation à un de ces recueils, car la *République* n'est pas destinée qu'aux lecteurs français mais Bodin lui donne une valeur universelle et de tels recueils ne sont pas répandus en dehors des milieux de praticiens. Des contemporains de Bodin rédigent déjà des sortes de répertoires chronologiques d'histoire, p. ex. Jean du Tillet. Le souci de publier d'une façon coordonnée les ordonnances des rois à la façon du Code de Justinien se manifeste notamment par la publication du Code Henri III de Barnabé Brisson.

Les coutumes françaises constituent une source qui ne doit pas être négligée: on sait que dans «La réponse de Jean Bodin à M. de Malestroit», l'auteur a dépouillé en historien les vieux textes législatifs et les vieux procès, comme le remarque Henri Hauser dans la préface de son édition et qu'il a utilisé les coutumes comme source de l'histoire des prix. Dans la *République* Bodin va se référer à des textes des coutumes pour illustrer ses raisonnements. Il est intéressant de remarquer que l'existence même des coutumes est rattachée aux compétences reconnues aux trois Etats du Royaume et que Bodin rappelle les modalités de rédaction officielle des coutumes (Liv. I, chap. 8, p. 137); il a soin de souligner que ce mode d'établissement n'est pas contradictoire avec l'autorité royale qui peut modifier les coutumes, notamment dans le cas de coutumes injustes (Livre I, chap. 8, p. 142). Il envisage aussi la coutume dans la hiérarchie des sources du droit et dans celle des actes juridiques (Livre I, chap. 8, p. 150).

La diversité des coutumes est pour lui une manifestation des changements de la règle de droit en fonction des climats: p. ex. à propos de la fixation de l'âge de la majorité (Liv. V, chap. I, p. 682); la diversité même des coutumes ainsi constatée (v. Liv. I, chap. 6, p. 72) est nous semble-t-il la cause de leur peu de force comme témoignage de règle de droit et justifie qu'elles ne soient alléguées qu'à titre d'exemples.

Nous relevons des citations précises à divers sujets: à propos de la saisie des biens vacants (Liv. I, chap. 10, p. 247) Touraine, Berry, Nevers, Blois, Bordeaux, Poitou; à propos de la succession des filles, (Liv. V, chap. 2, p. 720) coutumes d'Anjou, Maine et Montdidier; la coutume de Vendôme est mentionnée avec la remarque qu'il s'agit d'une ancienne Chatellenie d'Anjou. On trouve mention pour la Bretagne de l'Assise du Comte Geoffroy, et il est fait mention de la coutume du pays de Caux et de la coutume de Béarn (Liv. IV, chap. 7, p. 646); signalons encore des mentions de la Coutume de Vermandois (Liv. I, chap. 9, p. 171) de celle de Hainaut (Liv. I, chap. 9, p. 238). Nous ne considérons pas comme des citations de coutumes les références à des auteurs coutumiers qui donnent leur opinion à propos de dispositions d'une coutume: c'est essentiellement le cas de Du Moulin auquel Bodin se réfère souvent, en alléguant notamment son commentaire des fiefs de la coutume de Paris. Bodin qualifie d'ailleurs Du Moulin l'honneur des Jurisconsultes (Liv. III, chap. V, p. 441), même si parfois il est en désaccord avec lui; Bodin cite également D'Argentré sur la coutume de Bretagne, par exemple à propos du vassal (Liv. I, chap. 9,

p. 168), Chasseneuz sur la coutume de Bourgogne (Liv. I, chap. 10, p. 245;
Liv. III, chap. 6, p. 470), Gui Pape sur la coutume du Dauphiné (Liv. I,
chap. 9, p. 238; Liv. I, chap. 10, p. 248).

II. La jurisprudence

En ce qui concerne les arrêts, on remarquera le développement très net de
Bodin sur la portée de la jurisprudence au Livre VI, chap. 6, pp. 1025–1026
et la possibilité de juger selon l'équité. Les arrêts des parlements sont souvent cités par l'intermédiaire des auteurs qui les citent: Gui Pape pour
Grenoble, Aufrère pour Toulouse. La valeur historique de la jurisprudence
est parfaitement comprise par Bodin qui se réfère aux Olim et à des arrêts
d'époques diverses: il cite par exemple les Questiones Johannis Galli
(Livre V, chap. 6, p. 787; Liv. I, chap. 8, p. 154 et p. 158; Liv. I, chap. 10,
p. 241). On ne trouve aucune référence aux recueils de Papon ou de Du
Luc déjà publiés; mais on sait que les praticiens avaient des Mémoriaux,
des Recueils de décisions établis en fonction de leur activité propre ou de
la fréquentation du Palais. Certes les textes des Coutumes sont allégués à
propos des questions qui peuvent se rattacher au droit privé, mais Bodin
remarque combien certaines des dispositions les plus fréquemment réglées
par la coutume se rattachent à des problèmes qu'il étudie, p. ex. les relations vassaliques, les droits du Roi en matière de fief. Une preuve des liens
entre les questions de droit public et certaines dispositions du droit coutumier nous est fournie par des témoignages de l'influence de Bodin: ainsi
Pierre Delommeau dans ses *Maximes générales du droict françois* parues
en 1612 se réfère avec éloge à Bodin à plusieurs reprises dans le commentaire des maximes du premier Livre consacré aux Droits royaux (maxime
II, III, V, VI, IX, XII, maxime numérotée par erreur XV étant en réalité
la seizième, la même erreur se retrouvant encore dans la cinquième édition
de 1619, la numérotation étant décalée d'un numéro, XVI, XIX); les
renvois à Bodin sont plus rares au Livre II «Des Droits seigneuriaux»
(maxime XIX, XXIX); le Livre III, «Des droits des particuliers», ne
contient aucune référence à Bodin, alors qu'à plusieurs maximes, les références coincident avec des références données en notes par Bodin.

III. Les auteurs

Les auteurs constituent une des sources les plus importantes de Bodin;
nous n'envisageons que les auteurs juridiques à proprement parler, ceux
que Bodin lui-même appelle «Iurisconsultes» ou «Docteurs en loix» ou
seulement «docteurs». Bodin ne considère pas les multiples autorités seulement comme destinées à appuyer un développement, mais par une critique

interne de leur témoignage, il fait des opinions des jurisconsultes une manifestation d'une sorte de consensus des hommes compétents. Grâce à plusieurs passages de Bodin, nous pouvons voir quelles réserves il formule sur la valeur de ces opinions: Bodin reproche le caractère scolaire ou théorique de nombreux jurisconsultes: Liv. III, chap. 2, p. 378: «quant aux Iurisconsultes qui ne bougent des escholes, ils sont excusables...»; Liv. VI, chap. 2, p. 855 «...il y a plusieurs grands Docteurs en matière d'imposts, qui sçavent beaucoup de moyens de faire fonds aux finances, mais ils n'ont iamais eu la vraye science d'honneur, ny la prudence politique...»; Liv. V, chap. 6, p. 803 «...quelques docteurs ont soutenu, aussi mal informés de l'estat des Républiques comme des histoires anciennes, et du fondement de la vraye iustice, discourant des traictés faicts entre les Princes, comme des conventions et contracts faicts entre les particuliers...»; cet éloignement de la réalité pratique fait qu'ils donnent des avis intéressés et pour celui qui les leur demande (Liv. V, chap. 6, p. 807). «Les autres, qui ne peuvent trouver occasion véritable, ny vraysemblable de fausser la foy, demandent les advis et délibérations des Iurisconsultes et Canonistes» et Bodin leur reproche de ne pas se préoccupper de la loy de Dieu et de nature sous des prétextes équivoques de droit naturel (Liv. III, chap. 4, p. 415).

Par opposition Bodin dit aussi quel doit être le vrai jurisconsulte: Liv. I, chap. 5 (de la puissance seigneuriale), p. 49: «Mais les Iurisconsultes qui ne s'arrestent pas tant aux discours des Philosophes qu'à l'opinion populaire, tiennent que la servitude est directement contre nature et font tout ce qu'ils peuvent pour maintenir la liberté contre l'obscurité des loix, des testaments, des arrests, des contracts...» Bien qu'il y ait lieu de distinguer le philosophe et le juriste il y a des liens entre eux: p. ex. à la fin du chap. 5 du livre VI il note que «Platon a intitulé ses livres de la République, livres du droit ou de la iustice, combien qu'il en parle plustost en Philosophe qu'en Législateur ou Iurisconsulte».

Le jurisconsulte a donc une mission élevée et Bodin note que parfois il se trompe: ainsi Liv. III, chap. 4, p. 416 nous lisons «...car la iustice et raison qu'on dit naturelle n'est pas tousiours si claire qu'elle ne trouve des adversaires: et bien souvent les plus grands Iurisconsultes s'y trouvent empeschés et du tout contraires en opinions.» Il convient que le jurisconsulte soit au courant de tout ce qui peut contribuer à l'application de la loi; il peut tenir compte des circonstances particulières de la question: «...car, quoy que die Balde, que la raison et l'équite naturelle n'est pas bornée ni attachée aux lieux, cela reçoit distinction, c'est à savoir quand la raison particulière des lieux et des personnes reçoit une considération particulière» (Liv. V, chap. 1, p. 666); et, à propos de la dispute entre Lothaire et Azon (Liv. III, chap. 5, p. 432) il remarque «La difficulté est venue de ce que Lothaire et Azo n'ont pas eu connaissance de l'estat des

Rommains, desquels ils exposoient les loix et ordonnances, ny pris garde au changement survenu sous les Empereurs». On peut rapprocher ce qu'il expose à propos de l'équité Liv. VI, chap. 6, p. 1022. Si le jurisconsulte doit tenir compte des changements qui surviennent, il n'en convient pas moins de réduire ces changements le plus possible: (Liv. IV, chap. 3, p. 575) «Tout changement de loix qui touchent l'estat est dangereux: car de changer les coutumes et ordonnances concernans les successions, contracts ou servitudes de mal en bien, il est aucunement tolérable: mais de changer les loix qui touchent l'estat, il est aussi dangereux comme de remuer les fondements ou pierres angulaires qui soustiennent le faux du bastiment.»; et un peu plus loin (Liv. IV, chap. 4, p. 591): «La décadence des Républiques vient des nouveaux magistrats qui apportent nouveau conseil, nouveaux desseins, nouvelles loix, nouvelles coustumes, nouveaux édicts, nouveau stile, nouveaux jugements, nouvelles façons, nouveau changement de toutes choses.»

Certains jurisconsultes sont particulièrement appréciés. Dans l'Epistola Vido Fabro sont qualifiés de «principes iuris scientiae» Bartole, Balde, Alexandre, Faure, Paul et Du Moulin; dans divers passages de la *République* nous pouvons récolter des appréciations individuelles: ainsi Alexandre (Liv. I, chap. 9, p. 183) est qualifié le premier jurisconsulte de son âge (voir aussi Liv. III, chap. 3, p. 395 et. Liv. VI, chap. 6, p. 1023) de même Oldrade, dit le premier de son âge Liv. I, chap. 3, p. 21 et Bartole est dit, l'un des premiers jurisconsultes (Liv. III, chap. 7, p. 479), le premier jurisconsulte de son âge (Liv. V, chap. 6, p. 808).

Indépendamment de ces appréciations de valeur, Bodin relève certains éléments d'appréciation de telle ou telle opinion d'un jurisconsulte: ainsi Balde est dit «Iurisconsulte italien et subiect de l'empire» (Liv. I, chap. 9, p. 209) ce qui permet de renforcer l'intérêt de son opinion sur la situation du roi de France; les jurisconsultes italiens sont opposés aux Français, p. ex. Liv. I, chap. 4, p. 37 ou aussi Liv. I, chap. 3, p. 22.

Les termes employés sont ceux de «docteurs en droit» ou «docteurs en loix» ou encore «anciens docteurs»; les romanistes sont les plus souvent cités mais parfois les canonistes en sont distingués et cités à part ou même opposés aux romanistes. Il y a lieu de remarquer d'ailleurs que ces «docteurs» ne sont pas allégués seulement comme commentateurs de textes des compilations de Justinien et pour l'interprétation de ces textes romains, mais aussi pour leurs opinions sur des problèmes propres à leur temps; ils deviennent alors des éléments de documentation sur l'évolution des institutions ou même de droit comparé.

Les auteurs cités sont des auteurs de diverses époques; néanmoins, parmi ceux que nous appelons actuellement les glossateurs, nous ne trouvons qu'Accurse; les références qui le mentionnent nous paraissent se reporter à des opinions de lui dans la glose.

On trouve ensuite, fréquement cités, les maîtres de Bartole: Cinus, Butrigarius, Oldradus et Jacobus de Belvisio, puis Bartole luimême et Balde. Comme auteurs plus récents nous relevons principalement Decius et Alexander (c'est à dire Tartagni); ces deux auteurs sont en premier lieu auteurs de Consilia; or la littérature des Consilia est une des sources fondamentales de Bodin.

On peut se demander si les énumérations de références sont bien le résultat de consultations directes des auteurs; nous pensons que Bodin se reportait à des ouvrages dans lesquels figurent en notes des renvois nombreux. Nous possédons par exemple un recueil de traités «De statutis» imprimé à Lyon en 1552 qui comporte des œuvres d'Alberic de Rosate, de Balde, de Bartole et d'autres auteurs encore; chacun d'eux cite ses prédecesseurs et la présentation de certains de ces écrits (not. en ordre alphabétique) permet de comprendre l'utilisation de tels ouvrages par les auteurs qui disposent d'un arsenal de références et d'opinions très important. C'est là la seule manière d'expliquer les multiples références éparses à certains auteurs.

C'est la littérature des Consilia qui nous paraît constituer le lien entre l'interprétation ou le commentaire des lois romaines et les solutions de la pratique de l'époque de chaque jurisconsulte: ainsi Alexandre est cité comme référence, par un renvoi à un consilium à propos des coutumes de Milan et de Ferrare (Liv. I, chap. 6, p. 95), à propos des commissions rogatoires (Liv. I, chap. 6, p. 99), de même Bartole, Balde, Angelus, Salicetus, Alexandre sont cités sur les villes et communautés d'Italie (Liv. I, chap. 9, p. 183), Alexandre l'étant par un renvoi à un Consilium.

En ce qui concerne les auteurs récents, les citations en sont peu nombreuses et ont plus le caractère de références de droit comparé (p. ex. Zasius: Liv. V, chap. 3, p. 729) ou de références techniques (Choppin, renvoi au *de domanio*, Liv. VI, chap. 2, pp. 860, 863, et 864) ou polémiques (cas d'Hotman, Liv. III, chap. 1, p. 370 et surtout de Cujas à propos d'interprétations textuelles). Les seuls auteurs cités chacun une ou deux fois à titre documentaire et scientifique sont Connan et Tiraqueau. Nous laissons à part Du Moulin qui est allégué comme commentateur du droit des fiefs, comme auteur du traité des usures et annotateur des consilia de Decius. Il est l'auteur contemporain qui se rapproche le plus des préoccupations de Bodin, bien que s'étant surtout attaché au commentaire des coutumes et au droit des fiefs et non aux principes du droit politique.

En conclusion nous pouvons constater l'ampleur de l'information de Bodin sur les matières juridiques: pour lui le droit est la science de la vie en société sous toutes ses formes; toutes les manifestations de la vie des collectivités sociales trouvent leur écho dans les œuvres et les opinions des juristes ou les mesures des législateurs. Cela est vrai pour les siècles passés comme pour l'époque actuelle. Pour les siècles passés les textes juridiques contrôlés et appuyés par tous les témoignages concernant la civilisation d'une époque constituent des sources essentielles et particulièrement digne de foi. Le juriste et le philosophe politique ne doivent pas se contenter de décrire les situations de leur temps mais on doit rechercher les causes des transformations et des évolutions; c'est dans cette recherche que les commentateurs des textes anciens, notamment romains, se révèlent d'une importance essentielle car, partant de texte anciens, ils montrent la permanence de la pensée juridique, le souci de la justice dans des institutions en apparence différentes, mais qui répondent à des soucis analogues de ceux de l'époque même des textes.

Les multiples références ne sont certes pas toutes vérifiées par l'auteur, mais elles proviennent de sources effectivement consultées, elles sont le résultat d'une information très étendue accompagnée d'un travail critique précis et méthodique; il faut se garder de ne les considérer que comme un étalage d'érudition et une simple recherche d'autorités.

IV. BODINS POLITISCHE PHILOSOPHIE

Janine Chanteur

L'Idée de Loi Naturelle dans la République de Jean Bodin

Dès la première définition qui ouvre le livre I, chapitre 1 des «Six Livres de la République», et dont l'ouvrage entier n'est qu'un long commentaire, Jean Bodin pose dans toute sa difficulté, le problème de la *Loi naturelle*. L'affirmation d'un «*droit* gouvernement» renvoie en effet, au niveau même du jugement de valeur qu'elle implique, à un critère, à un «étalon» (pour employer l'expression de M. Léo Strauss),[1] qui ne saurait être de convention. Quelle autorité autre que *naturelle* pourrait servir de référence pour distinguer absolument et sans risque de contradiction le caractère *droit* d'un gouvernement, caractère qui oppose la société politique à toute forme d'association de brigands par exemple, et lui donne cette spécificité qui la sacralise? «Droit gouvernement de plusieurs ménages et de ce qui leur est commun», la République est naturelle à l'homme. Bodin, ce disant, n'innove pas: les théoriciens classiques de la loi naturelle le reconnaîtraient pour l'un de leurs héritiers.

Plus inquiétante, par rapport aux théories antiques ou médiévales, est l'affirmation de la *puissance souveraine*. Certes, elle renvoie à *l'imperium* romain, mais les analyses du chapitre 8 du livre I lui donnent une étendue et une densité telles, qu'évoquer contre elle le droit romain lui-même y est qualifié de «crime de lèse-majesté».[2] En fait, les attributs de la transcendance – cause première, unité principielle des Anciens, ou Dieu des chrétiens, – ne sont-ils pas décernés au pouvoir temporel, en dépit de la finitude de l'homme et de la reconnaissance d'une référence du politique à ce qui n'est pas lui?

Bodin vit une des époques les plus tourmentées de notre histoire. Les guerres d'Italie n'ont provoqué que des désastres, les guerres de religion déchirent le royaume, les horreurs de la Saint-Barthélémy toute proche, les abus de la Ligue, la violence des ouvrages protestants, tout concourt à l'exigence d'un gouvernement juste et fort dont la formule politique soit clairement mise en forme. Plus subtilement peut-être, les influences

---

[1] Léo Strauss, Droit naturel et histoire, Paris 1954, 108.

[2] *Rép.* I, 8, p. 155

culturelles qui ont marqué Bodin – une mère vraisemblablement juive espagnole que lui a légué une parfaite connaissance de l'hébreu, une adhésion possible à la religion réformée en dépit de son rattachement forcé à la Ligue, mais aussi une forte imprégnation catholique tradition-nelle et une longue familiarité avec les auteurs grecs et latins – le situent à une sorte de croisée des chemins: sa conception de la loi de nature est encore celle de ce que l'on peut appeler en gros la tradition classique. Mais déjà elle s'en sépare et elle ouvre la voie à des philosophies qui s'y opposeront. Dans ce XVIᵉ siècle où la brillante unité de doctrine de la Chrétienté achève de se défaire, où surgit un monde nouveau au sein des luttes les plus déchirantes, la philosophie politique de Jean Bodin, telle qu'elle apparaît dans les *Six Livres de la République,* nous pose le pro-blème d'une rupture, d'une conservation et d'un dépassement. Est-il possible d'accepter les prémisses que posaient les théories politiques tradi-tionnelles et d'en tirer des conséquences qui ne sont pas les leurs? Peut-on à la fois définir un *droit gouvernement* qui se réfère à la loi de nature, déchiffrée dans la contemplation des vérités éternelles, révélatrices de l'ordre et de la justice et, toujours au nom de la loi de nature, affirmer la souveraineté absolue et perpétuelle du pouvoir temporel? Quelles en seront les conséquences pour la pensée politique? Ne sera-t-elle pas amenée, par suite de ce glissement de perspectives qui en transforme le sens, à opter pour l'une ou l'autre de ses significations, finissant par nier les implications essentielles de la première, en élaborant une théorie radicalement différente de la loi de nature elle-même, qui porte en germe les futures définitions qu'en donneront les penseurs du XVIIᵉ et du XVIIIᵉ siècles? Jean Bodin serait alors à la charnière de deux mondes, pensant en maintenir l'unité, mais en hâtant l'irrémédiable déchirure. C'est ce que nous voudrions essayer d'étudier à travers les *Six Livres de la République* qui furent une tentative de conciliation, mais peut-être déjà l'annonce et même en partie la théorie de la doctrine nouvelle.

I

Si nous ne trouvons pas à proprement parler de définition explicite de la loi de nature dans la *République,* l'expression elle-même est souvent employée. Bodin parle tantôt de *la* loi de nature, tantôt *des* lois de nature, dans un sens très voisin, en tout cas, sans chercher à noter une différence significative entre l'emploi du singulier et celui du pluriel. Ainsi les «lois sacrées de nature» sont-elles immédiatement affirmées comme discrimina-tives du bien et du mal de la même façon que «le grand Dieu de nature» est défini dans ses attributs «très juste et très sage». Ce qui donne aux lois de nature leur caractère sacré, c'est qu'elles expriment la volonté de Dieu, la «loi éternelle par lui établie». Les deux termes sont à ce point synonymes qu'ils se retrouvent dans le même paragraphe de la Préface.[3] La référence à une *lex aeterna* rattache la *République* à la tradition classique de la loi naturelle et d'ailleurs, dans ce passage, son rôle est à la fois clair et sans originalité: la loi de nature fonde la hiérarchie universelle dans laquelle la politique s'insère harmonieusement: «Car tout ainsi que le grand Dieu de nature très sage et très juste, commande aux Anges, ainsi les Anges commandent aux hommes, les hommes aux bêtes, l'âme au corps, le Ciel à la terre, la raison aux appétits, afin que ce qui est moins habile à commander soit conduit et guidé par celui qui le peut garantir et préserver pour loyer de son obéissance. Mais au contraire, s'il advient que les appétits désobéissent à la raison, les particuliers aux magistrats, les magistrats aux princes, les princes à Dieu, alors on voit que Dieu vient venger ses injures et faire exécuter la loi éternelle par lui établie.»[4] Notons en passant la relation de protection et d'obéissance qui est la raison de toute hiérarchie et qui jouera un rôle important et complexe dans la politique de Jean Bodin.

Comment l'homme connaît-il cette hiérarchie et en vue de quoi Dieu l'a-t-il instituée? En d'autres termes, comment pouvons-nous suivre sans risque d'erreur la loi de nature? D'une part, Bodin ne met pas en doute la Révélation, manifeste à tout homme, et les références aux Tables de la Loi sont très nombreuses, d'autre part la raison humaine, dont il ne fait pas une étude originale et approfondie pour elle-même, est affirmée «conforme à la volonté de Dieu», à condition d'être éduquée pour pouvoir s'exercer. «Nous appelons liberté naturelle, de n'être sujet après Dieu à homme vivant et ne souffrir autre commandement que de soi-même, c'est-à-dire de la raison qui est toujours conforme à la volonté de Dieu. Voilà le premier et le plus ancien commandement qui soit, à savoir de la raison sur l'appétit bestial. Et auparavant qu'on puisse bien commander aux autres, il faut apprendre à commander à soi-même, rendant à la raison la puissance de commander et aux appétits l'obéissance.»[5]

L'homme est libre, d'une liberté naturelle, ce qui revient à dire qu'il est capable de raison, terme qui recouvre ici la maîtrise de soi et le discernement des commandements divins. La pensée de Bodin est proche de celle de Saint-Thomas pour qui «la créature raisonnable est soumise à la divine providence d'une manière plus excellente par le fait qu'elle participe elle-même à cette providence... C'est précisément cette participation à la Loi éternelle qui, dans la créature raisonnable, est appelée

---

[3] *Rép.*, Préface, V f.
[4] *Rép.* Préface, V f.
[5] *Rép.* I, 3, p. 19 f.

la loi naturelle».[6] Il n'y a pas rupture entre le monde et Dieu, la raison humaine est d'essence divine et, comme telle, apte à reconnaître la loi de nature.

Il est vrai qu'elle peut aussi la refuser: si «de leur propriété les choses naturelles suivent l'ordonnance de Dieu immuable», Dieu a «donné à l'homme le choix du bien et du mal, il contrevient le plus souvent à la défense et choisit le pire, contre la loi de Dieu et de nature. Et l'opinion dépravée en lui a tant de pouvoir, qu'elle passe en force de loi qui a plus d'autorité que la nature, de sorte qu'il n'y a si grande impiété ni méchanceté qui ne soit estimée et jugée vertu et piété.»[7] Le fait même que l'homme choisit, implique qu'il peut connaître la loi de nature, il n'est pas condamné à se conduire en aveugle, dans une existence tragique et déchirée parce qu'elle serait ignorante de ses fins. La raison a des repères qui lui permettent d'accéder à la vérité, elle peut toujours les retrouver. C'est pourquoi «le bien en tout ce monde est plus fort et plus puissant que le mal».[8]

Dans un univers ordonné, hiérarchisé, où l'homme occupe une place définie par une transcendance créatrice et organisatrice, dont il peut connaître l'existence par sa raison, le problème politique pose des difficultés plus pratiques que théoriques. Dès que le penseur aura nettement indiqué les fins du politique, qu'il reconnaît en faisant usage de la raison qui éclaire chacun de nous, l'ensemble de la conduite politique sera par là-même discernable elle aussi. Aussi Bodin s'empresse-t-il d'analyser les fins de la République et d'en définir nettement la portée: «Nous mettons cette définition en premier lieu, parce qu'il faut chercher en toute chose la fin principale, et puis après les moyens d'y parvenir. Or la définition n'est autre chose que la fin du sujet qui se présente... Mais qui ne sait la fin et définition du sujet qui lui est proposé, celui-là est hors d'espérance de trouver jamais les moyens d'y parvenir.»[9] L'importance que Bodin assigne à cette fin puisque c'est en la reconnaissant que seront trouvés «les moyens d'y parvenir», c'est-à-dire l'ensemble des différentes relations politiques, la lui fait étudier avant d'avoir analysé l'origine des Républiques. La cause finale est plus déterminante que la cause effective, c'est elle qui donne son sens au corps politique et qui permet d'en découvrir la loi.

La fin de l'Etat politique est en même temps sa félicité; l'adéquation de l'action politique à la fin qu'elle vise (qu'elle ne se donne pas elle-

---

[6] Saint THOMAS D'AQUIN, Somme théologique. La Loi. Q. 91. art. 2. p. 34 Traduction Laversin. Desclées. Paris

[7] *Rép.* I, 5, p. 51.

[8] *Rép.*, Préface, V.

[9] *Rép.* I, 1, p. 1.

même, mais dont elle découvre l'exigence en déchiffrant la loi de nature,
que peut connaître la raison humaine) est plénitude de vie bienheureuse
à la fois pour l'individu et pour l'Etat, qui, dans cette perspective, participent d'une essence identique. Perspective classique de l'unicité d'une
fin qui est reconnaissance et contemplation du principe, de l'unité originelle, de la transcendance qui confère à l'homme et à la société des
hommes même nature parce que même visée du Souverain Bien. L'analyse
évoque celle de Platon, les petites lettres et les grandes lettres de l'alphabet
à travers lesquelles on déchiffre plus aisément la montée ascétique du
sensible à l'intelligible, ascension dont le terme révèle dans la contemplation, l'ordre auquel doit obéir la cité terrestre pour que les hommes
puissent s'ordonner de même, en accord avec leur fin véritable. «Or si
la vraie félicité d'une République et d'un homme seul est tout un, et
que le Souverain Bien de la République en général, aussi bien que d'un
chacun en particulier, gît és-vertus intellectuelles et contemplatives,
comme les mieux entendus l'ont résolu, il faut accorder que ce peuple-là
jouit du Souverain Bien, quand il a ce but devant les yeux, de s'exercer
en la contemplation des choses naturelles, humaines et divines, en
rapportant la louange au grand Prince de nature. Si donc nous confessons
que cela est le but principal de la vie bienheureuse d'un chacun en particulier, nous concluons aussi que c'est la fin et félicité d'une République...
Puisque l'homme sage est la mesure de justice et vérité et que ceux-là qui
sont réputés les plus sages demeurent d'accord que le Souverain Bien
d'un particulier et de la République n'est qu'un, sans faire différence
entre l'homme de bien et le bon citoyen, nous arrêterons là le vrai point
de félicité et le but principal auquel se doit rapporter le droit gouvernement d'une République.»[10] De la finalité métaphysique se déduisent
l'éthique et la politique qui ne s'opposent pas dans un combat sans issue.
Le même homme, capable d'aimer Dieu et de contempler les vérités
éternelles, est homme de bien et bon citoyen. Cette perspective harmonieuse qui définit l'homme et ses activités essentielles par leur fin est
bien celle d'un ordre du monde dont la raison peut connaître le principe
qui est en même temps sa fin, car cet ordre est la loi même de sa nature.

Plus complexe est l'analyse de l'origine de l'Etat politique. Elle est
double et contradictoire.

Les théories antiques d'une unité principielle organisant le monde
envisagent logiquement les phases du devenir politique comme un éloignement progressif du principe. Les sociétés historiques, d'abord très proches
du principe qui leur donne sens, sont telles que ceux qui sont capables
de déchiffrer au mieux l'ordre du monde, ont aussi la charge du pouvoir
temporel ou de l'éducation de ceux qui peuvent l'exercer en vue de sa fin.

---

[10] *Rép.* I, 1, p. 5.

Au point de départ, les conflits sont si peu possibles dans le respect presque parfait de l'ordre, que les mythes de l'Age d'or expriment l'harmonie et le bonheur d'hommes dont les désirs sont en définitive orientés vers la contemplation. La paix nécessaire à cette contemplation a à peine besoin d'être assurée par un gouvernement, la hiérarchie des fonctions et des êtres se conformant aisément à la nature connue des choses. Au fur et à mesure que se déroule le devenir, alors que toute la sagesse de l'Age d'or consiste à conserver une sorte d'immobilité presque a-temporelle, a-politique, l'histoire apparaît comme la dégénérescence de la connaissance et de l'application du principe, c'est pourquoi les philosophies politiques pour lesquelles la loi de nature est assimilable à la raison, définie comme l'aptitude à connaître le principe ordonnant toute chose et visant à le contempler grâce à l'organisation d'une Cité politique qui le reflète dans sa hiérarchie, non seulement ne peuvent concevoir l'histoire comme un progrès, mais au contraire l'envisagent en général comme une lente détérioration à travers des régimes qui s'engendrent l'un l'autre, de plus en plus éloignés de la connaissance principielle. Le seul progrès possible, dans une vision de ce genre, et c'est bien celui que Platon conçoit, – mais il y faut, selon les termes de la lettre VII, «une longue vie d'efforts» – c'est l'ascèse propre au philosophe, capable de redécouvrir le principe, d'acquérir ainsi la «science du gouvernement» dont parlent la *République* et le *Politique* et, grâce à elle, de réinstituer dans le monde l'ordre perdu. La pensée du Moyen-Age va bien dans le même sens puisque, selon la déclaration expresse de Saint-Thomas «les fonctions humaines sont subordonnées à la contemplation comme à une fin supérieure de sorte que, à les considérer comme il faut, toutes semblent au service de ceux qui contemplent la vérité, et que le gouvernement tout entier de la vie civile a, au fond, pour véritable raison d'être, d'assurer la paix nécessaire à cette contemplation.»[11]

Quelle origine Bodin découvre-t-il aux Républiques? Suit-il l'enseignement des Anciens et celui du Moyen-Age, de telle sorte que l'Etat politique, qui a pour fin, selon lui, la contemplation des vérités éternelles lorsqu'il est conforme à la loi de nature, ne soit aussi constitué qu'en référence à elle?

La même expression est employée deux fois dans le 1er livre de la *République*, mais elle désigne deux processus radicalement différents. Les mots «source et origine de la République» sont rapportés d'une part à la famille, qualifiée de «vraie source et origine de toute République et membre principal d'icelle»,[12] conforme à la «Loi de Dieu et de nature»,

---

[11] Cité par RENÉ GUÉNON,, *Autorité spirituelle et pouvoir temporel*, (Véga) Paris, 63.
[12] *Rép.* I, 2, p. 10.

d'autre part, Bodin constate que «la raison et lumière naturelle nous conduit à cela de croire que la force et violence a donné source et origine aux Républiques».[13] Un peu plus loin, commentant les conséquences de cette lutte sans merci qui fait des vainqueurs et des vaincus, des chefs et des esclaves, il insiste: «chose qui ne pouvait se faire que par violence extrême, forçant les lois de nature … Voilà l'origine des Républiques qui peut éclairer la définition du citoyen.»[14] L'homme, être de raison, doué par Dieu d'une liberté naturelle qui n'est autre que l'exercice de sa raison, «toujours conforme à la volonté de Dieu», peut être défini le citoyen de l'Etat politique, d'une part parce qu'il est membre naturel d'une famille, d'autre part, parce que, contre les lois de nature, il fait usage de la force et de la violence qui sont contraires à la raison.

De cette double origine de l'Etat politique vont découler ses caractères et en particulier l'affirmation vigoureuse d'un pouvoir politique aux attributs tels qu'ils nous invitent à concevoir une deuxième acception de la loi de nature qui ne sera pas sans altérer le sens de la finalité même du politique.

II

La famille est naturelle, parce qu'elle est instituée de Dieu, d'abord au niveau le plus élémentaire, mais nécessaire des liens du sang qui créent les affections réciproques. Bodin s'élève contre la communauté platonicienne non seulement parce qu'elle viole la loi de nature qui est le commandement même de Dieu, mais encore parce qu'elle est principe d'indistinction et par conséquent ruine, selon lui, la hiérarchie naturelle conforme à la reconnaissance de la loi de nature.[15] Avec plus de vigueur encore, il attaque les prétentions des anabaptistes dont l'abstraction égalitaire tue jusqu'aux sentiments les plus naturels et rend impossible toute conduite raisonnable qui ne peut que se référer à un ordre,[16] alors que «sous voile d'une exemption de charges et liberté populaire», elle «ouvre la porte à une licencieuse anarchie qui est pire que la plus forte tyrannie du monde».[17]

Mais surtout, la famille est naturelle parce qu'elle est l'expression concrète fondamentale de la loi de nature, de l'ordre du monde: le père «qui est la vraie image du grand Dieu souverain»[18] est hiérarchiquement le premier de la famille. Il en est le Chef, il en a la puissance. C'est aux textes sacrés que Bodin demande les références les plus explicites: «les Hébreux qui montrent toujours la propriété des choses par les noms ont

[13] *Rép.* I, 6, p. 69.
[14] *Rép.* I, 6, p. 69 f.
[15] *Rép.* I, 2, p. 15.

[16] *Rép.* I, 2, p. 16.
[17] *Rép.*, Préface, VII.
[18] *Rép.* I, 4, p. 29.

appelé famille du mot qui signifie chef, seigneur, prince, nommant la famille par le chef d'icelle.»[19] Et encore: «or la loi de Dieu et la langue sainte qui a nommé toute chose selon la vraie nature et propriété, appelle le mari Bahal, c'est-à-dire le seigneur et maître pour montrer qu'à lui appartient de commander.»[20] S'il est le maître, c'est qu'il représente le commandement «de l'âme sur le corps, de la raison sur la cupidité»,[21] dit Bodin, plaçant ainsi la femme sous la puissance maritale, avant de ployer les enfants sous la domination du père. Cette hiérarchie naturelle de la famille justifie *ipso facto* la puissance du père de famille et assure aux familles des droits dont certains seront imprescriptibles dans l'Etat politique.

La relation naturelle du Chef de famille et de ses sujets, posée déjà dans la définition du «ménage» comme «un droit gouvernement de plusieurs sujets sous l'obéissance d'un chef de famille et de ce qui lui est propre»,[22] (et c'est ainsi comprise que la famille est «la vraie source et origine de toute République»), est une relation de commandement et d'obéissance aux nuances multiples. Si le père, image de Dieu, commande et que les membres de la famille, (femme, enfants, serviteurs, voire esclaves) lui obéissent comme des *sujets*, c'est parce que «le droit gouvernement du père et des enfants gît à *bien* user de la puissance que Dieu a donnée au père sur ses enfants».[23] De nouveau, l'idée de *droit gouvernement* fait appel à une référence d'ordre transcendant, explicitement désignée. Le père connaît les commandements divins, il est le dépôt, l'interprète et le garant de la loi de nature pour ses sujets à la raison trop débile pour la déchiffrer, bien qu'elle s'impose à eux comme à lui. C'est pourquoi la puissance du père apparaît d'abord et essentiellement sous la forme d'une obligation, d'un devoir du Chef de famille envers ses sujets. «Et tout ainsi que nature oblige le père à nourrir l'enfant, tant qu'il est impuissant, et l'instruire en tout honneur et vertu...»[24] N'est-ce pas reconnaître implicitement, car Bodin ne le dit pas expressément, un *droit des sujets,* issu de l'obligation du Chef? «Aussi, continue Bodin, l'enfant est obligé, mais beaucoup plus étroitement, d'aimer, révérer, servir, nourrir le père, et ployer sous ses mandements en toute obéissance, supporter, cacher et couvrir toutes les infirmités et imperfections et n'épargner jamais ses biens, ni son sang, pour sauver et entretenir la vie de celui duquel il tient la sienne. Laquelle obligation, ores qu'elle soit scellée du sceau de nature, voire qu'elle porte exécution parée, si est-ce toutefois pour montrer combien elle est grande, il n'y en a point de plus certain argument que le premier commandement de la Seconde Table,

---

[19] *Rép.* I, 2, p. 12.
[20] *Rép.* I, 3, p. 27 f.
[21] *Rép.* I, 3, p. 20.

[22] *Rép.* I, 2, p. 10.
[23] *Rép.* I, 4, p. 29.
[24] *Rép.* I, 4, p. 29.

et seul en tous les dix articles du Décalogue qui porte son loyer: combien qu'il n'est dû aucun loyer à celui qui est obligé de faire quelque chose mêmement par obligation si étroite que toutes les lois divines et humaines en sont pleines.»[25] La relation du Chef de famille à ses sujets, celle des sujets au Chef de famille, est donc une relation d'obligation, de devoir réciproque. Seulement, tandis que deux lignes (dans l'édition de 1580) suffisent à Bodin pour énoncer l'obligation du père, douze suffisent à peine pour édicter celle du fils. Les mots eux-mêmes sont bien différents: le père est obligé envers l'enfant encore impuissant, le fils est obligé à vie. Certes les deux obligations sont «de nature», mais tandis que celle du père aura toujours pour «loyer» celle du fils, cette dernière a la forme d'un devoir pur et pour la rendre encore plus formidable, appel est fait au Décalogue. Qu'est-ce à dire, sinon que la relation d'obligation réciproque qui unit le Chef de famille à ses sujets est une relation foncièrement inégalitaire, parce que l'essence de la famille est d'être une hiérarchie, un ordre réglé par la loi naturelle? Bodin ira même jusqu'à invoquer «la loi de Dieu et de nature» pour demander le rétablissement de la puissance de la vie et de la mort qu'il souhaite voir rendue aux pères de famille.[26]

Au rapport du commandement et de l'obéissance, correspond celui de l'obligation à la protection et de l'obligation à la fidélité. Il s'agit donc d'un ordre dans lequel, à des fonctions différentes, correspondent des devoirs différents. La hiérarchie n'a rien d'arbitraire, sa raison est claire, c'est celle qui consiste à reconnaître, sous une essence spécifique, commune à tous les hommes – l'aptitude à la raison, la liberté de vivre selon la raison, mais aussi la liberté de choisir contre la raison – des différences concrètes dans les propriétés de chacun, et l'organisation de notre monde de la finitude ne respecte l'ordre immuable qu'exige la loi naturelle, que dans la mesure où elle respecte d'abord cette hiérarchie des fonctions et des personnes en vue d'accomplir la loi, autant qu'il est possible.

En première analyse, et dans la mesure où «la famille est la vraie source et origine de toute République», «les piliers d'icelle»,[27] le pouvoir politique peut relever de la même interprétation. Bodin a indiqué dès la Préface, qu'il a commencé à étudier la famille «et continuant par ordre à la souveraineté, discourant de chacun membre de la République ...»[28] Le plan qu'il a suivi procède par élargissement et attribution à l'Etat de ce qui est vrai pour la famille. Ils sont tous deux de même nature. L'homme de bien et le bon citoyen sont tout un. La puissance du Souverain, quelle que soit la forme du gouvernement, est le fait de sa fonction qui le place au som-

---

[25] *Rép.* I, 4, p. 29 f.
[26] *Rép.* I, 4, p. 32.

[27] *Rép.* I, 2, p. 10 et I, 4, p. 34.
[28] *Rép.*, Préface, III.

met de la hiérarchie. Seules, les démocraties, parce qu'elles sont égalitaires, ne sauraient avoir «un droit gouvernement», sinon dans la mesure où elles rétablissent des «états» comme le fit Platon: «Et quoi que Platon s'efforçât de faire tous les citoyens de sa République égaux en tous droits et prérogatives, si est-ce qu'il les a divisés en trois états, à savoir en gardes, en gens d'armes et laboureurs qui est pour montrer qu'il n'y eut oncques République soit vraie ou imaginaire, voire la plus populaire qu'on peut penser où les citoyens soient égaux en tous droits et prérogatives mais toujours les uns ont eu plus ou moins que les autres.»[29]

La relation du Souverain et des sujets est une relation de protection et d'obéissance. Parce que le souverain a un devoir de protection, les sujets ont un devoir d'obéissance. C'est encore le devoir du Souverain qui implique les droits des sujets à la sûreté et à la liberté. Cette relation est affirmée avec force. Elle seule permet l'harmonieuse réalisation de la loi de nature dans un Etat justement ordonné en vue de ses fins ultimes: «Le mot de protection en général, s'étend à tous sujets qui sont en l'obéissance d'un Prince ou seigneurie souveraine. Comme nous avons dit que le Prince est obligé de maintenir par la force des armes et des lois ses sujets en sûreté de leurs personnes, biens et familles, et les sujets par obligation réciproque doivent à leur Prince foi, sujétion, obéissance, aide et secours. C'est la première et la plus forte protection qui soit, car la protection des maîtres envers leurs esclaves, des patrons envers leurs affranchis, des seigneurs envers leurs vassaux est beaucoup moindre que des Princes envers leurs sujets.»[30]

Protection très différente de celle qui s'étend aux pays alliés et que garantissent les traités, laquelle est sans réciprocité, autre que l'honneur et la reconnaissance qu'en tire le Prince protecteur.

Mais l'analyse est en réalité plus complexe et fait intervenir un autre élément qui transforme grandement cette vision, somme toute féodale, d'un pouvoir dont la légitimité est fondée sur l'obligation à la protection des personnes et des biens en échange de l'obéissance des sujets et de leur fidélité. Les Républiques n'ont pas seulement une source pure, selon la loi de nature. Elles se sont instituées par force et violence, forçant la loi elle-même. Les chefs de famille, vivant dans un état pré-politique mal défini se sont battus. Il y eut des vainqueurs, il y eut des vaincus. Parmi les vainqueurs, un homme, quelques hommes à la rigueur, ont déterminé la victoire par la violence de leur action. Il est ou ils sont les chefs, car le succès les a imposés. «Car auparavant qu'il n'y eût ni cité ni citoyen, ni forme aucune de République entre les hommes, chacun chef de famille était souverain en sa maison, ayant puissance de vie et de mort sur sa

---

[29] *Rép.* I, 6, p. 100.
[30] *Rép.* I, 7, p. 101.

femme et sur ses enfants. Et depuis que la force, la violence, l'ambition, l'avarice, la vengeance eurent armé les uns contre les autres, l'issue des guerres et combats, donnant la victoire aux uns, rendait les autres esclaves. Et entre les vainqueurs, celui qui était élu chef et capitaine et sous la conduite duquel les autres avaient eu la victoire, continuait en la puissance de commander les uns comme aux fidèles et loyaux sujets, aux autres comme aux esclaves. Alors la pleine et entière liberté que chacun avait de vivre en son plaisir, sans être commandé de personne fut tournée en pure servitude et du tout ôtée aux vaincus et diminuée pour le regard des vainqueurs, en ce qu'ils prêtaient obéissance à leur chef souverain, et celui qui ne voulait quitter quelque chose de sa liberté pour vivre sous les lois et commandements d'autrui, la perdait du tout. Ainsi le mot de seigneur et de serviteur, de Prince et de sujet, auparavant inconnus, furent mis en usage. La raison et lumière naturelle nous conduit à cela de croire que la force et violence a donné source et origine aux Républiques.»[31]

Voilà la source impure des Etats politiques. Alors qu'ils sont fondés en droit sur une finalité qui hiérarchise la famille et les ordonne de même, suivant le modèle qu'elle présente, alors que cet ordre relève de la loi naturelle qu'il concrétise, ils sont fondés en fait contre la loi de nature, par la force et la violence qui caractérisent les hommes au moins autant que la raison: «Les premiers hommes n'avaient point d'honneur et de vertu plus grande que de tuer, massacrer, voler ou asservir les hommes.»[32]

Aussi l'état prépolitique n'a-t-il rien d'un Age d'or, l'histoire qu'il inaugure n'est pas l'éloignement progressif d'un paradis perdu: «En quoi il appert que Démosthène, Aristote et Cicéron se sont mépris, suivant l'erreur d'Hérodote qui dit que les premiers rois ont été choisis pour leur justice et vertu, aux temps qu'ils ont figuré héroïques.»[33] L'image du Monarque exerçant le pouvoir politique en même temps qu'il détient l'autorité spirituelle, ou de celui à qui cette même autorité confère le pouvoir parce qu'il est le plus apte à déchiffrer l'ordre du monde, s'efface.

Pour ces premiers hommes plus avides de massacres que soucieux d'obéir à la loi de nature, asservir et dominer est la fin primordiale. Ainsi dans un second temps de l'analyse que Bodin n'indique pas avec netteté, mais qu'il nous a paru possible de discerner, des attributs du père de famille est abstrait et porté à l'absolu un seul caractère: la puissance. Certes, c'est elle qui, dans la vision hiérarchisée selon le juste, fait déjà l'unité de la famille. Bodin n'a eu garde de l'omettre dans la définition même de la famille, mais sa légitimité était assurée, son étendue n'était pas arbitraire, elle était bornée par les sentiments d'affection naturelle qui naissent au sein d'une famille. La souveraineté du chef d'Etat ne peut se

---

[31] *Rép.* I, 6, p. 68/9.
[32] *Rép.* I, 6, p. 69.
[33] *Rép.* I, 6, p. 69.

défaire de son origine contre-nature, et si – nous le verrons – Bodin la rattache expressément à la loi de nature, elle perdra si peu le souvenir de sa source impure, que c'est la loi de nature elle-même qui changera de sens. Car le passage de l'état pré-politique à l'Etat politique est un passage violent. La puissance est d'abord arbitraire et due aux hasards des combats. Aucune intention organisatrice ne la confère.

Tout le système politique se ressent de l'usage de la force qui est à l'origine des Républiques. Le citoyen, d'abord défini comme le protégé naturel du souverain, ce qui impliquait puissance du souverain et obéissance du citoyen, mais aussi reconnaissance de ses droits, est désormais un sujet. «Franc sujet» car il n'est pas parmi les vaincus du combat qui ne sont jamais que des esclaves. Vainqueur, il s'incline devant la force de celui qui lui a permis la victoire et il est défini non plus à partir d'une relation hiérarchique qui a sa racine dans la loi de nature, mais à partir de la puissance elle-même qui s'intitule *souveraineté* et dont les deux attributs, nouveaux par rapport à la définition antérieure, et, il faut bien le dire, exorbitants, la qualifient d'«absolue et perpétuelle».[34]

Ainsi se limite la naturelle autarchie du Chef de famille, ainsi s'affirme l'omnipotence du Chef d'Etat: «Or quand le Chef de famille vient à sortir de sa maison où il commande, pour traiter et négocier avec les autres chefs de famille de ce qui leur touche à tous en général, alors il dépouille le titre de maître, de chef, de seigneur, pour être compagnon, pair et associé avec les autres: laissant sa famille pour entrer en la cité, et les affaires domestiques, pour traiter les publiques: et au lieu de seigneur, il s'appelle citoyen qui n'est autre chose en propres termes que le franc sujet tenant de la souveraineté d'autrui.»[35] Que la puissance souveraine fasse le citoyen est répété sans changement et analysé très longuement aussi bien au chapitre VI de la *Methodus ad facilem historiarum cognitionem* que dans les longs chapitres consacrés à la définition différentielle du citoyen dans la *République*.[36] Nous pourrions prendre au hasard n'importe laquelle des très nombreuses définitions, toujours revient comme un leitmotiv le requisit essentiel de la puissance souveraine qui fait le citoyen. Définition qui n'exclut pas la précédente selon laquelle ce qui fait le citoyen, c'est «l'obligation mutuelle du souverain au sujet, auquel pour la foi et obéissance qu'il reçoit, il doit justice, conseil, confort, aide et protection, ce qui n'est point dû aux étrangers».[37] Mais la nouvelle définition risque fort de l'emporter sur la première. En effet, les droits reconnus implicitement au citoyen par la définition «naturelle» se transforment explicitement en

---

[34] *Rép.* I, 8, p. 122.
[35] *Rép.* I, 6, p. 68.
[36] *Methodus* ch. VI 350. PUF. Paris, et *République* I, 6–7.
[37] *Rép.* I, 6, p. 85.

privilèges. «Est appelé citoyen qui a quelque privilège particulier.»[38] «Ce mot de citoyen a je ne sais quoi de plus spécial à nous que le mot de bourgeois et c'est proprement le sujet naturel qui a droit de corps et collège ou quelques autres privilèges qui ne sont point communiqués aux bourgeois.»[39] Et si Bodin ajoute quelques pages plus loin: «Si les prérogatives et privilèges que les uns ont par-dessus les autres faisaient le citoyen, les étrangers et alliés seraient citoyens . . .»,[40] c'est justement pour montrer que le privilège n'est pas la définition essentielle du citoyen, mais bien qu'il est octroyé à celui dont la définition même est de tenir de la souveraineté d'autrui: «C'est pourquoi nous avons dit que le citoyen est le franc sujet tenant de la souveraineté d'autrui.»[41] Ainsi se diversifient les citoyens, selon leurs prérogatives et privilèges qu'ils tiennent de la souveraineté: «Si nous suivions la variété des privilèges pour juger la définition du citoyen, il se trouverait cinquante mille définitions du citoyen pour la diversité infinie des prérogatives que les citoyens ont les uns sur les autres.»[42] Ces différences dans les privilèges s'ordonnent à leur tour selon des classes: «Quant aux différences des sujets entre eux, il n'y en a pas moins en plusieurs lieux qu'il y a entre les étrangers et les sujets. J'en ai remarqué quelques-uns des Nobles aux roturiers, des majeurs aux mineurs, des hommes aux femmes et de la qualité d'un chacun. Et pour le faire court, il se peut faire en termes de droit qu'entre les citoyens les uns soient exempts de toutes charges, tailles et impôts auxquels les autres seront sujets. Nous en avons une infinité d'exemples en nos lois, comme aussi la société est bonne et valable où l'un des associés a part au profit et ne porte rien du dommage. C'est pourquoi nous voyons la distinction des citoyens en trois états, à savoir l'Ecclésiastique, la Noblesse et le Peuple qui est gardée presque en toute l'Europe.»[43] Voici observée et légitimée la hiérarchie sociale, à partir des privilèges conférés par le Souverain. On est en droit de se demander si elle recouvre exactement la hiérarchie naturelle, si elle correspond à des devoirs, à des *officia* qui distinguent les personnes et les corps politiques selon leur aptitude à bien remplir leur fonction. Bodin réaffirme la relation mutuelle de protection et d'obéissance qui unit le souverain au sujet,[44] mais cette relation n'est plus qu'un aspect de la hiérarchie politique, l'autre aspect, par la théorie de la puissance absolue et des privilèges qu'elle octroie, risque fort de la dénaturer.

La définition que Bodin donne de la souveraineté au début du chapitre VIII du Livre I se réfère aux Latins, aux Grecs et aux Hébreux. Un des termes grecs qu'il transcrit signifie à la fois «commandement» et «com-

---

[38] *Rép.* I, 6, p. 73.
[39] *Rép.* I, 6, p. 73.
[40] *Rép.* I, 6, p. 84.
[41] *Rép.* I, 6, p. 83.

[42] *Rép.* I, 6. p. 92.
[43] *Rép.* I. 6, p. 100.
[44] *Rép.* I, 7, p. 101.

mencement». La souveraineté apparaît désormais comme le fondement de la République, sa «vraie source et origine», celle qui, faisant son unité, lui donne l'être et l'existence. C'est elle qui définit les différents éléments du corps politique et leurs relations. Sa marque la plus évidente, parce qu'elle n'est «limitée ni en puissance, ni en charge, ni à certain temps»,[45] c'est «cette même puissance de donner et casser la loi» sous laquelle «sont compris tous les autres droits et marques de souveraineté: de sorte qu'à parler proprement, on peut dire qu'il n'y a que cette seule marque de souveraineté, attendu que tous les autres droits sont compris en celui-là.»[46] Aussi les lois ne dépendent-elles que de «la pure et franche volonté» du souverain, lequel «ne peut se lier les mains, quand ores il le voudrait».[47] En dépit de l'importance reconnue aux «états de tout le peuple», «le point principal de la majesté souveraine et puissance absolue gît principalement à donner lois aux sujets en général, sans leur consentement».[48]

La théorie de la souveraineté entraîne celle des charges et magistratures: le Sénat par exemple ne peut que donner des conseils. «La raison principale pourquoi le Sénat d'une République ne doit pas avoir commandement est que s'il avait puissance de commander ce qu'il conseille, la souveraineté serait au conseil, et les conseillers d'état au lieu de conseillers seraient maîtres, ayant le maniement des affaires et puissance d'en ordonner à leur plaisir: chose qui ne se peut faire sans diminution, ou pour mieux dire, éversion de la majesté qui est si haute et si sacrée qu'il n'appartient à sujets quels qu'ils soient, d'y toucher ni près, ni loin.»[49] Il serait même contraire à la «raison naturelle» que la souveraineté fût compatible avec l'obligation pour le Prince d'être soumis à ses propres lois.[50] La souveraineté ne rencontre d'autre limite que «la loi de Dieu et de nature», dont personne, à part le Prince, ne semble pouvoir exiger le respect. En effet, si «tous les Princes de la terre sont sujets aux lois de Dieu et de nature»,[51] si «le Prince souverain ne peut donner grâce de la peine établie par Dieu, non plus qu'il ne peut dispenser de la loi de Dieu, à laquelle il est sujet»,[52] aucun homme n'a le droit ou le pouvoir de lui demander une justification quelconque, «il n'est tenu rendre compte qu'à Dieu».[53]

Volonté du Souverain d'une part, soumission des sujets de l'autre, le ressort de la hiérarchie politique, d'abord définie dans une relation de protection et de fidélité, légitimée par la finalité de l'Etat, se retrouve tout entier tendu par la volonté souveraine du Prince, qui est bien tenu à l'observance de la loi naturelle, mais qui, dans le monde politique lui-même

---

[45] *Rép.* I, 8, p. 124.
[46] *Rép.* I, 10, p. 223.
[47] *Rép.* I, 8, p. 132/3.
[48] *Rép.* I, 8, p. 142.
[49] *Rép.* III, 1, p. 371.

[50] *Rép.* I, 8, p. 145.
[51] *Rép.* I, 8, p. 131.
[52] *Rép.* I, 10, p. 240.
[53] *Rép.* I, 8, p. 125.

n'a aucune preuve à donner de sa propre fidélité, sinon au niveau de ses contrats – que Bodin distingue soigneusement des lois,[54] – du respect possible de certaines coutumes[55] et d'une reconnaissance du bien d'autrui qu'il est contraire à la nature de s'approprier, «vu que c'est plutôt impuissance, faiblesse et lâcheté de cœur».[56]

Le sujet n'a aucun droit de révolte, aussi légitime qu'il puisse paraître dans un monde qui ne dit la raison de son ordre que par la volonté légiférante d'un homme: «il n'est pas licite au sujet de contrevenir aux lois, sous voile d'honneur et de justice ... et ne lui appartient pas à fonder sa convention en l'équité naturelle ... car la loi qui défend est plus forte que l'équité apparente, si la défense n'était directement contraire à la loi de Dieu et de nature.»[57] Aucune «autorité spirituelle» n'est garante ici-bas de la droiture du pouvoir politique. L'Eglise est étrangement absente de l'œuvre de Jean Bodin. Le Sacre des rois de France ne le retient qu'autant qu'il lui permet d'affirmer une fois de plus que le Souverain n'est pas tenu à ses lois.[58] Il ne l'interprète pas comme une initiation par laquelle «l'oint du Seigneur» reçoit en dépôt la couronne des mains d'une autorité à laquelle il se soumettrait naturellement parce qu'elle serait en mesure de connaître le plus adéquatement le principe transcendant.

Certes, le Monarque tient de Dieu seul «le sceptre et la puissance», c'est pourquoi il ne doit serment qu'à Dieu.[59] Mais entre Dieu et lui, aucun intermédiaire ne s'interpose: une *volonté* qui doit reconnaître la loi de nature décide de son interprétation et l'impose dans les lois positives, aucun savoir d'origine spirituelle ne l'éclaire nécessairement. Certes, Bodin ne pouvait trouver pareille théorie de la souveraineté ni chez Platon, ni chez Aristote, ni chez les penseurs du Moyen-Age, ni même dans le droit romain, qu'il éprouve précisément le besoin d'éliminer après avoir rattaché sa théorie de la souveraineté à l'*imperium* romain.[60] Le Prince Souverain est «l'image de Dieu en terre» aussi «afin qu'on puisse connaître celui qui est tel, c'est-à-dire Prince Souverain, il faut savoir les marques qui ne soient point communes aux autres sujets»,[61] marques qui permettent d'éviter de confondre «celui qui donne la loi, avec celui qui la reçoit, celui qui commande avec celui qui doit obéissance».[62] Le rapport de commandement et d'obéissance ne trouve vraiment sa définition qu'ainsi institué par la souveraineté, ou volonté toute puissante et absolue de celui qui incarne le pouvoir politique. Et Bodin, selon la logique de sa pensée, note que si le pouvoir absolu et perpétuel est exercé «par force, cela s'appelle

---

[54] *Rép.* I, 8, p. 134/5.
[55] *Rép.* I, 10, p. 222.
[56] *Rép.* I, 8, p. 156.
[57] *Rép.* I, 8, p. 151/2.
[58] *Rép.* I, 8, p. 135/6.

[59] *Rép.* I, 8, p. 143.
[60] *Rép.* I, 8, p. 155.
[61] *Rép.* I, 10, p. 212.
[62] *Rép.* I, 10, p. 214.

tyrannie et néanmoins le tyran est Souverain, tout ainsi que la possession violente du prédateur est vraie et possession naturelle quoiqu'elle soit contre la loi».[63] Ne retrouvons-nous pas ici l'origine impure de l'Etat politique, celle qui a érigé le fait en droit, justement en faisant la théorie de la souveraineté effective du vainqueur s'exerçant sur des sujets et sur des esclaves?

Il est vrai que depuis, cette brutale affirmation du pouvoir a rencontré sa finalité. Reconnaissant la lex aeterna, le souverain est de droit le protecteur des sujets qui lui obéissent. Mais cette reconnaissance est laissée à sa volonté plus qu'à une science contrôlée, elle n'est efficace que parce qu'il possède la force. La Monarchie est de droit divin, mais absolue. Les intermédiaires naturels entre la fin des sociétés politiques et l'ensemble de leur organisation tendent à s'effacer. En dépit des survivances d'un monde qui disparaît, le pouvoir politique se centralise, attirant à lui les attributs auxquels il n'aurait pu prétendre, quand il les regardait comme appartenant à la seule transcendance.

Les conséquences qui s'ensuivent de la définition de la République par le moyen de la souveraineté transforment à tel point la vision du politique qu'on peut se demander si sa finalité garde la fonction que Bodin lui assignait, lorsqu'il en faisait le principe directeur de toute philosophie politique. «Si elle n'est bien fondée, tout ce qui sera bâti sur icelle, se ruinera bientôt après», écrivait-il dans les premières lignes du premier chapitre.[64] Or, le principe qui distingue les différents régimes n'est pas la fin de l'Etat politique. Bodin critique vigoureusement Platon, Aristote et leurs successeurs, qui ont classé les régimes selon le Juste. Pour lui, la seule distinction susceptible «d'éviter la confusion et obscurité qui provient de la variété des gouverneurs bons ou mauvais»[65] est la distinction selon le nombre de ceux «qui tiennent la souveraineté». Elle est donc désormais principe directeur, plus important pour l'intelligence du système politique que la finalité elle-même. Et Bodin écrit étrangement: «Puis donc que la qualité ne change point la nature des choses, nous dirons qu'il n'y a que trois Etats ou trois sortes de Républiques, à savoir la Monarchie, l'Aristocratie et la Démocratie.»[66] La considération de la qualité n'est réintroduite que secondairement et comme de biais, dans la distinction des «gouvernements» à l'intérieur des régimes, selon que le souverain gouverne ou non en fonction de la loi de nature établissant une hiérarchie selon la justice, qui attache aux diverses fonctions les compétences requises. Encore est-ce la souveraineté qu'il peut seul incarner, qui le permet. «Le Monarque souverain se peut joindre à la plus saine et meilleure partie et faire choix des hommes sages et entendus aux affaires d'état, où la nécessité

---

[63] *Rép.* I, 8, p. 126.
[64] *Rép.* I, 1, p. 1.

[65] *Rép.* II, 1, p. 252.
[66] *Rép.* II, 1, p. 252.

contraint en l'état populaire et aristocratique, de recevoir au conseil et aux états, les sages et fols ensemble. Aussi est-il impossible au peuple et aux seigneurs de commander par puissance souveraine, ni faire aucun acte qui ne se peut faire que par une personne.»[67] Et c'est encore la théorie de la souveraineté qui, en définitive, oriente la préférence de Bodin pour l'Etat monarchique de gouvernement royal: «Mais le principal point de la République, qui est le droit de souveraineté, ne peut être ni subsister à proprement parler, sinon en la monarchie, car nul ne peut être souverain en une République qu'un seul. S'ils sont deux, trois ou plusieurs, pas un n'est souverain, d'autant que pas un seul ne peut donner ni recevoir loi de son compagnon. Et combien qu'on imagine un corps de plusieurs seigneurs ou d'un peuple tenir la souveraineté, si est-ce qu'elle n'a point de vrai sujet ni d'appui, s'il n'y a un chef avec puissance souveraine, pour unir les uns avec les autres: ce que ne peut faire un simple Magistrat sans puissance souveraine.»[68] L'unité du corps politique, son existence véritable, a donc pour fondement premier la souveraineté, définie comme volonté d'un seul homme, plutôt que la relation des citoyens hiérarchisés par l'exigence de leur finalité.

Non que Bodin renonce à la finalité de l'Etat politique, mais elle a changé de caractère. Sous le nom de «justice harmonique», il entend «ces quatre points ensemble, à savoir Loi, Equité, Exécution de la loi et devoir du Magistrat, soit en la distribution de la justice, soit au gouvernement de l'Etat.»[69] Or «cela touche les droits de la majesté souveraine ... les Princes s'attribuèrent la déclaration et correction des lois, en ce qui serait douteux entre la loi et l'équité résultant de la vraie interprétation de la loi.»[70] C'est donc le Prince, et le Prince seul, qui institue la fin de la République, qui ordonne une hiérarchie: «Il faut donc que le sage Roi gouverne son Royaume harmonieusement, entremêlant doucement les Nobles et les roturiers, les riches et les pauvres, avec telle discrétion toutefois que les Nobles aient quelque avantage sur les roturiers: car c'est bien la raison que le gentilhomme aussi excellent en armes ou en lois comme le roturier, soit préféré aux états de judicature ou de la guerre. Et que le riche égal en autre chose au pauvre soit aussi préféré aux états qui ont plus d'honneur que de profit et que le pauvre emporte les offices qui ont plus de profit que d'honneur et tous deux seront contents, car celui qui est assez riche ne cherche que l'honneur et le pauvre cherche son profit.»[71] C'est «le Prince élevé par dessus tous les sujets, la majesté duquel ne souffre non plus de division, que l'unité qui n'est point nombre, ni au rang des nombres, jaçait que tous les autres n'ont force ni puissance que de

---

[67] *Rép.* VI, 4, p. 962/3.
[68] *Rép.* VI, 4, p. 961/2.
[69] *Rép.* VI, 6, p. 1020.

[70] *Rép.* VI, 6, p. 1024.
[71] *Rép.* VI, 6, p. 1054.

l'unité»[72] qui, après avoir défini sa souveraineté «absolue et perpétuelle», joue, comme unité qui n'est point nombre, le rôle du principe transcendant. Et Bodin conclut logiquement: «aussi un Prince souverain est nécessaire, de la puissance duquel dépendent tous les autres.»[73] N'est-ce pas affirmer, en dépit de la référence constante aux vérités éternelles, l'autonomie pleinement conquise du pouvoir politique? Quelque forme qu'il prenne désormais, il est devenu la référence suprême. La limite que Bodin lui impose encore, en rattachant la volonté du Prince à celle de Dieu peut s'estomper. Le pouvoir politique est, par lui, armé et défini pour organiser le royaume de ce monde. Il est «l'intellect indivisible pur et simple...» qui unit toutes les parties et les accorde ensemble.»[74] Certes, Bodin croit encore que la loi naturelle est la raison humaine, dans la mesure où elle participe de la loi éternelle, mais si la restriction disparaît, il ne restera que la raison humaine, ou, pour mieux dire, la volonté humaine dotée du plus formidable pouvoir législatif et contraignant qu'on puisse imaginer. La politique, œuvre de la finitude, pourra s'ériger en absolu. Dans les *Six Livres de la République*, la rupture n'est pas consommée, elle s'esquisse: la leçon sera entendue.

---

[72] *Rép.* VI, 6, p. 1056.
[73] *Rép.* VI, 6, p. 1057.
[74] *Rép.* VI, 6, p. 1057.

Jürgen Dennert

Bemerkungen zum politischen Denken Jean Bodins

Seit dem 1914 erschienenen Werk Roger Chauvirés über Jean Bodin[1] hat sich die Forschung zunehmend mit dem universalen Gelehrten beschäftigt. Im Mittelpunkt der meisten Untersuchungen steht Bodin als politischer Theoretiker oder als Rechts- und Geschichtslehrer. Der Schwerpunkt der Literatur liegt also in jenen Bereichen, in denen Bodin vor allem gearbeitet und veröffentlicht hat. Ein erheblicher Teil dieser Analysen bleibt immanent. Man kommentiert Teile seines Werkes, legt einzelne Begriffe aus oder stellt Einflüsse anderer Autoren auf Bodin, bzw. Bodins auf andere Theoretiker fest.

Ich möchte versuchen, einen kleinen Schritt darüber hinaus zu tun, nämlich darzustellen, in welcher Weise sich zwei spezifische Richtungen der Wissenschaft und ihrer Methoden in bestimmten Teilen seines politischen Hauptwerkes, der *République,* überschneiden: Einmal die aristotelische Politiktradition, zum anderen der methodische Einfluß der Neuzeit.

Der Wissenschaftsbegriff Bodins, das wissen wir spätestens seit der ausgezeichneten Analyse von Georg Roellenbleck, ist bei Bodin zunächst noch einheitlich im Sinne der auf Aristoteles zurückgehenden Tradition, er ist kosmisch oder organisch und damit universal. «Die Wissenschaft (bei Bodin, J. D.) ist *eine,* weil der Kosmos, ihr Gegenstand, ein von einheitlichen Gesetzen beherrschtes Ganzes ist. Es ist ein Bau aus einander ähnlichen Stufen, in dem das Niedere das Höhere widerspiegelt. Alle Verschiedenheit ist gefaßt in dem Gesetz der Harmonie»,[2] schreibt Roellenbleck.

Läßt sich schon der Gedanke einer derartigen Weltauffassung bis auf Aristoteles (und weiter zurück) verfolgen, so geschieht auch das Erfassen der Erscheinungen dieser Welt bei Bodin in einer Weise, die seit Aristoteles noetisches Denken heißt.[3] In den Worten Roellenblecks: «Infolge-

---

[1] ROGER CHAUVIRÉ [76], Jean Bodin, auteur de la République, Paris 1914.

[2] GEORG ROELLENBLECK [239], Offenbarung, Natur und jüdische Überlieferung bei Jean Bodin, Gütersloh 1964, 29. Vgl. auch sein Literaturverzeichnis, 155 ff. und seinen Literaturbericht in: *Der Staat* 2/3 (1963/4)[231].

[3] Über Einzelheiten vgl. KLAUS OEHLER, Die Lehre vom noetischen und dianoetischen Denken bei Platon und Aristoteles, München 1962; JÜRGEN DENNERT, Die aristotelisch-ontologische Politikwissenschaft und die rationale Philosophie von Descartes bis Kant, Berlin 1970.

dessen beherrscht Bodin der Gedanke, die Grundgesetze der Welt ließen sich in *einem* Zugriff erfassen, man werde dann der Elemente ansichtig, aus denen der Kosmos erbaut sei. Daß es bei seiner Welterkenntnis ganz und gar um das Erfassen des Sinns und Wesens der Erscheinungen geht ... daß sichtbar werden soll, was jede Eigentümlichkeit an den Dingen und Ereignissen *bedeutet*, das heißt also, welche theologischen, psychologischen, moralischen usw. Wahrheiten sie ausdrücken ... davon wird noch öfter zu reden sein.»[4]

Doch mit dieser Vorbemerkung ist erst die eine Koordinate im Denken Bodins gefunden: seine Bindung an die traditionelle, noch immer aristotelisch-universalistisch bestimmte Denkweise. Wie aber verhält sich sein Denken zu den Kategorien der heraufkommenden Naturwissenschaft, denen dann einige Jahrzehnte später Denker wie Descartes und Hobbes so hohen Tribut gezollt haben? Wir werden zu zeigen versuchen, daß sich einiges von der «Neuen Denkart», wie Kant sie genannt hat, schon bei Bodin findet, gewissermaßen noch unreflektiert, unkritisch, aber doch schon ausgeführt und mit nicht unbedeutenden Konsequenzen für seine politischen Gedanken und Begriffe. Roellenbleck bemerkt ebenfalls, daß sich bei Bodin die «in unserem Sinne naturwissenschaftliche Absicht und Methode immer wieder einschleicht».[5] Durch den Ramismus, der ja zu den Vorläufern der naturwissenschaftlichen Methode gehört, dürfte Bodin mit diesen Kategorien vertraut geworden sein, ohne daß er ihre methodischen Konsequenzen oder das Verhältnis seiner neuen zu seinen traditionellen Kategorien systematisch durchreflektiert hat.[6]

Ich stelle diese sehr allgemein gehaltenen Bemerkungen gerade deshalb voran, weil es keineswegs selbstverständlich ist, in Bodin so etwas wie einen Philosophen oder einen politischen Theoretiker der Neuzeit zu sehen. Seine Dämonenlehre,[7] aber auch seine historischen Schriften[8] spre-

---

[4] ROELLENBLECK [239], 30; ähnlich 33.

[5] ROELLENBLECK [239], 30.

[6] Vgl. GEORG ROELLENBLECK [231], 345: «Den Begriff von einer einheitlichen Wissenschaft, deren Methode allen Disziplinen angemessen ist, die in einem System genauer Definitionen und strenger Deduktion der Begriffe auseinander besteht, welchem wiederum eine vom Einfachen zum Komplizierten, vom Allgemeinen zum Besonderen führende pädagogische Darstellungsweise entspricht, mag B(odin), ... von Ramus, dem Urheber der neuen Denk- und Lehrmethode, selbst gelernt haben.» Vgl. dazu auch KENNETH D. McRAE [189], Ramist Tendencies in the Thought of Jean Bodin, *Journal of the History of Ideas* 16 (1955). Derselbe, A Postscript on Bodin's Connections with Ramism [228].

[7] JEAN BODIN, *Le Fleu des Demons et Sorciers*, Nyort 1616 [10.13] (deutsch Hamburg 1698: Daemonomia oder ausführliche Erzehlung des wütenden Teuffels in seinen damahligen rasenden Hexen und Hexenmeistern).

[8] JOANNIS BODINI, *Methodus ad facilem historiarum cognitionem*, Paris 1566

chen für seine starke Bindung an zeitgenössische und historische Ideen und Vorstellungen.

Ich will also wie gesagt versuchen, Bodin aus politischer Sicht zu interpretieren als einen Denker, der einerseits noch ganz in der traditionellen Wertbindung steht, wie sie seit Aristoteles den ethisch-politischen Wissenschaften eigentümlich war, bei dem sich aber andererseits doch schon spürbar jene spezifische Tendenz der Neuzeit ankündigt, die versucht, die Begriffe des Politischen rein und das heißt frei von jeder Bindung zu denken, funktional und wertneutral statt wertgebunden, moralisch oder ontologisch. Ohne ihn in unhistorischer Vereinfachung schon in die kantische Frage nach der Möglichkeit reiner Erkenntnis a priori oder in die Webersche Problematik der Wertfreiheit der Sozialwissenschaften hineinzuziehen, will ich zu zeigen versuchen, daß sich dieses spezifische Problem der Neuzeit, dem sich spätestens seit Descartes und Galilei jeder politische Denker stellen mußte, im Ansatz auch bei ihm findet, und daß er von dort her schon zur Neuzeit gehört, so sehr er auch in den historischen Bindungen seiner Zeit gefangen blieb: psychologisch, stilistisch und politisch-theoretisch. Als Interpretationsgrundlage dienen mir dazu einige ausgewählte Begriffe aus den *Six Livres de la République*.

Zunächst zu Aristoteles.

Es ist eine selten bemerkte Tatsache, daß schon bei der Gliederung der *République* starke Übereinstimmungen mit der aristotelischen *Politik* bestehen. Aristoteles beginnt beispielsweise mit der Definition der Politischen Gemeinschaft (polis) und der Hausgemeinschaft (oikos), leitet dann über zu den verschiedenen Arten der Führung der Oikosgemeinschaft (oikonomía), definiert den Begriff des Sklaven (doulos) und kommt dann auf die Unterschiede zwischen der Regierung der Hausgemeinschaft (despoteía) und der politischen Herrschaft (politiké) zu sprechen.[10]

Analog ist der Aufbau der ersten Bücher der *République*. Der erste Satz

---

[4.1] (Neuausgabe in Œuvres Philosophiques de Jean Bodin, ed. PIERRE MESNARD, Paris 1951 [4.20]) und andere kleinere historische Schriften.

An Literatur zu Einzelgebieten vgl. u. a. J. BASDEVANT [152], Contribution de Jean Bodin à la Formation du Droit International Moderne; HENRI BAUDRILLART [27], Jean Bodin et son temps, Paris 1853; F. v. BEZOLD, Astrologische Geschichtskonstruktionen im Mittelalter, *Deutsche Zeitschrift für Geschichtswissenschaft* 8 (1892); ders. [70], Jean Bodin als Okkultist und seine Demonomanie; ders. [75], Jean Bodins Colloquium Heptaplomeres und der Atheismus des 16. Jahrhunderts; MATHIAS ERNST KAMP [165], Die Staatswirtschaftslehre Jean Bodins, Bonn 1949; ERNST OBERFOHREN [80], Jean Bodin und seine Schule, Untersuchungen über die Frühzeit der Universalökonomik, Kiel 1914; JEAN DE BODIN DE SAINT-LAURENT [62], Les Idées monétaires et commerciales de Jean Bodin, Bordeau 1907.

[10] Vgl. ARISTOTOLES, *Politica* (Politik), 1252 a 1–1255 b 40.

definiert die Politische Gemeinschaft (République), und zwar in einer verknappten, aber eindeutig aristotelischen Weise: «République est un droit gouvernement de plusieurs mesnages, & de ce qui (l)eur est commun.»[11] Zum Gemeinwesen (République) gehört also, wie bei Aristoteles, die Definition des obersten und teleologisch verstandenen Zieles (agathon) oder, in der Sprache Bodins, des summum bonum. Es schließt sich an die Definition der Hausgemeinschaft (mesnage, famille) und ihrer verschiedenen rechtlichen und pädagogischen Implikationen. (Alles unter ständiger Zitierung der alten Theoretiker und vor allem des Aristoteles.[12])

In Kapitel fünf wird dann der Sklavenbegriff (esclaves) im Rahmen der wohlgeordneten Politischen Gemeinschaft erörtert (les esclaves en la République bien ordonnée).[13] Darauf folgt die Explikation des Unterschiedes zwischen den verschiedenen Formen des Untertanen und der politischen Herrschaft über Bürger, verbunden mit einer ausdrücklichen (und historisch begründeten) Kritik am aristotelischen Begriff des Bürgers.[14] Eine Gliederung, die im wesentlichen der der aristotelischen *Politik* entspricht.

Ich begnüge mich mit der Feststellung dieser Übereinstimmung in der Grundgliederung der ersten Teile beider Werke. Zumindest bis zu diesem Punkt könnte man Bodins *République* auch in der abendländischen Tradition der Aristoteles-Kommentare sehen.

Darüber hinaus weisen aber auch bestimmte Begriffe auf die theoretischgedankliche Übereinstimmung beider Denker hin. Zunächst wird – wie die Eingangsdefinition zeigt – der Satz aufgestellt, daß Herrschaft eine Herrschaft über Haushalte sei. Das ist keineswegs so selbstverständlich, wie es auf den ersten Blick scheint. Zeitgenössisch wäre viel eher der Gedanke, das politische Gemeinwesen als eine Art Rechtspyramide zu begreifen, die sich über dem Boden als unantastbar gedachter Lois Fondamentales erhebt: Eine Vorstellung, die ihre Herkunft dem mittelalterlichen Lehnsrecht verdankt. So heißt es z. B. bei dem Protestanten Gentillet, dessen *Discours d'Estat* im gleichen Jahr erschien wie die Erstausgabe der *République*: «Ne peut aussi le Prince abolir les loix fondamentales de sa principauté, sur lesquelles son Estat est fondé & sans lesquelles sondit Estat ne pouroit subsister ne durer: car ce seroit s'abolir la Loy Salique, ni les trois Estats, ni la Loy de non aliener les pays & provinces unies à la Couronne: car le Royaume & la Royauté sont fondez sur ces trois poincts, qui sont comme les trois colonnes qui soustinnent

---

[11] *République*, 1.
[12] *Rép.*, 1–46.
[13] *Rép.*, 46.
[14] *Rép.*, 68 ff.

le Royaume, le Roy & la Royauté.»[15] Wie der mittelalterliche König über und durch seine Vasallen regierte, so herrscht der französische König des 16. Jahrhunderts nach der landläufigen (im einzelnen allerdings mit erheblichen Unterschieden interpretierten) Meinung der Zeitgenossen durch und mit (zumindest aber mit Hilfe) der Magistrate, also politischer Subinstitutionen, deren Enumeration bei den einzelnen Theoretikern zwar unterschiedlich ist und deren Rangordnung unterschiedlich eingeschätzt wird (etwa die Bedeutung der Stände oder der Parlamente), ohne die aber politische und das heißt in dieser Zeit immer: rechtlich gebundene und rechtlich begründete Herrschaft nicht vorstellbar ist. Rechtliche Herrschaft aber ist nicht Herrschaft im Sinne des positiven Rechts (auch das spielt durchaus eine Rolle zu dieser Zeit), sondern stets Herrschaft nach Maßgabe historischer und sittlicher Normen, d. h. naturrechtlicher Bindungen.

So definiert etwa der berühmte Jurist Etienne Pasquier (und hunderte ähnlicher Zitate ließen sich beibringen): «Tous ceux qui ont voulu fonder la liberté d'une république bien ordonné, ont estimé, que c'estoit lors que l'opinion du souverain Magistrat estoit attrempee par la rémonstrance de plusiers personnes de marque, estans constituez en estat pour cest effect: & quand en contr' eschange, ces plusiers estoient controullez par la presence, commandement & maiesté de leur Prince.»[16] Noch stärker tritt der Gedanke der Bindung des Königs an die Grundgesetze bzw. an die von ihnen begründeten Institutionen in dieser Zeit bei den protestantischen Monarchomachen hervor.[17] Eine solche Betrachtungsweise aber setzte mehr voraus als eine Herrschaft über Haushalte. Der König herrscht über die Stände, die Mitglieder der Stände aber sind wiederum Repräsentanten verschiedener Gebiete oder auch Städte, und in jedem dieser Gebiete baut sich dann wieder pyramidal ein Herrschaftssystem auf: An der Spitze ein «Seigneur» und unter ihm dann andere Herren, die wiederum über bestimmte Dörfer «regieren», so daß der Haushalt (der sich dann ebenfalls patriarchalisch gliedert) erst die unterste Stufe bildet. Der Herrscherbefehl des französischen Königs erreicht im 16. Jahrhundert überhaupt nicht direkt die «Haushalte» oder «Familien», sondern nur über

---

[15] INNOZENZ GENTILLET, *Discours d'Estat sur les moyens de bien Gouverner et maintenir en bonne paix un Royaume, ou autre Principauté* (zitiert nach der Ausgabe von 1609), 45 f.

[16] E(s)TIENNE PASQUIER, *Des Recherches de la France, Livres premier et second*, Paris 1569 (Erstausgabe, Buch I: 1560, Buch II: 1565). Das Zitat findet sich S. 72 b. Eine Anzahl weiterer in die gleiche Richtung weisender Zitate vgl. bei DENNERT [237], Ursprung und Begriff der Souveränität, Stuttgart 1964, 22–55.

[17] Vgl. dazu DENNERT, Beza, Brutus, Hotmann – Calvinistische Monarchomachen, Köln/Opladen 1968 (Quellenteil).

ein überaus kompliziertes, von Landschaft zu Landschaft verschiedenes
System von politischen Institutionen und privilegierten Amtsträgern und
unter Berücksichtigung der nahezu unendlichen Rechtsvielfalt des Ancien régime. Von all dem aber sieht Bodin mit seiner Definition ab, indem
er Herrschaft als Herrschaft über Haushalte (an anderer Stelle Familien)
definiert und noch hinzusetzt: «avec puissance souveraine».

So ist die an Aristoteles anknüpfende Eingangsdefinition von Bodin
in ihrer Lösung von den zeitgenössischen Bindungen also nicht nur eine
Wiederaufnahme einer alten Tradition, sondern gleichzeitig auch ein
erheblicher Fortschritt in Richtung auf die Rationalisierung des Herr-
schaftsverhältnisses. Dennoch ist diese Rationalisierung nicht so vollständig und total wie später bei Thomas Hobbes. Schon im Rückgriff auf
Aristoteles bleiben zumindest implizite sittlich-ontologische Prinzipien
erhalten – auch in dem Gedanken, daß Herrschaft Herrschaft über Haushalte sei.[18]

Schon die Einteilung der Herrschaft in Haushalte setzt eine gegliederte
politische Ordnung voraus, wenn auch nicht der Art, wie sie historisch
im Frankreich des 17. Jahrhunderts besteht oder sonst irgendwo in
Europa – mit einer gewissen Ausnahme allenfalls der oberitalienischen
Städte. Subjekt im politischen Sinne sind nach Aristoteles allenfalls die
Despotikoi, also die Herren eines Hauses, aber auch sie nur nach Maßgabe der Verfassung und insofern diese Verfassung demokratisch ist, d. h.
insofern alle Freien auch an den politischen Entscheidungen teilhaben.[19]

Nun ist das Ziel (Telos) des menschlichen Lebens bei Aristoteles bekanntlich die Eudaimonia oder das Eu zen, und dieses teleologische Ziel
ist nur erreichbar in der sich selbst genügenden (autarken) und gegliederten Gemeinschaft, in der die physischen Bedürfnisse des gemeinsamen
und des individuellen Lebens im Hause (Oikos) befriedigt werden. Wenn
auch in einer gewissen Polemik gegen die zu starke Betonung des kon-
templativen Elements bei Aristoteles,[20] so entwickelt Bodin doch eine
sehr ähnliche Lehre der Félicité, wenn sie auch nach ihm stärker als bei
Aristoteles die praktische Seite des Lebens miteinbezieht und wenn zu
den geistigen Prinzipien der Erfüllung des menschlichen Lebens auch
die Übung der (christlichen) Religion gehört. Doch das ändert nichts am
Prinzip der grundsätzlichen Übereinstimmung mit der aristotelischen

---

[18] Die Bedeutung der Polis/Oikos-Unterscheidung für die europäische Geistes-
und die politische Begriffsgeschichte hat in jüngster Zeit Otto Brunner erneut
betont. Vgl. OTTO BRUNNER, Das «ganze Haus» und die alteuropäische «Ökono-
mik», in: Neue Wege der Verfassungs- und Sozialgeschichte, Göttingen ²1968.
[19] ARISTOTELES, Politik, 1253 b 1–20; 1254 a 20–1255 a 2; 1255 b 16–40; 1259
b 19–1260 b 8; 1275 a 30–1276 a 8.
[20] *Rép.*, 5 f.

Tradition in diesem entscheidenden und grundlegenden Gedanken. «Qui semble avoir donné occasion à Marc Varron de dire, que la félicité des hommes est meslee d'action, & de contemplation: & sa raison est à mon advis, que d'une chose simple la felicité est simple, & d'une chose double, composee des parties diverses, la felicité est double: comme le bien du corps gist en santé, force, allegresse, & en la beauté des membres bien proportionnés: & la felicité de l'ame inferieur, qui est la vraye liaison du corps & de l'intellect, gist en l'obeissance que les appetits doyvent à la raison: c'est à dire, en l'action des vertus morales: tout ainsi que le souverain bien de la partie intellectuelle gist aux vertus intellectuelles: c'est à sçavoir, en prudence, science, & vraye religion: l'une touchant les choses humaines, l'autre les choses naturelles, la troisieme les choses divines: la premiere monstre la difference du bien & du mal: la seconde, du vray & du faux: la troisieme, de la pieté & impieté, & ce qu'il faut choisir & fair: car de ces trois se compose la vraye sagesse, où est le plus haut poinct de felicité en ce monde.»[21]

Dieser Gedanke der sittlichen Grundlage des menschlichen Gemeinschaftslebens und damit der Verbindung von Moral und Erkenntnis (science), die zusammen damit die «vraye sagesse» oder das höchste Prinzip der Eudaimonia (félicité) ausmachen (die mit dem blassen deutschen «Glückseligkeit» keineswegs ihrer Bedeutung gemäß adäquat übersetzt ist), erfüllt das gesamte erste und für die weiteren Erörterungen grundlegende Kapitel.[22] Viel stärker als die meisten seiner Zeitgenossen und auch als viele politische Denker der folgenden Generation reflektiert Bodin zurück auf die ontologisch-sittliche Grundlage des politischen Gemeinwesens, und zwar anhand und in der Weise des Aristoteles, während in den zeitgenössischen Schriften sowohl bei den Katholiken als auch bei den Protestanten institutionelle Erörterungen im Vordergrund stehen, d. h. die historische Situation Frankreichs den Mittelpunkt des theoretischen Interessen bildet.[23] Damit ist nicht gesagt, daß nicht auch bei ihnen noch sittliche Erwägungen einen entscheidenden Teil der Überlegungen bildeten. Aber das Sittliche wird meist in Form der naturrechtlich-institutionellen oder historisch-institutionellen Betrachtungen explizit: bei der Analyse der Bedeutung und der vielfältigen Begründungen der bestehenden politischen Institutionen Frankreichs, wofür die Monarchomachen

---

[21] *Rép.*, 5 f.

[22] Vgl. *Rép.*, 1–40.

[23] Vgl. dazu u. a. Theodore Béza, *Du Droit des Magistrats*, 1574; François Hotman, *La Gaule Françoise*, Köln 1574; Philippe de du Plessis-Mornay, *De la Puissance Légitime du Prince sur le Peuple, et du Peuple sur le Prince*, 1581. (Alle drei Schriften finden sich in deutscher Übersetzung in dem von mir edierten und kommentierten Band: Beza, Brutus, Hotman, Köln/Opladen 1968); Jean

gute Beispiele abgeben. Das erste Kapitel Bodins aber ist demgegenüber
ein systematischer Abriß einer politischen Ethik auf anthropologisch-
ontologischen Voraussetzungen: Wobei der Ansatz seine Definition des
Menschen als eines spezifischen, mit intellektuellen und moralischen Tu-
genden begabten Wesens ist und in der der Begriff der Sagesse die intel-
lektuell-analytischen und die moralischen Begabungen zur Einheit zu-
sammenfaßt (Erkenntnis des Richtigen und des Falschen, des Bösen und
des Guten).

Zu einer derartigen Ordnung der Dinge gehört die Ungleichheit der
Menschen in bezug auf die Verfassung, da die einen für die äußeren
Notwendigkeiten zu sorgen haben und dadurch überhaupt erst anderen,
Ausgezeichneten, jene Haltung der Contemplation ermöglichen, die
allein zur Weisheit führt. Aus diesem Grunde unterscheidet Bodin dann
auch anhand der antiken Theoretiker in Kapitel sechs die Menschen
ihrer unterschiedlichen Qualität nach, wobei Qualität stets als Seinsqua-
lität und nicht als etwas Erworbenes zu verstehen ist. Auf den ersten
18 Seiten dieses Kapitels findet sich denn auch folgerichtig kein einziges
zeitgenössisches Beispiel,[24] um den Gedankengang zu stützen. Auch Bürger ist ja nicht jedermann, sondern nur der freie (und das heißt in Analogie zu Aristoteles der politisch aktive) Bürger; dieser aber ist – wiederum
wie bei Aristoteles – der Herr des Hauses (Despotes, lt.: Pater Familias):
«Or quant le chef de famille vient à sortir de sa maison où il commande,
pour traitter & negocier avec les autres chefs de famille (wobei ‹famille›
dem an anderer Stelle gebrauchten Begriff ‹mesnage› entspricht,[25] beides
sind Übertragungen des aristotelischen Begriffs oikos), de ce qui leur
touche à tous en general, alors il despouille le tiltre de maistre, de chef, de
seigneur, pour estre compagnon, pair & associé avec les autres: laissant
sa famille, pour entrer en la cité: & les affaires domestiques, pour traitter
les publiques: & au lieu de seigneur, il s'appelle citoyen: qui n'est autre
chose en propres termes, que le franc subject tenant de la souveraineté
d'autruy.»[26]

BOUCHER, *Sermons de la Simulée Conversion*, Paris 1594; PHILIPPE DE COMMYNES,
Les Mémoires, Paris 1579 (neu: Paris 1925, deutsch: Stuttgart 1952); GENTILLET,
Discours d'Estat, 1576; BERNARD DU HAILLAN, *De l'Etat*, Paris 1570; ders., *Con-
ditions sous lesquelles les Francois se sont donné un ROI* (Neuausgabe), Paris
1789; MICHEL L'HÔPITAL, *La Harangue*, 1560; ETIENNE PASQUIER, *Des Recher-
ches de la France* (2 Bde.), Paris 1569; BERNARD DE LA ROCHE-FLAVIN, *Treze
Livres de Parlemens de France*, Bordeaux 1617; CLAUDE DE SEYSSEL, *La
Grand'Monarchie de France*, Paris 1557 (neu Paris 1961).

[24] *Rép.*, 68 ff.
[25] So auch KENNETH DOUGLAS MCRAE [7.44], Jean Bodin, The Six Bookes
of a Commonweale, Cambridge 1962, A 74.
[26] *Rép.*, 68.

Der gesamte Kontext dieses Zitats zeigt, daß Bodin hier überaus allgemein spricht, und daß er keineswegs den französischen Citoyen im Auge hat, sondern den Bürger allgemein, wobei als Anschauungsmaterial die Antike dient. Denn dieser «freie Bürger», der aus seinem Oikos heraustritt, um mit anderen die öffentlichen Dinge zu verhandeln, kommt zeitgenössisch gar nicht zur Erscheinung, auch wenn hier Begriffe wie Seigneur oder Pair fallen. Der französische Adlige des 16. Jahrhunderts entspricht dem hier entworfenen Bild des Bürgers als des politischen Handelnden ebensowenig wie der französische Stadtbürger der Zeit.

Auf der anderen Seite ist deutlich, daß Subjekte im politischen Sinne nur diejenigen sind, die eben die politischen Angelegenheiten verhandeln, daß also alle übrigen Menschen zum Oikos gehören und sie in diesem Sinne also nicht gleich sind – wiederum in Analogie zur aristotelischen Definition. So ist es nur natürlich, daß Bodin auch die aristotelische Einteilung der Verfassungen ganz selbstverständlich übernimmt: Monarchie, Aristokratie und Politie (fälschlich oft: Demokratie), bei Bodin: Estat populaire oder Respublica popularis.[27]

Warum führen wir diese Bindung an Aristoteles bei Bodin in dieser Ausführlichkeit an? Weil uns scheint, daß gerade darin eine von der politischen Theorie und Ideengeschichte noch nicht hinreichend gewürdigte Besonderheit Bodins zum Ausdruck kommt. Der Einfluß der historischen Umstände, der Politik seiner Zeit, der nationalen politischen Institutionen auf Bodin ist – etwa verglichen mit den oben angeführten Werken anderer Autoren – gering, obwohl er nicht völlig fehlt. Bodin geht es nicht so sehr um das politische Selbstverständnis der Zeit und ihrer Parteiungen, ihrer Gegensätze und Ideen, obwohl diese Probleme von ihm keineswegs völlig vernachlässigt werden. (Gerade aus diesen vielfältigen Gegensätzen ist ja damals auch eine reiche und vielfältige politische Literatur entstanden: Von den Monarchomachen über die verschiedenen katholischen Theoretiker bis zu den Parlamentsjuristen.) Die Probleme und die Fragen der meisten zeitgenössischen Darstellungen und Untersuchungen bewegen Bodin – zumindest in seinem Hauptwerk – nur am Rande, was umso erstaunlicher ist, wenn man seine Vita bedenkt: die eines durchaus engagierten Mitgliedes der Partei der «Politiques». Ihm geht es vielmehr um die Definition politischer Grundbegriffe, und gerade diese Intention hebt ihn aus der zeitgenössischen Literatur hinaus und stellt ihn in die Reihe der großen politischen Theoretiker. Schon die Kapitelüberschriften machen dieses Ziel deutlich: «Quelle es la fin principale *de la republique bien ordonnee?*» «Du mesnage, et la difference entre la republique & la famille.» In dieser Allgemeinheit geht es weiter:

---

[27] Parallelstellen bei McRae [7.44], A 76.

«De la puissance maritale», «de la puissance paternelle» usf.[28] Man mag
einwenden, dies entspräche einer juristischen Denktradition. Aber juristisch waren im 16. Jahrhundert die Unterschiede zwischen den einzelnen
Nationen längst erheblich, waren englische, französische, spanische oder
deutsche Rechtsinstitute keineswegs mehr in der Allgemeinheit römischer
Rechtsvorstellungen zu interpretieren, sondern nur noch auf nationaler
Basis. Die Wendung vom römischen zum nationalen Rechtsdenken fällt
ja nicht zufällig in diese Zeit, Franz Hotman ist, wie man weiß, einer der
entscheidenden Vertreter dieser neuen wissenschaftlichen Richtung.

Nein, das Ziel Bodins ist politisch-theoretisch. Seine Intention ist gerichtet auf die Definition politischer Grundbegriffe. Unter den vielfältigen
historischen Erscheinungen und Bewegungen der Politik soll das All-
gemeingültige und das Verbindliche des menschlichen Gemeinschaftslebens in Begriffe gefaßt werden: Was ist ein Gemeinwesen, was ist Herrschaft, was ist Recht?

Mit dem Hinweis auf den aristotelischen Bezug im Denken Bodins
und damit auf das Transzendieren der historischen Begriffe der Zeit ist
das Besondere an der politischen Theorie Bodins noch nicht hinreichend
gekennzeichnet. Denn wenn auch noch verborgen und wenig expliziert
kündigt sich – wie eingangs schon kurz bemerkt – bei Bodin schon jener
methodische Ansatz der Neuzeit an, der in ganz anderer Weise definiert
als die Tradition: der Rationalismus.

Um dies zu verdeutlichen, darf ich auf Descartes verweisen: Nicht
um zu zeigen, daß Descartes etwa von Bodin beeinflußt ist, sondern um
deutlich zu machen, daß jener neuzeitlich-rationale Zug des Denkens,
der bei Descartes zum Durchbruch kommt und der von da an die Philosophie und auch die politische Theorie der Neuzeit ganz entscheidend
geprägt hat, sich in gewisser Weise schon bei Bodin feststellen läßt –
wenn auch noch nicht systematisch expliziert. Auf den inneren Zusammenhang von Bodin und Descartes hat in jüngster Zeit wieder Imboden
aufmerksam gemacht.[29] In Kürze: Geleitet von dem neuen Methodenideal
der Naturwissenschaften [30] leugnet Descartes die Möglichkeit der Erkenntnis auch von Körpern durch die Sinne: «Denn da ich jetzt weiß,

---

[28] *République*, Sommaire des Chapitres.

[29] MAX IMBODEN [227], Johannes Bodinus und die Souveränitätslehre, Basel
1963, 5: «So ganz anders sich das Werk des Bodinus darstellt, so unförmig und
barock es, verglichen mit der Schlichtheit des Discours de la Méthode erscheint,
so stark ist doch die innere Gemeinsamkeit, die Bodinus mit dem zwei Gene-
rationen nach ihm lebenden Descartes verbindet ... Wie Descartes bemühte sich
auch Bodinus vor allem um methodische Klarheit. Er ordnet, er sucht nach
Exaktheit der Fragestellung, er mißt die von alters her mitgeführten Anschauungen an letzten Prinzipien.»

[30] Ich beschränke mich hier auf wenige Bemerkungen und verweise zur Li-

daß ja selbst Körper nicht eigentlich durch die Sinne oder durch die Einbildungskraft, sondern einzig und allein durch den Verstand erkannt werden ...»[31] Dieses Wissen bedingt eine neue Erkenntnismethode, über die er sich selbst vier Vorschriften gegeben hat, die bekanntlich folgendermaßen lauten:

«Die erste besagt, niemals eine Sache als wahr anzuerkennen, von der ich nicht evidentermaßen erkenne, daß sie wahr ist: d. h. Übereilung und Vorurteile sorgfältig zu vermeiden und über nichts zu urteilen, was sich meinem Denken nicht so klar und deutlich darstellte, daß ich keinen Anlaß hätte, daran zu zweifeln.

Die zweite, jedes Problem, das ich untersuchen würde, in so viele Teile zu teilen, wie es angeht und wie es nötig ist, um es leichter zu lösen.

Die dritte, in der gehörigen Ordnung zu denken, d. h. mit den einfachsten und am leichtesten zu durchschauenden Dingen zu beginnen, um so nach und nach, gleichsam über Stufen, bis zur Erkenntnis der zusammengesetztesten aufzusteigen, ja selbst in Dinge Ordnung zu bringen, die natürlicherweise nicht aufeinander folgen.

Die letzte, überall so vollständige Aufzählungen und so allgemeine Übersichten aufzustellen, daß ich versichert wäre, nichts zu vergessen.»[32]

Da ich an anderer Stelle die neue Methode und ihre Bedeutung für die moderne Wissenschaft ausführlich gewürdigt habe,[33] kann ich mich hier kurz fassen. Was Descartes wie Hobbes und andere unter wissenschaftlicher Erkenntnis verstehen, ist die zweifelsfreie Erkenntnis. Zweifelsfrei aber ist nur jene Erkenntnis, der zugrundeliegt ein einsehbares und jederzeit verifizierbares Erkenntnisprinzip. Ein solches Prinzip kann die Meßbarkeit im Sinne der Geometrie sein, es kann eine mechanisch gedachte Bewegung sein (wie bei Hobbes) oder das Gesetz der Kausalität. Entscheidend ist für unseren Gedankenzusammenhang zweierlei. Erstens, daß es sich bei diesem Erkenntnisprinzip um ein Prinzip des eigen Denkens handelt und zum zweiten, daß nach diesem Prinzip in der Weise, wie es hier Descartes sagt, alle Dinge geteilt werden müssen bis zu den «einfachsten und am leichtesten zu durchschauenden», in der Art, wie auch die Mathematiker vorgehen, die von den einfachsten Größen aus konstruierend die zusammengesetzten aufbauen und damit gleichzeitig erkennen. «Denn schließlich enthält die Methode, die der rechten Ordnung zu folgen und alle bedingenden Umstände des Gesuchten genau auf-

---

teratur und zur weiteren Explikation des Problems auf mein Buch: Die aristotelisch-ontologische Politikwissenschaft.

[31] Descartes, Meditationes de Prima Philosophia, Hamburg 1959, 59.
[32] Descartes, Von der Methode, Hamburg 1960, 15 f.
[33] Vgl. Dennert, Politikwissenschaft.

zuzählen lehrt, alles, was den arithmetischen Regeln ihre Sicherheit gibt»,[34] wie Descartes folgerichtig in diesem Zusammenhang sagt. In den Worten von Karl Jaspers: «Wenn also alle Erkenntnis dasselbe ist, dann gibt es nur eine *Methode*: dann muß eine Wissenschaft alles Wissen tragen. Es ist die mathesis universalis.»[35] Können wir Bodin bereits in diesem Zusammenhang neuzeitlicher Methodentheorie und Wissenschaftsphilosophie interpretieren? Sicherlich nicht vom methodischen Ansatz her. Nirgends wird eine ähnliche, auf eine universale Methode abzielende Denkweise bei ihm sichtbar. Seine Intention ist nicht die mathesis universalis. Aber historisch gesehen liegt diesem Gedanken der universalen, nach verifizierbaren Denkschritten vorgehenden Wissenschaft, dieser Erkenntnis «clare et distincte» ein langer Prozeß der Ablösung von scholastischen Denkkategorien zugrunde, ein Prozeß, der vor Bodin beginnt und der nach ihm bei Galilei einerseits, bei Descartes und bei Hobbes andererseits seinen ersten Höhepunkt erreicht und von dem aus dann eine gänzlich neue Entwicklung des Denkens beginnt.

An diesem Prozeß der Erneuerung des Denkens durch eine Ablösung von den hergebrachten Kategorien hat Bodin, wie mir scheint, einen entscheidenden Anteil gehabt, und zwar auf jenem Gebiet, das damals vom Umfang der Lehr- und Forschungstätigkeit her noch immer zu den wichtigsten Gebieten gehörte: auf dem der Politischen Wissenschaft oder, um es weniger speziell zu sagen, auf dem Gebiet der Wissenschaften, die die öffentlichen Angelegenheiten im Sinne des Bodinschen Begriffs «République» betreffen, wozu, wie sein Hauptwerk zeigt, philosophische, juristische, historische und ökonomische und in gewisser Weise noch theologische Überlegungen gehörten. Mit anderen Worten: Bodin ist kein Vorläufer Descartes im Sinne einer historischen Abfolge und Beeinflussung verschiedener Systeme. Aber er hatte Anteil an jener Rationalisierung des Denkens, die in der impliziten oder expliziten Kritik der überkommenen Denkweise das Mittelalter auch auf dem Gebiet der Wissenschaften ablöste und der Neuzeit den Weg bahnte. Ihm geht es um die methodische Klarheit und darum muß er sich von dem traditionellen Ballast des Denkens befreien – so sehr sein Werk äußerlich auch noch von dieser Last der Tradition befrachtet ist. Dies wird, wie mir scheint, exemplarisch deutlich an seinem Begriff der Herrschaft oder Souveränität. Dieses Wort ist damals durchaus gebräuchlich und zwar in einem sehr weiten Sinne, wie es ja auch bei Bodin in verschiedenen Bedeutungen

---

[34] DESCARTES, Methode, 17; vgl. auch das Kapitel Descartes, in: DENNERT, Politikwissenschaft, ebenso das Kapitel Kant.

[35] KARL JASPERS, Descartes und die Philosophie, (4. erw. Aufl.) Berlin 1966, 42.

vorkommt.[36] Souverän kann alles genannt werden, was in seiner Weise herausragend oder auch nur besonders ist.[37]

---

[36] Wie sehr die «Unklarheiten» des Bodinschen Souveränitätsbegriffs bis heute die Forschung beschäftigt haben, wird an der jüngst geführten Diskussion zwischen Imboden und Quaritsch erneut deutlich. (Vgl. IMBODEN [227], 12 ff., HELMUT QUARITSCH, Besprechung des Vortrages von Imboden, *Der Staat* 5 (1966), 112 ff.). Während Quaritsch schreibt: «Ob es sachlich richtig und terminologisch empfehlenswert ist, die Erdenschwere von Text und System eines klassischen Autors abzustreifen und die in grundverschiedenen Ebenen wurzelnden Komplexe: Souveränität und ‹la vraye iustice› in das auf einen Nenner zurückgehende Begriffspaar «Rechtssouveränität und Machtsouveränität» einzufangen, wird man bezweifeln dürfen» (S. 113), heißt es u. a. bei Imboden: «Daß man in diesem Werke (der *République* – J. D.) vor allem die These von der Einheit der souveränen Gewalt unterstrichen sieht, ist eine der großen verfälschenden Vereinfachungen, die in der Geschichte des Denkens über den Staat vollzogen worden sind. Viel eher muß Bodin der Verfechter der Lehre eines *doppelten* Souveränitätsgedankens genannt werden (S. 20, ähnlich auch ff.).» Da ich selbst mit meinem Buch über die Souveränität versucht habe, einen Beitrag zur Diskussion zu liefern, sei mir hier eine etwas ausführlichere Anmerkung gestattet.

Im Gegensatz zur traditionellen Souveränitätsdiskussion hat sich mit der Auseinandersetzung zwischen Imboden und Quaritsch und anderen Beiträgen begrüßenswerterweise nun auch in der Rechtswissenschaft die Diskussion stark in den historischen Bereich verlagert. Sie litt, wenn man das etwas vereinfacht sagen kann, bislang sehr wesentlich daran, daß mit Termini, die ihrem Gehalt und ihrem juristisch-kasuistischen Kontext nach in spätere Zeiten gehörten, ständig auf Bodin und auf noch frühere Zeiten zurückgegangen wurde, woraus sich dann so abstrakte Fragen entwickelten wie die, ob Bodin einen konservativen oder einen liberalen Souveränitätsbegriff entwickelt habe, ob es sich hier um Rechts-, Staats-, Stände-, Fürsten- und andere Arten von Souveränität gehandelt habe. Alle solche Fragestellungen – so sehr sie im Zusammenhang geschlossener juristischer Fragestellungen des 19. und des 20. Jahrhunderts ihren Platz haben mögen – tun der Quelle insofern Gewalt an, als Bodin ja überhaupt noch nicht in derartigen Kategorien und Fragestellungen denken *konnte* und er ja auch nur von einer «puissance souveraine» spricht und er dann genau definiert, was seiner – von ihm selbst als neu empfundenen – Auffassung nach Souveränität sei. Es ist eindeutig, daß Souveränität nach ihm *ein* Begriff ist, der einem Herrscher zukommt, weil sonst die Momente der Absolutheit und der Ständigkeit nicht erfüllt sind und damit die Definition hinfällig wird. Alle übrigen Probleme müssen eben in diesem begrifflichen und historischen Zusammenhang gesehen werden, ihrer sind wahrlich genug.

Doch auch in der historischen Auseinandersetzung gibt es Probleme, die die Diskussion zusätzlich belastet haben und belasten. Sie bestehen m. E. vor allem darin, daß Souveränität (oder davon abgeleitete adjektivische Formen) in der Zeit Bodins und vor allem auch schon in den Jahrhunderten davor ein allgemein gebräuchliches Wort ist, das eben *nicht* in einem begrifflichen Sinne verwendet

Das politische Gemeinwesen («République») ist nach der Bodinschen Definition «un droit gouvernement de plusieurs mesnages, & de ce qui leur est commun, avec puissance souveraine.»[38] Die Souveränität aber definiert er als «la puissance absolue & perpetuelle d'une République».[39] Dies ist – zeitgenössisch gesehen – eine kühne und neue Definition und Bodin ist sich der Tragweite dieses Schrittes, der Einmaligkeit seines Vorgehens durchaus bewußt, denn er fährt fort: «Il est icy besoin de former la definition de souveraineté, par ce qu'il n'y a ny iurisconsulte, ny philosophe politique, qui l'ayt definie: iaçoit que c'est le poinct principal, & le plus necessaire d'estre etendu au traitté de la République.»[40]

---

wird wie bei Bodin – darin besteht ja gerade das Neue der Definition, wie Bodin selber sagt. Da ich an anderer Stelle dazu bereits das Wichtigste gesagt habe (vgl. DENNERT [237], 101 ff.) kann ich mich hier kurz fassen. Es gibt bis in die Zeit Bodins praktisch überhaupt nichts, was nicht souverän genannt werden könnte, wenn es nur einzig in seiner Art ist: Von der Schönheit einer Frau bis zur Macht des Kaisers, von den Befugnissen der Rechnungskammer bis zur Position eines Abtes oder bis zum Mut eines Kastellans, der «souverän» voranschreitet. Jeder Dictionnaire der französischen Sprache oder der alten französischen Sprache bringt eine Fülle von Beispielen dieser Art, von denen ich in meiner Souveränitätsuntersuchung nur eine kurze, aber wie mir scheint, ausreichende Auswahl zusammengestellt habe. Es macht einem Autor damals überhaupt nichts aus, etwa im gleichen Atemzug einen Vasallen und auch gleichzeitig dessen König souverän zu nennen (DENNERT [237], 103).

Bei dieser geradezu universellen Anwendung des *Wortes* Souveränität oder des Adjektivs souverän ist es nur selbstverständlich, daß es besonders häufig dort gebraucht wird, wo es sich um die Betrachtung eines gegliederten Gebildes handelt: beim Gemeinwesen. Die jeweilige Spitze – vom voranschreitenden Kastellan über den Führer eines Heereszuges bis zum «Herren», auf welcher Stufe der Lehnspyramide oder der Herrschaftsausübung er auch immer stehen mag – wird daher ganz selbstverständlich souverän genannt. Die historische Diskussion leidet meiner Ansicht nach bis heute daran, daß immer neue Autoren «entdeckt» werden, bei denen «schon» von Souveränität die Rede ist, sei es eine des Kaisers oder des Königs oder der Stände oder sonst irgendeine, von welcher Entdeckung aus dann mit viel Scharfsinn die kühnsten Brücken zu neuzeitlichen und auf einem ganz anderen theoretischen Boden erwachsenen Begriffen geschlagen werden. Der Begriff der Volkssouveränität ist ein Beispiel dafür. (Auch Imbodens glänzende Rede vor der Universität Basel ist nicht frei davon. Bei ihm sind es nun Aeneas Silvius Piccolomini und Peter von Andlau, die zur «Prägung der Souveränitätslehre» beigetragen haben.) Ich würde, um den Tatbestand einmal in aller Schärfe deutlich zu machen, etwas überspitzt sagen: Es wäre eine Entdeckung, wenn man einen politischen Theoretiker in den drei oder vier Jahrhunderten vor Bodin ausfindig machen würde, der *nicht* in irgendeiner Form oder Verbindung das Wort Souveränität oder eine Ableitung von ihm verwendet. Gerade darum sollte die Aufmerksamkeit der Wissenschaft dem *neuen* Definitionsgehalt dieses alten Wortes bei Bodin gelten.

Nun liegt das Neue nicht nur im Inhalt dieser Definition – darüber
gleich –, sondern schon in der Art und Weise, in der hier definiert wird.
Bis zum Nominalismus war in der Regel definiert worden an Hand des
Objektes, waren bestimmte Seiten des zu betrachtenden Gegenstandes
prädikatisiert worden. Hier aber macht sich der denkende Verstand selber zum Autor und das heißt zum Ursprung der Definition, und zwar
nicht irgendwelcher Definitionen irgendwelcher sekundärer Gebilde, sondern des Gemeinwesens selbst und das heißt noch immer: des außerhalb
der Theologie fundamentalsten Gegenstandes der Reflexion.
Diese Methode des Hervorbringens der Dinge aus dem Verstand, wie

---

Andererseits gibt die Gedankenführung Bodins in der Tat Anlaß zu Miß-
verständnissen. Denn so rational seine Souveränitäts-Definition auf der einen
Seite ist, so sehr sie sich löst von überkommenen, qualitativ bestimmten Bindungen, so sehr bleibt ein erheblicher Teil der *übrigen* und begleitenden Gedankenführung noch eingebettet in die ontologisch-ethische Tradition des politischen Denkens einerseits, in zeitgenössische naturrechtliche oder göttlich-
rechtliche Bindungen andererseits. In diesem Punkt stimmen ja Imboden und
Quaritsch überein. ROELLENBLECK hat im zweiten Teil seiner Literaturübersicht
[231], 234 ff. anhand der verschiedenen Untersuchungen nachdrücklich auf
diese meist als «widersprüchlich» empfundenen Gegensätze hingewiesen, die
fast allen neueren Interpreten Bodins, aus welcher Perspektive sie immer schrie-
ben, aufgegangen sind.
Aber diese Widersprüchlichkeit ist nicht eine des Souveränitätsbegriffs bei
Bodin selbst oder irgendeines Begriffes: Sie fließt aus der Zweischichtigkeit des
Bodinschen Denkens. Auf diese Doppelbödigkeit hinzuweisen und sie zu analy-
sieren ist deshalb das Ziel dieser meiner Untersuchung. Die Widersprüchlichkeit
– wenn man schon diesen Terminus verwendet – ist nicht ein logischer Defekt
Bodins, ein Mangel an Klarheit, sondern umgekehrt: Das sich aus den traditionellen Bindungen zur Klarsicht emporringende Denken gerät mit sich selbst
in einen Gegensatz und muß in ihn geraten, solange es sich noch auf einen (zudem historischen) Gegenstand bezieht (die République, das Gemeinwesen) und
sich nicht in der Weise Descartes' oder Kants die Prinzipien des «klaren» oder
«reinen» Denkens vorher selbst entwickelt. Ehe das nicht geschieht, muß die Gedankenführung notwendig doppelbödig werden, «widersprüchlich». Aber daß
überhaupt ein zweiter «Boden» des Denkens gefunden wird, daß der traditionelle Grund des politischen Denkens nicht mehr unbezweifelt als alleiniger bestehen gelassen wird: darin liegt das Verdienst von Jean Bodin. Ob – nebenbei
bemerkt – Descartes und Kant die «reinen» und universalen Prinzipien «des»
Denkens in allen Teilen ihres Werkes durchgehalten haben, ob sie vor allem eine
Politische Wissenschaft auf diesen Prinzipien begründen konnten, kann hier
nicht untersucht werden. Auch das ist an anderem Ort ausführlich geschehen.

[37] Einzelheiten und Belege dafür in: DENNERT [237], 101 ff.
[38] *Rép.*, 1.
[39] *Rép.*, 122.
[40] *Rép.*, 122.

sie Kant dann später in der Vorrede zur zweiten Auflage der Kritik der reinen Vernunft [41] ausführlich analysiert hat, erreicht hier bei Bodin einen ersten Höhepunkt, wenn auch noch nicht im Zusammenhang von Überlegungen über die Logik dieser Methode und ihrer Implikationen. République ist für Bodin nicht mehr allein etwas Seiendes, ein Universale, das zu beschreiben ist, ein Gebilde naturrechtlicher Art, in seinen letzten Prinzipien nur metaphysisch zu begründen (das ist die République in anderen Gedankenzusammenhängen bei Bodin *auch*): es ist eine eindeutig und rational zu definierende Größe, wobei sich Bodin bewußt ist, mit seiner Definition etwas gegenüber der Tradition vollständig Neues zu sagen. Es ist der unabhängige, sich selbst als autonom setzende Verstand des Individuums, der den Dingen ihre Namen (und damit ihr Sein) gibt. Die Dinge sind nicht mehr etwas an und für sich, sondern das sich selbst als denkendes setzende Individuum sagt ihnen, was sie sind – denn nur auf dieser Voraussetzung ist ja eine neue Definition alter Gegenstände der wissenschaftlichen Betrachtung möglich.

Dies wird an anderer Stelle noch deutlicher, etwa wenn Bodin sich selbst als Ursprung der Definition nennt, inhaltlich gesehen ohne Rücksicht auf jede Tradition: «i'appelle iustice le droit partage des loyers, & des peines, & de ce qui appartient à chacun en termes de droit.» [42] Dieses «Ich nenne», dieses Hervortreten des den Gedankengang nach eigener Vollmacht führenden Subjektes wird nicht überall so deutlich wie hier, aber es ist das Prinzip des gesamten Werkes, meistens sprachlich eingekleidet in Pluralformen wie «appellons» oder andere. J'appelle – das ist bereits der Ton der Neuzeit. Man zähle einmal nach, wie oft in Max Webers Wirtschaft und Gesellschaft eine Definition mit einer solchen (oder ähnlichen) Formel eingeleitet wird, die ihrem Inhalt und ihrem Sinn nach etwas völlig anderes ist als das platonisch-aristotelische (und vorsokratische) legitai – man sagt. Das «Man sagt» der traditionellen Denkweise ist immer das Aussagen eines Seienden, denn nur darum kann man es sagen, ist es dem Denken als Gedachtes anwesend und gegenwärtig. Das Bodinsche «Ich sage» aber ist das Gegenteil, bedeutet eine radikale Wendung gegen das Man: Ich definiere neu, weil sich nur die neue Definition in den frei von mir gewählten Denk- und Darstellungsrahmen einordnen läßt.

Das bedeutet nicht, daß Bodin von hier aus schon eine systematische Denkmethode entwickeln wollte. Seine Erklärungen selbst sind meist durchaus noch inhaltlich, richten sich weniger auf die Methode als auf die Dinge. Insofern, das zeigte ich ja einleitend, bleibt er der Zeit und der Tradition verhaftet.

---

[41] IMMANUEL KANT, Kritik der reinen Vernunft, Hamburg 1956 (Philosophische Bibliothek), 2. Aufl., 14 ff.
[42] *Rép.*, 1014.

Aber mit diesen Bemerkungen ist noch nicht alles über die Bedeutung seiner Definitionen von République und Souveränität gesagt, wobei wir diese beiden Begriffe als besonders wichtige für das Gesamtwerk herausgegriffen haben. (Unser Gedankengang ließe sich auch an anderen Begriffen verifizieren, da der Vorgang stets der gleiche ist.) Das Gemeinwesen ist also «un droit gouvernement de plusieurs mesnages... avec puissance souveraine», die Souveränität «la puissance absolute & perpetuelle d'une République».

An der Neuheit dieser Definition ändert auch nichts, daß Bodin im Stil der Zeit Übersetzungen griechischer, lateinischer und sogar hebräischer Definitionen gibt, die das gleiche besagen sollen: – ein im Grunde etwas unlogischer Vorgang, nachdem er vorher ausdrücklich erklärt hat, niemand hätte die «République» bisher in dieser Weise definiert. (Möglicherweise wollte er damit der Kritik durch die traditionalistischen Fakultäten entgehen.)

Worin liegt also das Neue? Bodin hat das selbst ausgeführt. Die Souveränität, im Sinne seiner von ihm selbst als neu verstandenen Definition (er wiederholt hier ausdrücklich noch einmal die Eingangsdefinition der République als «droit gouvernement de plusieurs familles [mesnages]»[43]) kennzeichnet einige Merkmale, die nach traditioneller Auffassung keiner rechtlichen Herrschaft zukommen. In den Worten Bodins: «I'ay dit que ceste puissance est perpetuelle: parce qu'il se peut faire qu'on donne puissance absolue à un ou plusieurs à certain temps, lequel expiré, ils ne sont plus rien que subiects: & tant qu'ils sont en puissance, ils ne se peuvent appeller Princes souverains.»[44]

Auf den folgenden Seiten versucht Bodin dann, durch eine breit und ganz im barocken Stil der Zeit angelegte Argumentation, jeden möglichen Einwand gegen die Dauer der Souveränität auszuschalten. Wann immer eine Herrschaft temporär ist, und sei sie noch so umfassend, ist sie nicht perpetuelle und damit nicht souveräne Herrschaft. Das ist das Fazit des Gedankens.

Das gleiche gilt für das zweite Merkmal der Definition: die Absolutheit. Jede Bedingung, unter der einem Fürsten die Herrschaft gegeben wird, läßt den Begriff Souveränität deshalb hinfällig werden, weil Bedingungen das Moment der Absolutheit aufheben. «Aussi la souveraineté donnee à un Prince sous charges & conditions, n'est pas proprement souveraineté, ny puissance absolue.»[45] Bodin ist sich klar darüber, wogegen sich diese Definition richtet: Gegen das in seiner Zeit noch weithin selbstverständliche göttliche Recht bzw. gegen das Naturrecht: also gegen jeden metaphysisch oder ontologisch begründeten Herrschaftsanspruch, wobei ja

---

[43] *Rép.*, 122.
[44] *Rép.*, 122.
[45] *Rép.*, 128.

auch die Heiligung eines ursprünglich gesetzten Rechtes durch die lange
Dauer seiner Gültigkeit im Verständnis der Zeit der Norm das Siegel
einer höheren Qualität aufgeprägt hat. Bodin sagt ausdrücklich: «si ce
n'est que les conditions apposees en la creation du Prince, soyent de la loy
de Dieu ou de nature . . .»[46]

Nie zuvor hat es einen politischen Theoretiker gegeben, der Herrschaft
im Sinne dieses Begriffs von Souveränität definiert hätte – und das ist es
ja, was Bodin mit seiner Bemerkung über die Rechtsgelehrten und politischen Philosophen selber ausspricht. Es hat Herrschaften von un-
beschränkter Dauer gegeben – und gibt sie zur Zeit Bodins bekanntlich im
eigenen Land –: nämlich dynastische Herrschaften. Aber es hat nie eine
Herrschaft von zeitlich unbegrenzter Dauer gegeben, die nicht an göttliche oder an natürliche Gesetze gebunden gewesen wäre, eine Bindung,
die zeitgenössisch im allgemeinen sich ausspricht im Begriff der Lois Fondamentales, des göttlichen oder des Naturrechtes, was dann wieder einschließt die Bindung des Herrschers an den Rat der bestehenden politischen Institutionen (etwa des Parlamentes oder der Stände) usw.[47] Der
Herrscher auf Lebenszeit ist nur Herrscher im Rahmen des Rechtes. Bestehen keine derartigen Rechtsvorschriften oder hält er sich nicht an sie,
dann heißt er eben seit der Antike nicht Herrscher, sondern Tyrann. Eine
Tyrannenherrschaft aber ist weder ethisch-politisch noch rechtlich eine
res publica oder République.[48] In der Sprache der Zeit: Tyrannenherrschaft – sei sie die des tyrannus absque titulo oder die des tyrannus quoad
exercitionem – ist nicht legitim, d. h. sie ist rechtlose Machtausübung,
Nichtherrschaft.[49] Dieser Unterschied, der für die traditionelle Lehre
fundamental gewesen war, fällt mit der Definition Bodins – auch wenn
er an anderen Stellen durchaus noch gesehen wird, ein Grund mehr, bei
Bodin «Widersprüche» festzustellen.

Wie aber steht es um die legitime, d. h. in bestimmten Rechtsregeln ins
Amt gesetzte absolute Herrschaft auf Zeit, wie sie etwa die römische
Diktatur darstellte, ein Rechtsinstitut, das Bodin durchaus bekannt war?
Auch sie ist durch die Definition ausgeschlossen – denn die absolute Herr-
schaft soll ja gleichzeitig auch ständig sein, und das heißt: Niemals zu
widerrufen.

Damit aber ist der Herrscher – oder besser: der Souverän – theoretisch
auch aus der letzten noch möglichen Begrenzung gelöst, aus der zeitlichen.
Was uns entgegentritt, ist der absolute Herrscherwille, der im Leviathan

---

[46] *Rép.*, 128.
[47] Vgl. dazu die Bemerkungen bei IMBODEN [227], 20 ff.
[48] Einzelheiten und entsprechende Literatur bei DENNERT [237], 15 ff.
[49] Zur historischen Komponente dieses Begriffszusammenhangs vgl. DENNERT
[237], 8 ff; vgl. ders., in: Beza, Brutus, Hotman, LV ff.

des Thomas Hobbes dann seine konsequente methodische Begründung erfahren wird, der an nichts mehr gebundene Wille einer Person an der Spitze des Gemeinwesens.[50]

Ich bin mir, indem ich auf diesen Zusammenhang hinweise, bewußt, daß Bodin dieses Prinzip der bindungsfreien oder der schrankenlosen Herrschaft gedanklich keineswegs über die gesamte *République* durchgehalten hat, daß sich bei ihm zahlreiche Stellen finden, die das Gegenteil besagen (wie, nebenbei bemerkt, auch bei Hobbes). Aber im ersten Teil des achten Kapitels des ersten Buches tritt dieses Prinzip der absoluten Herrschergewalt in einer Klarheit und in einer Totalität hervor, daß dagegen der historische Hochabsolutismus im 18. Jahrhundert als rechtlich gebundenes Herrschaftssystem erscheint. Kein französischer König des Ancien régime hat je auch nur entfernt jenen Grad von Absolutheit erreicht, den Bodin zum Prädikat seiner Souveränitäts-Definition macht. Aber das gehört in die Historie – uns beschäftigt hier ausschließlich die Theorie, das Problem des Begriffs.

Unter welchen Umständen ist Bodin zu dieser Definition gekommen? Der Historiker wird auf die Umstände der Zeit hinweisen, möglicherweise unter besonderer Betonung der Vita des Bodin, die ihn nach einem Prinzip suchen lassen mußten, um der Selbstzerfleischung des Reiches ein Ende zu machen – und dieses Prinzip konnte dann nur in der omnipotenten (absoluten) Gewalt des Herrschers bestehen, einer Gewalt, die der französische König eben nach der Auffassung sowohl der protestantischen als auch der katholischen Theoretiker der Zeit nicht besaß, die er aber hätte besitzen *müssen*, um die Kämpfe und Parteiungen der Gegenwart zu beenden.

Das alles ist richtig. Aber darüber hinaus gilt eins: Es handelt sich hier um einen aus der Autonomie des denkenden Individuums geborenen Akt, der mit einem neuen und alle Historie übergreifenden, mit einem absoluten Gedanken das Gemeinwesen als Gemeinwesen neu definiert, es theoretisch ablöst von allen überkommenen Begriffen, Werten, Rechtsbindungen und es in Gedanken neu gründet auf nichts als auf das Individuum, auf den Herrscher. Das hat Bodin getan. Dem freien Gedanken entspricht der freie, der absolute und ständige Wille des Souveräns. Über die methodischen Voraussetzungen dieses Sprunges in die Neuzeit haben dann Spätere nachgedacht. Mit anderen Worten: Die Definition der Souveränität ist bei Bodin noch nicht eingebettet in allgemeine logische oder methodische Überlegungen, sie ist ein isolierter Akt in einem Kontext, der schon stilistisch noch stark traditionell ist, rezeptiv und memorierend. Damit soll im übrigen keineswegs die Leistung der Ramisten und anderer geschmälert werden, die Bodin vorangegangen sind. Aber wenn man sich

---

[50] Vgl. Thomas Hobbes, Leviathan, New York/London 1959, 89 f.

die noch weithin gültige Einbettung aller politischen Begriffe in das Natur-
rechtsdenken der Zeit vergegenwärtigt, wird der nahezu revolutionäre
Schritt deutlich, den der Vorgang dieser Definition für die Geschichte
der politischen Theorie bedeutet. Seine Konturen treten noch schärfer
hervor, wenn man Bodin mit den Augen des Historikers *und* des Aristo-
telikers liest: denn beides war der Autor der *République* in einem derartigen Maße, daß er auf beiden Gebieten als Autorität gelten könnte.
Diese auch heute noch längst nicht überall gesehene geistige Spannweite
Bodins deutlich zu machen, war der Sinn dieser Bemerkungen.

Horst Denzer

Bodins Staatsformenlehre

I

Die Staatsformenlehre steht in der Geschichte des politischen Denkens zwischen zwei Frageansätzen. Da ist einmal die Frage «nach dem Staate, was er wohl sein mag»,[1] die Frage nach Ziel, Zweck und Aufgabe des Staates, nach der Erfüllung des menschlichen *telos* in der Gemeinschaft. Wie kommt das in den verschiedenen Verfassungen zum tragen? Letztlich führt diese Fragereihe zur Frage nach dem besten Staat.

Zum andern findet jeder politische Philosoph in der Geschichte und in seiner Gegenwart eine Fülle konkreter Staaten vor, deren Verfassung und Entwicklung er studieren kann. Daher die weitere Frage: wie beurteile ich die Verfassung dieser Staaten und wie klassifiziere ich sie in einer Typologie der Staatsformen? Diese Frage zielt auf die historischen Bedingungen der Staatsformen und ihres Wandels und kann in eine Geschichtsphilosophie münden.

Die beiden Frageansätze sind dadurch charakterisiert, daß für den einen der Beginn des Fragens ist, was für den anderen das Frageziel, und umgekehrt. Die erste Frage geht von einer philosophischen und/oder theoretischen Überlegung aus und versucht damit die Vielfalt der Wirklichkeit zu erfassen, die zweite will von der historischen Vielfalt zu einer theoretischen Klassifikation vordringen. Beide Frageansätze bedingen sich wechselseitig. Welchen Ausgangspunkt und welche Intention jeder der beiden Frageansätze hat und wie die beiden Ansätze miteinander korrelieren: das bestimmt die spezifische Gestalt der Staatsformenlehre eines politischen Denkers.

Der Zugang zur Staatsformenlehre vom Wesen des Staates her ist in der klassischen politischen Philosophie von Plato bis Cicero relativ gleichförmig. Die verschiedenen Staatsformen werden danach gewertet, ob sie das Gute als solches in der Form der Gerechtigkeit verwirklichen (Plato), ob sie das gute Leben des Menschen in der Gemeinschaft ermöglichen (Aristoteles) oder ob sie auf Anerkennung des Rechts und auf die Gemeinsamkeit des Nutzens angelegt sind (Cicero). Die Forderung, was der Staat sein *soll*, gewinnt unmittelbare Bedeutung für die Staatsformen-

---

[1] Aristoteles, *Politik*, Beginn des dritten Buches.

Horst Denzer

lehre, indem die Verfassungen geschieden werden in die, die das *telos* des Staates verwirklichen und die es verfehlen. Den richtigen Verfassungen[2] werden die Entartungsformen[3] gegenübergestellt. Da nun alle Verfassungen den Bazillus der Entartung in sich tragen, entwickelt die klassische politische Theorie zur Verwirklichung des Staatszwecks das Paradigma des besten Staates, der eine aus den Staatsformen gemischte Verfassung ist. Bei Plato soll die Zusammenfügung der «Mutterverfassungen» Monarchie, die das Prinzip der herrscherlichen Autorität vertritt, und Demokratie, die auf dem Prinzip der Freiheit gründet, das rechte Maß *(metrion)* bilden. Während bei Aristoteles die rechte Mischung des besten Staates sich nicht ausdrücklich auf die Zusammenfügung der Staatsformen bezieht, erhält bei Polybios und Cicero die Lehre der Verbindung monarchischer, aristokratischer und demokratischer Elemente in der Mischverfassung ihre klassische Darstellung. Bei Polybios soll die Mischverfassung den fatalen Kreislauf der Staatsformen aufhalten, Cicero schätzt die gemischte Verfassung, weil in ihr alle Bürger nach ihrer *dignitas* an der Regierung des Staates teilhaben.

Auch bei den politischen Denkern der Neuzeit bewirkt der postulierte Staatszweck eine Bewertung der Staatsformen. Der Hobbes'sche Staat der Sicherheit ruft nach der Monarchie. Der freie und zu sich selbst kommende Mensch Rousseaus kann nur in der Demokratie gedeihen. Montesquieus Ziel der bürgerlichen Freiheit ist nur in seinen Staatsformen Republik und Monarchie, nicht aber in der Despotie zu verwirklichen. Auch der Gedanke der Mischverfassung, dem Bodin mit seiner Souveränitätslehre den Boden entzogen hat, lebt unter anderen Vorzeichen vereinzelt fort. Montesquieus Gewaltenteilungslehre etwa hat durch die Verknüpfung der Gewalten mit den sozialen Machtträgern: Königtum, Adel, Bürgertum Elemente der alten *status-mixtus*-Lehre aufgenommen.[4]

Freilich sind diese Gedanken nur mehr Restbestände der klassischen Tradition, der auch das politische Denken der Neuzeit verpflichtet ist. Das entscheidend Neue ist aber, daß die Staatsformenlehre nun nicht mehr an das Paradigma von Ziel und Zweck des Staates, sondern an die Theorie der Staatsentstehung anknüpft. Mit dem Herrschaftsvertrag wird auch die Staatsform festgelegt. Pufendorf, der zwischen Gesellschafts- und Herrschaftsvertrag ein Dekret über die Staatsform einschiebt, ist da-

---

[2] In Platos *Politeia:* Basilie und Aristokratie, bei Aristoteles: Basilie, Aristokratie und Politie, bei Cicero: Königtum, Optimatenherrschaft und Volksstaat.

[3] Bei Plato: Timokratie, Oligarchie, Demokratie und Tyrannis, bei Aristoteles und Cicero: Tyrannis, Oligarchie und Demokratie bzw. Ochlokratie.

[4] Vgl. HANS MAIER, Montesquieu und die Tradition, in: Epimeleia (Festschrift für Helmut Kuhn), München 1964, 277 f.; MAX IMBODEN, Montesquieu und die Lehre der Gewaltentrennung, 1959, 17 f.

für das charakteristischste Beispiel. Staatsform bedeutet damit nicht mehr der Boden, auf dem das gute Zusammenleben der Menschen im Gemeinwesen verwirklicht oder verfehlt werden kann. Sie wird instrumental gesehen als Organisationsform des Staates, als Bezeichnung für die Entscheidung darüber, durch wen der Wille des Staates verkörpert wird.

Die Art, die Staatsformenlehre von der Wirklichkeit der Staatenwelt anzugehen, läßt sich naturgemäß weniger typisieren. Es gibt politische Denker, die die historisch vergleichende Methode angewandt haben und eine Fülle von Staaten auf ihre Verfassung untersucht haben. Aristoteles und Montesquieu gehören dazu, und Bodin ist wegen seiner Materialfülle wohl der herausragendste Vertreter dieser Gattung. Andere politische Philosophen haben sich von einer einzigen Verfassung faszinieren lassen.

Maßgebend ist aber nicht diese Unterscheidung, sondern die Frage, welchen Einfluß die Beobachtung der Staatenwirklichkeit auf die theoretischen Überlegungen zu den Staatsformen gehabt hat. Aristoteles verändert und modifiziert wiederholt die Klassifikation in die drei guten und drei schlechten Staatsformen unter dem Eindruck der wirklichen Staaten.[5] Auch Montesquieu hätte wohl nicht die Staatsformen in Republiken, Monarchien und Despotien eingeteilt, wenn er nicht aus seinen geschichtsvergleichenden Studien die Staatsformen in bestimmten Weltteilen hätte lokalisieren können: in Asien und Afrika die Despotie, in Europa die gemäßigten Staatsformen Monarchie und Republik.

Besonders frappierend ist, wie stark eine einzige aus dem traditionellen Staatsformenschema herausfallende Staatsform zu Veränderungen Anlaß gegeben hat. Gerade hier setzen die entscheidenden Brüche in der Tradition der Staatsformenlehre an. Die klassische Ausformung der Mischverfassungstheorie bei Polybios und Cicero ist ohne das Beispiel der römischen Verfassung nicht denkbar. Ebenso unbestreitbar ist Pufendorfs Einteilung in reguläre, irreguläre Staatsformen und Staatenbünde aus der komplizierten Verfassung des Deutschen Reiches abgeleitet. Montesquieus Gewaltenteilungslehre schließlich entstand aus dem Bild, das er sich von der englischen Verfassung machte.

II

Wie entwickelt nun Bodin seine Staatsformenlehre aus der Spannung von theoretischer Ableitung und empirischer Beobachtung?

Bodins theoretische Reflexion über den Staat beginnt nicht mit der anti-

---

[5] *Politik*, Buch 3, 1279 b 11 ff., 1284 b 35 ff., 1286 b 8 ff., 1288 a 32 ff.; im 4. Buch eine weitere Differenzierung der Staatstypen, ebenso im 5. Buch und im ersten Teil des 6. Buches.

ken Frage nach dem *telos* des Staates, sie fragt auch nicht nach der Entstehung des Staates und seiner Legitimation durch den Herrschaftsvertrag.

Am Anfang steht die *Definition*: «Republique est un *droit gouvernement de plusieurs mesnages, et de ce qui leur est commun, avec puissance souveraine*» (1).[6] Die Staatsformenlehre entwickelt Bodin, wenn auch nicht allzu systematisch, aus der Auffaltung der in der Staatsdefinition enthaltenen Prinzipien *souveraineté, droit gouvernement, communauté*.[7] Dieses methodische Vorgehen ist in Anbetracht der traditionellen politischen Philosophie überraschend und neu. Bodin scheint hierin und im Pathos der Wissenschaftlichkeit, mit der er sein Vorgehen begründet, von der Methodenreform des Petrus Ramus beeinflußt zu sein. In dessen formaler Logik gibt es das Verfahren der *inventio*, der deduktiven Ableitung des Besonderen aus den allgemeinen Prinzipien, das mit der Definition beginnt und dann formal den definierten Gegenstand in seine wesentliche Bestandteile unterteilt.[8] Diese Absicht bekundet auch Bodin: man dürfe sich bei der Unterscheidung der Staatsformen nicht bei den unzählbaren Zufällen *(accidents qui sont innumerables)* aufhalten, sondern müsse auf die wesentlichen und formalen Unterschiede *(differences essentielles et formelles)* schauen. Denn mit indifferenten Dingen beschäftigt sich die Wissenschaft nicht (252). Und an anderer Stelle bemerkt er: «wenn die Prinzipien schlecht begründet sind, ist es unmöglich, etwas sicher aufzubauen» (339).

Bodins erstes und wesentliches Prinzip zur Unterteilung der Staatsformen ist die Souveränität. Auf die Frage, wer die Souveränität inne hat, gibt es nur drei quantitative Unterscheidungen: die Monarchie, wenn einer allein die Souveränität hat, die Aristokratie, wenn die Minderheit des Volkes als Körperschaft souverän ist, und die Demokratie oder Volksherrschaft, wenn das ganze Volk oder seine Mehrheit als Körperschaft die Souveränität hat (252). Diese drei sind für Bodin die einzigen Staatsformen; denn es kommt bei einer formalen Unterscheidung nicht auf die Erfassung einer Unzahl möglicher Staatsgestaltungen an, sondern auf die Klassifikation nach ihrem formalen Prinzip. Dafür ist die Wertung nach guten und schlechten Staatsformen akzidentiell. «Wenn man auf die Qualitäten der Herrscher abhebt, ob sie gut oder schlecht sind, schön oder kriegerisch oder reich oder gerecht, dann ergibt sich eine Unendlichkeit an Staatsformen» (252). Aber «la qualité ne change point la nature des

---

[6] Die Zahlen im Text beziehen sich auf den Nachdruck der Ausgabe der *Six Livres de la République*, Paris 1583 bei Scientia Aalen, 1961 [7.26].

[7] Zum ersten Mal gewürdigt von PIERRE MESNARD [129], L'essor de la philosophie politique au XVIᵉ siècle, Paris ²1951, 496 ff.

[8] Vgl. KENNETH D. MCRAE [189], Ramist Tendencies in the thought of Jean Bodin, *Journal of the History of Ideas* 16 (1955), 309 f.

choses» (252), sie ändert nichts an der prinzipiellen Unterscheidung in die
drei Staatsformen.

Indem die Souveränität Unterscheidungskriterium ist, kann es auch
keine gemischte Verfassung und keine beste Staatsform neben diesen drei
Typen geben, denn die Attribute der Souveränität sind unteilbar (253,
266).[9] Bodin setzt der Autorität der antiken Philosophen die vernünftige
Begründung *(vives raisons)*[10] entgegen, die eine Vernunft der formalen
Unterscheidung ist.

Die Formalität der Unterscheidung und die dadurch bedingte Gleich-
wertigkeit der drei Staatsformen hat Bodin aber in der *Republique* nicht
durchgehalten. Das kommt daher, daß er nicht durchgängig zwischen der
Souveränität des Herrschaftsorgans und dem Herrschaftsträger unterscheidet. Wohl differenziert er bei der Frage der Unveräußerlichkeit des
Kronguts (857 ff.) zwischen Herrscher und Königreich. Aber er kann sich,
und das ist entscheidend, nicht vorstellen, daß bei einer Mehrzahl von
Herrschenden die Souveränität ungeteilt bleibt. Er kennt noch nicht die
spätere Lehre (etwa bei Pufendorf), daß mehrere natürliche Personen eine
zusammengesetzte moralische Person ergeben können und so einen einzigen Willen haben, der die Souveränität im Staat verkörpert. Bodin meint:
«Das Hauptmerkmal des Staates, das Souveränitätsrecht, kann im eigentlichen Sinne nur in der Monarchie bestehen, denn niemand kann im Staat
souverän sein als nur ein einziger. Wenn es zwei, drei oder mehrere sind,
ist keiner souverän, weil keiner seinem Mitregenten Gesetz geben oder sich
von ihm geben lassen kann. So sehr man sich auch einen Körper von mehreren Herrschern oder ein Volk als Träger der Souveränität vorstellen
kann, gibt es doch kein eigentliches Subjekt, wenn nicht ein Oberhaupt
mit souveräner Gewalt alle miteinander eint» (961 f.). Im *Methodus* behauptet er sogar: «Die Demokratie ist nichts anderes als die Aufteilung
der Souveränität in gleiche Teile. Es ist weniger absurd, alle Reichtümer
von allen als die Herrschaft gleichmäßig aufzuteilen. Denn den Reichtum
kann jeder besitzen, die zum Herrschen notwendige Klugheit ist dagegen
nur sehr wenigen von Natur zuteil geworden».[11] Zusammen mit der
Analogie zwischen der monarchischen Gewalt und Gott als Herr der
Ordnung der Natur[12] kündigt sich hier aus der Inkonsequenz der
ursprünglichen formalen Unterscheidung bei Bodin die Möglichkeit an,
ein Staatsideal aufzustellen.

---

[9] Zur Ablehnung der Mischverfassung siehe auch *Methodus ad facilem historiarum cognitionen,* Œuvres Philosophiques de Jean Bodin, ed P. Mesnard,
Paris 1951, 177 A 19 ff.
[10] Vgl. *Methodus,* 167 B 29 ff.
[11] *Methodus* 214 B 53–58.
[12] *République,* 161, 1060, *Methodus,* 215 B 50 ff.

Um seine Staatsformenlehre sicher aufzubauen, ist für Bodin die Unterscheidung von Regierungsweise und Staatsform notwendig (339).[13] Das bedeutet, daß zu dem Prinzip der Souveränität das der Regierungsform hinzukommt. Jede Staatsform kann demokratisch, aristokratisch oder monarchisch regiert sein. Die neun möglichen Kombinationen sammelt Bodin zwar nicht systematisch, sie sind aber alle vorhanden.[14] Die Allokation der Souveränität wird dadurch nicht berührt. «Denn es gibt wohl einen Unterschied zwischen Staat und Regierung. Das ist eine Regel der Politik, die noch von niemand behandelt worden ist. Denn der Staat kann eine Monarchie sein, dennoch wird er demokratisch regiert, wenn der Fürst an den Stellen, Behörden, Ämtern und Belohnungen alle teilhaben läßt ohne Ansehen des Adels, des Reichtums oder der Tüchtigkeit. Die Monarchie kann auch aristokratisch regiert sein, wenn der Fürst die Stellen und Pfründen nur an die Adligen oder an die Reichsten oder an die Tüchtigsten gibt. Ebenso kann die aristokratische Herrschaft ihren Staat demokratisch regieren, wenn sie die Ehren und Belohnungen an alle Untertanen gleichmäßig verteilt; ebenso aristokratisch, wenn sie sie nur an die Adligen oder die Reichen verteilt. Dieser Unterschied in der Regierung hat bei denen den Irrtum erzeugt, die die Staaten vermischt haben, ohne den Unterschied zwischen der Staatsform und der Regierung oder Verwaltung dieser zu sehen» (272 f.).

Ist die Unterscheidung nach der Regierungsform genauso formal wie nach der Staatsform, so kann Bodin doch die neun Kombinationen nach dem Gesichtspunkt des *droit gouvernement* werten, ohne das Prinzip der Unteilbarkeit der Souveränität aufgeben zu müssen. Gute Regierung ist für ihn gemäßigte Regierung, die alle sozialen Gruppen oder Stände harmonisch zusammenschließt und entsprechend ihrer Leistung und Bedeutung für den Staat an der Regierung beteiligt. In der gemäßigten Regierungsform sollen im Idealfall Elemente monarchischer, aristokratischer und demokratischer Regierung verbunden sein.[15] Das Prinzip der

---

[13] Diese Unterscheidung ist im *Methodus* noch nicht ausgeprägt. Er kennt nur bei der Monarchie den Unterschied zwischen einer rechtmäßigen und nicht rechtmäßigen (186 B 1–4). Beim rechtmäßigen Königtum unterscheidet Bodin außerdem zwischen dem König, der an keine Gesetze gebunden ist und dem, der auf Grundgesetze seines Reiches eingeschworen ist (186 B 19 ff.). In der letzten Unterscheidung klingt auch hier schon die Frage des Eigentums mit, besonders im Zusammenhang mit dem Seneca-Zitat: «Ad reges potestas omnium pertinet, ad singulos proprietas» (188 A 26 ff.).

[14] *République*, 273, 269, 338 f., 1050.

[15] Freilich hat Bodin das Korrektiv der Mäßigung der Staatsform durch eine komplementäre Regierungsform nicht durchgängig akzeptiert. Bei dem Vergleich der Vor- und Nachteile der drei Staatsformen hat er der Demokratie Nachteile zugeschrieben, die nur bei der demokratisch regierten Demokratie

gemischten Verfassung, das der Souveränitätsbegriff aus der Staatsformenlehre verbannt hat, kommt bei der Erörterung der Regierungsweise zu
seinem Recht.

Freilich wird hier auch der Abstand zur klassischen Mischverfassungs-
lehre sichtbar. Denn die Verwirklichung der gemäßigten Regierung ist
dem Souverän, sprich: dem Monarchen und dessen Willkür anheim-
gegeben. Er soll für Gerechtigkeit sorgen durch das formale Prinzip der
proportion harmonique. Wie formal dieses Prinzip ist und wie wenig es
von einem inhaltlichen Gerechtigkeitsbegriff hat, zeigt sich daran, daß es
die Verbindung von der *proportion arithmétique,* dem demokratischen
Prinzip der Gleichheit der Zahl, und der *proportion géometrique,* der
aristokratischen Gleichheit des Zuwachses, ist und daß dies an den formalen Spielereien einer Zahlentheorie und Harmonielehre exemplifiziert
wird.[16] Wie die Zahlentheorie auf der Zahl eins und die Harmonielehre
auf dem Grundton basiert, so ist auch die *proportion harmonique* auf das
monarchische Prinzip zugeschnitten. Auch hier wird die Ordnung der
Natur als Vergleich und Vorbild herangezogen. Zusammen mit der Natür-
lichkeit der monarchischen Souveränität kommt Bodin damit zu seinem
Staatsideal, der legitimen Monarchie mit einer gemäßigten Regierung,[17]
obwohl von den formalen Kriterien der Souveränität und der Regierungsweise her ein bester Staat sich nicht ergibt. Aus der Analogie der Ordnung der Natur kommt Bodins Staatsformenlehre ein Wertprinzip zu, das
die ursprüngliche Formalität aufhebt.

Allein die Monarchie kann alle drei Regierungsprinzipien in sich auf-
nehmen und zur ausgewogensten Verfassung werden, weil sie die einheit-

---

vorhanden sind (939 ff.). Die monarchisch oder aristokratisch regierte Demokratie scheint er geradezu auszuschließen, indem er Pericles und Lorenzo de
Medici als Monarchen bezeichnet, während ihre Staaten nur noch zum Schein
demokratisch waren (945 f.). Ebenso verwirft er die demokratisch regierte Aristokratie, denn es sei unmöglich, das Volk zu den Staatsämtern zuzulassen, ohne
die Aristokratie in eine Demokratie umzuwandeln (955). Dies alles ist ein Zeichen dafür, wie sehr Bodin die Mäßigung durch die Regierungsweise auf die
Monarchie zugeschnitten hat.

[16] Vgl. dazu den Beitrag von Michel Villey.

[17] Vgl. *République,* 1013 f.: «Es genügt nicht zu sagen, daß die königliche
Monarchie die beste Staatsform ist. Man muß hinzufügen, daß sie gemäßigt werden muß durch die aristokratische und demokratische Regierungsform, d. h.
durch die harmonische Gerechtigkeit, die aus der distributiven oder geometrischen und der kommutativen oder arithmetischen Gerechtigkeit zusammengesetzt ist, die der aristokratischen und demokratischen Staatsform eigen sind.
Dadurch ist es möglich, daß die Staatsform Monarchie einfach ist, die Regierungsweise dagegen zusammengesetzt und gemäßigt, ohne irgendwelche Ver-
mischung der drei Staatsformen.»

lichste und einfachste Staatsform ist. Sie ist zudem die natürlichste Staatsform, weil sie die Harmonie der Lebensgesetzlichkeiten, des Universums
und Gottes am vollkommensten abbildet (961 ff.). «Tout ainsi que par
voix et sons contraires il se compose une douce et naturelle harmonie,
aussi des vices et vertus, des qualitez differentes des elements, des mouvements contraires, et des sympathies et antipathies liees par moyens invio-
lables, se compose l'harmonie de ce monde et de ses parties: comme aussi
la Republique est composée de bons et mauvais, de riches et de poures, de
sages et de fols, de forts et de foibles, alliez par ceux qui sont moyens entre
les uns et les autres: estant toujours le bien plus puissant que le mal, et les
accords plus que les discords. Et tout ainsi que l'unité sur les trois premiers
nombres, l'intellect sur les trois parties de l'ame, le poinct indivisible sur
la ligne, superficie et le corps: ainsi peut on dire, que ce grand Roy eternel,
unique, pur, simple, indivisible, eslevé par dessus le monde elementaire,
celeste et intelligible, unit les trois ensemble, faisant reluire la splendeur
de sa majesté et la douceur de l'harmonie divine en tout ce monde, à
l'exemple duquel le sage Roy se doit conformer et gouverner son
Royaume» (1060).

Bodin kennt gemäß seiner Staatsdefinition noch ein drittes Prinzip der
Einteilung von Staatsformen, nämlich den Grad des Gemeinsamen im
Staat und der Wahrung von Freiheit und Eigentum der Untertanen. So
sind die Erscheinungsformen der Monarchie die *monarchie royale, seigneuriale und tyrannique* (273). Diese Unterscheidung ist nur in der
Monarchie durchgeführt, sie gilt aber ausdrücklich auch für Demokratie
und Aristokratie (273).[18] In der *Monarchie royale* bleibt den Bürgern ihre
natürliche Freiheit und ihr Eigentum (273, 279). In der *monarchie seigneuriale* sind die Untertanen und ihr Besitz Eigentum des Herrschers; er hat
sich dieses Recht durch den Sieg in einem gerechten Krieg erworben und
nach dem Völkerrecht herrscht er über seine Untertanen wie ein Familien-
vater über seine Sklaven (273 f., 278). In der *monarchie tyrannique* gibt
es überhaupt keinen Eigentumsbegriff mehr, ebenso kein Recht und keine
Gerechtigkeit (273, 294).

Mit dieser Unterscheidung wird zum erstenmal der Zusammenhang von
Herrschaft und Eigentum[19] für die Typologie der Staatsformen relevant.
Das Problem selbst ist freilich älter. Bodin beruft sich auf Aristoteles, der
schon den *roi seigneurale* erwähne.[20] Aristoteles behandelt in der Aus-
einandersetzung mit Plato grundsätzlich die Frage des Eigentums im
Staat und meint, «in gewissem Sinne müssen die Güter gemeinsam sein,

---

[18] Vgl. auch *République*, 313, wo Bodin die Aristokratie einteilt in *seigneurale,
legitime ou factieuse*, und *Rép.* 295, wo Bodin Cicero zitiert, daß es auch in der
Volksherrschaft Tyrannei gibt.

[19] Dazu den Beitrag von WALTER EUCHNER.

[20] Vgl. *République*, 282.

im allgemeinen dagegen privat».[21] Bodin zitiert auch im Souveränitätskapitel Seneca: «Ad reges potestas omnium pertinet, ad singulos proprietas.»

Das Prinzip des Gemeinsamen im Staat unterscheidet sich nun von den
anderen Einteilungskriterien grundsätzlich dadurch, daß es nicht formal
gleichwertige Typen nebeneinander stellt, sondern nur für die rechte
Regierung von Staaten ein zusätzliches Kriterium bildet: die Wahrung
von Freiheit und Eigentum der Untertanen. Dagegen fallen Staaten, die
das verfehlen, die Seigneurie und die Tyrannis, streng genommen aus der
Staatentypologie überhaupt heraus. Bodin sagt nämlich, daß «ce n'est pas
Republique s'il n'y a rien de public» (14) und das Dein und Mein die
Grundlage für den Staat ist (948). In der Polemik gegen Platos Güter-,
Frauen- und Kindergemeinschaft kritisiert er Plato, «daß in diesem Fall
das einzige Merkmal des Staates verloren geht, denn es gibt nichts Öffentliches, wenn es kein Eigentum gibt. Ebenso wenn alle Bürger Könige
wären, gäbe es keinen König, und es gäbe keine Harmonie, wenn alle
Töne auf einen einzigen reduziert würden ... Es ist offenkundig, daß die
Staaten so von Gott eingerichtet sind, daß dem Staat das Öffentliche gehört, und jedem einzelnen, was ihm eigen ist. Die Gemeinsamkeit aller
Dinge ist unvereinbar mit dem Recht der Familien: denn wenn die Familie
und der Staat, das Eigentum und das Gemeinsame, das Öffentliche und
das Private vermischt sind, gibt es weder einen Staat, noch eine
Familie» (15). Die *monarchie seigneuriale* und *tyrannique* kennen das
Privateigentum aber ebenso wenig wie die totale Demokratie (948), sie
sind deshalb keine eigentlichen Staatsformen.

III

Wir haben gesehen, daß Bodin eine differenzierte Theorie der Staatsformen entwickelt hat. Seine drei Unterscheidungsprinzipien mit jeweils
drei Ausfaltungen können alle miteinander korreliert werden. So ergeben
sich 27 Typen der Staatsgestaltung. Dieses differenzierte theoretische In-
strumentarium ist deshalb viel geeigneter als das antike Schema der drei
guten und drei schlechten Staatsformen, die empirische Vielfalt der
Staatenwelt zu subsumieren. Dies auch deshalb, weil die Einordnung in
Bodins formales Schema nicht von der subjektiven Bewertung durch den
einzelnen Staatsphilosophen zu sehr abhängt, welche ja von anderen
politischen Denkern schwer nachzuvollziehen ist. Welchen Einfluß hat
unter diesen Umständen Bodins Beobachtung der Staatenwelt auf sein
theoretisches Schema?

---

[21] *Politik* 1263 a 1 ff.

Eines steht von Anfang an fest: das empirische Material, das Bodin in seinen *Six livres de la Republique* ausbreitet, ist schlechthin erdrückend. Er überblickt die Geschichte der Staaten von den Persern über die jüdischen Staatsbildungen, den Kosmos der griechischen Staaten, das Alexanderreich und Rom bis hin zu der spätrömischen Entwicklung und den Anfängen germanischer Staatenbildungen. Er analysiert auch die Verfassungen der Staaten seiner Gegenwart: die großen Monarchien Europas und das türkische Reich ebenso wie die italienischen Stadt- und Kleinstaaten, die schweizer Städte und Kantone und die freien Reichsstädte. Mit Äthiopien, Moskau und Peru bringt er für seine Zeitgenossen sogar ein paar exotische Farben in die Beschreibung der Staatenwelt.

Allem Anschein nach bedient sich Bodin des historischen Materials aber im Hinblick auf die Staatsformenlehre nur, um durch Beispiele seine Staatsformentheorie abzustützen. Das zeigt sich augenfällig bei all den Staaten, die wegen der Ausgewogenheit und Differenziertheit ihrer Verfassung nicht in das antike Staatsformenschema paßten und deshalb als Mischverfassungen bezeichnet wurden. Bodin sieht in all diesen Staaten, notfalls unter einseitiger Interpretation des ihm vorliegenden historischen Materials, eine einfache Staatsform, einen einzigen Träger der Souveränität, auch wenn die Regierungsweise diese Eindeutigkeit mildert und relativiert. Venedig und das Deutsche Reich sind Aristokratien (260 f.; 262, 117), Rom ist seit der Vertreibung der Könige eine Demokratie (267 f.). Aus der Staatsformentheorie fällt dadurch aber der historische Wandel heraus. Rom ist in den Anfängen der Republik für Bodin ebenso eine Demokratie wie zur Zeit des Prinzipats (269). Auch die Kräfteverschiebungen im Römischen Reich Deutscher Nation zwischen Kaiser, Kurfürsten, Fürsten, Reichstagen und Reichsstädten bleiben unberücksichtigt (320 f.).

Freilich macht Bodin auch Zugeständnisse an die geschichtliche Wirklichkeit, besonders wenn ihn die Leistung großer Führerpersönlichkeiten beeindruckt. Der Staat der Athener ist zwar eine Demokratie, aber «Pericles estoit vray Monarche d'icelle, ores qu'en apparence elle fust populaire» (945). Florenz ist eine Demokratie, aber «du temps de Laurens de Medicis, la Republique en apparence estoit populaire et en effect une pure tyrannie, par ce que Laurens gouvernoit tout seul» (946).

Außerdem kann man einwenden, daß angesichts der Vielfalt der geschichtlichen Staaten Bodin erst zu seiner differenzierten Staatsformenlehre veranlaßt worden ist. Mir scheint jedoch, daß die theoretische Ableitung der Staatsformenlehre und die Souveränitätstheorie über die Berücksichtigung der geschichtlichen Wirklichkeit dominieren.

Eine größere Bedeutung gewinnt die Beobachtung der Staatenwelt, wenn Bodin erörtern will, was rechte Regierung eines Staates heißt. Dies kann er nur an historischen Beispielen zeigen: an der römischen Republik

(1050), der venezianischen Aristokratie (955 ff.) und der französischen Monarchie (262 f., 860, 891). Alle Staatsformen bieten nämlich die Möglichkeit einer gemäßigten Regierung. Deshalb kann bei der Bevorzugung der einen oder anderen Verfassung die geographische Lage, die historischen Voraussetzungen und der Nationalcharakter des Volkes berücksichtigt werden. Die *monarchie royale* ist nur das abstrakte Staatsideal; das konkrete Staatsideal für den jeweiligen Staat kann durchaus ein anderes sein: die demokratisch regierte Aristokratie für Venedig, die aristokratisch regierte Demokratie für Rom. Die Theorie der Souveränität stellt keinen absoluten Imperativ auf, sondern nur einen nuancenreichen Optativ (Mesnard). Zwischen dem Determinismus der Naturgesetze und den Möglichkeiten der Institutionen liegt der Bereich des praktischen Handelns des Herrschers, der Anpassung an die natürlichen Gegebenheiten.

Den größten Einfluß hat Bodins historische Einsicht aber bei dem Problem, wie die politische Dynamik des Staates und der Wandel der geschichtlichen Situation durch *altérations*, Anpassung an die Umstände, Variationen des Regierungsstils und Reformen aufgefangen und Revolutionen vermieden werden können. Dazu muß das Naturell der Völker, die geographische Lage und das Klima berücksichtigt werden. Bodin sagt: «Jusques icy nous avons touché ce qui concernoit l'estat universel des Repliques, disons maintenent ce qui peut estre particulier à quelques-unes pour la diversité des peuples, afin d'accommoder la forme de la chose publique à la nature des lieux, et les ordonnances humaines aux loix naturelles» (663). Der hier gebrauchte Begriff des Naturgesetzes läßt an eine Gesetzmäßigkeit im Sinne der Naturwissenschaft denken. In der Tat ist der Nationalcharakter eine Frucht der dauernden Wirkungen der Geographie und der Geschichte. Lang erörtert Bodin, wie das Klima die Eigenart der Völker des Nordens und des Südens, des Westens und des Ostens, der Berge und der Ebenen geprägt hat (666 ff.). Deshalb solle der Herrscher «gouverner d'après le naturel des peuples»; denn «plusieurs ... s'efforçans de faire servir la nature à leurs édicts, ont troublé et souvent ruiné de grands estats» (663). Aber die Gegebenheiten des Klimas, des Ortes und der Geschichte determinieren den Menschen nicht, sie können durch Sitten und Gesetze korrigiert werden. «La discipline peut changer le droit naturel des hommes» (666). Ja, es ist geradezu die Pflicht des Gesetzgebers und Herrschers, die schlechten natürlichen Anlagen des Volkes durch Kultur zu korrigieren, um einen geordneten Staat errichten zu können. Als Beispiel für die kulturelle Veredelung eines Volkes dienen die Deutschen: «Qui voudra voir combien la nourriture, les loix, les coustumes ont puissance à changer la nature, il faut que voir les peuples d'Allemagne, qui n'avoyent du temps de Tacite ny loix, ny religion, ny science, ny forme de Republique, et maintenant ils ne cedent point aux autres peuples en tout cela» (697). Dagegen haben die Römer durch ihren

Müßiggang und ihre Dekadenz selbst ihren Untergang herbeigeführt (698). Bodins Staat verwirklicht seine rechte Verfassung immer wieder aufs neue, indem sich *l'estat universel des Republiques* anpaßt an *la diversité des peuples* (663) und die natürlichen Gegebenheiten der Geographie, der Geschichte und der Völker ihre Norm finden an den allgemeinen Prinzipien des wohlgeordneten Staates. Bodin steuert zwischen der Skylla des geschichtslosen Idealstaates und der Carybdis der zyklischen Geschichtsdynamik. Zwischen Dogmatismus und Determination ist ihm Staat der Ort, wo jede Nation, mehr oder weniger bewußt, nach der Verwirklichung ihrer besonderen Individualität strebt.

Robert Derathé

La Place de Jean Bodin dans l'Histoire des Théories de la Souveraineté

I

Voici tout d'abord, en guise d'introduction, quelque remarques préliminaires sur la notion de souveraineté chez Bodin.[1]

1. La première concerne l'importance que l'auteur attache à cette notion. Pour lui, on ne peut, en effet, concevoir l'Etat sans y inclure la souveraineté, comme le montre la définition célèbre (I, 1, p. 1): «République est un droit gouvernement de plusieurs ménages, et de ce qui leur est commun, avec puissance souveraine». Contrairement à ce que l'on pourrait croire, cette définition ne va pas de soi, car la plupart, pour ne pas dire tous les penseurs libéraux, refusent d'inclure la notion de souveraineté dans la définition de l'Etat. C'est ainsi, par exemple, qu'Emile Faguet écrivait en 1902: «Il n'y a de libre qu'un peuple où *il n'y a pas de souveraineté*, où il n'y a pas de volonté qui commande et où l'on n'obéit qu'à la Raison exprimée par la Loi» (Politique comparée de Montesquieu, Rousseau et Voltaire, p. 41).

2. Il faut, en second lieu, rappeler que Bodin prend soin de souligner combien son entreprise est nouvelle pour son époque: «Il est ici besoin de former la définition de souveraineté, parce qu'il n'y a ni jurisconsulte, ni philosophe politique, qui l'ait définie: jaçait que c'est le point principal et plus nécessaire d'être entendu au traité de la République» (I, 8, p. 122). Même si l'on ne doit pas aujourd'hui prendre à la lettre cette déclaration, on admet généralement que Bodin fut le premier théoricien de la souveraineté, qu'avec lui commence l'histoire de ce concept. Ainsi Bluntschli: «Bodin war der Erste, welcher die Idee der Souveränität zu definieren suchte und einer einläßlichen Untersuchung unterwarf» (Geschichte des Allgemeinen Staatsrechts und der Politik, 2. Auflage, München, 1867, p. 22). De même plus récemment Rudolf von Albertini: «Diese sich in der politischen Wirklichkeit ausbildende souveräne Staatsgewalt hat in Bodins *Six Livres de la République* ihre erste systematische Darstellung gefunden» (Das politische Denken in Frankreich zur Zeit Richelieus, Marburg,

---

[1] Nous citons *Les six livres de la République* d'après l'edition in – 8°, Paris 1583 [7.11].

1951, p. 34). Pourtant on a pu soutenir que la théorie bodinienne de la souveraineté provenait du droit romain: «N'oublions pas, écrit par exemple J. Moreau-Reibel, que les chapitres sur la souveraineté de Bodin condensent le Traité *De imperio et jurisdictione* du Digeste des Bartolistes» (Bodin et le droit public comparé dans ses rapports avec la philosophie de l'histoire, Paris, 1933, p. 140).

3. Nous devons enfin nous demander quelles furent les intentions de l'auteur en écrivant et en publiant les *Six livres de la République.*

Bodin est certes un savant, mais c'est aussi un «politique». Les visées scientifiques ou théoriques de l'ouvrage ne doivent pas nous faire oublier les préoccupations pratiques de l'auteur. Il s'agit pour lui, comme il le dit clairement, de prouver que la France est une monarchie véritable et que le roi de France est un «Prince souverain»: «On a voulu dire et publier par écrit que l'Etat de France était aussi composé des trois Républiques, et que le Parlement de Paris tenait une forme d'Aristocratie, les trois états tenaient la Démocratie, et le roi représentait l'Etat royal: qui est une opinion non seulement absurde, mais aussi capitale. Car c'est crime de lèse-majesté de faire les sujets compagnons du Prince souverain» (II, 1, pp. 262/3). C'est donc moins contre François Hotman, l'auteur de la *Franco-Gallia* (1573) que contre Claude de Seyssel, l'auteur de *La Grande Monarchie de France* (1519) qu'écrit Jean Bodin. Il pouvait d'autant plus facilement réfuter la thèse de Seyssel qu'il n'admettait pas les Etats mixtes.

Ainsi, l'exposé de la souveraineté reste lié, chez Bodin, à une préoccupation pratique, celle de la monarchie française. Bodin ne cesse de répéter que le Roi est seul souverain en France. C'est pourquoi un historien comme Bluntschli a pu lui reprocher d'avoir bâti sa théorie en se basant uniquement sur le cas français.[2]

Comme plus tard Grotius, Bodin est le théoricien de la souveraineté des rois, sans pourtant chercher sérieusement à montrer comment ceux-ci ont acquis la souveraineté. Si certains passages laissent entendre qu'ils l'ont

---

[2] BLUNTSCHLI écrit (Geschichte des allgem. Staatsrechts und der Politik, 25): «Offenbar hat unter den historischen Motiven die Rücksicht auf sein französisches Vaterland wie an sehr vielen anderen Stellen seines Werks am stärksten auf seine Meinung eingewirkt. Diese absolute, auf die Autorität des *corpus juris* gestützte Gewalt des Königstums war die Lieblingsidee nicht bloß des französischen Hofes, sondern vorzüglich auch des dritten Standes und seiner Juristen, weil sie von dieser Kraft aus die Beseitigung der feudalen Schranken, die Unterordnung der kleinen Herrschaften, die Bändigung der confessionellen Parteien, die Einigung der ganzen Nation, ein gleiches französisches Recht und eine energische französische Politik erwarteten. Der französische Gedanke erhob aber den Anspruch, eine allgemeine Wahrheit zu sein; das war der verhängnisvolle Irrtum Bodins, der so viele Nachfolger bis auf den heutigen Tag mißleitete.»

obtenue du consentement du peuple, d'autres, par contre, affirment que la souveraineté a été imposée par la force, comme le texte suivant (I, 6, p. 69): «La raison et lumière naturelle nous conduit à cela, de croire que la force et violence a donné source et origine aux Républiques.» C'est vraisemblablement sur ce texte que s'appuient Lerminier[3] et plus récemment Allen,[4] pour dire que, selon Bodin, l'origine de l'Etat, c'est la force.

II

Si, comme nous l'avons dit, Bodin s'est proposé de plaider pour la souveraineté des rois, s'il a voulu montrer à ses compatriotes que le roi de France est un Prince souverain, son exposé doctrinal n'est pourtant pas lié à une forme de gouvernement. Pour lui, dans tout Etat ou dans toute espèce régulière de République, il doit y avoir un pouvoir souverain. Les trois espèces de République se distinguent par le titulaire de la souveraineté, mais celle-ci est partout et toujours la même: «Puis donc que la qualité ne change point la nature des choses, nous dirons qu'il n'y a que trois Etats, ou trois sortes de Républiques, à savoir la monarchie, l'Aristocratie et la Démocratie: la Monarchie s'appelle quand un seul a la souveraineté, comme nous avons dit, et que le reste du peuple n'y a que voir; la Démocratie ou l'Etat populaire, quand tout le peuple, ou la pluspart d'icelui en corps a la puissance souveraine; l'Aristocratie, quand la moindre partie du peuple a la souveraineté en corps, et donne loi au reste du peuple, soit en général, soit en particulier» (II, 1, p. 252).

Nous avons vu également que Bodin ne s'est guère préoccupé de rechercher l'origine de la souveraineté. Ce qui l'intéresse, par contre, c'est d'en préciser la nature, de dire ce qu'elle est, et c'est en cela surtout que consiste sa contribution à la théorie de la souveraineté, contribution majeure, sinon exemplaire, à laquelle ses successeurs devront beaucoup, même s'ils ne se réfèrent pas explicitement à lui.

On connaît la définition célèbre (I, 8, p. 122): «La souveraineté est la puissance absolue et perpétuelle d'une République.»

1. Nous ne nous attarderons pas sur l'épithète *perpétuelle* qui disparaît d'ailleurs dans la traduction latine. Par perpétuelle Bodin veut dire que la souveraineté ne peut pas être conférée pour un certain temps seulement et qu'en ce sens ni le dictateur romain, ni le grand Archon d'Athènes, ni le lieutenant général et perpétuel d'un Prince avec puissance absolue ne sont princes souverains. Ils sont investis de la puissance comme «déposi-

---

[3] *Introduction générale à l'histoire du droit,* 2ᵉᵐᵉ éd., Paris, 1835, 74.

[4] J. W. ALLEN [97] *A History of Political Thought in the Sixteenth Century,* nouvelle édition, London 1961, 414.

taires de la puissance d'autrui» et en disposent «par forme de prêt ou de précaire».

2. Plus importante est l'épithète *absolue*, à laquelle Bodin attache une signification particulière. Sans doute entend-il par là que «la souveraineté donnée à un Prince sous charges et conditions n'est pas proprement souveraineté ni puissance absolue» (p. 128). Mais, pour lui, disposer de la puissance absolue, c'est avant tout être «absous de la puissance des lois». Il faut toutefois faire une réserve: il s'agit seulement des lois civiles et non des lois de Dieu et de nature: «Si nous disons, écrit Bodin, que celui a puissance absolue, qui n'est point sujet aux lois, il ne se trouvera Prince au monde souverain, vu que tous les Princes de la terre sont sujets aux lois de Dieu et de nature, et à plusieurs lois humaines communes à tous peuples» (I, 8, p. 131). Aussi Bodin précisera-t-il sa pensée en disant que «la puissance absolue n'est autre chose que dérogation aux lois civiles» (I, 8, p. 156). De là la définition de la souveraineté qui figure dans l'édition latine: «Majestas est summa in cives ac subditos legibus soluta potestas.»

3. Positivement parlant, la souveraineté devient la puissance de donner loi aux sujets *sans leur consentement*: «On voit, dit Bodin, que le point principal de la majesté souveraine et puissance absolue gît principalement à donner loi aux sujets en général sans leur consentement» (I, 8, p. 142).

Cette formule s'inscrit manifestement dans le cadre de la souveraineté des rois. A l'époque de Bodin, le consentement des sujets s'exprimait par l'approbation donnée par les états du peuple. On sait l'importance que Bodin, comme tous les politiques de son temps, attache aux collèges, communautés et états du peuple. Il n'hésitera pas à écrire au livre III, chapitre 7 (p. 499), que ce sont toujours les tyrans qui les suppriment. Même en la royauté, les états sont indispensables: «La juste royauté n'a point de fondement plus assuré que les états du peuple, corps et collèges: car, s'il est besoin de lever deniers, assembler des forces, maintenir l'Etat contre les ennemis, cela ne peut se faire que par les états du peuple, et de chacune province; ville ou communauté» (p. 500). Mais ces états du peuple sont entièrement soumis à la puissance du Prince souverain qui n'est pas tenu de suivre leur avis: «En cela se connaît la grandeur et majesté d'un vrai Prince souverain, quand les états de tout le peuple sont assemblés, présentant requête et supplications à leur prince en toute humilité, sans avoir aucune puissance de rien commander, ni décerner, ni voix délibérative: mais ce qu'il plaît au Roi consentir ou dissentir, commander ou défendre, est tenu pour loi, pour édit, pour ordonnance. En quoi ceux qui ont écrit du devoir des Magistrats, et autres livres semblables, se sont abusés de soutenir que les états du peuple sont plus grands que le prince: chose qui fait révolter les vrais sujets de l'obéissance qu'ils doivent à leur prince souverain» (I, 8, pp. 137/8). Le Prince souverain n'est donc aucunement tenu d'obtenir l'assentiment des états du peuple et la loi émane de sa seule autorité: «La première marque du prince souverain, c'est la puissance de donner loi à tous en général, et à chacun en particulier: mais ce n'est pas assez, car il faut ajouter, sans le consentement de plus grand, ni de pareil, ni de moindre que soi: car si le prince est obligé de ne faire loi sans le consentement d'un plus grand que soi, il est vrai sujet; si d'un pareil, il aura compagnon; si des sujets, soit du Sénat ou du peuple, il n'est pas souverain» (I, 10, p. 220).

4. Aussi, parmi les diverses marques de la souveraineté, la puissance de donner et casser la loi occupe-t-elle une place privilégiée, au point qu'elle englobe toutes les autres. Si Bodin peut dire que «les marques de la souveraineté sont indivisibles» ou encore que «la souveraineté est chose indivisible» (II, 1, pp. 266 et 254), c'est parce que la vraie marque de la souvraineté est de donner et de casser la loi. Nous reviendrons plus longuement sur ce point quand nous comparerons la théorie de Bodin à celle de Rousseau.

Après cet exposé, qui est relativement simple et cohérent, venons-en maintenant aux difficultés, qui ont fait dire à Allen[5] que la conception de la souveraineté n'était, chez Bodin, ni claire ni complète.

Ces difficultés viennent des limites que Bodin assigne à la souveraineté, dans le cadre de la souveraineté des rois ou, plus exactement, dans le cas de la souveraineté du Roi de France.

Ces limites, on le sait, sont au nombre de trois: 1. Le souverain est tenu de se soumettre aux lois de Dieu et de nature; 2. Il ne peut enfreindre les lois fondamentales du royaume *(leges imperii)* ni les changer sans le consentement des états du peuple; 3. Il doit enfin respecter la propriété privée de ses sujets, laquelle est, selon Bodin, un droit naturel et sacré, donc ne pas lever sur eux d'impôts ou de taxes sans leur consentement.

Examinons sucessivement ces trois points.

1. Nous passerons vite sur le premier, car il y a peu de théoriciens de la politique qui ne soient d'accord avec Bodin sur ce point. «Quant aux lois divines et naturelles, dit Bodin, tous les princes de la terre y sont sujets, et n'est pas en leur puissance d'y contrevenir, s'ils ne veulent être coupables de lèse-majesté divine, faisant guerre à Dieu, sous la grandeur duquel tous les Monarques du monde doivent faire joug, et baisser la tête en tout crainte et révérence. Et par ainsi la puissance absolue des princes et seigneuries souveraines ne s'étend aucunement aux lois de Dieu et de nature» (I, 8, p. 133).

Nous n'avons pas à nous préoccuper de ce qui arrive dans l'autre monde aux princes coupables de lèse-majesté divine. Politiquement parlant, le problème est de savoir si les sujets et particulièrement les magistrats doivent exécuter les ordres du prince, lorsque ces ordres sont contraires à la loi naturelle. Comme le dit Allen,[5] Bodin n'élude pas cette ques-

---

[5] ALLEN [97], 414.

tion primordiale, mais l'examine avec autant de clarté que de franchise au livre III, chapitre 4 *(De l'obéissance que doit le magistrat aux lois et au Prince souverain)*: «Or, écrit Bodin, si le sujet d'un seigneur particulier ou justicier, n'est pas tenu d'obéir en termes de droit, si le Seigneur ou le magistrat passe les bornes de son territoire, ou de la puissance qui lui est donnée, ores que la chose qu'il commande fût juste et honnête, comment serait tenu le magistrat d'obéir, ou d'exécuter les mandements du Prince en choses injustes et déshonnètes? car, en ce cas, le Prince franchit et brise les bornes sacrées de la loi de Dieu et de nature» (pp. 413/4). Selon Bodin – et il est très ferme sur ce point – le magistrat n'est donc pas tenu d'exécuter un ordre injuste et doit plutôt se démettre que d'agir contre sa conscience. C'est donc admettre, en certains cas, le devoir de désobéissance, mais non le droit à la rébellion. Aussi Bodin n'adopte-t-il pas l'attitude radicale des *Vindiciae contra Tyrannos* (1579) ni celle du livre de Théodore de Bèze, *Du Droit des magistrats sur leurs sujets* (1575), et cela, parce qu'il ne partage pas leur conception de la souveraineté. Bodin développe toutefois une casuistique habile pour préciser les cas où l'opportunité et le salut de l'Etat doivent l'emporter sur les scrupules de conscience. De toute façon il faut reconnaître, avec Allen,[6] que, pas plus que les penseurs médiévaux attachés à la notion de loi naturelle, Bodin ne peut admettre une souveraineté strictement illimitée.

2. Les lois fondamentales forment une seconde limite à l'exercice de la souveraineté du roi: «Quant aux lois qui concernent l'état du Royaume et de l'établissement d'icelui, dit Bodin, d'autant qu'elles sont annexées et unies avec la couronne, le Prince n'y peut déroger» (I, 8, p. 137). Ces lois fondamentales sont au nombre de deux: la loi salique qui règle la succession à la couronne et celle qui interdit l'aliénation du domaine. Cette dernière est sans doute la plus importante, puisque Bodin écrit au livre VI, chapitre 2, au moment où, abordant la question des finances publiques, il traite du domaine: «Le domaine appartient à la République ... la République l'apporte au Prince, comme dot à son époux, pour la tuition défense et entretenement d'icelle ... les Rois ne se le peuvent approprier en sorte quelconque» (p. 859). Bodin souligne en termes particulièrement vigoureux le caractère inaliénable du domaine public, caractère qui n'est pas, à ses yeux, uniquement propre à la monarchie française: «Afin, dit-il, que les Princes ne fussent contraints de charger d'impôts leurs sujets, ou chercher les moyens de confisquer leurs biens, tous les peuples et Monarques ont tenu pour loi générale et indubitable, que le domaine public doit être saint, sacré, et inaliénable: soit par contrats, soit par prescription» (p. 857).

On le voit, la souveraineté se trouve ici bornée non plus seulement par

---

[6] ALLEN [97], 417.

les lois de nature, mais par des lois constitutionnelles. Manifestement, Bodin a voulu concilier sa conception de la souveraineté avec ce qu'on a appelé la constitution du royaume. Certes l'absolutisme royal en France s'est toujours accommodé de ces lois du royaume, que les juristes ont distingué des lois du roi.[7] Mais on peut se demander si cette concession au constitutionalisme n'est pas préjudiciable à la notion même de souveraineté définie comme puissance absolue. On sait que Rousseau rejettera plus tard les lois fondamentales. Bodin déclare que la souveraineté ne peut être conférée «sous charges ou conditions» (I, 8, p. 128), formule qui n'est guère compatible avec les obligations qu'imposent au souverain les lois fondamentales. D'autres questions se posent: Qu'est-ce qui impose au souverain le respect des lois fondamentales? et surtout d'où proviennent-elles? Comme le dit Allen,[8] elles ne peuvent devoir leur origine à un acte du souverain, puisque le souverain ne peut se lier lui-même, ni lier son successeur. Elles ne peuvent non plus provenir d'un contrat qui lierait le roi au peuple. Ce ne sont, en fait, que des lois coutumières, plus importantes sans doute que les autres, mais qu'il est difficile d'appeler saintes ou sacrées, à moins d'admettre qu'elles font partie de ces lois humaines communes à tous les peuples que Bodin assimile aux lois naturelles. Le texte que nous avont cité plus haut pourrait suggérer une telle interprétation.

3. Le troisième point est relatif au respect du droit de propriété. C'est sans doute le plus important, car il concerne le droit d'imposition.

Pour Bodin, le droit de propriété est un droit naturel dont le Prince est tenu d'assurer l'exercice aux particuliers, sans pouvoir lui-même y porter atteinte: «Dire que les Princes sont seigneurs de tout, cela s'entend de la droite seigneurie et justice souveraine, demeurant à chacun la possession et propriété de ses biens. Ainsi disait Senèque (*De Beneficiis*, lb. VII, cap. 4 et 5): *Ad Reges potestas omnium pertinet, ad singulos proprietas*; et peu après: *Omnia Rex imperio possidet, singuli dominio*» (I, 8, p. 157).

Aussi le souverain n'a-t-il pas le droit de prélever sur les sujets, sans leur consentement, des impôts, des tributs ou des taxes: «Il n'est en la puissance de Prince du monde, de lever impôts à son plaisir sur le peuple, non plus que prendre le bien d'autrui; comme Philippe de Commines remontra sagement aux états tenus à Tours, ainsi que nous lisons en ses Mémoires» (I, 8, p. 140). Certes le fonctionnement de l'Etat exige des dépenses, mais les revenus du domaine doivent normalement suffire pour y faire face. Si le domaine public est inaliénable, c'est préciment pour éviter aux Princes de charger d'impôts leurs sujets.

---

[7] Cf. Fr. Olivier-Martin, Les lois du roi, *Cours d'Histoire du Droit public* 1945–1946, 4.

[8] Allen [97], 418.

Mais il peut arriver que les dépenses publiques excèdent les recettes du domaine et que le Prince soit dans la nécessité, comme le dit Bodin, de lever derniers. En ce cas, le Prince doit obtenir le consentement des états: «S'il est besoin de lever deniers, dit Bodin, cela ne se peut faire que par les états du peuple, et de chacune province, ville et communauté» (III, 7, p. 500). Il y a cependant une réserve: «Toutefois, si la nécessité est urgente, en ce cas le Prince ne doit pas attendre l'assemblée des états, ni le consentement du peuple, duquel le salut dépend de la prévoyance et diligence d'un sage Prince» (I, 8, p. 140). C'est pourquoi Bodin dira plus clairement encore au livre VI, chapitre 2 (pp. 877/8): «Le septième moyen [de faire fonds aux finances] est sur les sujets, auquel il ne faut jamais venir, si tous les autres moyens ne défaillent, et que la nécessité presse de pourvoir à la République: auquel cas, puisque la tuition et défense des particuliers dépend de la conservation du public, c'est bien la raison que chacun s'y emploie: alors les charges et impositions sur les sujets sont très justes, car il n'y a rien plus juste, que ce qui est nécessaire, comme disait un ancien sénateur romain.»

On le voit, l'attitude adoptée par Bodin à l'égard des impôts est claire, même si elle est complexe. Elle se résume en trois points: 1. Le mieux serait de ne jamais taxer les sujets et de subvenir aux besoin de l'Etat avec les revenus du domaine ou autres ressources. 2. S'il est néanmoins besoin de lever deniers ou d'établir des impôts, il faut, en droit, le consentement du peuple exprimé par l'approbation ou l'autorisation donnée par les états. 3. Enfin, «en cas de nécessité urgente», le Prince, invoquant le salut de l'Etat, peut se passer du consentement des états.

Quoi qu'on puisse penser de cette attitude, on peut s'étonner avec Allen, que Bodin n'ait pas jugé utile de la mettre en relation avec sa théorie de la souveraineté. Il en résulte toutefois qu'à la différence de Hobbes et de Pufendorf, Bodin n'a pu faire figurer parmi les marques de la souveraineté le droit de lever des taxes ou des impôts[9] sans se contredire. Sur ce point

---

[9] Comme, par exemple, dans le texte suivant, signalé au cours de la discussion: «Sous cette même puissance de donner et casser la loi, sont compris tous les autres droits et marques de souveraineté: de sorte qu'à parler proprement, on peut dire qu'il n'y a que cette seule marque de souveraineté, attendu que tous les autres droits sont compris en celui-là: comme décerner la guerre ou faire la paix: connaître en dernier ressort des jugements de tous magistrats, instituer et destituer les plus grands officiers; *imposer ou exempter les sujets de charges et subsides;* octroyer grâces et dispenses contre la rigueur des lois; hausser ou baisser le titre, valeur et pied des monnaies; faire jurer les sujets et hommes liges de garder fidélité sans exception à celui auquel est dû le serment, qui sont les vraies marques de souveraineté, comprises sous la puissance de donner la loi à tous en général, et à chacun en particulier, et ne la recevoir que de Dieu» (I, 10, pp. 223–224). Bodin ajoute un peu plus loin (p. 244): «Quant au droit de mettre sur

précis, il se trouve certainement plus proche d'un libéral comme Locke que des authentiques théoriciens de la souveraineté.

C'est pourquoi Allen a pu écrire non sans quelque sévérité: «Dire que la principale contribution de Bodin à la pensée politique est sa conception d'une souveraineté absolue et illimitée, laquelle est logiquement incluse dans la conception de l'Etat, est à la fois ambigu et inexact. Car il n'est pas vrai que Bodin ait conçu la souveraineté comme un droit illimité.»[10]

Nous ne pensons pas toutefois qu'on puisse soutenir, comme le fait Allen,[11] que l'originalité de la conception de Bodin consiste essentiellement, pour son époque du moins, dans le fait qu'il n'a pas lié la souveraineté ni spécifiquement ni directement à la volonté de Dieu. Il nous paraît beaucoup plus important que Bodin ait dit que «la souveraineté est chose indivisible»[12] et que le pouvoir de faire la loi en est le caractère essentiel.

III

Si nous voulons maintenant indiquer avec plus de précision la place de Jean Bodin dans l'histoire des théories de la souveraineté, nous aurons à examiner successivement quelle a été son influence sur le constitutionalisme français (A) et sur les conceptions ultérieures de la souveraineté formulées par des juristes ou philosophes, sans référence au cas français (B).

---

les sujets tailles et impôts, ou bien en excepter quelques-uns, cela dépend aussi de la puissance de donner la loi et les privilèges: non pas que la République ne puisse être sans tailles, comme le Président le Maistre écrit que les tailles ne sont imposées que depuis le Roi Saint Louis en ce royaume; mais s'il est besoin de les imposer, ou les ôter, il ne peut se faire que par celui qui a la puissance souveraine».

Ces textes ne s'accordent guère avec ceux que nous avons cités et qui ne donnent au prince souverain que conditionnellement et dans certains cas le droit d'imposer les sujets. Pour Bodin, l'idéal serait que le prince ne fût jamais dans la nécessité de lever des impôts sur ses sujets et que la République pût être «sans tailles». Manifestement Bodin n'a pas réussi à mettre en harmonie sa théorie de la souveraineté avec sa conception de la propriété, considérée comme un droit absolu et sacré. Sur l'ensemble de la question des impôts chez Bodin, cf. M. Wolfe [265], Jean Bodin on Taxes: The Sovereignty – Taxes Paradox, *Political Science Quarterly* 83 (1968) 268–284.

[10] Allen [97], 422.

[11] Allen [97], 423.

[12] Cf. J. Moreau-Reibel [116], Jean Bodin et le droit public comparé dans ses rapports avec la philosophie de l'histoire, Paris 1933, 153: «Entre tous les caractères que doit posséder la souveraineté, il en est un qui dirige la pensée de Bodin ..., il s'agit de l'indivisibilité.»

Ce sont manifestement deux vastes sujets sur lesquels nous ne pourrons que rappeler l'essentiel en posant quelques jalons pour orienter la discussion.

A

L'étude de Landmann (Der Souveränitätsbegriff bei den französischen Theoretikern von Jean Bodin bis Jean-Jacques Rousseau, Leipzig, 1896) laisse de côté les écrivains politiques ou légistes du XVIème et du XVIIème siècle. Cette lacune a été heureusement comblée par ce qu'ont écrit successivement sur ce sujet William Farr Church (Constitutional Thought in sixteenth-century France, Cambridge, Harvard University Press, London 1941) et Rudolf von Albertini (Das politische Denken in Frankreich zur Zeit Richelieus, Marburg, 1951). Nous lisons dans ce dernier ouvrage (p. 35): «Die Bedeutung Bodins für die theoretische Formulierung des französischen Absolutismus und damit im weiteren Sinne für das staatliche Bewußtsein des 17. Jahrhunderts überhaupt ist außerordentlich groß.»

L'influence de Bodin s'est exercée plus particulièrement sur deux écrivains d'inégale importance et d'inégale rigueur: Charles Loyseau[13] et Cardin Le Bret.[14]

Au début du *Traité des Seigneuries* (1608), au moment où il aborde le problème de la souveraineté, Charles Loyseau se réfère à Bodin «duquel, dit-il, j'ai été bien aise d'emprunter contre ma coutume partie de ce chapitre, afin d'avoir un garant en une matière si importante» (*Œuvres*, 1701, p. 14, texte cité par Albertini, *op. cit.*, p. 35, note 1). Pour Loyseau, la souveraineté est inséparable de l'Etat, elle est la forme qui lui donne l'être: «Cette souveraineté, dit-il, est la propre seigneurie de l'Etat. Car, combien que toute seigneurie publique dût demeurer à l'Etat, ce néanmoins les seigneurs particuliers ont usurpé la suzeraineté: mais la souveraineté est du tout inséparable de l'Etat, duquel si elle était ôtée, ce ne serait plus un Etat, et celui qui l'aurait, aurait l'Etat en tant et pour tant qu'il aurait la seigneurie souveraine, comme quand le Roi français quitta la souveraineté de Flandre, la Flandre fut, par conséquent, distraite et ôtée de l'Etat de France, et devint un Etat à part. Car enfin la souveraineté est la forme qui donne l'être à l'Etat et même l'Etat et la souveraineté prise *in concreto* sont synonymes, et l'Etat est ainsi appelé, pour

---

[13] «Loyseau, écrit CHURCH, fut, sans aucun doute le plus grand juriste de toute la période qui fait l'objet de cette étude, supérieur même à Bodin» (Constitutional Thought in Sixteenth-Century France [145], 317, note 33).

[14] Sur Le Bret, on peut consulter la thèse de GILBERT PICOT [163], Cardin Le Bret (1558–1655), et la Doctrine de la Souveraineté, Nancy 1948.

ce que la Souveraineté est le comble et période de puissance, où il faut que l'Etat s'arrête et établisse» (*Seigneuries,* chap. 2, §§ 4–6). Ce texte rappelle manifestement celui où Bodin déclare que l'Etat s'étend jusqu'où s'exerce la puissance souveraine: «De plusieurs citoyens . . . se fait une République, quand ils sont gouvernés par la puissance souveraine de un ou plusieurs seigneurs, encore qu'ils soient diversifiés en lois, en langue, en coutumes, en religions, en nations» (I, 6, p. 72). Loyseau distingue, en outre, selon la direction indiquée par Bodin entre Office et Seigneurie publique. Sans examiner ici en détail le sens de cette distinction, rappelons seulement que, pour Loyseau, la souvereineté est «la propre seigneurie de l'Etat» et qu'en fin de compte, cet écrivain se prononce en faveur de l'absolutisme royal: «Le Roi, dit-il, est parfaitement Officier, ayant le parfait exercice de toute puissance publique: et est aussi parfaitement Seigneur, ayant en perfection la propriété de toute puissance publique. Mais je dis qu'il est officier et feudataire tout ensemble, et à l'égard de Dieu, et à l'égard du peuple» (*Œuvres, Les cinq livres du droit des Offices,* p. 100; texte cité par Albertini, *op. cit.,* p. 38).

Cardin Le Bret, l'auteur de l'in-quarto intitulé *De la Souveraineté du Roi* (Paris, 1632), n'est pas un théoricien de la valeur de Charles Loyseau, c'est un esprit plus concret, plus pratique, plus soucieux de se référer à la tradition. Aussi ne trouve-t-on pas, comme on l'a dit,[15] «dans son analyse de la notion de souveraineté, une parfaite unité de vues».

Pourtant il consacre un chapitre de son livre – le chapitre 2 du livre I – à préciser ce «que c'est que la souveraineté».

1. Le Bret la définit «une suprême puissance déférée à un seul, qui lui donne droit de commander absolument et qui n'a pour but que le repos et l'utilité publique» (*De la souveraineté,* I, 1, p. 1). La souveraineté est ici définie par rapport à la monarchie, quoique Le Bret ne conteste pas que la souveraineté puisse aussi se trouver dans les Etats non monarchiques. Mais il partage l'opinion de Bodin, qui déclarait au livre VI, chap. 4, de la République (pp. 961/2): «Le principal point de la République, qui est le droit de souveraineté, ne peut être ni subsister, à proprement parler, sinon en la Monarchie, car nul ne peut être souverain en une République qu'un seul: s'ils sont deux, ou trois, ou plusieurs, pas un n'est souverain, d'autant que pas un seul ne peut donner, ni recevoir loi de son compagnon: et combien qu'on imagine un corps de plusieurs seigneurs, ou d'un peuple tenir la souveraineté, si est-ce qu'elle n'a point de vrai sujet ni d'appui, s'il n'y a un chef avec puissance souveraine, pour unir les uns avec les autres: ce que ne peut faire un simple Magistrat sans puissance souveraine.»

2. Nous avons vu que, pour Bodin, le caractère essentiel de la souverai-

---

neté était son indivisibilité. Ce caractère d'indivisibilité, Le Bret le souligne à son tour dans une formule frappante que Richelieu citera dans ses
Mémoires: «Mais l'on demande, si le Roi peut faire tous ces changements
de lois et d'ordonnances de sa seule autorité, sans en communiquer à son
Conseil ni à ses Cours souveraines. A quoi l'on répond, que cela ne reçoit
point de doute, pource que le Roi est le seul souverain dans son royaume;
et que la souveraineté n'est non plus divisible que le point en la Géome-
trie...»[16] (*De la Souveraineté*, p. 71). Si Le Bret se prononce pour un
gouvernement centralisé, c'est en raison de l'indivisibilité de la souveraineté. Il écrit, en effet, que l'on doit réserver à la seule personne du roi
«les choses qui concernent l'administration et le gouvernement de l'Etat,
dont la connaissance est réservée à la seule personne du Roi, sans qu'aucun
autre s'en puisse entremettre que par son ordre et sa commission, suivant
la loi fondamentale de la Monarchie, qui veut que le souverain commandement rèside en la personne d'un seul et l'obéissance en tous les
autres» (*De la Souveraineté*, IV, 4, p. 139).

3. Pourtant, pour mieux légitimer la souveraineté, Le Bret, à la différence de Bodin, se réfère au droit divin des Rois. Si les sujets leur doivent
obéissance, c'est que, «depuis que Dieu a établi des Rois sur les peuples,
ceux-ci ont été privés des droits de souveraineté, et l'on n'a plus observé
que les commandements des Princes» (*De la Souveraineté*, I, 9, p. 18).

Si nous voulions maintenant revenir sur certaines questions traitées par
Bodin, nous aurions à en examiner trois.

La première est le principe que le prince est absous des lois (*Princeps
legibus solutus est*). Ce principe se retrouve chez la plupart des théoriciens
de l'absolutisme et s'exprime par la formule bien connue: «Si veut le Roi,
si veut la Loi.»

Pourtant, tous admettent que le Roi de France doit observer les lois
fondamentales ou lois du royaume, sans préciser d'où ces lois tirent leur
origine et leur autorité. Ainsi, Loyseau dira, à peu près dans le même sens
que Bodin: «Les lois fondamentales bornet la puissance du souverain...
pource que le Prince doit user de la souveraineté selon la propre nature

---

[16] Rudolf von Albertini fait sur cette formule la remarque suivante: «Diese
treffende Formulierung, die selbst von Richelieu in seinen Memorien übernom-
men wurde, wird jeweils auf Le Bret zurückgeführt. Nun enthält aber die vene-
zianische Relation aus dem Jahre 1610 folgenden Passus: «Non può la regia
autorità da alcuno esser limitata, nè circonscritta, poichè la monarchia è come
il punto che non riceve divisione...» Barozzi e Berchet, Relazioni degli Stati
europei Serie II, Bd. I, S. 462. Es muß angenommen werden, daß sowohl die
Formulierung des venezianischen Gesandten, wie diejenige von Le Bret auf eine
dritte, gemeinsam benutzte zurückgehen. Um wen es sich handelt, konnten wir
nicht feststellen» (Das politische Denken in Frankreich zur Zeit Richelieus [176],
Marburg 1951, 40, note 3).

et en la forme et aux conditions qu'elle est établie» (*Des Seigneuries*, II, 8).
Dans son livre *De l'excellence des Rois et du Royaume de France* (Paris,
1610, p. 298), Bignon n'hésitera pas à écrire: «On a raison de dire, que
l'on ne trouve ni commencement ni écriture de cette loi Salique, car c'est
une loi de nature, née avec les hommes et un droit non écrit.»
Reste enfin la question si importante des impôts. Sur ce point les théoriciens ultérieurs se sont écartés de la thèse de Bodin, selon laquelle le Roi
était tenu d'obtenir le consentement des états pour lever deniers. Ainsi
La Roche-Flavin: «La principale cause d'assembler les Etats, dit-il, était
pour avoir leur consentement à quelque nouvelle levée . . . Mais, à présent,
le contraire s'observe partout ailleurs: et n'y a quasi plus d'autres Princes
souverains, voir même de Princes sujets . . . qui n'aient prescrit droit de
lever deniers sur le peuple» (*Treize livres des Parlements de France*,
Bordeaux, 1617, p. 804). Le Bret dira dans le même sens: «Depuis que la
guerre, comme un feu dévorant, a consommé la plupart du fonds de leur
domaine, les Rois ont été contraints d'user absolument de leur autorité, et
de lever sur leurs peuples des tailles et des subsides, même sans leur consentement; qui est un des droits plus remarquables de la Souveraineté des
Rois; et qui leur est si particulier, que l'on a tenu toujours pour maxime,
qu'il n'y a qu'eux qui aient le pouvoir dans leurs royaumes, de lever des
impositions sur les peuples de leur obéissance» (*De la Souveraineté*,
p. 396). On peut constater, d'après ce texte, l'évolution qui s'est faite dans
les esprits depuis Bodin, puisque, pour Le Bret, lever des impôts sur le
peuple sans son consentement est «un des droits plus remarquables de la
souveraineté des rois». Au reste, sur les états du peuple, Le Bret se borne
à reproduire la doctrine de Bodin: «Il est aisé de voir par la suite de ce
discours, dit-il, que, puisque l'on ne tient les Etats que par la permission
et le commandement de sa Majesté, que l'on n'y délibère et n'y résout rien
que par forme de requêtes et de très humbles supplications, et encore pour
le repos et le bien général de tout le Royaume; que ces assemblées ne sont
point contraires à la souveraineté des Rois, ne diminuent point leur
autorité, et ne combattent en aucune façon les maximes fondamentales de
la monarchie» (*De la Souveraineté*, p. 646).

B

Si l'influence de Bodin a été décisive sur le constitutionnalisme et l'absolutisme français, elle est certainement moins nette et plus difficile à évaluer
sur les théories générales de la souveraineté.

1. L'école du Droit naturel, qui lie la théorie de la souveraineté à celle
du contrat social, ne s'inspire pour ainsi dire pas de Bodin et ne le cite
guère. Grotius n'y fait, à ma connaissance, aucune allusion quand il traite

de la souveraineté. Pufendorf, par contre, le mentionne à deux reprises, mais sur des points secondaires. a) Se posant la question de savoir «s'il y a de véritables Rois, qui ne le soient que pour un temps» (*Droit de la nature et des gens*, liv. VII, chap. VII, § 15), Pufendorf rapelle que Grotius répond affirmativement en donnant pour exemple les Dictateurs romains. Mais il se range à l'avis de Bodin, qui refusait au dictateur romain la puissance souveraine, parce que celle que celui-ci detenait n'était pas perpétuelle: «Enimvero, et ante illum (Grotius), Bodinus, *de Republica*, lib. I, cap. 8, et post eruditi viri dictatorem non monarcham, sed magistratum duntaxat extraordinarium fuisse ostenderunt». b) Sur la liaison naturelle des parties de la souveraineté (liv. VII, chap. IV, § 12), Pufendorf renvoie à Bodin: «De quelque autre manière, dit-il, qu'on veuille diviser les Parties de la Souveraineté, les mêmes difficultés reviendront toujours.» Et il renvoie à Bodin, *De Republica*, Lib. II, Cap. I, p. 287, Ed. de Francfort, sans d'ailleurs citer le texte.

2. Je laisserai de côté la question des rapports de Bodin et de Hobbes, puisqu'elle sera traitée par Raymond Polin. Je tiens seulement à rappeler que pour Allen, la conception hobbienne de la souveraineté est radicalement différente de celle de Bodin: «The assertion that the legal Sovereign, dit-il, cannot tax without consent is no doubt inconsistent with the Hobbesian conception of sovereignty. Between Hobbes and Bodin is no mere difference of degree, but rather a great gulf fixed».[17]

3. Reste Rousseau. De tous les théoriciens de la souveraineté, c'est celui qui est le plus proche de Bodin.

Rousseau ne cite Bodin que dans l'*Economie politique*, au sujet des finances publiques. On sait que Rousseau est hostile aux impôts et, curieusement, leur préfère les corvées. Comme Bodin, il pense que l'Etat doit subvenir à ses dépenses à l'aide du domaine public: «Quiconque, dit-il, aura suffisamment réfléchi sur cette matière, ne pourra guère être à cet égard d'un autre avis que Bodin, qui regarde le domaine public comme le plus honnête et le plus sûr de tous les moyens de pourvoir aux besoins de l'Etat».[18]

Si l'on examine maintenant les deux théories de la souveraineté, on sera peut-être plus frappé des différences qui séparent les deux auteurs que de ce qui les rapproche.

1. Certes Bodin se propose essentiellement de légitimer et d'exposer la souveraineté des rois, alors que Rousseau la nie et n'admet que la souveraineté du peuple. Bodin parle sans cesse du Prince souverain, alors que Rousseau établit une distinction entre le Prince qui n'est qu'Officier et le

---

[17] Allen [97], 422.
[18] Œuvres complètes de J.-J. Rousseau, Bibliothèque de la Pléiade, Paris (Gallimard) Tome III, 1964, 265.

souverain. Mais précisément, cette distinction entre le Prince et le souverain, Rousseau a pu l'emprunter à Bodin pour la retourner contre lui. Mais ce n'est là qu'un aspect secondaire de l'influence de Jean Bodin.

2. La seconde différence – plus importante à mon sens – concerne les limites constitutionnelles de la souveraineté. Rousseau rejette les lois fondamentales, que Bodin, et plus tard Montesquieu, considéraient comme la base de la vraie monarchie: «Il faut remarquer encore, dit-il, que la délibération publique ... ne peut ... obliger le souverain envers lui-même, et que, par conséquent, il est contre la nature du corps politique que le souverain s'impose une loi qu'il ne puisse enfreindre. Ne pouvant se considérer que sous un seul et même rapport, il est alors dans le cas d'un particulier contractant avec soi-même; par où l'on voit qu'il n'y a ni ne peut y avoir nulle espèce de loi fondamentale obligatoire pour le corps du peuple, pas même le contrat social» (*Contrat social*, I, 7). C'est l'application stricte du principe *Princeps legibus solutus*, auquel ont dérogé tous les théoriciens de l'absolutisme, lorsqu'ils ont admis des lois fondamentales. Comme nous l'avons montré naguère,[19] l'argumentation de Rousseau est empruntée à Hobbes. Mais Bodin lui-même avait dit que «en l'Etat populaire, le peuple ne fait qu'un corps et ne se peut obliger à soi-même» (*République*, I, 8, p. 143).

3. Le point de jonction entre Bodin et Rousseau est la conception de la nature de la souveraineté et de son indivisibilité.

Pour Rousseau, comme pour Bodin, la puissance de donner loi constitue l'essence de la souveraineté et les autres marques de la souveraineté ne sont que des droits subordonnés.

On connaît le passage célèbre du *Contrat social* (liv. II, chap. 2), où Rousseau compare les écrivains politiques à des charlatans, parce qu'ils divisent la souveraineté en verses parties, pour ensuite reconstituer le tout. Ce passage ne vise pas Montesquieu, comme on l'a dit trop souvent, mais bien Hobbes et Pufendorf, car ces deux auteurs ont admis que la souveraineté se compose de divers droits, même s'ils ont déclaré qu'il y avait entre ces parties de la souveraineté «une liaison indissoluble» et qu'elles devaient se trouver réunies dans les mêmes mains.

Contre cette conception que l'on pourrait qualifier de pluraliste, Rousseau déclare: «Cette erreur vient de ne s'être pas fait des notions exactes de l'autorité souveraine, et d'avoir pris pour des parties de cette autorité ce qui n'en était que des émanations ... En suivant de même les autres divisions, on trouverait que, toutes les fois qu'on croit voir la souveraineté partagée, on se trompe; que les droits qu'on prend pour des parties de cette souveraineté lui sont tous subordonnés, et supposent toujours des

[19] Jean-Jacques Rousseau et la Science politique de son temps, Paris 1950, 335–336.

volontés suprêmes, dont ces droits ne donnent que l'exécution» (*Contrat social*, liv. II, chap. 2).

Or, ce que dit Rousseau est très proche de ce qu'écrivait Bodin au livre I, chapitre 10 de la *République* (pp. 221 et 223): «La première marque du prince souverain, c'est la puissance de donner loi à tous en général, et à chacun en particulier ... Sous cette même puissance de donner et casser la loi, sont compris tous les autres droits et marques de souveraineté: de sorte qu'à parler proprement, on peut dire qu'il n'y a que cette seule marque de souveraineté, attendu que tous les autres droits sont compris dans celui-là». Ce texte est confirmé par un autre, au moins aussi explicite du livre II, chapitre I (p. 266): «Les marques de souveraineté sont indivisibles: car celui qui aura puissance de donner loi à tous, c'est-à-dire commander ou défendre ce qu'il voudra, sans qu'on en puisse appeler, ni même s'opposer à ses mandements: il défendra aux autres de faire ni guerre ni paix, ni lever tailles, ni rendre la foi et hommage sans son congé: et celui à qui sera due la foi et hommage lige, obligera la noblesse et le peuple de ne prêter obéissance à autre qu'à lui.»

Le rapprochement s'arrête là, car Rousseau et Bodin ne se font pas la même conception de la loi. Pour le second, la loi «signifie le droit commandement de celui ou de ceux qui ont toute puissance par dessus les autres sans exception de personne» (*République*, I, 10, p. 216). Pour Rousseau, la loi est la «déclaration de la volonté générale» et l'on sait que, pour être telle, celle-ci doit générale dans sa source comme dans son objet, provenir de tous pour s'appliquer à tous, si bien qu'il ne peut y avoir de loi sur un objet particulier et qu'on ne peut légiférer que sur des objets généraux. A vrai dire, Bodin l'avait pressenti, puisqu'il écrit: «A parler plus proprement, loi et le commandement du souverain touchant tous les sujets en général, ou de choses générales» (*République*, I, 10, p. 216). Mais ce qui n'était chez Bodin qu'une formule, devient chez Rousseau toute une théorie.

Cette étude n'a pour but que d'attirer l'attention sur l'importance de la théorie de la souveraineté chez Bodin. L'influence de cet écrivain a été d'autant plus grande qu'elle s'est exercée en divers sens, en raison même de la complexité et de la richesse de sa doctrine, même si celle-ci n'est pas toujours rigoureuse ni parfaitement cohérente.

Walter Euchner

Eigentum und Herrschaft bei Bodin

In der Geschichte der politischen Theorien tritt das Eigentum zumeist dann ins Blickfeld, wenn es um die Genesis von Herrschaft, die Verfassungsprinzipien eines politischen Körpers und um die Triebkräfte des sozialen Wandels geht. Dabei ist zu beobachten, daß sich Bestimmung und Funktion des Eigentums in den verschiedenen Epochen der Sozialgeschichte des Westens verändern: Das Eigentum des über einen Haushalt gebietenden Familienvaters der Feudalgesellschaft schlägt sich in der politischen Theorie anders nieder als das im Dienste des Profitinteresses stehende Eigentum des Kapitalisten. Nicht zuletzt am Problemzusammenhang, in dem das Eigentum diskutiert wird, läßt sich die Position eines politischen Denkens in der theoretischen Bewältigung des sozialen Prozesses, der die «bürgerliche Gesellschaft» ausgebildet hat, erkennen – jener Gesellschaftsstruktur also, die in den nichtkommunistischen Ländern des Westens, wenn auch nicht ohne einschneidende Wandlungen, fortbesteht.

Bodin ist jenen Denkern zuzurechnen, die sich von der durch die Antike und christliche Scholastik geprägten Tradition abzukehren beginnen, aber noch nicht in der Lage sind, eine von der Tradition mehr oder weniger abgehobene Theorie der bürgerlichen Gesellschaft zu entwickeln, wie etwa jene von Locke, der schottischen Moralphilosophen oder von Hegel. Eine Untersuchung der Rolle des Eigentums bei Bodin kann, so darf man annehmen, dazu beitragen, die Eigenart seiner Zwischenposition zu erhellen – eine eigenständige Theorie des Übergangs, die traditionelle, an den fortbestehenden feudalistischen Organisationsformen des politischen Körpers orientierte Inhalte bewahrt und doch zugleich – Bodins Modernität ausmachend – Antworten auf Probleme der sich ausbildenden bürgerlichen Gesellschaft gibt. Dabei scheint folgender Gang der Untersuchung angezeigt: Zunächst soll ein Blick auf die Herleitung des Eigentums, sodann auf dessen Funktion bei Bodin und der aristotelischen Tradition geworfen werden. Dies kann zur Untersuchung der – wie hier angenommen wird – widersprüchlichen Kritik Bodins an der aristotelischen Trennung zwischen Ökonomie und Politik und, damit zusammenhängend, zu Einzelfragen wie der Staats- und Herrschaftsformenlehre, dem Bürgerbegriff und dem sogenannten Steuerparadoxon überleiten; hier anschließend soll die Idealform der Bodinschen Republik, soweit sie vom Eigentum und den Privilegien ihrer Bürger sowie vom Wirtschaftsprozeß beeinflußt wird, und endlich die Rolle, die das Eigentum Bodin zufolge beim sozialen Wandel spielt, betrachtet werden.

I

Bodin besitzt, obwohl das Eigentum in seinem politischen Denken unbestritten eine zentrale Stellung einnimmt, keine ausgeführte Eigentumstheorie wie etwa Locke; selbst bei scholastischen Autoren findet man mehr an grundsätzlichen Erwägungen über Entstehung und Wesen des Eigentums. Als ursprünglichen Entstehungsgrund betrachtet er offenbar die Okkupation, dagegen nicht, wie Locke und andere frühbürgerliche Theoretiker, Arbeit und Tausch. Im Naturzustand, in «ces fameux siècles d'or et d'argent», wie Bodin ironisch sagt, «les hommes y vivaient dispersés dans les champs et dans les bois comme de vraies bêtes sauvages, et ne possédaient en propre que ce qu'ils pouvaient conserver par la force et par le crime.»[1] Nach den Vorstellungen, die Bodin in den «Six livres de la Republique» äußert, waren die Menschen im Naturzustand in Familienclans organisiert. Als Motive des Streits, der zwischen den einzelnen Familien entbrennt, nennt er «la force, la violence, l'ambition, l'avarice, la vengeance».[2] Der Anführer eines solchen Clans oder eines Bündnisses zwischen einzelnen Familien unterwirft schließlich andere Clans, deren Mitglieder versklavt werden; die Angehörigen der siegreichen Familien erhalten in diesem – mit dem Sieg zusammenfallenden – Akt der Staatsgründung («la raison & lumiere naturelle nous conduit à cela, de croire que la force & violence a donné source & origine aux Republiques», *Rép.*, 69) bürgerliche Freiheiten und das politisch gesicherte Eigentumsrecht. Der wohlgeordnete Staat gleicht ja, wie Bodin an verschiedenen Stellen wiederholt, einem großen Haushalt, in dem die Familienoberhäupter sich zum Souverän wie die freien Familienmitglieder sich zum Vater verhalten. Die «femmes, & enfans de famille, qui sont francs de toute servitude», besitzen «leurs droits & libertés, & la puissance de disposer de

---

[1] *Methodus ad facilem historiarum cognitionem*, VII, 5, 428. Auf die Nähe zur Hobbesschen Schilderung des Naturzustandes braucht nicht besonders aufmerksam gemacht zu werden.

[2] *Six Livres de la Republique* I, 6, 68. Der dortige Wortlaut («depuis que la force, la violence, l'ambition (...) eurent armé les uns contre les autres (...)») läßt den Schluß zu, daß auch Bodin den alten, bereits bei Platon, der Patristik und der Scholastik auftauchenden Topos von der ursprünglichen Friedlichkeit des Naturzustandes (oder des Zustandes vor dem Sündenfall) angehangen hat, eines Zustands, der dann allerdings mit dem Aufkommen der Begehrlichkeit und des Eigentums immer unfriedlicher wurde.

leurs biens» – kurz, der Bürger dieses Staates ist «subiect, estant quelque peu de sa liberté diminuee, par la maiesté de celuy auquel il doit obeissance» (*Rép.*, 70).

Das Streben des Menschen zur «liberté», wenn nicht zur «pleine liberté sans frein ni mors quelconque» (II, 7, S. 340), und damit verbunden nach Besitz und Eigentum (deren Aufgabe ja ist, diese Freiheit zu sichern), scheint eine Grundannahme des Bodinschen Menschenbildes zu sein. Dieses Streben, das wesentlich auf den freien Genuß der irdischen Güter und weniger auf rechtlich gesichertes Privateigentum gerichtet ist, kann zur Forderung nach Gütergleichheit und Gemeineigentum und schließlich zu anarchistischen Konsequenzen führen (und Anarchie ist nach Bodin schlimmer als Tyrannis, VI, 4, S. 937). Auf der anderen Seite resultieren aus dem Streben nach Eigentum aber Kräfte, die bei der Schaffung und Erhaltung einer wohlgeordneten Republik nutzbar gemacht werden können. Sie sorgen nämlich dafür, daß die für eine harmonische Ordnung des Gemeinwesens konstitutive Pluralität von Haushalten, deren – im Medium des Gemeinsamen der Republik und der integrierenden Souveränität organisierter – Verkehr das Leben der Republik erzeugt, überhaupt erst entsteht. Vielleicht ist diese Konstruktion eine Reminiszenz an die patristische und augustinische Tradition, wonach das Streben nach Herrschaft und Eigentum zwar sündigen Ursprungs ist, beide aber, Herrschaft und Eigentum, nach göttlichem Plan dazu dienen, diese sündigen Bestrebungen niederzuhalten. Doch im Gegensatz zu dieser Tradition bewertet Bodin das Eigentum ohne Abstriche positiv. Daß aus der Eigensucht und dem Gewinnstreben der einzelnen Harmonie und Wohlfahrt des Gemeinwesens entspringen, scheint im übrigen zu einer Grundfigur der bürgerlichen Sozialphilosophie, die in fast allen Klassikern dieses Denkens nachzuweisen ist, geworden zu sein: Mandeville hat sie auf die Kurzformel «Private Vices, Publick Benefits» gebracht. Bodin soll hier keineswegs – um Mißverständnisse zu vermeiden, muß es betont werden – zu einem frühbürgerlichen Denker stilisiert werden. Gleichwohl fällt aus der späteren ausgebildeten bürgerlichen Sozialphilosophie Licht auf die Bodinsche Lehre, in der – unbeschadet ihrer prinzipiellen Eigenständigkeit – bürgerliche Theoreme in rudimentärer Form enthalten sind.

II

Nach Aristoteles kommt den Eigentum im politischen Leben eine ausschließlich dienende Funktion zu: «Reichtum ist nichts anderes als eine Menge von Werkzeugen für die Haus- oder Staatsverwaltung» (Politik, 1256 b). Die Erwerbskunst ist ein Teil der Haushaltungskunst (Ökonomie), die jedoch «nichts Großes und Ehrwürdiges an sich» hat, weshalb der Herr «diese Ehre dem Hausmeister» überläßt und «sich selbst mit den Staatsangelegenheiten oder der Philosophie» beschäftigt (1255 b). Haushalt *(Oikos)* und *Polis* sind klar unterschieden (1252 a). Nur der Staat ist eine vollkommene Gemeinschaft, und zwar eine Gemeinschaft von Gleichberechtigten, die um der Selbstbestimmung und des tugendhaften und damit glückseligen Lebens – und nicht wie der Haushalt nur um des bloßen Lebens – willen besteht (1280 a; 1328 b). Nach diesem Gesichtspunkt unterscheidet sich auch die Herrschaft in Oikos und Polis: Im Haushalt herrscht *einer*, an der Herrschaft in der Polis partizipiert jeder Bürger (1275 a ff.).

Bodin, dem es um eine pluralistische, die Interessen der gesellschaftlichen Stände und Gruppen wahrende und zugleich stabile Organisation der modernen Großstaaten geht, kann mit dem auf politische Partizipation gerichteten Polis-Modell des Aristoteles nichts anfangen. Für ihn sind Herrschaft und Ökonomie politische Grundkategorien, die für den Haushalt genauso wie für die Republik gelten. Aristoteles und Xenophon haben deshalb nach Bodins Ansicht ohne Grund die Ökonomie von der Politik getrennt: Man müsse aber, wie die Juristen, «les loix & ordonnances de la police, des colleges, & des familles en une mesme science» behandeln, und die Ökonomie, die «science d'acquerir des biens», «est commune aux corps & colleges aussi bien comme aux Republiques» (I, 2, S. 10 f.).[3] Bodins von Aristoteles abweichender Politikbegriff wird deutlich sichtbar: Politik ist nicht Gemeinschaftshandeln der Bürger, sondern Obrigkeitshandeln.

Ist eine Familie gut regiert, so ist sie «la vraye image de la Republique, & la puissance domestique semble à la puissance souveraine: aussi est le droit gouvernement de la maison, le vray modelle du gouvernement de la Republique» (I, 2, S. 11). Bodin unterscheidet im Haushalt vier Herrschaftsverhältnisse, je nachdem, ob es sich um die Frau, die Kinder, das Gesinde oder um Sklaven handelt (I, 3, S. 19), wobei er der an der römischen patria potestas orientierten «puissance paternelle» rigorose Voll-

---

[3] Von diesem Ansatz her wird leicht verständlich, wie Bodin in seinen ökonomischen Schriften *(La Response aux paradoxes de M.de Malestroit touchant l'enchérissement de toutes choses et des monnoies, 1568; Discours sur le rehaussement et la diminution des monnoies, pour réponse aux paradoxes du sieur de Malestroit, 1578)* zu einem Vorläufer der modernen Nationalökonomie werden konnte. Zu Bodins Stellung in der Geschichte der Nationalökonomie vgl. ERNST OBERFOHREN [81], Die Idee der Universalökonomie in der französischen wirtschaftswissenschaftlichen Literatur bis auf Turgot, Jena 1915; zum Übergang von der Ökonomie als Haushaltswissenschaft zur «Nationalökonomie» vgl. SIEG-FRIED LANDSHUT, Der Begriff des Ökonomischen, in: Kritik der Soziologie und andere Schriften zur Politik, Neuwied am Rhein und Berlin 1969 (= Politica, 27), 131–175.

machten einräumt (I, 3–5). Er geht sogar soweit, die Wiedereinführung
der väterlichen Gewalt über Leben und Tod der Kinder zu verlangen
(I, 4, S. 32). Die Bemerkungen, die Bodin über die Eigentumsrechte der
Frau und der Kinder innerhalb der Ökonomie eines solchen «ganzen
Hauses»[4] macht, ergeben allerdings kein klares Bild. In den einschlägigen
Kapiteln (I, 3–4) lassen gewisse Hinweise darauf schließen, daß Frau und
Kinder Sondereigentum besitzen können, an dem der Vater das Nieß-
brauchsrecht hat; das Verfügungsrecht über dieses Eigentum ist jedoch
von der allgemeinen Befehlsgewalt des Paterfamilias beschränkt. In Fällen des Mißbrauchs der väterlichen Gewalt steht der Rechtsweg offen –
eine Entwicklung zur Aushöhlung der patria potestas, über die Bodin
lamentiert (I, 3–4, S. 22–41). Andererseits hat Bodin ausdrücklich die
Analogie zwischen Staat und Familie hergestellt: Wie die freien Untertanen im Staat Eigentum besitzen können, so auch die freien Familienmitglieder in der Familie: Die freien Ehefrauen und Kinder, so heißt es
an einer anderen, oben bereits zitierten Stelle, haben das Recht, über ihre
Habe zu verfügen (I, 6, S. 70). Wie es sich mit dem Sondereigentum von
Frau und Kindern im Haushalt auch verhalten mag – die Analogie zwischen dem Haushalt mit dem rigiden Herrschaftsrecht des Familienvaters
und dem Staat macht jedenfalls deutlich, daß das Eigentum der Untertanen im Unterschied zu Aristoteles trotz der überragenden Rolle, die es
in Bodins politischem Denken spielt, der Theorie nach nicht die Funktion
hat, die Unabhängigkeit zu gewährleisten, die den Bürger zur Partizipation am politischen Leben berechtigt und befähigt (vgl. Aristoteles,
Politik 1329 a). Es wird zu zeigen sein, daß in Bodins Konstruktion der
Monarchie royale jedoch Tendenzen angelegt sind, welche die in der be-
haupteten Wesensgleichheit von Familie und Staat implizierte politische
Unmündigkeit der Bürger überwinden.

Die Idealrepublik der Monarchie royale, angeblich orientiert am Modell des Haushalts mit seinen strengen Herrschaftsverhältnissen, besitzt
bei Bodin die Gestalt der Denkfigur einer «Einheit in der Vielheit». Die
Vielheit, das Besondere (le particulier) der Haushalte, vereinigt sich zur
Allgemeinheit (le commun) im Medium des materiellen und geistigen Gemeinsamen [wobei die letztliche «causa efficiens» die Souveränität ist
(I, 2, S. 12; 14 f.)]. «(...) outre la souveraineté, il faut qu'il ait quelque
chose de commun, & de public: comme la domaine public, le thresor pub-

---

[4] Vgl. dazu OTTO BRUNNER, Das ‹ganze Haus› und die alteuropäische ‹Öko-
nomik›, in: Neue Wege der Sozialgeschichte, Göttingen 1956, 33–61, sowie MAX
WEBER, Zur Geschichte der Handelsgesellschaften im Mittelalter, Stuttgart 1889.
Weber weist darauf hin, daß die Rechtsform der Familienunternehmen die Güter-
gemeinschaft mit hervorgehobenem Verfügungsrecht des Familienvaters gewesen
sei.

lic, le pourpris de la cité, les rues, les murailles, les places, les temples, les marchés, les usages, les loix, les coustumes, la iustice, les loyers, les peines, & autres choses semblables, qui sont ou communes, ou publiques, ou l'un & l'autre ensemble: car ce n'est pas Republique s'il n'y a rien de public.» Genauso konstitutiv für die Republik wie die Souveränität und das Gemeinsame ist das Private oder Besondere: «(...) il n'y a point de chose publique, s'il n'y a quelque chose de propre: & ne se peut imaginer qu'il y ait rien commun, s'il n'y a rien particulier» (I, 2, S. 14 f.). Ohne die Wechselbeziehung von Besonderem und Allgemeinem könnte die wohlgeordnete Republik nicht bestehen.

Das die Republik konstituierende Besondere hat seine materielle Substanz im Eigentum der Haushalte. Deshalb wird der Schutz des Privateigentums zum Staatszweck, da er mit dem Schutz des Staates überhaupt zusammenfällt: «(...) en ostant ces deux mots Tien & Mien, on ruine les fondements de toutes Republiques, qui sont principalement establies pour rendre à chacun ce qui luy appartient (...)» (VI, 4, S. 948); «(...) la conservation des biens d'un chacun en particulier, est la conservation du bien publique» (I, 2, S. 17). Das Gesetz Gottes und der Natur, denen der Souverän, wie Bodin mehrfach versichert, untersteht, haben deshalb angeordnet, daß das Eigentum eines jeden bewahrt werden müsse (VI, 4, S. 948; I, 2, S. 15; vgl. auch V, 2, S. 706).

Ohne gesichertes Privateigentum kann es also nach Bodin keine harmonische Organisation des Gemeinwesens geben. Deshalb benützt er das Kriterium des Eigentums zur Differenzierung seiner *Staats- und Regierungsformenlehre*.[5] Sowohl Monarchie, Aristokratie wie Demokratie können royal, seigneurial und tyrannisch verfaßt sein. Bodin spielt die Prinzipien einer royalen usw. Verfassung nur am Beispiel der Monarchie durch: «(...) la Monarchie royale, ou legitime, est celle où les suiects obeissent aux loix du Monarque, & le Monarque aux loix de nature, demeurant la liberté naturelle & proprieté des biens aux suiects. La Monarchie seigneuriale est celle où le Prince est faict Seigneur du biens & des personnes par le droit des armes, & de bonne guerre, gouvernant ses suiects comme le pere de famille ses esclaves. La Monarchie tyrannique est où le Monarque mesprisant les loix de nature, abuse des personnes libres comme d'esclaves, & des biens des suiects comme des siens» (II, 2, S. 273). Die Monarchie seigneuriale, in welcher den Untertanen anscheinend eine mehr oder weniger rechtlich gesicherte Verwaltung ihres Besitzes bleibt – Bodin ist in diesem Punkte nicht sehr klar –, widerspricht keinesfalls dem Gesetz der Natur, wie man auf Grund der Sätze über den naturrechtlichen Eigentumsschutz, auf die oben hingewiesen wurde, annehmen könnte. Eine iusta causa, etwa ein gerechter Krieg, berechtigt nämlich durchaus

---

[5] Über die Staatsformenlehre vgl. den Beitrag von Horst Denzer.

zur Versklavung und Enteignung freier Menschen (II, 2, S. 278). Die seigneuriale Monarchie, übrigens die historisch erste Form der Monarchie,
besitzt dazu noch den Vorteil, stabiler zu sein als die royale Monarchie,
denn sie macht die Menschen feige und servil. Menschen dagegen, die frei
und Herrn ihres Eigentums sind, neigen rasch zur Rebellion, «ayant le
coeur genereux, nourri en liberté (II, 2, S. 279). Dieses elementare Streben
der Menschen nach Unabhängigkeit und Gleichheit, was den Genuß der
irdischen Güter betrifft, muß sich in der *Demokratie* besonders auswirken: Die Menschen verlangen dort nach zügelloser Freiheit, Gütergleichheit oder sogar nach Gemeinbesitz. Doch mit der Beseitigung von MEIN
und DEIN werden sie keinesfalls die Quellen des Konflikts unter den
Menschen, wie die Gleichmacher meinen, austrocknen: Im Gegenteil, nirgends herrscht so viel Streit wie unter Gleichen – so wird durch die Gütergleichheit die Freundschaft, die Grundlage einer jeden Republik, zer-
stört. Schließlich können jene, die auf Gleichheit und schrankenlose Freiheit drängen, keine Männer von offenkundiger Tugend dulden, und müssen so deren Dienste entbehren – kurz, eine auf Gütergleichheit beruhende
Demokratie wird nicht lange dauern. Deshalb gilt: «(...) la vraye liberté
populaire ne gist en autre chose sinon à iouir de ses biens en seureté (...)»
(I, 2, S. 15; II, 7, S. 340; VI, 4, S. 937 ff.).

III

Eine nähere Betrachtung der Bodinschen Idealrepublik, der Monarchie
royale, scheint die in der Literatur gelegentlich geäußerte Ansicht zu bestätigen, daß Bodins wiederholter Vergleich dieser Herrschaftsform mit
der Struktur der Familie – so, wie er diese nach dem Vorbild des römischen Rechts dargestellt hat – zu Unstimmigkeiten führt.[6] Bereits oben,
bei dem Versuch, die entscheidende Rolle des Eigentums in Bodins politischem Denken zu erklären, wurde darauf hingewiesen, daß die Monarchie royale eine von der Wechselwirkung zwischen dem Souverän, den
materiellen und geistigen Grundlagen der Republik (Gebiet, Institutionen, Normen) und den besonderen Haushalten konstituierte «Einheit
in der Vielheit» sei. Diesem Modell mag die Familienstruktur noch entsprechen, obwohl der bei Bodin von der patria potestas eingeschränkte
Freiheitsspielraum der Familienmitglieder eine solch pluralistische Organisation des Gemeinwesens eigentlich ausschließt. Sobald sich aber zeigt,

---

[6] Vgl. Jean Moreau-Reibel [116], Jean Bodin et le droit publique comparé
dans ses rapports avec la philosophie de l'histoire, Paris 1933, 183; Pierre Mesnard [129], L'essor de la philosophie politique au XVIe siècle. Paris 1951, 488;
Henri Baudrillart [27], Bodin et son temps (1853), Aalen 1964, 234.

daß es in der Monarchie royale eine politisch wirksame Ebene zwischen den Familien und dem Staat gibt, gebildet aus den in gewissen Verkehrsformen zueinander in Beziehung tretenden Familienväter, kann die Analogie zwischen Staat und Familie nicht mehr aufrecht erhalten werden, denn in der Familie fehlt ein solches Forum: «(...) quand le chef de famille vient à sortir de la maison où il commande pour traitter & negotier avec les autres chefs de famille, de ce qui leur touche à tous en general, alors il despouille le titre de maistre, de chef, de seigneur, pour estre compagnon, pair et associé avec les autres: laissant sa famille, pour entrer en la cité: & les affaires domestiques, pour traitter les publiques: & au lieu du seigneur, il s'appelle citoyen (...)» (I, 6, S. 68). Dieses Zitat scheint quer zum patriarchalischen Ansatz der politischen Theorie Bodins zu stehen.

Mit «traitter & negotier» sind eindeutig keine bürgerlichen Rechtsgeschäfte, sondern Verhandlungen über öffentliche Angelegenheiten gemeint: Offenbar hat der Bürger das Recht, mit Seinesgleichen darüber zu beraten. Diese Kommunikationsebene der Bürger ist also eine öffentliche und somit politische. Deshalb kann sie nicht als das bezeichnet werden, was in der späteren bürgerlichen Sozialphilosophie «bürgerliche Gesellschaft» genannt wurde, denn deren Kennzeichen war gerade ihr durch private Rechtsgeschäfte (Tausch, Arbeitsvertrag) gestifteter Zusammenhang.[7] Doch es ist plausibel anzunehmen, daß das im Zitat erwähnte öffentliche Recht der Bürger Ausfluß ihrer vorgängigen privaten, durch den Markt vermittelten Beziehungen beruht; hierauf weisen die Ausdrücke «traitter & negotier» hin. Wie die Bürger im Sinne von «Bourgeois» in ihren ökonomischen Marktbeziehungen – und in den Marktbeziehungen sind die «Gleiche» – ihren Vorteil und zugleich den der Gesellschaft realisieren, so erzielen die «Citoyens», in dieser Eigenschaft wie in ihren Marktbeziehungen «pair», indem sie mit ihren Mitbürgern «de ce qui leur touche à tous en general» verhandeln, das ihnen allen politisch Zuträgliche.[8] Es ist die für Bodins Idealmonarchie schlechthin konstitutive Stellung der Privateigentümer, die hier dieses Modell der bürgerlichen Öffentlichkeit, wenn auch nur im Grundriß, hervorgetrieben hat: Ist der Privateigentümer-Paterfamilias im politischen System unverzichtbar, so muß dies öffentlich, seis durch Privilegien, seis durch politi-

---

[7] Vgl. dazu MANFRED RIEDEL, Der Begriff der ‹Bürgerlichen Gesellschaft› und das Problem seines geschichtlichen Ursprungs, in: Studien zu Hegels Rechtsphilosophie, Frankfurt a. M. 1969, 135–166.

[8] Zu diesem Modell der bürgerlichen Gesellschaft und ihrer politischen Formen grundsätzlich JÜRGEN HABERMAS, Strukturwandel der Öffentlichkeit. Untersuchungen zu einer Kategorie der bürgerlichen Gesellschaft, Neuwied 1962 (= Politica, 4).

sches Mitspracherecht, honoriert werden. Zwar betont Bodin, gegen Aristoteles gewandt, ausdrücklich, daß es ein großer Fehler sei zu behaupten, Bürger könne nur sein, wer an obrigkeitlichen Institutionen partizipiere (I, 6, S. 77) – doch immerhin kommt das Mitspracherecht der Bürger in der Frage der Besteuerung vermittels der Ständevertretung, das Bodin hartnäckig verficht, einer Beteiligung am politischen Prozeß nahe.

Bürger im Sinne von Citoyen bedeutet für Bodin seiner generellen Definition zufolge «freier Untertan»: «franc subiect tenant de la souveraineté d'autruy» (I, 6, S. 68). In einem spezielleren Sinn bezeichnet Citoyen jedoch mehr als «non-esclave» (Mesnard), nämlich eine durch öffentlich relevante Privilegien ausgezeichnete und somit vom bloßen Bourgeois unterschiedene Stellung des Untertans: «(...) ce mot de citoyen a ie ne sçay quoy de plus special à nous, que le mot de bourgeois, & c'est proprement le subiect naturel, qui a droit de corps & college, ou quelques autres privileges qui ne sont point communiquez aux bourgeois» (I, 6, S. 73). Bodin sieht also zwei Arten von Untertanen, den Citoyen und den Bourgeois, wobei «Bourgeois» einfach «nichtprivilegierter Untertan», «non-esclave», bedeutet. Diese Unterscheidung nimmt bei ihm also noch nicht die theoretisch explizite Form an, in der sie in späteren Theorien der bürgerlichen Gesellschaft auftaucht, nämlich daß ein- und derselbe Bürger in zweierlei Rollen auftritt: als der seine Geschäfte betreibende Bourgeois und als der am politischen Leben partizipierende Citoyen.[9] Bei Bodin sind Citoyen und Bourgeois noch zwei voneinander unterschiedene Gruppen. Doch die oben zitierte Auffassung, daß der Untertan die Sphäre des Haushalts verlasse und in der öffentliche Angelegenheiten betreffenden Verhandlung mit seinen Mitbürgern zum Citoyen werde, scheint die spätere Vorstellung von der zweifachen Funktion des Bürgers bereits in nuce zu enthalten.

Die Bestimmung des Citoyens durch Korporationsrechte und Privilegien erinnert zweifellos mehr an die feudalistische Gesellschaftsstruktur als an die durch Rechtsgleichheit der Bürger charakterisierte ausgebildete bürgerliche Gesellschaft. Aber dennoch fallen die Privilegien des Citoyen nicht mit feudalen Privilegien zusammen. Trotz dem Überleben vieler institutioneller Elemente des Feudalismus wie Privilegien, Monopole, Stände, Zünfte usw. ist die gesellschaftliche Basis des Bodinschen Idealstaates nicht mehr feudalistisch: Sie ist die idealtypische Konstruktion einer Republik, die zwischen einem feudalistischen Gemeinwesen und einer ausgebildeten bürgerlichen Gesellschaft mit zentraler Staatsgewalt steht – eine Konstruktion, in der die gesellschaftlichen und politischen Kräfte so ausbalanciert sind, daß sozusagen eine transitorische Phase der Entwicklung von der feudalen zur bürgerlichen Gesellschaft im Modell

---

[9] Dazu RIEDEL, Begriff der ‹Bürgerlichen Gesellschaft›, 150.

institutionell fixiert wird. Das Recht des Citoyen bezeichnet eine hervor-
gehobene Stellung im Organismus dieser Republik, deren Strukturprinzip
weder die allgemeine Rechtsgleichheit noch die feudalistische komplexe
Herrschaftspyramide ist.

IV

Aus der Konstruktion der Idealrepublik Bodins, die – soll sie nicht zu
einer seigneurialen oder gar tyrannischen Herrschaftsform herabsinken –
einen ausgegrenzten, durch Eigentum und Privilegien abgesicherten Freiheitsspielraum der Bürger fordert, ergeben sich auch Gesichtspunkte zur
Klärung des sogenannten Bodinschen Steuerparadoxons. Bodin habe sich,
so wird gesagt, in einen Widerspruch verwickelt, wenn er behaupte, der
Fürst sei seinen Untertanen gegenüber absolut souverän, und zugleich
unter den Kennzeichen der Souveränität das Recht auf Steuererhebung
nicht nur weglasse (vgl. I, 10, S. 247), sondern dazu noch mehrfach und
nachdrücklich die Zustimmung der Stände für Steuererhebungen ver-
lange. Es sei kaum zu verstehen, daß Bodin, der doch den modernen
Großflächenstaat der europäischen Staatenwelt zur Zeit des heraufziehenden Absolutismus propagiert habe, die Notwendigkeit einer unein-
geschränkten Steuererhebung durch den Souverän nicht gesehen habe
(wie etwa Hobbes).[10] Mit den Mitteln aus den öffentlichen Domänen
allein – der Haupteinnahmequelle des Staates nach Bodin (VI, 2,
S. 856 ff.) – habe ein solcher Großflächenstaat nicht unterhalten werden
können. Zur Beantwortung dieses Paradoxons werden häufig politische
Gründe genannt: Etwa der, daß Bodin dem König das Geld, das dieser
zur Kriegsführung gegen die Hugenotten benötigte, als Verfechter des
ausgleichenden Kurses der «Politiques» verweigern wollte. Doch es
scheinen nicht nur pragmatische, sondern auch innertheoretisch notwendige Gründe vorzuliegen: Die Besteuerung tangiert das Grundrecht des
freien Untertanen, das Eigentum, dessen konstitutive Funktion in Bodins
politischem Denken bereits erörtert worden ist.[11] «Ie respons, que les
autres Rois n'ont pas plus de puissance que le Roy d'Angleterre: parce
qu'il n'est en la puissance de Prince du monde, de lever impost à son plaisir sur le peuple, non plus que prendre le bien d'autruy» (I, 8, S. 140,
vgl. auch VI, 2, S. 880). Mehrfach stellt Bodin illegitime Besteuerung

---

[10] Vgl. Leviathan, Kap. 18, Punkt 9.

[11] Vgl. Martin Wolfe [265], Jean Bodin on Taxes: The Sovereignty-Taxes-
Paradox, *Political Science Quarterly* 83 (1968), 268–284 (270); J. W. Allen
[97], A History of Political Thought in the Sixteenth Century, London, New
York 1961, 421.

und Konfiskation auf eine Stufe. Weder Papst noch Kaiser können ohne iusta causa ihre Untertanen enteignen. Die absolute Gewalt des Fürsten ist kein ausreichender Rechtstitel: Dies behaupten hieße dem Gesetz Gottes zuwider sich auf das Recht des Stärkeren und der Räuber berufen. Ein dringender Staatsnotstand ist zwar ein Rechtsgrund, der die Untertanen verpflichtet, ihr Vermögen dem Wohl des Staates zu opfern: Doch bevor der Fürst zu Konfiskationen berechtigt ist, muß er versuchen, den Notstand auf andere Art auszuräumen, etwa durch Friedensschluß mit dem Feind, oder dadurch, daß er sich die nötigen Mittel durch eine Anleihe oder durch Rückgriff auf seine eigenen Ersparnisse beschafft. Und ist dies nicht möglich, so muß er sich darum bemühen, den Verlust der geschädigten Untertanen auzugleichen (I, 8, S. 155 ff.). Auf jeden Fall gilt das Wort Samuels: «Voulez vous sçavoir (...) la coustume des tyrans: c'est de prendre les biens des suiects pour en disposer à leur plaisir» (I, 10, S. 212). Kurz – eine illegitime, von den Untertanen als konfiskatorisch empfundene Steuer würde MEIN und DEIN, die Grundlage der Republik, zerstören; es entstünden Herrschaftsformen, in welchen die Dialektik von Besonderem und Allgemeinem nicht mehr oder nur noch rudimentär besteht: eben jene politische Einheit in der Vielfalt selbständiger Haushalte, welche die Harmonie der idealen Republik ausmacht. Deshalb entspricht es der Logik des Bodinschen politischen Systems, daß die Untertanen der Besteuerung ihres Eigentums zustimmen müssen.

Das Privateigentum als fundamentale Institution der Republik gehört sozusagen zu jenem Bereich politischer Grundwerte, die durch Konsens zwischen Souverän und Bürgern abgesichert sind. Sie sind dem Bereich der Gesetzgebung des Souveräns – worin Bodin zufolge allein der – vom natürlichen und göttlichen Gesetz begrenzte – Wille des Souveräns herrscht (I, 8, S. 131; 155), entzogen – sie gleichen vertraglichen Abmachungen, die der Souverän nicht brechen darf, weil er dadurch das für den Bestand der Republik entscheidende Vertrauen des Bürgers in den Souverän erschüttern würde (I, 8, S. 134 ff.; 153). Zwar wird dieses Argument, das dem angelsächsischen Konsens-Denken entnommen ist, bei Bodin nicht entfaltet, doch es ist seinem Denken nicht fremd. Die Einführung des Gemeineigentums, der Gütergleichheit oder die Aufhebung von Schulden hätten gerade diese Zerstörung des Vertrauens und damit des Staates zur Folge: «(...) on peut dire, que l'equalité de biens est tres-pernicieuse aux Repliques, lesquelles n'ont appuy ni fondement plus asseuré que la foy, sans laquelle ni la iustice, ni societé quelconque ne peut estre durable: or la foy gist aux promesses des conventions legitimes. Si donc les obligations sont cassees, les contracts annullez, les debtes abolies, que doit-on attendre autre chose que l'entière eversion d'un estat?» (V, 2, S. 704).

Die Mitwirkung der Bürger an politischen Entscheidungen, die ihr

Eigentumsrecht, ein wesentliches Fundament des Staates, berühren, ist kein Fremdkörper im politischen System Bodins. Sie ist vielmehr eine aus diesem ableitbare Konsequenz, die allerdings über die von Bodin behauptete Wesensgleichheit von Oikos und Polis hinaustreibt. Die Zustimmung zur Besteuerung war das Recht privilegierter feudaler Stände; in der bürgerlichen Gesellschaft ist sie zum Element der Selbstbestimmung des aus freien Bürgern bestehenden Gemeinwesens geworden; in der Republik Bodins, in der feudalistische Strukturen und solche der heraufziehenden bürgerlichen Gesellschaft eine eigenständige Synthese bilden, soll sie das hieraus entstehende komplexe System von Allgemeinem und Besonderem erhalten.

V

Diese Zwischenstellung der Idealrepublik Bodins zwischen der feudalistischen und der ausgebildeten bürgerlichen Gesellschaftsstruktur, auf die in diesem Beitrag oftmals angespielt worden ist, ist nunmehr näher zu bestimmen. Im idealtypischen Modell der liberalen Gesellschaft stellte sich der Zusammenhang des Gemeinwesens dadurch her, daß jeder seine privaten Interessen verfolgte: Aus der Betätigung der besonderen Interessen ergab sich, durch die «invisible hand» im Sinne von Adam Smith, das Allgemeininteresse von selbst – und zwar nicht nur ökonomisch, vermittelt durch die Gesetze des Marktes, sondern auch politisch, durch die Auseinandersetzung der politischen Meinungen im Medium der Öffentlichkeit. Nach Bentham zum Beispiel treffen im Zentrum der politischen Willensbildung, dem Parlament, die Ideen aufeinander, die «Berührung der Ideen schlägt Funken» und führt zur Evidenz des politisch Richtigen, des Allgemeininteresses. Die Obrigkeit, die dieses im Willensbildungsprozeß der Bürger erkannte Allgemeininteresse verwirklichen soll, ist keine Institution mit eigener Legitimationsbasis, sondern sie untersteht dem Willen des sich selbst politisch bestimmenden Bürgertums. Die Voraussetzungen dieses bürgerlichen Systems, die Prinzipien der Gleichheit und Selbstbestimmung der Staatsbürger, fehlen in Bodins Konstruktion oder sind höchstens in den ersten Ansätzen vorhanden – zum Beispiel, wie gezeigt, dort, wo er von den ihre gemeinsamen Angelegenheiten beratenden Bürgern spricht. Der Souverän, der das Gemeinwesen zusammenhält, muß also mehr sein als ein Gremium, das von den Bürgern zur Verwaltung ihrer gemeinsamen Angelegenheiten eingesetzt worden ist. In der Tat besitzt der Souverän in der idealen Monarchie royale eine eigenständige Macht kraft originären Rechts, das aus der Unterwerfung seiner Untertanen entsprang. Bodin fordert bereits ein öffentliches Eigentum des Gemeinwesens – ein modernes Prinzip, denn der Feudalismus kannte die Unterscheidung von öffentlichem und privatem Eigentum nicht. Der Souverän darf nach Bodin über die öffentliche Domäne nicht wie über sein Privateigentum verfügen: Aber er soll doch «en qualité de particulier« einen privaten Schatz (fisque) und private Domänen haben (I, 10, S. 247). Der Souverän des Bodinschen Gemeinwesens ist dies kraft eigenständiger, originärer, durch umfangreichen Eigenbesitz abgesicherter Macht – die Obrigkeit der bürgerlichen Gesellschaft soll dies gerade nicht sein.

Dieser hervorgehobenen, nicht bloß öffentlich-rechtlichen, sondern gleichzeitig privaten, auf originärem Recht der Unterwerfung gestützten Machtstellung des Souveräns entsprechen andere gesellschaftliche Strukturen, die dem Feudalismus näher stehen als der bürgerlichen Gesellschaft. Bodin anerkennt feudale Vassallenverhältnisse, gekennzeichnet durch «foy & hommage», die der Lehens(fief)-Träger seinem Lehensherr schuldet. Bodin unterscheidet sechs Typen solcher Lehensverhältnisse. Fünf davon bestehen zwischen Personen, zwischen denen kein staatsrechtliches Untertanenverhältnis besteht; der sechste Typ ist jedoch derjenige Vassall, der zugleich Untertan seines Souveräns und damit dessen Jurisdiktion unterworfen ist (I, 9, S. 162 f.). Unter den Haushalten, den kleinsten gesellschaftlichen Einheiten des Staates, gibt es Standes- und Rangunterschiede, die vor allem in Privilegien bestehen: «(. . .) il n'est pas inconvenient, que les familles ayent quelques statuts particuliers pour eux & leurs successeurs, faicts par les anciens familles, & ratifiez par les Princes souverains» (I, 2, S. 17); «il se peut faire en termes de droit, qu'entre les citoyens, les uns soyent exempts de toutes charges, tailles, & imposts, ausquels les autres seront subjects» (I, 6, S. 100). Die Einteilung der Stände in «l'Ecclesiastic, la Noblesse, & le peuple» sei in ganz Europa vorherrschend. Selbst Platon könne in seiner Republik, die Bodin als «populaire» ansah, auf Stände nicht verzichten, so daß Bodin die generelle Feststellung trifft: «(. . .) qu'il n'y eut onques Republiques, soit vraye ou imaginaire, voire la plus populaire qu'on peust penser, où les citoyens soyent egaux en tous droits, & prerogatives, mais tousiours les uns ont plus ou moins que les autres» (I, 6, S. 100). Bodin ist also noch weit vom bürgerlichen Prinzip der Rechtsgleichheit entfernt.

Auch die intermediären Organe der «corps & colleges» weisen auf eine vorbürgerliche Gesellschaftssturktur hin. Dies soll nicht heißen, daß dies Korporationen (Kommunen, Stände und Zünfte) Elemente einer Herrschaftspyramide im Sinne des mittelalterlichen Feudalismus waren: Dieses gesellschaftliche Organisationsprinzip ist bei Bodin derart durchbrochen, daß davon keine Rede sein kann. Die Korporationen sollen als Organisation legitimer partikularer Interessen zur «amitié sacree & bienvueillance charitable» in der Republik beitragen; sie sollen verhindern, daß sich die Partikularinteressen in «coniurations & conspirations des uns envers les autres» zuspitzen; ihr Zweck ist die gesellschaftliche *Integra-tion* des Gemeinwesens zu einem harmonischen Ganzen (III, 7, S. 482; 495 ff.).[12] Da die Standes- und Zunftinteressen durch Erteilung von Pri-vilegien befriedigt werden (III, 7, S. 481), sind die Korporationen eine weitere Quelle von Rechtsungleichheit.

Obwohl also gesellschaftliche Ungleichheit zu den Strukturprinzipien der Bodinschen Republik gehört, ist in den «Six Livres» die Tendenz zu erkennen, die Rolle der Privilegien innerhalb des Rechtswesens abzu-schwächen. Zwar spricht sich Bodin nicht gegen die patrimoniale Gerichts-barkeit aus; doch sind die «seigneurs particuliers», ja der Souverän selbst, der strengen «voye de iustice» unterworfen, vor allem was den Eigen-tumsverkehr betrifft (III, 5, S. 446). Auch gegen den Fürsten muß der Rechtsweg offenstehen (I, 8, S. 158). Hier zeichnet sich offenbar das Prin-zip der Gleichheit vor dem Gesetz ab. Max Weber hat das Entstehen eines auf Rechtsgleichheit beruhenden generalisierten und rationalisierten Rechts mit den ökonomischen Bedürfnissen der «Markterweiterung» und der sich entwickelnden kapitalistischen Wirtschaftsweise zusammen-gebracht.[13] Diese These kann mit dem Werk Bodins nicht unmittelbar belegt werden, doch an Hinweisen fehlt es nicht. In seinen ökonomischen Schriften erweist er sich als Verfechter der von Weber angeführten «Markterweiterung». Die Lebenskraft und der Reichtum der Republik beruhen auf dem Gewerbe und dem Handel (I, 5, S. 67), weshalb die ökonomische Betätigung nichts Ehrenrühriges an sich hat und auch dem Adel, ja dem Fürsten, erlaubt ist: «Toutesfois est-il plus seant au Prince d'estre marchand que Tyran; & au gentilhomme de traffiquer que de voler» (VI, 2, S. 873). Die mittelalterliche Standesmoral ist hier einer Haltung zum Erwerbsleben gewichen, die als bürgerlich bezeichnet wer-den kann. In dieses Bild paßt auch Bodins Stellung zur Sklaverei. Im Grunde entspricht die traditionelle Rechtfertigung der Sklaverei seinem Weltbild: Die Menschen sind ungleich, daher ist die Sklaverei natürlich, und Kriegsgefangene können versklavt werden. Bodins Haupteinwand ist deshalb auch nicht strikt theoretischer Natur, sondern entstammt der christlichen Moral: Die Sklaverei ist grausam. Ein für Bodin dem An-schein nach wesentlicher Grund bleibt jedoch an der Stelle, wo Bodin die Sklaverei ablehnt, unausgesprochen: Die Sklaverei ist ökonomisch unren-

---

[12] Eine ähnliche Rolle spielen die Korporationen bei HEGEL. Vgl. *Rechts-philosophie* §§ 251, 252, 256. Die Elemente, durch die hindurch der objektive Geist bei Hegel den Staat hervortreibt, die Familie, das Eigentum, die «bürger-liche Gesellschaft» (in statu nascendi) und die Korporationen, sind bei Bodin bereits vorhanden, freilich nicht in dialektischen Schritten auseinander hervor-gehend, aber doch, was das Private und das Öffentliche angeht, einander be-dingend.

[13] MAX WEBER, Rechtssoziologie, Neuwied 1960, 138 ff. und passim.

tabel. Häufig haben die Sklaven keinen Beruf erlernt; sie verhungern nach ihrer Freilassung. Das Mittel, dies zu verhindern, «c'est devant les affranchir, leur enseigner quelque mestier», und zwar in Arbeitshäusern wie jenen, die in Paris, Lyon usw. für die Kinder der Armen eingerichtet worden sind, um ihnen ein Handwerk beizubringen (I, 5, S. 49 ff.; 67).[14] Zweifellos wäre es verfehlt, in Bodin den Verfechter einer ungehemmten kapitalistischen Dynamik sehen zu wollen. Wiederholt spricht er sich gegen Wucher, Bankgeschäfte und die Beteiligung mit Kapital an kaufmännischen Unternehmungen aus, um Profit zu erzielen[15] (V, 2, S. 710 ff.; VI, 2, S. 891 ff.). Die Besitzverhältnisse und ökonomischen Bewegungen in der Republik sollen offengelegt und kontrolliert werden. Zu diesem Zwecke führt Bodin nach antikem Vorbild das Amt der *Zensur* ein. Der Zensor soll den Besitz eines jeden schätzen. Es gibt zahllose Vorteile der Zensur: Sie trägt zur Steuergerechtigkeit bei, «on sçauroit aussi par ce moyen qui sont les prodigues, les cessionaires, les banqueroutiers, les riches, les povres, les saffraniers, les usuriers: & à quel ieu les uns gaignent tant de biens, & les autres dependent tout, pour y remedier; (...) aussi les tromperies qu'on fait aux mariages, aux ventes, aux marchez, & en toutes les negociations publiques & privees, seroyent descouvertes & cognuës» (VI, 1, S. 842). Lichtscheues Gesindel werde bei so strenger Überwachung sicherlich aus dem Lande verschwinden. Die «gens de bien» könnten also gegen die Zensur gar nichts haben, höchstens die «trompeurs», «pipeurs», «usuriers», «larrons du public», «cessionaires», «voleurs des particuliers», «banquiers», die schon in der Antike «ont eu en haine la censure, & empesché tant qu'ils ont peu, que le denombrement des biens ne se fist (...)» (VI, 1, S. 835; 840; 842 ff.). Bodin wird pathetisch, wenn er die Vorzüge der Zensur schildert. Beifällig zitiert er die Ansicht der Alten, welche die Zensur als «chose divine» angesehen hätten. Mit dem Zensurkapitel scheint man sich im Herzen der politischen Vorstellungen Bodins zu befinden. Denn die Zensur kontrolliert nicht nur den Besitzstand der Bürger, sie überwacht auch die Sitten des Volks, deren Niedergang die Gesetze allein nicht verhindern können. Wie sie darauf achtet, daß die Regeln der Musik, Symbol aller Harmonie, erhalten bleiben, so schützt sie auch die Harmonie der wohlgeordneten Republik (VI, 1, S. 847 ff.). Sie wacht darüber, daß die «peste de la Republique», nämlich das Thea-

---

[14] Zur Sklavenbefreiung vgl. MAX WEBER, Rechtssoziologie, 132 ff., der auf die schwindende Rentabilität der Sklaverei hinweist.

[15] Geschäfte «de sorte que le marchand, pour la douceur du proffit, devient casanier, l'artisan mesprise sa boutique, le laboureur quitte son labeur, le berger son bestail, le noble vend ses heritages, pour tirer quatre ou cinq cens livres de rentes constituees, au lieu de cent livres de rent fonsiere: & puis la rente constituee s'estaint, & l'argent s'en vole en fumee» (V, 2, 710 f.).

ter, «un apprentissage de toute impudicité, lubricité, paillardise, ruse, finesse, meschanceté», nicht die «bonnes meurs, & la simplicité & bonté naturelle d'un peuple» zerstöre (VI, 1, S. 848). Bodin beschwört hier den Geist eines tugendhaften Volkes, wobei er von den späteren Theorien des «Volksgeistes», wie sie sich bei Montesquieu, Rousseau und Hegel finden, nicht weit entfernt ist. Das Gemeinwesen, im Feudalismus in mannigfaltige, durch Rechtsbeziehungen verbundene politische Einheiten zersplittert, soll nicht nur durch die Souveränität und die gemeinsamen Gesetze und Institutionen, sondern auch durch einen «Gemeingeist» zur individualisierten politischen Allgemeinheit werden.[16]

Die Republik Bodins, die aus der Dialektik zwischen den gemeinsamen Grundlagen des Staates und dem besonderen Eigentum der Haushalte lebt, gibt den Partikularinteressen – denen des Adels und des an Bedeutung zunehmenden Bürgertums – so viel Raum, daß die harmonischen Proportionen des staatlichen Aufbaus mit Leben erfüllt, aber nicht gefährdet werden. Die «sciences liberales, & arts mechaniques» Handel und Gewerbe, müssen blühen, doch eine unkontrollierte ökonomische Dynamik kann nicht zugelassen werden: Sie würde die Freundschaft zwischen den sozialen Schichten, ohne welche die Republik keinen Bestand haben kann, untergraben. Die sozialen Gruppen sind nicht gleichwertig: Bodin zitiert Menenius Agrippa, um darzutun, daß die Republik wie der menschliche Körper von seinen edelsten Teilen gelenkt werden müsse (VI, 4, S. 950). Soll aber in der Idealrepublik tatsächlich Freundschaft zwischen den Ständen und Schichten bestehen, so darf nicht die Gerechtigkeitsvorstellung eines einzigen Standes vorherrschen – das heißt weder jene des Adels und der Reichen, die sich in der «geometrischen Proportion», noch die des einfachen Bürgertums (roturiers) und der Armen, die sich in der «arithmetischen Proportion» ausdrückt.[17] (Die erste Proportion ist die der Hierarchie, die zweite die des Tausches, weshalb sie auch «commutative» heißt.) Es muß vielmehr ein Ausdruck von Gerechtigkeit gefunden werden, der den Gerechtigkeitsbegriff der beiden wesentlichen sozialen Gruppen, des Adels und des Bürgertums, vereint. Bodin erblickt ihn in seiner «proportion harmonique» – diese ist gewissermaßen die kürzeste Formel der Zwischenstellung Bodins zwischen Feudalismus und bürgerlicher Gesellschaft (VI, 6, S. 1015 f.). Bodin illustriert ihre institutionellen Konsequenzen an seinem Bankett-Beispiel: Wie man seine Gäste an der Tafel so placiert, daß sich die Geschlechter, Stände und Berufe mischen,

---

[16] Bekanntlich gehört die Zensur auch zu den entscheidenden Institutionen bei Rousseau. Vgl. *Contrat social* IV, 8.

[17] Die «proportion arithmetique» schreitet durch Addition immer derselben Zahl fort (3, 9, 15, 21), die «proportion geometrique» im Kubus einer Zahl (3, 9, 27, 81). Vgl. den einschlägigen Kongreßbeitrag.

so «le sage Roy gouverne son Royaume harmoniquement, entremeslant doucement les nobles & roturiers», und zwar derart, daß «les nobles ayent quelque avantage sur les roturiers». Die Ämter in den Gerichtshöfen und anderen Körperschaften müssen mit Leuten aus allen Schichten besetzt werden, und der Tüchtige aus der Unterschicht muß eine Chance zum Aufstieg erhalten. Eine Republik, deren gesellschaftliche Glieder auf diese Weise zum harmonischen Zusammenklang gebracht werden, befindet sich in Übereinstimmung mit den Gesetzen des göttlichen Kosmos (VI, 6, S. 1054 ff.). Bodins Idealrepublik stellt ein ausgefeiltes Modell gesellschaftlicher Integration dar, das theoretische Versuche zur Lösung von Integrationsproblemen in späteren Entwicklungsstufen der bürgerlichen Gesellschaft (ständestaatliche Modelle) vorweggenommen hat.

VI

Bodin hat den sozialen Wandel, der zur Veränderung der Staats- und Regierungsform oder der gesellschaftlichen Verhältnisse einer Republik führt, vor allem im IV. und V. Buch der «Six Livres» behandelt. Unter «changement d'une Republique» versteht er ein «changement d'estat», eine Veränderung der Staatsform, die vorliegt, «quand la souveraineté d'un peuple vient en la puissance d'un Prince: ou la seigneurie des plus grands au menu peuple: ou bien au contraire» (IV, 1, S. 504). Ändert sich die Regierungsform, so spricht Bodin von einem «changement imparfaict», «c'est à sçavoir, d'estat Royal en seigneurial, de seigneurial en tyrannic, de tyrannic en Royal, de Royal en tyrannic, de tyrannic en Royal», usw. (IV, 1, S. 507). Ein bloßer sozialer Wandel, der die Staats- und Herrschaftsformen unberührt läßt, eine Veränderung der Gesetze, der Bräuche, der Religion usw., ist eine «alteration» (IV, 1, S. 504).

Die Gründe, die zum sozialen Wandel führen, können «humaines, ou naturelles, ou divines» sein. Zu den natürlichen Gründen gehören auch die «causes celestes, & plus esloignees» (IV, 2, S. 542), vor allem die Einflüsse der Gestirne und Zahlenkonstellationen, die Veränderungen an gewissen Daten erwarten lassen. Bodin, als «Klimatheoretiker» bekannt, mißt besonders natürlichen Faktoren wie der Beschaffenheit der Landschaft und dem Klima einen entscheidenden Einfluß auf das politische und soziale Verhalten eines Volkes bei: Diese Faktoren sind Konstanten, die auch beim sozialen Wandel in Rechnung gestellt werden müssen. Gebirgsvölker wie die des Nordens zum Beispiel neigen zur demokratischen Staats- und Regierungsform und werden darum ringen; es genügt aber auch schon, seinen Wohnsitz auf einem Berge zu haben, um demokratisch gesinnt zu sein. So hat Plutarch beobachtet, daß die Bewohner der hoch gelegenen Stadt Athen die Demokratie forderten, während die Bewohner der tiefer gelegenen Gebiete zur Oligarchie und jene des Piräus zur Aristokratie neigten (V, 1, S. 664; 694). Der Einfluß des Meeres weckt den Händlergeist, «la ruse de negotier, (...) tromper, mentir, & abuser les moins fins pour gaigner, qui est le but de plusieurs marchands» (V, 1, S. 696).

Zu den «causes humaines» des sozialen Wandels gehören auch jene, die unmittelbar mit der Sozialstruktur und der Eigentumsverteilung zusammenhängen. So treiben etwa konfiskatorische Steuern das Volk zum Aufruhr: «(...) il ne se trouve point de changemens, seditions, & ruines de Republiques plus frequentes, que pour les charges & imposts excessifs» (VI, 2, S. 881). An einer anderen Stelle faßt er die «causes que donnent changement aux estats & Republiques» zusammen: «des mesmes causes procedent les seditions & guerres civiles: le deny de iustice, l'oppression du menu peuple, la distribution inegale des peines & loyers, la richesse excessive d'un petit nombre, l'extreme povreté de plusieurs, l'oisiveté trop grande des subiects, l'impunité des forfaits» (IV, 2, S. 659). Bodin kritisiert an mehreren Stellen der «Six Livres» die Polarisierung von Reichen und Armen in heftigen Worten (z. B. V, 2, S. 704); doch er ist aus den bereits oben gezeigten Gründen ein scharfer Gegner einer Sozialreform, die auf Gütergleichheit, Umverteilung von Grund und Boden und Aufhebung von Schulden hinausliefe. Denn nicht die Ungleichheit – es sei denn, sie ist extrem –, sondern die Gleichheit ist die Ursache von Streit und Aufruhr: «(...) il est bien certain qu'il n'y a iamais haine plus grande, ni plus capitales inimitez, qu'en entre ceux-là qui sont esgaux: & la ialousie entre esgaux est la source des troubles, seditions & guerres civiles» (V, 2, S. 704). Eine Umverteilung der Güter, die Enteignung voraussetzte, würde das Vertrauen, das die Bürger in den Staat als den Beschützer ihres Eigentums haben, zerstören; das gleiche gilt für die Aufhebung von Schulden, die außerdem zur Folge hätte, daß die Bezieher von Renten aus angelegtem Kapital, also auch Waisen und einfache Leute, ruiniert werden, was weder Arm noch Reich, höchstens den Spekulanten, nützt (V, 2, S. 704). Die Güterverteilung muß dem Grundprinzip der Bodinschen Politik, der harmonischen Proportion, worin die Teile eines wohlgeordneten Gemeinwesens zu einander stehen, entsprechen.

Bodin wiederholt, wenn er auf die Beziehungen zwischen sozialer Struktur, politischen Anschauungen und sozialem Wandel zu sprechen kommt, vor allem Topoi aus der antiken Literatur (Platon, Aristoteles, Plutarch, usw.), und vergleicht sie mit seinem überreichen historischen Material (wo er sie zumeist bestätigt findet). Er ist jedoch hinter der Energie, mit der Platon und Aristoteles soziale Regelmäßigkeiten hinsichtlich des Zusammenhangs zwischen sozialer Schichtung, politischer Einstellung, Verfassungsstruktur und sozialem Wandel erforscht hatten, zurückgeblieben: So eindringliche Analysen wie die des aristokratischen, timokratischen, oligarchischen usw. Charakters in Platons «Politeia» und entsprechende Untersuchungen in der «Politik» des Aristoteles sind bei Bodin nicht zu finden. Die auf menschlichem Willen beruhenden Gründe des sozialen Wandels sind für ihn prinzipiell «muable & incertaine» (IV, 2, S. 542), kosmischen und göttlichen Einflüssen unterworfen, so daß sie die Formulierung von soziologischen Gesetzmäßigkeiten kaum zulassen. Es hat den Anschein, als hätten ihn die natürlichen und übernatürliche Gründe stärker interessiert als die menschlichen. In seinem zum Teil von magischen Vorstellungen beherrschten Renaissance-Weltbild hatte der Gedanke einer weltimmanenten, allein auf den ökonomischen und moralischen Triebkräften der Gesellschaft beruhenden Gesetzmäßigkeit, wie sie spätere bürgerliche Theoretiker, etwa Harrington und die schottischen Moralphilosophen (John Millar, Ferguson, Adam Smith) entwickelten, noch keinen Platz. Dies verbietet es auch, Bodin als einen Vorläufer der Soziologie anzusehen.

Ernst Hinrichs

Das Fürstenbild Bodins und die Krise
der französischen Renaissancemonarchie

Kaum ein politischer Theoretiker der frühen Neuzeit hat seinen Lesern einen so umfassenden Eindruck von dem Krisenbewußtsein seiner Zeit vermittelt, kaum ein Autor ist dem Vorgang der staatlich-politischen Veränderung (changement) mit einem so differenzierten System erfahrungs- und realitätsbezogener Verhaltensvorschriften zu Leibe gerückt wie Jean Bodin. Als typischer Vertreter des nordalpinen juristischen Humanismus mit den institutionellen, politischen, sozialen und ökonomischen Problemen seines Heimatlandes vertraut, hat Bodin in seinem politischen Hauptwerk[1] Reformvorstellungen entwickelt, die nach seinen eigenen Worten den von der politischen Wissenschaft erarbeiteten «Regeln» entsprachen und daher für eine Anwendung geeignet erschienen.[2] Immer wieder die polemische Auseinandersetzung mit Plato und Morus suchend, deren «republique en idee sans effet»[3] ihm als negatives Modell seines eigenen, radikal un-utopischen Entwurfs diente, hat Bodin allen staatstheoretischen Überlegungen implizit und explizit das Bild der französischen Monarchie zugrunde gelegt, von dessen Vorbildlichkeit er wie fast alle französischen Juristen seiner Zeit überzeugt war.

In welche Richtung die Reformideen Bodins zielten, wie tiefgreifend sie angelegt waren – darüber besteht bis heute keine Einigkeit.[4] Bodin selbst hat zu dem wechselvollen Schicksal seiner Wirkungsgeschichte sicher nicht unerheblich beigetragen. Die gigantischen Ausmaße seines Traktats, die erdrückende Last seines Belegapparats, die vielen scheinbaren und tatsächlichen Widersprüche seiner Argumentation,[5] die Text-

---

[1] JEAN BODIN, *Les six livres de la république*, Paris 1576, zitiert nach einem Faksimiledruck der Ausgabe von 1583 (Aalen 1961).

[2] *République*, 4.

[3] *République*, 4.

[4] Ein ausführlicher Forschungsbericht bei G. ROELLENBLECK [231], Zum Schrifttum über Jean Bodin seit 1936 (II), *Der Staat 3* (1964), 227–246. Nach der «Logik» von Bodins Souveränitätsbegriff fragt J. U. LEWIS [261], Jean Bodin's «Logic of Sovereignty», *Political Studies* 16 (1968), 202–221.

[5] Ein vieldiskutiertes Beispiel ist Bodins Steuertheorie. Vgl. dazu M. WOLFE [265], Jean Bodin on Taxes: The Sovereignty-Taxes Paradox, in *Political Science Quaterly* 83 (1968), 268–284.

veränderungen, welche der Autor an den in rascher Folge erscheinenden
Neuauflagen vornahm – all das hat den Versuch einer konsistenten Ge-
samtinterpretation erschwert. So kam es, daß Einzelaspekte seiner Theorie aus ihrem Zusammenhang herausgelöst und mit dem Blick auf die
«Modernität» Bodins unangemessen stark betont wurden. Besonders der
Begriff der Souveränität und seine verfassungspolitischen Implikationen
traten im Zuge verabsolutierender staatsrechtsgeschichtlicher und etatisti-
scher Betrachtungsweisen derart in den Vordergrund, daß sie lange Zeit
als der zentrale Anlaß für das Entstehen der *République* Bodins erscheinen mußten.

Demgegenüber richtet sich die heutige Bodin-Deutung wieder stärker
auf die gesamte Staatslehre dieses Autors und darüber hinaus auf seine
übrigen, zumeist unterschätzten Werke zur Theorie des Rechts, der Geschichte, der Religion und der Erkenntnis. Der konservative Grundzug
seines politischen Denkens, der heute als erwiesen gilt[6] und in einem gewissen Widerspruch zur Neuartigkeit seiner Souveränitätstheorie steht,
hat zudem das Bedürfnis nach einer genaueren theoriegeschichtlichen
Einordnung der *République* geweckt. Der häufig angestellte Vergleich
Bodins mit Aristoteles auf der einen, Hobbes auf der anderen Seite hat
sich dabei in vieler Hinsicht als fruchtbar erwiesen. Weitgehend unbeach-
tet blieb jedoch die Frage, in welchem Verhältnis die Staatslehre Bodins
zur politischen, sozialen, wirtschaftlichen und geistigen Realität ihrer
Zeit selbst steht. Wenn Bodin in seiner Auseinandersetzung mit Plato und
Morus den «imaginativen» Zug dieser Autoren verwirft, so muß der
Frage, was er im Vergleich dazu als normative Faktizität begreift und
bei der Abfassung seiner Theorie voraussetzt, eine besondere Bedeutung
zukommen.

Im vorliegenden Beitrag soll dieser Frage an ausgewählten Beispielen
aus der Argumentation Bodins nachgegangen werden. Er verschließt sich
bewußt einer idealtypischen Betrachtungsweise[7] und faßt die Aussagen
Bodins in ihrer konkreten Zeitgebundenheit ins Auge. Sein Gegenstand
ist Bodins Staatsideal der Monarchie Royale, das für ihn die höchste Stufe
seiner Staatsformenlehre und in gewisser Weise die einzig brauchbare,
harmonische Herrschaftsform darstellte.

Wann immer Bodin die Funktionsweise der Monarchie Royale in der
République näher erläutert, nimmt er eine Fülle spätmittelalterlicher und
humanistischer Maximen zur Fürstenlehre in sein Werk auf, die einen

---

[6] Vgl. z. B. E. HASSINGER, Das Werden des neuzeitlichen Europa 1300–1600,
Brauschweig 1959, 384.

[7] Ich verweise auf den Beitrag von W. EUCHNER in diesem Band S. 261 ff., in
dem Bodins Staatsideal der Monarchie Royale mit dem Blick auf eine Einordnung der sozialen Ideen Bodins in die Geschichte der politischen Theorie analysiert wird.

seltsamen Kontrast bilden zu den rationalen, abstrakten Konstruktionen seiner Souveränitätslehre. Aus diesem Grunde sollen einige Bemerkungen über die Funktion der Fürstenethik in der *République* Bodins vorweggeschickt werden (I). Im Anschluß daran sollen die Strukturprinzipien seiner Monarchie Royale beschrieben werden (II). Ein dritter Abschnitt enthält eine kurze Skizze der Herrschaftsbedingungen in der französischen Renaissancemonarchie und der Wandlungen, von denen sie im Zeitalter der religiösen Bürgerkriege bedroht war. Ihre Wirkung auf Bodins Monarchieverständnis bildet den Inhalt des vierten und letzten Abschnittes.

I

Bodin hat, im Gegensatz zur Tradition der Fürstenspiegel, die politischen Handlungsnormen des Herrschers als Inhabers der Souveränität nicht zum Gegenstand einer systematischen Analyse gemacht. Er hat dagegen Anmerkungen zu Fürstenherrschaft und Fürstenethik über sein ganzes Werk verstreut und vor allem in den vielen historischen Exkursen, mit deren Hilfe er seine staatstheoretischen Thesen zu veranschaulichen suchte, immer wieder auf konkrete Herrscher der Vergangenheit und seiner eigenen Gegenwart Bezug genommen.[8]

Gerade Bodins Aussagen zur Fürstenethik wird nun von Interpreten, denen es um eine Darstellung des Neuartigen, Modernen bei Bodin geht, eine traditionelle, ins Mittelalter zurückweisende Tendenz nachgesagt.[9] In der Tat nähert sich Bodin häufig dem Vorbild der traditionellen Fürstenspiegel, wenn er auf die Pflichten des Monarque Royal eingeht. So in dem Kapitel II, 3 (De la Monarchie Royale), wo er – in sprachlicher Parallelität zu dem Souveränitätskapitel (mit seinen «vrayes marques de souveraineté») – von den «vrayes marques d'un grand Roy» spricht und dabei alle Kriterien des überkommenen Ideals des «princeps perfectus» oder «princeps optimus» zusammenstellt.[10] Auch der in der europäischen Fürstenethik so vielfach variierte Imperativ Ciceros «salus populi suprema lex esto» wird von Bodin an hervorragender Stelle als «allgemeine Maxime» der Gesetzgebung aufgenommen, die «keine Ausnahme zulasse».[11]

---

[8] Im Zusammenhang mit anderen Publizisten und der Politik Heinrichs IV. untersucht bei E. HINRICHS [266], Fürstenlehre und politisches Handeln im Frankreich Heinrichs IV. (= Veröffentlichungen des Max-Planck-Instituts für Geschichte 21) Göttingen 1969.

[9] Als Beispiel J. DENNERT [237], Ursprung und Begriff der Souveränität (= Sozialwissenschaftliche Studien, 7) Stuttgart 1964, 69.

[10] Vgl. z. B. *République*, 280, 614.

[11] *République*, 576.

Nun überraschen solche Äußerungen kaum bei einem Autor, der, wie die meisten juristischen und politischen Publizisten seiner Zeit, das Ideal der Monarchie Royale keineswegs mit der Absicht grundsätzlicher Neuerungen formulierte. In der Ideenwelt der politisch Gebildeten Frankreichs im 16. Jahrhundert waren Vorstellungen von einem monarchischen Verfassungsideal lebendig, das auf dem überkommenen Verständnis einer hierarchischen Weltordnung beruhte, in der dem Fürsten wie den Untertanen ihre fest umrissenen Positionen und Aufgaben zugewiesen waren.[12] Gab es auch zwischen Autoren unterschiedlicher politischer Intention gegensätzliche Auffassungen über das Gewicht und die Bedeutung einzelner Bestandteile der Hierarchie, so herrschte doch weitgehende Einigkeit über die Einordnung des Fürsten und die Definition seiner Pflichten und Rechte. Mit Ausnahme der Publizisten, die auf dem Höhepunkt des Bürgerkriegs nach 1585 den ligistischen Extremismus vertraten und dabei Auffassungen formulierten, die erst wieder vom Radikalismus der Pariser Sektionen in der Revolution artikuliert wurden, blieb für das politische Denken Frankreichs in der zweiten Hälfte des 16. Jahrhunderts die traditionelle Vorstellung einer idealen monarchischen Verfassung Frankreichs zentraler Bezugspunkt. Denis Richet hat jüngst darauf hingewiesen, daß Bodin gerade deshalb so wenig Mühe hatte, seine monarchomachischen Gegner zu widerlegen, weil sie – in ihrer Auseinandersetzung mit Machiavelli – mit dem ständigen Verweis auf die christliche Zielsetzung der königlichen Macht, auf die Grenzen, die ihr durch Gesetze und Gewohnheitsrecht gesteckt seien, grundsätzlich den Rahmen der absoluten Monarchie nicht sprengten. Sie stellten zwar die «Funktionsfähigkeit der französischen Monarchie in einem besonderen Fall in Frage»[13] und formulierten institutionelle Möglichkeiten der Vorsorge für den Fall, daß sich ein Herrscher vom Monarque Royal in einen «tyran d'exercice» verwandelte; doch blieb damit für die Monarchomachen – und bis zu einem gewissen Grad auch für Bodin – die Amtsführung des Herrschers das Zentrum ihres politischen Denkens. Auch gemäßigte Ligisten hätten, so sagt Richet, einen einzelnen Fürsten angefochten, nicht aber das System als solches.[14]

Hier wird nun die Bedeutung der traditionellen Fürstenethik für die französische politische Theorie im 16. Jahrhundert, ja bis in die Zeit Ludwigs XIV. hinein, deutlich.[15] Blieb der Fürst, als raison d'être der

---

[12] Vgl. z. B. *République*, Préface.

[13] D. RICHET, Autour des origines idéologiques lointaines de la Révolution française: Elites et Despotisme, Annales *E.S.C.* 24 (1969), 1–23, hier 15.

[14] RICHET, Origines idéologiques, 16.

[15] Dazu insgesamt G. LACOUR-GAYET, L'Education politique de Louis XIV, Paris 2. Aufl. 1923; zu Fénelon jetzt die wertvolle Studie von F. GALLOUÉDEC-GENUYS, Le prince selon Fénelon, Paris 1963.

Monarchie Royale, Zentrum des Verfassungsbildes, so mußten zwangsläufig Traditionen der politischen Meinungsäußerung gepflegt werden,
denen es um einen Einfluß auf den Herrscher als wirksamstes Element dieser Verfassung ging. Erst am Ende des 17. und zu Beginn des 18. Jahrhunderts, als im Reflex auf die Amtsführung Ludwigs XIV. der neuzeit-
liche Despotismusbegriff geboren wurde, als die sich ausbildende Theorie
einer elitären Kontrolle des Herrschers durch Adel und andere Zwischen-
gewalten einem neuen Verständnis der französischen Verfassung Raum
gab,[16] war die Zeit der Fürstenethik in Frankreich vorüber. Für Montesquieu steht fest, daß die monarchische Regierungsform nicht mehr der
«vertu» bedarf – weder beim Herrscher, noch im Volk: «Dans les états
monarchiques et modérés la puissance est bornée par ce qui en est le
ressort, je veux dire l'honneur, qui règne, comme un monarque, sur le
prince et sur le peuple.»[17] Solchen und ähnlichen Aussagen Montesquieus
liegt ein neues Staatsverständnis zugrunde, das die Interdependenz von
politischer Herrschaft und Sozialstruktur als eine «historische und natürliche Gesetzmäßigkeit»[18] begreift und daher zwangsläufig den Herrscher in eine relative, abhängige Position rückt; der Adel gehört für Montesquieu als Zwischengewalt «irgendwie zum Wesen der Monarchie».[19]

Dieses auf eine «bestimmte soziale Kontrolle des Staates»[20] hinauslau-
fende Verfassungsverständnis lag Bodin wie seinen monarchomachischen
Kontrahenten fern. So sehr sich diese auch bemühten, durch ihre verschiedenen Vertragskonstruktionen juristische Bindungen des Herrschers zu
fixieren, so wurden mögliche Kontrollen der fürstlichen Regierungsweise,
mögliche Formen des Widerstandes doch ausschließlich institutionell definiert. Sie wurden nicht als permanent wirksamer, sozial determinierter
Mechanismus begriffen, sondern als institutionelles Therapeutikum für
den Grenzfall, daß der Fürst den Schritt vom «bon et iuste Roy» zum
Tyrannen tat. Institutionell nicht gebundene Gruppen blieben vom Widerstandsrecht kategorisch ausgeschlossen, und die Aversion der Monarchomachen gegen die «populace» entspricht vollkommen Bodins abwer-
tendem Urteil über das Volk als «Tier mit den vielen Köpfen».[21] Wenn
Bodin trotzdem in aller Schärfe gegen die monarchomachischen Theorien
des Widerstands Stellung nahm, so spielt hier, neben seiner grundsätzlich
staatsbezogenen, legistischen Tradition, die zur Ausbildung seines Souveränitätsbegriffs führte, vor allem sein andersartiges Verhältnis zu Fra-

---

[16] RICHET, Origines idéologiques, 19.
[17] MONTESQUIEU, *De l'esprit des lois*, in der Ausgabe der Sammlung L'Intégrale Paris 1964, 540.
[18] RICHET, Origines idéologiques, 19.
[19] RICHET, Origines idéologiques, 19.
[20] RICHET, Origines idéologiques, 19.
[21] So z. B. *République*, 649 u. 940.

gen der politischen Praxis, zu den Bedingungen von Macht und Herrschaft, eine Rolle.

Denn wenn Bodins Auffassung von der fürstlichen Herrschaft auch,
wie eingangs betont wurde, von dem traditionellen Verständnis der französischen Monarchie als einer unter dem Recht stehenden, mit der Gesellschaft in Harmonie befindlichen Institution abgeleitet erscheint, so
darf doch nicht übersehen werden, daß er diese Tradition nicht, wie
manche der monarchomachischen Publizisten, idealisiert und mystifiziert.[22] Der Fürst Bodins hat zwar seine feste Position in einem an überkommenen Ordovorstellungen orientierten Weltbild, sein politisches
Handeln wird zwar ständig an seiner Fähigkeit gemessen, gemäß den
Traditionen einer (allerdings national-institutionell, nicht universell-reli-
giös gesehenen) Verfassung zu regieren; doch der Staat Bodins ist weder
Institution zur Wiederherstellung einer transzendenten Heilsordnung,
noch säkulare Utopie,[23] sondern institutionelle Wirklichkeit, die Wandlungen ausgesetzt ist und von Bodin mit den Kriterien erfahrener (und
erlebter) Wandlungen analysiert wird. Sein Fürst ist daher nur noch par-
tiell Träger von Gesinnungen, wie die Herrscher der mittelalterlichen
Fürstenspiegel,[24] ebenso aber politisch Handelnder im materiellsten Sinn
des Wortes, Leiter der «affaires d'estat», der die Regeln der «science politique» kennt, über die geographischen, klimatischen, institutionellen und
sozialen Bedingungen seiner Herrschaft informiert[25] und darum optimal
gerüstet ist, den drohenden Wandlungen zu begegnen.

Hier liegt die Ursache dafür, daß in der *République* Bodins im Grunde
drei sehr unterschiedliche Fürstenbilder gezeichnet werden. Wir finden
einmal den «bon et iuste Roy», den «princeps perfectus», der sich dem
Gottes- und Naturrecht unterwirft, der die überkommenen Grundrechte
des Königreichs (die «lois fondamentales») respektiert, die Rechte und
Privilegien seiner Untertanen schützt, der die zeitgenössischen Darstellungen des «tyrannischen» Regiments kennt und seine Amtsführung so

---

[22] Vor allem dort, wo Bodin den «Roy tresiuste» dem Tyrannen gegenüber-
stellt, läßt er durchblicken, daß eine schematische Trennung beider Herrscher-
typen nicht immer möglich ist. Vgl. *République*, 294: «Voila les differences les
plus remarquables du Roy et du tyran: qui ne sont pas difficiles à congnoistre
entre les deux extremités d'un Roy tresiuste, et d'un tyran tres-meschant: mais
il n'est pas si aisé à iuger, quand un Prince tient quelque chose d'un bon Roy et
d'un tyran. Car le temps, les lieux, les personnes, les occasions qui se presentent,
contraignent souvent les Princes à faire chose qui semblent tyranniques aux uns,
et louables aux autres.»

[23] Vgl. Th. Nipperdey, Thomas Morus, in: Klassiker des politischen Denkens,
Bd. 1 München ³1969, 222–244, hier 233.

[24] Nipperdey, Morus, 233.

[25] *République*, 574.

einrichtet, daß den Untertanen kein Zweifel kommt an der Reinheit und Redlichkeit seiner Absichten.[26] Sodann den «absoluten» und «souveränen» Fürst. Zwar steht er unter dem «Recht», doch hat er – als einziger in seinem Staat – die Möglichkeit, Gesetze aufzuheben, zu verändern und zu erlassen, und damit in die gewohnheitsrechtliche Verfassung seines Reichs einzugreifen. Schließlich den «prince habile», den «klugen» und «geschickten» Fürst, in dem sich der Realist, ja Machiavellist Bodin spiegelt. Sein Bild wird vor allem in jenen Teilen der *République* gezeichnet, welche das aristotelische Thema der Staatsveränderungen aktualisieren. Hier, wo es nicht mehr um die Beschreibung der Monarchie Royale geht, ihrer «normalen» Funktionen, ihrer Institutionen und ihrer Gesellschaft, hier ist ein Fürst erforderlich, der nach der Maßgabe des Staatsnutzens (nécessité) handelt, drohenden Veränderungen rechtzeitig zu begegnen sucht, die Ursachen möglicher Umstürze analysiert und zu beseitigen trachtet. Ein Blick in die Kasuistik Bodins in den Büchern 4 bis 6 könnte uns einen plastischen Eindruck *seines* Principe vermitteln.[27]

II

Gerade die unterschiedlichen Farbgebungen seines Fürstenbildes und die Theorie der Wandlungen, deren Ursachen und Folgen Bodin so ausführlich zu ergründen sucht, stellen sein Werk in den politischen, sozialen und ökonomischen Kontext seiner Zeit, der nicht nur ein Anlaß für das Entstehen der *République,* sondern auch einer ihrer wesentlichen Gegenstände wurde. Im Gegensatz zu vielen Interpreten Bodins, welche der Geschichte Frankreichs nach dem Eindringen der Reformation nur insofern Bedeutung beimaßen, als sie zur Deutung Bodins beitrug, hat Ch. Morazé in einer frühen Schrift[28] über den Ursprung des französischen Staatsbegriffs diese dialektische Interdependenz von Staatstheorie und Geschichte zu erfassen versucht. Ausgehend von wirtschafts-, sozial- und finanzgeschichtlichen Beobachtungen, sieht Morazé in Jean Bodin einen Autor, der in seiner *République* die um 1576 sichtbar werdende Divergenz zwischen der politischen Verfassung Frankreichs und seiner Sozial- und Wirtschaftsverfassung zum Ausdruck bringt. Indem Bodin einerseits die Achtung vor dem Eigentum zum Prinzip der Monarchie Royale erhebe, andererseits dem Fürsten mit dem Souveränitätsbegriff ein Instru-

---

[26] Vgl. vor allem *République* Buch II, K. 3.

[27] Der Machiavellismus Bodins gut herauspräpariert bei G. CARDASCIA [150], Machiavel et Jean Bodin, *Bibliothèque d'humanisme et renaissance* 3 (1943), 129–167.

[28] CH. MORAZÉ, La France Bourgeoise, 18e–20e siècle, Paris 1946, 152 ff.

ment in die Hand gebe, das sich gegen die Inhaber wohlerworbener Rechte verwenden ließ, versuche er die französische Gesellschaftsordnung den im 16. Jahrhundert rapide fortgeschrittenen wirtschaftlichen Bedingungen anzupassen, ohne das Prinzip des privaten Eigentums zu verletzen, auf dem auch die neue Gesellschaft mit ihrem «liberaleren» Wirtschaftsverhalten beruhen müsse. «Parce que les conditions du commerce, du travail appellent une réglementation neuve ... le roi doit avoir le droit, ce droit qu'on lui refusait jusque-là, de changer la législation en vigueur, d'agir en arbitre des coutumes et des lois. Mais aussi parce que la puissance des hommes nouveaux s'appuie sur la richesse matérielle, sur le droit de chacun à jouir du fruit de son travail pendant sa vie et d'en disposer à l'heure de la mort, toute entrave au droit de propriété ... est considérée comme une survivance des principes arbitraires absolus.»[29] Morazé, der sich der Problematik einer allzu generalisierenden Interpretation Bodins bewußt ist, versucht hier, die Souveräntitätslehre Bodins mit jenen Definitionen der *République* in einen historischen Kontext zu bringen, die eine Bindung des absoluten Monarchen an die bestehenden Eigentumsverhältnisse erkennen lassen. In der Tat erscheint das Eigentumsargument bei Bodin mehrfach an hervorragender Stelle. «Le Monarque Royal est celuy – so beginnt Bodin seine Betrachtungen über sein Staatsideal – qui se rend aussi obeissant aux loix de nature, comme il desire les subjects estre envers luy, laissant la liberté naturelle, et la propriété des biens à chacun.»[30] Nun geht Bodin nirgends darauf ein, was er unter «natürliche Freiheit» und «Eigentum» versteht und verzichtet somit auf eine theoretische Untermauerung dieser Definition. Insofern läßt sich Morazés Interpretation des Staatsbegriffs Bodins am Text der *République* nur schwer nachvollziehen. Insbesondere die Frage, inwieweit Bodin als Protagonist bestimmter gesellschaftlicher Gruppen und ihrer Eigentumsformen betrachtet werden kann, muß angesichts mancher Unklarheiten seiner Argumentation m. E. offenbleiben.[31] Bodins Blick bleibt, auch wenn er für die Achtung von Freiheit und Eigentum des einzelnen eintritt, immer auf die Funktionsweise der Monarchie Royale

---

[29] MORAZÉ, France Bourgeoise, 154.

[30] *République*, 279.

[31] Morazé ist durchaus zuzustimmen, wenn er betont, daß die Ämterpolitik für die französische Monarchie ein Instrument darstellte, das es den Königen erlaubte «de satisfaire d'une manière permanente les ambitions des plus favorisés des roturiers»; MORAZÉ, France Bourgeoise, 156. Fraglich erscheint jedoch, ob Bodin die Tendenz der Monarchie billigte, diese Ämterpolitik mittels der Vergabe der Ämter als Eigentum ihrer Inhaber zu betreiben. Bodin hat sich zwar, insbesondere für die Beamten der Cours souveraines (*République*, 600 f.), für eine Einsetzung der Beamten auf Lebenszeit ausgesprochen, doch muß er dabei nicht, wie Morazé vermutet, das Ziel verfolgt haben, «de sauvegarder une forme

insgesamt gerichtet. Die Achtung von Freiheit und Eigentum, was immer Bodin darunter im einzelnen versteht, durch den Fürsten impliziert die Anerkennung bestehender Verträge und Rechtsverhältnisse. Die Monarchie Royale kann – im Gegensatz zur Monarchie Seigneuriale – nur «funktionieren», wenn in ihr Rechtssicherheit gewährleistet ist. Nicht zufällig erhebt Bodin dieses Postulat anläßlich der Frage, ob die in der Antike praktizierten Verfahren einer egalitären Neuverteilung von Eigentum in seiner Zeit Anwendung finden sollen. Bodin bestreitet ihre Nützlichkeit nicht grundsätzlich, er lehnt sie aber ab für einen bestehenden Staat, in dem sich die vorhandenen Eigentumsformen auf der Grundlage und mit Hilfe des Vertrauens in die bestehenden Gesetze ausgebildet haben. «On peut dire, que l'equalité des biens est tres pernicieuse aux Republiques, lesquelles n'ont appuy ny fondement plus asseuré que la foy, sans laquelle ny la iustice, ny societé quelconque ne peut estre durable: or la foy gist aux promesses des conventions legitimes. Si donc les obligations sont cassees, les contracts annullés, les debtes abolies, que doit-on attendre autre chose que l'entiere eversion d'un estat? Car il n'y aura fiance quelconque de l'un à l'autre.»[32]

Dieses Zitat wirft ein bezeichnendes Licht auf Bodins Definition der Monarchie Royale. Nicht die natürliche Freiheit und das Eigentum *als solche* sind das Ziel seiner Argumentation, sondern die rechtlichen Kommunikationsformen, die sich zu ihrer Wahrung ausgebildet haben und die als Element der Stabilität des bestehenden Staatswesens begriffen werden. Diese Auffassung Bodins tritt noch deutlicher hervor, wenn er sich über den staatlich dekretierten Schuldenerlaß äußert: «Quant à l'abolition des debtes, c'estoit chose de mauvais exemple ... non pas tant pour la perte des creanciers, qui ne seroit pas fort considerable quand il y va du public, que pour l'ouverture qui se fait de rompre la foy des iustes conventions, et pour l'occasion que les mutins empoignent, pour troubler un estat, sous l'esperance qu'ils ont tousjours de la rescision des debtes.»[33] Hier wird dem Fürsten, wie übrigens an anderen Stellen auch,[34] recht freimütig – «quand il y va du public» – ein Eingriff in die individuelle

---

nouvelle de la propriété» (MORAZÉ, France Bourgeoise, 156). Verfolgt man Bodins eigene Argumentation in dem Kapitel IV, 4, so zeigt sich, daß er vor allem aus Nützlichkeitserwägungen für die Monarchie Royale eine Einsetzung der breiten Schicht mittlerer und kleiner Beamten auf Lebenszeit empfiehlt. Dagegen gehört Bodin, wie das von Morazé völlig übersehene Kapitel V, 4 zeigt, zu den entschiedensten Gegnern der Ämterkäuflichkeit.

[32] *République*, 704.

[33] *République*, 707.

[34] Vgl. z. B. *République*, 157. «Mais la raison naturelle veut que le public soit preferé au particulier, et que les subiects relaschent non seulement leurs iniures et vengeances, ains aussi leurs biens pour le salut de la Republique.»

Eigentumssphäre zugestanden. Nicht *er* bildet Bodins Problem, sondern die möglichen gefährlichen Konsequenzen solcher Akte für die allgemeine Rechtssicherheit und damit für den Bestand der Monarchie Royale.

Der Gedanke der allgemeinen Rechtssicherheit und des sich daraus ergebenden Vertrauensverhältnisses zwischen dem Herrscher und den Untertanen taucht bei Bodin nicht nur im Zusammenhang mit staatlichen Eingriffen in die Eigentumsverhältnisse auf. Er ist vielmehr das Strukturprinzip der Monarchie Royale schlechthin. Immer wieder findet Bodin zu eindringlichen Formulierungen, wenn er im Rahmen seiner Typologie der Staatskrisen auf die Gefahrenmomente für die Monarchie Royale hinweist, die sich aus einem Schwinden des allgemeinen Konsensus zwischen Herrscher und Untertanen, aus einer Verunsicherung der bestehenden Rechtsverhältnisse ergeben. Ein besonders plastisches Beispiel bietet Bodin in dem Kapitel über die Stellung der Beamten (officiers) in der Monarchie Royale. Die Frage, ob die Beamten auf Lebenszeit eingesetzt werden sollen, ist für Bodin durchaus Anlaß für pragmatische, unter dem Gesichtspunkt der Staatsnützlichkeit stehende Erwägungen. Nicht zweifelhaft darf aber für die Beamten selbst sein, daß Einstellung und Entlassung nicht auf fürstlicher Willkür beruhen, sondern durch Gesetze geregelt werden. «En la Monarchie Royale ... il est besoin de reigler les choses par loix le plus qu'on pourra: autrement, si le Roy sans cause deboute d'un estat plustost l'un que l'autre, celuy qui sera forclos se tiendra iniurie, et sera mal content de son Roy, qui doit estre armé des subjects: et pour ce faire il faut oster toute occasion de mal-talent qu'on pourroit avoir contre luy; or il n'y a moyen plus grand que d'en laisser la disposition aux loix et ordonnances.»[35] Hier zeigt sich, wie stark Bodin jene Entscheidungen des Fürsten, die einen Eingriff in die bestehende Rechtsordnung nach sich ziehen, und daher die Loyalität einzelner (oder ganzer Gruppen) zum bestehenden Staatswesen negativ beeinflussen können, an einen Kalkül der möglichen Folgen bindet. Insofern bleibt die Rolle des Fürsten bei Bodin, solange die Stabilität der Monarchie Royale lediglich von der Entscheidungsklugheit des Herrschers abhängt, weitgehend auf die Funktion der Rechtsbewahrung beschränkt.

Nun ist aber die innerstaatliche Rechtssicherheit, auf der das Vertrauensverhältnis zwischen Fürst und Untertanen basiert, keinesfalls nur durch «tyrannische» Entscheidungen des Fürsten selbst bedroht. In seiner Typologie der Staatskrisen nennt Bodin eine ganze Reihe von Ursachen, die zu der gefürchteten «ruine des republiques» führen können.[36] Neben inneren Parteiungen, Nachfolgekämpfen, Veränderungen der bestehenden Gesetze, Religionsunruhen mißt Bodin der mangelnden Harmonie der

---

[35] *République*, 599.
[36] *République*, 503 ff.

Eigentumsverfassung – «la pauvreté trop grande de la plus part des subjects, et richesses excessives de peu de gents»[37] – eine so große Bedeutung
bei, daß er ihr ein eigenes Kapitel widmet.[38] Hier nähern wir uns dem
zentralen Problem Bodins. Innerstaatliche Wandlungsvorgänge, die nicht
durch fürstliche Fehlentscheidungen provoziert werden, sondern sich aus
der eigenen Dynamik des politischen, sozialen und wirtschaftlichen Lebens
ergeben, gefährden die Stabilität und Harmonie der Monarchie Royale
ebenso wie unangemessene fürstliche Eingriffe in die bestehende Rechts-
sphäre und lassen eine Entscheidungsinstanz notwendig erscheinen, welche
den hier auftretenden Gefahren begegnen kann. Konfrontiert man Bodins
rationale Maximen zur Souveränität mit seinen Anschauungen über die
fürstliche Verhaltensweise in Krisenzeiten, so drängt sich die Vermutung
auf, daß der absolute «Souverän» Bodins vor allem als Antwort auf diese
Krisenkonstellation der Monarchie Royale gedacht war. Denn so sehr
Bodin mit der Theorie des «legibus solutus» den Herrscher als Träger der
Befehls- und Gesetzgebungsgewalt gegenüber allen übrigen Untertanen
verabsolutiert, so sehr bindet er ihn an die Funktionsbedingungen der
Monarchie Royale, in der Rechtssicherheit, und das heißt Vertrauen
(fiance) in die gleichbleibende Gültigkeit der bestehenden Gesetze (der
königlichen Edikte und Ordonnanzen wie der «coutumes») herrschen
muß. Es erscheint daher bedeutsam, wenn Bodin in seinen Erläuterungen
zu den monarchischen Souveränitätsrechten nicht die Möglichkeit der *Gesetzgebung*, sondern die der *Veränderung* und *Korrektur* betont: «Car il
faut que le Prince souverain ait les loix en sa puissance *pour les changer,
et corriger selon l'occurence des cas.*»[39] Das Kapitel IV, 3 mit seiner zentralen Maxime, «que les changements des loix ne se doivent faire tout à
coup»,[40] bringt anschauliche Belege für die Regierungspraxis des absoluten
Souveräns Bodins in konkreten innerstaatlichen Krisenfällen.

III

Sicherheit von Freiheit und Eigentum als Rechtssicherheit auf der einen
Seite, absolutes, souveränes Königtum als Institution der Modernisierung
der Rechtsordnung auf der anderen – hier tritt die grundlegende Widersprüchlichkeit der Staatslehre Bodins zutage, die nicht auf seiner Un-
fähigkeit zur konsequenten Konstruktion beruht, sondern die Bindung
seiner Betrachtungsweise an die in seiner Zeit herrschenden politischen,

---

[37] *République*, 511.
[38] Das Kap. V, 2 *République*, 701 ff.
[39] *République*, 142; Sperrung vom Verfasser.
[40] Im Titel des Kapitels *République* IV, 3, S. 572.

sozialen und ökonomischen Verhältnisse spiegelt. Die französische Renaissancemonarchie war noch zur Zeit Bodins ein weitgehend dezentralisierter Staat.[41] Die königliche Bürokratie wuchs zwar ständig, war aber nicht in der Lage, eine straff durchrationalisierte Verwaltung aufzubauen. Viele Beamten und Institutionen, besonders in den von Paris entfernt gelegenen Regionen, hatten zudem die Neigung, sich so weit wie möglich von der Krone zu lösen. Eine Fülle von Funktionen war vom König in der Form von Privilegien vergeben und in das Patrimonium ihrer Inhaber eingegangen. Die militärischen Machtmittel des Königs reichten bei weitem nicht aus, so daß er im Kriegsfall auf die Hilfe großer Adliger und ihrer Klientel und auf ausländische Söldner angewiesen blieb. Das Steuersystem wies erhebliche Schwächen auf. War es der Monarchie auch im Laufe der Jahrhunderte gelungen, die regelmäßige Erhebung der «taille» ohne Zustimmung der Generalstände auf dem Wege der Verjährung zu sichern, so blieb die Einführung neuer Steuern, außer in Notfällen, an ihr Einverständnis gebunden.[42] Die Generalstände jedoch hatten sich nicht zu einer regelmäßig tagenden Institution entwickelt, so daß der König auf andere Mittel der Geldbeschaffung – auf Anleihen und auf Manipulationen mit dem Gewicht der Gold- und Silbermünzen – ausweichen mußte. [43]

Die Partizipation regionaler und lokaler ständischer Institutionen an allgemeinen Verwaltungsaufgaben war dagegen in der Mitte des 16. Jahrhunderts noch in hohem Maße gewährleistet. Vor allem die Provinzialstände in den großen Provinzen und die «parlements» in Paris und in den Provinzialhauptstädten bildeten feste institutionelle Organisationen mit eigenem Korpsgeist, deren Bedeutung für die Verwaltung eines institutionellen Flächenstaates wie Frankreich in der Zeit unterentwickelter Kommunikationsformen nicht unterschätzt werden darf.[44] Das Kapitel III, 7 der *République* Bodins mit seinen eindringlichen Formulierungen über die Stellung der «corps» in der Monarchie Royale ist ein deutlicher Reflex auf diesen Tatbestand.

---

[41] Ich folge hier den grundlegenden Untersuchungen von J. RUSSELL MAJOR, The Limitations of Absolutism in the «New Monarchies», in: The «New Monarchies» and Representative Assemblies. Medieval Constitutionalism or Modern Absolutism?, Hg. von A. J. Slavin, Boston 1964 77–84 (Nachdruck eines in dem Emory University Quarterly 1957 112–124 abgedruckten Aufsatzes.) DERS., The Crown and the Aristocracy in Renaissance France, *American Historical Review* 69 (1964), 631–645. DERS., The French Renaissance Monarchy as seen through the Estates General, *Studies in the Renaissance* 9 (1962), 113–125.

[42] PH. DUR, The Right of Taxation in the Political Theory of the French Religious Wars, *The Journal of Modern History* 17 (1945) 289–303, hier 300 ff. und WOLFE [265], 275.

[43] MORAZÉ, France Bourgeoise, 159 ff.

[44] RUSSELL MAJOR, Limitations of Absolutism, 81.

Dem französischen Königtum stand demnach im 16. Jahrhundert eine Gesellschaft gegenüber, die zwar nur beschränkte institutionelle Möglichkeiten einer Kontrolle ihrer Regierung besaß, deren Führungsschichten aber durch eine Fülle faktischer Autonomien gegenüber dem Königtum abgesichert waren. Man denke etwa an die breite Schicht Pariser Bürger, die durch die Zeichnung königlicher Anleihen praktisch zum Gläubiger der Krone geworden waren und deren Wohlverhalten im Staat davon abhing, ob die Krone ihnen die regelmäßige Zahlung ihrer Renten garantierte;[45] oder an die vielen «officiers», die ihre Ämter bereits käuflich erworben hatten und deren Loyalität sich naturgemäß danach bemaß, ob die Krone ihnen einen ungestörten Genuß ihrer Amtspfründen gewährleistete oder ob sie von dem ihr an sich zustehenden Recht einer Rücknahme von Ämtern Gebrauch machte.[46] Auch hierfür bietet Jean Bodin einen anschaulichen Kommentar, wenn er die Politik Karls IX. rühmt, der angesichts der Unzahl von Ämtern nicht mit der «force en main» vorgegangen sei, sondern den Tod von Beamten abgewartet habe, um ihre Ämter einzuziehen. «Car outre la difficulté du remboursement qui faire se doit, encore est-il plus à craindre que ceux-là remuent l'estat, qui sont despouillés de l'honneur qui plus est cher aux ambitieux que les biens ny la vie.»[47]

J. Russell Major hat in einem instruktiven Artikel gezeigt,[48] wie stark die Struktur der französischen Renaissancemonarchie, auch wenn die großen Feudalherren seit der früheren Renaissanceperiode aus dem Blickfeld verschwanden, von einer neuen Aristokratie aus Landadel, höherer Bürokratie und geadelten bürgerlichen Patriziern geprägt wurde, einer Klasse, die trotz mannigfacher Spannungen zwischen älterem Adel und den «homines novi» aus den Städten kraft ihrer auf dem Landbesitz beruhenden, ständig sich verbessernden wirtschaftlichen Position zum Erben des alten Feudaladels wurde. Parallel zu dieser neuen Klasse bildeten sich im Frankreich der Renaissance neue, an das Lehnswesen erinnernde Abhängigkeitsformen aus, die, auf einem rein persönlichen Patron-Klienten-Verhältnis beruhend, dem Einfluß bedeutender Herren – von ihrer privaten Miliz bis hinauf zur Stellenbesetzung am Hof – einen wirksamen Hintergrund geben konnten.[49] Wenn Bodin in seiner Polemik gegen

[45] R. Pillorget, Les problèmes monétaires français de 1602 à 1689, *XVIIe siècle* 70/71 (1966), 107–130, hier 114; B. Schnapper, Les rentes au XVIe siècle. Histoire d'un instrument de crédit (Ecole pratique des Hautes Etudes, VIe section, Affaires et gens d'affaires 12) Paris 1957, 169 ff.

[46] L. Romier, Le royaume de Cathérine de Médicis. La France à la veille des guerres de religion, Bd. 2 Paris 1925, 23 f.

[47] *République*, 579 f.

[48] Russell Major, The Crown and the Aristocracy, 631 ff.

[49] Russell Major, The Crown and the Aristocracy, 635.

Plato und Morus die «équalité» als gesellschaftliches Bindeglied, als «nourrice d'amitié», verwirft und dagegen die Behauptung stellt, (que) «le pauvre, le petit, le foible, ploye et obeit volontiers au grand, au riche, au puissant, pour l'aide et proffit qu'il en espere»,[50] so zeigt sich hier erneut seine intime Vertrautheit mit den realen Verhältnissen seiner Zeit. In dieser Situation hatte der französische König nur zwei wirksame Machtmittel: Das Vertrauen der Untertanen, die in der erbrechtlich legitimierten Dynastie den Garanten für ihre eigene Sicherheit sahen,[51] und die Vergabe von Ämtern und Würden in Kirche, Verwaltung und Militär, wodurch er sich seinerseits, als bedeutendster Patron Frankreichs, eine Klientel schaffen konnte. Hören wir auch hierzu Bodin, der die Bedeutung dieses königlichen Machtinstruments einzuschätzen wußte; mehrfach, und besonders nachdrücklich, empfiehlt er seinem Fürsten, «(de se reserver) la distribution des loyers, qui sont les estats, honneurs, offices, benefices, pensions, privileges, prerogatives, immunités, exemptions, restitutions, et autres graces et faveurs.»[52]

Das Ansehen der vom König vergebenen Ämter, die Kreditwürdigkeit des Hofes, der auf die Anleihen der Untertanen angewiesen war, hatten somit einen Konsensus zwischen Herrscher und Untertanen zur Voraussetzung, zu dessen Bewahrung der König im Grunde mehr beisteuern mußte als die Untertanen. Bodins Forderung nach der Respektierung von Freiheit und Eigentum, seine ständigen Verweise auf die Rechtssicherheit im Staat und auf die unerläßliche «Liebe» der Untertanen zu ihrem König,[53] seine differenzierten Äußerungen zur Steuerfrage, in deren Zentrum die Warnung vor exzessiven Steuern als einer Gefahr für die «république» steht,[54] bezeugen die weitgehende Abhängigkeit der französischen Renaissancemonarchie von einer ständisch gegliederten, regional äußerst differenzierten Gesellschaft. Die Ratsgremien des Königs, so hat J. Russell Major[55] gezeigt, erwiesen in ihren Entscheidungen den Privilegierten einen größeren Respekt als die normalen Gerichte und sicherten sie häufig sogar gegen die Übergriffe der königlichen Bürokratie. Glanzvolle Demonstration des Vertrauensverhältnisses von König und Untertanen wurden im 16. Jahrhundert die wenigen Versammlungen der Generalstände, die in den Augen des Volkes von dem Willen des Königs kündeten, den Rat seiner Untertanen einzuholen.[56]

---

[50] *République*, 704.
[51] Russell Major, Limitations of Absolutism, 80 ff.
[52] *République*, 625.
[53] Vgl. z. B. *République*, 641, 599.
[54] *République*, 881 f. Vgl. M. Wolfe [265], 279.
[55] Russell Major, Limitation of Absolutism, 80.
[56] Vgl. die berühmten Äußerungen Bodins über Ständeversammlungen *République*, 137 f. u. 141 f.

Es zeigt sich damit, daß die Stabilität der französischen Renaissancemonarchie (wie die der Monarchie Royale Bodins) auf einem prekären
Status quo beruhte, dessen Wahrung von einem weitgehenden Konsensus
zwischen dem Königtum und den Untertanen abhing. Seit dem Tod
Heinrichs II. (1559) verschlechterten sich die Bedingungen für diesen
Konsensus zunehmend. Einmal erfüllten die herrschenden Könige nicht
mehr die unerläßlichen Voraussetzungen für einen «bon et iuste Roy». Die
minderjährigen Söhne Heinrichs II. standen der Reputation ihres Vaters
und vor allem Franz' I. (Bodins Herrscherideal) um vieles nach. In ihnen
und durch sie diskreditierte sich die Monarchie und legte einmal mehr ihre
strukturelle Schwäche – die Notwendigkeit von großen Herrscherpersön-
lichkeiten – bloß, die noch klarer in den Regentschaftskrisen des 17. und
frühen 18. Jahrhunderts sichtbar wurde. Zum anderen wurde Frankreich
von Wandlungen erfaßt, die auch bedeutenderen Monarchen Schwierigkeiten bereitet hätten. Das Eindringen der Reformation führte zur Glau-
bensspaltung, zugleich auch zu einer sozialen Krise und zu Veränderungen
in der Eigentumsverfassung.[57] Neue soziale Gruppen und Schichten
kamen zu Besitz und Ansehen,[58] stießen auf den Widerstand vorhandener
Rechts- und Besitzordnungen und forderten daher die Anpassung der
staatlichen Gesetzgebung an die neuen Verhältnisse. Nicht erst im Jahr
1789 begann in Frankreich der Druck auf das Kirchengut; wie in anderen Ländern (vor allem England und Schweden) setzte er auch in Frankreich schon im Verlauf des 16. Jahrhunderts ein.[59] Der wachsende Zu-
strom amerikanischer Edelmetalle ließ die Preise in die Höhe schnellen
und zwang den Staat seinerseits zu einer Verstärkung des Steuerdrucks.[60]
Die latent seit Jahrhunderten vorhandenen, in Krisenzeiten offensichtlich werdenden Finanzprobleme der französischen Monarchie trugen
zu einer Akzeleration des inneren Wandlungsprozesses[61] und zu einer
zunehmenden Unterminierung des Vertrauensverhältnisses zwischen
König und Untertanen bei. Die Geldpolitik litt unter der «anarchie
monétaire» mit ihrem Dualismus von nominellem und realem Geld-
wert, ohne daß Reformen, wie sie 1577 von Heinrich III. eingeleitet
wurden, zu dauernden Ergebnissen führten.[62] Da das Instrument der
staatlichen Steuerpolitik bei weitem nicht ausreichte, mußte der König

---

[57] G. Livet, Les guerres de religion (Que sais-je? Nr. 1016), Paris 2. Aufl.
1966, 90 ff.

[58] Livet, Guerres de religion, 92 ff.

[59] Livet, Guerres de religion, 91 f. und Russell Major, The French Renaissance Monarchy as seen through the Estates General, 121.

[60] Russell Major, Limitations of Absolutism, 82.

[61] Unter diesem Aspekt steht Bodins Kapitel über die Finanzen; vgl. *République*, 855 ff.

[62] Vgl. Livet, Guerres de religioi, 75 f.; Pillgrget, Problèmes monétaires, 113.

fortwährend gegen eine der «lois fondamentales» des Reiches verstoßen und Teile seiner Domäne veräußern. Spätestens seit der Zeit Heinrichs II. wurde die Ämterkäuflichkeit als ein Krebsübel des französischen Staats gebrandmarkt; doch stand die Heftigkeit der literarischen Kritik an diesem «expédient» in einer direkten Relation zur Häufigkeit seiner Anwendung.[63] Wandlungserscheinungen, wie sie hier nur in groben Umrissen beschrieben werden konnten, führten die französische Monarchie im späteren 16. Jahrhundert in eine Übergangsphase, die man als Krise der französischen Renaissancemonarchie bezeichnen könnte. Es war keine Staatskrise im modernen Sinne, da ein «moderner Staat» in Frankreich nicht bestand. Ein Großteil der Funktionen und Rechte, die später «öffentlich» genannt werden sollten, gehörte zum privaten Eigentum der Untertanen. Die Institutionen bestanden fort; die Generalstände wurden sogar häufiger einberufen als in früheren Zeiten, sie brachten allerdings spätestens seit 1576 weit mehr die Konflikte zwischen Königtum und Gesellschaft zum Ausdruck als das traditionelle Vertrauensverhältnis.

So scheint die Vorstellung einer Vertrauenskrise der Wirklichkeit näher zu kommen. Zwar gab es im politischen Denken Frankreichs seit dem Ende Heinrichs II. in zunehmendem Maße Tendenzen und Auffassungen, welche die Umwälzungen der Zeit zum Anlaß nahmen, nach den «Grundlagen des sozialen und politischen Lebens»[64] überhaupt zu fragen, doch in der Praxis blieben Reformvorschläge auf offensichtliche Mißstände beschränkt, deren Korrektur als Aufgabe des Königs betrachtet wurde.[65] So trafen die unmittelbaren Auswirkungen der Vertrauenskrise vor allem den König selbst, von dem die Untertanen immer dringender eine Reform seiner «police» erwarteten. Bodin gab seine *République* gerade zu einer Zeit heraus, als sich alle Hoffnungen Frankreichs auf Heinrich III. richteten, der sein Amt nach langen Jahren des Bürgerkriegs und nach dem von der Politik Katharinas von Medici bestimmten «Interregnum» seiner Brüder angetreten hatte.[66]

---

[63] Zur Kritik an der Ämterkäuflichkeit vgl. Romier, Le royaume de Cathérine de Médicis, Bd. 2, 29 ff.

[64] W. F. Church [145], Constitutional Thought in Sixteenth-Century France. A Study in the Evolution of Ideas, Cambridge 1941, 75.
Der gesamteuropäische Aspekt dieser Vertrauenskrise wird behandelt bei H. R. Trevor-Roper, The General Crisis of the Seventeenth Century, in: Crisis in Europa 1560–1660, hrsg. v. Trevor Aston, Garden City, N.Y. ²1967, 63–102 und in dem Sammelband: Preconditions of Revolution in Early Modern Europe, hrsg. v. Robert Forster u. Jack P. Greene, Baltimore u. London 1970.

[65] A. Karcher, L'Assemblée des notables de Saint-Germain-En-Laye (1583), *Bibliothèque de l'Ecole des Chartes* 114 (1957), 115–162, hier 117.

[66] Vgl. Karcher, L'Assemblé, 117. Bodins optimistisches Urteil über Hein-

IV

Daß Jean Bodin die unterschiedlichen Aspekte dieser Vertrauenskrise erfaßt und seine Auffassung von der fürstlichen Amtsführung darauf eingestellt hat, zeigen die letzten drei Bücher seiner *République*. Sie haben zunächst Fragen zum Gegenstand, die sich auf die Stellung des Fürsten und sein politisches Verhalten in einem von inneren Wandlungen bedrohten Gemeinwesen beziehen (das Verhältnis des Fürsten zu den Beamten, die Formen seiner Rechtsprechung, seine Stellung in den Parteikämpfen, die Vergabe von Ämtern);[67] sie zeichnen sodann die Grundzüge einer allgemeinen Reformpolitik (im Rechtswesen, in den Finanzen, im Militär, im Geldwesen).[68] Hier zeigt sich nun, daß die unterschiedlichen Schattierungen seines Fürstenbildes, von denen wir gesprochen haben, in einer direkten Relation zu den gegensätzlichen Aufgaben stehen, die der Fürst bei der Lösung der Vertrauenskrise bewältigen muß. Wenn er z. B. seine Finanzpolitik reformieren und dabei die Ungerechtigkeit des bestehenden Steuersystems durch eine gerechte Verteilung der «taille» mildern sollte,[69] wenn er zugleich das Ansehen der Monarchie bei den Untertanen sichern sollte, deren führende Gruppen von diesem Steuersystem profitierten, so mußte die fürstliche «habileté» zum entscheidenden Signum seines politischen Handelns werden. Wenn der Fürst, im Interesse einer Rationalisierung seiner Bürokratie, bestimmte Ämter abschaffen, zugleich aber nicht «Tyrann» sein sollte, der in die wohlerworbenen Rechte seiner Untertanen eingriff, so ließ sich eine solche Aufgabe nur mit Methoden lösen, die auf dem Wege der «Anpassung» allenfalls Teilerfolge ermöglichten, für grundsätzliche Änderungen der herrschenden Verhältnisse aber nicht ausreichten. Die Regierungszeit Heinrichs III., dessen Reformbestrebungen neuerdings betont werden, bietet eine Reihe von eindrucksvollen Belegen für die Schwierigkeit einer konsequenten königlichen Reformpolitik, die sich in jedem Fall gegen bestimmte Gruppen mit wohlerworbenen Rechten wenden mußte.[70]

So zeigt uns Bodins Argumentation das Bild eines Fürsten, der sein Verhalten ständig an einem Erfolgskalkül mißt, das den im Prinzip unvereinbaren Aufgaben seiner Amtsführung Rechnung trägt: der Fürst

---

rich III. findet sich auch noch in der Ausgabe von 1583. Vgl. *République*, 863: «Vray est que le paix asseuree depuis quinze ans, a bien servi pour maintenir l'estat d'Angleterre, et la guerre pour ruiner la France, si Dieu n'eust envoyé du ciel nostre Roy Henri III pour le restablir en sa premiere splendeur.»

[67] Vgl. die Kapitel *République* IV, 6, 7 u. V, 4.

[68] Vgl. die Kapitel *République* IV, 3; V, 5 u. VI, 1–3.

[69] *République*, 877 ff.

[70] Vgl. z. B. LIVET, Guerres de religion, 81.

soll vornehmster Repräsentant und Garant der bestehenden Ordnung
bleibt und zugleich die offensichtlichen Mißstände dieser Ordnung, die
Ursachen für Wandlungen, Bürgerkriege und Revolution, beseitigen.
Wichtigster Bestandteil dieses Erfolgskalküls bei der Planung und Durch-
führung von Reformen bleibt daher die Abschätzung ihrer Wirkung bei
den Untertanen. Die Legitimität des Souveräns bei Bodin erweise sich, so
formuliert es Morazé, weniger in seiner rechtmäßigen Herkunft als in der
Art seiner Amtsführung. «C'est dans l'attitude du monarque qu'il faut
voir le témoignage du juste pouvoir.»[71] Der Fürst, als Reformer immer
ein potentieller Tyrann, ist abhängig von der Meinung der Untertanen
über ihn.[72] Das Fortleben aller traditionellen Maximen der Fürstenethik
in der politischen Publizistik Frankreichs im 16. Jahrhundert ist der
literarische Reflex auf diesen Tatbestand.

Im Gegensatz zu vielen Autoren seiner Zeit sieht Bodin nun aber sehr
genau, daß die Lösung dieser Aufgaben die politischen Fähigkeiten eines
einzelnen Herrschers übersteigen konnte. Mehrfach stellt er einen Vergleich an zwischen der «simplicité» Heinrichs II., die zu einem Niedergang Frankreichs geführt habe, und der «sévérité» Franz' I., in dessen
letzten Regierungsjahren das Land auf dem Gipfel seiner politischen
Größe gestanden habe.[73] Zudem könne, und hier spielt die Geschichte
Frankreichs unter Heinrich II. und seinen Söhnen in Bodins Argumentation hinein, nicht ausgeschlossen werden, daß die Monarchie Royale in die
Hände unfähiger Fürsten gerate, deren mangelhafte Amtsführung sich auf
das Verhältnis der Institution Königtum zu den Untertanen auswirken
könne.[74] Nicht ohne Grund ergeht sich Bodin in langen Erörterungen
über die persönliche Rechtsprechung des Fürsten und über seine direkte
Kommunikation mit den Untertanen.[75] Mögen viele seiner Erwägungen
über das Pro und Kontra einer solchen Regierungsweise aus heutiger Sicht
obsolet erscheinen, so darf ihre eminente Bedeutung für die Struktur der
Renaissancemonarchie nicht übersehen werden: Bodin sammelt hier im
Rahmen einer ganz konkreten Argumentation eine Fülle von Beobachtungen, die den in seiner Zeit einsetzenden Prozeß der «Verobjektivierung
der Fürstenrolle zum ‹Staat›» (M. Draht)[76] und damit eine Aufgabe des
personalistischen Herrschaftsprinzips der Renaissancemonarchie erkennen
lassen. Gerade wenn das Königtum der Integrationsfaktor des Gemeinwesens, d. h. der Garant der bestehenden Rechts- und Sozialordnung blei-

---

[71] Morazé, France Bourgeoise, 153.
[72] Dazu Hinrichs [266], 68 ff.
[73] Vor allem *République*, 296 f. u. 744.
[74] *République*, 614 f.
[75] *République*, Kapital IV, 6, S. 610 ff.
[76] Evangelisches Staatslexikon, Artikel «Staat», Sp. 2120.

ben sollte, mußte es in einen «verobjektivierten» Raum gestellt werden,
von dem aus es, unabhängig von den politischen, religiösen und vor allem
rechtlichen Konflikten der Untertanen und ihrer Parteien, diese Funktion
angemessen erfüllen konnte.[77] So entscheidet sich Bodin nach einer aus-
führlichen Darlegung der Vorteile einer persönlichen Rechtsprechung, in
deren Verlauf der Theoretiker der absoluten Monarchie noch einmal das
Bild des Lehnskönigtums beschwört,[78] gegen die persönliche Rechtsprechung und gegen ein zu häufiges Auftreten des Fürsten in der «Öffentlichkeit» und schließt seine Erörterungen mit einem Postulat ab, das eher
im Versailles Ludwig XIV. als im Louvre Heinrichs III. Wirklichkeit geworden ist: «Si donc le sage prince doit au maniement de ses subjects
imiter la sagesse de Dieu au gouvernement de ce monde, il faut qu'il se
mette peu souvent en veue des subjects, et avec une maiesté convenable
à sa grandeur et puissance: et neantmoins qu'il face chois des hommes dignes, qui ne peuvent estre qu'en petit nombre, pour declarer sa volonté au surplus, et incessamment combler ses subjects de ses graces et faveurs.»[79]

Das ist nicht mehr der durch das Land ziehende Renaissancefürst, der
«premier gentilhomme», dessen intimes Verhältnis zu seinen Untertanen
die venetianischen Gesandten in Erstaunen versetzte.[80] Hier erscheint
vielmehr das Bild einer zu allen Untertanen in gleichmäßige Distanz
tretenden Institution, deren nach außen wirksame Funktion vor allem
darin besteht, eine Rolle zu erfüllen, die ihr von den Untertanen zugeschrieben wird. Mehrfach fordert Bodin, der Fürst möge sich die Vergabe von Ämtern und Würden vorbehalten, Bestrafungen, Konfiskationen
u. ä. jedoch seinen zuständigen Institutionen überlassen. «Car la plus belle
reigle qui peut entretenir l'estat d'une monarchie, c'est que le Prince se
face aimer de tous sans mesprit, et haï de personne, si faire se peut.»[81] Und
der weitgehende Verzicht des Fürsten auf die persönliche Rechtsprechung,
auf seine alte Rolle als «roy en son conseil», wird von Bodin unter anderem auch mit dem Begnadigungsrecht des Fürsten motiviert, das mit
seiner Aufgabe als höchstem Richter kollidieren müsse, für das Ansehen

---

[77] Wesentliche Teile seines Fürstenbildes entwickelt Bodin in dem Kapital
IV, 7 (*République*, 634 ff.), das die Stellung des Fürsten zu Parteikämpfen und
sein Verhalten bei Aufständen zum Thema hat.

[78] *République*, 610 f.

[79] *République*, 617; vgl. auch 514.

[80] Russell Major, Limitations of Absolutism, 82.

[81] *République*, 625; vgl. auch 730. Besonders eindringlich 626: «Je pense
quant à moy, que c'est l'un des plus beaux secrets qui a maintenu si longuement
ceste Monarchie, et que nos Rois ont tresbien sceu pratiquer de toute ancienneté:
c'est à sçavoir d'ottroyer tous les bienfaicts et loyers, et laisser les peines aux
officiers, sans respect des personnes».

der Monarchie aber unerläßlich sei; denn «l'un des principaux poincts de la maiesté souveraine gist à donner la grace aux coulpables.»[82] Diese Äußerungen zeigen noch einmal sehr deutlich, aus welchem Grund Bodin den Fürsten in eine Distanz zu den Untertanen setzt. Sein historischer Ausgangspunkt ist das Versagen der personalistischen Herrschaftsform der Renaissancemonarchie, das in einer Zeit innerer Krisen zu einer Gefahr für den Bestand der Monarchie Royale werden konnte. Bodin schafft die Distanz nicht, um den Herrscher als Träger einer allgewaltigen Staatsräson von den Untertanen abzuheben;[83] er mystifiziert den Staat nicht, wie es in der Zeit Heinrichs IV. in zunehmendem Maße geschieht.[84] Sein einziges Ziel ist die Sicherung einer durch innere und äußere Krisen bedrohten Institution in ihrer *traditionellen Funktion*.

Von diesem Maßstab wird auch der Charakter der institutionellen und finanzpolitischen Reformvorstellungen bestimmt, die Bodin in den letzten beiden Büchern der *République* skizziert.[85] Bodin schreibt keine Reformschrift im Sinne eines Vauban oder eines Boisguilbert. Er hebt nicht *ein* Element der institutionellen oder ökonomischen Struktur heraus und macht es zum Gegenstand einer in alle anderen Bereiche hineinwirkenden Reform; er betrachtete alle Aspekte der zeitgenössischen politischen Wirklichkeit und analysiert sie mit dem Blick auf ihre spezifische Bedeutung für die verschiedenen Staatsformen. Sofern er von der Monarchie Royale spricht, bleiben ihre Strukturmerkmale – die Sicherung von Freiheit und Eigentum, die Wahrung der Rechtssicherheit und des Vertrauens zwischen Herrscher und Untertanen – seine zentralen Bezugspunkte, denen er institutionelle und finanzpolitische Reformvorstellungen unterordnet.

Analysiert man daher die Reformideen Bodins mit dem Blick auf die Strukturprobleme des neuzeitlichen, absolutistischen Staates, wie sie auch im Frankreich Bodins schon sichtbar wurden, so tritt in ihnen ein seltsam ambivalenter, ja anachronistischer Zug zutage. Sie sind nicht auf die spezifischen Erfordernisse konkreter staatlicher Entwicklungen in der Zeit Bodins zugeschnitten, sondern sie zeigen, unter welchen optimalen institutionellen, finanz- und wirtschaftspolitischen Bedingungen Bodins Staatsideal, die Monarchie Royale, ohne die Gefahr einer Wandlung der Staats- oder Regierungsform bestehen kann. Wenn Bodin etwa gegen die Ämterkäuflichkeit, gegen zinsbare Staatsanleihen, gegen die staatliche «Münzfälschung» oder gegen eine zu hohe Besteuerung der Bevölkerung Stellung nimmt, so vor allem, weil die exzessive Anwendung dieser Mittel zur Ver-

---

[82] *République*, 622; vgl. auch 630.
[83] Zum Eindringen der Staatsräson in das politische Denken Frankreichs jetzt E. Thuau, Raison d'état et pensée politique à l'époque de Richelieu o. O. u. J. (Paris 1967).
[84] Dazu Church [145], 306 ff.
[85] Vgl. vor allem die Kapitel *République* V, 2; V, 4; VI, 1–3.

trauenskrise beiträgt und die Wandlung der Herrschaftsform einleitet.[86] Daß die Monarchie auf diese Mittel angewiesen sein kann, läßt Bodin demgegenüber nicht als Argument gelten, wie seine Erörterungen über den Ämterhandel zeigen.[87] Und wenn Bodin in seinem Kapitel über die «Finanzen» das Modell einer «ehrenwerten» staatlichen Finanzplanung entwirft («des moyens honnestes de faire fonds aux finances»), in dem sich Ansätze zu einer staatlichen Budgetplanung verbergen,[88] und dabei den Fürsten immer noch auf die Domanialeinkünfte als wichtigste Geldquelle verweist,[89] so stellt er sich auch hier ganz konsequent auf die Basis seiner üblichen Forderung nach innerstaatlichem Vertrauen, ohne zu berücksichtigen, in welchem fast schon grotesken Mißverhältnis solche Vorschläge zu den in Frankreich (und in anderen Ländern) herrschenden Bedingungen und Bedürfnissen standen.

Diese Ambivalenz der institutionellen und finanzpolitischen Reformvorstellungen läßt sich gewiß zu einem Teil aus der Bindung Bodins an die immanenten Traditionen der abendländischen politischen Theorie erklären; sie spiegelt mehr noch seine realitäts- und zeitbefangene Sehweise, die sich utopischen Entwürfen im Sinne von Morus ebenso versagt wie radikalen Reformplänen, deren Realisation nur unter Aufgabe des Konsensus von Herrscher und Untertanen, und das heißt mit dem bewußten Risiko grundsätzlicher Staatsveränderungen, möglich gewesen wäre. So beschreibt Bodin, wenn er die Forderung nach Freiheit und Eigentum, nach innerstaatlicher Rechtssicherheit und nach «Vertrauen» zwischen Herrscher und Untertanen als den Strukturprinzipien der Monarchie Royale erhebt, letztlich die Funktionsweisen einer ständisch-hierarchischen Gesellschaftsordnung, deren Freiheitsraum im wesentlichen durch die Sicherung ihrer wohlerworbenen Rechte bestimmt war. Der Fürst als politisch Handelnder tritt bei Bodin nur insoweit in Erscheinung, sein Fürstenbild nimmt im Vergleich zum Fürstenideal des Mittelalters und der Renaissance nur insofern neue Züge an, als diese Voraussetzungen für den Bestand der Monarchie Royale gefährdet erscheinen. Die absolutistischen Theoretiker Frankreichs im 17. Jahrhundert haben diese Position Bodins ebenso verlassen wie die Praktiker in Staat und Verwaltung. Gerade die Regierung Ludwigs XIV. sollte zeigen, daß der Konsensus zwi-

---

[86] Zur Ämterkäuflichkeit vgl. *République*, 742 f.; zu den Anleihen S. 893; zum Problem der Münzpolitik das ganze Kapitel VI, 3; zur Steuerpolitik S. 877 ff. Zu den wirtschafts- und finanzpolitischen Anschauungen Bodins vgl. M. E. KAMP [165], Die Staatswirtschaftslehre Jean Bodins, Bonn 1949, hier bes. 33 ff.

[87] *République*, 743.

[88] *République*, 855 ff.

[89] *République*, 856: «Quant au premier (moyen de faire fonds aux finances), qui est le dommaine, il semble estre le plus honneste et le plus seur de tous.»

schen Herrscher und Untertanen, zwischen dem absoluten Monarchen und der Gesellschaft der wohlerworbenen Rechte, nur unter größten Gefahren für die bestehende Ordnung verletzt werden konnte. Erst im Reflex auf den exaltierten Herrschaftsstil Ludwigs XIV., der dem überkommenen Fürstenbild im französischen politischen Denken so gründlich widersprach, wuchs in Frankreich die Erkenntnis, daß die von Bodin immer wieder beschworenen Kautelen zur Wahrung des Konsensus zwischen Herrscher und Untertanen nicht unbedingt ausreichen mußten und daher konstitutionelle Sicherungen neuer Art erforderlich waren.

R. W. K. Hinton

Bodin and the Retreat into Legalism

It goes without saying that Anglo-Saxon commentators have had difficulties with Bodin. From Dunning (1896) to Sabine (1937) the English-
thinking world has found in this majestic French and European writer
inconsistency, difficulties, lapses and ‹serious confusion›. He glimpsed,
they said, the idea of sovereignty – but failed to understand it completely.
For that achievement one had to wait for Hobbes, whom some considered
as Bodin's ‹disciple› – but a more far-sighted and accurate thinker than
his master. To Hearnshaw Bodin presented himself as ‹a curious mixture
of the sublime and the ridiculous ... of the wise and the otherwise ... As
a rule, turning his face towards the future, he beholds with the clear eye
of the Renaissance the reality of things as they are; but ever and anon he
turns his face backward and sees things through a mist of superstition.›
(The superstition lay in his talk of divine and natural law.) Allen,
referring especially to the *leges imperii* which prohibited the sovereign
from taxing at will, remarked that ‹Bodin does not seem to see that a
strictly unlimited right must include all other conceivable powers›. The
fundamental difficulty for these commentators was that Bodin postulated
sovereignty but set limits to it, limits which the greater and later Hobbes
swept aside. Either, then, according to this tradition of commentators,
the limitations were not to be taken as serious – in which case Bodin was
verbally careless though fundamentally sound – or (if they were taken
seriously) he was verbally conclusive but doctrinally inconsistent. Of
course both comments were misleading. The error lay in considering Bodin
from the standpoint of Hobbesian or Austinian sovereignty, as if the
history of political philosophy was the record of ideas leading up to that
ultimate truth. It hardly needs saying that Bodin cannot be judged as a
stepping-stone on the way from Machiavelli towards Hobbes and is not
to be accounted confused or inconsistent on the ground that he did not
advance at one step towards the Hobbesian concept. It is clear that Bodin
himself did take very seriously his limitations on sovereignty, and generations of readers took them seriously too. They were precisely, in Bodin's
view, what *prevented* the sovereign from lapsing into the unspeakably
horrid state of Hobbesian sovereignty. To regard what presented itself to
Bodin as an essential safeguard as a fault or inconsistency was clearly

to misunderstand him completely and to distort him beyond recognition.[1]

But neither is the corrective interpretation, which is largely an American interpretation and which owes so much to the inspiration of Professor McIlwain, entirely illuminating.[2] The fault of this interpretation is exactly the opposite, namely to have set Bodin too firmly in a supposedly medieval intellectual context. In preserving – indeed exagerating – the elements of continuity in Bodin, possibly too in overemphasising the place of law and custom in the medieval mind, this tradition of commentary has done justice and more than justice to Bodin's limitations on sovereignty only at the cost of whittling down his concept of sovereignty itself

---

[1] W. Dunning [50], Jean Bodin on Sovereignty, *Political Science Quarterly* 11 (1896); History of Political Theories from Luther to Montesquieu, New York 1905. F. J. C. Hearnshaw [94], Bodin and the Genesis of the Doctrine of Sovereignty, in: Tudor Studies, ed. R. W. Seton-Watson, London 1924. J. W. Allen [96] in: Social and Political Ideas of Some Great Thinkers of the Sixteenth and Seventeenth Centuries, ed. F. J. C. Hearnshaw, London 1926; A History of Political Thought in the Sixteenth Century, London 1928 [97]; G. H. Sabine [134], A History of Political Theory (London, 1937). I cite the passage from Hearnshaw because it represents a point of view which is exactly the opposite of what I take to be the truth, namely that it is the ‹superstition› in Bodin that is ‹modern› and the clarity that is old. Allen rightly recognized a ‹great gulf› between Bodin and Hobbes but still speaks of ‹serious confusion› in his thought. Sabine finds ‹a great amount of confusion› and even echoes Hearnshaw at one point. Let me say at once that I think there *is* difficulty in Bodin, but not confusion. The purpose of this paper is to suggest that we understand Bodin best by acknowledging the difficulty, but that the older tradition of Anglo-Saxon interpretation got it the wrong way round.

[2] Especially Max A. Shepard [110], Sovereignty at the Crossroads, *Political Science Quarterly* 45 (1930), 580 ff. Shepard emphasises the practical effectiveness of Bodin's limitations on sovereignty: in my opinion overemphasises them. And note the extreme swing of the pendulum in Beatrice Reynolds [113], Proponents of Limited Monarchy in Sixteenth Century France: François Hotman and Jean Bodin, New York 1931. There is not much left of sovereignty here. C. H. McIlwain in his papers Sovereignty (1926), A Fragment on Sovereignty (1933) and Whig Sovereignty and Real Sovereignty (1934), reprinted in his Constitutionalism and the Changing World, Cambridge 1939, went a step further than Shepard. Shepard had concluded that the last word on Bodin was that he was attempting to reconcile irreconcilables. Of course the overriding belief of McIlwain's life was that political power *ought* to be checked by the rule of law, that in general it had been so checked till relatively recent times, that the idea of unlimited Hobbesian sovereignty was a dangerous modern heresy, and in short that there was no question of irreconcilability in Bodin because the notion of sovereignty checked by law is after all mankind's normal and appropriate idea.

to an extent which Bodin himself would not have accepted. The *Six Livres* after all was not a book about the rule of law whether of divine law, natural law, the law of nations or the law of the realm. Bodin speaks of these laws and intends them to be taken so seriously that he says that an officer of the commonwealth in case of a clash between the law and the sovereign's command will preserve the law and disobey the command, but he is writing a treatise of sovereignty, not a treatise of law. He is emphasising what a sovereign *can* do, not what he cannot do. The sovereign is at the centre of his picture and the gist of his doctrine is not that the sovereign is limited – although he is limited – but that he is powerful, that he is in fact a political master (like a father) and that obedience to him is the main thing, not obedience to the laws.

Indeed Bodin's historical significance as the towering sixteenth century figure which he was may be best understood by developing not the similarity of his thought to his predecessors' but the contrast between them. In this connection Seysell stands out as the corresponding French writer of an earlier generation. Like Bodin Seysell emphasised, indeed exulted in, the king's power, like Bodin Seysell took seriously the limitations on that power. He is not a tyrant, this great king, says Seysell proudly: he *cannot* be a tyrant: he is not even ‹absolute›. But the famous three bridles which restrain him from this disgrace are not the law (as in Bodin) but what we would call public opinion, and public opinion backed by force. If the king does not show himself zealous for the Christian religion, says Seysell, the people as a whole will obey him badly. He is incapable of acting unjustly, because the *parlements,* which have been principally instituted as a restraint on the king, consist of such great personages (Seysell says) that kings have always been subject to them. Similarly if he attempts to break ‹la police› – i.e. the rules of government themselves, the constitution itself – he will simply be disobeyed not only by the ‹sovereign courts of the *parlements*› but by the king's own chamber of accounts itself. These bridles were certainly not moral bridles and although some of them can be called legal they were clearly not wholly or essentially legal. Seysell is to be understood as saying in effect that the king of France is *physically* prevented from using his admittedly great power at his own pure will (which would be tyranny) by the corresponding and countervailing great power of the people of France in the very regional and institutional organizations whose unification under the crown constituted (he thought) the nation's crowning glory and the crown's great achievement. The people have acquiesced in and welcomed the king's power, but at the same time they remain firmly entrenched behind their ancient customs and institutions and they can and will resist the king's power in case of need, and resist it successfully, not because laws and ordinances are legally binding (though no doubt they are legally

binding) but because they themselves, i.e. the people as a whole and the
great personages who hold high positions, are many and strong.

How different from Bodin, even though we shall say that Bodin is in
many respects Seysell brought up to date! Seysell's king is not sovereign,
or at any rate no more sovereign that the *parlements*; and Seysell's
effectual limitation is not law but force, not a legal limitation but a
political or physical limitation. And yet Seysell has his affinities with
Machiavelli and Guiccardini too. The contrast is not simply between two
Frenchmen of different generations but between Bodin and what we may
call the whole scheme of political philosophy of the renaissance. The
renaissance was optimistic, pragmatic, realist. Bodin was pessimistic,
legalistic, idealist.[3]

Gentillet attacked Machiavelli on the ground of his ignorance, saying
that he did not understand the law. It was a true criticism. Machiavelli
conceived of political life *without* law:[4] for Machiavelli as for all the
characteristic Italian humanists of that time the state existed by instinct
and politics, that is to say by the operation of reason and force. By God-
given reason, Machiavelli thought – following Aquinas and many
medievalists – men were led by nature – since reason was natural – to
create and live and find their psychological fulfilment in civil society
under government, that is to say in the state. The state therefore was

---

[3] This may be thought a bold contrast, especially in view of Professor
MESNARD's characterisation of Machiavelli (in: L'Essor de la philosophie politique au XVI Siècle [129]): En un mot, *l'anarchie règne*. Machiavelli was therefore fighting a defensive battle for stability in a dissolving world. But we may
also say that Machiavelli took a surprising amount of instability for granted.
He condoned violence and chicanery, e.g. in Romulus and Numa as well as in
the contemporary prince. He welcomed internal political tensions as generating
social dynamism. He assumed self-interest, ambition, wickedness in political
life, in spite of which the state would work unless and until it was taken-over
by another state. And even then, we must remember in the Italian context, the
city would stand even though it lost its statehood. There was no question of
anything approaching a reversion to a state of nature. Machiavelli's text possibly
does not quite bear out the extent to which Mesnard considered that he saw
anarchy everywhere. – On the other hand in regard to Bodin, Professor Mesnard
can be said to have passed over too easily what may be termed the disciplinary
and dogmatic aspect of Bodin's thought. In this aspect one seems to find elements
of Platonism and Ramism, and the notion of harmonic justice calls for attention.
And does the text really bear out all the implications that Professor Mesnard
read into the phrase ‹droit gouvernement›?

[4] Wise legislators and good laws were of course very important for Machiavelli, but he did not suppose that laws had a coercive power over political life.
He expected men to behave like politicians, not like lawyers.

reasonable and natural, a product of will and instinct (as we would call it) at the same time: in short a product of God. Similarly the operations of political life within the state were therefore reasonable and natural and a work of God too, and this must be true in general however evil men were and however wicked their actions: evidently God could turn evil to account. We may perhaps say that the renaissance humanist was amoral because he was religious. If God and nature were behind everything one saw, then everything one saw must be in some sense right and proper. Let God judge sins, men must accept history. Men must accept whatever God had arranged for them, even human nature. In politics all action, even action which God would probably punish, contributed therefore – no doubt – to the life of the state.

The renaissance humanist was a political opportunist because he was also at heart a political optimist. He could hardly conceive of the state dissolving of its own accord. In Italy he saw cities which would live in spite of changes of government, in France, England and Spain (France being incomparably the most important example) he saw nations in the achievement of statehood. Men could therefore be evil, but human life was so arranged that statehood was pre-ordained. This belief encouraged the thought that man (in society) was selfsufficient, however bad; that even the prince could contribute to the life of the republic; that the assassin had a part to play, even in a principality; that the prince must manage his government by astuteness (not right); that the people could rebel legitimately if they felt themselves to be downtrodden; in short that all regimes and all successful political devices were legitimate. On these assumptions a pragmatic view of politics was indicated inevitably, to such an extent that the renaissance can easily be accused (though falsely) of superficiality. Almost deliberately the renaissance thinker took political things at face value. One of the things he took at face value was power. Accordingly he saw power everywhere, in the greatness of the prince, in the wealth of the rich, in the passions of the discontented, in the multitude of the poor. Power, he saw, was dispersed throughout society: it was everywhere that men had the will to mobilise it.

Power is what one feels, authority is what one recognises, but the recognition of authority creates power and pure power in the sense of brute force is very rare in politics, commonly authority and power merge. The renaissance humanist saw this very clearly. If the people of Florence accepted a prince they conferred power on him; if they refused to accept him they took it away. If Pisan republicans were conquered by a Florentine prince they could either submit or escape. If they escaped (or died) they quitted the state: if they submitted they recognised the authority of the prince. Or they could rebel: in that case they recreated the Pisan state which they could reconstitute as a republic or a principality as they

willed. This is why *respublica* and *principatus* are to a modern ear
astonishingly interchangeable terms. We must conclude in the end that the
renaissance humanist conceived of all governing power as conferred and
of all governing authority as revocable. In other words he saw that
government was a product of consent.

Machiavelli's Prince was not Seysell's King of France but they had at
least this in common, that they could command only while they could
command consent. We may say that government by consent was a cardinal
principle of renaissance thinking. It was a matter of physical necessity in
renaissance eyes that there could be no government at all without consent,
and government without consent in renaissance texts was often called
tyranny.

Bodin of course insisted that consent was immaterial. He required us to
obey whatever sovereign had been placed over us and to do (unless in
some cases we were an officer of the commonwealth) whatever that
sovereign commanded. For by Bodin's time the world had changed.
Religion had introduced the divisive force of ideology into politics, reason
and nature were no longer evidently sufficient for the efficient running of
political life, in France especially the state seemed to be on the verge of
dissolution – France in which young men had been brought up to pride
themselves on their successful reunification. And this was held to have
come about not merely through the addition of religion to politics, for the
religious motivation for political actions was easily recognized as a
pretence, but because – or so it seemed – reason and nature had proved to
be not an adequate basis for political life after all. We enter what Friedrich
has truly called the age of the baroque. The optimism and the simplicity
of the renaissance were lost.[5]

In France many new solutions were offered and all had one thing in
common: they replaced power by authority and they regarded authority
as a power that belonged rather than as a power that was conferred. The
author of *Vindiciae contra Tyrannos* placed this authority in the people,
or rather in the persons who held office. Others placed it fairly and square-
ly in the king: if supreme power originally resided with the people they

---

[5] If I were writing of Francis Bacon, whose views in England, *mutatis mutan-
dis,* correspond rather closely to Bodin's in France, it would be necessary to
invoke another factor, namely the development of an administrative system
and an administrative spirit. One knows how easily frustrated administrators
recoil on authority. Possibly this factor should be mentioned in Bodin's case too.
But I think that the traditional suggestions are sufficient. Or rather, I suspect
that they may not go quite far enough. For example, was it entirely unreasonable
in 1575 to fear the actual disintegration of France into some of its component
parts? Burgundy and Navarre had pretensions to independence, and by analogy
Britanny and Orange.

had transferred it once for all to the king, if not the king hat possessed it from all time from God. Others again attempted to place it in the king and the states jointly, which was Hotman's solution; or in the king and the *parlements*, which was perhaps the natural solution of the lawyers. For obvious reasons none of these solutions could command general assent. Frenchmen were accustomed to think that they obeyed the Valois king but not a Valois Grand Turk; and in a dissolving state a single focus of obedience was an evident necessity. It is clear that Bodin's solution was the only one likely to command general assent. All must obey the king alone, says Bodin; because (firstly) to obey more than one master is to invite disaster and (secondly) to obey a true king is not in any case to submit oneself to a tyrant. This accorded with normal French beliefs. It was Seysell. But it was Seysell brought up to date. In place of the power which Seysell allowed the King of France to exercise by virtue of the recognition of his authority by the French people, Bodin placed an authority which belonged to him intrinsically. In place of the power (literally understood) of public opinion which Seysell ascribed to the people and in virtue of which the king was physically incapable of affronting the people, Bodin placed a set of laws.

This kingly authority Bodin called sovereignty. In fact the king of Bodin's world in face of the Guises and the Huguenots was powerless. Bodin urged his readers to recognise the authority of this powerless king in order that the general recognition of the king's authority should confer on the king not the power to render himself a tyrant but the power to reunify the once-united but now-divided nation of France against both the Guises and the Huguenots. But his argument was that the king should be obeyed *de jure*, of right, because his status intrinsically entitled him to obedience; not as a voluntary act of will.

Bodin's famous concept of sovereignty was thus the child of disillusion. But it was only, after all, a concept of logic.[6]

We cannot fail to recognise that the whole structure of the *Six Livres* depends on a series of logical propositions and distinctions. Sovereignty, Bodin pronounces, is indivisible: because supreme power *by definition* can have neither equal nor superior. Since sovereignty is indivisible it must *logically* reside either in a single person, in the majority voice of the few or in the majority voice of the whole. *By definition* there are three distinct

---

[6] Bodin's empiricism is often stressed, but I think that as far as his method is concerned the important point is the way everything hinges on distinctions. The doctrine depends entirely on distinctions and definitions. These definitions and distinctions do not emerge from the data. The *absolute* distinction between monarchical states and aristocratic or democratic states was quite new: hitherto this distinction had been a matter of degree. One may say that the absoluteness of this distinction is Bodin's novel point and the crux of his doctrine.

sorts of sovereign, namely the seigneurial or lordly sovereign, the lawful
or royal sovereign and the illegitimately tyrannical sovereign. Most
important distinction of all, for which Bodin rightly claimed the honour
of novelty – the form of the government and the nature of the state are
completely different things. That is, appearances are illusory. *What we
see does not matter.* Reality lies below the surface. I shall ask, how can
Bodin's elaborately conceived structure possibly stand the test of real life,
constructed as it is not only on a least three undemonstrable propositions
which we are asked to take as axiomatic but on propositions which are
thus confessedly unverifiable by observation?

I think that Bodin's position can well be termed a retreat from reality.
Appearances had played men false. Reason and nature had betrayed
them. The state was falling to pieces. The ordinary selfinterest of mankind
had turned out to be a faulty foundation for political life. The overriding
necessity was for a unifying idea. Abandoning appearances, Bodin sup-
plied an idea which was striking in its novelty, its precision, its elaboration and its inner consistency as well as in the impressive length of the book
in which it was developed; and which captured the imagination of its age
because it answered so accurately to the social needs of the time. In
retreating from the realism of Seysell and Machiavelli he had no doubt
advanced – into what? Not quite, I think, into philosophy. Better to say,
perhaps, into legalism. For Bodin necessarily the observations of lawyers
carried more authority than the chaotic political facts which he saw
around him.

Even if we take Bodin strictly in his own terms the gap between his
abstract fiction of a lawful sovereign and what he conceived to be the
reality of the actual constitutional position of the king of France remains
astonishingly and revealingly wide. We learn from what he says in brief
passages that this position was a product of historical circumstances.
Nimrod the cruel oppressor and mighty hunter created the first state,
Bodin says, which was therefore a lordly monarchy. States in general, he
affirms, had their origin in violence. But in course of time and as men
became more civilised, and especially in Western Europe where the
climatic conditions were such – we must always remember Bodin's
climatic theory – that the inhabitants of this region could not abide to be
slaves, the nature of states changed. The Huns who came from Scythia
practised lordly monarchy as conquerors, but Odovacer took only a third
part of the lands of Italy. Similarly the Germans, the Lombards, the Franks,
the Saxons, the Burgundians, the Goths, the Ostrogoths, the Angles and
other conquerors, although they took their example from the conquering
Huns, left the major part of the conquered land to the inhabitants, con-
tenting themselves with certain feudal rights. And these feudal relics
«show that the shadow of the ancient lordly monarchy as yet remaineth,

although greatly diminished».[7] In short western monarchy including French monarchy is a product of conquest and Henri III inherits in some sense the rights of a conqueror, which are lordly or despotic rights. At the same time his predecessors have foregone some of these rights, so that the French people are free and he himself is now a lawful or royal sovereign. How this has taken place is not explained. We must admit that there remains in this historical process an ambiguity which Bodin does nothing to resolve, and above all there is no proof that Henri III and the lawful sovereign are one and the same person. Proof indeed is impossible in view of Bodin's explicit dismissal of the significance of outward appearances.[8]

Bodin's logic does not contradict the facts but neither do the facts support his logic to the exclusion of alternative logics. The real king is so far away from the fictional sovereign that we can bridge the gap only by a leap of the imagination.

This of course does not detract from the grandeur of Bodin's logic in itself. On the contrary. But I venture to suggest in conclusion that

---

[7] Thus in the English translation by Richard Knolles, 1606 [7.43]. It should be noticed that the modern abridged English translation by Miss Tooley is misleading at this point. *République*, Book II, chapter 2. The distinction between lordly *(seigneuriales)* monarchies and royal *(légitimes)* monarchies is therefore relative. This is very important. The royal monarch *can legitimately* do lordly things from time to time and subjects ought to give the sovereign the benefit of the doubt in such cases..

[8] Conquest does not account for the *origin* of sovereignty, which presents itself to Bodin as a functional necessity. Sovereignty is created when the state is created and can therefore originate either in conquest *or* in the extension of the family *or* in mutual agreement. Mutual agreement will have operated, for example, whenever a popular state was set up. e.g. Sweden, Denmark, Poland – that is, when a popular state was set up *ab initio* or when a monarchy was transformed into a popular state by a revolution. (Bodin was certainly an empirical thinker to the extent that he allowed states to change by political accident. But so also did Hobbes who can hardly be termed an empiricist). Strictly speaking, conquest, for Bodin, merely defined (1) the *location* of sovereignty, i.e. in a monarch, and (2) the *kind* of sovereignty, i.e. lordly. But he also was sure that monarchy was the most ‹natural› form of a state, that most states had in fact been founded by conquest, and that in any case all the important western states had been founded by conquest. All this was and is easily acceptable. The gap is the gap between the original lordly sovereign and the present lawful sovereign. Bodin wants continuity on the one hand so that the monarch always has in reserve, so to speak, the lordly power of his predecessor, and real change on the other hand so that the lawful monarch *cannot* be a tyrant. Constitutional history is therefore of crucial importance for Bodin. He virtually ignores it.

however useful that legalistic logic may have been in the immediate circumstances of France in the second half of the sixteenth century the central concept has done harm in Europe because it has persuaded us to believe a lie. Sovereignty as Bodin presented it does not exist. This indictment may be laid against it not on the ground that Bodin's ideas failed to attain the clarity of Hobbes's ideas but on the contrary on the ground that they departed too far from the ideas of Seysell and Machiavelli. The renaissance was right. Power *is* dispersed throughout society. Government *does* stand on consent. The proposition that supreme power must reside in some single place is not only not necessary, it is false.[9]

Hobbes attempted the same task as Bodin, namely to appeal to a nation's reason in order to urge them to acknowledge the full extent of their obedience. It was again magnificent but it was not true, it was not believed. In the nineteenth century John Austin lectured on the principles of jurisprudence. His enunciation of the doctrine of parliamentary sovereignty proved to be influential, but the lectures were very poorly attended. These instinctive renunciations were soundly based. At the turn of the century an arrogant Anglo-Saxon tradition adopted the Austinian concept as the ultimate stage in the history of democracy.[10] Almost immediately however one of the great names of our time, Professor McIlwain, saw the dangerous connection between the doctrine of sover-

---

[9] The objection to this stricture on Bodin had already been made by McIlwain in his papers referred to above (note 2). Bodin's sovereignty, according to McIlwain, was *legal* sovereignty, the only proper sovereignty: it had nothing to do with political supreme power, which resides always and necessarily in the last resort in the popular will: legal sovereignty was therefore a legal fiction (of immense value) and for that very reason susceptible to legal limitations. Hence no difficulty or confusion in Bodin, and the sovereignty which McIlwain attacked was Bodin's legal sovereignty *misunderstood* as political power. I can only answer that in relation to Bodin I find it difficult to accept this distinction. I think Bodin was writing about politics, therefore about political sovereignty; but in the manner of a lawyer under the compulsion of unpleasant political facts, therefore legalistically.

[10] McILWAIN recorded Maitland's doubts in 1910 about Austin (Constitutionalism and the Changing World, 61). They were destructive. Maitland thought that Austin ‹was too ignorant of the English, the Roman and every other system of law to make any considerable addition to the sum of knowledge›. But Maitland was a leader of ideas and a heretic. Note J. N. FIGGIS's apology in his preface to the second edition of his Divine Right of Kings that the book had ‹the defect of being written beneath the shadow of the Austinian idol›; the first edition was published in 1896, the second in 1914. In the thirties of this century McIlwain could still assume that Austin was the Anglo-Saxon lawyer's idol, also that Maitland had condemned Austin for the wrong reasons (Constitutionalism and the Changing World, 85).

eignty and fascism. The subjugation of the political will, the abnegation of political responsibility – easy but fatal relapses into barbarism! Professor McIlwain was however wrong (I venture to suggest) on two counts. Firstly he found the answer to this overwhelming sovereignty (like Bodin) in the power of the law, whereas it really lies in the stubborn wills of individuals. Secondly, as to the historical origin of the doctrine of sovereignty, he averred that it was the *damnosa hereditas* of the English civil wars in the middle of the seventeenth century;[11] but I think it can more truly be laid at Bodin's door amid the French civil wars of the sixteenth century. If we are now learning in our universities that the authority which belongs by law is a poor substitute for the authority which is conferred by consent, and in Vietnam that pure power in the sense of armed might is no substitute for consent at all, it is perhaps as well that we should not allow our admiration of Bodin to be a barrier to our admiration of the truer and more worthy ideas of the renaissance, so that human dignity and civil responsibility may once more go hand in hand.

---

[11] C. H. McILWAIN, The Growth of Political Thought in the West, New York 1932, 387: «the fatal identification of sovereignty [a legal fiction] with might [force] is the *damnosa hereditas* of the English civil wars».

Rudolf Hoke

Bodins Einfluß auf die Anfänge der Dogmatik des deutschen Reichsstaatsrechts

I

Als Bodins Bücher über den Staat gegen Ende des 16. Jahrhunderts auf das europäische Staatsdenken einzuwirken begannen,[1] traf dies in Deutschland zeitlich zusammen mit dem Vorabend eines grundlegenden Wandels in der wissenschaftlichen Behandlung des Reichsverfassungsrechts.[2] Hier hatte die Rechtswissenschaft bisher das Verfassungsrecht des Heiligen Römischen Reiches Deutscher Nation in der Regel nur am Rande anderer Fragenkomplexe berücksichtigt, sei es bei der Exegese von Digesten und Codex unter dem Titel der *jurisdictio*, sei es bei der Interpretation der Libri Feudorum unter dem Regalientitel oder in der Kanonistik im Zusammenhang mit dem kirchlichen Verfassungsrecht. Im Grunde sah man das Staatsrecht gar nicht als Sache der Jurisprudenz an, sondern als zur Politikwissenschaft gehörend, und man ist daher auch bei der Diskussion der aristotelischen Politik auf Fragen der Reichsverfassung eingegangen. Wo immer aber auch Probleme des deutschen Verfassungsrechts angeschnitten wurden, da wurden sie nicht in erster Linie aufgrund der relevanten Fakten der deutschen Verfassungsgeschichte beurteilt, sondern aufgrund des Corpus Juris Civilis, des Kirchenrechts, der Heiligen Schrift oder der Politik des Aristoteles. Bei der Universalität der herangezogenen Quellen konnte es dann nicht ausbleiben, daß die für verfassungsrechtliche Probleme von der Wissenschaft gebotenen Lösungen mehr oder weniger

---

[1] In Deutschland hauptsächlich in der hier den Gelehrten sprachlich besser zugänglichen lateinischen Fassung, von der auch in Frankfurt am Main Auflagen veranstaltet wurden. Ich zitiere daher im folgenden nach der lateinischen Ausgabe, und zwar in erster Linie nach der 2. Auflage von Frankfurt 1591 [7.30]. Vom 2. Kapitel des 2. Buches an gebe ich jedoch der 6. Auflage von Frankfurt 1622 [7.37] den Vorzug vor der 2., weil letztere ab p. 289 falsch paginiert ist.

[2] Zu Folgendem vgl. R. HOKE, Die Reichsstaatsrechtslehre des Johannes Limnaeus. Ein Beitrag zur Geschichte der deutschen Staatsrechtswissenschaft im 17. Jahrhundert (= Unters. z. deutschen Staats- und Rechtsgeschichte, NF. Bd. 9), Aalen 1968, 17 ff. [260].

auf jeden Staat des Abendlandes paßten, daß sie aber den Besonderheiten der deutschen Verfassungsentwicklung nicht Rechnung trugen. Eine Änderung der Situation ergab sich mit der Wende vom 16. zum 17. Jahrhundert aus dem Zusammenwirken verschiedener Faktoren: An dem Konfessionskonflikt im Reich hatte sich der Verfassungskonflikt zwischen Kaiser und Reichsständen entzündet, der grundlegende Fragen des Reichsverfassungsrechts aufwarf. Sie drängten die Rechtswissenschaft zur Stellungnahme. Zwei neue Richtungen der philosophischen Erkenntnistheorie machten sich im Geistesleben geltend. Empirisch erkannte man, daß die tradierten gesamteuropäischen Rechtsquellen für die deutsche Verfassungswirklichkeit nur noch toter Buchstabe waren, daß diese vielmehr durch die Fakten der eigenen Verfassungsgeschichte bestimmt war. Die spezifisch deutschen Verfassungsdokumente wurden nun mit Sammeleifer gesichtet und ediert.[3] Und die Wirkung des Empirismus wurde unterstützt durch die des Rationalismus, unter dessen Einfluß sich die Rechtswissenschaft in Fragen der Reichsverfassung von der Autorität der aus der Spätantike überlieferten Texte emanzipierte.

Seit der Jahrhundertwende war das Reichsstaatsrecht in der Literatur Gegenstand eigener Untersuchungen, und auch im juristischen Hochschulunterricht wurde es nun um seiner selbst willen behandelt. Dabei ging man allerdings zuerst noch von den alten Anknüpfungspunkten der *jurisdictio* und der Regalien aus. Die ersten Bearbeitungen des deutschen Verfassungsrechts standen daher auch noch mehr oder weniger unter dem Einfluß der traditionellen Rechtsquellen.

Kristallisationspunkte der publizistischen Forschung und Lehre in Deutschland waren die lutherischen Universitäten Gießen und Jena. Jede von ihnen wurde zur Hochburg für eine der beiden großen, in der reichsverfassungsrechtlichen Kernfrage des Verhältnisses von Kaiser und Reichsständen zueinander konträren Richtungen innerhalb der nun als eigenständige wissenschaftliche Disziplin entstehenden Reichsstaatsrechtswissenschaft. In der Gießener Universität, der Gegengründung der mit dem Kaiser sympathisierenden lutherischen Darmstädter Linie des landgräflichen Hauses in Hessen gegen die Landesuniversität Marburg der calvinistischen Kasseler Linie, trat der *professor primarius* der Juristenfakultät, Gottfried Antonius, literarisch für die von dem Marburger Rechtslehrer Hermann Vultejus bestrittene absolute Monarchenstellung des deutschen Kaisers ein. In Jena etablierte Dominicus Arumaeus, Professor der Rechtsfakultät, erstmalig das Staatsrecht im juristischen Wissenschaftsbetrieb als ein an der deutschen Verfassungspraxis orientiertes,

---

[3] Goldast und Freher haben sich dabei hervorgetan. S. R. HOKE, Artikel Goldast und Freher, in: Handwörterbuch zur deutschen Rechtsgeschichte, hrsg. von A. Erler u. E. Kaufmann, 1. Bd., Berlin 1963 ff.

eigenständiges Fach. Er gilt daher als der Begründer der eigentlichen deutschen Staatsrechtswissenschaft und sein Jenaer Hörerkreis als die «Pflanzschule der deutschen Publizistik».[4] Arumaeus lehrte, daß der Staat dem Herrscher vor- und übergeordnet ist und daß deshalb dem Kaiser die hoheitliche Gewalt nur in dem Ausmaß zusteht, wie sie von den Kurfürsten als den Repräsentanten des Reiches in der Wahlkapitulation bestimmt wurde.[5]

Die von Antonius in Gießen ausgehende streng monarchistisch gesinnte, prokaiserliche Richtung der deutschen Reichsstaatsrechtslehre in der ersten Hälfte des 17. Jahrhunderts erreichte in seinem Nachfolger Theodor Reinking (1590–1646) ihren Höhepunkt.[6] Diesem stand als überragender wissenschaftlicher Gegner der aus der das aristokratische Element in der Reichsverfassung betonenden, reichsständisch gesinnten Schule des Arumaeus[7] hervorgegangene, deren Lehren mit seinem Werk krönende Johannes Limnaeus (1592–1663) gegenüber.[8] Reinking und in noch größerem Maß Limnaeus haben jeder von seinem wissenschaftlichen Standpunkt aus eine Dogmatik des Reichsstaatsrechts geschaffen. Reinkings *Tractatus de regimine seculari et ecclesiastico*[9] und die *Juris publici Imperii Romano-Germanici libri IX*[10] des Limnaeus waren in jener Anfangszeit der deutschen Publizistik die meistverbreiteten Lehrbücher des Reichsstaatsrechts. Es empfiehlt sich daher, die gestellte Frage nach dem Einfluß Bodins auf die Anfänge der Dogmatik des deutschen Reichsstaatsrechts exemplarisch am Werk dieser beiden Autoren zu untersuchen.

---

[4] Vgl. u. a. R. STINTZING, Geschichte d. deutschen Rechtswissenschaft, 1. Abt., München-Leipzig 1880, 720, 667, 670.

[5] Vgl. HOKE [260], 81 ff.

[6] Zu Reinkings Biographie s. R. STINTZING, Geschichte d. deutschen Rechtswissenschaft, 2. Abtl., hg. von E. Landsberg, München-Leipzig 1884, 189 ff. Eine Würdigung seiner wissenschaftlichen Bedeutung s. ebda. sowie bei E. WOLF, Idee und Wirklichkeit des Reiches im deutschen Rechtsdenken des 16. und 17. Jahrhunderts, in: K. LARENZ, Reich und Recht in der deutschen Philosophie, 1. Bd., Stuttgart-Berlin 1943, 94 ff.

[7] Zu ihr gehörte u. a. auch Benedict Carpzov. Zu den Schülern des Arumaeus s. HOKE, Reichsstaatsrechtslehre [260], 30 ff.

[8] Seine Biographie s. HOKE [260], 7 ff.

[9] Gießen 1619. Das Werk erschien 1651 in Frankfurt bereits in der 5. Auflage. Ich zitiere im folgenden nach der 1. Auflage.

[10] 3 Bde., Straßburg, 1. Aufl. 1629/1632/1634, 2. Aufl. 1645, 3. Aufl. 1657; dazu: Additiones, 2 Bde., Straßburg, 1. Bd., 1. Aufl. 1650, 2. Aufl. 1666, 2. Bd., 1. Aufl. 1660, 2. Aufl. 1670. Ich zitiere im folgenden nach den 1. Auflagen.

II

Ein für Reinkings Lehre grundlegendes Kapitel am Anfang seines Buches beschäftigt sich mit der Staatsform des Reiches.[11] Bereits in der Überschrift kündigt Reinking an, es werde hier, wenn er für die Auffassung eintritt, daß die Staatsform des Reiches *monarchisch* sei, hauptsächlich darum gehen, die Argumente Bodins zurückzuweisen.[12] Solche Argumente, die Bodin für seine These von der *aristokratischen* Staatsform des Reiches beibringt, gibt Reinking im Anschluß wieder.[13] Dabei inseriert er aber nicht etwa den Bodinschen Text Wort für Wort, wie das bei den Autoren jener Zeit gelegentlich des Eingehens auf gegnerische Meinungen auch vorkam. Reinking trifft vielmehr eine Auswahl, wobei er sich als guter Kenner Bodins erweist. Er stützt sich, ganz sachgemäß, in erster Linie auf Kapitel 6 des 2. Buches der *Respublica*, wo Bodin seine Lehre von der Staatsform des Reiches zusammenhängend formuliert, er berücksichtigt aber auch die Kapitel 8, 10 und 9 im 1. Buch, in denen Bodin seinen Souveränitätsbegriff definiert, die Souveränitätsrechte behandelt und er dem deutschen Kaiser die Eigenschaft des Souveräns abspricht. Reinking führt im wesentlichen zwei Argumentationsreihen Bodins vor. Die eine bezieht sich auf das Subjekt der staatlichen Hoheitsrechte im Reich. Die Hoheitsrechte im Reich stehen nach Bodins Anschauung nicht dem Kaiser zu, sondern der Gesamtheit der auf dem Reichstag versammelten Reichsstände. Das gälte für die Gesetzgebung, für die Entscheidung über Krieg und Frieden, für die Steuerausschreibung wie für die Aufstellung der Richter an dem die höchste Rechtsprechungsgewalt ausübenden Reichskammergericht. Die andere Argumentationsreihe zielt auf das Fehlen wesentlicher Merkmale der Souveränität in der Rechtsstellung des Kaisers ab. Nach der Reichsverfassung habe der Kaiser weder die höchste Gewalt im Reich. Seine Gewalt sei der der Reichsfürsten, die ihn einsetzen und die ihn auch absetzen können, untergeordnet. Noch treffe die *legibus solutio* für die Gewalt des Kaisers zu. Denn der Kaiser werde durch die von den Reichsständen auf dem Reichstag erlassenen Gesetze verpflichtet. Und auch stehe die kaiserliche Gewalt ihrem Inhaber nicht dauernd und nicht zu eigenem Recht, sondern nur prekaristisch zu. Die staatlichen Hoheitsrechte sind nach Bodin in der Staatswirklichkeit die Symptome der souveränen Gewalt, an denen man diese erkennt.

---

[11] REINKING, *Tractatus*, Lib. 1, class. 2, cap. 2, p. 15–30.

[12] De Sacri Imperii Rom. statu ubi rejectis Bodini et aliorum argumentis immotis fundamentis defenditur, statum Imperii nostri Romano-Germanici esse monarchicum.

[13] REINKING, *Tractatus*, Lib. 1, class. 2, cap. 2, nr. 6–51, p. 15–17.

Sie sind die Souveränitäts- oder Majestätsrechte.[14] Die Souveränität oder Majestät ist höchste irdische Gewalt, die ihrem Subjekt dauernd eigen und in bestimmtem Sinne[15] nicht an die Gesetze gebunden ist.[16] Aus seiner von Reinking wiedergegebenen Argumentation zieht Bodin daher den Schluß, daß, was das Heilige Römische Reich Deutscher Nation anlangt, die Souveränität nicht beim Kaiser ist, sondern bei der Gesamtheit der auf dem Reichstag versammelten Reichsstände. Und da für Bodin, je nachdem, ob in einem Staat ein Individuum oder ein Kollektiv Subjekt der Souveränität ist, in Übernahme der aristotelischen Unterscheidung die Staatsform im ersten Fall monarchisch, im zweiten polyarchisch ist, diagnostiziert er in weiterer Konsequenz die Staatsform des Reiches als eine aristokratische.[17]

Reinking zitiert die Meinung Bodins.[18] Er verurteilt sie mit besonders harten Worten,[19] ja wegen seiner der Rechtsstellung des deutschen Kaisers abträglichen Lehre wird paradoxerweise der französische Theoretiker der Fürstensouveränität von Reinking gar ein Monarchomach geheißen.[20] Als Reinking dann seine eigene Lehre entwickelt, zeigt sich jedoch sowohl in materieller wie in formaler Hinsicht seine Abhängigkeit von Bodin.

Den in der Staatslehre seit jeher verwendeten Begriff der höchsten Gewalt, der *summa potestas* oder des *summum imperium,* hat Bodin unter der Bezeichnung als Souveränität oder Majestät als erster juristisch präzisiert. Dieser Bodinsche Souveränitätsbegriff hat für Reinking bereits das Gewicht eines Axioms erlangt. Ausdrücklich und unter Berufung auf Bodin übernimmt er dessen Definition der Souveränität als der *summa et legibus soluta potestas in cives ac subditos,*[21] und unter Zitierung des Autors der *De republica libri sex* erläutert er mit dessen Worten,[22] daß höchste Gewalt nur der habe, der selbst keiner anderen irdischen Instanz untertan ist, der aber seinerseits allen anderen Angehörigen der staatlichen Gemeinschaft, als Individuen wie in ihrer Gesamtheit, zwingend befehlen kann.[23] Bodins Souveränitätsbegriff hat mit einer der staatlichen Gemeinschaft immanenten höchsten Gewalt nichts zu tun. Die Souveräni-

---

[14] *Respublica* [7.30], I, 10. Zu den einzelnen Souveränitätsrechten s. E. Hancke, Bodin. Eine Studie über den Begriff der Souverainetät (= Unters. z. Deutschen Staats- und Rechtsgeschichte, Heft 47), Breslau 1894, 51 ff. [48].

[15] S. Hoke [260], 56.

[16] Vgl. *Respublica* [7.30], I, 8, p. 123, 125, 127, 129.

[17] Vgl. *Respublica* [7.30], I, 9, p. 191, II, 1, p. 283, [7.37], II, 6, p. 348.

[18] Reinking, *Tractatus,* Lib. 1, cl. 2, c. 2, nr. 5, p. 15.

[19] Reinking, *Tractatus,* Lib. 1, cl. 2, c. 2, nr. 4, p. 15.

[20] Reinking, *Tractatus,* Lib. 1, cl. 2, c. 2, nr. 11, p. 15.

[21] Reinking, *Tractatus,* Lib. 1, cl. 2, c. 2, nr. 54, p. 17.

[22] Aus *Respublica* [7.37], II, 2, p. 292.

[23] Reinking, *Tractatus,* Lib. 1, cl. 2, c. 2, nr. 64, p. 18.

tät, wie er sie auffaßt, ist nicht Staatssouveränität. Subjekt seines Souveränitätsbegriffes ist vielmehr der individuelle oder kollektive Herrscher im Staat. Bodin versteht die Souveränität als Herrschersouveränität, die er in der Staatspraxis nur durch einen Einzelherrscher, einen Fürsten, d. h. als Fürstensouveränität dauerhaft verwirklicht sieht.[24] Genau wie Bodin so vermag sich auch Reinking als das Subjekt des Souveränitätsbegriffes einzig und allein den Herrscher in einem Staate vorzustellen. Dabei hat er noch stärker als Bodin, schon in der Theorie, vor allem den Einzelherrscher im Auge. So setzt er in einem der späteren Kapitel seines Buches die Rechte des Fürsten schlechthin gleich mit der *summa et absoluta potestas*,[25] und bezeichnet er die Rechte des Fürsten schlechthin als die Souveränität: «jura principis uno verbo dici possunt majestas».[26]

Der Bodinschen Lehre von der Herrschersouveränität hatte zu Beginn des 17. Jahrhunderts Johannes Althusius[27] seine, die alte Lehre, welche die höchste irdische Gewalt dem Volk zuschreibt, neu fassende Doktrin von der Souveränität des dem Herrscher übergeordneten staatlich organisierten Volkes entgegengesetzt.[28] Reinking verschließt sich den Konsequenzen dieser Doktrin nicht völlig. Unter Berufung auf Althusius[29] erkennt er an, daß gegenüber einem *tyrannus exercitio*, der die Grundgesetze des Staates[30] verletzt, die Ephoren im Staat ein Absetzungsrecht haben,[31] und er verweist ausdrücklich auf die Voraussetzungen, die Althusius für die Ausübung dieses Rechtes nennt.[32] Auch gesteht er unter dem Einfluß dieser Doktrin an anderer Stelle zu, daß die Autorität von Herrscher und Optimaten zusammen größer sei als die des Herrschers allein.[33] Als es aber darum geht, hinsichtlich des Reiches das Subjekt der Souveränität zu erkennen und aufgrund dessen das rechtliche Verhältnis von Kaiser und Reichsständen abzugrenzen, da erweist sich Reinking als im Banne der Bodinschen Souveränitätslehre stehend. Da verwahrt er sich gegen die von ihm zitierte Meinung, für die er u. a. Althusius[34] namhaft macht,

---

[24] Vgl. *Respublica*, VI, 4, p. 1111: «Maiestas autem imperii praeterquam in uno principe vere ac proprie consistere nullo modo potest.»

[25] REINKING, *Tractatus*, Lib. 1, cl. 3, c. 11, nr. 2, p. 81.

[26] REINKING, *Tractatus*, Lib. 1, cl. 3, c. 11, nr. 4, p. 81.

[27] *Politica methodice digesta*, Herborn 1603; 3. Aufl. ebda. 1614. Reinking benützte die 3. Aufl.

[28] Vgl. HOKE [260], 65 ff. mit Literaturhinweis in Anm. 76.

[29] *Politica*, 3. Aufl., XXXVIII.

[30] Diese werden von REINKING, Lib. 2, cl. 2, c. 6, p. 247 s definiert und im Hinblick auf das Reich aufgezählt.

[31] REINKING, *Tractatus*, Lib. 1, cl. 1, c. 5, nr. 39 s, p. 10.

[32] REINKING, *Tractatus*, Lib. 1, cl. 1, c. 5, nr. 58, p. 12.

[33] REINKING, *Tractatus*, Lib. 1, cl. 5, c. 9, nr. 15, p. 203 s.

[34] Mit *Politica* XIX, 12.

wonach das *extremum superioritatis* nicht beim Herrscher, sondern beim Staat selbst sei.[35] Da bekennt er sich unter Hinweis auf seine früheren Aussagen nochmals ganz eindeutig zu dem Begriff der Herrscher-, ja der Fürstensouveränität.[36]

Wo sich in einem Staat die Souveränität befindet, daran liest Reinking mit Bodin den Charakter der jeweiligen Staatsform ab. Unter Berufung auf die einschlägigen Ausführungen des französischen Staatstheoretikers[37] doziert er im Hinblick auf die monarchische Staatsform, und auf die staatlichen Hoheitsrechte als die Auswirkungen der Souveränität abstellend, daß es sich bei einem Staat dann um eine Monarchie handelt, wenn ein einziges Individuum die Majestätsrechte hat.[38]

Wissenschaftlicher Gegner Bodins ist Reinking nur in der Frage nach dem Souveränitätssubjekt und der Staatsform des *deutschen Reiches*. Im Gegensatz zu Bodin sieht er den Kaiser als Souverän an und das Reich daher als eine Monarchie. Zu dieser Ansicht gelangt er, hierin noch ganz an der alten, aus dem Mittelalter überkommenen Methode festhaltend, teilweise auf metajuristischem Wege, durch eine Verknüpfung der Auslegung des Buches Daniel mit der Translationstheorie. Als gläubiger Lutheraner vertraut er auf die Weissagung des Propheten Daniel von den vier Weltmonarchien.[39] Deren letzte ist für ihn das römische Reich, das, durch die Translatio Imperii von den Römern auf die Deutschen übergegangen, in Gestalt des Imperium Romano-Germanicum bis ans Ende der Welt dauere.[40] Aus der formalen Tatsache, daß in der Prophezeiung Daniels von «Königreichen» die Rede ist, schließt Reinking, daß es sich bei den vier Weltreichen und damit auch beim römisch-deutschen Reich nur um Monarchien handeln könne.[41] Überdies ergibt sich für ihn aus der Translatio Imperii von den Römern auf die Deutschen, daß das römische Kaisertum im deutschen Kaisertum fortbesteht und deshalb auch die römische *lex regia* nach wie vor gültig ist. Durch diese aber hatte das römische Volk einst die gesamte hoheitliche Gewalt auf den Vorgänger der Kaiser übertragen. Somit sei diese Gewalt noch immer beim Kaiser.[42]

Als Reinking diese seine gegensätzliche Auffassung zu Bodin dann

---

[35] REINKING, *Tractatus*, Lib. 1, cl. 5, c. 9, nr. 1, p. 202.

[36] REINKING, *Tractatus*, Lib. 1, cl. 5, c. 9, nr. 11, p. 203.

[37] *Respublica* [7.30], II, 1, p. 273.

[38] REINKING, *Tractatus*, Lib. 1, cl. 2, c. 2, nr. 52, p. 17.

[39] Daniel 2 und 7.

[40] REINKING, *Tractatus*, Lib. 1, cl. 2, c. 1, nr. 3, p. 14. Zur Translationstheorie s. WERNER GOEZ, Translatio Imperii, Tübingen 1958, der 353 ff. auf Reinking und 366 ff. auf das Verhältnis der Translationstheorie zur Vier-Weltmonarchienlehre eingeht.

[41] REINKING, *Tractatus*, Lib. 1, cl. 2, c. 2, nr. 1–3, p. 15.

[42] REINKING, *Tractatus*, Lib. 1, cl. 2, c. 2, nr. 55 s, p. 17.

aber auch noch nach der mit der Jahrhundertwende aufgekommenen, spezifisch publizistischen Methode aus dem deutschen Verfassungsrecht begründet und seine Lehre im einzelnen darlegt, steht er in formaler Hinsicht selbst da unter dem Einfluß Bodins. Die Diskussionsweise der Frage, um die es geht, ist durch Bodin bestimmt. So vermag Reinking seine Lehren über das Subjekt der Souveränität und, damit verbunden, über die Kompetenzen für die obersten Staatsfunktionen sowie über die Staatsform des Reiches nun nur als Antithesen zu Bodin zu konzipieren und zu formulieren.

Er zielt darauf ab, Bodins Lehre zu widerlegen, daß das Subjekt der staatlichen Hoheitsrechte, die er mit Bodin als die Majestätsrechte anspricht, im Reich die Gesamtheit der auf dem Reichstag versammelten Reichsstände sei. Indem er sich an der Argumentation Bodins orientiert und immer wieder auf sie eingeht, untersucht er die Kompetenz für jedes der von Bodin angeführten Hoheitsrechte.[43] In der Absicht, die Kompetenz für die obersten Staatsaufgaben im Reich dem Kaiser zu vindizieren, tut er dabei den Anteil, den die Gesamtheit der Reichsstände faktisch an den staatlichen Hoheitsrechten hat, als unwesentlich und jedenfalls für die in diesem Kaiptel seines Buches zu entscheidende Frage der Staatsform des Reiches bedeutungslos ab. So versucht er den Nachweis zu führen, daß im Reichsgesetzgebungsverfahren der Anteil des Kaisers gegenüber dem der Reichsstände der maßgebende sei («potissimas... partes Imperator in legum constitutione obtinet»).[44] Die Reichsgesetze kämen auf dem Reichstag durch das gemeinsame Handeln von Kaiser und Reichsständen zustande. Der Kaiser aber sei es, der den Reichstag einberufe, der auf diesem den Vorsitz führe, der allein das Recht der Gesetzesinitiative habe und unter dessen Autorität, und nicht unter der der Reichsstände, die Reichsgesetze verkündet würden.[45] Aufgrund seiner Beweisführung hält sich Reinking für legitimiert, der These Bodins die seine entgegenzusetzen: «jura majestatis resident penes Imperatorem unum et solum in imperio.»[46]

An dem Bodinschen Souveränitätsbegriff mißt Reinking die Rechtsstellung des Kaisers. Er meint feststellen zu können, daß Bodins Definition der Souveränität als der *potestas summa et legibus soluta in cives ac subditos* auf die Gewalt des Kaisers genau zutrifft: «Talem... potestatem habet Imperator.»[47] Entgegen der Behauptung Bodins sei nach der Reichsverfassung die Gewalt des Kaisers höchste Gewalt im Reich und nicht der

---

[43] Reinking, *Tractatus*, Lib. 1, cl. 2, c. 2, nr. 106–217, p. 20–28.
[44] Reinking, *Tractatus*, Lib. 1, cl. 2, c. 2, nr. 120, p. 21.
[45] Reinking, *Tractatus*, Lib. 1, cl. 2, c. 2, nr. 114–134, p. 21 s.
[46] Reinking, *Tractatus*, Lib. 1, cl. 2, c. 2, nr. 53, p. 17.
[47] Reinking, *Tractatus*, Lib. 1, cl. 2, c. 2, nr. 54, p. 17.

der ihn einsetzenden Reichsfürsten untergeordnet. Vielmehr würden die Kurfürsten mit der Kaiserwahl ihrem Amt Genüge tun, damit ihre Gewalt niederlegen und sich dem Kaiser durch Eid unterwerfen und zu Gehorsam verpflichten.[48] Auch passe daher die Kennzeichnung des Souveräns durch Bodin als desjenigen, der keiner anderen irdischen Instanz untertan ist, selbst aber allen anderen Angehörigen der staatlichen Gemeinschaft, als Individuen und in ihrer Gesamtheit, zwingend befehlen kann, sowohl was das erste, als auch was das zweite Merkmal angeht, bestens auf die Rechtsstellung des Kaisers («primum membrum» und «secundum membrum definitionis Bodinianae optime convenit Imperatori»). Unter Hinweis auf entsprechende Formulierungen in Reichsverfassungsgesetzen führt Reinking zur Begründung an, daß der Kaiser «nullius tenetur imperio et neminem nisi Deum et Ensem superiorem cognoscit» und «non solum omnibus et singulis imperat, sed etiam omnes et singulos coercet, in omnes et singulos animadvertit».[49] Entgegen der Behauptung Bodins gelte folglich für den Kaiser sehr wohl die *legibus solutio*. Durch die von Kaiser und Reichsständen gemeinsam beschlossenen Gesetze werde der Kaiser nicht zwangsweise *(ex imperio),* sondern vertraglich *(ex conventione)* verpflichtet.[50] Schließlich widerspricht Reinking der Behauptung Bodins, daß die kaiserliche Gewalt ihrem Inhaber nur prekaristisch zustehe. Dabei befindet er sich mit seinem Einwand gegen das von Bodin hier ins Treffen geführte Absetzungsrecht, das die Kurfürsten in bezug auf den Kaiser haben, in einer Linie mit der auch sonst in der Reichspublizistik vertretenen Lehre,[51] wonach der Kaiser, der seine hoheitliche Tätigkeit nicht mehr den Grundgesetzen gemäß ausübt, sich selbst seiner Stellung begibt. Reinking hält Bodin entgegen, daß der Kaiser, der die Grundgesetze verletzt, nicht als Kaiser, sondern als ein *fidei et juris temerator* entfernt werde.[52] Aus allen seinen Entgegnungen auf Bodins Thesen zieht Reinking dann, indem er sich des Bodinschen Souveränitätsbegriffes bedient, das Fazit, daß die Souveränität im Reich nur dem Kaiser zusteht.[53]

Damit ist für Reinking auch die Frage entschieden, auf die sich seine antithetische Stellungnahme zu Bodin konzentriert: Da er die Souveränität im Reich einzig und allein in der Institution des Kaisers lokalisiert, erscheint ihm in weiterer Konsequenz die Staatsform des Reiches nicht als aristokratisch, wie Bodin sie sieht, sondern als rein monarchisch.

---

[48] REINKING, *Tractatus*, Lib. 1, cl. 2, c. 2, nr. 184, p. 26.
[49] REINKING, *Tractatus*, Lib. 1, cl. 2, c. 2, nr. 64 s, nr. 69 ss, p. 18 ss.
[50] REINKING, *Tractatus*, Lib. 1, cl. 2, c. 2, nr. 115 s, p. 21.
[51] So von Limnaeus; vgl. HOKE [260], 145 ff.
[52] REINKING, *Tractatus*, Lib. 1, cl. 2, c. 2, nr. 187, p. 26.
[53] REINKING, *Tractatus*, Lib. I, cl. 3, c. 11, nr. 9, p. 81: «Competit ... majestas ... soli imperatori.»

In der Verfassungswirklichkeit jener Zeit aber hatten, im Reich wie anderswo, die Stände sehr wohl Anteil an der Staatsgewalt. Dem faktischen Dualismus von Herrscher und Ständen auch in der Reichsverfassung suchte eine Richtung in der Staatstheorie dadurch Rechnung zu tragen, daß sie solche Verfassungen als aus dem monarchischen und dem aristokratischen Element gemischt ansah. Es war dies die Theorie von der gemischten Staatsform oder gemischten Verfassung (vom *status mixtus*), wie wir ihr noch in der Lehre des Limnaeus begegnen werden.[54] Bodin lehnte diese Theorie ab,[55] und Reinking folgt ihm darin, freilich aus dem genau entgegengesetzten Motiv. Wollte Bodin damit im Hinblick auf das Reich die theoretische Möglichkeit einer Beteiligung des Kaisers an der Souveränität ausschließen,[56] so wird Reinking bei seiner Ablehnung der Lehre vom *status mixtus* von der Absicht geleitet, die Souveränität gerade dem Kaiser, unter Ausschluß der Reichsstände, theoretisch vorzubehalten. In der Argumentation jedoch schließt sich Reinking an Bodin an, den er in diesem Zusammenhang auch zitiert.[57] Mit Bodin[58] hält er eine Mischung der Staatsformen für theoretisch unmöglich. Seine Auffassung begründet er wie Bodin damit, daß die Souveränität unteilbar sei. Sie dulde per definitionem keine gleichgeordnete Gewalt neben sich.[59]

Nun war freilich der faktische Dualismus von Herrscher und Ständen nicht zu übersehen. Um ihn in seine Staatstheorie einzupassen, nahm Bodin die Unterscheidung zwischen Staatsform *(status reipublicae)* und Regierungsform *(ratio imperandi* oder *gubernatio)* vor.[60] Er lehrt, daß in einem Staat die Staatsform einerseits und die Regierungsform andererseits differieren können. So kann nach seiner Lehre ein Staat, dessen Staatsform monarchisch ist, aristokratisch oder auch demokratisch regiert werden. Diese Bodinsche Lehre greift Reinking auf. Sie dient ihm dazu, für das in der Verfassungswirklichkeit des Reiches bestehende Nebeneinander von Kaiser und Reichsständen in seinem System wenigstens irgendeine Erklärung geben zu können. Unter wiederholter Berufung auf Bodin, allerdings im Zusammenhang seiner in der Frage der Staatsform des Reiches gegen diesen gerichteten Polemik, vertritt auch Reinking die Lehre,

---

[54] S. dort auch zu der synonymen Verwendung von status, Staatsform und Verfassung.

[55] *Respublica* [7.30], II, 1, p. 273 ss.

[56] Vgl. *Respublica* [7.30], II, 1, p. 283.

[57] REINKING, *Tractatus,* Lib. 1, cl. 2, c. 2, nr. 231, p. 29.

[58] *Respublica* [7.30], p. 275.

[59] REINKING, *Tractatus,* Lib. 1, cl. 2, c. 2, nr. 226 ss, p. 29.

[60] *Respublica* [7.37], II, 2, p. 295: «admonendi sumus, reipublicae statum ab imperandi ratione distare plurimum». In der französischen Ausgabe von Paris 1583, jetzt Aalen 1961, p. 273, wird von der Regierungsform als gouvernement et administration gesprochen.

daß der *status reipublicae* etwas anderes sei als die akzidentielle Regierungsform. Daher könne die Staatsform eines Staates monarchisch sein, wenn auch die Regierungsform aristokratische Elemente enthalte.[61]

III

Die wissenschaftliche Gegenposition, die der »Patriarch« oder »Erzvater« der deutschen Reichsstaatsrechtswissenschaft, wie Limnaeus apostrophiert wurde,[62] zu Reinking einnimmt, wird auch und gerade an dem unterschiedlichen Verhältnis der beiden Gelehrten zu Bodin deutlich. Das System des Reichsstaatsrechts, das Limnaeus in seinem großen Lehrbuch, in seinen Kommentaren zu den Wahlkapitulationen der deutschen Kaiser und Könige[63] und zur Goldenen Bulle[64] und nicht zuletzt in seiner *Dissertatio apologetica de statu Imperii Romano Germanici*[65] entwickelt, ist, anders als das von Reinking, nicht auf den Souveränitätsbegriff und die Staatsformenlehre Bodins gegründet. Nichtsdestoweniger haben die Bodinschen Theorien, zusammen mit anderen Faktoren, auch für die Hauptlehren dieses deutschen Publizisten erst den Anlaß gegeben, und sie gehören in diesem Sinne zu den Voraussetzungen auch der Reichsstaatsrechtslehre des Limnaeus.

Die in der wissenschaftlichen Diskussion zu Beginn des 17. Jahrhunderts einander gegenüberstehenden monistischen Souveränitätstheorien, die Bodinsche Lehre von der Herrschersouveränität und die zuletzt von Althusius formulierte Lehre von der Souveränität des staatlich organisierten Volkes, suchte eine dritte Theorie miteinander zu verknüpfen. Sie stellt insofern eine Synthese der beiden anderen Theorien dar. Scheinbar handelt es sich bei ihr um eine dualistische Souveränitätstheorie. Ihrem Inhalt nach ist sie aber nichts anderes als eine Variante der Lehre von der höchsten Gewalt des staatlich organisierten Volkes. Ihre Bedeutung liegt auf terminologischem Gebiet. Sie bezeichnet nicht nur die staatliche Gemeinschaft, der nach ihrer Auffassung die höchste irdische Gewalt eigen

---

[61] REINKING, *Tractatus*, Lib. 1, cl. 2, c. 2, nr. 104 s, p. 20: «Distinguendum inter ipsum reipub. statum et imperandi seu administrandi formam ac rationem accidentalem, quae inter se distant plurimum, ipso Bodino rursus fatente, d. c. 2. Potest itaque status ipse regalis et monarchicus esse, licet gubernandi forma aristocratis rationibus sit temperata. Bodin d. loc.»

[62] S. die Belegstellen bei HOKE [260], 53.

[63] *Capitulationes Imperatorum et Regum Romanogermanorum*, Straßburg 1651.

[64] *In Auream Bullam Caroli Quarti Imperatoris Romani observationes*, Straßburg 1662.

[65] Ansbach 1643.

ist, als Subjekt der Majestät und macht damit eine Aussage im Sinne der
Lehre von der Souveränität des staatlich organisierten Volkes. Sie bezeichnet ebenfalls den Herrscher im Staat, den sie wie diese Lehre als denjenigen auffaßt, der die der staatlichen Gemeinschaft eigene Gewalt ausübt, als Subjekt von Majestät. Damit aber formuliert sie genauso wie die
Vertreter der Bodinschen Lehre von der Herrschersouveränität. Im ersten
Fall spricht sie von realer Majestät, im zweiten von personaler Majestät.
Indem sie sowohl die staatliche Gemeinschaft als auch den Herrscher mit
der Bezeichnung eines Subjekts der Majestät bedenkt, stellt sie eine Parallele zu der späteren Staatstheorie dar, die die Termini der Staatssouveränität und der Organsouveränität prägte.

Der zuerst von Hermann Kirchner[66] vorgetragenen Lehre von der
realen und der personalen Majestät hing auch Limnaeus an.[67] Limnaeus
stellt sich bewußt in Gegensatz zu der Staatstheorie, die mit Bodin Majestät und Souveränität als Synonyma auffaßt und dem darunter verstandenen Begriff als wesentliches Merkmal höchste Gewalt zuschreibt. Majestät schlechthin bedeutet für ihn nicht *summa potestas*, sondern nur eine
hervorragende Gewalt – *potestas aliqua egregia* –, die es in verschiedenen
Abstufungen gibt.[68] Sie ist daher auch nicht auf ein einziges Subjekt beschränkt. Ihre verschiedenen Spezifizierungen sind vielmehr bei verschiedenen Subjekten. Diese sind die staatliche Gemeinschaft und der Herrscher im Staat. Nur eine der Spezifizierungen des Majestätsbegriffes ist
nach Limnaeus höchste, von keiner anderen irdischen Instanz abhängige
Gewalt, Souveränität: diejenige, die er als *majestas realis* bezeichnet und
als deren Subjekt er die staatliche Gemeinschaft erkennt. Die andere
Spezifizierung des von Limnaeus vertretenen Majestätsbegriffes, deren
Subjekt der Herrscher ist, die *majestas personalis*, sie ist dagegen nur,
wenn man die Gewalten der einzelnen Angehörigen der staatlichen Gemeinschaft miteinander vergleicht, unter diesen Gewalten die höchste. Die
personale Majestät wird von der realen Majestät konstituiert und hängt
dauernd von ihr ab.

Diese Lehre bezieht Limnaeus auf das deutsche Reich. Da nach seiner
Auffassung das Reich von der Gesamtheit der Reichsstände repräsentiert
wird, sieht er hier das Subjekt der realen Majestät von der Gesamtheit
der Reichsstände verkörpert – somit für das Reich zu dem gleichen Resultat kommend wie Bodin. Von der Gesamtheit der Reichsstände hat nach
Limnaeus der Kaiser, aber nicht einmal ausschließlich, die personale
Majestät, und von ihr ist er als Subjekt der personalen Majestät während

---

[66] *Respublica*, Marburg 1608, disp. 2, thes. 3. Zu Kirchner s. HOKE [260], 78.
[67] Zur Lehre von der realen und der personalen Majestät bei Limnaeus vgl.
HOKE [260], 98 ff. Andere Vertreter s. 78 ff.
[68] *Capitulationes*, p. 526 s.

der Dauer seiner Funktion abhängig. Die Konsequenz, die Limnaeus in denjenigen Teilen seiner Dogmatik des Reichsstaatsrechts, die sich dieser seiner beiden Hauptlehren zuordnen lassen, herausarbeitet, ist, daß der Kaiser im Reich keine andere Stellung als die eines an die Grundgesetze gebundenen Organs hat.[69] Als er in diesem Zusammenhang den Amtscharakter der kaiserlichen Stellung aufzeigt, schließt er sich an den in der Nachfolge Bodins stehenden Charles Loyseau[70] an. Mit Loyseau, der sich seinerseits hier auf Bodin beruft,[71] meint Limnaeus, daß der deutsche Kaiser die souveräne Gewalt nicht zu eigenem Recht wie ein Eigentümer hat, sondern daß er sie lediglich als Amtsträger, als der erste Amtsträger des Staates ausübt.[72]

Die Theoretiker der realen und der personalen Majestät wollten mit ihrer Lehre von der Staatssouveränität die Bodinsche Lehre von der Herrschersouveränität überwinden. Aber selbst bei diesen wissenschaftlichen Gegnern Bodins stand der französische Staatstheoretiker in so großem Ansehen, daß sie gerade auch ihn für die Stützung ihrer Theorie in Anspruch nahmen. Wie schon Kirchner[73] so meint auch Limnaeus aus einer Äußerung im 7. Kapitel des 1. Buches der *Respublica* herauslesen zu können, daß Bodin neben der *majestas regnantis* eine Majestät des Staates selbst, eine *majestas regni*, kenne.[74] Limnaeus wie Kirchner berufen sich daher bei der Begründung ihrer Lehre von der realen und der personalen Majestät auch auf diese angebliche Meinung Bodins. Freilich erfolgt die Inanspruchnahme Bodins hier zu Unrecht. An der genannten Stelle spricht Bodin zwar einmal davon, daß der Kaiser dem Reich untergeordnet sei.[75] Eine ausdrückliche Unterscheidung von *majestas regnantis*

---

[69] Vgl. HOKE [260], 117 ff.
[70] *Traité des seigneuries*, Paris 1608, Kap. 2. S. dazu HOKE [260], 125 f.; F. H. SCHUBERT, Französische Staatstheorie und deutsche Reichsverfassung im 16. und 17. Jahrhundert, in: LUTZ-SCHUBERT-WEBER, Frankreich und das Reich im 16. und 17. Jahrh., Göttingen 1968, 56 f., Anm. 10 [264].
[71] *Traité des seigneuries*, Kap. 2, nr. 32, 31, nr. 90, 42.
[72] *Capitulationes*, p. 129, nr. 3; *Jus publ.*, Add. 1. Bd., zu I, 10, p. 113, und insbes. *In A. B. observationes*, p. 42 s.
[73] *Respublica*, disp. 2, thes. 3, b.
[74] *Jus publ.*, I, 12, nr. 24; ebenso Althusius, vgl. HOKE [260], 62, 76 f. Offenbar unter dem Einfluß des Althusius vertreten in der neueren Literatur die gleiche Auffassung LUDWIG WALDECKER, Allgemeine Staatslehre, Berlin 1927, 650, und CARL JOACHIM FRIEDRICH, Politica methodice digesta of Johannes Althusius with an introduction (= Harvard political classics, vol II), Cambridge (USA) 1932, Introduction, S. XXXI und XC Anmerkung 5. Friedrich glaubt deshalb sogar, daß sich die Theorie von der realen und der personalen Majestät auf Bodin zurückführen ließe.
[75] *Respublica*, 120.

und *majestas regni* trifft er aber weder hier noch anderswo. Sein Majestäts-
begriff läßt die Existenz einer Gewalt, die über der Souveränität des
Herrschers stünde, auch gar nicht zu. Außerdem meint Bodin in seiner
von Limnaeus und Kirchner herangezogenen Äußerung mit dem «Reich»
überhaupt nicht den deutschen Staat, sondern gerade den Herrscher in
diesem Staat. Mit «Reich» bezeichnet er nach einem zu seiner Zeit aufkommenden Sprachgebrauch die Gesamtheit der Reichsstände. Das ergibt
sich eindeutig daraus, daß dort, wo im lateinischen Text vom *imperium
Germanicum* die Rede ist, zu dem der Kaiser in einem Abhängigkeits-
verhältnis steht, die französische Version von den *estats de l'Empire*
spricht, denen der Kaiser unterworfen ist.[76] Die Gesamtheit der Reichsstände aber ist nach Bodins Anschauung der wahre Herrscher und das
Subjekt der Souveränität im deutschen Reich.

Dagegen stützt sich Limnaeus in einer anderen Frage völlig zu Recht
auf den französischen Autor. Auf dem Boden der Theorie von der realen
und der personalen Majestät entwickelt Limnaeus die Lehre, daß der
deutsche Kaiser an die Grundgesetze als die für seine hoheitliche Tätigkeit
von dem Subjekt der realen Majestät des Reiches aufgestellten Normen
gebunden ist.[77] Demgegenüber betont er die sonstigen rechtlichen Bindungen, die für den Kaiser bestehen, weniger stark. Er begnügt sich damit,
die in der Staatstheorie seiner Zeit fest verankerten Thesen von der Bindung des Herrschers an die *leges divinae, naturae* und *gentium* vorzutra-
gen, und hier ist es u. a. Bodin mit seinem 8. Kapitel des 1. Buches, auf
den er sich beruft.[78]

Während die Synthese, die die Lehre von der realen und der personalen
Majestät darstellt, formaler Art ist, handelt es sich bei der anderen
Hauptlehre des Limnaeus um eine inhaltliche Verknüpfung von zwei
gegensätzlichen, zu jener Zeit vertretenen Doktrinen, die auf diese Weise
überwunden werden sollen. Davon ist die eine wieder eine Doktrin des
Bodin. Diese zweite Hauptlehre des Limnaeus ist die bereits erwähnte
Lehre von der gemischten Staatsform oder gemischten Verfassung (vom
status mixtus) des Reiches.

Staat im technischen Sinn, *status* in des Wortes primärer Bedeutung,
gibt es für Limnaeus nur in einer Daseinsform: nämlich als Organisation
der Volksgemeinschaft, die wie nach außen so auch im Innern der Organisation selbst Subjekt der souveränen Gewalt, der realen Majestät, ist.
Diese Daseinsform des Staates ist nach seiner Auffassung, wenn er es auch
nicht ausdrücklich sagt, gleichsam die einzige Staatsform. Etwas anderes
ist für ihn die Organisationsform der obersten Organgewalt im Staat, also

---

[76] *Respublica*, 119.
[77] Vgl. Hoke [260], 134 ff.
[78] *Jus publ.*, II, 8, nr. 55.

die Organisationsform der personalen Majestät. Sie versteht Limnaeus als die zweite Bedeutung des Wortes *status*. Sie ist die von dem Subjekt der realen Majestät in den Grundgesetzen geschaffene Verfassung des Staates. Die personale Majestät kann von dem Subjekt der realen Majestät einem oder mehreren Individuen zugewiesen sein, und je nachdem ist die Organisationsform der personalen Majestät, also der *status* des Staates, monarchisch oder polyarchisch. Limnaeus weist darauf hin, daß der *status* als die Organisationsform der personalen Majestät in der Wissenschaft auch Staatsform *(forma reipublicae)* genannt wird. Da es sich beim *status* aber um die Organisationsform der obersten Organgewalt im Staat handelt, die in der Regierung besteht, ist er seinem Wesen nach nicht Staatsform, sondern Regierungsform *(forma regiminis)*. *Status* in des Wortes zweiter Bedeutung, Staatsform und Regierungsform faßt Limnaeus daher als kongruente Begriffe auf. Und da sich der *status* nur in der Regierung manifestiert, ist von dieser auf den *status* zu schließen. Je nachdem, ob in einem Staat die Regierung monarchisch, aristokratisch oder demokratisch geführt wird, bezeichnet man dessen *status* als Monarchie, Aristokratie oder Demokratie.[79]

Seine Lehre von der Kongruenz der Begriffe Staats- und Regierungsform entwickelt Limnaeus im Rahmen einer Auseinandersetzung mit Bodin. Er trägt zunächst vor, wie der französische Staatstheoretiker und dessen Anhänger, darunter Reinking, die Staatsform von der Regierungsform unterscheiden.[80] Bei dieser Gelegenheit erfahren wir von ihm auch, daß er selbst die Frankfurter lateinische Ausgabe der *Respublica* von 1594 benützt hat.[81] Er bezieht sich auf das 2. Kapitel des 2. Buches, aber auch, seine gute Kenntnis des Bodinschen Werkes unter Beweis stellend, auf die anderen Kapitel, in denen Bodin seine Lehre wiederholt. Die Tatsache dieser Wiederholung durch Bodin nimmt er bereits zum Anlaß zu einer abfälligen Äußerung über die Unterscheidung von Staatsform und Regierungsform – «Bodinus ... hanc crambem coquit et recoquit».[82] Dann teilt er mit, daß ihm diese Unterscheidung schon, als er ihr das erste Mal begegnete, suspekt erschienen sei. Dabei läßt sich seinen Worten entnehmen, daß an der Jenaer Universität, die Limnaeus bis zu seinem 22. Lebensjahr besuchte,[83] die Lektüre der *Respublica* des Bodin offenbar zum Pensum der Studenten seines Faches gehörte: «Ego ab ea statim aetate, qua occoepi politico me addicere studio et lectioni Bodinianae

---

[79] Vgl. HOKE [260], 165 ff.

[80] *Jus publ.*, I, 10, nr. 23, 20; *Diss. apolog.*, sect. 2, nr. 1–4, 6 = *Jus publ.*, Add. 1. Bd., zu I, 10, p. 98–101.

[81] *Jus publ.*, Add. 1. Bd., zu I, 10, p. 98.

[82] *Jus publ.*, I, 10, nr. 23.

[83] Danach bezog er die Universität Altdorf. Vgl. HOKE [260], 8.

accingere, suspectam habui distinctionem eam».[84] Nun in seinen Publi-
kationen zum Reichsstaatsrecht weist er die Bodinsche Unterscheidung
gänzlich zurück. Seine ablehnende Meinung findet er bei Althusius bestätigt, dessen negatives Urteil über diese Theorie des Bodin er zitiert –
«male, meo judicio, ita Bodinus distinguit»[85] – und dem er sich, auch in
der Argumentation, anschließt.[86] Aufgrund seiner Auffassung kann er in
der Lehre Bodins die drei *status* Monarchie, Aristokratie und Demokratie
allein als Formen der Regierung verstehen: «Firmiter credo, statum eo
sensu, quo Bodinus utitur, nihil esse aliud, quam ipsius reipublicae (quae
status est et dicitur) regiminis formam.»[87] Die Bodinsche Theorie einer
vom *status* verschiedenen Regierungsform erscheint ihm daher als eine
gedankliche Konstruktion, die mit der Staatswirklichkeit nicht in Einklang steht.[88]

Neben den reinen *status*-Typen Monarchie, Aristokratie und Demokratie kennt Limnaeus in Übernahme der alten Lehre vom *status mixtus*[89]
Mischtypen, die aus Elementen von zwei oder allen drei Grundtypen
bestehen. Den Gegnern der Lehre vom *status mixtus*, zu denen Bodin und
Reinking gehören, die hier von Limnaeus allerdings nicht namentlich genannt werden, hält er vor allem entgegen, daß es im Belieben der souveränen staatlichen Gemeinschaft steht, welchen *status* sie sich gibt.[90]
Folglich kann sie sich auch für einen *status mixtus* entscheiden. Die Verfassung eines Staates kann daher so beschaffen sein, daß die oberste
Organgewalt, die personale Majestät, hinsichtlich mancher Staatsaufgaben von einem Einzelnen, also auf monarchische Weise, hinsichtlich anderer dagegen von diesem Einzelnen in Gemeinschaft mit den
Optimaten des Staates, also auf aristokratische Weise, wahrgenommen
wird.[91]

In diese Kategorie stuft Limnaeus die Verfassung des Heiligen Römi-

---

[84] *Jus publ.*, I, 10, nr. 24.

[85] *Politica*, XXXIX, 3.

[86] *Jus publ.*, Add. 1. Bd., zu I, 10, p. 101: «mihi eadem cum Althusio mens est»;
vgl. auch *Diss. apolog.*, sect. 3, nr. 3.

[87] *Jus publ.*, Add. 1. Bd., zu I, 10, p. 101.

[88] *Jus publ.*, Add. 1. Bd., p. 102: «Bodinum itaque quod tangit, notandum
venit, eum in abstracto et in republica quae cerebri limitibus terminatur, ita mis-
cuisse statum gubernationis, ut in concreto talis a rerum primordiis nec fuerit nec
ulibi esse possit.»

[89] S. zu den Vorläufern des Limnaeus, an die er sich hier anschließt, HOKE
[260], 158 ff.

[90] *Diss. apolog.*, sect. 6, nr. 5 = *Jus publ.*, Add. 1. Bd., zu I, 10, p. 96: «Volun-
tatem status liber habet, quae formam regiminis pro libitu sibi eligere potest,
quam voluerit.»

[91] Vgl. HOKE [260], 169 ff.

schen Reiches Deutscher Nation ein.[92] Die Interpretationen der Reichsverfassung, die diese einseitig entweder als eine aristokratische, wie es durch Bodin geschieht, oder als eine monarchische deuten, welche Richtung in Reinking ihren Hauptvertreter hat, lehnt er ab. Als er hier gegen Bodin Stellung nimmt, wirft er diesem vor, er sei zu seiner Einschätzung des Reiches als Aristokratie deshalb gekommen, weil er die Rechtsstellung des Kaisers nur teilweise berücksichtigt habe.[93] Limnaeus sieht die der Wirklichkeit Rechnung tragende Deutung der Reichsverfassung in der Synthese der beiden Auffassungen, deren Protagonisten Bodin und Reinking sind. Er stellt diesen beiden Gelehrten und ihren Anhängern seine Auffassung entgegen: «Illis autem omnibus calculum nostrum subducimus, Imperiumque mixtum ex monarchia et aristocratia arbitramur».[94] Dabei tritt nach seiner Ansicht das aristokratische Element gegenüber dem monarchischen stärker in Erscheinung. Diese zweite Hauptlehre des Limnaeus vom *status mixtus* des Reiches findet ihre Bestätigung in den ihr zuzuordnenden Teilen seiner Dogmatik des Reichsstaatsrechts, in denen er darlegt, welche Kompetenzen im Reich dem Kaiser nur gemeinschaftlich mit den Reichsständen oder mit den Kurfürsten zustehen und welche allein.[95] Für seine Ansicht vom Überwiegen des aristokratischen Elements in der Reichsverfassung will er aber auf die zusätzliche Stütze, die ihm die Autorität Bodins hier bieten kann, nicht verzichten. Allerdings ohne Bodin beim Namen zu nennen, jedoch eindeutig auf ihn gemünzt, weist er darauf hin, daß nur, weil in der Reichsverfassung das aristokratische Element ganz offensichtlich überwiegt, gewisse Autoren, die diese Verfassung nicht zur Gänze kannten, zu der Anschauung gelangt sind, es handele sich dabei um eine rein aristokratische. Wenn das monarchische Element stärker wäre, dann hätte dieser Eindruck nie entstehen können.[96]

IV

Am Beispiel zweier Juristen aus der ersten Hälfte des 17. Jahrhunderts, von denen jeder für eine der beiden großen gegensätzlichen Richtungen in der jungen deutschen Reichsstaatsrechtslehre repräsentativ war, hat die Untersuchung folgendes Resultat ergeben: Die Bodinsche Staatstheorie

---

[92] Vgl. Hoke [260], 171 ff.

[93] *Jus publ.*, I, 10, nr. 39: «Ut plane hinc inciviliter Bodinum, non toto statu et jure Imperatorio inspecto, sed una particula proposita judicasse pateat, Imperium nostrum puram esse aristocratiam.»

[94] *Jus publ.* I, 10, nr. 12.

[95] Zur Kompetenzlehre des Limnaeus s. Hoke [260], 175 ff.

[96] Vgl. *Jus publ.*, Add. 2. Bd., zu I, 10, p. 156.

war in jener Zeit geistiger Besitz der Reichsjuristen, dessen Erwerb, wie die Äußerung des einen von ihnen annehmen läßt, sogar zum juristischen Studienprogramm gehörte. Die Autorität, die der französische Staatstheoretiker selbst bei einem wissenschaftlichen Gegner wie Limnaeus genoß, war so groß, daß auch dieser, wo immer er nur konnte, sich auf ihn berief, um damit seine eigenen Auffassungen zu stützen. Für den anderen deutschen Gelehrten, Reinking, war der Bodinsche Souveränitätsbegriff bereits zum Axiom geworden. Wie Bodin verstand Reinking die Souveränität als Herrschersouveränität, noch stärker sogar als jener, schon in der Theorie als Fürstensouveränität. Limnaeus dagegen lehnte, in der Tradition der zuletzt von Althusius formulierten Doktrin von der Souveränität des staatlich organisierten Volkes stehend, die Bodinsche Herrschersouveränität ab. Nichtsdestoweniger ist die Souveränitätslehre Bodins ein maßgeblicher Faktor für die Ausbildung der Staatssouveränitätslehre des Limnaeus gewesen. In seinen Büchern über den Staat hat sich Bodin mit der deutschen Reichsverfassung besonders eingehend beschäftigt.[97] Da konnte es bei dem Gewicht seines Wortes gar nicht ausbleiben, daß Reinking wie Limnaeus in den reichsverfassungsrechtlichen Kernfragen, zu denen er Stellung genommen hatte, genötigt waren, ihre eigene Meinung in einer Auseinandersetzung mit Bodin zu entwickeln. Das gilt für Reinkings gegen Bodin verteidigte These vom monarchischen Charakter der Reichsverfassung ebenso wie für die von Limnaeus mittels einer Synthese beider Lehrmeinungen aufgestellte Doktrin von der gemischten Verfassung des Reiches. Reinking hat sich dabei allerdings auch die Diskussionsweise völlig durch Bodin aufdrängen lassen. Das Beispiel beider Autoren jedoch zeigt, daß die Thematik der jungen deutschen Reichsstaatsrechtswissenschaft weitgehend durch den französischen Staatstheoretiker bestimmt war.

---

[97] Vgl. auch SCHUBERT [264], 23 ff.

Kenneth D. McRae

Bodin and the Development of Empirical Political Science

I

Broadly speaking, one can study Bodin from the standpoint either of specific concepts or of methodological contributions to various disciplines. It seems a fair comment that up to now the bulk of scholarly interest in Bodin has focussed upon concepts, upon his views of sovereignty, natural law, climate, religious toleration, and so on. The present conference – to judge from the preliminary list of topics – appears to lean in the same direction. Of course there are a few substantial exceptions in the literature,[1] but these have emphasized primarily his contributions to the methodology of history and law. His contribution to the development of the discipline of political science has so far attracted rather little attention. Nevertheless, there would appear to be a fairly widely held view – at least in North American universities – that Machiavelli and Bodin are to be reckoned among the founders of «modern» political science. This paper will probe for the basis for this rather vague view.

The methodological contributions of Machiavelli are identified easily enough, and in my opinion they overshadow any of his conceptual innovations. To put the matter in its simplest form, Machiavelli separated his observations on political power from the considerations of morality traditionally associated with it by his predecessors. This divorce between politics and morality was a giant step in the evolution of Western political inquiry, but it should not overshadow the fact that in other respects Machiavelli's methodology reveals notable weaknesses. There is, indeed, very little formal scientific method to Machiavelli's writings; rather they are the fascinating product of his acute observation of human conduct based on half a lifetime of challenging diplomatic work. Even his use of

---

[1] I am thinking particularly of the studies by J. MOREAU-REIBEL [116], Jean Bodin et le droit public comparé dans ses rapports avec la philosophie de l'histoire, Paris 1933; J. L. BROWN [141], The Methodus ad facilem historiarum cognitionem of Jean Bodin, Washington 1939; and J. H. FRANKLIN [226], Jean Bodin and the Sixteenth-Century Revolution in the Methodology of Law and History, New York and London 1963.

Roman history in the *Discourses* serves mainly to illustrate insights into human nature that were derived as much from his own diplomatic experience as from his perusal of classical authors. All in all, Machiavelli is one of the least methodologically oriented of all the political thinkers of first rank.

My concern here, however, is not with Machiavelli but with Bodin, and more particularly with his methodology of political inquiry. Of course some of the theory text books, while recognizing Bodin's central position as the first major theorist of the modern nation-state, do not comment on his methodology at all. Others, while recognizing that there are methodological aspects – after all, any book as formidable to read as the *République* must have *some* contribution to make to the methodological debate – retreat into simple generalizations about the comparative method of politics, or Bodin's encyclopedic mind, or the dull repetitiveness of his style. Despite the inadequacy of most of the textbook comments, there is a real theme here that is worthy of exploration. What exactly *was* Bodin's technique of political inquiry? To what degree was it an improvement over that of his contemporaries and predecessors? What were its limitations? These questions deserve to be explored, not only in the sixteenth-century context, but also from the standpoint of the longer-run development of political science as a branch of intellectual inquiry.

II

To understand Bodin's methodology, one must first consider the intellectual setting. First and foremost, he lived in an age of the explosion of knowledge, and this explosion had both historical and geographical dimensions. The rediscovery and printing of many works of antiquity, combined with the expansion of geographical horizons occasioned by travellers' accounts of distant and little known lands, opened up sweeping new vistas. European man in the sixteenth century came face to face with an enormous expansion of his intellectual horizons in relation to those of his mediaeval forebears, who had lived within the limits of a closed European civilization. It was a revolution not unlike that of our own lifetime – or perhaps of our children's lifetime – as we seriously contemplate for the first time the expansion of human activity beyond this small planet.

The Renaissance European mind, facing this apparently limitless horizon of strange civilizations and different customs, reacted instinctively and strongly with an attempt to reimpose order. The late Professor Mesnard, in his *Essor de la philosophie politique au seizième siècle,* has shown admirably the relationship between religious divisions and subsequent efforts to rebuild a new unity. In a wider sense I believe it can be shown that the first reaction to the unfolding diversity of intellectual horizons was to seek to synthesize anew, to rebuild the shattered systems of medieval thought on broader, stronger foundations. Bodin was in the forefront of this effort, but he did not work alone.

From roughly the mid-point of the sixteenth century, the synthesizers and system-builders had a ready philosophical instrument for their purpose in the logic of Peter Ramus. Elsewhere I have indicated how extensively Bodin was influenced by the Ramist methods of logical analysis,[2] and there is no need to review the evidence in detail here. Nor does space permit me to describe in full the basic procedures of Ramist logic. However, to state the central point briefly, I think it is evident that these Ramist foundations are a central component of Bodin's intellectual system, and that they accordingly constitute both strengths and weaknesses in Bodin's political methodology.

As is well known, Bodin developed in his early years a systematic approach to the whole of knowledge. The foundations are to be seen in his first major publication, in the opening pages of the *Methodus*. The materials of human history, fitted into a framework suggested by jurisprudence, are to form the basis for a science of man, or human history. But this was to be merely the first phase in a vast tripartite intellectual odyssey that would lead on towards a science of nature and eventually of things divine. The grand design embraced the whole of knowledge, and when we speak of Bodin's contribution to politics, law, history, or any other discipline, we must in some sense abstract that portion of his thought from the total system to which it belongs.

In the case of the *République*, where we find the core of Bodin's political thought, the more immediate setting also exerted some influence on the form of the work. Since the publication of the *Methodus* in 1566, France had seen four outbreaks of civil war, which helps to explain the vastly increased emphasis in the later work upon authority and stability. Similarly, the prescription for royal monarchy is less a universalist formula than the political remedy of the *Politiques* for the current ills of France. Besides, by this time Bodin was active at least in a minor way in the royal administration and clearly fascinated by the problems of political power. In all likelihood he was the shadowy «secrétaire nommé Bodin» who was implicated in the La Molle-Coconat plot while Charles IX lay dying in the spring of 1574. It is no coincidence that the year 1576, date of the first French edition of the *République*, marks the high tide of

---

[2] See Ramist Tendencies in the Thought of Jean Bodin, *Journal of the History of Ideas* 16 (1955), 306–323 [189], and also A Postcript on Bodin's Connections with Ramism, *Journal of the History of Ideas* 24 (1963) 569–571 [228].

Bodin's leaning towards a Machiavellian political realism,[3] and this tendency, which is contrary to some of the more lasting elements in his thought, was to recede a few years later when he retired from active public life.

It might even be argued that it is this more immediate setting of the *République* which is chiefly responsible for Bodin's special significance in the history of *political* thought. It was above all the crisis in France that focussed his attention on things political, and especially on the concept of authority. The *République* accordingly became a treatise directed towards the problems of political science, though somewhat overlaid with legal and sociological materials. What we might have had under more peaceable circumstances, had the earlier indications of the *Methodus* and the *Juris universi distributio* been followed more exactly, is an even larger sociological-legal treatise, the projected science of human society, of which the political elements would have been a smaller component.

III

It is against this general and special background that we must study Bodin's methodology of political science. Perhaps the first and most striking characteristic of this methodology is that it is synthesizing. Above all else, it strives to deal in universals. In the field of law Julian Franklin has shown how Bodin represents the culmination of the movement away from the authority of Roman Law towards the establishment of a universalist and comparative discipline.[4] Much the same can be said of his system of politics, though here it is not only the lawyers but the constitutional historians of France and other countries that constitute the point of departure. The great innovation of the theory of sovereignty is the development of a general definition of authority potentially applicable to all peoples, regardless of their form of state, degree of development, or climatic situation.

This universalist tendency can be viewed as the natural reaction of a generation that lived in the shadow of a lost medieval unity. But it also had specific roots in contemporary philosophy. The Ramist procedure – which rested on solid Aristotelian foundations despite Ramus' attacks on the Philosopher – was to move from simple definitions of the most

---

[3] For its expression in the *République*, see G. Cardascia [150], Machiavel et Jean Bodin, *Bibliothèque d'Humanisme et Renaissance*, 3 (1943), especially 151–167; and also *The Six Bookes of a Commonweale*, ed. K. D. McRae [7.44], Cambridge, Mass. 1962, A 37.

[4] Franklin [226], ch. 4.

general aspect of the matter under study, by divisions or dichotomies, to the study of its subordinate parts. It began from universals, and the mark of a true science in Ramist eyes was that its precepts be universally and necessarily true. Writing the Preface to the Latin version of the *République* in 1584, Bodin echoes the same idea: «For long ago in my youth I learned from the philosophers that common saying: that there is no science of individual things.»[5]

A second major feature of Ramism was its rejection of the precepts of the Schoolmen and its passionate concern to discover the real world. Ramists frequently emphasized that they were interested in «things», not «words». The real test of the validity of general definitions was their capacity to accommodate the facts of daily experience into the logical framework that they developed. There was, however, a weak spot in these procedures: the general definitions did not proceed from the individual data by a process of induction, but rather were formulated independently and prior to the consideration of detailed data. They then became the starting point for a deductive process that progressed by division from global concepts to the smallest components, which would be, hopefully, the raw, factual data of the real world. In all fairness, it should be noted that Ramus himself developed his system primarily as an expository technique, an educational reform, rather than as a scientific method in itself.

These two central aspects of the Ramists movement, its universalism and its concern with the «real» or day-to-day world, bring us to the heart of Bodin's problem as a political scientist. On the one hand he sought to develop a concept of authority and principles of government having universal validity, as the only basis for a true science. On the other hand, he embraced avidly the vast mass of empirical evidence that was opening up to the rapidly expanding intellectual world of his time. The complex adjustment of this vast mass of incredibly diverse data into his universalist framework is at once a central problem of Bodin's system of politics and a measure of his stature as a social scientist. It is also, be it noted, the source of his long-windedness.

The problems of reconciling empirical and conceptual elements can perhaps be seen best in relation to sovereignty itself. The first stage, in Book I, Chapter 8, is the presentation of a short, simple definition of sovereignty in conceptual terms. The bulk of this chapter and the following one then proceed to discuss some of the complexities that arise in applying the terms of this definition to concrete situations. Already Bodin is moving

---

[5] *The Six Bookes*, [7.44], A 73. The same idea is restated in relation to jurisprudence in the *Methodus*. See: Œuvres Philosophiques (ed. P. MESNARD), Vol. I, 107.

in an empirical direction, but the next stage is even more clearly so. In Chapter 10, he goes on to identify the characteristic «marks» or «rights» of sovereignty, and here he attempts to distinguish between those rights which are characteristic of one or a few sovereigns only and those which are universal – or almost universal. Unlike his definition, which was a great innovation, this kind of approach had been used by previous writers, usually for the discussion of individual countries, but Bodin has his criterion of universality clearly in view as he examines each right, and certain rights are excluded precisely because they do not satisfy this criterion.[6]

Thus for Bodin the formulation of universal definitions represents a first stage only in the construction of valid theory. The theoretical process includes the application of these definitions to the real world. Only when all the marginal, difficult or doubtful cases are satisfactorily disposed of is the job complete. This is of course completely in accordance with the tenets of Ramism.

In dealing with sovereignty the basic issue was to determine who ultimately exercised the various marks of sovereignty, with special emphasis on the first and foremost mark, the law-making power. The determination of this question in specific instances gave rise to a whole series of special problems. Some of these problems illustrate the transition between medieval and modern authority of the world in which Bodin lived. Others illustrate more aptly the special problems of his methodology, and it is these which are of interest here.

In the case of the German Empire Bodin had little difficulty in deciding that it was an aristocracy ruled by the Imperial Estates; it was almost policy for French writers to dispute the position of the Emperor as part of their assertion of the independence of the French monarchy. But there was a second question as to whether the Empire was one state or many, and here Bodin makes the comment that in times of internal strife among factions, the individual cities and principalities behave like so many aristocracies and monarchies, and every member itself becomes a sovereign state.[7] This remark is interesting. Although Bodin values stability, and although he does not elsewhere seriously criticize the Empire as unstable

---

[6] «Quant au droit des regales, il est bien propre aux Princes souverains qui en usent: mais d'autant qu'il y en a peu qui ayent ce droit, il ne doit pas estre mis au nombre des marques de Souveraineté.» *Les six Livres de la République*, 248; «Je laisse icy plusieurs menus droits, que les Princes souverains chacun en son pays pretend, qui ne sont point marques de Souveraineté qui doyvent estre propres à tous Princes souverains, privativement à tous autres seigneurs justiciers, magistrats, & subjects.» *République*, 250.

[7] «Et neantmoins quand il advient que l'Empire est divisé en factions & partialités, & les Princes bandés les uns contre les autres, ce qu'on a veu assez sou-

(as he does certain other countries), yet he clearly recognizes an important *de facto* change of sovereignty as taking place in times of stress. The analysis does not proceed further, but in this brief comment his concern for empirical reality becomes stronger than his sense of theoretical tidiness.

More elaborate difficulties arose in the case of Poland and the Scandinavian monarchies. In the original edition of the *Methodus,* Bodin qualifies all of them as monarchies. The second edition adds an interesting passage suggesting that Denmark and Poland might be considered aristocracies in view of some of the powers of the nobility.[8] The allocation of the marks of sovereignty is then taken up more carefully in the *République* and the new point is an emphasis on instability. Their classification as monarchies or aristocracies will vary from time to time according to the balance of political forces.[9] Further on, in analysing political change, he finds that these alternating periods of royal and aristocratic supremacy correspond to elective and hereditary phases of the kingship, the nobility gaining strength when an outside line is elected to the throne.[10] In his analysis of these northern countries, then, Bodin not only subordinates his constitutional and legal framework of analysis to the tracing of the real locus of power, but even offers explanations of why this locus changes, based on political history.

In some of his other examples, however, Bodin shows himself less flexible. In the cases of Venice and Rome he holds out forcibly against the notion of a mixed sovereignty, concluding after an analysis of the marks of sovereignty that Venice was an aristocracy and republican Rome a democracy. Where other writers had found elements of a mixed constitution in these states, Bodin found only institutions subordinate to the sovereign authority. In some instances he treats the exercise of various rights of sovereignty at Rome by these subordinate authorities as cases of delegation or tacit consent by the sovereign assembly of the *populus.* But at least twice, as in the case of magistrates exempting men from the laws, or the Senate's use of the power of life and death, Bodin associates himself with the dictum of Papinianus that one should be concerned not with

---

vent, alors l'estat municipal des villes, & jurisdiction subalterne des Princes, se trouve en plusieurs estats Aristocratiques & Monarchies particulieres: & de chacun membre se fait un corps particulier de Republique souveraine.» *République,* 326.

  [8] *Methodus,* 212.

  [9] «Nam regna Polonorum, Danorum, Suevorum, Norvegiorum cum incerta sunt ac paulo momento mutabilia, prout nobilitas principe, aut princeps nobilitate potentior sit . . .» *De republica libri sex,* s. l. 1591 [7.28], 207.

  [10] *République,* 539–540.

what was done at Rome but what ought to be done.[11] In these examples the empirical facts – which Bodin does not dispute – are clearly subordinated to constitutional norms.

The same normative tendencies can be traced requently enough in his consideration of the constitutional development of France. He admits that many of the marks of sovereignty, such as the powers of pardon, of issuing coinage, of determining weights and measures, and even of taxation, had been exercised by various feudal lords at various times. But there is never the slightest suggestion that sovereignty thereby changed. Bodin makes it quite clear that he regards these practices as illegal abuses. Furthermore, he insists that no prescription can run against the Crown, and no amount of successful usurpation can extinguish these rights of sovereignty.[12] In the discussion of France in particular the existential world recedes ignominiously before the exposition of received constitutional doctrine. We are back to the dictum of the lawyer Papinianus.

After considering the above examples we are in a better position to resolve a basic question raised by the late Professor C. H. McIlwain, namely, whether Bodin's sovereignty is a concept of legally constituted authority or of physical mastery.[13] McIlwain himself contends that Bodin's sovereignty, building upon the Roman legal tradition of *potestas,* is a concept of legally constituted authority. However, it is now possible to distinguish two distinct levels of analysis in Bodin. As a universal theorist – and this includes both his general definition of sovereignty and its elaboration as a group of distinguishing characteristics – Bodin is clearly thinking of a formally constituted authority. On this point the ambiguities of the French version are clarified in the Latin: *puissance* becomes the more explicit *potestas* and the *marques* of sovereignty become *jura.* However, as an avid observer of the real world, he shows a strong tendency – though not a consistent one – to look for the locus of real power.[14] Behind the more general conflict between universal theory and empirical inquiry, therefore, there lies a further unresolved conflict between a theory of constitutionally or legally constituted authority and an analysis of political power. In my opinion Bodin never really resolves this issue, but moves repeatedly from the one level of analysis to the other.

---

[11] «Non quid Romae fiat, sed quid fieri debeat, spectandum esse.» *De Republica* [7.28], 201, and repeated 210.

[12] *De Republica* [7.28], 216–222.

[13] C. H. McIlwain, Constitutionalism and the Changiig World, Cambridge 1939, 26 ff.; and also his Growth of Political Thought in the West, New York 1932, 132–133.

[14] Though some of the evidence that he cites in his quest for the location of sovereignty is of a rather formalistic or symbolic kind, for example, the arrangement of seals on treaties.

Furthermore, it is the continuing tension between universal concepts and empirical inquiry in his methodology which provides the clue as to why he does so.

So far we have looked only at Bodin's central concept of authority or sovereignty. It may be briefly noted, however, that the same conflict between universal principles and empirical exceptions to them may be found in other aspects of Bodin's political system. To cite one striking example only, the procedure of the fifth chapter of the *Methodus* is to construct a body of theory about national characteristics, the validity of which will rest upon the stable and immutable laws of nature, and this theoretical structure is then to serve as a criterion for evaluating the trustworthiness of various historians. In other words, if the theory, once established, conflicts with the testimony of any given historian, it is the testimony which is to be rejected, at least if there is testimony by others which coincides with theory.

IV

It is easy to point to deficiencies in Bodin's handling of empirical materials. It can hardly be disputed that his capacity for dispassionate analysis varies in proportion to distance from his own country and French interests. Reasons for this selective application of empirical technique may be seen clearly enough. In analysing France he was undoubtedly strongly influenced by the constitutionalism of his predecessors and contemporaries. His own delicate political position was also an important factor, and unconscious bias also appears from time to time. Beyond this we should remember the very strong programmatic elements in the *République*. It was not only a general treatise on politics but a political programme of the Politiques, a remedy for the contemporary crisis of authority in France. All these factors make serious inroads on Bodin's attempt at objective analysis of his world.

Yet all of these defects, visible as they are, should not blind us to Bodin's very substantial contribution to the empirical study of politics. Because of the Ramists' concern for the «real world», because of their preference for «things» over «words», the systematic collection and rational presentation of empirical data was recognized as part of the organization of knowledge. Although Bodin did not invent this methodology, but only absorbed it as part of his early education, he was the first to apply it systematically and extensively to the study of politics. Consequently, if Machiavelli first emphasized the importance of basing policy on how men behave instead of on how they ought to behave, Bodin made notable advances not only in seeking out this information systematically, but in integrating empirical data with his universalist framework.

In the last analysis, however, the two worlds of concepts and empirical data remain distinct. The young Bodin of the *Methodus* and *Distributio* appears to have expected his study of the laws and customs of all peoples to yield not only a universally valid scientific analysis of human society, but normative precepts as well,[15] so that the study of *leges* would yield an ultimate *jus*. By the time that he wrote the Latin version of the *République* in the 1580's, there are more frequent comments on the variability of human behaviour and values, as well as a recognition that the chasm between «is» and «ought» is unbridgeable.[16] In the light of his growing disillusionment with the prospects for a true science of human affairs, it is not surprising that he turned increasingly to natural science and religion in his closing years.

Yet even if Bodin ultimately failed in his attempt to integrate his universal concepts and the real world to the extent that his methodology required, the two remain linked with each other in a double relationship. For just as his political system reflects at many points the influence of empirical data gathered from all quarters of the Renaissance world, so also did his universal concepts in turn shape the subsequent development of that world. If he interpreted his evidence as to the location of sovereignty with a certain leaning towards the emerging nation-state and against older tendencies of universal empire and feudal particularism, so also did his concept of sovereignty help the transition to become complete. Bodin certainly shows bias in his handling of the empirical data of his own world, but it is a bias that has four centuries of later history ranged on its side.

---

[15] See the *Methodus*, 107. The idea is attributed to Plato but Bodin cites him with obvious approval.

[16] «For if anyone should wish to open the folded tablets of his own mind, he would learn at once that a good man is one who assists whom he can, and injures no one unless provoked by injustice. These things are not included in the laws of any nation. Indeed we see many destructive and ruinous commands and prohibitions, which no more deserve the name of laws than if a madman had decreed them of his own authority.» *The Six Bookes* [7.44], A 155; cf. also A 36–A 37. The passage quoted is from the Latin version (*De Republica* [7.28], 934); such remarks are scarcely to be found in any of the French editions.

Raymond Polin

L'Idée de République selon Jean Bodin

Dans la France de ce temps là, entre la mort de Henri II et l'avènement de Henri IV, l'autorité royale vacille et se désagrège. Les liens politiques se défont. Les troubles civils répondent aux luttes religieuses. Partout se développe l'insécurité des vies, des fonctions, des biens et des honneurs. Dans l'état de guerre endémique qui s'installe, chacun se fie de plus en plus à sa force, à son plaisir, à l'arbitraire, à la violence. Les Grands retrouvent des moeurs féodales. Les combats et leurs séquelles sont menés de façon cruelle: la justification de la terreur comme moyen de succès habitue à la pratique des pires atrocités. La misère grandit, dont Bodin témoigne, cependant que la concussion et le vol se répandent au grand jour. En même temps que les moeurs politiques, la moralité tombe dans tous les désordres de l'égoïsme sans foi, du caprice, de l'arbitraire. Les scandales ont cessé d'être considérés comme des scandales. Parfois on les voile en se prétendant disciple de Machiavel. En vérité, c'est une anarchie politique et morale qui tend à s'instaurer de toutes parts.

Elle fait écho à cet anabaptisme qui, à Münster, avait installé l'anarchie avec la prétention de pratiquer l'égalité absolue dans la liberté absolue, et qui n'avait abouti qu'à la débauche et au désordre avant de se trouver anéanti par des forces extérieures.

Cette dispersion et cette dissolution des institutions et des liens politiques, cet émiettement semblent conduire à la réapparition d'une sorte d'état de nature, où chacun aurait la liberté «de vivre à son plaisir, sans être commandé de personne»[1] de n'être «sujet, après Dieu à aucun homme vivant».[2] A bien des égards, c'est à la revendication et au renouveau de cette «liberté naturelle» que se rattachent les théories des droits de l'homme qui vont bientôt se développer et qui vont s'efforcer de démontrer que les droits inhérents à la nature de l'homme doivent former l'objet et le ciment des sociétés humaines.

Mais Jean Bodin sait de reste que «la pleine liberté que chacun a de vivre à son plaisir, sans être commandé de personne», se tourne bientôt en servitude. C'est pourquoi il combat si directement «ceux qui, sous voile d'une exemption de charges et liberté populaire, font rebeller les sujets

---

[1] *République*, Livre I, chap. 6, p. 68.
[2] *Rép.* I, 3, p. 19.

contre leurs Princes naturels, ouvrant la porte à une licencieuse anarchie, qui est pire que la plus forte tyrannie du monde.»[3] Contre cette dispersion, contre cet émiettement, contre cette licence anarchique, Bodin lutte en affirmant la nécessité humaine de l'ordre politique, d'un ordre commun, public, c'est-à-dire, d'une communauté politique, d'une chose publique, d'une République.

La *République,* la conservation de la République, voilà le vrai thème d'un livre bien nommé. On pouvait l'oublier quand «le navire de notre République avait en poupe le vent agréable et qu'on ne pensait qu'à jouir d'un repos ferme et assuré, avec toutes les farces et mascarades que peuvent imaginer les hommes fondus en toutes sortes de plaisirs. Mais, depuis que l'orage impétueux a tourmenté le vaisseau de notre République et que certains prendraient un singulier plaisir à son naufrage»,[4] il faut bien que les passagers viennent en aide au Patron et aux Pilotes. Les passagers, c'est, en particulier, Bodin, en son temps; n'est-ce pas aussi nous-mêmes aujourd'hui? La République, voilà le thème de Bodin et le nôtre.

I

Délibérément, Bodin s'inscrit dans la tradition classique qui fondait la communauté politique sur la poursuite du bien commun[5] . . . Dès les premiers mots de sa préface, il désigne d'emblée la fin de toute République: «réussir au bien de tous en général et de chacun en particulier»,[6] ce qui implique d'abord la conservation de la République elle-même. Nous n'insisterons pas sur la définition équilibrée, inspirée d'Aristote,[7] que Bodin donne de ce bien commun, dont la fin principale réside dans l'exercice des vertus éthiques et, par dessus tout, des vertus contemplatives. La réalisation de cette fin suppose, comme des conditions *sine qua non,* dans une République bien ordonnée, les actions politiques ordinaires, «la voie de justice, la garde et défense des sujets, les vivres et provisions nécessaires à l'entretènement d'iceux, non plus que l'homme ne peut vivre longuement, si l'âme est si fort ravie en contemplation, qu'on en perde le boire et le manger.»[8] Ce qui importe, c'est que ce bien soit commun.

---

[3] *Rép.* Préf. p. VII.

[4] *Rép.* Préf. p. Is.

[5] Aristote, *Politique,* III, IX, 1280 b 33. «L'Etat, c'est la communauté du bien-vivre, et pour les familles et pour les groupes de familles, en vue d'une vie parfaite qui se suffise à elle-même.»

[6] *Rép.* Préf., p. I.

[7] Aristote. *Politique,* VII, I à III.

[8] *Rép.* I, 1, p. 9.

Pour Bodin, ce bien est commun pour deux raisons: d'une part, pour une raison spécifique du politique, parce que «République est un droit gouvernement de plusieurs ménages et de ce qui leur est commun»,[9] par opposition au ménage «qui gouverne ce qui lui est propre»;[10] d'autre part, parce que «le souverain bien d'un particulier et de la République n'est qu'un.»[11] Le bien d'un particulier est inséparable du bien commun et ne peut être recherché sans lui. Bodin ne parle jamais d'individus, mais de sujets ou de citoyens. Et l'homme de bien est identifié au bon citoyen. C'est la communauté qui est la seule réalité concrète, même au niveau infra-politique du «ménage, droit gouvernement de plusieurs sujets, . . . et de ce qui lui est propre», de ce qui est propre au ménage, ce qui serait propre aux sujets n'étant évidement pas pris en considération.

Une communauté politique, une République, est un rassemblement de communautés, de ménages, et, en aucune façon, un rassemblement d'individus.

C'est pourquoi Bodin se montre si hostile à toute doctrine d'égalité parmi les hommes. L'erreur de l'égalité, c'est d'impliquer la détermination de réalités particulières, tenues, en tant que telles, pour égales: des hommes tous égaux et même, à la limite, tous semblables. En dépit de Platon, «il n'y eut jamais de République, soit vraie ou imaginaire, voire la plus populaire qu'on peut penser, où les citoyens soient égaux en tous droits et prérogatives, mais toujours les uns ont plus ou moins que les autres.»[12] On a eu bien tort de croire que l'égalité pouvait être tenue pour la «mère nourrice de paix et amitié».[13] Non seulement l'entreprise d'établir une société où règne une égalité absolue est impossible, mais une insuffisante inégalité est pernicieuse aux Républiques. A chaque fois, se sont détruites d'elles mêmes celles dans lesquelles on s'efforçait d'établir à un moment donné, une trop parfaite égalité des biens.[14] L'égalité n'entretient pas l'amitié, mais la jalousie et la haine, propices aux séditions et aux guerres civiles. Platon lui-même, dans sa *République*, a établi quatre classes de citoyens suivant le cens: pourquoi prôner alors l'égalité dans les droits politiques *(imperii aequationem)*? Il était moins absurde d'égaliser la richesse que le droit à la souveraineté, dont si peu d'hommes sont capables.[15]

---

[9] *Rép.* I, 1, p. 1.
[10] *Rép.* I, 2, p. 10.
[11] *Rép.* I, 1, p. 5.
[12] Méthode pour faciliter la connaissance de l'histoire, Paris, 1952, trad. Mesnard, chap. 412 A. (*Methodus ad facilem historiarum cognitionem*, Paris 1566) et *Rép.* L. VI, 47.
[13] *Rép.* V, 2, p. 702 et VI, 4, p. 938.
[14] *Rép.* V, 2, p. 704.
[15] *Meth.* VI, 412 B.

Certes, les excès de l'inégalité dans les conditions ou dans la richesse, forment, eux aussi, la cause de bien des haines, de bien des troubles et entraînent souvent la ruine des Républiques.[16] Mais le meilleur des Etats politiques se conserve par l'heureuse combinaison des inégalités. L'inégalité, la compensation des différences, est le meilleur ciment, quant à la solidité d'une République et à sa longue durée. «La différence des gouvernants, et des gouvernés, des maîtres et des serviteurs, des riches et des peuvres, des bons et des méchants, des forts et des faibles un certain mélange d'esprits opposés sert à maintenir la République ferme et inébranlable.»[17] Grâce aux classes supérieures et inférieures, et à un ordre intermédiaire, l'Etat trouve dans une heureuse combinaison des contraires un admirable accord.

Il en va de l'ordre de la République comme de l'ordre du monde, car il doit «imiter la nature, comme il est nécessaire». Le monde, œuvre admirable de Dieu, n'est-il pas composé de parties inégales et d'éléments qui se combattent entre eux à un haut degré? Les mouvements des astres ne sont-ils pas si nécessaires à le maintenir que sans cette discorde harmonique, tout périrait? Le sage Roi se doit conformer et gouverner son royaume à l'exemple de l'harmonie instituée par Dieu en ce monde, où toujours de justes milieux concilient les contraires.[18] La correspondance à établir, selon la justice et puisqu'il s'agit d'un droit gouvernement, entre l'ordre de la République et l'ordre du monde, montre à quel point la conception de la République est proche, chez Jean Bodin, de celle profondément inégalitaire, de la cité antique.

L'ordre de la République résulte, comme l'ordre du monde, d'une *«discorde harmonique»*. «Le discord donne grâce à l'harmonie.»[19] Cette expression révélatrice montre bien que la solidarité et la solidité qui résultent de la compensation des différences ne sont pas seulement le produit d'une complémentarité ou logique, ou physique, ni même le produit de l'assimilation et intégration de l'ordre politique à l'ordre universel. L'ordre de la République relève du même principe qui a présidé à la mise en ordre du monde, c'est-à-dire de la justice, qui est la loi de Dieu et de nature. Bodin fait, ainsi, la théorie d'une «justice harmonique» comme de la seule justice qui convienne à la République.[20]

La justice harmonique est, en effet, le principe de la discorde harmonique. La justice harmonique assure la concorde et l'amitié, donc l'ordre de la République, par la juste organisation des éléments complémentaires qui la composent. «Le riche roturier s'accorde mieux avec la pauvre damoiselle et le pauvre gentilhomme avec le riche roturier; et celui qui a

[16] *Rép.* V, 2, p. 702.
[17] *Meth.* VI, 412 B.
[18] *Rép.* VI, 6, p. 1059–1060.
[19] *Rép.* VI, 6, p. 1060.
[20] *Rép.* VI, 6, p. 1020/1.

quelque perfection d'esprit avec celle qui a la grâce du corps, que s'ils étaient égaux en tout et partout.»[21] Pour faire que la société soit bien assurée, un Prince habile doit assortir «doucement les nobles et les roturiers, les riches et les pauvres, avec telle discrétion toutefois que les nobles aient quelque avantage sur les roturiers. Car c'est bien la raison que le gentilhomme aussi excellent en armes ou aux lois comme le roturier soit préféré aux estats de judicature ou de la guerre: et que le riche égal en autre chose au pauvre soit aussi préféré aux estats qui ont plus d'honneur que de profit; et que le pauvre emporte les offices qui ont plus de profit que d'honneur: et tous deux seront contents: car celui qui est riche cherche l'honneur et le pauvre cherche le profit.»[22] Ainsi la République sera bien conservée.

II

On le voit, les fonctions de chacun sont attribuées en raison des services qu'il est capable de rendre et elles lui sont conférées par voie d'autorité. C'est l'obéissance, en effet, et l'obéissance plus encore que l'obligation, qui constitue, dans la République, le lien politique et le ressort de la conduite de chacun.

Certes «si la Justice est la fin de la loi, la loi, œuvre du Prince, le Prince est image de Dieu et il faut par même raison que la loi du Prince soit faite au modèle de la loi de Dieu.»[23] L'autorité souveraine a pour premier fondement la Justice, c'est-à-dire la loi de Dieu et de nature, et l'obéissance, pareillement. «C'est une loi divine et naturelle d'obéir aux édits et ordonnances de celui à qui Dieu a donné puissance sur nous.»[24]

Certes, autorité et obéissance ont pour second fondement la prise en considération «de tout ce qui touche à tous en général». C'est bien là le sort qui advient aux chefs de familles qui traitent et négocient les uns avec les autres, qui laissent là leur famille pour entrer en la Cité, et les affaires domestiques pour traiter les publiques.[25]

Mais la République, naissant de la violence et de la guerre, «la liberté naturelle que chacun avait auparavant de vivre à son plaisir est diminuée, pour ce qui regarde les vainqueurs, en ce qu'ils prêtent obéissance à leur chef souverain.»[26] «Et celui qui ne voulait quitter quelque chose de sa liberté pour vivre sous les lois et commandements d'autrui, la perdait du tout.» L'obéissance est une condition de liberté naturelle diminuée: elle est la condition des citoyens, «francs sujets tenant de la souveraineté

[21] *Rép.* VI, VI, 730.
[22] *Rép.* VI, 6, p. 1054.
[23] *Rép.* I, 8, p. 161.
[24] *Rép.* I, 8, p. 152.
[25] *Rép.* I, 6, p. 68.
[26] *Rép.* I, 6, p. 68/9.

d'autrui», «fidèles et loyaux sujets», ce n'est pas une condition d'esclave.
Il n'en reste pas moins que le premier ressort de l'obéissance réside dans
la contrainte exercée dans une situation de domination indéfiniment re-
nouvelée dans la République, née de l'assujettissement des uns par force
et violence des autres.[27] Les premiers Rois n'ont point été choisis pour
leur force et vertu, mais ils se sont imposés par la force et la ruse à l'o-
béïssance des autres. Et l'origine des Républiques, aux yeux de Bodin,
illustre clairement la nature de l'obéïssance que doit le sujet à son Prince
souverain.

Néanmoins, une République étant fondée sur la Justice, la contrainte
ne peut être le seul ressort de l'obéissance: la contrainte suffit à établir
des relations de maître à esclave, mais, d'homme à homme, «la servitude
est droitement contre nature».[28] Bodin la condamne sans réserves, aussi
bien sur le plan de la Justice que sur le plan de l'utilité. Il faut donc que
la contrainte soit assortie d'un second ressort, qui s'adjoigne à elle en la
justifiant. Ce second ressort, c'est la foi (au sens où les modernes parlent
par exemple de la foi jurée): «Les Républiques n'ont appui ni fondement
plus assuré que la foi, sans laquelle ni la justice ni société quelconque ne
peut être durable; or la foi gît aux promesses des conventions légitimes.»[29]

Le terme de «foi» est directement emprunté au vocabulaire féodal.
«Quand je dis foi et hommage, j'entends, écrit Bodin, le serment de fidélité, la submission, le service et devoir du vassal envers le seigneur.»[30]
Quels que soient les liens de soumission qui sont établis sur la foi, ils sont
fondés sur un serment et constituent un devoir, une obligation. En aucune
façon, l'idée de droit ne se trouve évoquée. Mais Bodin insiste sur la
double idée d'un service et d'un devoir garantis par un serment, en
échange d'un service rendu par le seigneur, qui est la terre allouée, le fief
ou la protection accordée. Le service réciproque qui concerne une conduite à tenir en échange de la jouissance actuelle d'un bien, s'appuie
naturellement sur la forme d'une promesse pour l'avenir et d'un engagement à quoi l'on s'oblige. Tant qu'il s'agit d'un lien féodal, comme celui
qui unit un Prince à un autre, le Prince tributaire, le Prince en protection
ou le Prince vassal pour quelque fief, ou même le simple vassal pour
quelque fief, tous ceux-ci ne doivent à leur Suzerain que le service et
hommage pour lequel ils ont prêté serment, une fois pour toutes.[31] C'est
un service bien déterminé, dont le vassal peut s'exempter en quittant son
fief sans fraude.

Au contraire, dans la République, il n'y a plus de Suzerain et de vassaux, mais un Souverain et des sujets. Foi et hommage, serment de fidélité

---

[27] *Rép.* I, 6, p. 68/9.   [30] *Rép.* I, 9, p. 162.
[28] *Rép.* I, 5, p. 49.   [31] *Rép.* I, 9, p. 162–163.
[29] *Rép.* V, II, 545. V, 2, p. 704.

et soumission subsistent, mais le sujet, quel qu'il soit, «est toujours tenu de prêter le serment, toutes et quantes fois qu'il plaira à son Prince souverain.»[32] «Chacun en particulier et tout le peuple en corps doit jurer de garder les lois et faire serment de fidélité au Monarque, qui ne doit serment qu'à Dieu.»[33] Ainsi le serment de chacun est redoublé par le serment du peuple en corps. Mais ce n'est pas d'un *pactum subjectionis,* qu'il s'agit, car, si l'obligation est réciproque, le serment est unilatéral, il va seulement du sujet au Souverain.[34]

En tant que sujet, le sujet ne doit pas seulement un service déterminé, il doit obéissance, c'est-à-dire tout service réclamé par son Prince Souverain, «réservée la majesté de Dieu, qui est Seigneur absolu de tous les Princes du monde.»[35] «Il n'y a que le sujet qui doit obéissance, et il ne peut s'exempter de la puissance de son Souverain sans son vouloir et consentement.» L'autorité du Souverain sur ses sujets est une autorité absolue, et il n'est pas licite aux sujets de contrevenir aux lois, sous voile d'honneur et de justice. Le sujet se trouve lié par une obligation irrévocable car elle se trouve inscrite dans la loi divine et naturelle qui prescrit aux sujets d'obéir aux lois de celui à qui Dieu a donné puissance sur eux. L'obligation politique répond à une loi naturelle et à une loi divine: c'est pourquoi elle s'exprime dans un serment, à travers lequel elle devient consciente d'elle-même. Ce serait donc un contre-sens de faire de l'obligation le résultat d'un libre consentement. N'est-ce pas d'ailleurs un principe de droit qui proclame *«nulla obligatio consistere potest, quae a voluntate promittentis statum capit.»*[36] Le franc sujet a renoncé à sa liberté naturelle: il n'est plus que le tenant de la souveraineté d'autrui. C'est dire qu'il est tenu irrévocablement par tout ce qu'il tient d'elle.

III

Les magistrats ont beau être les dépositaires provisoires d'un fragment de la puissance souveraine, en eux aussi, l'obéissance l'emporte sur la puissance. Ce sont, eux aussi, des sujets.

Leur pouvoir est tout entier composé de leur obéissance et de l'accomplissement de leur devoir, qu'il s'agisse de l'officier, c'est-à-dire de celui qui, en tant que personne publique, a charge ordinaire, limitée par édit, ou qu'il s'agisse du commissaire, c'est-à-dire de celui qui, en tant que personne publique, a reçu une charge extraordinaire, limitée par une simple commission.

---

[32] *Rép.* I, 9, p. 164.
[33] *Rép.* I, 8, p. 143.
[34] *Rép.* I, 8, p. 143.

[35] *Rép.* I, 8, p. 152.
[36] *Rép.* I, 8, p. 132.

Son devoir consiste dans l'obéissance au Souverain, mais, en tant que magistrat, il soutient «plusieurs personnes»; pour s'acquitter de sa charge, il faut qu'il sache comment «obéir au Souverain, ployer sous la puissance des Magistrats supérieurs à soi, honorer ses égaux, commander aux sujets, défendre les petits, faire tête aux grands et justice à tous.»[37]

Son devoir consiste, on peut tout aussi bien le dire, dans le commandement public, c'est-à-dire dans la puissance publique de contraindre ceux qui ne veuient pas obéir à ce qu'il enjoint ou ceux qui contreviennent à ses défenses.[38] Comme le dit Bodin d'étonnante façon: «le Magistrat est la vive loi.» La loi elle-même, elle, est muette. C'est-à-dire qu'en soi la loi est illusoire, si le magistrat n'intervient en son nom et dans ses limites, pour commander, défendre, permettre ou punir. «Toute la force des lois gît en ceux qui ont le commandement, soit le Prince Souverain, soit le Magistrat»,[39] puisqu'ils disposent seuls de la puissance publique, qui est une puissance de contraindre.

La puissance publique souveraine de commander est «absolue, infinie et par dessus des lois, les magistrats et les particuliers», tandis que la puissance des Magistrats «est légitime, sujette aux lois et au Souverain». C'est du Souverain que le Magistrat tient sa légitimité et ses lois.[40] C'est donc par rapport au Souverain qu'il est obligé, plus encore que par ses lois. Cette obligation est, comme telle, un devoir; elle n'est pas fonction de la puissance actuelle du Prince Souverain sur le Magistrat. Celui-ci y doit obéir, quand même les commandements du Prince iraient contre les lois civiles, puisqu'ils en tiennent lieu, voire contre le droit des gens, puisque celui-ci peut être changé et altéré par la loi civile, chaque fois que celle-ci concerne, non la justice naturelle, mais le profit et l'utilité publics.[41]

Bodin va plus loin encore et déclare que le Magistrat a pour devoir d'obéir à son Prince Souverain, même si celui-ci contrevient à son serment, lorsqu'il s'est obligé envers son peuple par serment, ou aux lois de la République. C'est donc un principe général que la Magistrat a pour devoir «de ne contrevenir aucunement à la volonté de son Prince, ès lois humaines auxquelles le Prince peut déroger.»[42] C'est tout juste si le Magistrat est en droit d'introduire quelques délais dans l'exécution des ordres reçus et de faire remontrance à son Souverain à la condition que l'urgence de l'action le permette.

En revanche, et c'est là la seule limite à son obligation d'obéir, «le Magistrat, pas plus que le sujet, n'est tenu d'obéir ou d'exécuter les mandements du Prince ès choses injustes et déshonnêtes, car, en ce cas, le Prince brise les bornes sacrées de la loi de Dieu et de nature, auxquelles tout

---

[37] *Rép.* III, 4, p. 409.
[38] *Rép.* III, 5, p. 429.
[39] *Rép.* III, 5, p. 430.

[40] *Rép.* III, 5, p. 431.
[41] *Rép.* III, 4, p. 414/5.
[42] *Rép.* III, 4, p. 415.

Prince est tenu par son devoir irrévocable».[43] «Il vaut mieux quitter l'Etat que d'obéir à choses qui soient contraires à la loi de nature.» Encore faut-il bien prendre garde à ne s'y décider que si la controverse peut être résolue de façon claire et aux yeux d'un nombre suffisant d'hommes sages et entendus.[44] Car toute désobéissance assumée dans la République introduit une situation pleine de périls; on risque de faire «une périlleuse ouverture à tous les sujets de refuser et rejeter les édits du Prince» et d'abandonner l'Etat dans le danger à la tempête. Car le but de toute politique doit être de conserver la République dans sa stabilité, sa prospérité et sa grandeur.

Une fois de plus, dans une communauté politique conçue comme un système de services et d'obligations assurés par l'obéissance et la contrainte, la Justice demeure le cadre transcendant qui garantit et légitime l'exécution des uns et des autres.

IV

Il n'est pas jusqu'au pouvoir absolu et infini du Souverain qui ne soit, lui aussi, encadré et limité par des obligations très strictes.

On a fait volontiers de Jean Bodin le fondateur le plus éminent de la théorie moderne de la souveraineté. On a été frappé à juste titre, par sa définition fameuse de la souveraineté comme «puissance absolue et perpétuelle d'une République»,[45] puissance que Bodin affirme infinie et irrévocable.[46] Elle ne comporte ni charge, ni condition,[47] sous peine de n'être pas proprement souveraineté ni puissance de donner lois à tous en général et chacun en particulier,[48] pouvoir de décréter la guerre et de traiter de la paix,[49] pouvoir d'instituer les principaux officiers,[50] droit de grâce,[51] droit de décider en dernier ressort.[52] Bodin prend bien soin de marquer que le souverain n'est pas obligé par les lois humaines:[53] un Prince qui jurerait de garder les lois ne serait pas un Prince Souverain.[54] Il ne saurait d'ailleurs y avoir d'édits perpétuels et irrévocables.[55] Tout au contraire, le Prince peut changer les lois pour des raisons de justice, d'honneur et de profit.[56] Il n'est pas tenu à prêter de serments vis à vis de ses vassaux ou de ses sujets.[57]

---

[43] *Rép.* III, 4, p. 414.
[44] *Rép.* III, 4. pp. 416–418.
[45] *Rép.* I, 8, p. 122.
[46] *Rép.* I, VIII, 129–130.
[47] *Rép.* I, X.
[48] *Rép.* I, 10, p. 221.
[49] *Rép.* I, 10, p. 224.
[50] *Rép.* I, 10, p. 228.

[51] *Rép.* I, 10, p. 236.
[52] *Rép.* I, 10, p. 231.
[53] *Rép.* I, 8, p. 152.
[54] *Rép.* I, 8, p. 144 et 154.
[55] *Rép.* I, 8, p. 145.
[56] *Rép.* I, 8, p. 150/1.
[57] *Rép.* I, 8, p. 143.

La théorie de Bodin culmine dans l'idée que «le Prince ne se peut lier les mains, ores quand il le voudrait»:[58] ce qui revient à dire que son droit souverain est, avant la lettre, un droit inaliénable. (N'est-ce pas en usant de cette formule que l'on expliquera, un siècle plus tard, que la liberté est, pour tout homme, cette fois, un droit inaliénable?) Bodin est ainsi amené à faire de la formule «car tel est notre bon plaisir» la maxime de la puissance souveraine: ce qu'elle veut dire, en effet, c'est que la décision du Souverain n'a pas besoin d'être justifiée pour être légitime. Elle est légitime parce qu'elle est la décision du Souverain. «Les lois du Souverain ores qu'elles fussent fondées en bonne et vive raison, néanmoins, elles ne dépendent que de sa pure et franche volonté.»[59] C'est à ce prix seulement que le Souverain peut légitimement et inconditionellement décider en dernier ressort, ses décisions échappant radicalement à toute contestation, puisqu'elles n'ont besoin d'aucune justification, d'aucune argumentation, d'aucune preuve pour être légitimes et suffisantes.

Néanmoins, le primat de la Justice est si fort dans la pensée de Bodin et la nécessité de maintenir un ordre juste est si évidente à ses yeux que cette puissance parfaitement absolue ne s'exerce jamais que dans le cadre des obligations qui lui sont inhérentes. Le Prince, en devenant le Souverain, n'en reste pas moins le sujet de la Divinité et reste soumis à la loi naturelle et divine. En aucun cas, il n'est admissible qu'il l'enfreigne, et il n'en saurait avoir l'occasion, puisque c'est la loi de nature et de Dieu qui lui confère sa puissance en même temps qu'elle la règle.[60] Il peut tout faire, pourvu qu'il ne fasse rien contre la loi de Dieu. Et Bodin formule

---

[58] *Rép.* I, 8, p. 132.

[59] *Rép.* I, 8, p. 133.

Peut-être faut-il saisir l'occasion de cette formule «Cat tel est notre bon plaisir» pour lever un préjugé courant sur l'idée de «pouvoir absolu». Il faut éviter de confondre «pouvoir absolu» et «pouvoir arbitraire».

L'idée de pouvoir absolu n'exclut pas, en effet, celle de lois fondamentales. Car le pouvoir absolu peut être un pouvoir limité, comme chez Bodin. Les lois fondamentales servent alors de limites et de conditions au pouvoir du Souverain. Mais elles ne fondent pas sa légitimité, ni la légitimité de ses décisions souveraines. Une décision du Souverain est légitime parce qu'elle est absolue, *ab-soluta*, séparée de tout fondement extérieur au Souverain, parce qu'elle trouve son uniquement fondement dans la volonté du Souverain qui, dans la communauté, s'exerce en dernier ressort.

Je suis bien d'accord avec M. Michel Villey, qui rapproche la formule «Car tel est notre bon plaisir» du *Placuit* du droit romain qui marque que, les parties entendues, l'Empereur prend en dernier ressort sa décision et sa responsabilité.

De même chez Hobbes, le pouvoir absolu répond à des calculs rationnels et s'exerce, s'il est absolu, conformément à la raison (Cf. notre Politique et Philosophie chez Hobbes, 74 et 245).

[60] *Rép.* I, 8, p. 152.

ainsi la règle de son action: «si la justice, image de Dieu, est la fin de la loi, la loi, œuvre du Prince, le Prince est image de Dieu; il faut par suite de même raison que la loi du Prince soit faite au modèle de la loi de Dieu.»[61] Cette obligation est universelle et irrévocable.

La loi naturelle et de Dieu est la loi à laquelle tous Rois et Princes sont sujets,[62] et «il n'est pas en leur pouvoir d'y contrevenir, s'ils ne veulent pas être coupables de lèse-Majesté divine, faisant guerre à Dieu sous la grandeur duquel tous les Monarques du monde doivent faire joug et baisser la tête en toute crainte et révérence.» Il y a dans la toute puissance du Souverain une sorte de perfection comme dans la toute puissance de Dieu, qui permet à Bodin d'affirmer que «c'est une incongruité en droit de dire que le Prince peut quelque chose qui ne soit honnête.»[63] Il ne faut pas oublier que voler et mal faire, ce n'est pas puissance, mais impuissance, faiblesse et lâcheté de cœur. En ce sens, le Prince ne peut rien qui soit injuste. «Son pouvoir doit toujours être mesuré au pied de justice.»

Certains ont estimé qu'en marquant ainsi la subordination du Prince Souverain à la loi naturelle et divine, Bodin n'avait lié celui-ci que d'une obligation toute théorétique et sans efficace. Certes, le Souverain est le seul dans la République sur lequel ne pèse aucune contrainte temporelle engendrée par la loi des hommes. Mais quelle contrainte légale pourrait peser sur un Prince disposant d'une souveraineté indivisible? En revanche, quelle menace plus redoutable peut être dirigée contre le Souverain que l'affirmation de l'illégitimité de son pouvoir et la constatation qu'il se trouve déchu de sa souveraineté? Le Prince qui franchit et brise les bornes sacrées de la loi de Dieu et de nature fait contre le devoir du Prince. Or, déclare Bodin, «celui perd le titre et l'honneur de Prince qui fait contre le devoir de Prince.»[64] Bodin n'hésite même pas à user d'un argument sophistique et à proclamer qu'on ne trouvera pas de Prince si mal appris, qu'il voulût commander choses contre loi de Dieu et de nature, puisque le Prince qui le fait cesse de l'être par là même. Sophisme mis à part, il n'en reste pas moins que le Souverain se trouverait dans le plus extrême péril le jour où ses sujets se trouveraient ainsi déliés de leur foi et de leur serment d'obéissance. La République ne peut être durablement conservée par la contrainte seule et sans la foi.

L'obligation et soumission du Prince Souverain à la loi naturelle et divine est la première des obligations du Souverain. Elle n'est pas la seule, mais elle est le principe de toutes les autres.

---

[61] *Rép.* I, 8, p. 162.

[62] *Rép.* I, 8, pp. 133 et 156.

[63] *Rép.* I, 8, p. 156. Hobbes retrouvera plus tard la même argumentation. Cf. notre étude Justice et Raison chez Hobbes, *Rivista critica di Storia della filosofia*, 1962, p. 467.

[64] *Rép.* III, 4, p. 414.

Elle sert en particulier de principe à la théorie du serment. On sait que, dans la relation du vassal au Suzerain l'obligation est réciproque, mais le serment est le fait du seul vassal.[65] Il en va de même, *a fortiori*, dans la relation de sujet à Souverain. Il n'empêche que le Souverain peut s'engager par serment, même envers ses sujets; que cette convention est mutuelle et qu'elle lie les deux parties et les oblige réciproquement.[66] L'une des parties ne peut y contrevenir au préjudice de l'autre et sans son consentement. «Le Prince, en ce cas, n'a rien par-dessus le sujet.» Il s'ensuit que le Souverain est en mesure de contracter et que ses contrats, qui sont valides, l'obligent, tout comme l'autre partie contractante. «Le Prince Souverain est tenu aux contrats par lui faits»,[67] bien qu'ils ne soient que de droit civil et non de droit naturel. Le Souverain est garant des conventions passées entre ses sujets. A plus forte raison est-il «débiteur de justice» de son fait. Le Souverain est obligé par ses contrats, cela est juste et raisonnable, alors qu'il n'est pas obligé, nous le savons, par ses lois. Et, de plus il a intérêt à ce que sa parole soit crue et considérée «comme un oracle».

C'est pourquoi Bodin approuve sans réserve, par exemple, le serment prêté par les Rois de France au moment de leur sacre. Voici le texte de l'un d'eux: «je jure au nom de Dieu tout puissant et promets de gouverner bien et dûment les sujets commis en ma garde, et de faire en tout mon pouvoir jugement, justice et miséricorde.»[68] Ce n'est en aucune façon un contrat social, mais c'est le type d'un serment qui, par son existence même, par l'invocation de la divinité et de la justice qu'il comporte, rend possible et valide l'engagement du Prince Souverain et constitue ainsi le principe d'un système d'obligations positives, essentielles à la conservation de la République.

Quant aux «lois qui concernent l'état du royaume et de l'établissement d'icelui», c'est-à-dire, quant aux lois fondamentales de la République, même si le Souverain ne s'y engage pas par serment, il est tenu, selon Bodin, de les respecter; il ne peut les modifier selon son bon plaisir. Elles sont situées au-dessus de son pouvoir, elles l'obligent. Le Prince n'y peut déroger. Telle est la loi salique dans le Royaume de France.[69] Bodin n'en donne pas davantage de raisons, mais on les voit bien s'imposer d'elles-mêmes: l'avènement de chaque nouveau Prince Souverain ne peut s'accompagner de la reprise à zéro de toute la législation positive. La tâche conservatrice du Souverain n'a de chances d'efficacité que si elle s'insère dans la continuité de la République. Celle-ci s'exprime, par excellence, dans les règles qui président à la transmission des pouvoirs souverains et qui sont

---

[65] *Rép.* I, 8, p. 143.
[66] *Rép.* I, 8, p. 133.
[67] *Rép.* I, 8, p. 152/3.

[68] *Rép.* I, 8, p. 136.
[69] *Meth.* VI, 403 B.

beaucoup moins des lois que des coutumes, rendues sacrées et efficaces par leur usage et leur pérennisation. Ces coutumes fondamentales imposent au Souverain des obligations que les lois positives ne sont pas capables, en tant que telles, de lui imposer. C'est le but même de la République, c'est-à-dire sa propre conservation, qui oblige le Souverain et fait de lui-même le moyen propre de son accomplissement. Pour se conserver, il doit conserver.

A cet égard, il est remarquable que Bodin impose au pouvoir souverain une dernière catégorie d'obligations, celles qui respectent la propriété privée aussi bien que la propriété publique. Il est clair que pour lui, la propriété privée est primordiale, antérieure à la République et intégralement de droit naturel. Il fait remarquer qu'il n'y a de République, de «chose publique» qu'à la condition qu'il y ait des «choses privées».[70] La République est elle-même le gouvernement de plusieurs ménages qui, par définition, ont, chacun pour eux-mêmes, à gouverner «ce qui leur est propre». La «communauté de toutes choses ‹serait› impossible et incompatible avec le droit des familles.» En condamnant la confusion du *tien* et du *mien* Bodin condamne non seulement Platon qui avait voulu que tous les biens fussent communs «en sa première République», mais aussi toutes les tentatives communautaires. La dernière en date, celle des anabaptistes de Münster, l'avait empli d'horreur. Loin de contribuer à l'amour réciproque des citoyens, la communauté des biens engendre la haine et la discorde. «La nature d'amour est telle que plus elle est commune, et moins a de vigueur.»[71] L'amour épars à toute personne et à toute chose perd sa force et sa vertu. Il retrouve toute sa force et toute sa vertu de lien social au sein des familles, et dans la jouissance de ce qui leur est propre. La propriété privée des biens est non pas le but, comme Locke le dira plus tard, mais la condition d'existence de la communauté politique.

«Les Républiques sont aussi ordonnées de Dieu, pour rendre à la République ce qui est public et à chacun ce qui est propre.»[72] «Il s'ensuit qu'il n'est au pouvoir de Prince au monde de lever impôt à son plaisir sur le peuple pas plus que de prendre le bien d'autrui.»[73] La levée de l'impôt doit être soumise au consentement du peuple. Quant au domaine public, qui est la source la plus stable des finances publiques, du temps de Bodin, il doit être, quant au fonds, tenu pour saint, sacré et inaliénable.[74] Ce sont là des obligations qui portent leurs sanctions avec elles car le Prince qui ne les honorerait pas risquerait fort de voir ruinés tous les moyens financiers de sa puissance et, par là sa puissance elle-même. Bodin n'hésite pas à en faire luire la menace, en révélant qu'il n'est pas de

---

[70] *Rép.* I, 2, p. 15.
[71] *Rép.* I, 2, p. 17.
[72] *Rép.* I, 2, p. 15.
[73] *Rép.* I, 8, p. 140.
[74] *Rép.* VI, 2, p. 857.

causes plus fréquentes de sédition que la charge des impôts et le mauvais usage des biens publics.

De quelque côté que l'on considère son pouvoir, on voit bien que le Prince Souverain a autant d'obligation qu'il a de puissance et que sa puissance est, en vérité, fonction de son obligation, au plan du droit aussi bien qu'au plan de la réalité.[75]

V

Et cependant, il s'agit d'une puissance souveraine, dont Bodin va répétant qu'elle est absolue, infinie, perpétuelle. Mais depuis trois siècles au contraire, on s'est évertué à nous apprendre à considérer qu'une République est un système de droits réciproquement compensés et consentis, n'ayant d'autre but que la sauvegarde des libertés, des pouvoirs et des biens de chacun, le bien commun n'étant rien d'autre que la somme des biens de tous. On nous a d'ailleurs aussi appris, subsidiairement, qu'un système d'obligations correspondantes sous-tendait ce système de droits et en assurait le respect. Et cette deuxième leçon, nous avons eu tendance à l'oublier le plus possible ou à la déformer, voire à nous en moquer.

Pour un peu, nous serions surpris d'entendre Bodin affirmer qu'une République n'est stable et capable de durer en paix et prospérité que si le bien commun l'emporte sur le bien des particuliers et si le bien des particuliers réside, non dans leur bonheur, mais dans leur vertu, et si la République tout entière est composée d'un système de services réciproques pourvoyant au bien commun, et redoublé d'un système d'obligations également réciproques. La justice qui préside à la durée et prospérité de la République de Bodin ne sert pas de principe à une exacte répartition de droits. Son principe réside dans la loi de nature et de Dieu, qui impose avant toute reconnaissance de droits, le système des obligations qui font de la République un ordre solidaire, solide et stable. C'est à ce prix que la République peut encore être un droit gouvernement, l'autorité publique fondée et assurée, la Justice harmonieusement réalisée.

Bodin avait trouvé, lui, «une forme de gouvernement qui mette la loi au dessus de l'homme». Mais nous, nous préférons proclamer indéfiniment, après Jean-Jacques, que c'est là «la quadrature du cercle»[76] et réclamer à

---

[75] Ajoutons que l'appréciation des obligations qui pèsent sur le Souverain ne sont pas laissées à sa discrétion. Bodin insiste sur la thérie des freins qu'il convient d'imposer à l'autorité royale, par exemple, en accordant aux magistrats des charges inamovibles (*Methodus,* VI, 405 B): «Plus on freine l'autorité du Prince (et il est difficile de dépasser sur ce point une juste limite) plus le pouvoir tendra vers la justice et vers la stabilité».

[76] J. J. Rousseau. *Lettre à Mirabeau,* 26 Juillet 1767.

tout les vents, à tous les nuages, «une forme d'association» par laquelle chacun s'unissant à tous n'obéisse pourtant qu'à lui-même et demeure aussi libre qu'auparavant.[77] N'avons-nous pas décidé, une fois pour toutes, de nous moquer, nous autres modernes, de ceux qui prétendent qu'il n'y a de libertés qu'autant qu'il y a des lois et qu'il n'y a des droits que parce qu'il y a des obligations? N'exigeons-nous pas de parler en termes de droit et non en termes de nature, en termes de désirs et non plus en termes de nécessité?

A moins qu'il ne convienne, malgré tout, de voir, dans le désordre de l'université et dans la dissolution des mœurs que nous subissons, dans la menace de l'anarchie généralisée, prodrome des pires tyrannies, qui pèse sur nous, le résultat de notre incompréhension et les premières conséquences de notre erreur.

---

[77] Rousseau. *Contrat social,* Livre I, chap. VI, éd. Halbwachs, p. 90.

J. H. M. Salmon

Bodin and the Monarchomachs

I. *Seventeenth-century Associations*

For a century after its first publication in 1576 Bodin's *Six Livres de la République* occurred in the marginalia of every notable political controversy. But it was not always cited to the same effect. During the turbulent events in mid-seventeenth century England, for example, Bodin's opinions were marshalled to support such a diverse collection of causes as the sovereignty of the Long Parliament, the prerogative of Stuart monarchy, the rights of the Cromwellian army against the parliament, the execution of Charles I, and the defence of Cromwell against the radical elements that had once supported him. In some instances Bodin's views were palpably distorted, and in many others they were set beside those of the Huguenot critics of absolute monarchy, the so-called monarchomachs, whom Bodin had ostensibly set out to refute.[1]

To find the *République* a bed-fellow with Hotman's *Francogallia*, Beza's *De Jure Magistratuum*, and Mornay's *Vindiciae contra Tyrannos* is less surprising than it might seem. Within a decade of Bodin's death in 1596 the great jurist Althusius had turned him upon his head, and assimilated his definition of sovereignty to the opposing doctrine of the sovereignty of the community. If sovereignty were to be supreme and indivisible, as Bodin had argued, then its only possible repository must be the whole community. Althusius quoted the monarchomachs in support of the proposition that the community had agreed upon certain fundamental laws as conditions under which the administration and exercise of the rights of sovereignty were entrusted to the ruler. Althusius could then suggest that, since Bodin had distinguished between the sovereignty of the kingdom and that of the ruler *(inter majestatem regni et regnantis)*, and since he had admitted the subordination of the ruler to the fundamental laws, he had meant to show the ruler had no proprietary claim to the sovereign rights he exercised. By such subtle inferences Althusius could conclude that Bodin's premises were really those of his opponents.[2]

---

[1] J. H. M. SALMON [201], The French Religious Wars in English Political Thought, Oxford, 1959, 83–106.

[2] SALMON [201], 40–50.

Other jurists within the Empire attempted to synthesize the opposing
theories that had emerged from the French Wars of Religion, but their
methods and conclusions differed from those of Althusius. The exponents
of double sovereignty postulated a balance between *majestas realis,*
reposing in the community, and the *majestas personalis* of the ruler.
Besoldus of Tübingen cited Althusius and another monarchomach, Lam-
bert Daneau, to demonstrate that the *leges imperii* were the fundamental
laws safeguarding a commonwealth against tyranny. Bodin's account of
the *leges imperii* as intrinsic to the sovereignty but beyond the reach of
the actual sovereign suggested to Besoldus that Bodin had circumscribed
the ruler's jurisdiction with a similar purpose in mind. Besoldus, however,
was as anxious to defend the rights of the ruler as he was to defend those
of the community, while another celebrated jurist, Arnisaeus, believed
that Bodin had made too many concessions to the monarchomachs.[3]

How is it possible that the ruler may be *legibus solutus* and yet limited
by constitutional law? How can a theory of legislative sovereignty, containing all the implications of interest of state, accept effective moral
restraint through principles of natural law? Modern discussion of such
issues in Bodin's thought has not always been aware that seventeenth
century commentators attempted to answer their own equivalent of these
questions by establishing the relationship between Bodin and the
monarchomachs. In the hope that the relationship may offer fresh insight
into Bodin's thinking, this paper sets out to discover where precisely he
refuted their ideas, and where, if anywhere, he stood with them upon
common ground.

II. The Prefaces to the République

Bodin's general purpose in writing the *République,* and his attitude to the
theorists of resistance, are set out in the various prefaces to the work. They
reveal a marked contrast to the views he had expressed in the sixth
chapter of his *Methodus ad facilem historiarum cognitionem,* which
served as a preliminary sketch for the *République.* The *Methodus* was
first published in 1566, and certain additional remarks in the revised
edition of early 1572 displayed Bodin's belief in the stability of the
French monarchy during the early phases of the religious wars. Bodin
declared that the imposition of peace amid such conflicts demonstrated
the splendour and prestige of French institutions and the magnanimity
of the race of Valois.[4] The *République* was composed after the massacre

---

[3] SALMON [201], 50–54.
[4] *Methodus ad facilem historiarum cognitionem,* cap. VI, p. 210.

of St. Bartholomew and in the course of a new war, where Catholic *politiques* fought beside the Huguenots against the crown. Bodin's view of the contemporary scene was entirely transformed. The first preface in the *République* proclaimed the book an anodyne for anarchy. It declared the impending wreck of the ship of state and suggested that, when the captain and crew were exhausted by the force of the storm, it was time for the passengers to lend a hand. «C'est pourquoy de ma part (Bodin wrote), ne pouvant rien mieux, j'ay entrepris le discours de la République.»[5]

This preface denounced two kinds of men who had «prophané les sacrez mysteres de la Philosophie Politique: chose qui a donné occasion de troubler et renverser de beaux estats.» The first were disciples of Machiavelli who supposedly extolled impiety and injustice. Although the second were critics of the Machiavellians, they constituted a more dangerous threat to the commonwealth. They were men «qui, soubs voile d'une exemption de charges et liberté populaire, font rebeller les suiets contre leurs princes naturels, ouvrant la porte à une licentieuse anarchie, qui est pire que la plus forte tyrannie du monde.» Bodin unquestionably had the Huguenot libels of the years 1573–1575 in mind when he wrote this passage, for the attack upon the Machiavellian policies of Catherine de Medici was an established theme in Huguenot literature well before Gentillet published his *Anti-Machiavel* in 1576.[6] Moreover, the phrases «exemption de charges» and «liberté populaire» were apt descriptions of the *De Jure Magistratuum* and the *Francogallia* in the eyes of a hostile critic. Bodin tempered his own asperity by remarking that such authors were moved by ignorance of affairs of state, rather than by malice. The purpose of the *République*, he declared in the preface, was to correct these dangerous errors.

In 1577 the *République* was republished at Geneva without Bodin's authority.[7] The editor, Claude de Juge, added a preface of his own to correct Bodin's errors of fact and interpretation. The first category concerned references to the Genevan constitution, its association with Berne, and the use of excommunication as a political weapon by the consistory.[8]

---

[5] *Les Six Livres de la République*, Préface à Monseigneur du Faur, Seigneur de Pibrac, Conseiller du Roy en son privé Conseil. (unpaginated).

[6] E.g. *Dialogi ab Eusebio Philadelpho – compositi*, «Edimburgi», 1574 (better known by its French title *Le Reveille-Matin des François*), Dialogue I, p. 98.

[7] G. CARDASCIA [135], Sur une édition genévoise de la République de Jean Bodin, *Humanisme et Renaissance* 4 (1937), 212–214; and M. REULOS [180], L'édition de 1577 de la République, *Bibliothèque d'humanisme et renaissance* 13 (1951), 342–354.

[8] *Les Six Livres de la République*, s.l. (Geneva) 1577 [7.3], Advertissement au lecteur (unpaginated).

The second kind of supposed error was said to be contained in the chapter of the *République* which discussed the question of resistance to a tyrant. There Bodin had advocated that the penalties stated in the *Lex Julia* for counselling the murder of a magistrate should be applied to those who, «par livres imprimez», suggested «les suiets peuvent iustement prendre les armes contre leur Prince tyran, et le faire mourir, en quelque sorte que ce soit.»[9] Bodin had claimed that both Calvin and Luther denied the legality of regicide or rebellion unless there was an indubitable command from God, as in the case of Jehu's divine mission to exterminate Jezebel and the race of Ahab. The author of the Genevan preface called upon Bodin to name the alleged works that counselled armed resistance and tyrannicide by private men. In fact the *Reveille-Matin* had suggested the latter remedy, but the *De Jure Magistratuum* had explicitly forbidden resistance to a tyrant with legitimate title by private citizens, and it had refused to discuss the question of a special divine mandate.[10]

The Genevan preface answered Bodin by quoting in full the celebrated penultimate paragraph in the fourth book of Calvin's *Institutes* where resistance to oppression was allowed through constituted ephoral authority, which, in contemporary terms, Calvin had cautiously designated as residing in «les trois estats quand ils sont assemblez». Calvin, the author argued, had said in his commentary on St. John XVIII,[11] that armed resistance was forbidden except where it was specifically permitted by «le droit public et les loix». Hence legitimate opposition to a tyrant need not await Jehu's divine summons. France was listed by Claude de Juge among a number of European states where institutions such as the estates existed for the very purpose of restraining tyrants. Bodin's terminology was vague and evasive. He was mistaken, too, about Luther, for if Bodin had read further in Sleidan's history, whence he had derived his information, he would have seen that Luther later acknowledged the possibility of resistance to the emperor under the provisions of the constitution.[11] The Genevan preface concluded by ridiculing Bodin's astrology, and defending past Huguenot armed action, not as conspiracy, but as an endeavour to deliver the king from those who had usurped his authority. The *République*, in the writer's opinion, consisted of a series of dubious speculations where Bodin had «manié à son plaisir les historiens et Iurisconsultes».

---

[9] *République* [7.3], II, 5, p. 389.

[10] *Dialogi ab Eusebio Philadelpho – compositi*, II, p. 67. *De Jure Magistratuum*, published with the *Vindiciae contra Tyrannos*, s.l. 1580, VI, p. 242. It may be noted that the *Vindiciae*, which, since it was not published until 1579, was not a target for the remarks in *République*, II, 5, was less cautious about a divine mandate (*Vindiciae*, II, pp. 59–64).

[11] Préface à Monseigneur du Faur etc. Cf. *République* [7.3], II, 5, p. 390.

Here, appended to a pirated edition of Bodin's own work, was a refutation of the very principles which he claimed had impelled him to compose it. Bodin responded with a second preface, published with the 1578 and subsequent editions.[12] His Paris publisher, Jacques du Puy, added a note of his own in which he indignantly assailed the commercial motives and professional antecedents of the Genevan editor.[13] Bodin's reply was far more moderate: indeed, it was wholly defensive. He had praised, he said, the very institutions which his Genevan critic professed to admire. He was amazed that it could be thought he had conceded too much to the authority of a single ruler. He had taken pains to dissociate himself from those who exalted the power of royal prerogative. The authority of kings was subjected in his book to divine and natural law. No king in a royal monarchy could impose taxes without the consent of his subjects, and he was as closely bound by his covenants as they. These, said Bodin, were principles he had always held, and he had made them manifest in his book. What he had opposed were doctrines which would have expelled princes under pretence of tyranny, and which taught that kings held their thrones not by hereditary right but by the choice of the people. These were the voices of anarchy the *République* had been intended to refute.[14] Bodin pointed out that he himself had lost the favour of the king by supporting the constitutional interests of the commonwealth at the Blois estates general of 1576.[15] He made no alteration to the text of *République* II, 5, which the Genevan preface had found objectionable, save to add the precise reference to Calvin's *Institutes* in the margin.[16] The remainder of his second preface was devoted to answering objections of a different kind from Cujas.

When Bodin withdrew to his office in Laon in 1584 he composed a third prefatory letter, which was to be published with the first Latin edition of the *République* in 1586.[17] Here he again referred to the political crisis and the need to dispel ignorance about affairs of state. He did not,

---

[12] *République*, Io. Bodinus Vido Fabro Curiae Parisiorum Praesidi (second preface to Du Faur – unpaginated).

[13] *République*, Iacques du Puys, Libraire, au lecteur (unpaginated).

[14] *République*, Second Preface. «Sed cum viderem ubique subditos in principes armari, libros etiam, veluti faces ad rerum publicarum incendia, palam proferri, quibus docemur principes, divinitus hominum generi tributos, tyrannidis obiecta specie de imperio deturbare: reges item non a stirpe, sed a populo arbitrio peti oportere: easque disciplinas, non solum huius imperii, verum etiam rerum omnium publicarum fundamenta labefactare.»

[15] Bodin also added an account of his role at the Blois estates to the text: *République* III, 7, pp. 485–486.

[16] *République* II, 5, p. 305.

[17] *The Six Bookes of a Commonweale*, ed. K. D. McRae [7.44], A 72.

however, mention the Protestant monarchomachs, whose ideological role was about to be assumed by the polemicists of the Catholic League. Instead, he concentrated upon the «incurable folly» that had beset the royal policies, and suggested, in apparent despair, that the realm had almost «withered away through its own antiquity». A few years later, when his office and security were threatened by the League's occupation of Laon, he was to sign the notorious statement in which he appeared to reverse all he had said in favour of absolute monarchy and to accept the now-Leaguer doctrine of popular sovereignty.[18]

III. The Estates, the Coronation Oath, and the Attributes of Sovereignty

If Bodin's prefaces are taken at face value, it would appear that he discerned in monarchomach thought something novel and subversive, and it was against this, rather than the «Machiavellian» lapses, the weakness and the folly of royal policies, that he directed the *République*. Yet the prefaces also reveal extreme caution. His reply to the Genevan attack was cast in the mould of conservative constitutionalism, and he refused the Genevan challenge to cite chapter and verse of the works he claimed to assail. Except for a brief reference to Hotman, who is not quoted in the capacity of the author of the *Francogallia*,[19] no monarchomach author is named throughout the entire text and the substantial marginal apparatus of the *République*. Nevertheless, it is possible to find certain passages and chapters where Bodin appears to answer his professed enemies directly. One such, the chapter on whether resistance to a legitimate tyrant was lawful, was identified by Claude de Juge. Some of the other instances involved a substantial modification, or even a contradiction, of views earlier expressed by Bodin in the sixth chapter of the *Methodus*. These examples have a particular significance, for it is possible to see in them how the novel elements in the *République* are developed in reaction to monarchomach ideas.

The first two examples occur in the chapter on sovereignty (I, 8), and are separated by a remark in which Bodin comes close to citing the title of the *De Jure Magistratuum*: «En quoy ceux qui ont escrit du devoir des

---

[18] J. MOREAU-REIBEL [124], Bodin et la Ligue d'après des lettres inédites, *Humanisme et Renaissance* 2 (1935) and S. BALDWIN [137], Jean Bodin and the League *Catholic Historical Review* 23 (1937/38).

[19] *République* III, 3, p. 402. Bodin cites Hotman's opinion that the Roman censors had *potestas* but not *imperium* as a contradiction in terms. The description of Hotman as «a most skilfull antiquary» in the English version is an addition by the translator, Knolles, and is not to be found in the original text (*The Six Bookes* [7.44], 304).

Magistrats, et autres livres semblables, se sont abusés de soustenir que les estats du peuple sont plus grands que le Prince: chose qui fait revolter les vrais subiects de l'obeissance qu'ils doyvent à leur Prince souverain.»[20] In the *Methodus* Bodin stated, quite unequivocally, not merely that the king was powerless to change fundamental law, but also that he required the consent of the estates to change long established national or provincial custom.[21] In the *République*, where, of course, the inviolability of the *leges imperii* was reaffirmed, Bodin argued that, although it was usual to obtain the consent of the estates for alterations to custom, the king need not do so and might reject the advice of the estates if natural reason and justice suggested such a course.[22]

Bodin's rejection of consent, and his diminution of the role of the estates, were the consequences of his new doctrine of sovereignty. If the king were subjected to the authority of the estates, the form of state was not a monarchy but an aristocracy. The possibility of shared authority was removed by the denial of the mixed form. If an English monarch used parliament, or a French king the court of parlement, to verify their edicts, this was merely to ensure the survival of the legislation after their death. It was the sovereign who convoked and dissolved the estates. They existed merely to provide subjects with an opportunity to present their humble requests. The only active role left to the estates (and this only by implication) was to give consent to taxation, and even here the king could dispense with consent in circumstances of necessity.[23] Bodin concluded that the sovereignty of the monarch, far from being diminished by the estates, was exalted by their presence, since it was then that his sovereignty was explicitly recognized.[24] There followed the well known passage where absolute legislative sovereignty was specifically defined to

---

[20] *République* I, 8, pp. 137–138.

[21] *Methodus* VI, 187. «Leges autem totius imperii proprias convellere princeps non potest, nec de moribus civitatum & antiqua consuetudine quicquam immutare, sine trium ordinum consensu.»

[22] *République* I, 8, p. 137. «Mais quant aux coustumes generales, & particulieres, qui ne concernent point l'establissment du royaume, on n'a pas accoustumé d'y rien changer, sinon apres avoir bien & deuement assemblé les trois estats de France en general, ou de chacun Bailliage en particulier: non pas qu'il soit necessaire de s'arrester à leur advis, ou que le Roy ne puisse faire le contraire de ce qu'on demandera, si la raison naturelle, & la iustice de son vouloir luy assiste.»

[23] *République* I, 8, p. 140, Another circumstance when the estates had an active role, according to Bodin, was when the king was a minor, insane, or a captive in a foreign war (*Rép.* I, 8, p. 138). This was not included, however, in the 1576 and Genevan editions (*République* [7.3], 205). It was a point constantly affirmed by the theorists of resistance.

[24] *République* I, 8, p. 141.

exclude consent: «Par ainsi on void que le poinct principal de la maiesté souveraine, & puissance absolue, gist principalement à donner loy aux subiects en general sans leur consentement.»[25]

In their view of the estates the monarchomach writers began with the ephoral argument of Calvin and depicted the institution in the essentially defensive role of protecting the fundamental laws against tyranny. This was not very different from the constitutional opinions of Claude de Seyssel's *Grand' Monarchie de France* (1519). The trend to give the estates a much more active part in government was noticeable in Beza's *De Jure Magistratuum*. He argued that the sovereign was subject to law, and it was the sovereignty, not the sovereign, that obliged inferior magistrates to enforce the law. In the event of manifest tyranny these magistrates should resist by force until the estates, who held supreme authority over the laws and government of the kingdom, should decide what had to be done.[26] The estates were the protectors of the rights of sovereignty. They could hold the sovereign to his duty and correct and punish him, if the need arose.[27] They appointed an administrator in a royal minority. They had the power to elect and depose kings, and, were it not so, Carolingian and Capetian kings must have held the crown unlawfully. The estates had once appointed the chief officers of the commonwealth, and should supervise the king's control of them. They could impose taxes, and all the great affairs of state in peace and war were their concern.[28] The old authority of the estates had gradually been attenuated, and in the time of Louis XI tyranny had supervened.[29]

---

[25] *Rép.* I, 8, p. 142.

[26] *De Jure Magistratuum*, 249–250. «Dico igitur si eo necessitatis fuerint adacti, reneri ipsos omnino adversus manifestam Tyrannidem salutem eorum procurare (etiam armata manu si possunt) qui ipsorum fidei & curae sunt traditi: tantisper dum ex communi, vel νομοφυλάκων (id est eorum penes quos est omnis legum Regni illius, aut imperii de quo agitur, authoritas) consilio, melius rebus publicis consultum sit, & ut decet provisum.»

[27] *De Jure Magistratuum*, 254: «Constituti sunt defensores ac protectores iurium ipsius supremae potestatis, ut summos Magistratus in officio retineant, eosque, si opus erit & coerceant, & mulctent.»

See also 286: «Ordines vero vel status Regionis quibus haec authoritas a legibus est collata eatenus sese tyranno opponere atque adeo ipsi iustas, & promeritas poenas, si opus erit, irrogare & possunt & debent, donec Res in pristinum statum restitutae sint.»

[28] *De Jure Magistratuum*, 281: «Porro quod attinet eorundem ordinum authoritatem, qua vel Regni praecipuas dignitates & officia conferebant, adimebantque: vel saltem sollicte animadvertebant, quomodo se reges tam in iis conferendis, adimentisve, quam in tributis exigendis, aut in aliis Regni praecipuis negotiis, quum belli tum pacis tempore gerent.»

[29] *De Jure Magistratuum*, 283.

Beza made explicit the lessons implied in Hotman's historical account of the role of the estates in the *Francogallia*. There the functions of the estates in early times were described as appointing and deposing kings, declaring war and peace, controlling public laws, distributing important offices of the kingdom, assigning appanages to the sons of a deceased king and dowries to his daughters, and, finally and in general, supervising all major affairs of state.[30] In his violent replies to his critics, Papire Masson and Antoine Matharel, Hotman vigorously repudiated the accusation that the *Francogallia* suggested a return to the election of kings by the estates – a practice which, he admitted, had been replaced by hereditary succession for the past six centuries. At the same time, Hotman clearly believed that the authority of the estates ought to be superior to that of the king, and quoted Seyssel to this effect.[31]

If Hotman hid his political opinions under the guise of antiquarianism in the *Francogallia* (though in fact his general reflections upon politics in that work often betrayed him), the *Reveille-Matin* proclaimed his book to be explicit proof of the rightful sovereignty of the estates.[32] *Summa rerum* lay not with the king but in the estates, from which the author of the second dialogue, like Hotman and Seyssel, excluded the clergy. The estates had deposed eight Merovingian and Carolingian kings and ought to depose Charles IX. In comparatively recent times they had been wrongfully deprived of their authority by ambitious ministers on the royal council and venal judges in the parlement. But prescription had no force against the rights of the community, as represented by the estates, and it was upon them that the election and authority of a king depended.[33] It is understandable that Bodin regarded such opinions as an advocacy of elective kingship and popular liberty, for they went far beyond the defensive, constitutionalist position, and, with the *Reveille-Matin* at least, seemed to support the active sovereignty of the estates. Hence Bodin applied his own definition of absolute sovereignty against this body of doctrine. and in so doing radically departed from his earlier, constitutionalist attitude.

The same conclusion may be drawn from a second specific change of front between the *Methodus* and the *République*. In the *Methodus* he expressed his admiration for the coronation oath, where the kings of France swore to do justice and thereafter were as closely held by the laws as were private citizens.[34] The monarchomachs repeatedly cited coronation oaths

---

[30] *Francogallia*, Cologne 1574, XI, p. 82.

[31] *Matagonis de Matagonibus – Monitoriale*, s.l. 1575, 13, 22, 59. *Strigilis Papirii Massoni*, s.l. 1578 (2nd ed.), 19.

[32] *Dialogi ab Eusebio Philadelpho – compositi*, II, pp. 88, 134.

[33] *Dialogi ab Eusebio Philadelpho – compositi*, II, pp. 65–66, 91, 135.

[34] *Methodus* VI, 187. «Formula quidem initiationis regum nostrorum, non

as express formulations of the conditions under which kings held authority. The *Reveille-Matin* recalled the oaths of David and Joshua. The latter's was depicted as a contract made with the people in the presence of God, and similar oaths were said to have been sworn by Christian kings in every age. That for the French monarchy could be found in the Frankish chronicle of Aimoin de Fleury. Should the king break his oath, as had Charles IX in ordering the massacre of his people, the community no longer owed obedience.[35] The *De Jure Magistratuum* quoted the fictitous oath of the kings of Aragon in a passage which stressed the supremacy of the cortes over the king, the conditional nature of royal authority, and the overriding powers of the Justicia. This, Beza stated, was indeed the way kings should be treated, and he went on to cite oaths sworn by the German emperors.[36] The fictitious Aragonese oath was also included in the *Francogallia,* where Hotman regarded it as evidence of the practice of all peoples who lived under legitimate monarchy to hold public councils and to preserve liberty.[37]

The authors of the *De Jure Magistratuum* and the *Francogallia* knew each other's books before either was published. Bodin noted references to coronation oaths, and especially to the Aragonese oath, in at least one of the two, and he seems to have used the French *Du Droit des Magistrats* for the text of the oath of Aragon which he reproduced in the *République.*[38] He cited it, of course, to refute the claim that the oath presupposed the election of kings: «En quoy s'est abusé celuy qui a escrit que le Roy estoit alors esleu du peuple, chose que jamais ne se fit.» In any event he had learnt from «un chevalier Espagnol» that the oath was no longer used.[39]

Bodin proceeded to undermine the monarchomach position, and also to contradict his own opinion in the *Methodus*. In the *De Jure Magistratuum* and the *Reveille-Matin* the oath was associated with a theory of contract. Bodin distinguished between the law of a sovereign prince

---

modo verborum & antiquitatis eximia specie, sed etiam pondere & gravitate sententiarum pulcherrima visa mihi est: in eo maxime, quod Princeps ante Pontifices per Deum immortalem jurat, se omnibus ordinibus, debitam legem ac justitiam redditurum: & quanta poterit integritate ac religione judicaturum. Neque vero juratus fidem violare facile potest, aut si possit, nolit tamen. Jus enim illi dicitur ut privato cuique, & iisdem legibus tenetur.»

[35] *Dialogi ab Eusebio Philadelpho – compositi,* II, pp. 62–63.

[36] *De Jure Magistratuum,* 276–277.

[37] *Francogallia* (1574) X, pp. 75–77.

On the use of the fictitious oath by Beza, Hotman and Bodin, see RALPH E. GIESEY, If Not, Not, Princeton 1968, 20–24, 220–222.

[38] GIESEY, If Not, Not, 221.

[39] *République* I, 8, pp. 129–130.

and the contracts to which he became a party. The laws were his commands, and they could not bind him since they depended upon his will. A contract did bind the king, but if the equity within it, of which the king was the sole interpreter, should lapse, he might reject it, and break his oath or promise. This Bodin illustrated from Aragonese history. Sovereign princes were never advised to swear to uphold the laws of their predecessors, for thereby they renounced sovereignty. A German emperor might so swear, but since the empire was an aristocracy he was not sovereign in any case. Some might advance other examples of royal oaths, such as those sworn by the kings of Epirus: «Ie dy que non obstant tous ces serments, le prince souverain peut deroger aux loix, ou icelles casser & annuler cessant la iustice d'icelles. Aussi le serment de nos Rois, qui est le plus beau, & le plus bref qui se peut faire, ne porte rien de garder les loix & coustumes du païs, ny des predecesseurs.» Bodin cited various forms of the French coronation oath to show that kings swore merely to do justice. Moreover, the ancient Hebrew kings had taken no oaths.[40] The argument and the examples chosen constituted a direct reply to the monarchomachs, and, once again, the case which Bodin presented was an application of his new doctrine of sovereignty. It is tempting to think that, when Hotman added to his 1586 Latin edition of the *Francogallia* several pages describing the role of the Aragonese *Justicia* in support of his view of the oath,[41] he did so to rebut Bodin's remarks on the subject in the *République*.

A third instance of a contradiction between the *Methodus* and the *République* concerns the definition of the attributes of sovereignty. Like the first two examples, the distinction is based upon Bodin's revised concept of sovereignty, but unlike them, there is no specific textual evidence that Bodin was simultaneously refuting the monarchomach ideas. The list which Bodin provided in the *Methodus* of the ways in which supreme authority could be exercised comprised: appointing the high magistrates and defining their office; ordaining and abrogating laws; declaring war and peace; hearing final appeals; and exercising the power of life and death.[42] The first three of these attributes were included in the list provided by Hotman in the 1573 edition of the *Francogallia* as having former-

---

[40] *Rép.* I, 8, pp. 133–136.

[41] *Francogallia*, Frankfort 1665, XII (ch. X of the first edition), pp. 148–156.

[42] *Methodus* VI, 175. «Video summam Reipublicae in quinque partibus versari. Una ac praecipua, in summis magistratibus creandis, & officio cujusque definiendo: altera in legibus jubendis aut abrogandis: tertia in bello indicendo ac finiendo: quarta in extrema provocatione ab omnibus magistratibus: postrema in potestate vitae ac necis, cum lex ipsa nec facilitatis ullum, nec clementiae locum relinquit.»

ly been included in the powers of the estates.[43] Hotman wished to repose
in the estates all, and more than all, the attributes which Bodin in the
Methodus confided in the king.

In the *République* Bodin referred to the practice of ancient and modern
writers (and it would not seem that he here had the monarchomachs in
mind) of composing long lists of regalian rights which they believed to
be marks of sovereignty. All these writers, Bodin declared, were mistaken.
Anything that was communicated by a sovereign prince to a subject was,
ipso facto, not an attribute of sovereignty. The rights of jurisdiction, the
appointment of magistrates, the infliction of penalities, the award of
honours, and the taking of counsel – none of these were marks of sovereignty. There was really only one attribute from which all others were
derived, the power to make law: «Sous ceste mesme puissance de donner
& casser la loy sont compris tous les autres droits & marques de souveraineté: de sorte qu'à parler proprement on peut dire qu'il n'y a que ceste
seule marque de souveraineté, attendu que tous les autres droits sont compris en cestuy là...»[44] Moreover, law made by the sovereign was superior to custom, which had binding force only in so far as the sovereign
was pleased to authorize it.[45]

In their tendency to give supreme authority to the estates, as representing the superiority of the kingdom as a whole over the king, the theorists
of resistance lacked Bodin's precise definition of legislative sovereignty.
They respected custom in its own right, and they believed that the exercise of authority ought to be shared. Hence the efficacy of Bodin's argument as a mine to destroy the defences of the monarchomachs. Through
the power to make law a sovereign prince was supreme in every aspect
of political authority. He could share this power with no one, nor was
he obliged to obtain consent, for if he did so he was no longer sovereign,
and the commonwealth no longer a monarchy.[46]

But Hotman, for one, remained unpersuaded. Just as he added the
passages of Aragonese history to the 1586 version of the *Francogallia,*
so, too, he added a new list of constitutional laws which had once limited

---

[43] See note 30.

[44] *République* I, 10, p. 223/4. The passage goes on to define the subordinate
attributes as follows: «Comme decerner la guerre, ou faire la paix; congnoistre
en dernier ressort des iugements de tous magistrats, instituer & destituer les plus
grands officiers: imposer ou exempter les subiects de charges & subsides: ottroyer
graces & despenses contre la rigueur des loix: hausser ou baisser le titre, valeur &
pied des monnoyes: faire iurer les subiects et hommes liges de garder fidelité sans
exception à celuy auquel est deu le serment –» These attributes are discussed in
detail in the remainder of the chapter.

[45] *Rép.* I, 10, p. 222.

[46] *Rép.* I, 10, p. 221.

the French crown. Nor were they all defensive, for the first declared that it was unlawful for the king to determine anything concerning the whole commonwealth without the authority of the estates. He now had reason to include the laws of hereditary succession, which, together with the inalienability of the domain (which he also cited), remained limitations on the sovereign accepted by Bodin. But he also added laws which seemed to answer the subordinate attributes of sovereignty listed in the *République*. These laws included the inability of the king to remit punishment for a capital crime, the irremoveability of an officer of the commonwealth without trial by his peers, and the need for the estates to sanction any change in the monetary system.[47]

IV. Mixed Monarchy, Magistrates, and Election

Three other major sections of the *République* appear to be aimed at the Huguenot monarchomachs, but none of them represent any notable departure from ideas expressed in the *Methodus*, and only in one *(République* VI, 5, on the superiority of hereditary succession by male primogeniture over election and female inheritance) is it beyond doubt that Bodin was attacking the theorists of resistance.

Bodin denied the existence of the mixed or Polybian form of state in the *Methodus*, but there he found it difficult to show why the marks of sovereignty could not be distributed among different institutions.[48] In *République* II, 1, the new concept of indivisible legislative sovereignty found a dogmatic answer to the problem: «On a voulu dire & publier par escrit que l'estat de France estoit aussi composé des trois Républiques, & que le Parlement de Paris tenoit une forme d'Aristocratie, les trois estats tenoyent la Democratie, et le Roy representoit l'estat Royal: qui est une opinion non seulement absurde, ains aussi capitale. Car c'est crime de leze maiesté de faire les subiects compagnons du Prince souverain.»[49] In the 1586 Latin edition Bodin inserted beside this passage a marginal reference to Du Haillan's *De l'estat et succez des affaires de France.*[50]

---

[47] *Francogallia* (1665), XXV, pp. 283–300. Cf. Bodin's list in note 44.

[48] *Methodus* VI, 177–181.

[49] *République* II, 1, pp. 262–263. It may be noted that Bodin's denial of the mixed form was not quite as simple as this. In *République* II, 2, p. 272, Bodin distinguished between the form of the state and the method of its administration. A monarchy could therefore be governed aristocratically or in a populer fashion. ARNISAEUS *(De Jure Majestatis,* Argentorati 1635, I, 3, p. 33) was to condemn Bodin for weakening his denial of the mixed state. But Bodin had done no such thing, for he did not admit the sharing of sovereignty, which was the principle underlying the doctrine of mixed monarchy.

[50] *The Six Bookes* [7.44], A 117 (note to p. 191).

Bodin may possibly have noticed two approving references to Du
Haillan's book in Hotman's reply to Matharel. The second reference
associated Du Haillan with Seyssel, and remarked that Du Haillan had
discussed the election of kings, the fallibilities of queen mothers and the
corruption of the parlement.[51] Hotman provided the most persuasive
exposition of mixed monarchy among the monarchomachs. He described
the estates as originally a mixture of monarchic, aristocratic and popular
elements, in which each tempered the others and the whole rested in harmonious balance. He cited Plato, Aristotle, Polybius, and Cicero on such
a form of commonwealth.[52] In the second (1576) version of the *Francogallia* he added a long passage from Seyssel supporting his interpretation.[53]

Bernard de Girard, sieur du Haillan, represented a constitutionalist
position with which Bodin and Hotman had some points in common and
some of radical divergence. In his *Histoire de France* (1577) he paid tri-
bute to his fellow constitutionalist historians, such as Jean du Tillet and
Etienne Pasquier, but he seemed to have Hotman in mind when he denounced those plagiarists who had allowed respect for historical truth
to be distorted by political passion: «Leur imposture a esté descouverte
au bastiment de leurs œuvres: car outre leur crime de blasmer nos Rois,
ils ont esté si impudens que d'emprunter, en ce qui est bon en leurs edifi-
ces, la main et l'œuvre des meilleurs massons qu'eux pour les faire.»[54] Du
Haillan mentioned Bodin with respect in the preface to the second (1580)
edition of *De l'estat,* but in the text of his 1594 edition he indignantly
repudiated Bodin's assertion that his support of mixed monarchy was a
treasonable statement. Later in the text he argued that French kings were
accustomed to submit themselves voluntarily to the laws and the magistrates, and to accept limitations. The aristocratic and popular elements
in French government did not detract from royal authority. Some audacious writers, remarked Du Haillan, had denied this proposition, and
one of them (presumably he meant Bodin) had himself committed treason
by joining the Catholic League.[55]

Du Haillan quoted Seyssel's views on the estates and on the three
«freins» on kingship: *la religion, la justice* and *la police.*[56] Like the

---

[51] *Matagonis de Matagonibus – Monitoriale,* 55, 60.

[52] *Francogallia* (1574), X, pp. 69–71.

[53] *Francogallia* (1665), X, pp. 134–135. Cf. CLAUDE DE SEYSSEL, *La Monarchie
de France,* ed. Jacques Poujol, Paris 1961, 127–128.

[54] *L'Histoire de France,* 2 vols., Paris 1577, vol. I, Preface (unpaginated).

[55] *De l'estat et succez des affaires de France,* Paris 1613, (containing the dedi-
cations of the 1580 and 1594 editions – the first edition appeared in 1570),
Préface au lecteur (unpaginated) and pp. 191 recto, 191 verso.

[56] *De l'estat,* 190 verso, 195 verso. Cf. *La Monarchie de France,* 113–128.

Francogallia, he saw the public council as controlling important affairs of state under the Merovingian and Carolingian dynasties, but he held all the existing institutions to have been fashioned by the Capetians.[57] Like the monarchomachs, he censured Louis XI for introducing tyranny.[58] A true constitutionalist, he saw the king as absolute within a sphere narrowly defined by law and custom, and voluntarily limited outside that sphere.[59] The paradox of a ruler at once absolute and restrained by law is a paradox only to modern minds, accustomed to the «logic» of legislative sovereignty. The passages in which Du Haillan refers to Hotman and Bodin, and those in which they mention him, indicate that the two extremes had drawn apart in opposing directions from the constitutionalist position.

The role of lesser magistrates to resist a prince who broke the conditions under which authority was entrusted to him, and flagrantly oppressed his subjects, was a major principle of monarchomach theory. Beza declared in the *De Jure Magistratuum* that lesser magistrates shared authority, albeit in an inferior capacity, with the prince. The ruler was not the source of their rights, for upon his death they remained in possession of their offices. The prince could discipline or dismiss a magistrate for failing to administer his office according to the law, and, equally, the magistrate had to resist a prince who acted as a tyrant.[60] Unlike the author of the *Vindiciae contra Tyrannos*[61] Beza did not allow the lesser magistrates to resist an idolatrous prince for religious reasons. He merely permitted resistance to a prince who tyrannically revoked edicts tolerating the exercise of true religion.[62] Like Beza, Hotman distinguished between officers of the king and those of the kingdom, and maintained that the latter had once been appointed by the estates and could not be dismissed without just cause. He did not, however, develop the idea of lesser magistrates as leaders of resistance.[63]

---

[57] *De l'estat*, 201 recto, 190 recto.

[58] *De l'estat*, 186 recto – 187 verso.

[59] *De l'estat*, 190 verso. «Premierement il y a le Roy qui est le Monarque souverain & absolu, aimé, reveré, crainct & obey: & bien qu'il ait toute puissance & authorité de commander & faire ce qu'il veut, si est-ce que ceste grande & souveraine liberté est reiglee, limitee & bridee par bonnes loix et ordonnances, & par la multitude & diversité des officiers qui sont tant pres de sa personne, qu'establis en divers lieux de son Royaume: ne luy estant tout permis, ains seulement ce qui est iuste & raisonnable, & prescrit par les ordonnances, & par l'advis de son conseil.»

[60] *De Jure Magistratuum* VI, pp. 245–254.

[61] *Vindiciae contra Tyrannos* II, pp. 67–68.

[62] *De Jure Magistratuum* X, pp. 322–323.

[63] *Francogallia* (1665), XIX, pp. 237–239.

The section on the magistrate *(Quid magistratus)* in *Methodus* VI had discussed the relative meanings of *potestas* and *imperium* in no very conclusive fashion. The old issue of whether *merum imperium* should be possessed by a magistrate, or by the prince alone, had been treated in the following section concerning supreme authority *(Quid summum imperium)*.[64] In the *République* the five chapters of the third book (III, 2–6) devoted to officers and magistrates were generally concerned with a more extensive treatment of such topics, without particular reference to the concept of sovereignty. Bodin's statement that office belonged to the commonwealth, and merely its provision to the prince,[65] made his position equivocal, and only in his discussion of the obedience owed by the magistrate to the laws and the prince *(République, III, 4)* is it possible to sense oblique reference to the monarchomach doctrine. Bodin went as far as his professional conscience would permit in denying the right of the magistrate to disobey the command of the sovereign. Although he conceded the right of the parlement to remonstrate against an edict sent to it for registration, he opposed the frequent use of this right, since it encouraged public disobedience and led to rebellion.[66] Nevertheless, he retained from the *Methodus* the example of the fearless president of the parlement, La Vacquerie, who told Louis XI he would rather be put to death than register the king's unjust edicts.[67] Bodin admitted that a magistrate might resign when confronted by an unjust command from his sovereign, but generally he should set an example of submission, for matters of equity were often complex and his own opinion might be in error. The chapter concluded with the remark that conscience and religion should not be alleged by the magistrate as grounds for disobedience.[68] It is possible to construe this as a reference to what he supposed the monarchomach doctrine of the role of lesser magistrates to be, but it does not seem likely that Bodin's other chapters on magistrates were written with this theory in mind.[69]

---

[64] *Methodus* VI, 173–175.

[65] *République* III, 5, p. 436.

[66] *Rép.* III, 4, p. 427.

[67] *Rép.* III, 4, p. 417. Cf. *Methodus* VI, 208.

[68] *République* III, 4, p. 429. «Mais aussi faut-il bien prendre garde, que le voile de conscience et de superstition mal fondee, ne face ouverture à la rebellion: car puis que le Magistrat a recours à sa conscience sur la difficulté qu'il fait d'executer les mandemens, il fait sinistre iugement de la conscience de son Prince.»

[69] Another instance which at first sight suggests the contrary occurs at *République* III, 5, p. 445. «Mais il n'y a loy divine ny humaine qui permette de revanger ses iniures de faict et de force contre les Magistrats, comme quelques uns ont pensé: qui font ouverture aux rebelles pour troubler tout un estat: car

In his criticism of certain monarchomach doctrines Bodin neither referred to the particular works in which they were expounded nor provided any accurate account of what he was refuting. His method was the more effective because he accepted vulgar misrepresentations of these ideas, in terms of popular liberty or elective monarchy, as the targets he chose to attack. Thus in the chapter he directed against election (*République*, VI, 5) he wrote: «Ce qu'il est besoin d'esclaircir par raisons necessaires, & par exemples, pour lever l'opinion que plusieurs impriment aux subiects d'autruy, & par ce moyen entretiennent les rebellions pour changer les monarchies bien ordonnees, & remuer ciel & terre. Et tout cela se fait sous le voile de vertu, de pieté et de iustice. Et mesmes il s'en trouve qui osent publier livres, & soustenir contre leur Prince naturel venu à la couronne par legitime succession, que le droit de chois est meilleur en la Monarchie.»[70] The particular example he gave to support this opinion was an Oxford disputation on the relative merits of election and hereditary succession debated before Queen Elizabeth in 1566 – perhaps the prototype of more celebrated Oxford disputations on defence of king and country. Bodin's real target would appear to have been the *Francogallia*, or its vulgarisation in the second dialogue of the *Reveille-Matin*. Since the latter work was addressed to the estates, princes, nobles and people of Poland,[71] its title would fit Bodin's remarks about encouraging rebellion against foreign rulers.

Apart from discussing European precedents for the inevitable growth of factions and conspiracies associated with royal election, Bodin assailed Hotman and his imitators upon their own ground, and reviewed the course of Frankish history. He began this section of the chapter by referring to the opinion that «les Rois de France estoyent electifs, & que le royaume tomboit en chois anciennement; cela se fust faict sous la lignee des Merovingues, ou des Carlingues, ou des Capets.»[72] It was his aim to show that each of these dynasties used rules of hereditary succession. It

---

s'il est permis au subiect de se revanger de faict et de force contre les Magistrats, on usera de mesmes arguments pour resister aux Princes souverains, & fouler les loix aux pieds.» The marginal references, however, are to civilians, and any chance of connection with the theory of magisterial resistance appears extremely remote.

[70] *Rép.* VI, 5, p. 973.

[71] «Ordinibus, principibus, proceribus, baronibus, nobilibus, ac populo Poloniae Eusebius Cosmopolitanus salutem ac perpetuam foelicitatem exoptat.» Preface to *Dialogi ab Eusebio Philadelpho – compositi*. It was, of course, common practice for Huguenot writers after the massacre of St. Bartholomew to address their tracts to foreign rulers. The *Francogallia* was dedicated to the Elector Palatine.

[72] *République* VI, 5, p. 983.

was an impossible task for him to demonstrate the practice of primogeniture, but he did his best. The wars between the sons of Louis the Pious, he declared, were caused by the illegal grant of the better part of the kingdom to Charles the Bald, in preference to his elder stepbrothers, Lothar and Louis.[73] Since France had been partitioned between the claimants (a practice which Bodin deplored but could hardly deny),[74] the example was not a happy one. He was also obliged to admit that Louis the Pious himself had obtained his kingdom by force of arms rather than the right of succession, for Bernard of Italy was the son of Pepin, Louis' deceased elder brother, and had the better claim by primogeniture.[75] Disputed successions between uncles and nephews in Frankish history were an awkward problem for Bodin, and he lamely concluded that more nephews had made good their claim than had uncles.[76]

Bodin need not have followed the monarchomachs into this morass, for he concluded that the Capetians had established the sole rights of the eldest son and the exclusion of bastards.[77] It was his purpose, however, to demonstrate in universal terms, and not merely in the context of modern France, the advantages of monarchy by male primogeniture. He also argued that the maxim «the king never dies» and the form of the royal funeral ceremony indicated that the French monarchy had never been elective.[78] Further, the text of the ceremony for the coronation of Philip I in 1058 showed that both the Archbishop of Reims and the Pope claimed the right to appoint a king. Their claims were to be rejected, but the text did, at least, show the error of those who maintained the popular election of kings.[79] When Bodin came to discuss the advent of the

---

[73] *Rép.* VI, 5, pp. 985–986.

[74] *Rép.* VI, 5, p. 995.

[75] *Rép.* VI, 5, p. 993.

[76] *Rép.* VI, 5, p. 994. Bodin provided a long discussion of the respective rights of uncles and nephews, concluding in favour of the latter, and mentioning the likely relevance of the issue to the succession problem of his own day.

Hotman discussed the issue at length in *Quaestionum illustrium liber,* (2nd ed. 1576, III, pp. 27–34). He concluded in favour of the uncle, but after 1584 he changed his mind and in his works on the succession supported the claim of Henry of Navarre against his uncle, the Cardinal de Bourbon (*Disputatio de controversia successionis regiae inter patruum et fratris praemortui filium,* 1585: *Consilia,* 1586: *De Iure successionis regiae in regno Francorum,* 1588: *Ad tractatum Matthaei Zampini – responsio,* 1588).

[77] *République* VI, 5, p. 995.

[78] *Rép.* VI, 5, p. 986. Reference to the funeral ceremony is a later addition. (*The Six Bookes* [7.44], 733).

[79] *République* VI, 5, pp. 984–986. The document on the coronation of Philip I had already been quoted at I, 8, p. 136.

Carolingians and Capetians he asserted that it was the consent of the nobility, and not of the estates, that had enabled Pepin the Short and Hugh Capet to establish their respective lines.[80]

The *Reveille-Matin* had exhibited the same distaste for gynaecocracy as did Bodin's chapter on male primogeniture and the perils of election, but in every other respect its views were clearly anathema to Bodin. In addition to its list of deposed kings, it argued that the best form of monarchy was a combination of heredity and election. Preferably the crown should remain in one family, but the best representative should be chosen, and minorities should be avoided. The Capetians were declared to be usurpers.[81] Some of these opinions were at variance with the views of the *Francogallia*, but Hotman's historic vision proved no more acceptable to the author of the *République* than did the *Reveille-Matin*.

Although the *Antitribonian* and the *Methodus* adopted identical viewpoints on the fallibility of Roman Law and the need to combine history and jurisprudence,[82] the actual history written by their authors was in most respects mutually incompatible. Each writer originated a fruitful historical myth. Bodin exalted the prowess of the Celts, and represented the Franks as Gallic colonists established east of the Rhine five centuries before Caesar.[83] Hotman glorified the Franks as the Germanic standard-bearers of liberty (although the *Francogallia* actually gave some credit to ancient Gallic institutions). Hotman's thesis that a public council, similar to the modern estates, had elected and deposed kings at will, and had divided the kingdom among them, was a wilder distortion than Bodin's. Hotman massed his citations with far greater skill (but with less objectivity) than Bodin employed in the *République*, where examples were constantly being introduced which contradicted the case they were meant to support. As already mentioned, Hotman did not intend to imply that the French monarchy should be restored to an elective form. His reference to Plutarch's remark on choosing a horse or a dog for its personal qualities rather than its breeding was merely a piece of rhetoric.[84] His stress upon Frankish election was meant to demonstrate the former sovereignty of the estates, and when he referred to the need to return to the pristine constitution, it was this he had in mind.

It was in this respect, rather than upon the issue of elective monarchy, that the *Francogallia* represented the most powerful challenge to the

---

[80] *Rép.* VI, 5, p. 983.

[81] *Dialogi ab Eusebio Philadelpho – compositi*, II, pp. 63–65.

[82] Cf. JULIAN H. FRANKLIN [226], Jean Bodin and the Sixteenth-Century Revolution in the Methodology of Law and History, New York, 1963, 68.

[83] *Methodus* IX, 244–251.

[84] *Francogallia* (1574), VI, p. 42.

République. Accepting political change in historical terms, Bodin provided an empirical answer to Hotman's fundamentalism; yet he developed a fundamentalism of his own in rational and universal terms. Each of the two moved away from a constitutionalism to which they had once adhered in a comparable but not identical form. Traces of their former similarity remained in their writings to confuse later commentators.[85] But Bodin's doctrine of an absolute sovereignty reposed in the French crown seems to have been enunciated in reaction to the concept of the sovereignty of the community through the estates, as implied in the works of Hotman and his fellow monarchomachs.

For all this, those sections of the *République* in which Bodin has been shown to have been following one of the purposes declared in his prefaces, and correcting the supposed errors of the Huguenot polemicists, constitute but a small proportion of the massed erudition in the book. The relationship between Bodin and the monarchomachs does not suggest that the *République* as a whole was a *livre de circonstance*: what it does suggest is that the concept of sovereignty was a *thèse de circonstance*.

---

[85] For example, both Hotman and Bodin quoted with approval the maxim of Cicero, «Salus populi suprema lex esto», and that of Seneca, «Omnia rex possidet imperio, singuli dominio.» *République*, IV, 3, p. 576; and I, 8, p. 157: *Francogallia* (1665) XII, pp. 138, 156; and VIII, p. 99.

Ulrich Scheuner

Ständische Einrichtungen und innerstaatliche Kräfte in der Theorie Bodins

I

Das Bild Jean Bodins und seiner Stellung im Rahmen der Entwicklung der politischen Theorie hat in der neueren Forschung gewisse Wandlungen erfahren. Wurde früher seine Rolle für die Ausbildung des Souveränitätsbegriffes und damit seine Position innerhalb der Anhänger des absolutistischen Fürstenregiments betont, und zuweilen diese Seite seiner Lehre isolierend zum Ausdruck gebracht, so wird Bodin in der Gegenwart stärker in den Zusammenhang der gesamten Strömungen des 16. Jahrhunderts als einer vielschichtigen Periode des Übergangs gestellt. Dadurch ergibt sich ein differenzierteres Bild, in dem die Züge sichtbar werden, die Bodin auch mit der Lehre eines konstitutionellen und gemäßigten Staatsdenkens verbinden.[1] Es bleibt richtig, daß in den Auseinandersetzungen des Zeitalters Bodin mit Entschiedenheit sich zum Verfechter einer starken und geschlossenen monarchischen Gewalt gemacht hat, und daß seine Stellung und auch seine Einwirkung auf die Nachwelt hiervon entscheidend bestimmt wird. Aber seine Lehre enthält – wenn man sich nicht zu sehr an eine Vereinzelung einiger hervortretender Thesen hält – eine Reihe von Aussagen, die die absolute Macht des Fürsten begrenzen und ausgleichen, und die es nicht erlauben, den Verfasser der *Republik* dem unbeschränkten Absolutismus zuzurechnen. Inmitten der Gegensätze der religiösen Wirren erblickte Bodin wie manche andere in der königlichen Herrschaft den einzig möglichen Ansatz zur Wiederherstellung von Einheit und Frieden.[2]

---

[1] Eine Hervorhebung der Elemente in Bodins Theorie, die einer einseitigen Zuweisung der *Republik* zur Lehre des absoluten Regiments entgegenstehen und die Bodin eher als Vertreter einer durch feste Grenzen umrissenen, wenn auch jeder Teilung der Herrschaft fremden Monarchie erscheinen lassen, bei Hans Ulrich Scupin [245], *Der Staat* 4 (1965), 22 ff.; Ernst Hinrichs [266], Fürstenlehre und politisches Handeln im Frankreich Heinrichs IV (= Veröffentlichungen des Max Planck Instituts für Geschichte, 21) Göttingen 1969, 48 f., 73, 92 f.

[2] *Six Livres de la République* IV, 7, S. 636: «Or si les factions et séditions sont pernicieuses aux Monarchies, encores sont-elles beaucoup plus dangereuses

Er gab aber – und hierin zeigen sich bestimmte, wenn auch schwächere Verbindungen zu der konstitutionellen Theorie des 15. und 16. Jahrhunderts – der *monarchie royale*, die die Rechte ihrer Bürger schützt und achtet, den Vorzug vor der unbeschränkten Gewalt der *monarchie seigneuriale*. Für jeden Monarchen fordert er freilich, daß er *absolument souverain* sei.[3] Die Momente dieser Bindung auch des souveränen Herrschers an bestimmte Begrenzungen, denen wir bei Bodin begegnen, weisen in verschiedene Richtung. Der Herrscher bleibt für ihn dem göttlichen und natürlichen Recht unterworfen, und er vermag sich auch nicht über Fundamentalgesetze seines Landes hinwegzusetzen. Er kann sich durch Verträge binden. Dagegen erscheinen in der *Republik* weder das französische Parlament noch die ständischen Versammlungen als solche Begrenzungen oder als Gegengewicht der königlichen Macht. Das würde zu einer Hauptthese des Werkes in Widerspruch treten, nach der die souveräne Gewalt nicht geteilt werden kann[4] und die Form einer gemischten Verfassung, in der sich Elemente der verschiedenen Staatsformen verbinden, abgelehnt wird, da sie keinen dauerhaften Frieden herbeizuführen vermag.[5] Aber die ständischen Einrichtungen werden doch nicht einfach abgelehnt oder beiseitegerückt, wenn ihre Einschätzung auch gelegentlich Zweifel erwecken kann. So wird für England unternommen nachzuweisen, daß das Parlament keinen entscheidenden Anteil an der Herrschaft habe.[6] Es wird aber die Bedeutung der Stände für den geordneten Staat anerkannt, ihre Rolle im Rahmen eines aristokratischen Regiments unbefangen gewürdigt, und ihre Rechte werden auch im Zusammenhang des französischen Rechts, wie man an der Stellung zur Steuerbewilligung sehen kann, nicht übergangen. Damit bestätigt sich auch an

---

és estats populaires, et Aristocraties: car les Monarques peuvent maintenir leur maiesté, et décider comme neutres les quérelles, ou, se joignans à l'une des parties, amener l'autre à la raison, ou l'opprimer du tout: mais le peuple estant divisé en l'estat populaire, n'a point de souverain: non plus que les seigneurs en l'aristocratie divisés en partialités, n'ont personne qui leur puisse commander.» Vgl. auch S. 652: «Mais s'il advient au Prince souverain de se faire partie, au lieu de tenir place de Juge souverain, il ne sera rien plus que chef de partie, et se mettra au hazard de perdre sa vie.»

[3] *République* II, 3, S. 284.

[4] Die Unteilbarkeit der souveränen Gewalt wird betont. Vgl. *République* II, 1, S. 266: «Les marques de la souveraineté sont indivisibles.» Ebenso II, 7, S. 339: »Car tousiours la souveraineté indivisible et incommunicable est à un seul, ou à la moindre partie de tous ou à la pluspart.»

[5] Die gemischte Staatsform ruft, so meint Bodin, Unruhen und Aufstände hervor, bis die Souveränität auf der einen oder anderen Seite stabilisiert wird. Als Beispiel wird auf Dänemark unter Christian II. hingewiesen. Vgl. *République* II, 1, S. 266/67.

[6] *République* I, 8, S. 139, 141.

dieser Stelle, daß es Bodin in seiner großen Darstellung nicht nur um bestimmte grundlegende Thesen, sondern um eine weitergreifende Erfassung der aus Geschichte und Gegenwart für die Staatsbetrachtung zu gewinnenden Beispiele und Einsichten geht. Es hängt mit dieser beschreibenden und abwägenden Seite des Werkes zusammen – das insoweit den ersten Ansatz des *Methodus* in breiterem Rahmen wieder aufnimmt – daß die Folgezeit Bodin zuweilen ebenso wegen seiner absolutistischen Tendenzen tadelte[7] wie sie ihn auch in Zusammenhang mit konstitutionellen Lehren brachte.[8]

Die Position der Souveränitätslehre der *Republik* wird vor allem deutlich, wenn sie auf dem Hintergrunde der gesamten Entwicklung der theoretischen und politischen Auseinandersetzungen des 16. Jahrhunderts betrachtet wird. Als die *Republik* erschien, waren allerdings die beiden politischen Hauptrichtungen, die monarchische und die ständische Theorie, schon klar auseinandergetreten. Die ständische Auffassung wandte sich nun einer Ableitung der politischen Gewalt aus dem Volke zu, auf der Grundlage vertraglicher Vorstellungen, ordnete den Fürsten dem Ganzen unter und machte dieses zum Richter über die Einhaltung der Grenzen fürstlicher Gewalt; im Lager der französischen Protestanten und in den Niederlanden hatte diese Seite einen deutlich kämpferisch-revolutionären Charakter gewonnen.[9] Unter den Anhängern der monarchischen Gewalt, die die Tradition der französischen Legisten aufnahm, gewannen auf der anderen Seite jene die Oberhand – und zu ihnen darf man Bodin rechnen –, die über das Bild der konstitutionellen Theorie der ersten Jahrhunderthälfte hinausgingen.

Die Gegensätze des 16. Jahrhunderts entstammten nicht erst dieser Periode. Sie haben ihre Wurzeln schon im späteren Mittelalter. Hier bildeten sich die zwei Richtungen aus, von denen die eine den Gedanken der populären Herrschaft, begründet auf die Vorstellung einer Ableitung der Macht vom Volke her, vertrat, währenddem die andere die Stärkung der fürstlichen Macht vor Augen hatte.[10] Beide Strömungen, von denen die eine die Superiorität des Ganzen über seine Teile wie über sein Haupt

---

[7] Vgl. die Beurteilungen bei J. H. M. SALMON [201], The French Religious Wars and English Political Thought, Oxford 1959, 47, 139.

[8] SALMON [201], 47.

[9] Zur Entwicklung der oppositionellen Kräfte in diesen beiden Ländern zur eigentlichen Organisation revolutionärer Bewegungen siehe KÖNIGSBERGER, The Organization of Revolutionary Parties in France and the Netherlands during the Sixteenth Century, *Journ. of Modern History* 27 (1955), 335 ff.

[10] Zu diesen Gegensätzen siehe OTTO V. GIERKE, Johannes Althusius und die Entwicklung der naturrechtlichen Staatstheorien, 1880 (6. Aufl. 1929), 123 ff.; ferner WALTER ULLMANN, Principles of Government and Politics in the Middle Ages, London 1961, 264 ff. (über populare Theorie und die Bedeutung des Konsenses).

und die Bindung des Herrschers an den Konsens des sozialen oder kirchlichen Körpers, die andere die *suprema potestas* des Papstes und die ihr angeglichene auf die Verleihung durch Gott begründete monarchische Stellung vertrat, wurden in den innerkirchlichen Kämpfen des 15. Jahrhunderts auch zum Ausdruck eines Ringens innerhalb der ganzen Christenheit und gewannen damit eine besondere Bedeutung.[11] Im Kreise der politischen Theorie begegneten sich die gleichen theoretischen Positionen in der Lehre des 16. Jahrhunderts, und diese Diskussion vollzog sich vielfach noch im Schatten der geistigen Gegensätze der Epoche der konziliaren Theorie, auf die auch die Autoren des nächsten Jahrhunderts oftmals Bezug nahmen.[12]

Im späteren 15. und 16. Jahrhundert bildete sich bei einer Reihe von Autoren – man mag für England Sir John Fortescue, für Frankreich Seyssel und Hotman nennen – eine Theorie der gemäßigten Monarchie aus, die den Typ des sich an Recht und Gerechtigkeit bindenden Herrschers dem nach absoluter Macht strebenden Fürsten und vollends dem Tyrannen gegenüberstellte.[13] In ihr waren auch Elemente der Lehre von der gemischten Staatsform lebendig. Es wäre überhaupt unrichtig für die erste Hälfte des 16. Jahrhunderts von einem allgemeinen Gegensatz fürstlicher und ständischer Tendenzen auszugehen. Gewiß waren die Fürsten stets bestrebt, die ständische Mitwirkung in Grenzen zu halten, aber sie

---

[11] Zur Betonung der Überordnung des Ganzen über die Teile in der konziliaren Theorie siehe BRIAN TIERNEY, Foundations of Conciliar Theory, Cambridge 1955, 157 ff., 179 ff.; M. J. WILKS, The Problem of Sovereignty in the Later Middle Ages, Cambridge 1963, 479 ff.; MARIO D'ADDIO, L'Idea del Contratto Sociale dai Sofisti alla Riforma, Mailand 1954, 360 ff.
Umgekehrt siehe zur Auswirkung der päpstlichen Suprematie gegenüber Kaiser und Konzil auf die fürstliche Gewalt TIERNEY, Foundations, 141 ff.; WILKS, Problem of Sovereignty, 184 ff.

[12] Bezugnahmen auf die konziliaren Auseinandersetzungen sind nicht selten. So berufen sich die *Vindiciae contra Tyrannos* (hier benutzt nach der Ausgabe Frankfurt 1608) für den Satz, daß der einzelne dem König untergeordnet sei, dieser selbst aber der Gesamtheit, auf die Konstitutionen des Baseler Konzils (S. 37). BEZA, *De iure magistratuum in subditos* (Ausgabe v. KLAUS STURM, Neukirchen 1965), 75 verweist auf die Überordnung des Konzils über den Papst. Vgl. hierzu FRIEDRICH HERMANN SCHUBERT [252], Die deutschen Reichstage in der Staatslehre der frühen Neuzeit, Göttingen 1966, 388. Allgemein zur Einwirkung der konziliaren Theorie J. W. ALLEN [97], A History of Political Thought in the Sixteenth Century, London ²1951, 281.

[13] Zu Fortescue's Unterscheidung zwischen *dominium politicum* und *dominium regale* siehe R. WILKINSON, Constitutional History of England in the Fifteenth Century, London 1964, 167, 194 ff. Zur französischen konstitutionellen Theorie siehe WILLAM F. CHURCH [145], Constitutional Thought in Sixteenth Century France, Cambridge (Mass.) 1941, 194 ff.

waren sich wohl bewußt, daß den Ständen für die Zusammenfassung und
Einigung des Landes eine Bedeutung zukam und daß sie durch ihre Prä-
senz sich einer breiteren Basis der Zustimmung versichern konnten. Die
burgundischen Herzöge haben die Zusammenfassung der ständischen Ein-
richtungen ihrer Besitzungen als Mittel der Einigung verwendet, und in
England hat das Tudor-Regime für die administrativen und religiösen
Neuerungen der Epoche aus der parlamentarischen Billigung entschei-
dende Kraft gezogen.[14] Das gilt auch in gewissem Umfang für Frankreich.
J. Russell Major hat auf diese Seite der ständischen Entwicklung zu
Recht hingewiesen.[15] Sie hat freilich gerade in Frankreich nicht zu einer
Stärkung der Stände geführt. Teils wegen der mangelnden Fähigkeit der
Generalstände mit ihren Beschlüssen bereits die Stände der einzelnen
Regionen verbindlich zu verpflichten,[16] teils wegen der oft geringen Be-
reitschaft zur Bewilligung von Mitteln,[17] haben die Generalstände in der
zweiten Hälfte des 16. Jahrhunderts nicht den von ihnen erstrebten
Anteil an der Regierung Frankreichs gewinnen können.[18]

---

[14] Für Burgund siehe J. Russell Major, The Estates General of 1560,
Princeton 1951, 9 f., der auch auf die spanische Monarchie der katholischen
Könige verweist. Zu der (nicht erfolgreichen) Verwendung der Ständeversammlung für die gesamten burgundischen Gebiete für die Einheit des Landes siehe
auch Hermann Heimpel, Festschrift für Gerhard Ritter, Tübingen 1950, 149 ff.,
155 ff. Philipp II griff hingegen in Abwehr der aufkommenden Opposition wieder auf eine getrennte Befragung der Stände aus den einzelnen Gebieten zurück.
Vgl. G. Griffiths, Representative Government in Western Europe in the Sixteenth Century. Commentary and Documents for the Study of Comparative
Constitutional History, Oxford 1968, 391 f. (Brief an Margarete von Parma v.
15. 7. 1562). In England war entgegen der Auffassung Bodins das Parlament
schon ein wesentlicher Bestandteil der Verfassungsordnung und wurde (in seiner
Bedeutung als *King in Parliament*) schon als *absolute power in the realm* angesehen. Vgl. G. R. Elton, The Tudor Constitution. Documents and Commentary, Cambridge 1960, 230 f.

[15] Vgl. auch J. Russell Major, Representative Institutions in Renaissance
France 1421–1559, Madison 1960, 15 ff. Siehe auch die Äußerungen in der An-
sprache des Kanzlers L'Hospital vor den Ständen zu Orleans am 13. 12. 1560
(Text bei Griffiths, Representative Government, 147): «Car, de vouloir dire
que toutes grandes assemblees sont a craindre, et devoient estre suspecte: ouy, aux
tyrans; mais non, aux princes légitimes, comme est le nostre. Et si nous regardons
au temps passe, pour nostre instruction a l'advenir, nous touverons que tous les
estats qui ont ete tenueus, ont apporte profict et utilite aux princes, les ont
secourus a leur grand besoing; comme apres la prinse du roy Jean, et en aultre
temps, que je tairay de peur d'estre long.»

[16] J. Russell major, The Estates General, 119 f.

[17] J. Russell Major, The Estates General, 120.

[18] Zum Niedergang der Stände siehe (zu kritisch) R. Doucet, Les institutions
de la France au XVIe siècle, Paris 1948 Bd. I, 325 ff.

Das 16. Jahrhundert ist auf der einen Seite ein Zeitalter bedeutender Macht der ständischen Einrichtungen, die sich vor allem im Deutschen Reiche, in England und in Polen eine starke Position sichern konnten. Auf der anderen Seite leitet diese Periode in manchen anderen Ländern den Niedergang der Stände ein. Das gilt – abgesehen von den aragonesischen Territorien – für Spanien (Kastilien)[19] wie auch für Frankreich. Hier hatten die Stände von Tours 1484 dem König gegenüber nachdrücklich ihren Anspruch auf Mitwirkung, auf einen Anteil an der Gesetzgebung (durch die Übertragung ihrer cahiers in Normen) und auf die Bewilligung der Steuern erhoben. Sie waren im Ergebnis damit nicht durchgedrungen.[20] In der Zeit bis 1558 begnügten sich dann die Monarchen mit der Hilfe anderer Versammlungen, teils der provinziellen Stände, teils von Notabeln oder Vertretern der Städte.[21] Die finanzielle Krise und zu einem gewissen Umfang die religiösen Wirren führten dann in der zweiten Jahrhunderthälfte zu mehrfacher Berufung von Generalständen. Stets war damit in deren Kreise eine Betonung des Gedankens der Rechte des ganzen Volkes, als deren Repräsentanten die Stände auftraten,[22] verbunden. Aber die eigentliche Entfaltung der ständischen, gegen die absolute Macht gerichteten Haltung hatte nicht hier ihre Wurzel. Sie formte sich vielmehr im Rahmen der kämpferischen Bewegungen der Zeit. Die Literatur des protestantischen Lagers, sich rasch verschärfend nach der Bartholomäusnacht, und das Beispiel des niederländischen Kampfs sind hier maßgebend.

In diesem Rahmen entstand eine Lehre, die ihre Thesen wesentlich schärfer ausformte und zuspitzte. Auf dem Gedanken der Überordnung des Ganzen über dem Fürsten ruhend, stellte sie den Gedanken vertraglicher Bindungen zwischen Fürst und Volk in den Mittelpunkt und ge-

---

[19] Siehe JOHN LYNCH, Spain under the Habsburgs Bd. I, Oxford 1964, 192 ff., Bd. II 1969, 86 ff.

[20] RUSSELL MAJOR, Representative Institutions, 66 ff.

[21] RUSSELL MAJOR, Representative Institutions, 117 ff. Erst mit den Ständen von Paris 1558 beginnt eine neue Reihe von Versammlungen der Generalstände bis zu ihrem letzten Zusammentreten von 1614/15. Siehe die Übersicht bei RUSSELL MAJOR, Repräsentative Institutions, 152 f. und denselben zu den Ständen von Pontoise in: *Speculum* 29 (1954), 460 ff.

[22] Die repräsentative Stellung der Stände ist vor allem in den Niederlanden betont worden. Wilhelm von Oranien schreibt den Ständen 1576 «que vous tenez, en représentant le corps universel de tout le peuple, duquel vous avez la liberté et salut comme en depost...» (vgl. bei GRIFFITHS, Representative Government, 432). Vgl. auch in den *Vindiciae contra tyrannos*, 69: «Porro quod de universo populo dicimus, de iis etiam ut in secunda quaestione, dictum volumus qui populum universum in omni Regno, urbeve legitime representant, qui quidem vulgo Regni, non Regis officiarii censentur.»

langte auf dieser Grundlage zur Annahme eines in der Hand der berufenen Stände und Magistrate liegenden Widerstandsrechts gegen den ungerechten Herrscher. Von den bekannten Zeugnissen dieser Richtung, die in den Schriften der sog. Monarchomachen ihren besten Ausdruck fand, lagen bei dem Erscheinen der *Republik* schon einige vor.[23] In diesem Kreise, der im niederländischen Gebiet und unter den Hugenotten eine kämpferisch-revolutionäre Prägung erhielt, wurde eine Doktrin der ständischen Gegengewalten ausgearbeitet. Zwar gewährte man dem einfachen Bürger *(privatus)* kein Recht zum Widerstande, wohl aber den Ständen und Magistraten des Landes, die als Wächter über Recht und Herkommen gegenüber einem seine Bindung mißachtenden Regenten hierzu berufen erscheinen.[24] Überschreitet der Herrscher die Grenzen des Rechts, wendet er sich insbesondere gegen göttliches Gebot, wird er damit zum Tyrannen, so kann er von den hierzu befugten Trägern eines Amtes so wie Christian II von Dänemark oder Erich XIV von Schweden abgesetzt werden.[25] In diesem Rahmen wird den Ständen auch das Recht auf Teilhabe an der Gesetzgebung zugesprochen und ihr Recht betont, die Steuern zu bewilligen. So findet sich in dieser Literatur ein ganzes Arsenal von Gedanken und Argumenten, das großenteils von Bodin ausdrücklich abgelehnt wird, wenn er es auch im allgemeinen vermeidet, die Gegner selbst namhaft zu machen, deren Thesen er bekämpft. Es handelt sich hier aber nicht nur um bloße Theorie. Die Anschauung fand auch einen staatsrechtlichen Ausdruck in der Deklaration der Generalstaaten über die Absetzung Philipps II. Dem König wird hier, da er für die Untertanen, nicht diese für ihn da seien, und da er nicht als ein echter Hirte sondern als ein ungerechter Herrscher und Tyrann sich dargetan hat, kundgetan, daß damit rechtliche Ursache gegeben ist, ihm aufzusagen *(te verlaten)* und ihm alle Rechte der Herrschaft zu nehmen. Er wird seiner Herrschaft für entsetzt erklärt.[26]

---

[23] Es genügt hinzuweisen auf den *Reveille-Matin* (1573) und Beza's *De iure magistratuum* (1574).

[24] In den *Vindiciae* wird die Duldung des gegen das göttliche Gesetz verstoßenden Fürsten durch die Mitverantwortlichen als *negligentia* oder *conniventia* zur Mitschuld (32 ff,). Da die Gesamtheit über dem Fürsten steht, kann sie ihn absetzen (37). Dazu sind die Seniores oder Principes durch den Bund des Volkes mit Gott legitimiert (43, 125). Der einfache Bürger hat kein Widerstandsrecht (165 f.), wohl aber die Stände, die das ganze Volk vertreten (71 f., 161 f.).

[25] Die Beispiele werden in den *Vindiciae* (159) und bei Beza (54) angeführt. Diese gemeinsamen Berufungen weisen ebenso wie andere gemeinsame Anführungen (z. B. den Hinweis auf den Sachsenspiegel für den Krönungseid der deutschen Könige bei Beza, 60, den *Vindiciae*, 128) auf die gegenseitige Berührung dieser Schriften.

[26] Vgl. den Text der Erklärung vom 26. Juli 1581 bei Griffiths, Representative Government, 510 ff.

In diesen Auseinandersetzungen und Kämpfen liegt der Hintergrund, von dem aus Bodin die Stellung der Stände und anderer innerpolitischen Kräfte betrachtet. Er selbst war an ständischen Einrichtungen 1576 als Vertreter des Vermandois zu Blois beteiligt. Und seine ganze Lehre spiegelt die Gegensätze der Zeit deutlich wieder. In vielen Dingen hält er den Gegenpart zu der Auffassung, die uns in den *Vindiciae* und ähnlichen Schriften begegnet. Dennoch werden die Stände in einer positiven Bedeutung von ihm gewürdigt und nicht etwa in ihrem Recht und ihrer Aufgabe negiert.

II

Werfen wir, bevor wir uns im besonderen der Stellungnahme Bodins zu den ständischen Einrichtungen zuwenden, einen kurzen Blick auf die Beschränkungen, die er in seiner Lehre der Souveränität für die fürstliche souveräne Gewalt überhaupt anerkennt. Es wird sich dann zeigen, daß der in der *Republik* entwickelte Begriff der Souveränität keineswegs Schrankenlosigkeit der Machtübung bedeutet, sondern nur Unteilbarkeit und Lösung von der Unterordnung an einen fremden Willen oder den Konsens der Untertanen. Wiewohl Bodin es liebt, der Souveränität die Attribute der absoluten und unbeschränkten Macht zu geben,[27] so nimmt er doch mit dieser Ausdrucksweise keine Lösung von allen rechtlichen Schranken und Begrenzungen vor. Nur im Rahmen dieser bestehenden Bindungen ist die monarchische Gewalt souverän.[28] Die wichtigste dieser Schranken stellt die Bindung des Souveräns an das natürliche und göttliche Recht dar. Sie wird in dem Werke unseres Autors immer wieder nachdrücklich hervorgehoben.[29] Diese Begrenzung muß auch im echten Sinne als eine rechtliche Limitation verstanden werden. Ein Verstoß gegen das natürliche Gebot nimmt der Anordnung des Fürsten ihre Verbindlichkeit. Das wird zwar von Bodin nirgends klar ausgesprochen, er-

---

[27] *Puissance absolue* vgl. *République* I, 8, S. 122, 124; *illimitée* vgl. *Rép.* I, 8, S. 124.

[28] So sagt Bodin (*République* I, 8, S. 156): «La puissance absolue n'est autre chose que derogation aux lois civiles, comme nous avons monstré ci dessus, et qui ne peut attenter aux lois de Dieu ...» Hier kommt klar zum Ausdruck, daß der Begriff der Souveränität bei Bodin nicht rechtliche Bindungslosigkeit bedeutet. Diese Deutung des Begriffes der Souveränität als Lösung von rechtlichen Grenzen gehört erst der Staatslehre des 19. Jahrhunderts an. Die Fürsten des 16.–18.-Jahrhunderts haben niemals eine Lösung vom göttlichen oder natürlichen Recht beansprucht. Auch für das englische Parlament wurde eine Bindung an das Naturrecht angenommen (vgl. ELTON, The Tudor Constitution, 231).

[29] *République* I, 8, S. 133/34, 156. Insbesondere S. 150: «Aussi les loix des Princes souverains ne peuvent alterer, ni changer les loix de Dieu et de la nature.»

gibt sich aber, wenn man den Blick auf die allgemeine Anschauung der Zeit richtet. Die höheren Normen des natürlichen und göttlichen Rechts werden von ihr als rechtliche Regeln, nicht bloß als moralische innere Prinzipien angesehen.[30] Es erscheint daher als eine Vorwegnahme späterer Entwicklungen seit dem 18. Jahrhundert, wenn man sich diese Bindung des Fürsten nur als eine moralische innere Grenzlinie vorstellt.[31] Die rechtliche Bedeutung des übergeordneten Rechts wird vor allem in einer speziellen Anwendung bei Bodin deutlich, die bei ihm erhebliche Aufmerksamkeit findet. Zu den Regeln des göttlichen Rechts zählt er auch den Grundsatz, daß niemand in das Gut eines anderen eingreifen dürfe.[32] Daher bleibt auch dem Fürsten die Wegnahme des Gutes seiner Untertanen ohne besondere Ursache verschlossen. Nur im Falle besonderer Not darf er für die *conservation de l'estat* d. h. für das Wohl der Gesamtheit[33] privates Gut an sich ziehen oder verwenden.[34] Denn die Unter-

---

[30] Vgl. zur Einordnung des positiven Rechts in das Naturrecht FERDINAND VAZQUEZ, *Controversiarum Illustrium Libri Tres* (Ausg. Frankfurt 1572), Lib. I, cap. 47 § 11, S. 121. Hier wird als Folge vor allem die Verwandlung des Fürsten in einen Tyrannen hervorgehoben. Siehe ferner FRANCISCO DE VITORIA, *Relectio de Indis* (Ausgabe: L. Perena y J. M. Perez Prendes, Corpus Hispanorum de Pace, Vol. V, Madrid 1967), Lib. I sect. 3, 1 in fine: «Si autem lex humana esset quae prohiberet sine aliqua causa a iure naturali et divino, esset inhumana nec esset rationabilis, et per consequens non haberet vim legis.»

[31] Nur als moralische Bindung sieht das natürliche Recht an W. H. GREENLEAF [238], Order, Empiricism and Politics, Oxford 1964, 133 f. Dagegen wird zutreffend der rechtlich bindende Charakter des göttlichen Rechts betont von HINRICHS [266], 46. Der Unterschied rechtlicher und moralischer Bindung darf aber überhaupt für das 16. Jahrhundert nicht zu sehr betont werden. Vgl. J. W. GOUGH, Fundamental Law in English Constitutional History, Oxford 1955, 17, 45.

[32] *République* I, 8, S. 156/57.

[33] An dieser Stelle wird von Bodin das Wort *estat* gleichgesetzt mit der politischen Gesamtheit, der *République,* die nach seiner Definition (*République* I, 1, S. 1) durch die *puissance souveraine* geformt wird. Sonst tritt der Ausdruck *estat,* abgesehen von seinem Gebrauch zur Bezeichnung der Stände, bei Bodin aber auch in der Sinngebung als fürstliche Machtorganisation und Hoheit auf. Vgl. zur Bedeutung des Ausdrucks «Staat», Estat: WOLFGANG MAGER [262], Zur Entstehung des modernen Staatsbegriffs (= Akademie der Wissenschaften und der Literatur Mainz, Abhandlungen Jahrg. 1968 Nr. 9) Wiesbaden 1968, 455 ff. 489 f.

[34] *Rép.* I, 8, p. 157. Bei diesem Grundsatz handelt es sich um einen allgemein im 16. und noch am Beginn des 17. Jahrhunderts anerkannten Satz, der Freiheit und Eigentum der Untertanen schützt und zu den anerkannten Schranken der fürstlichen Gewalt zählt. Vgl. RUDOLF VON ALBERTINI [176], Das politische Denken in Frankreich zur Zeit Richelieus (= Beihefte zum Archiv für Kulturgeschichte, 1) Marburg 1951, 52.

tanen sind schuldig, auch mit ihrem Gut für das Wohl des Staates ein-
zustehen. Aus dieser Darlegung Bodins, die eng mit der Überordnung des
natürlichen Rechts verbunden ist, erhellt klar, daß hier von rechtlichen
Schranken die Rede ist, die das höhere Rechtsgebot zieht.

Man muß von dieser rechtlichen Beschränkung des Souveräns den
Grundsatz unterscheiden, nach dem der Fürst dort, wo er über das Recht
verfügen kann, dies im Blick auf das Gemeinwohl und in Wahrung der
Gerechtigkeit tun soll. Hier geht es dann in der Tat um innere Schranken
seines Handelns. Es ist eine der wichtigsten Beiträge Bodins zur Theorie
der höchsten Gewalt, daß er über die ältere Deutung der fürstlichen Aufgabe als der eines Richters hinausgeht,[35] die Verfügung über das Gesetz
an die erste Stelle rückt und in ihr eine entscheidende *marque de souveraineté* erblickt. Damit wird der überkommene Rechtsbestand der Gestaltung durch das Gebot des Monarchen unterstellt, und es wird zugleich der Anspruch der Stände zurückgewiesen, daß ohne ihren Konsens
kein neues Recht zustandekommen könne.[36] Man muß dabei im Auge behalten, daß der Begriff des Gesetzes im 16. Jahrhundert noch ein sehr
weiter ist, der nicht nur allgemeine Normen umschließt, sondern auch
Privilegien und Erlasse für den Einzelfall in sich begreift.[37] Wenn diese
Befugnis des Fürsten, Recht zu setzen, die ein entscheidendes Merkmal
seiner Souveränität bildet, für Bodin auch das Recht einschließt, den
Untertanen Steuern und Abgaben aufzuerlegen, so tritt ihre grundlegende
Bedeutung um so deutlicher hervor.[38] In der Frage des Besteuerungsrechts
bleibt die Stellungnahme Bodins im Rahmen jener Unsicherheit, die die
französische Entwicklung auf diesem Gebiet im 16. Jahrhundert kennzeichnet.[39] Er gibt zu, daß in anderen Staaten Steuern nicht ohne stän-

---

[35] Zu der Ansicht, den Fürsten vor allem als Richter zu beschreiben, siehe
CHURCH [145], 199 f.
[36] *République* I, 8, S. 142. «Par ainsi on void que le poinct principal de la
majesté souveraine, et puissance absolue, gist principalement à donner la loy aux
subjects en général sans leur consentement. ... Car il faut que le prince souverain
ait les loix en sa puissance pour les changer, et corriger selon l'occurence des cas.»
[37] *République* I, 8, S. 224. Hier wird als *vraie marque de souveraineté* die
Befugnis bezeichnet «de donner la loy à tous en general et à chacun en particulier.»
[38] *République* I, 8, S. 244: «Quant au droit de mettre sur les subjects tailles et
imposts, ou bien en exempter quelques uns, cela depend aussi de la puissance de
donner la loy et les privileges: non pas que la Republique ne puisse estre sans
tailles, comme le President de Maistre escrit que les tailles ne sont imposées que
depuis le Roy S. Louys en ce royaume: mais s'il est besoin de les imposer. ou de
les oster. il ne peut se faire que par celuy qui a la puissance souveraine.» Bodin
verweist hier dann auf das Edikt von Moulins von 1566.
[39] Zu dieser Unsicherheit siehe R. DOUCET, Les Institutions de la France auf

dische Bewilligung beschlossen werden und verweist auf ältere französische Erklärungen in diesem Sinne, vor allem die Begehren der Stände von Tours im Jahre 1484.[40] Auf der anderen Seite aber erkennt der Autor der *Republique* in dringenden Fällen dem Fürsten das Recht zu, Einnahmen zu erheben.[41] In diesen Stellungnahmen wird es jedenfalls deutlich, daß Bodin an diesem Punkt keineswegs einen strengen Standpunkt zugunsten der fürstlichen Gewalt vertritt.

Die ständischen Rechte werden von ihm hier wohl in Erwägung gezogen. Was die allgemeine Schranke anlangt, die die Pflicht, Gerechtigkeit zu üben und dem Gemeinwohl zu dienen, dem Souverän zieht, so werden hiermit in der Tat bei Bodin nur innere Verpflichtungen ausgesprochen. An ihrer Befolgung, darin liegt eine Verstärkung dieser Pflichten – scheidet sich – entsprechend der Unterscheidung Bodins zwischen der Staatsform und der Regierungsweise, zwischen «estat» und «gouvernment[42] – die Art des fürstlichen Regiments. In der *monarchie royale,* für die die *Republique* eintritt, hält der Fürst diese innere Begrenzung ein und achtet die natürliche Freiheit wie das Eigentum seiner Untertanen, während er in der *monarchie seigneuriale* wie ein Eroberer über Person und Gut seiner Untertanen verfügt.[43] In der recht geordneten Monarchie entscheidet hingegen zwischen Fürst und Untertan das Recht. Der Tyrann endlich aber tritt die Gebote des natürlichen Rechts mit Füßen, behandelt seine Untertanen als Sklaven und folgt nur seiner Willkür.[44] Gegen den Fürsten läßt Bodin für den Untertanen kein Widerstandsrecht zu, das jede Herrschaft gefährden würde.[45] Wohl aber kann

XVIe siècle Bd. I 1948, 323 ff. sowie C. Soule, Le rôle des Etats Généraux et des assemblées de notables dans le vote de l'impôt, in: Etudes sur l'histoire des Assemblées d'Etats herg. v. F. Dumont (Travaux et Recherches de la Faculté de Droit et des Sciences Economiques de Paris, Série Sciences Historiques No. 8) Paris 1966, 98 ff. Siehe auch G. Oestreich, Der Staat 6 (1967), 64 ff.

[40] *Republique* VI, 2, S. 863, 880. Hier wird der Grundsatz, daß keine Steuer ohne Zustimmung der Stände erhoben weden soll, von Bodin erwähnt, den die französischen Stände immer wieder geltend gemacht haben (vgl. Soule, Rôle des Etats Généraux, 98 ff.).

[41] *Republique* VI, 2, S. 863: «Car les Monarques, qui n'ont revenu plus assuré que du dommaine, et qui n'ont droit de mettre impost sur les subjects, sinon de leur consentement, ou en cas de necessite urgente, ne sont pas si prodigues de leur dommaine.»

[42] Zur Unterscheidung von *estat* und *gouvernement* (*Republique* II, 2, S. 272) siehe Greenleaf [238], 131 f. Diese Unterscheidung gab Bodin die Möglichkeit, eine gewisse Differenzierung der Staatstypen vorzunehmen, ohne den Grundsatz der Unteilbarkeit der souveränen Gewalt aufzugeben.

[43] *Republique* II, 3, S. 279.

[44] Vgl. *Republique* II, 4, S. 287, 289.

[45] *Republique* II, 5, S. 298.

gegen den Tyrannen, der seine Macht usurpiert hat, ein fremder Fürst eingreifen, der das Recht wiederherstellt.[46] Mit der Zubilligung eines solchen Interventionsrechts eines anderen Fürsten zur Wiederherstellung der Rechte der Untertanen fügt sich Bodin in eine allgemeine Anschauung der Zeit ein. Nicht nur in den religiösen Kämpfen des Zeitalters, auch darüber hinaus hat diese Idee im Staatsleben eine Rolle gespielt und hat noch Richelieu Anlaß geboten, sein Eingreifen in den 30jährigen Krieg als Verteidigung der Freiheit der deutschen Fürsten gegen den Kaiser zu rechtfertigen.[47] Trägt die innere Bindung des rechten Monarchen an die Wahrung von Gerechtigkeit und Gemeinwohl die Natur einer Forderung im Stile der älteren Fürstenlehre, so entspringt eine zweite wichtige Bindung der fürstlichen Gewalt aus ihrer Gebundenheit an die Fundamentalgesetze des Königreichs. Hier nimmt Bodin eine Lehre auf, die sich langsam im späteren Mittelalter in vielen Ländern entfaltet hatte, als man im Deutschen Reiche ebenso wie in England, Frankreich oder Aragon einzelne niemals genau definierte Grundsätze des Gewohnheitsrechts oder der Gesetzgebung mit dem Charakter dauerhafter Grundlagen des Gemeinwesens versah. Während dieser Begriff im deutschen Reichsrecht schon im 16. Jahrhundert aufkam und weiten Umfang gewann, so daß er neben der Goldenen Bulle, der Wahlkapitulation auch die Reichsabschiede und später auch den Westfälischen Frieden umfaßte,[48] trug das *fundamental law* in England, abgesehen von der Magna Charta,

---

[46] *République* II, 5, S. 300; «Car il est bien difference de dire que le tyran peut estre licitement tué par un prince estranger, ou par le subject.» Ferner V, 6, S. 823 ff. Es ist bezeichnend, daß die Fälle Christians II von Dänemark und Erichs XIV von Schweden bei Bodin nicht wie in den ständischen Schriften als Beispiele der Absetzung vorkommen, sondern als Handeln ihrer fürstlichen Verwandten, die sie nicht töten, sondern in Gefangenschaft halten! Vgl. *République* II, 5, S. 312.

[47] Auf diese Bedeutung der Intervention für das Eingreifen und seinen Zusammenhang mit der Annahme eines Widerstandsrechts – ein Eingreifen, das Richelieu gegenüber einem wahren Souverän wie dem französischen König ablehnte – in seiner Bedeutung für das Handeln des Kardinals weist hin Fritz Dickmann, *Historische Zeitschrift* 196 (1963), 272 ff. Sie wird von Richelieu auch für sein Eingreifen in Katalonien herangezogen und verbindet sich bei anderen Autoren mit dem Kampf für die Freiheit der deutschen Fürsten, schon in einer mehr dem Gleichgewichtsdenken zuneigenden Sicht (vgl. de Silhon, *Le Ministre d'Estat*, Ausg. Paris 1654, Teil II discours 3, 460), wo er «la subsistance du Corps et la liberté des Membres» des Reichskörpers unter den Schutz Frankreichs stellt.

[48] Zu den *leges fundamentales* in der Reichsstaatslehre siehe Schubert [252], 148, 283 ff. Der Begriff bleibt auch bis ins 18. Jahrhundert in dieser Ausdehnung erhalten. Vgl. J. St. Pütter, Institutiones iuris publici Germanici, 6. Aufl. Göttingen 1802, §§ 39 ff., S. 43 ff.

die Natur des Gewohnheitsrechts und erhielt erst im beginnenden 17. Jahrhundert durch Sir Edward Coke eine eigentliche präzisere Anwendung.[49] Es hing mit diesem historischen Zug des englischen Grundgesetzes zusammen, daß sein Gehalt niemals genau bestimmt werden konnte und im wesentlichen die Elemente der parlamentarischen Mitwirkung deckte.[50] Auch in Frankreich wird der Begriff im 16. Jahrhundert verwendet. Er dient teilweise der Begründung ständischer Ansprüche, wird aber in der der Monarchie zugewandten Literatur – zu der wir Bodin rechnen müssen – auf zwei traditionelle Grundsätze beschränkt. Einmal das salische Gesetz, das klarlegt, daß der französische Monarch seine Stellung nicht aus Wahl oder ständischer Mitwirkung gewinnt, sondern aus diesem Prinzip, und daher weder durch Vertrag noch durch Krönungseide verpflichtet wird.[51] Zum andern erscheint hier der Grundsatz der Unveräußerlichkeit des königlichen Besitzes, der dem König untersagt, Territorien oder Rechte zu veräußern. Beide Grundsätze werden von Bodin anerkannt.[52] Sie sind Regeln, die der Fürst nicht zu ändern vermag. Denn, so darf man wohl die Argumentation verstehen, auf diesen Grundsätzen beruht eben seine Souveränität. Sie können freilich nach überwiegender Lehre jedenfalls im Falle der Unveräußerlichkeit des Besitzes durch Zustimmung der Stände beiseitegesetzt werden. Diese Möglichkeit wird aber bei Bodin nur kurz erwähnt, als er von der Möglichkeit spricht, daß das *domaine public* mit Bewilligung der drei Stände veräußert werden könne.[53]

---

[49] Zur Entwicklung des Begriffs in England siehe J. W. Gough, The Social Contract 2. Aufl., Oxford 1957, 95; Ders., Fundamental Law in English Constitutional History, Oxford 1955, 12 ff., 35 ff.

[50] Vgl. J. G. A. Pocock, The Ancient Constitution and the Feudal Law, Cambridge 1957, 48 ff. Von entscheidender Bedeutung war dabei der Satz, daß der consent der Untertanen für die Auferlegung der Steuern gefordert werde. Im Parlament von 1629 nannte Pym diesen Grundsatz «the ancient and fundamental law arising from the first frame and constitution of the Kingdom». Vgl. J. Rushworth, Historical Collections of Private Passages of State, London 1682–1721, Bd. I, 596; und dazu Perez Zagorin, The Court and the Country, London 1969, 83 f.

[51] Diese Richtung gegen eine Bindung des Fürsten wird deutlich bei Bodin hervorgehoben. Der Nachfolger des Königs kann nicht gebunden werden und tritt seine Herrschaft zu vollem souveränen Recht an kraft der salischen Folge. Vgl. *République* I, 8, S. 137. Beispiele aus der französischen Praxis werden angeführt, die solche Bindung ablehnen (*Rép.*, 159). Doch kann ein Vertrag, den der Vorgänger als Souverän abgeschlossen hat und der die Zustimmung der Stände hatte, wenn er dem Lande zum Vorteil gereicht, fortbestehen (*Rép.*, 160).

[52] Für die Entstehung des Begriffs der *lois fondamentales* in Frankreich siehe Albertini [176], 58 ff.; Hinrichs [266], 49.

[53] Vgl. *République* VI, 2, S. 859: «Car sur ce poinct là estoit fondée l'infrac-

Von diesem Fall abgesehen, kennt Bodin sonst keine verbindliche Mitwirkung der Stände[54] und lehnt es auch ab, den souveränen Fürsten an
seine im Krönungseid übernommenen Versprechungen zu binden.[55] Nur
dort, wo die Stände herrschen, wo mithin keine Monarchie, sondern ein
aristokratisches Regiment besteht[56] werden Bindungen der obersten Magistrate verbindlich, weil diese trotz der ihnen – wie dem deutschen König
oder dem Dogen – gespendeten königlichen Ehren in Wahrheit Magistrate
mit gebundener Vollmacht sind.[57]

Auch wenn mithin Bodin die souveräne Macht von den Bindungen
ständischer Mitwirkung oder von Verpflichtungen aus dem Krönungseid
unabhängig stellt,[58] liegt doch in dem Begriff der lois fondamentales für
die monarchische Stellung eine gewisse Beschränkung. Sie wird vor allem
bei dem Grundsatz der Unveräußerlichkeit des Besitzes sichtbar. Hier
kann der König nicht allein verfügen. Gewiß, auch diese Beschränkung
soll im Grunde seine Macht nicht vermindern, sondern sie soll ihrer Erhaltung dienen, indem sie Schmälerung oder Teilung der souveränen Ge-

---

tion du traicté de Madrid: d'autant que la coustume ancienne de ce Royaume
conforme aux edicts et aux ordonnances des autres peuples, requiert le consentement des trois estats, come il se fait encore en Polongne.» In der Staatspraxis hat
diese *inaliénabilité du domaine* den Grund für die Nichterfüllung des von Franz I
mit Philipp II in Madrid 1526 geschlossenen Vertrages geliefert. Der Präsident
de Selves erklärte auf der vom König 1527 berufenen Notabelnversammlung
den Punkt der Abtretung von Burgund in diesem Vertrage für unwirksam. Vgl.
J. Russell Major, Representative Institutions, 135 ff.

[54] Vgl. *République* I, 8, S. 239.

[55] *Rép.* I, 8, S. 130, 136. – Der Krönungseid wird als allgemeines Bekenntnis
zur Gerechtigkeit aufgefaßt.

[56] Für das deutsche Reich wird dies von Bodin mit dem Hinweis auf die Absetzung von Adolf von Nassau (1296) und Wenzel (1400) angenommen (*Rép.*
II, 5, S. 301). Aber eben diese Tatsachen bestätigen Bodin, daß der deutsche
König keine Souveränität besitzt, sondern diese bei den Ständen des Reiches
liegt (vgl. II, 2, S. 262 und II, 4, S. 320/21). Vgl. hierzu Schubert [252], 218,
269, 341, der zu Recht bemerkt daß diese Ansicht Elementen der Reichsverfassung wie dem Kurfürstenkollegium, den Deputationen und Kreisständen nicht
gerecht wird und auch der Sicht der Verfassung, soweit sie die kaiserlichen
Rechte betont, nicht entspricht (360 ff.).

[57] Vgl. *République* II, 6, S. 321.

[58] Ein anderes Bild ergibt sich in der ständischen Theorie. Hier bindet sich
der Fürst durch den Krönungseid und die Wahlkapitulation (*Vindiciae*, 126, 128,
130) und ist an alle Grundgesetze gebunden (z. B. in Brabant S. 130). Da ihm
das Volk die Herrschaft überträgt, wird er damit an die Schranken des Gesetzes gebunden (S. 94). Zur ständischen Theorie des Vertrages und des Dop-
pelbundes siehe Gerhard Oestreich, Die Idee des religiösen Bundes und die
Lehre vom Staatsvertrag, jetzt in: Geist und Gestalt des frühmodernen Staates,
1969, 168 ff.

walt verhütet.[59] Von diesem Gesichtspunkt her wird es zu verstehen sein, daß Bodin als Mitglied der Ständeversammlung zu Blois 1576 sich gegen den Vorschlag wandte, die Finanznot durch Veräußerung königlicher Güter zu beheben.[60] In der Tat hat der Grundsatz der Unveräußerlichkeit des Besitzes nicht nur im 16. Jahrhundert nach dem Vertrage von Madrid 1526 die Nichterfüllung einer Verpflichtung zu territorialer Abtretung begründen helfen. Er hat im 17. Jahrhundert im Kreise Richelieus dann, indem man unverjährbare königliche Ansprüche auf im Deutschen Reich liegende Gebiete annahm, dazu gedient, einer Begründung von Ansprüchen der französischen Herrscher auf Gebietserweiterung zu dienen.[61] Für den hier zu behandelnden Zusammenhang ist wichtig, daß sich diese ganze Materie mit der Anerkennung ständischer Einflüsse verbindet. Mit Zustimmung der Stände und unter Registrierung im Parlament konnte der König über den Besitz verfügen; das wurde stets in dieser Zeit anerkannt.[62]

Überblickt man im Zusammenhang diese Beschränkungen der souveränen Gewalt, die Bodin in seinem Werke annimmt, so zeigt sich nicht nur, daß echte Begrenzungen der Souveränität und schon aus diesem Grunde Elemente der Mäßigung in seiner Lehre vorliegen, diese Momente weisen auch an einzelnen Positionen Verbindungen zu ständischen Einrichtungen und der Stellung der Untertanen auf. Das natürliche Recht schützt deren Eigentum, und das Fundamentalgesetz über die *inaliénabilité du domaine royal* verweist geradezu auf ständische Mitwirkung für seine Durchbrechung. Das Gleiche gilt von dem Gedanken, daß der Fürst an Verträge seines Vorgängers gebunden bleibt, wenn sie das öffentliche Wohl betreffen, ständische Zustimmung besitzen und dem Lande Vorteil bringen.[63] Auch darin zeigt sich eine Begrenzung, daß Bodin an-

---

[59] Diese Deutung auch bei ALBERTINI [176], 62.

[60] In diesem Sinn versteht sein Eintreten in Blois OWEN ULPH [156], Jean Bodin and the Estates General of 1576, *Journal of Modern History* 19 (1947), 293 ff. Siehe auch ROELLENBLECK [231], *Der Staat* 4 (1964), 237. Eine bewahrende Rolle für die Erhaltung der französischen Territorien hat dies Prinzip anläßlich der Lossagung vom Madrider Vertrag mit Karl V von 1526 gespielt. Vgl. DICKMANN, *Historische Zeitschrift* 196 (1963), 303 und oben Anm. 53.

[61] Vgl. DICKMANN, *HZ* 196 (1963), 281 ff.

[62] Vgl. DICKMANN, *HZ* 196 (1963), 290, 294.

[63] Vgl. *République* I, 8, S. 160 Auf der anderen Seite zieht Bodin dem Einfluß der Parlamente Schranken. Er sieht in ihnen Gerichtshöfe, die indes ohne politische Zuständigkeiten sind, denen zwar das Recht der Remonstranzen gegen die königlichen Edikte und Ordonnanzen bleibt, die aber letztlich den königlichen Rechtssatz nicht endgültig aufhalten können, wenn auch ein kluger Monarch nicht gegen ihre Meinung handeln wird. Vgl. *République* III, 4, S. 418 und hierzu HINRICHS [266], 92 f. und J. H. SHENNAN, The Parliament of Paris, London 1968, 220.

erkennt, daß der Magistrat an sich zwar dem Fürsten Gehorsam schuldet, daß aber diese Pflicht entfällt, wenn der Fürst diese Gebote des Naturrechts verletzt; bei Nichtachtung der Fundamentalgesetze gewährt Bodin dem *officier* ein Remonstrationsrecht.[64]

III

Schon die bisherige Betrachtung hat gezeigt, daß die Lehre Bodins zwar durch den Grundsatz der Unteilbarkeit der Souveränität keinen Raum für eine entscheidende Mitbestimmung der ständischen Vertretungen läßt, daß er aber ihre Existenz anerkennt und in bestimmten Richtungen ihre rechtliche Mitwirkung als notwendig oder als bedeutsam ansieht. Wenn hierbei von ständischen Einrichtungen die Rede ist, so fallen hierunter nur Erscheinungen, die zu den verfassungsmäßig anerkannten Institutionen gehören. Hinsichtlich aller außerhalb dieses legalen Bereiches stehenden Gruppen und Zusammenschlüssen teilt Bodin die allgemeine negative Haltung seiner Zeit. Die Fixierung auf die hohe Bedeutung der Einheit für den Staat, besonders für die Monarchie, führt die Anschauung des 16. Jahrhunderts dazu, alle Verbindungen der Untertanen, die nicht in den vorgesehenen Formen erfolgen, als Faktionen und Quellen von Unruhe und Tumult zu verurteilen. Entsprechend wendet sich Bodin gegen die Bestrebungen des dänischen Adels, dem König seinen Willen aufzuzwingen.[65] Faktionen werden gleicherweise wie Aufstände als verderblich für alle Staatsformen bezeichnet. Dabei definiert Bodin die Faktion nicht als eine kleine Zahl von Personen, sondern als größere Zusammenschlüsse. Der Fürst soll sie, wenn er sie nicht im Guten beruhigen kann, mit Gewalt bekämpfen.[66] In der Gefahr der Bildung von Faktionen liegt auch der Grund für die negative Beurteilung der Wahlmonarchie.[67] Immer droht bei der Bildung solcher Parteiungen die Gefahr des Bürgerkrieges.

Diese Haltung entspricht auch der Stellungnahme des Autors der *Republik* zur religiösen Frage. Er lehnt hier – und das wird auch seine praktische Haltung in Blois 1576 bestimmen – die Anwendung von Gewalt zur Herstellung der Einheit ab.[68] Aber in der *Republik* tritt er für die Gewinnung einer religiösen Einheit ein. Es gibt, so sagt er, nichts Gefährlicheres, als wenn die Untertanen in ihren Anschauungen über den Staat, die Religion oder die Gesetze geteilt sind.[69] Auch hiermit befindet sich Bodin im Einvernehmen mit der herrschenden Richtung seiner Epoche,

---

[64] Vgl. *Rép.* III, 4, S. 414 f.
[65] *Républiqe* II, 1, S. 266.
[66] *Rép.* IV, 7, S. 636.

[67] *Rép.* VI, 5, S. 977.
[68] *Rép.* IV, 7, S. 654.
[69] *Rép.* IV, 7, S. 655.

die in der Einheit der Religion innerhalb des Staates die Grundlage für den Frieden erblickte.[70] Nur eine Minderheit, die für ihren Bestand kämpfte, trat in jener Zeit für eine allgemeine Toleranz ein.[71] Vom Standpunkt Bodins aus können ständische Vertretungen nicht an der obersten Entscheidung teilhaben, weil dadurch eine Teilung der Souveränität eintreten würde. Daher betont er, daß der Fürst auch ohne die Stände Gesetze erlassen kann.[72] Aber er hebt andererseits hervor, daß eine Anhörung der Stände und ihre Zustimmung zwar nicht eine Sache der *necessitas*, aber der *humanitas* sei.[73] Darüber hinaus tritt Bodin in zurückhaltender Form, aber immerhin erkennbar, für das Recht der Stände bei der Bewilligung von Steuern ein. Indem er die Anerkennung dieses Rechts in England, dem Reich und Spanien erwähnt, und zugleich ohne Ablehnung den Standpunkt der französischen Generalstände von Tours gegenüber Karl VIII (1484) berichtet, zeigt sich seine Haltung.[74]

Zeigt sich der Verfasser also bei der Bemessung der Rechte der ständischen Einrichtungen vorsichtig, so erkennt er ihre Bedeutung und ihren Nutzen für das Land in vollem Maße an. Er lehnt die Meinung derer ab, die wie Philipp von Commynes in den Ständen eine Gefahr erblickte. Es gibt vielmehr, so sagt er, für das rechte Königtum keine sicherere Grundlage als die Stände des Volkes, die Korporationen und Zünfte *(estats du peuple, corps et colleges)*. Sie dienen zu Schutz und Verteidigung des Fürsten, bewilligen ihm Steuern, sichern die Aushebung von Truppen. Sie ermöglichen, daß der Fürst die Beschwerden seiner Untertanen hört und die Schäden in seinem Lande erfährt. Das Volk wünscht, daß er diese Beschwerden hört, und es ist stolz, Zugang zu seinem Herrscher zu haben.[75] In den wohlgeordneten Aristokratien und Monarchien gehört die

---

[70] Zur allgemeinen Auffassung siehe HINRICHS [266], 115.

[71] So setzte sich 1562 SÉBASTIEN CASTELLION in seiner Schrift «Conseil à la France désolée» für die Toleranz ein (Ausgabe von MARIUS F. VALKHOFF, Genf 1967). Und 1588 wandte sich ESTIENNE PASQUIER in seiner Flugschrift Advis au Roy wiederum im gleichen Sinne an den König. (Ausgabe in «Ecrits Politiques» hrsg. von H. D. THICKETT, Genf 1966, Bd. I, 91 ff.).

[72] *République* I, 8, S. 142.

[73] *République* I, 8, S. 149.

[74] *République* VI, 1, S. 880. Vgl. zu dieser positiven, wenn auch zurückhaltenden Stellungnahme JEAN MOREAU-REIBEL [116], Jean Bodin et le droit public comparé, Paris 1933, 196 ff.; W. J. STANKIEWICZ, Politics and Religion in Seventeenth Century France, Berkeley 1960, 50.

[75] *République* III, 7, S. 500/01.: «Et néanmoins la juste Royauté n'a point de fondement plus asseuré que les estats du peuple, corps et colleges; car s'il est besoin de lever deniers, assembler des forces, maintenir l'estat contre les ennemis, cela ne se peut faire que par les estats du peuple de chacune province, ville et communauté.» (500).

Rücksicht auf die *corps et colleges* zu der in jedem Staat löblichen Mäßigung *(mediocrité)*. Denn alle solche Gemeinschaften und Korporationen aufzuheben, würde den Staat ruinieren und aus ihm eine barbarische Tyrannei machen.[76] Er warnt freilich, im Einklang mit der Stellungnahme zu den Faktionen, jede Art von *assemblees et confrairies* zuzulassen. Hält man sich diese Darlegungen vor Augen, so wird man nicht mehr von einer den Ständen gegenüber abweisenden Haltung Bodins sprechen können. Gibt er ihnen auch nicht den Platz, den ihnen die ständische Theorie erringen wollte, hält er an der Geschlossenheit der souveränen Macht des Fürsten fest, so räumt er ihnen doch einen wesentlichen, für das Wohl der Gesamtheit sogar bestimmende Position ein. Das Wort *mediocrité*, das wir mit Mäßigung übersetzen dürfen, das in diesen Zusammenhang fällt, kennzeichnet die Gesamttendenz deutlich. Auch hier ergibt die Untersuchung, daß Bodin starke Elemente einer gemäßigten Anschauung beibehält.

Mit dieser Feststellung geht dann auch seine eigene politische Haltung während der Stände in Blois im Grundsatz zusammen. Auf dieser Versammlung hat Bodin, wie wir wissen,[77] eine führende Rolle im Rahmen des Dritten Standes gespielt, dem er als Deputierter des Vermandois angehörte. Er trat dabei ebenso gewissen Vorschlägen der Berater des Königs wie auch den privilegierten Ständen energisch entgegen. In Sachen der Religion setzte er sich – hierin über die Äußerungen der *Republik* hinausgehend – für Toleranz ein. Er sah deutlich, daß die Wahl nur zwischen der Forderung religiöser Einheit, die von dem Pariser Advokaten Versoris (Pierre le Tourneur) vorgetragen wurde und die zum Bürgerkrieg führen mußte, und einer Politik der Duldung lag. So vermochte er eine Entscheidung für die erstere Linie zwar nur aufzuschieben, aber er blieb seiner Grundlinie treu.[78] In der Frage der vom König gewünschten Leistung der Stände vertrat Bodin einen Standpunkt, der durch die Verteidigung der Interessen des Dritten Standes bestimmt wurde. Er forderte, daß die Steuern gleichmäßig von allen Ständen getragen werden sollten und widersetzte sich daher auch der Bildung eines ständischen Ausschusses zur Zusammenstellung der Beschwerden der *cahiers*, der alle drei

---

[76] *Rép.* III, 7, S. 502: «J'ay dit que la mediocrité qui est louable en toutes choses, se doit aussi garder és estats Aristocratiques, et justes Royautés, pour le regard des corps et colleges: car d'oster tous les corps et communautes, c'est ruiner un estat, et d'en faire une barbare tyrannie.»

[77] Wir kennen diese Vorgänge aus seinem Selbstzeugnis: Recueil de tout ce qui s'est négocié en la compagnie du tier-état de France en assemblée générale des trois états, assignée par le Roi en la ville de Blois au 15. novembre 1576 (Des ètats généraux et autres assemblées nationales 13 hrsg. v. Cʜ. J. Mᴀʏᴇʀ Paris 1789, S. 212–313). Vgl. auch hierzu Hɪɴʀɪᴄʜꜱ [266], 92 f.

[78] Vgl. Owᴇɴ Uʟᴘʜ [156], *Journal of Modern History* 19 (1947), 289 ff.

Stände umfassen sollte, weil er Minorisierung des Dritten Standes besorgte. Hier machte er sich zum Anwalt einer in jener Zeit mehrfach erhobenen Forderung nach größerer Gerechtigkeit in der Verteilung der Steuerlast.[79] Dagegen hielt Bodin zurück, wo es sich um die wie bei früheren Versammlungen hervortretenden Forderungen nach stärkerer Mitbeteiligung der Stände an den Fragen der Regierung handelte. Das hätte seiner Auffassung widersprochen.[80]

Wir sehen dann Bodin in späteren Jahren noch ein letztes Mal diese Haltung beobachten, als er 1583 im Dienste des Herzogs von Anjou in Antwerpen weilt und die Verhandlungen des Herzogs mit den niederländischen Ständen beurteilt. Hier findet der von den Niederländern vorgeschlagene Vertrag seine Kritik. Da die Städte die Zitadellen nicht aufgeben wollen, würden sie Meister des Prinzen werden. Denn derjenige sei Herr im Staate, der über die Streitmacht *(puissance publique)* verfügt. Eine solche Regelung würde zur Teilung der Souveränität führen und den Ruin des Staates verursachen.[81]

Die Züge, die diese Untersuchung dem Bilde Bodins einzuzeichnen sucht, sind gewiß nicht unbekannt. Sie sollen auch nicht dessen Grundlagen verändern. Wohl aber erscheint es gegenüber der älteren, oft zu sehr allein auf die absolutistischen Neigungen des Autors abgestellten Würdigungen notwendig, heute dem Gesamtbild ausgleichendere und detailliertere Konturen zu geben. Neben seiner für die Folgezeit so entscheidenden Vertretung der fürstlichen Souveränität hat Bodin doch, entsprechend der umfassenden und breit dokumentierten Basis seines Werkes, auch den Erscheinungen des Ständetums erhebliche Beachtung und zu einem nicht geringen Maße auch Anerkennung geschenkt, ohne freilich in seiner Grundeinstellung den Standpunkt der monarchischen Seite zu verlassen.

---

[79] ULPH [156], 291 ff. Zu dem Verlangen nach Verteilung der Lasten auf alle Stände, die in jener Zeit weithin erhoben wurden, siehe DAVIS BITTON, The French Nobility in Crisis 1560–1640, Stanford 1969, 22 f.

[80] Bodin selbst hat seine Tätigkeit auch in der Folge für bedeutsam gehalten und betont. Während sich in den frühen Auflagen keine Erwähnung seiner Aktivität in Blois findet (vgl. *République* Ausgabe 1577 [7.4], III, 7, S. 388), wird seine Tätigkeit in späteren Auflagen (Ausgabe 1583, 486) eingefügt und mit Stolz vermerkt, daß der König gesagt habe «que Bodin auroit manié les Estats à son plaisir.»

[81] Brief vom 21. 1. 1583 an seinen Schwiegervater Trouillard, Auszug bei GRIFFITHS, Representative Government, 505.

R. J. Schoeck

Bodin's Opposition to the Mixed State and to Thomas More[1]

I. Preliminary Observations

Comparisons are not always odious; they may in fact be heuristic, as Hexter has recently shown with his comparison of Utopia and Geneva, for example.[2] They may be useful to explore differences, as with the conventional comparison so frequently made between Bodin and Machiavelli: «la perspective habituelle pour apprécier la porté de *la République*» (as Mesnard has written) «reste cependant la comparaison avec l'œuvre et les doctrines de Machiavel»;[3] and the comparison between More and the doctrines of Machiavelli works equally well.[4] In spatial terms, we might say that the use of two points of reference is most useful in establishing or locating a gap between them: simple to say, More is *here*, Machiavelli *there*. Bodin himself is of course fond of comparisons.

But in the very act of making a comparison, we must always be clear about what we are comparing. We should remind ourselves that we run the risk of being extractive – that the theme of Pride in More's *Utopia*, e.g., is only a part of the whole – and that we may be flattening out changes of tone or voice, a common failing with historians of ideas. For

---

[1] The definitive edition of More's *Utopia* is that by E. Surtz and J. H. Hexter in the Complete Works of St. Thomas More, volume 4 (New Haven: Yale University Press, 1965) – all page references will be to this edition. For an introduction to the continuing impact of Utopian thought in a wide spectrum of approaches, see Daedalus (Spring, 1965).

For English students of Bodin, a useful *accessus ad auctores* is provided by the early pages of E. William Monter's recent essay on Inflation and Witchcraft: The Case of Jean Bodin, in Action and Conviction in Rarly Modern Europe – Princeton: University Press 1969, 371–89, [268].

[2] J. H. Hexter, Utopia and Geneva.

[3] On Bodin and Machiavelli see P. Mesnard [129], L'Essor de la Philosophie Politique au XVe Siècle, 2me ed. Paris 1952, 538.

[4] There is an extended comparison by Gerhard Ritter, Machtstaat und Utopie... Die Daemonie der Macht, 2 Aufl. (1941), transl. by R. W. Pick as The Corrupting Influence of Power, London 1952; see also J. H. Hexter, The Loom of Language and the Fabric of Imperatives: The Case of *Il Principe* and Utopia, *The American Historical Review* 69 (1964), 945–968. Cf. *Utopia*, pp. XXVI–XXVII, XC, CI.

the diatribe against Pride is spoken by Raphael Hythloday, who is only a character within the total work, expressing one point of view with which the authorial character indicates at the very end that he does not in fact fully agree (and the etymologizing of *Hythloday* as ‹speaker of nonsense› may be taken as a key to the play of irony in the literary work).[5]

We might draw attention to parallels between the two authors: both are extraordinarily conscious of the rapidity of change in their own times, both acutely aware of the importance of economics. In both we find a bringing together of humanistic and legal education, and both served their kings in high legal office – More as King's Counsel, Chancellor of the Duchy of Lancaster, and Lord Chancellor of England; Bodin as King's attorney – and both played significant parliamentary roles. One could go on, but I do not intend to develop the biographical parallels, merely to call attention to them and to subtle differences and affinities in the humanism of the two men.[6] Yet I would urge two final vital points, the one of similarity and the other of difference: each had a strong element of conservatism in his writing and thought that is often masked by an originality or radicalism of another kind; and there is little in Bodin to compare with the core of spirituality that is so much of the essential More.

We might begin with Bodin's reference to More at the beginning of the *République*, for while this reference is well known it needs to be closely examined: «Toutefois, nous ne voulons pas aussi figurer une République en Idée sans effet, telle que Platon et Thomas le More, chancelier d'Angleterre, ont imaginé: mais nous nous contenterons de suivre les regles Politiques au plus près qu'il sera possible.»[7]

Like so many others, Bodin seems to have read More's *Utopia* univocally – I know of no evidence to the contrary – that is, he read it as a treatise or programme (albeit an imagined one), with no allowance for

---

[5] For my reading of *Utopia*, see: On reading More's Utopia as Dialogue: ‹A Nursery of Correct and Useful Institutions›, *Moreana*, 22 (Mai 1969), 19–32.

[6] Both combined humanistic and legal studies. Bodin's humanism was carried a step further than More's in that the Christian element was less conspicuous and the elevation of a more self-centered philosophy prepared for as Mesnard has characterized that humanism: «Bodin, on le voit, ne considère pas l'humanisme comme l'acquisition d'une simple forme littéraire, mais comme une philosophie véritable qui conduit l'homme à la sagesse par un contact de plus en plus vivifiant avec les oeuvres maîtresses de l'antiquité. Cf. dans le même esprit la leçon de Latomus au Collège des Trois langues, *De studiis humanitatis*, éditée par Gryphe, Paris 1534.» Œuvres Philosophiques, Paris 1951, Tome V, 3, p. 45 n.

[7] *République*, Préface, p. IV (édition 1579, DuPuys); cf. P. MESNARD [129], 476.

an ironic mirror or prism. For us today, Hexter has quite usefully put the several questions which this line of inquiry raises: «Is the More of *Utopia* the *real* More? Did More *really* believe what he wrote in *Utopia*? Did Machiavelli *really* believe what he wrote in *Il Principe*? Is the Machiavelli of *Il Principe,* that hasty chance tract, the *real* Machiavelli? Is not the real Machiavelli rather the author of the *Discorsi,* the work that represents the meditation of a lifetime?»[8] These are not questions which are likely to have disturbed Bodin, yet they are not only ‹modern› questions but questions germane to our present concerns, and we shall consider some of them later.

II. The Mixed State and More's Sources

There is no need, given the nature of this seminar, to attempt to sketch the traditional idea of the mixed state. What is important is to indicate what of that tradition was available to More – and perhaps to suggest lines of difference from that available to Bodin – and to analyse and evaluate its presentation in the *Utopia.*

That More knew both Aristotle and Plato first-hand is beyond dispute, and a considerable degree of influence of Plato's *Republic* in the *Utopia* has never been doubted.[9] Among classical authors, it is likely that More would also have known Xenophon's *Cyropaedia,* and (through Erasmus' modified translation of Isocrates' treatise published in 1516 with his own *Institutio principis Christiani*) Isocrates' *To Nicocles.* (We might also glance at the list of ‹great books› in *Utopia,* a list which includes Plato, Aristotle, Plutarch, Thucydides, Herodotus, and Herodian.) Surtz has suggested a number of parallels with Patrizi, who declared that everyone was now reading Isocrates in Italy, and there are other parallels, of course, suggested in his commentary to the *Utopia.*[10]

Lacking a synthetic statement on More's medieval heritage, we can profitably catalogue the obvious and established medieval sources and provide a provisional list of the less certain or problematic sources of More's political ideas. Certain sources would include Augustine's *City of*

---

[8] HEXTER, Loom of Language, 949.

[9] Still the most detailed study is LINA BEGER, Thomas Morus und Plato: ein Beitrag zur Geschichte des Humanismus, *Zeitschrift für die gesamte Staatswissenschaft* 35 (1879), 187–216, 405–83; cf. SURTZ, *Utopia,* pp. CLIX–CLX.

[10] For Patrizi, see esp. SURTZ, pp. CLXXVI–XLXXVII, on *De regno* and *De institutione statu* ... Other parallels and sources: Plutarch, Cicero, Seneca, Tacitus, and other classical writers; The Travels of Sir John Mandeville, Piers Plowman and other poems of social protest; Petrarch, Bracciolini, Pontano, and other humanists.

God, on which we know that he lectured quite early in his career; Aquinas, an established source in some areas (as with the *Catena Aurea* and some parts of the *Summa Theologiae),* but less certain in other areas; a considerable but as yet largely undefined body of writing by the commentators in canon law, theology, and scripture;[11] some conciliar writers, including certainly Gerson and Cusa[12] – the list will surely be enlarged as more analysis is done in this sector of More studies. It is likely that More knew the treatises of such writers as John of Salisbury and Aegidius Romanus, but the case has not yet been made with certainty; nor has more than a drawing of parallels been done with Beroaldo and Campano.[13] He would most assuredly have been familiar with Bracton, Glanvil, Littleton, the Year-Books, and other essential texts in the English common-law tradition which leads to Plowden and the enunciation of the king's two bodies.[14]

There is no evidence that More knew Dudley's *Tree of Commonwealth,* composed in 1509–1510 while the former minister of Henry VII was in prison awaiting his execution by Henry VIII; and while it is difficult to believe that More would not have known him personally (for a number of reasons), it must be remembered that the text was not printed before the nineteenth century and that More may not have been among those who read in manuscript that curiously conventional representation of an organic theory. A thorough study of More's political sources will

---

[11] It is of course dangerous to assume that one writer will always know firsthand the sources of an author he is using, but it is worth recording that among the sources of Bracton on kingship are Ambrose, Augustine, the Roman *Corpus iuris civilis,* Gratian's *Decretum,* the decretals of Gregory IX, Raymond of Pennafort, and Azo of Bologna: cf. FRITZ SCHULZ, *The English Historical Review* 60 (1945), 136–176.

[12] Even if More himself did not know the conciliar tradition before 1528 (which he did), he dealt with it in his controversies with St. German, whose materials included conciliar writings and Gerson. SABINE has reminded us that in the conciliar theory we find the idea of «a monarchy tempered by aristocracy in which the authority conceived to lie in the whole church was shared concurrently among its representative organs. Each organ had the right and the duty to keep the other organs in their places, while all were subject to the organic law of the whole body,' and decrees of the Council of Constance articulate this principle: A History of Political Theory, 3d ed. (1950), 323.

[13] BEROALDO, *De optimo statu,* and CAMPANO, *De regendo magistratu,* frequently appear in the commentary of Surtz's edition of *Utopia:* see Introduction, pp. CLXXVI f.

[14] See E. H. KANTOROWITZ, The King's Two Bodies: A Study in Mediaeval Political Theology, Princeton: University Press 1957, and T. F. T. PLUCKNETT, Early English Legal Literature, Cambridge: University Press 1958, with my review in *Natural Law Forum,* 4 (1959), 182–90.

include the writings of his opponents in a series of long polemical works: Luther, Tyndale, and Christopher St. German; and one must study as well as the vitally important prefaces to the Henrician statutes (which so often embody crucial modifications of political theory and doctrine), and a number of pamphlets (among which I would signal *A Glasse of the Truthe*, 1533, for its appeal to a General Council and for its citations of Gerson).[15] One would weigh carefully the influence of the 1522 Basle reprinting of Marsilius of Padua's *Defensor Pacis* and the preparation of an English translation under Cromwell's patronage (noting that the translation was completed some time before its release in 1535). But above all, one must read the several works of Christopher St. German, who is central to such a study and to the full history of Tudor political theory. For (in the words of Baumer)[16]: «As the statute book during these years introduced more and more radical innovations, St. German himself became more and more audacious, and in his last pamphlet, *An Answer to a Letter*, ended by ascribing to the king in parliament all the jurisdictional power formerly wielded by both pope and English clergy.»

It is patent that the histories cited by Bodin in *La Méthode* – Polydore Virgil and one or two others – were not adequate to give Bodin an understanding of the complexities of constitutional thought in England.

But for our understanding of More, the most neglected figure is the perhaps still shadowy John Fortescue, who like More had been a distinguished lawyer, before becoming chancellor in exile to Henry VI. Thomas More was educated in the same Inn of Court as Fortescue, and so was his father; and it is possible, indeed even probable, that John More would have known Fortescue. The common law traditions were very strong at that time; given the vigour of the educational system (in which all lawyers had to participate) and the particular institution of the readings, we are justified in thinking that Fortescue's ideas would have held sway more lastingly and more deeply in Lincoln's Inn than anywhere else in England.[17] I do not know that Bodin read any Fortescue (though his name is mentioned); and that is rather a pity, for Fortescue would have

---

[15] At present, these can best be identified in the appendices to Baumer's study of Tudor kingship – F. L. BAUMER, The Early Tudor Theory of Kingship, New Haven: Yale University Press 1940 – although a number are discussed by Julius King in his unpublished Cornell dissertation on the Royal Propaganda campaign of Henry VIII.

[16] FRANKLIN LE VAN BAUMER, The Early Tudor Theory of Kingship. See my forthcoming study of St. German.

[17] In a group of unpublished lectures on Thomas More and the Law (Yale 1968), I have stressed the importance of traditions in Lincoln's Inn. Cf. H. LÈVY-ULLMANN, The English Legal Tradition, London 1935.

provided an even more pronounced target of the theory of a *système equilibrée* than More in his treatise of *The Difference between an Absolute and a Limited Monarchy,* while *De Laudibus Legum Anglie* with its extolling of the English legal tradition and its institutions would have provided far more detail in constitutional areas than can be found in Polydore Virgil.

Let us take Fortescue's *De Natura Legis Naturae* for its explicit and vigorous statement of his ideas on kingship. Following the main lines of late medieval natural law thought, but reinforced by common law tradition, Fortescue strongly upheld the concept of the *dominium politicum et regale,* and he drew forth these conclusions: 1. that the king, either *solus* or in parliament, is subordinate to the natural law – he is ‹under God and the law›. Enunciated as early as Henry of Bracton *(Ipse autem rex non debet esse sub hominem sed sub deo et sub lege* fol. 5b), this concept was reaffirmed by innumerable judges in the Year-Books and by St. German in the *Doctor and Student.* 2. That the king, in formulating law (and *a fortiori* in changing the customary law or in levying taxes), must work in and with parliament. Or, in Fortescue's words, the «kynge may not rule his peple bi other lawes than such as thai assenten unto.»[18] 3. That the king must himself observe the law, for he is himself under God and the law.[19]

The Thomistic distinction between *dominium regale* and *dominium regale et politicum* (familiar in the *Summa,* Ia IIae, q. 17, a 7; q 56, a 4; q 58, a 2) is thus strongly reaffirmed in England by Fortescue, and in the opening chapter of his *De Monarchia* he stated: «There bith two kyndes off kyndomes, of the wich that on is a lordship callid in laten *dominium regale,* and that other is callid *dominium politicum et regale.* And thai diversen in that the first kynge may rule his peple bi such lawes as he makyth him self. And therefore he may sett upon thaim tayles and other imposicions such as he wol hym self, witowt thair assent. The secounde kynge may not rule his peple by other lawes than such as thai assenten unto. And therefore he may sett uppon thaim non imposicions withowt thair owne assent. This diversite is wel taught bi Seynt Thomas in his boke wich he wrote ad regem Cipri de Regimine Principum.»[20]

And in his pioneering (albeit at times perhaps primitive) comparative study, Fortescue notes that the *dominium politicum et regale* is the

---

[18] The Governance of England, ed. C. PLUMMER, Oxford 1885, 109 – cf. *Utopia,* Surtz ed., p. CLXIX.

[19] BAUMER, Early Tudor Theory of Kingship, 8 – cf. *Utopia,* CLXVIII f.

[20] See further S. B. CHRIMES, Sir John Fortescue, Cambridge: University Press 1942, and C. H. McILWAIN, Growth of Political Thought in the West (1932), 354 ff.

government of England and Scotland, whereas *dominium regale* is the government in France.²¹ Again and again in his *De Laudibus Legum Anglie*, Fortescue contrasts the English common law either to the Roman law or to contemporary practices on the Continent; and he elsewhere calls the French monarchy a tyranny.²²

In the author of the *Utopia*, then, we have a man who may not have been so prodigiously widely read as Bodin, perhaps only John Selden among English legal historians could be considered his rival in point of range of inquiry. But the sheer range of More's reading continues to surprize us as we learn more about it, and with Maitland we might well declare that it is unwise to speak too quickly about what he did not know or had not read. We can declare, however, that in his thought a number of traditions come together. It is clear that he knew Aristotle and Plato first-hand, and a considerable number of other classical and patristic authors, as well as medieval and renaissance writers commenting on or indebted to them. Equally clearly, he knew Aquinas and an as yet undetermined body of medieval writing on kingship, law, and the nature of the commonwealth. To this must be added a first-hand knowledge of a good deal of fifteenth- and sixteenth-century writing in political and related fields. Not least, he was deeply immersed in the common-law tradition from Bracton to Fortescue – and let us not forget that he had numerous canonists and civilians as friends and colleagues or correspondents (the names would include Tunstall, Peter Giles, Budé and Busleiden), and that the legal printer John Rastell was his brother-in-law. All of this was available to the author of the *Utopia,* and the commentary by Surtz to the Yale Edition of this work will quickly indicate how richly evocative More's thought and writing are.

---

²¹ *Governance,* ch. III, pp. 113–15; SURTZ, *Utopia,* p. CLXIX. Surtz has noted a number of points at which Fortescue seems to be following Aegidius Romanus, *De regimine principum* (Venice ed., 1498): *Utopia,* p. CLXIX.

²² *Governance,* IV, p. 117; SURTZ, *Utopia,* p. CLXX. Fortescue has quoted Saint Thomas to the effect that «whan a kynge rulith his reaume only to his owne profite, and not to the good off is subiectes, he is a tyrant»; but if he is as poor as English kings before Henry VII, «he shal bi necessite be arted [compelled] to fynde exquysite meanes of geytinge of good; as to putt defaute in some of his subgettes that bith innocentes, and vpon riche men more then the pore, by cause that he mey bettir pay» (Governance IX, p. 119).

²³ On Utopus, see *Utopia,* pp. 219–21, 385–7, 395, 449. I have commented on the Spartan and Plutarchan overtones of the allusion to the history of Utopia stretching back 1760 years; see: More, Plutarch, and King Agis: Spartan History and the Meaning of *Utopia, Philological Quarterly* 35 (1956), 366–75, and *Utopia,* pp. 395–6.

III. The Mixed State of Utopia

But how mixed a state is More's Utopia? Let us examine the work itself, for there have been many confusions about its structure and functions.

The commonwealth – and we speak of course only as we are permitted to see it through the eyes of that *enthousiaste* Hythloday – had originally been a monarchy, although we have only glimpses of the legendary founder, King Utopus.[23] Yet there is enough given to enable us to say that he came from outside the land and that he conquered the island (and in fact it was he who made it into an island), and that he laid down the regulations concerning religion and prescribed the punishments.[24] Utopia originally was structured, it follows, as a *dominium regale*, for we are given a number of examples of action from which we can infer the king's sole exercise of sovereignty and jurisdiction. It would be helpful if we had a fuller account of the transition from the presumably absolute monarchy under King Utopus to the kind of democracy described by Hythloday. But we do not. More seems to have given less thought than Bodin to the birth of a state and not to have been concerned to provide a very full or very clear account of the founding-process;[25] for that kind of interest we must turn either to More's contemporary, Machiavelli, or to the younger contemporary of Bodin, the Calvinist writer Joannes Althusius, who has given a clear statement of the contract theory, which is one of the possible lines for founding and development.[26]

---

[24] *Utopia*, pp. 219–221. It is quite interesting that the Utopian toleration of religious beliefs was by virtue of a royal command.

[25] In urging an emphasis on the *comprehension* of history, Bodin also spoke of a sense of process, of an inquiry into beginnings: «Et en réalité le meilleur du droit universel se cache bien dans l'histoire, si l'on pense que l'on y trouve cet élément si important pour l'appréciation des lois, à savoir les moeurs des peuples, sans compter l'origine, l'accroissement, le fonctionnement, les transformations et la fin de toutes les affaires publiques, c'est-à-dire le principal objet de cette méthode.» *La Méthode*, ed. MESNARD, 276.

Yet Allen is surely right in observing that despite Bodin's declared interest in origins, «he did not clearly see that recognition [of the true end of the State] as a process in time past. Never anywhere does he give any clear and coherent account of how or why the loose early associations of families were transformed into States.» J. W. Allen [97], A History of Political Thought in the Sixteenth Century, 2d ed. London 1951, 411.

[26] With Althusius we move to the notion that a contract «lies at the basis of every association or community of men. He distinguishes various types of community; the family, the *collegium or* corporation, the local community, the Province and the State.» F. COPLESTON, A History of Philosophy, III, Part II New York: Image 1963, 141.

When discovered by the sailor Hythloday – whose sailing, Giles tells More «has not been like that of Palinurus but that of Ulysses or, rather, of Plato» (*Utopia*, p. 49) – Utopia was an on-going society and government. What is described is in some functions closer to a constitutional monarchy than to a pure representative democracy, for the governor is more like a monarch than the president of most modern republics, especially with the provision of holding office for life. The political structure of Utopia, however, is by no means self-evident, having a number of ambiguities, and it would be well to remind ourselves of the details. Apparently there was a bicameral legislature, with assembly and senate. In the assembly there were 200 syphogrants (while we are told that phylarch is the newer term, the older is the term Hythloday favours), democratically elected by family-groups.[27] In the senate there were 20 photophylarchs (or tranibors, which again is the favoured term), plus two syphogrants – a different two being admitted each day, as an obvious device to broaden the base of representation and accountability. The senate consults with the governor at least every other day, and they take counsel about the commonwealth. Theirs is in part also a judicial function, for if there are disputes between private persons the matter is taken at once to the senate to be settled without delay. Its resemblance to the Roman Senate, even to the preparation of legislative bills brought before the people, has been remarked.[28] A balance-check is provided by the device of having whatever is considered important laid before the assembly of the syphogrants who, after informing their groups of families, take counsel together and report their decision to the senate.[29]

Such is the organization for each of the 54 city-states, all of which are reported by Hythloday as identical in language, traditions, customs, and laws. For all 54 form a loose federation, with one national senate at Amaurotum, to which three are sent annually from each city.[30] The final

---

[27] Each syphogrant is elected by thirty families, and a possible clue to this particular number, Surtz suggests, is in Aulus Gellius, a favorite of the humanists: see *Utopia*, p. 397, and my note in *Renaissance News* 13 (1960) 127–129.

[28] SURTZ, *Utopia*, p. 400.

[29] *Utopia*, 400–401. We may here note Marsilius' argument in favour of power belonging to the community, and the corollary (as put by D'Entrèves) that «only the whole community can adequately value what is just and consonant to the common good, and express it in the form of law; reciprocally, only what the community has laid down in the form of law can and must be supreme measure of justice» (on the strength of Dictio I, ch. xii: A. P. D'ENTRÈVES, The Medieval Contribution to-Political Thought Oxford 1939; rptd. New York 1959, 62.

[30] SURTZ, *Utopia*, 147/34.

picture, as Surtz remarks, is not so much one of looseness but «that of independently chosen governors enforcing one law, common and uniform throughout Utopia».[31]

The office of the prince of each city-state is held for life,[32] and he is chosen by the assembly by secret balloting. One of the four candidates named by the people (one out of each of the four quarters of the city) is commended to the senate, for confirmation as I take it. The marginal gloss comments: Mira ratio creandi magistratus.[33] The prince or governor then holds office for life, unless ousted on suspicion of aiming at a tyranny, for, as the gloss here comments, Tyrannis inuisa bene institutae reipublicae.[34] Little else is said of the duties of the governor (Hythloday is fond of saying ‹they› when describing authority and its operations), but we have these hints: a letter from the governor is needed for travel, the governor may apply compassion to pardon criminals, and the governor enjoys few ceremonials – all officials are called fathers – and he himself is distinguished not by a robe or a crown but by the carrying of a handful of grain.[35]

It would be somewhat misleading to call each city-state in Utopia simply a representative democracy: each is very much a mixed state, having free elections but with certain other safeguards. The island is a federation or confederacy of city-states.[36]

---

[31] *Utopia*, 387.

[32] Argument for lifetime term, on the strength of experience, had been made by Isocrates (Nic. 17–18); and against, by Patrizi, on the score that it provided an occasion for tyrants (Rep-., 3.5, fol. 39v) see SURTZ, *Utopia*, 400.

[33] *Utopia*, 122/117.

[34] *Utopia*, 122/118.

[35] *Utopia*, 194/2 & sqq. Cf. my reading of Utopia (cited in n. 5 above) for an echo of the grain metaphor.

On officials being called ‹fathers›, we may recall that Lucan styled Cato *urbi pater urbique maritus*, and for the history of the Roman title *pater patriae* we are directed by Kantorowicz to A. ALFÖLDI, Die Geburt der kaiserlichen Bildsymbolik: 3. Parens patriae, *Museum Helveticum* 9 (1952), 204–43, and 10 (1953), 103–24: see E. H. KANTOROWICZ, Mysteries of State – An absolutist concept and its late mediaeval origins, rptd. from *Harvard Theological Review* 48 (1955), 65–91 in: Selected Studies, Locust Valley, New York: J. J. Augustin 1965, 389 & sqq.

[36] If one were pursuing the sixteenth-century argument on constitutional monarchy, and looking for a defense of constitutionalism, Hooker might be taken as a reply to Bodin, for he continues, as D'Entrèves stresses, the traditional English view of the derivation of power from the community, «or, as he calls it, of ‹the King's dependency› on the ‹whole entire body, over the several parts whereof he hath dominion›, without accepting the ‹strange, untrue, and unnatural conceits, set abroad by seedsmen of rebellion›, «and Hooker is

IV. Comparisons and Contrasts

There are important implications for toleration in the writings of both More and Bodin, but they cannot be our concern at this point. But we must at least note some vital points of interface. In the *Méthode*, Bodin in dealing with the education of the king, stresses that «the elements of the true religion should be gently inculcated in the still pliable mind of the prince . . . On this one point depended in the end the salvation of the State and of all its laws.»[37] But More has given us nothing on the education of a Utopian prince with which to compare (although we note that there is much on education generally in Utopia, and that this is a subject of great interest to Thomas More himself); perhaps the *Utopia* is even egalitarian to the extent of having the prince receive the same potentials of education as anyone else – and inasmuch as he will be elected (and presumably only once every generation or so), no one could know who the prince might be: Hythloday might respond that everyone, therefore, should be educated as though he might become the prince. However, on the question of atheism within the commonwealth there is a common bearing; Hythloday would have completed the unamity of view that there is no room for atheism in a commonwealth. And the Thomas More of the later polemical works would have agreed with Bodin in *la République* that it was »impossible to put those subjects who despised all religions under obedience to the law».[38] The later More moved closer to Bodin's thought, not so much in providing a civic rationale for religion but in seeing that such a rationale was a significant part of the total rôle of religion.

Clearly the stress on the family is an important point of comparison. I have spoken of the role of the family – unit in providing a voting basis

---

thus, D'ENTRÈVES continues, directly condemning the doctrine of *the Vindiciae contra Tyrannos*, and in fact of the whole left wing of sixteenth-century political theory.» The Medieval Contribution to Political Thought (1959), 134.

[37] *La Méthode* VI. 424. It is in this passage that Bodin comments that «nombreux sont les rois d'Angleterre qui ont perdu la couronne pour ne pas avoir écouté la voix du peuple qui leur réclamait les lois de saint Édouard.» Cf. JOSEPH LECLER, Toleration and the Reformation, trans. by T. L. Westow, New York: Association Press 1960, II, 179. The only conclusion of the speakers in the *Heptaplomeres*, Lecler writes (II, 184), «was completely negative: let us no more discuss religious question. Each was left to his conscience; all should practise mutual tolerance and charity . . . Written when the civil war was at its worst, it expressed in its own way the disgust roused by interdenominational conflict and the desire to reach a peaceful solution which would leave freedom of conscience intact whilst restoring order in the State.»

[38] *République*, VI, 1, p. 890.

for the election of delegates to the assembly, and elsewhere in Book II the family is the focal unit. Bodin could have derived his stress on the family from a number of sources other than More, to be sure, but it is remarkable that both he and More virtually eradicate all structures between the family and the state. In Utopia, we must observe, the size of the family was strictly controlled: «... provision is made that no household shall have fewer than ten or more than sixteen adults ... Of children under age, of course, no number can be fixed. This limit is easily observed by transferring those who exceed the number in larger families into those that are under the prescribed number. Whenever all the families of a city reach their full quota, the adults in excess of that number help to make up the deficient population of other cities.»[39]

It would seem that in the *Utopia* the family had a greater political importance than social. In Bodin's view, the state was an association of families which recognized unlimited law-making power in some person. «There must be, says Bodin in substance, in every political society some supreme power to make the laws and invest the magistrates – a power which is itself subject to no law other than the laws of God and Nature.»[40] For Bodin, as for More in the *Utopia*, the family is the cornerstone of the political system (for More the politico-economy, for Bodin the state); and Bodin has to make special provisions for it in relation to his theory of sovereignty. The family must have property, and the king may not take this property without the consent of the father of the family; thus, the king may not tax (directly) without consent, and if direct taxation is necessary, he must ask for a grant. For both More's *Utopia* and for Bodin, the family is vital, but only a means to an end – scarcely an end in itself. (To More personally his family counted a great deal more, as we know from his letters and early biographers.)

For Bodin, it is clear, sovereignty must function as an entity, it must be conceived as a unit – a notion he might have derived from Marsilius of Padua: hii plures [the rulers] sunt unus principatus numero quantum ad officium.[41] I do not believe that there is much Marsilian thought in More, but it must be remembered that the great impetus for his generation came

---

[39] *Utopia*, 135–7. Surtz comments that «an essential difference between Plato's *Republic* and More's *Utopia* lies in the treatment of the family. By his communism of wives and children, Socrates abolished the individual family for the guardians» (p. 414). But by invading the absolute authority of a father over his family – in allowing for children and others to be moved – More has lessened the autonomy of the family; in Utopia it is not inviolable.

[40] Thus BERTRAND DE JOUVENEL, Sovereignty, Cambridge: University Press 1957, 183.

[41] *Defensor Pacis*, I, 17, § 2 – cf. discussion by D'ENTRÈVES, Medieval Contribution, 84–5.

from the 1522 (Basle) edition of the *Defensor*, that St. German picked up some of these ideas (as I have elsewhere argued) and More is not likely to have been receptive to those ideas, both because of the change in political climate and because of their appearance in the writings of St. German from about 1530 onwards. More, it is clear, thought in terms of an equilibrium of powers and forces. His ideas were important to Bodin by virtue of the stature of the *Utopia* itself and of the prestige of More everywhere in the sixteenth century; but they were ideas that cut across Bodin's thinking.

In writing on the constitution of republics (chapter 6 of *la Méthode*), Bodin spoke of the early work of Plato and Aristotle on the science of government: «Après Aristote, Polybe, Denys d'Halicarnasse, Plutarque, Dion, Tacite (pour ne pas mentionner ceux dont les ouvrages ont disparu) nous ont laissé, éparses dans leurs historiques, beaucoup de réflexions aussi brillantes que profondes sur le gouvernement des États. Enfin Machiavel, le premier... Après lui sont venus Patrizi, Thomas Morus, Robert l'Anglois, Garimberti, qui tous ont beaucoup écrit, avec sérieux et abondance, sur les réformes à établir, sur l'éducation des peuples et l'institution des princes, sur la consolidation des lois: mais ils n'ont guère parlé du gouvernment des empires et ont complètement omis d'étudier leurs révolutions...»[42]

V. Conclusion

I do not know of any evidence that Bodin had read More's *Richard III*, which paints tyranny black, or his epigrams, so large a proportion of which deal with tyranny – or if he had (one can never be certain that he had never read something) that Bodin weighs them in the balance. More would have agreed heartily with de Jouvenel's formulation that «the character of a State changes with the agencies and procedures whereby what has been said gets done.» [43] For the *Richard III* and the epigrams can help to explain the egalitarian cast of More's Utopian society and the emphasis on freedom of elections in Utopia. At a time when the idea that the king never dies was developing rapidly and about to flower fully in Plowden (and to be echoed in Bodin), the formulation in More's *Utopia* must be seen as a control of the mysteries of state and all those conflations and heightenings of political theology which were to bring forth the enunciation of the divine right of kings.[44] It must by now be evident

---

[42] *La Méthode*, VI, 349.
[43] The Pure Theory of Politics, Cambridge: University Press 1963, 145.
[44] E. H. KANTOROWICZ, The King's Two Bodies, cf. n. 14 above.

that I am urging a reading of *Utopia* not as a program or ideal commonwealth, but rather the model of a possibility: what reason might do.[45]

To write that More was among those who approved vigorously of the notion, got from Polybius, that sovereignty of the state resides in part in the people, in part in the Senate, and in part in the consuls,[46] is not an unfair reading of Hythloday's description of the Utopian commonwealth. But it does not of course allow for More's qualified response within Book II of the *Utopia*: «Meanwhile ... I cannot agree with all that he said ... But I readily admit that there are very many features in the Utopian commonwealth which it is easier for me to wish for in our countries than to have any hope of seeing realized.»[47]

---

[45] «Viewed rhetorically, More has presented an extended *declamatio,* that rhetorical form which posits an imagined situation and attempts by every device and means available to persuade the audience of its actuality, or potentiality ...» And, as the article continues, «small wonder that Budé felt that ‹our age and succeeding ages will hold [More's] account as a nursery of correct and useful institutions from which every man may introduce and adapt transplanted customs to his own city.» ‹A Nursery of Correct and Useful Institutions›: On Reading More's *Utopia* as Dialogue, *Moreana* 22 (Mai 1969), 19–28.

[46] *La Méthode*, Mesnard ed., 362.

[47] *Utopia*, 245–7.

TEIL II: DISKUSSION

I. PHILOSOPHIE UND RELIGION BEI BODIN

Zusammenfassung: Georg Roellenbleck

Roellenbleck (Zusammenfassung der Referate des ersten Themenkreises)
Il se dégagent les trois points de vue suivants: deux des rapports (Villey, Greenleaf) montrent Bodin comme penseur de l'ordre. Le cours de la Nature est immuable, de toute façon peut-il être aperçu par la raison humaine. Le nombre Un comme le Souverain sont transcendants à cet ordre des choses, bien entendu; mais il y a des œuvres où Bodin insiste particulièrement sur leur caractère d'être accessible à la raison.

Deux autres rapports (Chanteur, Isnardi Parente) soulignent l'idée contraire, l'absolue transcendance de Dieu, et l'analogie de cette transcendance dans la position que Bodin attribue au Souverain. Trois rapports enfin s'occupent de la question s'il y a un développement dans la pensée bodinienne (Isnardi Parente, Baxter, Roellenbleck); idée qui me paraît être niée chez Mme Parente, tandis qu'elle est affirmée dans les deux autres cas.

Je proposerais donc pour matière de ce débat de voir comment s'opère dans l'œuvre de Bodin la conciliation de ces notions opposées. Est-ce là plutôt une opposition entre l'analyse empirique de l'Etat, et la réflexion métaphysique de l'auteur sur les mêmes données? et qu'est-ce que nous révèle l'analyse des points de transition entre ces deux ordres de réflexion? Ou est-ce qu'on n'a affaire qu'à de la piètre philosophie? Où s'insère l'activité politique, donc la biographie, de Bodin, dans ce système? Est-ce qu'il y a une développement dans sa philosophie, et quel est le rôle de la pensée juive dans la formation de ses idées?

Isnardi Parente
Dans la pensée de Jean Bodin il faut reconnaître deux tendances virtuellement opposées: une tendance volontariste très poussée par rapport à la conception de Dieu et des lois qu'il impose à la nature, une tendance nécessitariste par rapport à l'histoire des hommes, qui est réglée par des lois de caractère géographique ou astrologique-numérique. Le lien entre ces deux tendances, qui pourraient aboutir à une véritable contradiction, est constitué par une conception de Dieu seigneur souverain, libre lui-même des lois et jouissant du pouvoir de les imposer à ses sujets. Une conception fortement pragmatique et assez naïve du point de vue philosophique.

Villey

De même que Mme Parente mais pas tout à fait de la même façon, je ne vois pas entre nos différents rapports et dans les différents aspects de l'œuvre de Bodin les opposition que vous venez de marquer. Je dois dire que je fais ici un peu une autocritique puisque si j'avais connu les quatre autres rapports de ce matin, au lieu d'insister sur l'influence du néo-platonisme, je crois que j'aurais marqué plus que je n'ai fait l'influence de la pensée religieuse de Bodin sur son système d'idées. Le judaisme me paraît vraiment une clef de la pensée de Bodin, et aussi l'influence qu'il a reçu du scotisme, c'est à dire de la scolastique de la fin du moyen âge à laquelle il est également lié.

Mais je vois une unité entre toutes ces sources; elles s'accordent toutes dans ceci qu'elles font ressortir la primauté de l'Un: l'Un, c'est Dieu, le nombre Un est le symbole de la divinité et de son gouvernement de l'histoire. Dieu est libre; il agit selon les nombres parce que c'est un Dieu sage, mais le Dieu de Bodin tient beaucoup à se réserver la possibilité du miracle; analogue la position du souverain vis-à-vis de l'état.

Je ne vois donc que peu d'opposition entre les aspects religieux de la pensée de Bodin et ses aspects philosophiques et, un peu différemment de Mme Parente, je vois une unité profonde dans toute la pensée bodinienne; et en outre je n'y vois pas tellement d'évolution, parce que cette même tendance à tout soumettre à l'unité de Dieu se retrouve dans toute l'œuvre de Bodin depuis la *Methodus* jusqu'aux dernières œuvres.

Greenleaf (stimmt zu)

I think that if there is any apparent antithesis between the concept of the unity and harmony and order on the one hand and a concept of independent occamist voluntarism on the other in Bodin's thought, then this antithesis is only apparent in so far as the whole philosophy of unity which, as I understand it, was implicit in the whole of Bodin's thinking, does contain the possibility not only of order but also of disorder. And any act of will on the part of the individual person might, well, would be in conformity with the fundamental god-given order of the world. And in this sense a disorder arising from acts of will is itself a part of the concept of order, which is fundamental of Bodin's thought. It would be possible, therefore, to find also in Bodin the concepts of a divine law and order as which he nominates monarchy and compatibility in human relations and at the same time the notion that you would find kings that are tyrannical or individuals who do not conform to the divine order. These are two different aspects of the same thing, not incompatible elements.

Franklin (stimmt zu)

«Ordnung» und «Voluntarismus» widersprechen sich nicht. Bodins Denken macht in diesem Punkt eine Entwicklung durch; auf jeden Fall aber ist bei ihm der Abstand von Souveränität zu Verfassungsstaat (constitutional law) geringer als dreißig, vierzig Jahre zuvor in der französischen Theorie. And so consequently in particular respect of Prof. Villey's paper, the harmonic order has to be imposed by the sovereign. He is artistic in creating this all, he must be terribly active all the time. The order is not stable, but it needs a constant effort of the sovereign to keep that balance in the state.

Baxter (unterstützt die These von Isnardi Parente)
I think, in the *Methodus* we have basically a self-regulating system without the concept of miracle and of constant intervention from above, we haven't got a concept of law revealed or imposed from above. This was changed by the time of the *République*. In beiden Werken ist neben Maimonides und Leo Hebraeus Philo als Quelle wichtig; er ist jedoch für die *République* wichtiger als für die *Methodus* – warum? I guess this is because in the *Methodus* the Philo which Bodin is using is the pseudo-Philo of *De mundo*, an Aristotelian tract which is supporting the eternity of the world. In the later work Bodin eliminates this side of Philo and goes to the correct Philo. – But the basic point, where I agree with Mrs. Isnardi Parente, is that the supernatural is missing in the analysis of the *Methodus* which is trying to concern itself only with what Bodin calls human history and not with the other two levels of natural and divine history.

Roellenbleck
Bodin lui-même n'a pas eu de difficultés avec l'unité de son système parce que, pour lui, le monde est «the great chain of being» qui part de l'Un, l'unité absolument transcendante, et qui va de «haut» en «bas» comprenant dans son unité l'esprit et la matière. – Mais est-ce qu'on ne retrouve pas la même contradiction apparente entre sa doctrine de l'état, où il est partisan de la plus absolue souveraineté, et son activité politique qui le montre extrêmement actif aux États de Blois pour faire voter le tiers état contre la volonté expresse du roi?

Baxter
I think that at the time of the *Methodus* Bodin is not very interested in direct political intervention and in the 1566 edition of the *Methodus* there are virtually no comments about the present political situation. In the 1572 edition however Bodin is beginning to make comments about the political situation, e.g. concerning the religious wars.

Franklin (stimmt zu)

Die Souveränitätslehre ist in der *Methodus* noch nicht in dem Maß ausgearbeitet, wie später; die Beziehungen König-Staat sind dort noch enger, und die königliche Gewalt wird viel stärker eingeschränkt gesehen.

Villey

Bodins System ist weit und idealistisch genug, die Begründung und Verteidigung sowohl der Einzelinteressen als auch des Staatsinteresses zu ermöglichen.

Freund

Il faut comprendre comme il faut le concept de souveraineté chez Bodin. Ce qu'il refuse, ce n'est pas qu'on ne puisse pour des raisons politiques, s'opposer au roi sur des problèmes pratiques. Ce qu'il refuse, c'est qu'on mette en cause la souveraineté comme telle qui est le principe même de l'unité de l'état. Mais au sein de cette unité vous pouvez avoir des opinions divergentes, vous pouvez être en opposition avec le roi, soit relativement aux différents ordres sociaux, soit même, en conseil privé, au nom de l'ordre général de l'état – toujours à condition que vous ne mettiez pas en cause la notion de souveraineté. Ce qu'il reproche aux monarchomaques, c'est précisément de mettre en cause cette notion de souveraineté et par là, de créer une division à l'intérieur de l'état, et cela non pas pour des raisons politiques mais pour des raisons autres que politiques. Je crois donc que les parties de cet ensemble se concilient sans qu'on puisse parler d'une scission dans la pensée de Bodin.

Scheuner

I agree entirely with Prof. Freund and if you take Bodin's idea of unity and sovereignty we must be sure that he defended it not only as a theoretical right but also as a politician, as the unity of the monarchy and the unity of the state of the *République* practically and theoretically. Therefore we find with him an idea of tolerance, but a tolerance only indivisible to it. He will never allow that the «indivisibilité de l'état» is compromised by tolerance. He would never accept for example a solution as had been accepted in Germany that the whole state was split into two by religious contract. When he suggested a compromise at the estates of Blois in 1576, at which he participated – it was only because he recognized that to demand unity of religion was equivalent to civil war. And he did not accept the possibility of a religious unity set forth by military force or at the cost of a civil war. He only advocated toleration at that time in order to defend the unity of the state. Bodin has always made a difference between his idea of sovereignty and his conception of monarchy beyond the person, beyond the present holder of the sovereignty and the monarch he had before him. So at Blois he opposed the king not because he opposed the sovereign, but because his idea of sovereignty was against that what the sovereign at this moment desired.

Franklin
One must keep in mind Bodin's very sharp and continuing distinction between despotic and royal monarchy. Royal monarchy is absolute – only in the sense that it is not responsible to any other agency. The despotic monarch is not responsible at all – he can do anything. One thing that a royal monarch cannot do is to tax without consent. The key position of Bodin at Blois is the refusal of taxation as a means of preventing civil war. And this is quite consistent with his documented use of sovereignty. Sovereignty does not include the power of taxe without consent.

Salmon (bezieht sich zustimmend auf Freund)
And I do think that there is a great difference in what Bodin has to say about the contemporary situation in the *Methodus* and what he says about it in the *République*. In the *Methodus*, you remember, he talks about the way institutions have survived in the early stages of the civil war; he says that the juridical system is so strong that the war would not be so important. But in the *République* everything is anarchy and I wouldn't like to see Bodin's comments of the *République* interpret the *Methodus* referring not so much to 1570 as Mr Baxter suggested, but I confess I see them rather in the context of the 1560es. All this cross is getting rather away from the philosophical and religious implications of Bodin's general thought. But with Bodin this is inevitable, I suspect.

Baxter
I suspect that the particular references that Mr Salmon thinks of are passages of the 1572 edition. The general distinction between the *Methodus* and the *République* seems to be that in the *Methodus* the limitations of royal power are basically immanent, strictly constitutional and political. In the *République* the stress is laid much more on the divine and supernatural limitations of the exercise of royal power; in part they are seen as deriving from the decalogue, as e.g. the private property. One cannot attack private property, one cannot for instance raise taxes without consent, without thereby infringing the decalogue, infringing positive revealed law. Another aspect of this supernatural level of explanation in the *République* is that it does allow for individuals who are aware of the purposes of god, rare individuals, to intervene directly political affairs if they have the status of prophets. This will occur very infrequently and Bodin doesn't say much about it. Bodin selbst scheint seine Rolle gelegentlich so verstanden zu haben, etwa bei seinen Voraussagen über den Tod

der Königin Elisabeth im Zusammenhang mit dem Barrington-Komplott.

We do know that in the *République* Bodin thinks of Henri III as of the 63rd king of France and therefore as of a person in great danger, and I have the impression that he thinks that Henri III is maintained on the throne by some divine intervention. In diesem Zusammenhang sind die Varianten lehrreich, die McRae in seiner Ausgabe der *République* verzeichnet: Bodins Wechsel von der Königspartei zur Liga schlägt sich in der Betonung bzw. dem Schweigen davon nieder, daß unter dem 63. König eine conversio reipublicae zu erwarten ist.

Hinrichs
Je suis très d'accord avec les vues de Mr. Baxter sur le rôle du surnaturel dans la *République* et dans tous les écrits de Bodin, mais je crois aussi que Bodin avait une conception très précise du fonctionnement politique d'un état. Toutes les notions théoriques de ses œuvres, y compris la notion de la souveraineté, sont influencées par une certaine conception de la réalisation de ces théories. Le fonctionnement politique de l'état n'est pas possible si les conditions pratiques ne sont pas données, si p.e. les relations entre le roi et le peuple ne sont pas bonnes. Selon M. Villey, un des éléments essentiels de ces relations, c'est le respect de la propriété individuelle. Or, ce n'est pas seulement du décalogue que dérive cette idée bodinienne, mais aussi de la condition de la propriété en France aux temps de Bodin. Le roi de France ne pouvait pas disposer de la propriété de ses sujets, mais les relations roi – sujets reposaient sur une espèce de confiance mutuelle, de la confiance p.e. que le roi respectât la propriété, les prêts, les emprunts d'Etat, étc.

Denzer
If I do understand right the paper of Mr. Baxter, then there is noted a distinction between the early Bodin and the late Bodin after his daemonic experiences. The difference is, that the early Bodin has an empirical approach and the late Bodin a metaphysical approach. The question is, whether this interpretation is right. It seems to me that in the *Methodus* and in the *République* both approaches are present: the empirical approach and the idea of order. For example in the *République*, especially considering the system of the forms of government, Bodin gathered the different forms of state empirically and logically, whereas the idea of the best state is influenced by the metaphysical approach, because the royal monarchy corresponds to the order of nature. That's the first problem.

The second problem is whether the idea of order is strictly connected with the influence of judaism and becomes more important, when the influence of judaism increases in Bodin's thought after the *Methodus*. I think, judaism is only one authority to support the idea of order. I agree with Prof. Isnardi Parente, that the authorities and sources: judaism, Maimonides, Scotus are interchangeable. But the position, which Bodin adhered to throughout all his works, is the idea of order, which is independent of the supporting sources.

Villey

Geht Bodins Verteidigung des Privateigentums und des Steuerbewilligungsrechts der Bürger wirklich letztlich auf den Dekalog zurück? Auf einen richtig verstandenen Dekalog gewiß nicht, parce que c'est une interprétation vraiment arbitraire du décalogue que celle qui avait du succès au XVIe et au XVIIe siècle. Je crois que M. Hinrichs a tout à fait raison de trouver le soutien de la position de Bodin à cet égard comme à beaucoup d'autres, dans la situation sociale réelle. Seulement, il y a une rencontre entre les idées politiques et les idées religieuses de Bodin; ce service politique que rendent les idées . . . – on entre vraiment à l'âge des idéologies. Je crois que malgré tout, tout le système religieux et philosophique de Bodin est un peu une superstructure.

Reulos

La préoccupation du Un, de l'unité chez Bodin se traduit en tout cas dans la réalité. Sur le plan politique, le Un est réalisé par la souveraineté susceptible de multiples modalités qui tiennent compte des réalités pratiques. Sur le plan religieux, Bodin – et c'est là que son effort est vraiment remarquable à son époque – a cherché cette unité dans un Dieu unique dont l'action est reflété par toute l'activité humaine, et cela indépendamment de la forme religieuse particulière. Sicher lag einer der wesentlichen Impulse seiner Theologie in der Absicht, die weitgehende Übereinstimmung des christlichen mit den anderen Gottesbegriffen nachzuweisen und zu zeigen, daß eine solche Auffassung der Verwirklichung der Wahrheit nicht entgegensteht. Genau so deckt der Souveränitätsbegriff die verschiedenen Spielarten politischer Wirklichkeit; er benennt eine Einheit, die sich in die verschiedensten Elemente zerlegen läßt. De même, la notion de *loi* se distingue en loi naturelle et loi positive, et par là même, Bodin montrait que cette notion de la loi ne pouvait pas être en contradiction avec la notion de la souveraineté, parce que la loi naturelle répondait à l'idée de l'unité de Dieu et à l'idéal de la souveraineté tout en admettant des coutumes diverses; tout comme la notion de loi positive admettait la distinction des cas idéeologiques et techniques du droit romain comme des droits coutumiers et des droits des ordonnances. C'est dans cette recherche constante d'un principe d'interprétation susceptible d'applications multiples à la réalité que je verrais la liaison qui a été évoquée, entre l'idée de l'unité et l'observation de la réalité qui est impressionnante dans toute l'œuvre de Bodin.

Isnardi Parente
Bodin n'est ni Giordano Bruno ni Spinoza; le centre unitaire de sa pensée est le Dieu de la Bible conçu sur le modèle du seigneur de l'Etat; ce n'est pas un Un conçu comme principe philosophique pur. Le centre de la pensée de Bodin est fortement pragmatique; Bodin n'est pas un philosophe, mais plutôt un savant et un humaniste qui ressent de plusieurs influences philosophiques et vise à donner une justification philosophique *a posteriori* de ses intérêts religieux ou politiques. La contradiction potentielle que j'ai signalée est simplement une entre plusieurs autres: par exemple on peut voir qu'il y a une contradiction potentielle aussi dans la conception bodinienne de la monarchie seigneuriale (d'un côté la plus naturelle, de l'autre côté celle qui ne reconnaît pas la loi naturelle de la propriété individuelle des sujets); ou, encore, dans la conception de la propriété (d'un côté vol et violence, du moins par rapport à son origine; de l'autre côté droit fondé dans la nature). Ce sont des contradictions qui n'éclatent pas ouvertement, mais qui subsistent quand-même.

Villey
Je suis tout à fait persuadé des dimensions religieuses de la pensée de Bodin, mais je ne vois pas ici une grande différence entre une conception de l'Un philosophique et religieuse, puisque toute la littérature philosophique qui a le plus influencé Bodin, à commencer par la pensée juive et arabe mais aussi néo-platonicienne et même platonicienne, est profondément religieuse. Donc je ne vois pas beaucoup de contradictions. – Den Anteil politischer, pragmatischer Faktoren in Bodins Werk hat Herr Hinrichs sehr richtig herausgearbeitet; mais il n'empêche que ces positions politiques, particulières de Bodin ne rentrent parfaitement dans son système qui est tellement ample puisque fondé sur la toute-puissance et la transcendance de Dieu.

Isnardi Parente
Il est vrai que Platon est aussi un esprit religieux, mais il est vraiment impossible de comparer la valeur théorique des idées de Platon, ou, si l'on veut, même de l'Un de Plotin, à la valeur éminemment pragmatique de cet Un-Dieu-roi qui est le centre spéculatif de la pensée de Bodin.

Derathé
Je ne crois pas qu'il y ait un véritable système chez Bodin ni philosophique ni même, j'ajouterai, politique. Dieses «System» mag außerordentlich weit und aufnahmefähig sein, aber es wird aus divergierenden Quellen

gespeist, die er schlecht und recht zu versöhnen bemüht war. Hierin stimme ich mit Frau Isnardi Parente überein. – En ce qui concerne la politique, je ne voudrais pas anticiper sur ce que nous dirons dans les discussions politiques, mais j'ai l'impression aussi que Bodin est plutôt un conciliateur, un homme de compromis qu'un véritable théoricien, en particulier dans sa théorie de la souveraineté, die außerordentlich schwache Stellen hat. Aber ich will nicht vorgreifen und stimme daher zu, wenn von einem gewissen Empirismus Bodins gesprochen wird. Auffallender als der Einfluß von Gegenwartsfragen scheint mir hier allerdings die Überfülle historischer, besonders antiker Belege und ihre Rolle als Argumente in der Diskussion.

Schnur

What is the meaning of «system» in the time when Bodin, after having written the *Methodus,* prepared a new thinking expressed in the *République?* What is the meaning of «order», the great chain of tradition having been interrupted? And if we have a certain idea of system and order, il will be very difficult to use these notions for a time of transition. But perhaps the contradictions are given in the reality? If we can clarify all these points, then we should be able to recognize more fully the difficulty of a thinker at such a time, a time between the old chain of being and the new subjectivism of the following century. And so I did not find any contradiction between the participants of this discussion but the attempt to find the right expression for the situation in which Bodin tries to find new notions of political science. In his situation he could not accept fully any of the traditional systems, nor did he have more confidence into the new calvinistic system. So to save order in these times of transition he must look around for arguments and take them where he found them.

Villey

Je ne me sens aucunement en opposition avec Mme Parente. Qu'est-ce qu'il y a chez Bodin comme système philosophique? Probablement pas grande chose, peut-être cette formule de l'harmonie que est parfois primauté de l'Un et présence des harmoniques, mais qui n'est au fond pas tellement originale et aussi extrêmement vague. De la primauté de l'Un, on peut en tirer beaucoup de choses, d'autant plus qu'il y a plusieurs «Un», il y a plusieurs souverains.

Polin (zustimmend zu Schnur)

Die Unterschiede der bisher geäußerten Meinungen werden nicht zuletzt daher rühren, daß die Einzelnen verschiedene Quellen des Bodinschen Werks studiert haben und ihn von daher verstehen wollen. Nun verarbeitet Bodin in seiner enzyklopädischen Gelehrsamkeit eine Unmasse von Material unterschiedlichster Herkunft; et il est naturel par conséquent que les historiens qui abordent Bodin soient particulièrement sensibles à la diversité des traditions qu'il rassemble dans sa mémoire. Mais d'autre part, je crois qu'il ne faut pas nous laisser impressionner trop par cette idée de système; c'est un fourre-tout que sa philosophie sous l'égide d'un dieu transcendant. Mit dem Begriff des Systems läßt sich das trotzdem vereinbaren, eben eines weitgespannten Systems, in dem notfalls alles unterzubringen ist. Man darf Bodin natürlich nicht als systematischen Philosophen im Sinn des 17. oder 18. Jahrhunderts verstehen. Mais ce qui me paraît important c'est de souligner le remarquable effort de compromis ou, pour le placer à un niveau plus élevé, l'effort extraordinaire de cohérence de sa pensée, l'effort de constituer l'ensemble des informations dans le corps d'une doctrine. Vielleicht sollte man also nicht von «System» sprechen, man darf aber – denkt man nur an die Idee der Ordnung, an der Bodin sein Leben lang gearbeitet hat – auf jeden Fall von einem zusammenhängenden Gedankengebäude («doctrine») sprechen. Cette doctrine, c'est une doctrine de l'ordre politique en conformité avec l'ordre universel, d'une justice qui sera harmonique, une recherche de l'harmonie qui tâche de définir les structures sociales, les fonctions sociales au sein de la communauté politique.

Greenleaf
I am somewhat worried by the way in which various participants were concerned rather to point out contradictions in Bodin's thought than to observe what he himself presumably thought. It is easy enough to point out contradictions or apparent contradictions in his doctrine, but this is only the superficies of the problem. The real question is how did these contradictions not appear to be contradictions? How was it that things that seem so obviously inconsistent to us were to him quite coherent? What we have to do therefore is to do determine the fundamental principle of coherence, the way of thinking which was inherent in his mind and in his writing, that makes of all these apparent inconsistencies a unity.

Scheuner
Nous ne devons pas oublier que pour Bodin, l'unité est toujours une unité née d'une certaine complexité, même d'une certaine discorde; ce n'est pas une unité abstraite. Hier ist auch nochmals auf die Stellung des Königs im Staat zurückzukommen. Bodin denkt keinesfalls an einen absoluten Monarchen, der sich über jede Beschränkung seiner Gewalt hinwegsetzen kann; er sieht ihn vielmehr in der französischen Tradition als an eine historische harmonische Ordnung gebunden an. Und in der

Tat hat sich die französische Monarchie bis zur Revolution nie von ihren Einschränkungen durch die Gesetze gelöst. Bodin ist kein Konstitutionalist im alten Sinn, er ist Parteigänger der königlichen Gewalt, aber eben einer geordneten Gewalt. Der französische König war immer ein König des Volks, das Volk hatte Zutritt zum Schloß, etwa bei Galadiners. Bei der alten Monarchie wurde der König nie ohne das Volk gesehen. Der König, heißt es in Bodins Überlegungen zu den Ständen und Körperschaften, hört das Volk an, spricht mit ihm. – Und so ist Bodins Voluntarismus zu verstehen: als Voluntarismus innerhalb eines harmonisch geordneten Ganzen.

Freund
Je crois que nous arrivons à un point crucial dans l'interprétation de Bodin. Il est tout-à-fait exact qu'il faut tenir compte des conditions sociales de l'époque qui étaient des conditions désordonnées. Et Bodin introduit la notion d'ordre, mais d'un ordre qui tient compte de la multiplicité; c'est pourquoi il l'appelle «harmonie» plutôt que «système». Il est également important de tenir compte des sources qui ont agi sur Bodin. Mais en même temps nous ne devons pas interpréter les notions de souveraineté ou d'absolutisme par la systématisation que ces concepts ont subi plus tard. Il ne faut pas oublier que Bodin a été le premier qui en quelque sorte a vulgarisé la notion de souveraineté. Par conséquent, il n'a même pas pu avoir systématisé – la systématisation évolue après. Ebenso darf man nicht vergessen, daß der Begriff «Absolutismus» damals nicht den heutigen negativen Sinn hatte. – Alors, si nous prenons cet ensemble et que nous posons de nouveau le problème de l'unité, il faut bien se rendre compte que Bodin savait très bien que l'unité n'est pas un concept de politique. On ne fait pas de la politique avec la simple unité. Il faut cette diversité que l'ordre va introduire. Car la politique qui ne travaille qu'avec la notion de l'unité est précisément ce que lui, Bodin, rejette, la tyrannie. Donc cette unité est vraiment une unité de doctrine parce qu'elle doit couvrir cette pluralité qu'il y a dans l'ordre; ainsi elle peut servir de concept opératoire pour des vues sur la politique, mais elle n'est pas un concept politique en elle-même.

Villey (zustimmend zu Scheuner)
Bodin geht von der Betrachtung der Realität aus; in diesem Sinn steht er noch dem Naturrecht der alten realistischen Schule nahe und vermag ein Abgleiten in idealistische Konstruktionen zu vermeiden. Il y a ceci de nouveau chez lui qu'il commence à observer la réalité avec le souci de méthode, de mise en système, que lui suggère un certain nombre de sources philosophiques et religieuses sur lesquelles on a insisté. Darin schließlich, daß er die Wirklichkeit zugleich in ihrer Komplexität nimmt

und sie zu ordnen versucht, zeigt sich seine Mittelstellung zwischen der alten und der modernen Zeit.

Schoeck

One or two times the discussion has alluded to Bodin as a humanist. It seems to me worth stressing that he was in some ways an oldfashioned humanist. By Bodin's time so many of the humanists had become very much specialized. Bei ihm ist das noch nicht so sehr der Fall. Wenn wir von Bodins Quellen sprechen, müssen wir uns nicht nur vor der Annahme hüten, er habe sie in der Weise, wie wir sie heute verstehen, gelesen, sondern auch bedenken, daß nicht jeder zu seiner Zeit sie in der gleichen Weise verstand. Es ist z. B. bekannt, welch orthodoxe Figur die Biographen Gian Francesco Pico und Thomas Morus aus Giovanni Pico gemacht haben. Bei Bodin und vielen anderen Autoren des Jahrhunderts hat er ein wenig voltairesche Züge. You have to ask who is reading Pico and how he is reading him, before we use the label of Pico as a coin.

Maier

Où est, dans l'œuvre de Bodin, le point culminant, la priorité logique: dans la théorie de la politique, ou dans la pratique? Appliqué au problème de la tolérance: est-elle, chez lui, sujette aux changements? doitelle se plier aux exigences de la réalité politique, ou est-ce qu'il y a des aspects qui n'en sont pas touchés? Est-ce là chez lui une conception qui cherche a posteriori une justification théologique ou philosophique? Faitelle partie intégrante de sa pensée ou est-elle stimulée par des causes extérieures?

McRae

Zwei gegensätzliche Betrachtungsweisen sind in der Diskussion auf Bodin angewandt worden, je nachdem, ob in seinem Werk mehr das normative oder mehr das analytische Vorgehen untersucht wurde. In die erste Gruppe gehören etwa die Begriffe der Ordnung, der harmonischen Gerechtigkeit. In der *République* findet sich beides; in der Beschreibung der Souveränität entfernt sich Bodin von der sonst von ihm auf die monarchie royale angewandten normativen Betrachtungsweise. Ich glaube, dieser Unterschied kommt daher, daß die normative Methode und die zugehörigen Themen in engem Zusammenhang mit Bodins religiösen und philosophischen Grundannahmen stehen, während die andere Seite zu seinem juristischen und politischen Denken gehört.

Greenleaf

Ein solche Unterscheidung kann allenfalls dazu dienen, Bodins Schriften genauer zu erklären, keinesfalls aber beantwortet sie die Frage, wo der

Autor selber den Zusammenhang zwischen der normativen und der analytischen Betrachtungsweise sah.

Baxter (stimmt zu)

Es ist ein auffälliger Zug an der *République*, daß Bodin zur Illustration seiner Vorstellungen und Empfehlungen immer wieder auf jüdische Autoritäten, besonders auf das Alte Testament verweist (Beobachtung des Sabbat, Recht des Vaters über Leben und Tod der Kinder, und dergleichen). Von daher möchte ich auf den bereits berührten Unterschied zwischen *Methodus* und *République* zurückkommen. In the *République* there seems to be an apriori that revelation and actual facts correspond; in the *Methodus* this is less the case. In the *Methodus* Bodin tries to keep the analysis at the level of the res humanae, of concrete empirical concern. But one notices a tension in the *Methodus;* increasingly towards the end Bodin is bringing in providential interpretations of history. In the *Methodus* he has not yet worked out how this actually occurs, but by the time of the *République* he has a system which involves the activity of demons who provoke civil war, famine, plague and the rest, when the monarch goes against divine law. Im großen und ganzen bleibt die Erörterung in der *République* zwar auf der Ebene der natürlichen und zwischenmenschlichen Bezüge; immer wieder aber kommen Bruchstücke des später in der *Démonomanie* ausgeführten Systems der übernatürlichen Einflüsse auf die Gesellschaft herein. Durchlaufend wird auf jüdische Belege und Autoritäten Bezug genommen, sogar in ökonomischen Zusammenhängen, besonders aber da, wo von der harmonischen Gerechtigkeit die Rede ist. – Auch in der Frage der wahren Religion glaube ich nicht, daß man Bodins Lösung als Kompromiß ansehen muß. Auf der einen Seite geht durch das ganze Werk der Gedanke, daß es verschiedene Religionen gibt, daß aber nur eine von ihnen die wahre ist. In den drei letzten Büchern des *Heptaplomeres* wiederum wird zunächst die Übereinstimmung der natürlichen Religion mit dem Judentum erwiesen, und dann wird gezeigt, daß der Islam im wesentlichen, die verschiedenen Spielarten des Christentums aber jeweils nur in dem einen oder anderen Zug, nicht aber im Grundsätzlichen, dieser wahren Religion entsprechen. Now I think that this is still a system of harmony, of «concordia discors». But in this «concordia discors» Bodin will include things that are actually wrong. He does think that to a certain extent even evil has to be included.

Kelley

Herrn McRaes Unterscheidung zwischen normativen und analytischen Seiten bei Bodin könnte dazu dienen, den Unterschied zwischen *Methodus* und *République* genauer zu fassen. Die *Methodus* scheint doch vor allem

ein analytisches Werk zu sein, ohne Reflexion auf die eventuelle Anwendbarkeit der Ergebnisse; die *République* dagegen hat es mit Problemen der
Praxis zu tun. – Aber das ist sicher eine untergeordnete Frage demgegenüber, wie Bodin über die Versöhnung dieser verschiedenen Ansätze
dachte.

Franklin
Herr Baxter bringt die Bodinsche Anschauung, nach der Verfehlungen
gegen das staatliche und religiöse Wohlverhalten schwere Strafen finden
müßten, mit seinem Judaismus in Verbindung. Könnte die alttestamenta-
rische Begründung dieser Strafordnung nicht ebensogut kalvinistischen
Ursprungs sein? Man denke etwa an Bodins Ausführungen über die Zensur
in Genf.

Baxter
I do think that the origin of Bondin's judaism is calvinistic. Virtually
everything he says about judaism comes from calvinistic sources. In the
Heptaplomeres Curtius, the calvinist, treats it very sympathetically indeed.
Für den Ursprung dieses Denkens wird man an eine – sehr frühe – pro-
testantische Phase in Bodins Leben denken müssen. Daß er jüdischer Her-
kunft war, ist inzwischen zweifelsfrei widerlegt. In seinem Artikel über
«La famille de Bodin» erwähnt Jacques Levron einen Umstand, dessen
Bedeutsamkeit ihm entgangen zu sein scheint: Bodin ist in demselben
Haus aufgewachsen wie einer der lecteurs royaux für Hebräisch, Jordanus.
Hier mag eine der Ursachen für Bodins frühes Interesse am Judentum zu
suchen sein. But this concern derives basically from a wish to return to the
sources. Everybody who is interested in the revelation must think that the
best version of it is the one which is nearest to its source. It inevitably
takes him back to Calvinism, to the Jewish interpreters of the Old Testament, because they are naturally closer to the original documents.

Schnur
Diese Diskussion ist in der Tat interessant für den Unterschied zwischen
Methodus und République. Die Unterscheidung normativ und analytisch
ist vielleicht nicht allzu bedeutungsvoll, denn alle Probleme der Gesellschaft sind normativer Art. Die Analysen der *Methodus* haben als Rahmen den juristischen Humanismus (legal humanism), der sich auf den
humanistischen Judaismus zubewegt; und Herr Giesey hat gezeigt, wie
sich dagegen in der *République* die Probleme der Gegenwart nieder-
geschlagen haben. Bodin muß sich darüber klar geworden sein, daß sein
in der *Methodus* entworfenes System unzureichend geworden, zerbrochen
war, und daß er vor der Aufgabe stand, eine neue Ordnung zu begründen. – Herr Hinton hat mit Recht bemerkt, die andere Lösung in einer

Zeit derartigen Umbruchs wäre der Ruf nach einem Diktator gewesen. Und von daher gesehen bekommt der Begriff «Dualismus» eine verschiedene Bedeutung, je nachdem, ob man ihn für eine Zeit der Stabilität oder für eine Zeit des Übergangs verwendet. Manche widersprüchlichen Kräfte, die sonst unerträglich schienen, konnte er in diesem kritischen Moment der französischen Geschichte zusammensehen und hoffen, aus ihnen eine neue, nicht von einem Diktator auferlegte Ordnung hervorgehen zu sehen.

Giesey
Welcher philosophische oder historische Zusammenhang besteht zwischen Bodins Dämonologie und seinem Voluntarismus? Diese beiden Elemente zusammen scheinen mir ein bedeutendes psychologisches Element des Bodinschen Werks auszumachen, auch darin, daß sie dem normalen Weltlauf irgendwie entgegenzulaufen scheinen. I am as much taken by the position of the voluntarists – the king as a voluntaristic nemesis of the divine – as I am by the position of Greenleaf regarding the natural order that must exist. This, it seems to me, is totally in the mediaeval tradition and Bodin has no good way of escaping from it. But the strong psychological element from within the divine order to be voluntaristic, does seem to be not entirely new per se; but as Bodin applies it to the real world he does introduce a new disturbing element different from the traditionally idea of the great chain of being.

Baxter
Yes, I think this is quite correct. But we see in the *République* this new twin notion of demons and divine voluntarism enter into Bodin's much neater and more methodical system of the *Methodus*. Die Rolle der Dämonen bleibt ein dunkler Punkt in seinem System, und ich glaube nicht, daß es ihm jemals gelungen ist, ganz klarzustellen, welches ihr Platz in seiner Unterscheidung zwischen dem Bereich der geordneten, vorhersagbaren normalen Abläufe und dem Bereich der göttlichen Freiheit ist. Dieses Verhältnis wird sich nicht restlos klären lassen; aber ich bin nicht Ihrer Meinung, daß sich beide Bereiche ohne weiteres ergänzen, vielmehr scheint Bodin nach der *Methodus* Schwierigkeiten gehabt zu haben, ein rational befriedigendes System zu konstruieren. Because his demons are so multipresent, they can be brought in to explain anything which Bodin has not been able to fix into a system of regular causation. But there is no intellectual control of saying what is and what is not demonically caused.

Giesey
(Wiederholt seine Frage nach dem Verhältnis zwischen Bodins Dämonologie und seinem Voluntarismus.)

Isnardi Parente

Malgré ce que j'ai affirmé dans ma communication, et qui a été souligné par M. Roellenbleck dans la présentation qu'il en a fait, c'est-à-dire que le cadre d'ensemble du volontarisme bodinien est déjà complètement formé dans l'interpretation de la démonologie dans la *Methodus*, je crois (et on peut le lire aussi dans ma communication, si l'on regarde bien) qu'il ne faut pas nier un certain développement dans la pensée de Bodin. Ce développement est dans le même sens que suppose M. Baxter, même si je ne suis pas tout à fait d'accord avec lui à propos d'une transformation radicale de la pensée de Bodin: il consiste dans l'accentuation de l'importance du merveilleux et de l'extraordinaire, qui joue encore un rôle très modeste dans la *Methodus* et devient très sensible dans les derniers ouvrages à partir de la *Démonomanie*.

Kelley

Eine Frage an Herrn Baxter: Gibt es einen Zusammenhang zwischen Bodins Dämon und der Zunahme seiner juristisch-politischen Reflexion und Aktivität nach der Erstausgabe der *Methodus*?

Baxter

Zunächst zu Frau Isnardi Parente: Zweifellos ist der Voluntarismus in der *Methodus* vorhanden – aber nur in embryonaler Form, als Einzelbeispiele voluntaristischer Geschichtsinterpretation, nicht jedoch ausgearbeitet in einem Mechanismus dämonischer Bezüge und Wirkungen. – Wenn Bodin gleich nach der Abfassung der *Methodus* seinem Dämon begegnete oder sich seiner bewußt wurde, so mußte er sich davon prophetische Erleuchtung, übernatürliche Einsicht in die Entwicklung der geschichtlichen Situation erwarten und sich das Recht zusprechen, aktiv in geschichtliche Zusammenhänge einzugreifen. Kurze Zeit später ist er in der Normandie als commissaire des eaux et forêts tätig, hat dann mit der Verschwörung von La Mole und Coconas zu tun, und beginnt in der Neuauflage der *Methodus* von 1572 seine Betrachtungen über die europäische und speziell die französische politische Lage. Ich sehe dies durchaus im Zusammenhang mit seiner Theorie der prophetischen Erleuchtung, die es dem Propheten zur Pflicht macht, den Fürsten vor gottlosen, d. h. den Staat schädigenden Entscheidungen zu warnen.

Hinrichs

Ich sähe gern noch die von Herrn Maier aufgeworfene Frage nach der Toleranz bei Bodin behandelt. Personnellement, je connais assez bien la théorie de la tolérance dans la *République*, mais je ne connais que peu la théorie du *Colloquium Heptaplomeres*, et je voudrais poser une question à M. Roellenbleck: Est-ce que vous croyez qu'au fond et en principe, les deux théories sont identiques? La théorie de la tolérance dans la *République*, je la conçois comme très pragmatique, très utilitariste, c'est-à-dire une théorie de tolérance politique. Croyez-vous donc que c'est la cas aussi du *Colloquium Heptaplomeres*?

Roellenbleck

Je crois qu'il s'agit au fond le la même théorie, mais que Bodin l'accepte d'abord – dans la *République* – plutôt comme une nécessité en vue du fonctionnement de l'état, tandis que dans l'*Heptaplomeres*, il se montre convaincu de l'historicité des formes des religions et accepte en conséquence le pluralisme des religions. J'ai cru pouvoir conclure cela de la forme du dialogue dans le *Colloque* où les sept partenaires (et j'aimerais demander à M. Villey de nous expliquer pourquoi ce dialogue comprend six livres et sept personnages, ce qui certainement n'est pas sans importance) sont absolument égaux en droit; bien qu'on puisse de préférence retrouver dans les interventions du juif Salomon et de Toralba les idées du Bodin des derniers écrits.

Hinrichs

Mais est-ce qu'on trouve dans le *Colloque* la même subordination de la religion sous les exigences de l'état, que dans la *République*, ou non?

Roellenbleck

La même, bien sûr. Le *Colloque* part de l'idée de la recherche de la vérité, de la vraie religion; on parle d'abord des démons et des matières traitées déjà dans les œuvres antérieures; puis au début du 4e livre, avant d'entrer dans la matière principale, on discute la question s'il est utile de parler des religions, vu que de pareils débats sont censés affaiblir les convictions religieuses, conséquence jugée à quasi-unanimité nuisible à l'état; pourtant le débat a lieu; avec l'issue que l'on sait. L'idée de l'harmonie qui ouvre le 4e livre et qui clôt le 6e, est motivée, surtout à la fin du débat, avec le souci principal d'intégrer la religion, la théologie et la pratique religieuse, dans le système des exigences de l'état.

Baxter

Yes, I do agree with this with one exception – and I think it is an important exception –, which is, that the *Heptaplomeres* is an intellectual debate. It is taking place in a group of privileged hearers in a we-group, it is not a public discussion; and personnally I think that the *Heptaplomeres* is still much closer to the *République* than, I think, you do, Mr. Roellenbleck. Das *Heptaplomeres* diskutiert die Verhaltensmöglichkeiten für den Fall, daß man nicht mit der im Staat praktizierten Religion übereinstimmt; grundsätzlich ausgeschlossen wird die Möglichkeit, die

Frage in der Art, wie sie im *Heptaplomeres* behandelt wird, öffentlich zu diskutieren. Bodin selbst hat diese Konsequenz gezogen und sich sein Leben lang nicht von der Praxis der katholischen Religion entfernt.

Roellenbleck
Ich bin völlig Ihrer Meinung. Gerade in einem nicht zur Veröffentlichung bestimmten Werk hätten abweichende, nicht realisierbare Ideen durchgespielt werden können; und es ist in der Tat ein starkes Argument für die Überzeugung Bodins, daß die Religion dem Staat untergeordnet werden müsse, daß er im *Heptaplomeres* die Debatte in dem oben beschriebenen Sinn verlaufen und enden läßt.

Baxter
Bodin begriff die persönliche Natur der religiösen Bindungen sehr gut, und die Debatten des *Heptaplomeres* finden auch aus diesem Grund keine endgültige Lösung. In fact, I would guess that the *Colloquium Heptaplomeres* is a very personal work in the sense that it articulates the various kinds of religious attitudes which Bodin held himself in various times of his life.

Schnur
Herr Baxter unterscheidet bei Bodin zwei Weisen, Debatten über religiöse Fragen zu beurteilen: die eine, wenn es sich um Gespräche im kleinen Kreis, unter Gelehrten, handelt, und die andere, die die Bedeutung der religiösen Überzeugung für den Zusammenhalt des Staats betrifft. Ich würde vorschlagen, den Toleranzbegriff auf den politischen Kontext zu beschränken und die Ideen des *Heptaplomeres* als dafür weniger bedeutsam beiseite zu lassen. – Über Toleranz kann nur schreiben, wer der herrschenden Konfession angehört. Bodin entwarf eine Theorie vom Pluralismus der Religionen im Staat, während die Kirche eine Lehre vom Staat, der mehrere Religionen umgreift und ihren Angehörigen Duldung gewährt, noch nicht akzeptieren konnte. Eine Schrift wie das *Heptaplomeres* setzt eine sehr präzise religiöse Überzeugung bei ihrem Verfasser voraus, denn es ist ein Unterschied, ob man vom Standpunkt des Staats aus für die Duldung anderer Religionen argumentiert, oder ob man für die eigenen Überzeugungen und Rechte spricht.

Isnardi Parente
J'ai l'impression que l'idée de tolérance, cela se voit aussi dans la *République*, est une idée de l'arbitrage royal entre les differents partis, non seulement politiques, mais aussi religieuses. Dans cette question, je pense, il y a une chaîne entre Bodin et la tradition juridique. Mais comme je ne suis pas juriste, ce n'est qu'une question que je pose.

Je suis d'accord avec M. Roellenbleck sur les limites politiques et pragmatiques de la conception de la tolérance, aussi dans l'*Heptaplomeres*.

Quant à la *République*, je me demande s'il ne faut pas y chercher, aussi à ce propos, une source de la pensée de Bodin dans certains schèmes juridiques médiévaux: car Bodin fonde sa conception de la tolérance sur une conception de l'impartialité du roi, due à sa position de supériorité aux divergences entre ses sujets, divergences politiques et religieuses.

Reulos

Je ne crois pas que l'on puisse aller jusque là où vous pensez. En effet, si le roi est arbitre entre les corps et les classes de son royaume, il ne peut le faire que dans une mesure très limitée en matière religieuse dès qu'il s'agira d'une question de foi. Donc s'il s'agit d'une question de discipline, d'organisation, le roi peut intervenir pour agir en qualité d'arbitre entre les classes et corps de son royaume, entre les corps et collèges, mais dès qu'il s'agit d'une question de foi, là la compétence du roi disparaît, et c'est une tradition constante dans la monarchie française.

Bien sûr, le roi de France a une situation très privilegiée parce que c'est un roi sacré et il a une situation privilégiée aussi sur le plan religieux. Mais ça ne peut pas aller en dehors d'établir, de maintenir la paix entre ses sujets; au maximum on pourrait fonder la réconcilitation des différentes religions sur une idée qu'on rencontre fréquemment, c'est-à-dire que la fin de la fonction du roi est d'amener tous ses sujets à la vie éternelle. Mais c'est une perspective qui n'appartenait plus au domaine de la réflexion politique proprement dite. Je pense que Bodin se plaçait sur un plan de paix, de la nécessité de maintenir la concorde entre les sujets, entre les corps et les classes du royaume, et qu'il n'allait pas jusqu'à attribuer au souverain un droit d'intervention dans le domaine de la foi, des notions religieuses.

Villey

In Herrn Roellenblecks Vorlage ist von der Einheit des Bodinschen Denkens die Rede, von den Zusammenhängen zwischen *République* und *Heptaplomeres*, und von der Entwicklung dieses Denkens von einem Werk zum andern. Einerseits führt das Harmonie-Denken, das in Gott, dem absolut Einen, gipfelt, Bodin zu dem Postulat der Einheit der Religion im Staat; er entwickelt es aber weiter zu einem großen Entwurf, der der politischen (und theologischen) Problematik der Epoche entsprach, nämlich der Verstärkung der weltlichen Gewalt auch circa sacra, weil ja der Versuch, die konfessionelle Spaltung durch Religionsgespräche zu überwinden, gescheitert war. Er ist damit ein Vorläufer wesentlicher Denkansätze des 17. Jahrhunderts, während ihn ein tiefer Graben von dem juridisch-politischen Denken des ausgehenden Mittelalters trennt.

McRae

Eine Frage an Herrn Roellenbleck: In der *Methodus* unterscheidet Bodin zwischen historia humana, naturalis und divina und spricht den Vorsatz aus, alle drei in Schriften zu behandeln. Sehen Sie nun im *Heptaplomeres* die Ausführung dieses dritten Projekts?

Roellenbleck

Nein, ich bin nicht dieser Auffassung, weil er sich hier vor allem mit den Fragen nach der wahren Religion und nach der Toleranz beschäftigt.

Maier

La question est donc la suivante: où sont les limites de l'arbitrage royal? Le roi peut-il disposer du contenu de la religion, du dogme, comme le législateur de Rousseau qui peut prescrire une religion civile, un minimum de dogmes, de lois fondamentales en matière de religion? Ou – et c'est là ce que je crois – l'idée de Bodin se borne-t-elle aux actes extérieurs de la religion comme, par exemple, de défendre aux partis confessionnels de se tuer mutuellement, etc.

Scheuner

Für das ganze 16. Jahrhundert ist es undenkbar, daß der Monarch Vorschriften über die Religion macht. Er soll die wahre Religion, angeleitet von den Theologen, verteidigen, er kann eventuell eine falsche dulden, aber Inhalte kann er unmöglich vorschreiben. Auch das «cujus regio, ejus religio» des Deutschen Reichs bedeutet nichts anderes.

Freund

Man muß Bodins Toleranzdenken wohl im Licht seines Pragmatismus sehen, und man sollte nicht vergessen, daß nicht er der Erfinder dieser Idee war, sondern daß es Etienne Pasquier gewesen war, der sie in der *Exhortation aux Princes* von 1561 in Umlauf gebracht hatte. Die *Exhortation* fand rasch eine große Verbreitung, wurde ins Deutsche und ins Lateinische übersetzt und sowohl von den liberalen Protestanten (etwa von Castellio) als auch von den politiques rezipiert. Ich möchte also die Hypothese wagen, daß Bodin unter dem Eindruck dieser Schrift in der Toleranz eine mögliche Lösung des politischen Problems des Bürgerkriegs sehen lernte – das wäre die Position der *République*; und daß der Schritt von der *République* zum *Heptaplomeres* der von einer Auffassung der Toleranz als Lösung des Problems zu einer Auffassung von Toleranz als einem politischen Instrument gewesen ist.

Hinrichs

Zu den Ausführungen von Herrn Reulos: ich glaube doch, daß in der

République für die Einheit der Religion plädiert wird. Natürlich ist für Bodin der Frieden im Staat die erste Forderung; danach aber kommt die, daß der Herrscher die wahre Religion kennen, und daß er seine Untertanen zu ihr hinführen muß; freilich sagt Bodin nicht, um welche es sich handelt. Dieses Hinführen soll nicht durch Zwang oder ähnliches geschehen, sondern durch Überzeugung, durch das Vorbild des Königs, der die Religion selbst praktiziert; da der König den Mittelpunkt des Denkens der ganzen Nation bildete, konnte Bodin dies für möglich halten. Im übrigen konnte es sich zu dieser Zeit nur um ein Plädoyer für ein katholisches Frankreich handeln. Noch die Politik der Folgezeit, denken Sie an das Edikt von Nantes, weist Züge dieses Bodinschen Denkens auf: etwa in gewissen, man möchte sagen machiavellistischen, Mitteln, die dieses «Überzeugen» unterstützen sollen, wie Pensionskassen für konvertierte protestantische Geistliche, und dergleichen.

II. BODINS HISTORISCHES DENKEN

Zusammenfassung: Julien Freund und Donald R. Kelley

Villey

pose la question de la traduction du terme *ars*. Comme l'a souligné Freund, la traduction de Mesnard ne semble pas correcte, car *ars* a une signification précise dans la jurisprudence du XVIe siècle et même du Moyen Age. C'est le sens que Cicéron lui donnait dans le *De Oratore*: mettre en ordre pour clarifier et simplifier une question. Il semble donc que Bodin suive exactement la tradition de la jurisprudence humaniste de son temps.

Freund

accepte cette interprétation, puisque Bodin associe constamment les notions d'*ars* et de *colligere*, au sens où il s'agit de rassembler des éléments épars pour les mettre en ordre.

Reulos

est à peu près du même avis, sauf qu'il faut tenir compte de certaines discussions de cette époque pour savoir si le droit et aussi la médecine étaient des *artes* ou bien des *scientiae*. Toutefois il ne semble pas que Bodin se soit préoccupé de cette distinction.

Pour *Roellenbleck*

l'art chez Bodin vise l'enseignement, il définit un mode de présentation.

Kelley

recalls that there was a juridical tradition of the term «art», namely, Ulpian's definition of *jus* as *ars boni et aequi*, which was voluminously discussed by jurists and was of major significance for Bodin. This definition emphasized the utilitarian aspect of «art».

Franklin

adds that *ars* as historical concept referred rather to *methodus legendi* than to *methodus scribendi* and so emphasizes the content and its orderly exposition. This fits in also with the juridical, utilitarian usage.

McRae

believes that the logical meaning of the term is primary and refers mainly to the systematic ordering of material.

Freund
propose de confronter le texte français et le texte latin des *Six Livres de la République* pour voir comment Bodin a lui-même traduit le mot *ars* en français. Il regrette de n'y avoir pas pensé plus tôt.

Franklin
asks if *ars* or *methodus* are equivalent to «apparatus», that is, to knowledge of such subjects as geography and political science, which are necessary for the understanding of history. More particularly, the *ars* corresponds to the *loci communes* into which history may be ordered.

Freund
estime que chez Bodin la notion de *methodus* implique l'idée de division, alors que celle d'*ars* implique l'idée de regroupement. On ne saurait donc identifier *methodus* et *ars*.

Giesey
remarks that some Bartolists accepted the traditional but false conception of *ars* as *imitatio naturae*, thus stressing the creative ordering of law by individual jurists so as to make a correspondence with the natural world.

Derathé
demande à Villey de lui indiquer la référence exacte du *De Oratore*. N'ayant pas l'ouvrage sous la main,

Villey
renvoie au livre I où on définit l'art par les termes d'*ordo et judicio dispensare atque componere*.

Reulos
aborde une autre question, celle de la signification de l'histoire chez Bodin. A son avis, il n'a pas voulu la cultiver pour elle-même, mais pour en faire la base des études ultérieures sur la politique et le droit. S'il a rassemblé *in artem* tant de faits historiques, c'est pour bâtir là-dessus sa théorie politique et juridique. L'histoire a donc chez lui un rôle accessoire et préparatoire.

Freund
est d'accord avec la première idée, mais non avec la seconde, qui ne semble pas correspondre à ce que Bodin déclare dans la dédicace et la préface du *Methodus*. On ne saurait donc dire que le *Methodus* a été écrit pour servir *Les Six Livres de la République*, car il est peu probable qu'en rédigeant cette œuvre de jeunesse Bodin savait quels ouvrages il écrirait plus tard.

La meilleure preuve en est que le chapitre VI qui annonce les *Six Livres de la République* est intégré dans l'ensemble du *Methodus*, comme un chapitre parmi d'autres, sans statut spécial.

Reulos
pose alors la question de savoir ce qu'on entendait à cette époque par histoire. Il semble qu'il faille se référer aux œuvres italiennes.

Suit une longue discussion entre *Reulos*, *Freund* et *Roellenbleck* sur la connaissance que Bodin avait de l'œuvre de Sleidan et sur la signification des derniers chapitres du *Methodus*.

Villey
remarque que le dernier chapitre consacré à la chronologie a une valeur purement instrumentale. Ce qui est essentiel, c'est que pour Bodin l'histoire est ordonnée pour donner des leçons de politique ou de droit. Il serait anachronique de lui attribuer une conception scientifique de l'histoire, au sens où nous l'entendons de nos jours: il ne traite pas de l'histoire pour elle-même, pour établir uniquement l'exactitude des faits. Ainsi que Cotroneo l'a montré dans son rapport il voit en elle, comme Machiavel, un ensemble de leçons.

Freund
intervient pour préciser que si Bodin cherche des leçons dans l'histoire, il y a lieu de tenir compte du fait qu'il emploie le terme au pluriel (historiae) et non au singulier, comme d'ailleurs aussi Machiavel ou Guichardin et plus tard Descartes.

Baxter
observe qu'il y a une tradition de l'histoire universelle au singulier depuis Saint Augustin et Dante, avant Bossuet.

Derathe
demande si l'histoire au singulier inclut l'histoire au pluriel ou si inversement l'histoire au pluriel inclut l'histoire au singulier.

Reulos
précise que lorsqu'on employait à cette époque l'histoire au singulier, c'était à propos d'une étude portant sur un sujet très particulier, par exemple l'histoire d'un diocèse ou d'une ville. L'histoire au pluriel concernait un ensemble plus vaste, y compris les institutions. Or, il est remarquable qu'à l'époque de Bodin l'humanisme ne s'intéresse pas seulement à la période classique, mais aussi aux antiquités nationales, aux coutumes franques, etc.

Hinrichs
indique que de grands historiens de cette époque employaient la notion
d'histoire au singulier, par exemple de Thou et de La Popelinière, sans
limiter leur étude à un sujet spécialisé.

A quoi *Reulos*
réplique que La Popelinière a écrit l'*Histoire des guerres civiles de notre
temps*, c'est-à-dire le sujet est limité et particulier.

Franklin
asks if «historiarum» in the title of the *Methodus* refers to events or to
written accounts. Probably the latter, as is the case with (Machiavelli's)
Istorie fiorentine, implying that numerous «histories» are linked together.

Villey
demande à Freund de mettre au point cette question du singulier et du
pluriel puisque dans d'autres écrits il a montré qu'on utilisait aussi le
pluriel pour désigner la liberté (les franchises) ou le droit *(iura)*.

McRae
adds that «historiarum trado» refers to authors rather than to separate
works.

Isnardi Parente
remarque que *historiae* est une façon très commune de nommer l'ouvrage
des historiens anciens dans la tradition humaniste et qu'elle n'oserait pas
donner tant d'importance à la différence entre historia et historiae. Elle
n'est pas non plus d'accord avec Freund à propos du concept de finalité
chez Bodin quand il se réfère à l'aristotélisme.

Freund
maintient que dans le chapitre I du *Methodus* la conception de la finalité
est aristotélicienne, puisqu'il y est question de la fin de chaque action
humaine.

Chanteur
indique que dans le livre I, chapitre I de la République Bodin se réfère
explicitement à Aristote à propos de la notion de la fin des actions. Elle
lit le texte en question.

Isnardi Parente
république que ce passage exprime au contraire une condamnation
d'Aristote. Si Bodin accepte la notion de finalité, c'est uniquement parce

qu'elle est commune et qu'on peut la trouver dans la tradition platonicienne comme chez Cicéron ou dans la Patristique.

Polin
observe que si dans ce texte Bodin polémique contre Aristote il ne le contredit pas, puisqu'il dit que la République doit rechercher à la fois la contemplation et un but pratique de satisfaction.

Chanteur
poursuit en montrant que si Bodin accepte la distinction aristotélicienne entre les vertus éthiques et les vertus contemplatives il ne lui donne pas la même signification. En tout cas les quatre références succesives à Aristote montrent qu'à propos de la finalité il se référait à la doctrine du Stagirite.

Suit une discussion entre *Isnardi Parente* et *Chanteur* ainsi que *Freund* sur les rapports entre Bodin et Aristote, mais aussi Saint Augustin.

Schnur
reviews some general themes in Kelley's and Giesey's papers and in Franklin's book. Legal humanists look at history and at law in the same way and from the same point of departure, that is, through a systematic use of divisions and subdivisions. In Toulouse a teacher of law tended to develop *Professorenrecht*; after gaining legal experience in Paris he would return more to *Juristenrecht*. As Kelley says, Bodin did not substitute one for the other but combined the best of both. Today this is still the crucial problem of constitutional history, to find a historical system that also, as Kelley says «views institutions, constitutional as well as religious, in a functional manner.» Bodin derived this view from his legal experience and from Bartolist inclinations, oriented to concrete problems. For Bodin the whole history of a constitution involved the concrete view of a society toward particular social problems in terms of private and public law, and it is the same with the historical approach today. This is also the main point of Moreau-Reibel's book, to compare similar models and similar groups of problems in order to find solutions. One difficulty for Bodin (and still for us) is that the problem of constitutional history cannot be solved in a way either strictly historical or strictly political. His great innovation was to approach this problem according to the method described by Walter Ullmann: «By viewing law as a social phenomenon, medieval jurisprudence was forced to elucidate some basic principles about society, and thus was led to consider topics which, under modern conditions, would be dealt with, not by the lawyer but by the sociologist.» One may contest this sharp distinction between lawyer and sociologist, but it is more useful than that between lawyer and law professor, and it describes the connection under discussion.

Kelley
adds that his subject was more the form and tendencies of Bodin's work
than his actual achievements. In some ways the humanist or historical
approach and the Bartolist approach are irreconcilable. Bodin created
further problems for himself by trying to reduce history to *loci communes*
and then apply these to social reality. This becomes more apparent in the
Republic. To what extent are these difficulties the result of applying the
method of jurisprudence to the material of history?

Hinton
points out that there is little about history an the *République,* although
Bodin was setting out in political fashion to demonstrate that the king of
France was a legal, royal monarch and should not have avoided the
historical question. He agrees with La Popelinière, quoted by Kelley, that
it is a pity Bodin did not do more history of particular countries. Implied
in the *République* is the view that all governments of Western Europe
had been conquered, that conquest created despotic rights in the conquerors, but that subsequently the conquerors had yielded their rights to
the people by some form of covenant, such that the king retained what
Bodin called the shadow of despotic monarchy. Bodin's inferred point is
that the historical process itself has created law. Other historians of that
time would have gone back to the origins to find that law and would not
have allowed anything to be added by the process of time. What Bodin
says is much the same as what Francis Bacon says in England a little
later, and this becomes typical of English Toryism at the end of the 17th
century. Finally, it is surprising that Bodin did not feel it necessary to
offer a demonstration of some of his assertions. Perhaps this is because
it is impossible, but it remains a weakness in his treatment that he did
not even make the attempt.

Salmon
believes that the one thing distinguishing Bodin from other contemporaries writing or reflecting on history is that he accepts the fact of change
and is not bound to some sort of thesis, political or otherwise, in the
Methodus. Second is the point about objectivity raised by Freund and
Kelley. Bodin does talk about the need to read historians of another
country, not a native historian, and this seems to distinguish him from
the chauvinist views of Charles Dumoulin and especially of François
Hotman in the *Franco-Gallia*. Yet the 9th chapter of the *Methodus* mentioned earlier by Baxter contains the myth of the Celts, who crossed the
Rhine from the east and then came back again. Bodin's Celticism is
crucial, though not much commented upon. How does this fit in with
Bodin's supposed objectivity?

Scheuner

remarks on the difficulty of determining the sort of work Bodin intended the *Methodus* to be. It is a juridical system, not a history or a comparative history of constitutional institutions. This system, inconceivable today, is in many ways medieval. It is a treatise *De regimine principum*, a moral treatise and not political in the manner of Machiavelli's *Prince*. In the *Discorsi* Machiavelli is a moralist (perhaps an a-moralist), treating practical statecraft and giving a mass of examples. In the *Methodus* Bodin reflects on the utility of history and also provides a mass of information, bringing it into systematic form. He was not successful in his attempts to give a history of constitutions, nor was anyone else for a long time. Other historians wrote old-fashioned world histories, but Bodin does not do this. He is too immersed in medieval categories and cannot think in concrete and positive terms. Positivistic history was not yet possible in the 16th century except for a mere chronologist, for there was no way of making a selection for a more developmental history. The big works of the 16th century also exhibit a great apparatus of Biblical citations and examples from antiquity but few from contemporary times. Bodin gives more of the latter than most. Even Grotius does not give many contemporary examples in his *De Jure belli ac pacis,* nor does Althusius. Bodin's method could only be eclectic, as Kelley says. He could not discuss sovereignty in general terms as today or in an empirical way, he could only give that curious mixture of historical examples and general reflections which is the *Methodus.*

Kelley

adds that this mixture is largely the result of Bodin's juristic approach and proposes this hypothesis about Bodin's general method. For legal allegations and citations he had all the sources of ancient and medieval jurisprudence, but these contained very little about public law, which ancient and even medieval jurists tended to avoid. So what Bodin had to do in the *Methodus,* especially in chapter 6, the forerunner of the *République,* was to supply material from historical sources. A test of this hyothesis is Bodin's use of history in the *République,* and this indeed seems to be equivalent to his use of legal allegations. In other words, Bodin had gathered together a mass of information drawn from very different legal and historiographical sources and applied according to one common method. Even the *Methodus* was not historical but rather an assemblage of information to be applied to problems, and specifically to the problem which he came to define in the *République.*

Franklin

adds to the remarks of Hinton and Salmon. The *République* may be understood as an elaboration through a comparative method of a system which Bodin then tried to exemplify and to prove as universal. Historical material is used simply for citations and allegation to build up his case. This may answer Hinton's question about the use of history and explain the universalistic tendency of Bodin's method ... So the juridical aim of the *Methodus*, although the book was not a conscious work on jurisprudence, does explain the peculiar use of history.

Schoeck

refers to McRae's view. In the early 1560's Ramism was being applied to nearly every field, and it seems likely that an ambitious man like Bodin would apply a new technique to an area not yet so treated. This throws light on the title he chose. The «art of» anything in the 16th century has a neo-scholastic overtone. It is a term used by everybody in education. *Methodus* is a title that Ramus and others used for their works and also with an emphasis on a way of learning. Bodin's aim also was to provide an easy way of learning history. His book is not so neatly diagrammatic as some Ramist works, but then history does not lend itself to this as easily as logic. Nevertheless, Bodin did move from conventional history to the *loci communes* as a simple way of preparing for the study of history The emphasis is indeed upon «enseignement» – not only writing but also teaching history.

Kelley

replies that, nevertheless, the method of the book, especially in the 6th chapter, was not simply to read history but also to resolve certain problems of law. One must account both for Bodin's decision to focus upon specifically public law and for the relation between the *Methodus* and the *République*.

Polin

soulève la question du déterminisme dans l'histoire chez Bodin. Il est d'accord avec Freund pour condamner ce terme, mais pour d'autres raisons. Ce n'est pas parce que Bodin accorde une grande importance à la décision individuelle qu'il n'est pas déterministe, mais parce que ce terme constitue un anachronisme, puisqu'il s'agit d'une doctrine de la fin du XVIIIᵉ siècle, dévelopée par Kant et Laplace. Pour la même raison on ne saurait qualifier Montesquieu de déterministe. De toute façon il faut proscrire le terme dans l'interprétation de Bodin.

Freund

est d'accord avec Polin et remarque que s'il a employé cette notion, c'est uniquement pour s'opposer à Mesnard qui l'a utilisé pour caractériser la philosophie de Bodin. Certes, Bodin emploie le terme de nécessité, mais non point dans un sens déterministe.

Derathé
reproche à Freund d'avoir employé par contre le terme de probabilisme, qui constitue également un anachronisme. On ne saurait appliquer à Bodin ce qui revient à Voltaire.

Freund
rétorque que Bodin utilise fréquement la notion de probabilitas à la fois dans un sens scientifique d'explication et dans un sens moral en liaison avec la prudence.

Derathé
reste opposé à l'emploi de la notion de probabilisme.

Isnardi-Parente
met ensuite sur le tapis la question du *ius gentium*. A son avis Bodin n'a pas tiré toutes les conséquences de cette notion dans le *Methodus*. Dans la *République* par contre il est surtout question du *ius naturae* et du *ius civile*, le *ius gentium* jouant un rôle moins important et tendant à s'identifier à l'un ou à l'autre de ces deux concepts.

Kelley
replies that by *ius gentium* he did not mean the specific body of law in the *Corpus Juris Justiniani* but rather a generic concept, namely, the law of all nations, modern as well as ancient, in Bodin's sense. This is illustrated in the *Iuris universi distributio* perhaps even more clearly than in the *Methodus*. The law of nations in this sense will of course also include feudal customs of European nations subsequent to Justinian's corpus.

Reulos
observe que Bodin emploie la notion dans le sens technique du droit romain, mais se trouve embarrassé du fait que cette signification ne correspond plus aux usages de son époque. On trouve déjà chez lui une approche du sens moderne du droit international.

Scheuner
pense qu'au XVᵉ siècle le *ius gentium* est ambigu, car d'une part il désigne la pratique commune aux nations dans l'application du droit positif, une sorte de *common law* pour toutes les nations, de l'autre il vise aussi les relations entre les nations et les républiques au sens que développera le siècle suivant.

Freund
constate que si Bodin n'a pas encore une notion claire du droit international, Guillaume Postel, un de ses contemporains, est déjà plus précis.

Scheuner
met en avant le fait qu'au Moyen Age déjà il y avait un problème à propos
de ce qu'on peut appeler le droit national et le droit des gens. Bien que l'on
ait parfois accordé une priorité au droit national, l'idée de la subordination
de ce droit à un autre plus général et supérieur a toujours était reconnue.

Reulos
trouve qu'il y a une autre difficulté chez Bodin qui vient du *ius commune*
des juristes médiévaux et italiens. S'agit-il d'un *ius* gentium? Bodin ne va
pas jusqu'à les confondre.

Selon *Isnardi Parente*
Bodin a sous évalué le *ius gentium* dans la *République*. Se référant au
canoniste Giovanni d'Andrea il permet au roi d'annuler ce droit s'il est
contraire à l'équité.

Reulos
note que le *ius gentium* n'est pas vraiment du droit chez Bodin, c'est plutôt
un ensemble de règles que les nations observent en fait, mais sans qu'on
puisse y attacher un caractère obligatoire.

Hinrichs
insiste sur le changement qu'on peut observer du *Methodus* à la *Républi*-
que. Dans ce dernier ouvrage il a abandonné l'universalisme qui est in-
discutable dans le premier. Il est devenu plus nationaliste et même mer-
cantiliste, sans doute sous la pression des événements.

Villey
refuse toutes ces distinctions, arguant du fait qu'à Rome comme au
Moyen Age le *ius gentium* était à peu près synonyme de droit naturel.

McRae
conteste l'interprétation de Mme Isnardi Parente en montrant l'importance du *ius gentium* dans la *République*, puisque Bodin déclare que le
roi ne saurait falsifier la monnaie, ce procédé étant contraire au droit
des gens.

Hinrichs
cite par contre un autre passage où Bodin admet que le roi peut en cas de

nécessité négliger le droit des gens, mais jamais les lois fondamentales du royaume.

Franklin
understands that the *ius gentium* was always subject to revision by positive law and gives the example of slavery, which Bodin disapproved of but did not deny was part of the *ius gentium*. In general the *ius gentium* consisted of supplements, corrections, and sometimes restrictions of the *ius naturale*, which was itself subject to control by positive legislation. Consider the distinction between despotic monarchy and royal monarchy. Despotic monarchy is a violent correction or restriction of the *ius naturale* of which he disapproves; but since so many people have accepted it, he will not reject it in so far as it serves the *ius naturale*.

Schnur
makes a summary statement. The discussion touches upon the same fundamental conception treated earlier, that is, the notion of order. Bodin discusses this in the *Republique*, chapter 4, book 4, concerning political and social change. How could a man find order in a time when the traditional system did not fit the concrete historical situation? This sometimes happens, as in the 16th and 17th centuries and at times before, though not afterwards. One answer might be that the situation was chaos and without explanation, but Bodin did not say this. For him there is always political and social change that cannot be controlled by men, and so specific institutions are needed to maintain human dignity and a minimum of order. This involved a conception of history that makes allowance for social policy. According to Bodin, «Il faut donc au gouvernement d'un estat bien ordonné suyvre ce grand Dieu de nature, qui procede en toutes choses lentement, et petit à petit . . .» This statement is not only factual but also normative. Perhaps it expresses for the first time a new idea of institutions –institutions which are living and developing. It ist important to note that men cannot live within such changing institutions if the rate of change exceeds his capacity to accept it. No one before Bodin had such clear ideas about social change. This seems quite in agreement with Kelley's interpretation.

Kelley
adds that Bodin approaches this problem of social change through the study of many specific relationships among the sovereign, officers, citizens, corporations, and a number of other groups; and that the study of this complex structure, which is the vehicle of social change, was in some ways more important than his more famous discussion of the theory of sovereignty.

Schnur
sees in this system of social change the clearest expression of Bodin's legal thought. In general the profession of jurisprudence is closest of all to the study of social change.

Greenleaf
finds a difficulty in this. If this were Bodin's aim, why did he not base his *République* on a historical introduction and derive his theory from history and the observed processes of social and political change instead of merely using examples? The reason is that if one tried at that time to derive a political theory from historical experience, one would arrive at some doctrine of limited or constitutional government, and Bodin did not want this. He wanted to expound the doctrine of absolute and unlimited sovereignty with only moral restrictions. Historical or inductive analysis would not support such a doctrine.

Salmon
adds that in the *Methodus* Bodin wanted to deny the possibility of mixed government, although he could not demonstrate this from his examples.

Franklin
answers that Bodin's position in the *Methodus* is nevertheless consistent with a certain kind of constitutionalism and does contain a historical and legal approach. It is true that the curious account of the Roman republic in the *Methodus* is unchanged in the *République*. The inference is that Bodin came to the concept of indivisible sovereignty before becoming an absolutist, and that his later absolutist position was a distortion of his concept of indivisible sovereignty.

Greenleaf
repeats that Bodin shows mixed government to be impossible.

Franklin
agrees but argues that unmixed government and undivided sovereignty is compatible with juridical limitations on sovereignty. In this respect Bodin's view very much resembles that of Pasquier.

Salmon
disagrees. Bodin will not have a mixed government, though he cannot say why.

Greenleaf
suggests that Bodin did have explanations, including the fundamental principle of unity and the incompatibility of mixed government with national human law. So there must be a single locus of power.

Hinton

poses the question of the idea of progress in Bodin's work. It seems that Bodin was among the first people in history to accept this idea, particularly in his application of history to politics, which showed the well ordered royal monarchy to have emerged from a state of despotism. But he did not quite understand the idea, whether because it was so new, or because there were logical difficulties in applying it to the politics of his time. He needed the idea to explain the government of the well ordered state, but he could not apply it absolutely since the well ordered state would then not retain the germ, the element of despotism that justified sovereignty.

Kelley

finds a difficulty in attributing the notion of «progress» (Bodin's term is *conversio*) to Bodin since his idea was organistic and also involved degeneration at some point.

Salmon

doubts that Bodin had a straight-line view of progress in the French monarchy since in the *République* he argued that royal succession had not changed and that generally the eldest son succeeded, though the examples he chose made a mess of his case. Bodin accepted the idea of change in a general and detached way in the *Methodus*, but in the *République* he did not accept change in that sense, nor did he have any clear idea of the evolution of the French monarchy.

McRae

finds nothing in Bodin inconsistent with the cyclical theory of change, although this idea sometimes obscured what he has to say about change in certain places.

Baxter

agrees that Bodin has no conception of progress within an individual state, which he interprets on the analogy of a human life, with its beginning, prime, and decline. At best on can try to conserve a state in its prime as long as possible, and in the end the *conversio*, the dissolution, is unavoidable. But on the history of individual states there seems to be imposed a sort of cultural progression or accumulation. This is an important distinction.

Franklin

asks if Bodin's view includes a kind of socio-psychological or moral progress underlying historical evolution.

Hinton

finds in Bodin a sense of general amelioration of life, especially in the West, perhaps over a long period of time, but on the whole there is a little sense of «progress».

Freund

soulève une dernière question à propos des rapports présentées par MM. Kelley et Cotroneo. Bodin était hostile à Machiavel, mais comme beaucoup d'auteurs du siècle suivant il cite avec faveur Tacite.

Kelley

thinks that the connections and congruence between Bodin and Machiavelli have been overemphasized at the expense of some fundamental differences. Bodin had been trained as a jurist and had all the intellectual habits and inhibitions of that profession. On the other hand Machiavelli, as Hinton remarked, tended to think of politics without law and to some extent without institutions. Although it by no means precludes significant influence, this contrast should be kept in mind.

Baxter

remarks on Bodin's «Tacitism». Bodin admires Tacitus not because he was a republican or a good stylist but because he was, as a pagan and a critic of Christianity, an honest historical witness.

Schoeck

points to the difference between Machiavelli's almost medieval use of analogies and Bodin's comparative method and in general their different qualities of mind.

Polin

conteste l'interprétation de Kelley. Machiavel n'est pas hostile aux lois. Pour le Florentin il y a deux manières d'agir, l'une par la force, l'autre par la loi. La différence c'est que chez Machiavel la loi n'est pas fondée comme chez Bodin sur la justice ou un ordre naturel.

Schnur

continues the comparison of Machiavelli and Bodin. The interest of Bodin and other French politiques was in the relation between politics and law and social institutions and in the stabilization of political change, an idea which does not appear in Machiavelli. The difference is not that Bodin is for natural law and Machiavelli against it, but that Bodin was concerned with the middle range, that is, the rule of law in the whole political system.

III. BODIN UND DIE RECHTSTRADITION

Zusammenfassung: Ralph E. Giesey

Reulos

Il me paraît nécessaire d'envisager la souveraineté dans Bodin d'une façon réelle: en effet Bodin traite au chapitre 6 du Livre premier *Des vrayes marques de souveraineté* les modalités d'exercice de celle-ci et les prérogatives qui y son rattachées. Il s'agit notamment de la possibilité de déterminer une loi, de prendre des édits et de constater la loi existante (cas important en France en raison du développement du droit coutumier et s'appliquant aussi à l'admission plus ou moins large du droit romain en pays de droit écrit) et enfin la possibilité d'exercer des attributions d'interprétation par la voie d'organismes délégués qui sont les parlements.

A l'époque de Bodin on compare certes le Parlement au Sénat Romain, mais il s'agit d'une tradition humaniste déja reconnue fausse par Budé; les avocats cherchent de leur coté à valoriser leur situation, en se qualifant «orator» et en exposant que le Parlement est le seul endroit où l'on puisse faire des discours et discuter des problèmes divers comme on pouvait le faire au sein des assemblées romaines et du Sénat. Je ne vois pas dans cette comparaison de grande portée politique; elle est honorifique et n'a que le but de valoriser l'institution et les professions qui s'exercent au sein du Parlement.

Certaines remarques de Bodin sur les décisions de justice sont interessantes: seules certaines juridictions statuent sans appel, ce sont celles qui se qualifient de souveraines et parlent au nom du roi, souverain; c'est là un rappel du sens étymologique de souveraineté, possibilité de prendre une décision sans aucun recours *(superioritas)*; d'autre part il ne faut pas oublier que, le roi présent, le Parlement n'a plus que le caractère d'organe de conseil, qu'il s'agisse de matière politique ou de matière de droit privé. Le roi tient beaucoup à manifester aux souverains étrangers de visite en France que la justice est rendue sur un terrain strictement judiciaire d'application de la règle de justice; il est de tradition de faire venir le souverain étranger à une audience du Parlement où il assiste àux plaidoiries et voit recueillir les voix. On comprend que Bodin conteste l'appellation de cour «souveraine» pour les Parlements car le Parlement exerce la justice souveraine du Roi mais n'a pas la jouissance de cette souveraineté selon la distinction traditionnelle de la capacité de jouissance et d'exercice.

En ce qui concerne les sources du droit, il faut noter que, par la notion de souveraineté, est mise en valeur l'unité de la création du droit, mais les modalités peuvent en être variées et Bodin se rend clairement compte de cette complexité; cette multiplicité des sources du droit n'est pas contraire à la notion de souveraineté créatrice du droit.

*

Hinrichs
One of the main questions raised today is that of controls. It is easy to say that *lois fondamentales* exist without specifying how people are able to insure that the king will govern in conformity with these laws. I have two questions for Mr. Franklin. I would ask, first, what possibilities of controls were recognized. Could a tyrannical king be legitimately deposed according to the tradition of the French monarchy? I would ask, secondly, how one should interpret the many possibilies of control of the king which Bodin insists on in many places of the *République*. One example is the right of private property; another is Bodin's insistence, quite in accord with traditional theory, that members of the Parlement were not removable.

Franklin
Professor Hinrichs rightly suggests that the power of deposing or resisting kings logically follows from the recognition of institutional restraints. This ultimate consequence had been left ambiguous in the French tradition of limited monarchy. But in the 1570's the right of resistance asserted by the Huguenots depended precisely upon this inference. If a king was subject to control, then those bodies established to control him could depose him for tyrannical behaviour. This, moreover, was the very connection of ideas that helps us to understand why Bodin was led to absolutism. One main purpose of the *République* was to exclude legitimate resistance by showing that the king was not controlled. I should again point out, however, that Bodin was not required to contend that a sovereign king was above the law of nature. He had merely to maintain that, for violations of the law of nature, a king was accountable to God alone.

I agree with Professor Hinrichs that Bodin did expect the courts and other agencies to exercise a moderating influence in practice. But this moderating influence lay in the domain of advice and dilatory tactics, not of formal veto.

A distinction must be drawn between the recognition of limitations and the recognition of institutional restraints. Almost all absolutists in the European tradition admit that the ruler is limited by natural and divine law, and also by certain fundamental laws of human provenance. The critical difference, then, between limited and absolute monarchy has to do with the presence or absence of institutional restraints. Using this criterion, I would say that the French tradition prior to Bodin was semi-constitutionalist. It persistently tended to assume that there were many things a ruler could not do without the consent of the Parlements or other agencies. On the other hand, I would say that Bodin's position in the *République* was distinctly absolutist, since in that work at least the existence of formal institutional restraints on royal power was systematically denied.

Scheuner

I might offer the following answer to Mr. Hinrich's question about the means of controlling the prince. Bodin is well aware of the fundamental political controversy dominating the sixteenth century. One side consisted of the social-contract theory developed in the doctrines of the so-called monarchomachs. They claimed that there existed one contract between God and the people, and another (not always clearly emphasized) between the prince and the people [*Vindiciae contra tyrannos,* cap. 1; ed. Frankfort, 1608, p. 10ff]. If the prince violated this contract, if he became a tyrant, it was not for the people but for the «digniores», the Optimates or Estates, to resist him and if need be to expel or depose him [*ibid.,* cap. 3; *ed. cit.,* 154f. Further, Beza, *De iure magistratuum,* quaest. V; ed. Sturm, Neukirchen, 1965, p. 46ff.]. This was not mere theory; it was practised several times in the sixteenth century. Three instances of these times (not to mention others of an earlier date) were Christian II. of Denmark (1523) who was deposed and died in old age as a prisoner; Eric XIV of Sweden (1568) who was held in prison by his brother, John III, and later murdered; and Mary of Scotland. These are cited in the literature defending the rights of the people [Beza, p. 54; Vindiciae, p. 159]. The same cases appear also in Bodin's chapter on resistance to tyranny [Book II, cap.V; ed. Paris, 1583, p. 312] but here as examples of an intervention of relatives against a prince who did only imprison him and not kill him. Bodin recognizes a right to act against a tyrant not on the part of the people or the estates but only by other princes. He writes [*ibid,* p. 300]: «Car il y a bien difference de dire que le tyran pour estre licitement tué par un Prince estranger, ou par le subiect.» That means that a Prince can be judged only by princes. Princes can intervene to release a people from a tyrant, but the people cannot act on their own behalf.

Greenleaf

In support of Professor Franklin's interpretation of Bodin's absolutism, I call your attention to the reputation Bodin had in early seventeenth-century Britain, where he was published by Knolles and continually cited, for example, by Filmer precisely in these terms. His authority was always invoked to maintain the doctrine of absolute sovereignty which admitted no right of resistance on the part of any institution or person, or group of persons, whatever. He may have been seen otherwise by some people, but the royalists whom I have in mind were always citing him in these terms. And whilst it may have been formally and theoretically acknowledged that no power could be without limitations, for example by divine or natural law, these limitations were in fact rather the conditions - the moral and prudential conditions – of sovereignty rightly exercised, and not limitations implicit in sovereign power as such. It was always possible for sovereign power to be exercised without regard to these conditions; that was despotical rule. It was also possible for this power to be exercised rightly, and such an exercise constituted royal monarchy as different from despotic monarchy.

*

Villey

Il y a quelque anachronisme à transporter au moyen-âge le terme de «constitutionnalisme.» Le «constitutionallisme» implique une philosophie du contrat social qu'est généralement absente (sauf dans l'école nominaliste surtout occamienne) de la pensée juridique médiévale.

Franklin

If «medieval constitutionalism» is deemed too strong a term, generally speaking, allow me to qualify what I mean. I think that it is correct to say that the subjection of the king to institutional restraints, which is one criterion of constitutionalism, existed in medieval thought – though most often in an ambiguous form. Recognition of this older «constitutionalism» together with its ambiguities is indispensable for understanding the historical significance of Bodin's later work. Responding to the radical challenge of the Huguenots, Bodin resolved all the ambiguities of the older tradition in favor of the royal power. This, I believe, is the precise content as well as the novelty of his developed theory of sovereignty.

Salmon

I, too, would like to be a little «anachronistic» and suggest that there are three types of «constitutionalism» in the sixteenth century. In this sense Professor Franklin's paper and my own paper are rather complementary. First, there is the kind of «constitutionalism» we find in Seyssel and later in Du Haillan, who is Bodin's contemporary. From them stem the two other kinds of constitutionalism. One is the kind developed by the monarchomachs, which stresses fundamental laws but goes beyond the earlier form to create a «rationale» of these laws, and attributes an overriding authority to the community, expressed through the estates general. The other is Bodin's, which, starting from the same point, proceeds to define the legislative sovereignty of the king in the terms which Mr. Polin describes. Like Mr. Franklin, I see Bodin's particular definition of sovereignty in the *République* as enunciated in contradistinction to that of the monarchomachs. Franklin explains why this should be so, and I hope my paper explains how it was so.

Apropos of Mr. Greenleaf's remarks, I do not think that one can make a straight transition from Bodin to English political theory in the mid-seventeenth century. One has first to look at what Dutch and German jurists in the intermediate period made of the attitudes both of Bodin and of the monarchomachs. Some of these jurists tried to compare them and to see what points they had in common. This created considerable confusion in the minds of Englishmen who were as familiar with Arnisaeus and Althusius as they were with Bodin and Hotman. In the English seventeenth-century conflicts Bodin is often quoted to support a variety of arguments, because of misinterpretations by the «intermediaries». He is used by the absolutist defenders of the Stuarts, by Griffith Williams and others as Mr. Greenleaf says, but he is also used by publicists such as Parker and Prynne defending the legislative sovereignty of the Long Parliament. He is even used by the «Fifth Monarchist», John Canne, to defend the execution of Charles I. And he is used again by writers justifying the régime of Cromwell, such as Marchamont Nedham. Much of this has to be explained by reference to the German and Dutch jurists who played such a crucial part in the seventeenth-century images of Bodin.

Isnardi Parente
Sans doute dans la distinction que Bodin fait entre loi et contrat il faut aussi voir une logique intérieure. Ça n'empêche pourtant pas que l'intérêt de cette position du point de vue historique soit dans sa dépendance de la tradition juridique médiévale (qu'on lise, par exemple, un passage de Baldo degli Ubaldi, ce juriste que M. Giesey dans sa relation a indiqué comme très important pour Bodin dans la *République,* un passage où l'on affirme que «Deus subiecit ei [= au prince] leges, sed non contractus».) La tradition juridique qui va du Moyen Age à la Renaissance est d'ailleurs très importante pour Bodin sous des autres aspects aussi, des aspects qui mériteraient d'être étudiés: par exemple Bodin donne une interprétation historique d'un fait social de grande importance, comme le ‹droit des fiefs›, en s'appuyant justement sur une longue discussion en cours entre les juristes, qui disputaient depuis longtemps si le féodalisme a son origine dans l'antiquité romaine ou est un phenomène dû aux invasions des barbares; il dit (et sa solution semble toute personnelle) que le féodalisme a

été emporté par les Huns ou les Hungars, qu'il a une origine dans la monarchie orientale, que c'est une phenomène qui se rélie à une organisation despotique de la société.

*

Villey

Pour revenir à ce rapport de M. Giesey: d'abord je crois qu'il est important d'avoir montré que Bodin était le continuateur de toute une tradition romanistique médiévale, de toute cette littérature médiévale qui interprétait «legibus solutus» en maintenant la soumission du roi au *droit naturel*. Bodin assume cette tradition, et le rappeler; c'est nous prévenir contre des erreurs d'interprétation, celles justement que nous a signalées le rapport de M. Hinton. On n'a souvent vu dans Bodin que le «souveraineté», en oubliant que dans ce temps là, la soumission au droit naturel, cela signifiait quelque chose. Toutefois, je pense que Bodin fausse cette doctrine romanistique traditionnelle, la prive de son sens. Parce que Bodin, volontariste, ne conçoit plus guère de loi naturelle que la loi divine ou comme le disait Mme. Chanteur, éthique. Elle avait été autre chose chez les romanistes. Prenons en exemple ce problème, en pratique si important (en pratique, il se pose toujours), de savoir si le prince est tenu à ses contrats, et en fait, nous savons qu'il abuse de sa puissance pour essayer de ne pas respecter ses contrats. Bodin, parce que sa «loi naturelle» est seulement éthique, ne peut plus apporter à ce problème une réponse satisfaisante, car c'est extrêmement vague et flou les conséquences qu'on peut tirer d'une règle simplement éthique: «on doit en principe tenir ses promesses», maxime morale qu'il est difficile de considérer comme dotée de valeur juridique. C'est une grande erreur de ce temps et du début du XVIIe siècle d'avoir cru pouvoir fonder le droit sur ces règles éthiques.

Ce qui est caractéristique de Bodin est qu'il a perdu la substance du droit naturel des romanistes et des penseurs du Moyen-Age, d'un droit naturel qui était substantiel, parce qu'il était autre chose qu'une loi morale: mais une méthode de discussion, de controverse pour aboutir à des solutions judiciaires en s'appuyant sur l'observation de la nature des choses.

Bodin a l'air d'être le continuateur de la tradition médiévale, comme vous l'avez relaté, en réalité il en a perdu l'esprit, ne le comprend plus.

Giesey

In full agreement with Professor Villey, I might add that Bodin's «medievalism» was like that of the Monarchomachs: one found what one wanted to find, but no one then had the sensibility (that all historians have today) that views on politics and jurisprudence had changed fundamentally from the fourteenth to the sixteenth centuries in France.

In addition to the effect of Bodin's voluntarism upon the conception of natural law, which Professor Villey has just pointed out, I find that Bodin's voluntarism affected his concept of the relationship of the royal office to the royal person. Office and person were kept quite distinct in the sophisticated juridical thought of the later Middle Ages. The royal office was a «real» entity in which authority was vested; the royal person was but the administrator of that authority. Bodin does not pursue this distinction in his ascription of authority: the king's will and the authority of the office are generally regarded as the same. The famous new abstration, «sovereignty», does not limit but rather enhances the king's power.

To put it yet another way (which, granted, suggests more than can be proven) the rôle of the king changes from that of a judge, maintaining a fixed order of things believed to be natural and immemorial, to that of a legislator voluntarily creating order in the state, which is regarded as changing and growing.

*

[In response to queries about the German sources of Bodin's thought, and the reciprocal influence of Bodin's thought in Germany.]

Isnardi Parente
Pour l'Allemagne, il ne faut pas oublier l'importance de l'ouvrage de l'evêque Julius von Pflug, *De Republica Germaniae,* que Bodin cite lui-même dans la *Methodus* et dont il a tiré de conséquences d'ordre constitutionnel. En général, on doit se méfier du manque de citation expresse dans l'œuvre de Bodin, surtout quand il s'agit de contemporains, qu'il ne nomme pas toujours; par exemple, pour les notices concernant les républiques italiennes, on pourrait croire que Bodin disposait d'informations directes, tandis qu'un curieux se faute dans l'interprétation de l'italien dénonce, par exemple, qu'il a emprunté a Francesco Sansovino la description de la constitution de Raguse, ainsi que d'autres villes comme on peut facilement supposer (Bodin, au lieu des mots «da Zara fino a Cattaro» = de Zara jusqu'à Cattaro, qu'il trouve chez Sansovino, lit le mot ‹Zarafino›, et il le reproduit comme ça en créant une phrase dépourvue de sens commun. C'est un exemple significatif qu'il faut rappeler pour être prudents dans nos affirmations au sujet de l'originalité absolue de l'information bodinienne).

Hoke
En Allemagne, il y avaient déjà au moyen-âge des auteurs qui traitaient le droit public – Peter von Andlau par exemple. Mais ce n'était qu'au commencement du 17e siècle que l'on s'est rendu compte en Allemagne que les vraies sources du droit public allemand étaient les lois publiques de l'Empire et les faits de son histoire. On s'est détaché des sources de l'anti-

quité maintenant. C'est dans la première moitié du 17ᵉ siècle que sont parues les premières grandes œuvres traitant le droit public de l'Empire. Dans cette littérature – dès le début – il y avaient deux tendances, dont une favorable au pouvoir de l'empereur, l'autre au pouvoir des états de l'Empire. Le protagoniste du deuxième groupe était Johannes Limnaeus. Il suit la théorie de la double majesté qui apparaît comme une synthèse formelle ou terminologique de la théorie Bodinienne et de la théorie de la souveraineté du peuple. Pour Limnaeus, comme pour les autres théoriciens de la double majesté, c'est uniquement la majestas realis qui est une vraie souveraineté et qui appartient au peuple organisé dans l'Etat dont dépend totalement l'autre majestas, la majestas personalis, qui dans l'Empire est le pouvoir de l'empereur. Le pouvoir souverain, la majestas realis du peuple organisé dans l'Empire, est exercé par les états de l'Empire. L'empereur, ayant la majestas personalis, n'est qu'un organe de ce souverain. L'autre théorie principale de Limnaeus est une vraie synthèse de la théorie de Bodin du caractère aristocratique de l'Empire et de la théorie monarchique de celui-ci. C'est la theorie du status mixtus. Pour Limnaeus le pouvoir souverain, la majestas realis, appartient toujours au peuple organisé dans l'Etat – represénté par les états. Mais la forme de l'Etat qui pour lui n'est rien d'autre que le gouvernement ou l'administration peut être différente selon que la majestas personalis – le pouvoir du suprême organe ou premier magistrat – est exercée par un seul ou par plusieurs ou par un prince et un collectif de nobles, c'est-èdire des états, ensemble. Dans ce dernier cas la forme de l'Etat, le status reipublicae, pour Limnaeus est un status mixtus.

*

Schoeck
I should like to offer two sets of reflections that have a bearing on Bodin and the context of his legal ideas. The first is a plea for more study of legal education in the sixteenth century. This should begin with the texts that were being used, and how they were being used. It is not enough to know that a man has studied at Bologna; we have know under which teacher he studied. As Stelling-Michaud has shown with respect to the Swiss lawyers who came to Bologna, there is a wide variation in the ideas they brought back for the interpretation of the same texts. And so, it is not enough to know that Bodin was using Bartolus; it is how he was reading Bartolus that counts. In respect of the situation in English, we find that Baumer's well-known study nowhere takes this very important fact of legal education into consideration. Nor does Zeeveld, in studying the foundations of Tudor policy, look to see where the counsellors of Henry VIII studied; but he assumed that everybody who studied at Bologna or Padua learned the same thing, which is simplistic. Related to the

same issue, let me recall the quotation in Giesey's paper from the second preface of the *République:* «I realized that a true and sound knowedge of the law lay not in law-college debates, but in courtroom battles.» We have a great deal to learn about these two different arenas of legal rhetoric. The recent thesis by Catherine Holmes on the eloquence of the French legal tradition does very little with the law-college debates, and there is all too little known about, or being done with, the law debates in England at this time – although we do know, for example, that the students at Oxford debated before the Queen for four hours on the inheritance of the crown.

The second set of reflections jumps off from some of our previous discussion of natural law. While the statement is true that for Bodin the major source for natural-law thinking lay in the civil law, we ought not to neglect those elements which developed and were transmitted in the canon-law tradition. Until roughly 1520 or 1530 every lawyer was trained in both laws – «canonista sine legibus parum valet, legista sine canonibus nihil!» Even after that, reformers as well as the Romanists continued to read and study the canon law, or at least to use it for its quotations from the Roman law. The effects of the disruption of the tradition were of several kinds. Very often the energy which previously was bound within the canon law tradition was released, perhaps for the kind of effort in the civil law which Giesey has pointed out. There is also a negative result: in general there is the lessening of access to the thought of the decretists and decretalists, so much of which had been available up until 1520. During the sixteenth century, citations and illustrations from the commentators are increasingly quoted second hand; this is a point that needs investigation. For very often the context of the canonical reference belonged traditionally to the citation of it, and if the sense of the context is lost, then we have a very different method and matter.

*

Schnur
Permit me to include references to Mr. Hinton's paper, because I see now the connections between it and those of Mr. Franklin and Mr. Giesey. Mr. Hinton has a difficult title for his paper: «Retreat into Legalism». What does it mean? He gives some clues when he says, further, that the Renaissance was optimistic, pragmatic, and realistic, while Bodin was pessimistic, legalistic, and – to my great surprise – idealistic! The problem may perhaps be but this way: what element of the system guarantees best the minimal order of the political system? If you have great confidence in all parts of the society, then you have small interest in concentrating the power of decision at one point. If, however, you are (as Mr. Hinton say) pessimistic, your confidence in the diverse parts of society is not very

great; then, however, there arises the problem of how to augment power at one point in the political system without inducing dictatorship or tyranny. You must construct limits. It is typical of legal reasoning at this juncture to sharpen the question of who decides when the political system is endangered. If the public order is threatened by conflict between two churches or two religions, what is to be done and who is to make the decision? Bodin's answer was to go back to certain mediaeval political theories. Bartolus and others had fought for the temporal power of the emperor against intervention from other rising powers. As a lawyer, Bodin has seen the problem more sharply than philosophers – optimistic philosophers – could have seen it. The monarchomachs may have lost confidence in the French monarchs, but Bodin remains confident that the monarch would find a solution to the religious problem. How could one limit the monarchy in a fashion agreable to the various religious parts of the nation, when these very parts of society had not been integrated with each other? One cannot resolve the discussion by reference to absolute standards. Certainly Bodin himself was not an absolutist in the seventeenth-century sense.

IV. BODINS POLITISCHE PHILOSOPHIE

Zusammenfassung: Horst Denzer

Polin

Pour la discussion, je veux attirer votre attention sur cinq thèmes qui me semblent se dégager des divers exposés, le thème de la définition de la souveraineté, le thème de la limite de la souveraineté, le thème des conditions d'exercice de la souveraineté dans la France du 16e siècle, le problème de la théorie de Bodin dans ses rapports avec les théories contemporaines ou antérieures et le problème de la théorie de Bodin dans ses rapports avec les théories qui lui ont succédé, son influence.

Freund

En partant de la définition de la souveraineté, c'est l'orginalité de Bodin, qu'il ne fonde pas cette souveraineté sur un contrat, contrairement aux grandes théories de la souveraineté qui le suivront, p.e. celles-ci de Hobbes et de Rousseau. D'autre part, il faut souligner, que précisément la théorie du contrat apparaît à l'époque de Bodin avec les monarchomaques. Pour l'histoire des idées ultérieures, nous voyons que finalement et Hobbes et Rousseau vont essayer de joindre ces deux thèmes du contrat et de la souveraineté qui étaient disjoints au 16e siècle. Par conséquent, en refusant la théorie du contrat Bodin aboutit à une conception hiérarchique de la vie politique, alors que ceux qui prendront pour base de la souveraineté le contrat en iront de plus en plus vers une conception égalitaire de la vie politique. C'est là à mon avis dans l'ensemble de ces idées qui nous viennent du 16e siècle et qui aujourd'hui sont encore discutées, le véritable problème: est-ce que la vie politique est établie hiérarchique ou égalitaire ou bien y a-t-il des aspects égalitaires *et* hiérarchiques, qu'il s'agit de respecter l'un et l'autre, et non pas de vouloir hiérarchiser ce qui est égalitaire ou égaliser ce qui est hiérarchique.

Derathé

pose la question: En disant que Bodin ne fonde pas la souveraineté sur un contrat, sur quoi fonde-t-il la souveraineté? Afin de modifier l'interprétation de Mme Chanteur, qui dit «la souveraineté c'est la force», il cite des textes de la *République*. Bodin dit (I, 6, p. 69): «La raison et lumière naturelle nous conduit à cela, de croire que la force et violence a donné source et origine aux Républiques.» Il n'a jamais dit «source et origine de la *souveraineté*». Mais il y a d'autres textes où Bodin pense que les rois ont acquis la souveraineté du peuple, sans contrat, mais néanmoins du peuple: «Disons que signifient ces mots, puissance absolue. Car le peuple ou les seigneurs d'une République, peuvent donner purement et simplement la puissance souveraine et perpétuelle à quelqu'un pour diposer des biens, des personnes et de tout l'état à son plaisir, et puis le laisser à qui il voudra, et tout ainsi que le propriétaire peut donner son bien purement et simplement sans autre cause que de sa libéralité, qui est la vraie donation et qui ne reçoit plus de conditions.» Alors Bodin montre ici que le roi a acquis la souveraineté du peuple sous forme de donation.

Chanteur
réplique: Quand même Bodin ne parle pas de l'origine de la souveraineté et quand il dit que la force et la violence sont la vraie source et origine des républiques, les républiques sont définies par la souveraineté. Le texte que vous citez d'ailleurs justement a pour but de définir la souveraineté et de montrer, qu'on ne peut parler de souveraineté du roi qu'à condition que le peuple en est éliminé complètement. Or, cette origine, il y avait par la force qui fait des vainqueurs, et ce sont les vainqueurs qui sont souverains. Cette interprétation cadre avec l'exercice du pouvoir souverain dans la république. Si le pouvoir absolu et perpétuel est exercé par force, cela s'appelle tyrannie, et néanmoins le tyran est souverain. Certainement, le souverain légitime n'est pas un tyran, mais si vous pensez au problème de source et d'origine, je crois qu'il faut montrer que la cause finale est plus importante que la cause effective. L'origine de la république par la force n'est pas une question du droit, mais du fait. Le vainqueur, c'est le souverain.

Salmon
It is an error, if we assume that Bodin was presenting us a systematic, complete and selfcontained theory of sovereignty. The explanation lies in the ambivalent purpose behind Bodin's composition of the *République*. Bodin was not aware of the full implications of some of the points he used. If you appraise the problem of limitations and absolute sovereignty compared with each other, you are bound to conclude that there are certain contradictions.

Greenleaf
contradicts Salmon. I would like to make a distinction between different levels of dealing with politics. The highest level is achieved by those who see politics as part of a general world imperium worked out on a philosophical level, but these, like Hobbes, are few in number. I don't want to suggest that Bodin is operating at this level. Nevertheless, I think that he does produce a more or less logical and complete theory of politics

without being a political philosopher. Therefore, it is necessary to determine the basis of his theory by observing the ontological overtone for the absolute presuppositions. He obviously defines political power in terms of sovereignty. And this concept of sovereignty is in fact logically implied in the metaphysical assumptions that he makes concerning his notion of order and hierarchy. During the Middle Ages the principle of unity was always a part of this world-view. Usually the temporal sovereignty, that applied in this world to the Pope, acquired a sort of divine plenitudo potestatis. Bodin simply transfers this concept of sovereignty which is implicit in the world-view of order to a temporal monarch. In that sense, the notion of sovereignty is derived from these metaphysical assumptions.

Now, this concept of sovereignty, of unified power can of course take on various forms. Hence, Bodin's discussion of the different kinds of state, which can be monarchical, aristocratic or democratic. It can also be administered in various ways. Hence his discussion of different forms of government. It can also be exercised in different fashions. Hence his discussion of the different types of monarchical state, for instance. You can have a king, exercising his power tyrannically who is nevertheless sovereign; or you can have a king exercising his power royally, i. e. he observes certain moral or conventional limitations in the exercise of the monarchical power. It seems to me therefore that the limits of Bodin's theory of sovereignty are not limits on the concept of sovereignty at all, but simply an observation of certain conditions or ways in which power may be exercised. These were the observations Bodin made to point out that a wise and moral monarch will exercise sovereign power in this way in France at this time. I do not see how this kind of observation implies a fundamental logical contradiction to his theory, it is simply a development of social aspects of it. Bodin's theory was not a philosophy on the highest level, but nevertheless an appropriate theory in general terms.

Salmon
differs from Greenleaf's theory: I think that Bodin's desire to associate his theory with the practicalities of how French government had proceeded in past and in his view proceeded in his own days, provides the key to our difference. He assumes that his theory is fully consistent with what actually happened in the government of France. This was not the case; consequently there must either be something wrong within his view of what actually happened or his system is not fully logical.

Franklin
I would like to comment on the discussion about contract in Bodin. A contractual theory in the grand style particularly in the seventeenth cen-

tury is an attempt by means of an examination of the terms or conditions of the contract to define the content and the limits of the sovereign power. Now, with Bodin one finds precise historical and precise contractual explanations of the origins of the state. There are fables and historical myths about the way the Hellenic state came into existence. But this does not establish for him the content of sovereignty or the limitations. The content of sovereignty, the limits of sovereignty are established purely by comparative historical analysis. If you want to know what the content of sovereignty is, you should study the Roman republic. If you want to know whether sovereignty is indivisible, you should examine many cases. If you want to know what the rights of resistance are or lack of rights of resistance, you should study French law or the Lex Iulia, etc. So it seems to me that it is proper to say that Bodin does not have a contractual theory and that the substitute for it is a highly precise empirical consideration of history.

Villey (se réfère à Chanteur et Derathé)
La question d'origine, des causes de la souveraineté ne se posait absolument pas pour Bodin comme elle se pose pour les modernes; parce que pour Bodin il n'y a pas à justifier la souveraineté. Simplement telle souveraineté *est*, mais parce qu'elle est, puisque Bodin croit à l'ordre naturel, elle est justifiée. Et c'est une toute autre question de se demander quels sont les moyens par lesquels cet ordre naturel se réalisait. Ces moyens peuvent être la force, la conquête et autre chose. Ça, c'est un petit peu comme ce que Hegel apprenne la ruse de la nature, la providence s'est servi de tel ou tel moyen pour arriver à réaliser cet ordre. Il ne s'agit pas là de cause justifiante. Bodin est fidèle tout simplement à l'ontologie classique pour laquelle l'être est bon. Par conséquent, c'est tout à fait un anachronisme de lui poser le problème de l'origine de la souveraineté, comme on le pose à partir de Hobbes ou de Locke.

Freund
Le problème de la légitimation se pose précisément au 16e siècle, étant donné les désordres qui régnaient et les théories qui combattaient la légitimité du pouvoir royal. Donc, c'est vrai, ce qui vient d'être dit, dans une certaine mesure, c'est faux dans la mesure où le 16e siècle avec les guerres de religion posait le problème de la légitimité du pouvoir. Il faut faire attention de quelle façon, mais le problème est posé.

Schnur
Bodin saw the problem of distinguishing between contract and consent. If power should be legitimatized, there must be consent. There are different forms to achieve consent. The more rational form is the contract.

But the concept of contract involves the danger of the dissolution of relations between the sovereign and the other members of the political society, the danger of instability of the political system. The only way for avoiding this danger is to identify the contract with the transference of all legal power on the sovereign, as Hobbes and his followers built up their theories in this way. The other form of consent arises from the historically developed relationship between the power and the individuals. The difficulty for Bodin is to connect the historical view of the growth of power and the analytical concept of sovereignty. The historical explanation cannot be logical, and the logical concept cannot explain the historical situation of power in a given state. Therefore Bodin saw the impossibility of questioning the historical origin of a given political power, and he tried to construct the republic on consent, that means in accordance with the historical reality. This dichotomy, I would like to emphasize, does not mean a contradiction in Bodin's thought, but it is a fundamental problem for all political theories.

Hinton (agrees with Chanteur)
For Bodin the state of Western Europe originated in conquest. He points out the development from Nimrod to the rise and decline of the Roman republic. During the Barbarian Invasions Europe again was a prey to conquerors who originated the states of Western Europe. Again after the revolutionary conquest the people became more peaceful, the kings became wiser, and royal monarchies emerged from despotic and potentially despotic monarchies. This conquest theory shows that Bodin is chiefly emphasizing sovereignty, not limitations. And the sovereignty is still the sovereignty of a conqueror. Obviously with the description of the different types of monarchy in book II, the chapter of the seigneural, the despotic monarchy precedes the chapter of royal monarchy. One notices that in the scheme of differentiating the states, there is even a distinction between the distinctions. The distinction between monarchy, aristocracy and democracy is absolute. The distinction between royal monarchy, despotic monarchy and tyranny is a distinction of degree. Bodin wishes to say, that if a royal monarch should behave in a way which is apparently tyrannical, still the subject with a doubt judgement of matters of this sort must accept this supposed tyranny in good part. Those who stress the limitations, can easily exaggerate their effectiveness, even in the mind of Bodin. Property, for example, can be taken away by royal monarch, and the subject has to accept the fact. And Bodin acknowledges that taxes which have been originally extraordinary become habitual. Therefore, I agree with Salmon, there *is* an inconsistency in Bodin. As a matter of fact, I think, he himself once thought, it was a correct and accurate system. However, if he had written under Henri IV,

not to mention Louis XIV or François I, he would not have been satisfied with the limitations which he put into the *République;* he would have followed, for example, Seysell where the limitations are much more formal.

On the occasion of *Derathé's* question, Hinton explains what he means by the inconsistency in Bodin concerning the limitations of sovereignty:

I think that the practical consequences would be for Bodin that he would have to accept a tax imposed by Henri III. I think the consequences for us are that we have to accept that the limitations were not so satisfactory as Bodin himself cared to believe. The indivisibility of the sovereignty is of paramount importance to Bodin, not the power of the sovereign. And since Bodin was operating under a very weak king, he did not very much concern himself with the question of limitation of the actual power of the king. However, it is natural that in the *République* Bodin does not offer a recipe for making the king more powerful. Similar writing – similar context: Fortescue in England a hundred years earlier would solve the problem by making the king rich and strong, by presenting him with force at his disposal. Bodin is content to give the king authority, so one cannot expect Bodin to be very clear or precise about the limitations. I think that Bodin's constant references to law as a limitation to the incorrect use of sovereignty are an attempt to assure his readers, that they can safely give the king the authority which, as Bodin says, is his right.

McRae
points out the double process of the origin of sovereignty and of legitimization. The sovereignty originates from force. At a second stage, force becomes authority by a process of legitimization. There are a number of different ways to legitimize this original force, through custom, lapse of time, succession, testament, and so on. To Bodin in his comparative aspect, there is no real need to assign any value to these different types of legitimization. They are all part of the process whereby sovereignty has emerged and become legitimately recognized authority.

Hinton (in response to Chanteur)
Time and need of processes will, no doubt, create authority and legality, but the conqueror's power and sovereignty is established simply by the law of nations.

Reulos
Bodin a employé un terme quelque peu nouveau qui était le substantif «souveraineté», alors que ce qui était d'usage général c'était l'adjectif «souverain». Pour bien dégager la définition de la souveraineté, il con-

vient d'opposer la souveraineté aux notions qu'il veut écarter, aux notions traditionnelles, qu'il trouvait dans toutes les littératures du 14ᵉ et 15ᵉ siècle: imperium avec les distinctions imperium maius et imperium inferior, la notion de iurisdictio avec ses différents niveaux qui correspondent à certains des individus attachés à la souveraineté, la notion de domaine, dominium, la notion de potestas et plenitudo potestatis, et il trouve aussi cette notion du contrat qui soulève tant de difficultés et de discussions, ce qui est en présence du sermon du sacre, c'est un engagement unilatéral qui est accepté par l'acclamation du peuple, et c'est ainsi que naît ce que l'on appelle le contrat. Cette excursion terminologique me paraît très importante pour situer Bodin au 16ᵉ siècle et évaluer son originalité. Le mot quelque peu nouveau adopté veut marquer qu'il y a une notion qui ne se rattache pas directement aux notions antérieures, mais qu'il veut extraire de ces notions antérieures, ce qui peut aboutir à une clarification et à une notion unitaire sur laquelle on pourra ensuite travailler. Et ce point me paraît également important pour expliquer les premières utilisations de Bodin, par exemple Loiseau et les *Maximes générales du droit français* de Pierre Delommeau.

Polin

Vous avez dit, ce mot «souveraineté» est quelque peu nouveau. Où apparaît-il avant Bodin?

Reulos

On trouve épisodiquement le mot «superioritas». Je n'ai pas d'exemples précis du mot «souveraineté» antérieur à Bodin, mais il est possible que ça existe. L'adjectif «souverain» existe et la formation d'un substantif nouveau abstrait n'est pas quelque chose d'exceptionnel dans la langue française du 16ᵉ siècle.

Villey

ne connaît pas le terme «souveraineté» avant Bodin.

Hoke

On entend souvent summum imperium, même superioritas, mais sans aucune définition originale. Et c'est Bodin qui le premier définit.

Je veux attirer votre attention sur les remarques de Bodin (I, 8, p. 127), suivant ce que disait Derathé sur l'origine de la souveraineté. A ce lieu-là, Bodin définit même le souverain comme celui-ci à qui le peuple a donné par sa propre volonté la souveraineté, comme celui-ci que le peuple a investi avec la puissance souveraine: «Que dirons nous donc de celui qui a du peuple la puissance absolue, tant et si longuement qu'il vivra? En ce cas il faut distinguer, si la puissance absolue lui est donné purement et simplement, sans qualité de magistrat ni de commissaire, ni forme de précaire, il est bien certain que celui-là est et se peut dire monarque souverain, car le peuple s'est dessaisi et dépouillé de sa puissance souveraine pour l'ensaisiner et investir . . .»

Chanteur

Bodin parle des sources et origines des républiques, et il définit bien la république à partir de la souveraineté, ce qui prouve que la souveraineté est logiquement le fondement des républiques. On parle des termes antérieurs qu'on peut trouver dans la littérature politique, mais Bodin nous donne lui-même des équivalents, puisque au début du chap. 8 il rappelle précisément les termes latins, grecs, italiens et hébreux. Or, un des termes grecs est significatif, la souveraineté est ἀρχή, c'est à dire qu'elle est le fondement, du fondement on ne demande pas son origine. On ne demande pas à un fondement, que c'est légitimé; c'est lui qui va légitimer l'état politique.

Derathé

n'est pas d'accord.

Franklin

has an objection to the view that Bodin's sovereignty is always introduced by conquest and subsequently legitimated. Apart from the former, at least two other accounts are given in the *République*. One, I think, which goes back to Polybius is the notion of a group of people getting together and rallying around the strongest or most distinguished person among them. An example is given: heads of households who get together for common protection. The other account is a conquest theory. Bodin says, that the conquered population approaches the sovereign in the status of slaves, and the ruler's relationship with them is of a seigneural nature; but with respect to his own barons, his relationship is based upon their own consent, and is therefore royal.

The basis of these three theories is not any droit naturel, ius naturale, where the consent would be general, but ius gentium derived from history.

Concerning the example of Hoke in which the language of consent is used very specifically to trace out what distinguishes the sovereign, it seems to me Bodin is using Roman law conceptions in terms of what constitutes an unconditional gift (don inconditionnel), and he uses the concept of donation under Roman law to show that a gift which is either not absolute or not perpetual, is conditional and therefore cannot be sovereign. I think, nowhere in his writings did Bodin adopt a method of deriving the *content* of sovereignty from any analysis of how the state began.

Kelley

agrees with Salmon and Schnur, that the paradoxes in Bodin are not
entirely of his own doing, but due to his attempt to stand on two legs, one
in the realm of theory and one in the realm of history.

Freund

Derathé et Hoke ont cité des textes sur la souveraineté étant pas un contrat, mais une donation venant du peuple. Mais on n'a pas fait attention à
un terme négatif, celui de commission. C'est un terme qui va avoir un
succès très grand puisque Rousseau va le reprendre dans le *Contrat social*
et dire que le gouvernement par rapport à la souveraineté est commission.
Or, ce qui est important chez Bodin quand il emploie le terme de commission, c'est que le souverain ne reçoit pas commission, il donne commission. Les officiers, ce sont les commissaires du souverain. Toute cette
théorie de la commission (le commissaire de la République Soviétique est
un exemple postérieur) toujours sert à comprendre qu'est-ce qui est le
souverain. Chez Bodin il n'est ni fondé sur un contrat ni commissaire.
Dans toute la théorie de Bodin, on n'a pas encore prêté assez attention au
terme de commission, qui est fondamental pour toute la pensée politique
postérieure.

Derathé

Mais la distinction entre officier et souverain est plus importante, plus
développée dans la littérature postérieure que chez Bodin.

Villey

Un mot sur la nouvauté du terme souveraineté chez Bodin. Au Moyen
Age et avant Bodin le mot souverain est employé de façon très relative à
des circonstances, il apparaît dans les discussions sur l'indépendance ou la
non-indépendance du roi vis-à-vis de l'empereur et de l'empereur vis-à-vis
du pape. Et au contraire, le mot souveraineté chez Bodin devient une pièce
intemporelle dans un système du cosmos tout entier. Je pense que c'est un
des éléments de la nouvauté.

Hinrichs

Dans la traduction allemande de la *République*, parue en 1592, on a
traduit le mot souveraineté avec le terme «Oberkeit», c'est plutôt la signification traditionnelle du mot souveraineté en France. On n'a pas compris
la modernité et la nouveauté du mot souveraineté chez Bodin, parce que
«Oberkeit» c'est une des possibilités d'être supérieur à un autre, mais non
la possibilité de souveraineté.

Scheuner

There are two schools of thought in this assembly. The one party likes to make of Bodin a philosopher who has a logically complete system of thought. But Bodin's theory has not only a philosophical and logical foundation, he also seeks for legal examples in history, he has always a tendency to recognize the facts of life, which the other party emphasizes. And it is on this side of Bodin that I insist too. For example, concerning the origin of sovereignty, Bodin presents «l'acquisition de la souveraineté du Royaume d'Arles» (*République* I, 9, p. 188). That sovereignty was bought by a contract with the empire, and Bodin points out that the documents are still in the royal archives. This example is not taken from a philosophical point of view, but from the facts of life he recognized. Therefore we should not stress too much the logical devolution.

Concerning Schnur's difference between consent and contract, I would say, that the theory of consent has a certain tendency towards the theory of contract. And that is a line Bodin never took. He never recognized that sovereign power is responsible.

As to the conception of the word «souveraineté», I would not underline the etymological side. The real expression in Latin is «suprema potestas», and this term is already used in the late Middle Ages quite correctly. Not only the Royal theory, but above all the Papal theory (Augustinus Triumphans and other authors of the Middle Ages) have already developed the conception, that the Pope is supreme and not bound by the council. This theory – at least in the conceptional and verbal sense – has developed the term sovereignty. The original contribution of Bodin is, that he defines the term more precisely and creates a new word for the existing conception. In the Middle Ages, sovereignty is never an abstract or absolute term; it is a relative term. Suprema potestas means in the Middle Ages «not dependent on anybody else». That means in the great discussion of the 15th century, that the council is not above the Pope; whereas the conciliar theory (and this is the thought of the later theory of the Estates, of the theory of contract) says that if the Pope fails against the divine law and the law of nature, he can be deposed, he can be judged by the council. Without recognizing this heritage we cannot grasp the discovery of the 16th century.

Hinrichs

montre à Derathé une contradiction. Chez Bodin (*République* I, 10, p. 223) dans l'énumération des droits qui sont compris en la seule marque de souveraineté (c'est-à-dire la puissance de donner et casser la loi) se trouve aussi le droit «d'imposer ou exempter les sujets de charges et subsides». Mais Derathé a écrit dans son rapport (p. 252): «Il en résulte toutefois qu'à la différence de Hobbes et de Pufendorf, Bodin n'a pu faire figurer parmi les marques de la souveraineté le droit de lever des taxes ou des impôts.»

Schnur

For Bodin the decisive point is – and he is the first to emphasize this – that sovereignty is a social fact for any political community which wants to survive. Only then follows the question of legitimating power and of the restrictions for legitimate power (not for sovereignty!). Therefore sovereign power has the right to impose taxes, but not the legitimate monarch, who needs the consent of his subjects.

Polin

Schnur, tout-à-l'heure, a employé à plusieurs reprises le mot «légitime». Il me semble qu'on ne peut pas dire que chez Bodin la souveraineté est légitime. C'est *un* certain usage de la souveraineté qui est légitime ou qui n'est pas légitime, par exemple l'usage que les magistrats commis par le souverain font de leur pouvoir. La légitimité est la conformité à la loi. Mais le souverain qui fait la loi et qui est au-dessus des lois, on ne peut pas dire qu'il est ou qu'il n'est pas légitime. La souveraineté est l'expression de l'ordre naturel des choses humaines.

Hinrichs

explique la contradiction montrée au sujet du texte cité concernant l'énumération des marques de souveraineté. Bodin implique dans ce texte le droit d'imposer et d'exempter les sujets comme une marque de souveraineté, parce qu'il veut le commandement sur les sujets; il le prend pour démontrer que les féodales, les grandseigneurs ne peuvent plus imposer leurs sujets, d'aucune manière.

Reulos

Je crois que le texte sur l'énumération des marques de souveraineté doit être mis en rapport avec le thème des conditions d'exercice de la souveraineté en France. Car il résume la pratique politique et administrative en France depuis la reconstruction du royaume par Charles VII. Bodin considère à très juste titre le droit d'imposer et d'exempter les sujets comme une marque de souveraineté, parce que cela vise précisément le droit du roi vis-à-vis des arrières-vassaux. Mais ce droit sera conditionné par certaines coutumes du royaume (je n'emploie pas le mot limitation). Il faut mettre cela en rapport avec les caractéristiques du droit des corps, des communautés; une de celles-ci est de pouvoir collecter et disposer des fonds. Par exemple, lorsque les églises réformées sont reconnues comme des unités de droit public (les églises locales bien entendu), on leur reconnaît le droit de recevoir des aumônes, mais pas le droit de s'imposer; cela ne sera admis que par l'Edit de Nantes. Mais c'est toujours très soigneusement précisé dans tous les édits de pacification. Donc le roi a comme marque de souveraineté le droit d'imposer des subsides sur ses sujets, et lorsque cette imposition est nouvelle, il y ait à consulter les états. C'est un des éléments sur lequel la position de Bodin en raison de circonstances politiques ou d'opportunités pourra varier. Cette possibilité est conditionnée par l'état et le bien commun du royaume. Tous les exemples sur la pratique des états présentent cette notion du bien commun. Encore les états du 16e siècle critiquent non pas le principe du roi d'imposer, mais l'emploi qu'il fait des deniers, et veut imposer un contrôle sur l'emploi des deniers. Je crois qu'à ce point de vue la théorie de Bodin est tout de même très cohérente. Il affirme un principe, mais l'exercice de ce droit est soumis à certaines conditions générales d'exercice et à la finalité du bien commun.

Franklin
asks Hinrichs: When you quote that passage of Bodin on the primacy of legislative power as the true and comprehensive mark of sovereignty, how do you interpret the meaning of comprehensive? Does this mean, that the other marks of sovereignty have an instrumental relationship to the legislative power, or are they additional examples of the same thing?

Hinrichs
There is a difference between the power of taxing, which is bound to the consent of the people, and the other instrumental powers of the sovereignty which are not bound to consent.

Franklin
What is the relationship, for example, of the power of «dernier ressort» to the power to make law? Is it a relationship of means to end or is the power of final appeal another example of the power to command?

Hoke
About the relationship between the power of taxing and the legislative power Bodin says (*République* I, 10, p. 244), that the power of taxing is «émanation» of the power to make law: «Quand au droit de mettre sur les sujets tailles et impôts, ou bien en exempter quelques uns, cela dépend aussi de la puissance de donner la loi et les privilèges.»

Franklin
defines precisely his question: whether there is in Bodin any distinction in the modern sense between legislative and executive power?

Kelley

I believe that in the *Methodus* there is a distinction between imperium, consilium and executio. But we should estimate the «esprit de système» of Bodin in this context; it is necessary for him to arrive at a single category, which is the notion of indivisible sovereignty. Certainly, the distribution of the marks of sovereignty in ancient institutions may form the subject, but the logical drive of Bodin makes this single category necessary, and logically the distribution of all these individual factors is the emanation of the power of legislation.

McRae

You cannot assume that Bodin has a clear idea of the distinction between executive and legislative power, because of the frequency with which he puts together the notion of law as a general law and privilege as a rule made in respect to a particular person.

Franklin

agrees with Kelley and McRae, but asks himself, why Bodin has such difficulties in explaining why sovereignty is indivisible.

Villey

Dans son rapport Chanteur a montré la position ambiguë, intermédiaire de Bodin entre la tradition classique, d'où il sort, et certaines conceptions modernes de la loi qu'il annonce. Il y a d'une part, un sens classique extrêmement large du mot loi: la loi c'est l'ordre du monde. Ça tient encore un grand rôle chez Bodin, puisque les souverainetés, par exemple, se rattachent à cette espèce de la loi comme ordre naturel informulé, et c'était là-dessus que se bâtissait le droit naturel. Mais je me demande si Bodin emploie souvent le mot loi naturelle dans ce sens très large. L'autre sens apparaît chez Bodin, quand il s'agit de limiter la souveraineté du roi temporel, du roi humain. La loi naturelle limite et là, on voit Bodin volontariste: la loi est commandement. Ici, nous sommes au cœur de la nouveauté de Bodin; il s'agit déjà d'une loi naturelle qui est éthique. Je n'était pas d'accord avec Scheuner quand il disait que cette conception de la loi naturelle comme éthique était seulement postérieure. C'est oublier toute une tradition théologique, qui à partir du commentaire de Saint Paul a développé ce sens-là de loi naturelle. Je crois que c'est celui qui l'emporte chez Bodin et c'est dans ce sens-là Bodin parle expressément de loi naturelle.

Alors, cela c'est l'abnégation du droit naturel, puisque le droit naturel qui pouvait vraiment apporter une limite au légalisme était bâti sur le premier sens, et on voit chez Bodin le sens large, classique, d'ordre informulé s'estomper devant le sens volontariste de loi-commandement de Dieu, de l'homme.

Scheuner

Si j'ai dit que chez Bodin la loi naturelle n'est pas conçue comme une loi morale, je ne voulais pas dire que la loi naturelle n'est pas aussi une loi, mais que cette séparation entre la loi naturelle dans le sens juridique et celle-ci dans le sens moral est une division des 17ᵉ et 18ᵉ siècles et cette distinction n'est pas encore chez Bodin.

Salmon

I would like to point out that the antithesis to the idea of natural law is «raison d'état». I cannot see anywhere in Bodin any consciousness or advocation of «raison d'état». Indeed, as far as one can trace a relationship between Machiavelli, interest of state and raison d'état, Bodin is fully opposed to this kind of very new tradition.

Schnur

Bodin describes the royal monarch (*République* II, 3, p. 279): «Le monarque royal est celui, qui se rend aussi obéissant aux lois de nature, comme il désire les sujets être envers lui, laissant la liberté naturelle et la propriété des bien à chacun.» Later, liberty and property become the two leading notions for the state of John Locke and then for the «société bourgeoise». In Bodin these notions are the normative elements in the system of «monarchie royale», and they are used to distinguish between the «monarchie royale» and the «monarchie seigneurale». In the «monarchie seigneurale» there is no guarantee for the protection of liberty and property, and the subject is not recognized as citizen in the political sense. Therefore Bodin favours the «monarchie royale», where the subjectivity and the human rights of the subject are granted and the citizen has the condition to give consent to the monarch. So, the royal monarch obeys the natural law. Bodin here is developing the concept of natural law in the modern sense, which will be fully constructed in the following centuries.

Franklin

Hinrichs emphasizes in his paper a dual motif in Bodin, the one element of conservation and preservation of property in «société bourgeoise», the other element: the emphasis of sovereignty in the condition of reform. I sympathize with that element in Bodin: strong king, but condition of reform. But all that puzzles me is that in the *Methodus* the concept of royal power is already formed and that there is a great emphasis upon limitation, civil law sense of limitation. Yet this is precisely the period when the reformists' impulse around the French monarchy is at its height. Bodin himself associated with L'Hôpital. L'Hôpital is invoking absolutist principles of the Etats de Blois. In part, Bodin pushed through a reformists' programme in the Estates and against the Royal Office. And yet there is no clue about Bodin having formed the concept of sovereignty in response to the Reformists' impulse à la L'Hôpital. Therefore I find myself forced to adopt the view that there is nothing particulary reformist about the concept of sovereignty even in the *République*, that's really an ideological reaction to the monarchomachs.

Hinrichs

You see, there are different aspects of reform in earlier times and in later times. There was the necessary reform concerning the excessive property within the church, of which Bodin speaks in book VI of the *République*. Some of the aspects of social or economic reforms had just developed at the time of the publication of the *Republique,* and therefore Bodin does include in the *République* a lot of aspects of reform which you cannot find in such an explicit manner in the *Methodus*, f.e. the great subject of «changement des tailles». The solution is that Bodin became conscious of all the political, social and economic implications of the reforms which were necessary at that time, in the period between *Methodus* and *République*, when he had gleaned much political experiences.

Salmon

The explanation is that Bodin, when he was writing the *République*, was not in the inside of the reformists' group, nor had he ever really been in that circle. It is the great Office of the Secretary of State who really made up the reform.

Hinrichs

At the time of Henri III most intensive work on reform was started within the assembly of notables, work which had never been done during the time of Michel de L'Hôpital. In an article of a member of Ecole de Chartres about the assembly of notables, published about 1582 or 1583, there appears for the first time a very intensive project of reform d'Etat for the council on financial problems. The real time of reform had begun in the seventies of the 16th century.

Franklin

I agree with you. But nevertheless the concept of sovereignty was born in 1566; though you cannot say, the concept of sovereignty was developed for the purpose of strengthening the position of the king in order to make reforms. Bodin developed the concept of sovereignty at a time when he was not yet interested in reforms.

Salmon

But I don't think that the concept of sovereignty *was* developed in 1566. Tax-reforms were denied; it is a very strange sovereignty which is not financed!

Franklin

Yes, what I was saying is that the absolutism of the *République* was a reaction to the political programme of the monarchomachs and not to the problem of giving the king sufficient power to carry through his own plans.

Hinrichs

agrees with Salmon (p. 474) that there is no notion of «raison d'état» in Bodin and that he does not use the word «necessitas» in the meaning of «raison d'état». But the following governor Henri IV and Richelieu were using the term «necessitas» in an exaggerated manner, which was possibly borrowed from Bodin. The king could tax without consent if there was a necessity. And it was very easy for the king to argue that there *was* a necessity.

Salmon

You support my point, that Bodin himself was not conscious of the implications of his theory.

Villey

accuse le rapport de Polin d'être trop bodinophil.

Polin

L'intention de mon rapport était plutôt d'approfondir une certaine conception de l'Etat. Non pas tellement avec le souci de faire le palégérique de Bodin, mais plutôt avec l'idée de montrer les déficiences d'un certain nombre de théories politiques et des régimes qui leur sont inféodés et dont nous souffrons, dans la mesure où on a une république fondée sur une structure inégalitaire et sur une répartition objective des fonctions des obligations. On tâche parfois de faire triompher une communauté politique fondée sur une soi-disant égalité et sur un soi-disant respect absolu de droits subjectifs dont on se préoccupe pas toujours de montrer s'ils sont ou non compatibles entre eux.

Freund

Dans le rapport de Polin, il ne s'agit pas de la souveraineté comme concept, mais de l'exercice réel d'une souveraineté dans la communauté politique. Et alors, là une chose est essentielle, c'est que la souveraineté est en fait la consécration de l'inégalité. Cette inégalité essaie de trouver l'équilibre entre les inégalités nécessaires dans la vie politique. Et sur ce point, Polin a très bien montré l'éloge de l'inégalité.

Schnur

Mais Bodin n'aime pas du tout l'esprit de l'inégalité, au contraire il dit que la première et principale cause des séditions c'est l'inégalité.

Freund

Dans ce texte là, Bodin traite le problème de l'inégalité sociale, donc une inégalité trop grande et excessive. Mais l'ensemble de l'œuvre comporte une nette prise de position pour la valeur politique de l'inégalité.

Polin

Bodin dit, que l'égalité n'est pas capable de constituer un ordre. Seule une structure inégalitaire peut être ordonnable. Mais il va sans dire qu'il peut y avoir, par conséquent, des inégalités extrêmes, comme dira plus tard Montesquieu, qui ne sont pas compatibles avec un ordre. Le propre d'une inégalité dans l'ordre, c'est qu'elle est ordonnée, limitée, relative et, par conséquent, liée à une harmonie. Le texte en question précisément montre une inégalité inharmonique.

Derathé

Je suis d'accord sur l'inégalité, mais pas sur les rapports que Freund établi entre inégalité et souveraineté. Je crois que Bodin pense dans le cadre de sociétés hiérarchisées, qui étaient celles de son temps, mais je pense tout de même qu'il est difficile d'introduire le concept de souveraineté, sans lui faire quelques accrocs, dans une société strictement hiérarchisée et limitée par un certain nombre de coutumes.

Freund

Je ne vois pas pourquoi il y a une affinité entre égalité et souveraineté.

Derathé

Parce que la souveraineté c'est tout de même la domination, enfin le pouvoir d'un seul. C'est beaucoup plus difficile de donner un pouvoir de souverain absolu, comme le font Hobbes ou Rousseau, dans une société hiérarchisée et limitée comme l'était celle de l'ancien régime.

Polin

C'est aussi le problème de la signification du caractère absolu du pouvoir qui intervient ici.

Derathé

Il y a une grosse difficulté chez Bodin, et il me paraît très difficile qu'un théoricien de la souveraineté absolue puisse accepter doctrinalement les lois fondamentales. Je dis pour un *théoricien* de la souveraineté absolue. L'absolutisme français les acceptait très bien, mais sans les fonder si ce n'est par la coutume.

Polin

L'absolutité du pouvoir définit le fait que ce pouvoir décide en dernier ressort et que cette décision n'est pas fondée ni sur des lois ni sur des raisons, mais elle n'exclut pas les conditions dans lesquelles le pouvoir s'exerce, qui peuvent être précisément les lois fondamentales.

Derathé

Et d'où vient l'autorité des lois fondamentales?

Polin

De la coutume, tout simplement.

Derathé

De la coutume! Alors, si vous donnez au souverain le droit de casser la coutume, il y a deux coutumes, s'il n'y avait que deux lois fondamentales en France!

Polin

Non, parce que la coutume tient à l'ordre devenu naturel de la communauté et l'exercice absolu du pouvoir n'a qu'une justification abstraite, si en la considère en général et non pas dans des conditions historiques et traditionnelles données. Il n'y a pas de pouvoir absolu en général, mais un pouvoir s'exerçant au milieu d'une communauté comportant une certaine structure et des traditions telles que si ce pouvoir absolu ne les respectait pas, il volerait en éclats. Il y a des textes où Bodin dit: si le souverain se permettait d'aller contre certaines lois ou contre la loi naturelle, il ne serait plus obéi. C'est là le meilleur des contrôles chez Bodin.

Freund

La souveraineté est absolue chez lui parce que, lorsqu'il y a conflit, c'est le souverain qui décide en dernier ressort.

Derathé

Il ne décidait pas en dernier ressort s'il y avait conflit sur les lois fondamentales.

Salmon

The fundamental laws are considered as custom, as many people have said. Up to this point! Because at this point Beza and others are rationalizing and associating them with the origin of the constitution. Therefore one can understand why Bodin is conservative, traditional, just as one can understand how his theory of sovereignty answers their theory.

Scheuner

We must always have in mind that law (lex) in the sense of the 16th century is not a general law, but a concrete law and identical with the term of supreme command. There are many passages where Bodin equates privilege with law. Quite natural! For the Middle Ages, the just law is not a general law, but a law for the single case. This is quite another conception of law than that of modern times. It is anachronistic to think that Bodin speaks of legislative power. For Bodin the prince has the power of a judge *and* of a legislator. Legislation and judicature are united in the thought of Bodin.

Concerning change, the new element in Bodin is that law can be made to change custom, whereas in the Middle Ages law is not made to change custom, but to restore custom in its old splendour. In this respect, Bodin is transcending the medieval thought. He gave a new content to legislation, but he does not speak of legislation in the modern sense.

When Hinrichs spoke of necessity (necessitas) in relation to taxes, we must see that this term goes back to a medieval tradition. In the Middle Ages, the king could impose a tax on these occasions: marriage of his daughter, imprisonment by an enemy and necessitas. Necessitas is an old term and does not mean ragione di stato.

Greenleaf

In fact, custom in terms of Bodin's theory precedes each legitimacy, not because it exists as custom, but because the sovereign chooses to accept it and wills its continuance. And that is the reason why I was a little perturbed by Polin's definition of the sovereign with reference to his function, his obligation and his duty, because even a tyrant who presumably by definition may be repudiating custom retains the essential marks of sovereignty in his own person and office. And in this sense, I think that by defining sovereignty in relation to the observance of custom and duty Polin is somewhat restricting the wider ambit of sovereignty in Bodin's conception.

Polin

répond à Greenleaf que le thème «le devoir du prince» est une citation de Bodin (*République* III, 4, p. 414): «Le prince qui franchit et brise les bornes sacrées de la loi de Dieu et de nature fait contre le devoir du prince. Celui perd le titre et l'honneur de prince qui fait contre le devoir du prince.» Et j'ai ajouté dans mon texte: «Bodin n'hésite même pas à user d'un argument sophistique et à proclamer qu'on ne trouvera pas de prince si mal appris qu'il voulût commander choses contre loi de Dieu et de nature, puisque le prince qui le fait cesse de l'être par là même.» Il y a une espèce de cohérence interne de la fonction du prince, d'exercice, conforme à son essence, de la fonction du prince.

Franklin
Il cesse d'être prince, mais il reste souverain.

Freund
Il a accompli ses fonctions de prince.

Villey
On retrouve la même chose chez Hobbes, avec une autre argumentation.

Polin
Cela correspond à mon interprétation de Hobbes, et à l'idée que la limite interne de pouvoir absolu chez Hobbes c'est précisément le fait que le souverain dans la situation dans laquelle il se trouve placé à l'intérieur du Commonwealth est un homme essentiellement raisonnable. C'est la raisonnabilité du souverain de Hobbes qui est sa justification, comme la fonctionnalité du souverain de Bodin l'est ici.

*

Greenleaf
criticizes with respect to the methodology of Hinton's and McRae's papers that they are both transgressing the fundamental principles in the historical discussion of ideas. McRae's attempt to discern Bodin's role for the development of modern science of politics involves a so-called representative modernism; that means that one casts one's searchlight back into the past, looking for developments of a particular kind of ideas which has now become dominant, and there is always the tendency that one might overlook other elements in a man's thought which do not contribute to the line of development which is under examination. If Bodin was indeed one of the founders of modern political science, then one would expect to find in Bodin at least some indication of the conceptional framework that one associates with Bacon f. i.. Hinton's approach involves what I would suggest to call moralism, and there is again the danger of anachronism. It is not the task of a historian to judge, to criticize, to assess, but sympathetically to understand.

McRae

One can discuss the significance of Bodin in the 16th century. At the same time one can quite differently look at the question whether Bodin had any significance for us today. If one recognizes the distinctness of this question, I see no reáson why it should not be discussed.

Schnur

asks Salmon for an explanation of the statement in his paper, that Bodin's concept of sovereignty is a «thèse de circonstance».

Salmon

Frequently one refers to the whole of *République* as being a «livre de circonstance». That is not a thesis of mine. Only a small part of the whole contents in the *République* has been influenced by Bodin's comprehension that the position of the monarchomachs is something new and subversive. Bodin departs from the constitutional tradition, changes the view that was held in *Methodus* in certain crucial passages and produces the theory of legislative sovereignty.

Franklin

agrees with Salmon that the monarchomachs represent a sharp caesura for Bodin and the entire French political tradition. Some people say that the idea of sovereignty was introduced into French political thought not by Bodin, but by the monarchomachs. They were raising the issue of people's sovereignty, of community sovereignty.

Salmon

This is true, but the monarchomachs have not got the concept of legislative sovereignty. Bodin once says, that the position of the monarchomachs contradicts legislative sovereignty.

Franklin

Regarding the importance of the monarchomachs, I am in complete agreement with you. What puzzles me is that at no place in the *République* Bodin has specifically mentioned Hotman, Beza and the others, and deliberately refuted awarenness of what their issues were. For instance, there is a crucial confrontation between Bodin and Hotman in the chapter, where Bodin is trying to prove that hereditary monarchy is a better form than elective monarchy or female inherited monarchy. But Bodin seems to have misread the issue and never met the argument of the monarchomachs directly.

Salmon

There is a simple explanation. Bodin deliberately omitted to mention the monarchomachs. He did not want to get involved in the change of political thought. He was trying to get above it and was deliberately misrepresenting it. For example, in the first preface he is talking about people who are not machiavellian, about people who counsel «exeption des charges et la liberté populaire». This is a reference to Beza's *De jure magistratuum*. But I think, «liberté du peuple» is a deliberate misrepresentation.

Freund

s'informe de l'auteur de *De jure magistratuum* et de *Vindiciae contra tyrannos*.

Salmon

Il n'y a pas de doute, que Théodore de Bèze soit l'auteur, parce que le Registre Français en fait mention. Sur le problème, à qui on attribue les *Vindiciae contra tyrannos*, j'indique l'article de Graham Jagger, On the Authorship of the Vindiciae contra tyrannos, *Durham University Journal*, March 1968, pp. 73–80.

Reulos

signale une nouvelle édition aux exemplaires limités et non mis dans le commerce *Du droit des magistrats* de Théodore de Bèze avec des notes et une introduction, où il y a une comparaison avec les passages parallèles du *Franco-Gallia*.

Freund

pose une question à Salmon sur les rapports entre Bodin et les monarchomaques catholiques. Vous n'avez pas abordé le problème des monarchomaques catholiques, comme par exemple presque votre homonyme Salamonius. Mais, lorsque Bodin était à Laon, il y a eu collusion entre Bodin et les monarchomaques catholiques, était-elle imposée ou y-a-t-il eu consentement de Bodin?

Salmon

J'en ai fait mention dans mon papier. Bodin a signé le document où il admet les doctrines des monarchomaques, le doctrine de la souveraineté populaire. Mais devant Bodin, la réponse est simple. C'est le même son, mais il a changé.

Freund

Vous dites que la théorie de la souveraineté dans la *République* était une thèse de circonstance. Or, le problème de la souveraineté est déjà posé dans le *Methodus*, où l'influence des monarchomaques n'agit pas encore, parce que les premiers ouvrages des monarchomaques commencent à paraître dans les années après 1570. Alors il y avait donc une préfiguration de la théorie de la souveraineté dans le *Methodus* et je ne pense pas que ce soit tout-à-fait une thèse de circonstance.

Salmon
Dans le *Methodus*, Bodin fond l'idée de la souveraineté sur l'impossibilité de l'état mixte. Mais j'insiste que la théorie de la soveraineté législative dans la *République* était une reponse aux monarchomaques.

Baxter
emphazises on a question of *Kelley* that in the 1572 edition of *Methodus* there is absolutely nothing new about sovereignty.

Franklin
La position nouvelle dans la théorie de la *République*, c'est l'absolutisme, parce que la théorie de l'indivisibilité de la souveraineté précède les guerres civiles. L'intention de la primatie du pouvoir législatif dans la *République* est de transformer l'indivisibilité de la souveraineté en une doctrine d'absolutisme.

Villey
Dans le *Methodus*, il y avait déjà clairement les principes logiques du système, il y avait l'analogie entre l'unité de Dieu et du souverain; si cela dépend des circonstances, c'est le climat général des guerres civiles avant la littérature des monarchomaques.

Baxter
The doctrin of sovereignty is part of the empirical, analytical apparatus which Bodin is using in the *Methodus* and in the *République*. And I myself cannot accept the thesis that the concept of sovereignty is a «thèse de circonstance». Now, in the *République* the notion of sovereignty applies to democracies, to aristocracies, as well as to monarchies. And those protestant readers who use Bodin to defend democratic systems of government comprehend rightly the analytical language which Bodin is using. But the new view in the *République* stems from the induction of a very new sonant of conservatism and from the use of the idea of divine law and revelation. There are two levels, the empirical, analytical level and on top of this very heavily a normative note in the *République*. All the affirmations for the normative note given so far refer to the situation of France at that time. I want to make the suggestion, that the affirma-

tion may be biographical, at least in part. A demon had appeared to Bodin and he had a strong likeness to his father. His father died in 1566. Ever since then, Bodin stressed the image of the all-powerful Father.

Reulos

Le rapport de Euchner sur la propriété et la domination chez Bodin donne un «coup de pouce» à la théorie de Bodin en parlant de propriété dans le sens moderne du mot, il emploie le terme allemand «Eigentum», c'est la propriété au sens romain, le droit étant pris absolu. Mais Bodin parle des choses que chacun a en propre, et se place dans la structure de son époque, et notamment des structures féodales qui comportaient des droits conditionnés et superposés, et il ne parle pas de la propriété dans le sens romain du mot, dans le sens que donnaient les compilations de Justinien, le sens moderne de droit individuel et total sur les biens. Il ne faut pas oublier que tout de même au 16e siècle la notion de la propriété romaine n'est encore que sur le plan des théories juridiques, que les juristes romanistes essaient de faire passer dans le droit de leur temps.

Derathé

Mais il y a chez Bodin une citation qui se réfère à Sénèque, et Sénèque oppose l'imperium du prince au dominium du particulier: «Dire que les princes sont seigneurs de tout, cela s'entend de la droite seigneurie et justice souveraine demeurant à chacun la *possession* et *propriété* de ses biens. Ainsi disait Sénèque: *Ad reges potestas omnium pertinet, ad singulos proprietas.*» Et peu après: «*Omnia Rex imperio possidet, singuli dominio.*» (*République* I, 8, p. 147) Je crois que Bodin a opposé très nettement la propriété à l'imperium.

Reulos

Je suis parfaitement d'accord, mais là, il s'agit d'un texte où Bodin se réfère à Rome. Et dans les textes où il parle de la situation de son époque, il nous parle des choses qui sont propres, et il se garde bien d'employer propriété ou un terme technique dérivé de la terminologie romaine. Il y a une distinction nette dans les textes de la *République*.

Derathé

Tantôt Bodin se réfère au droit romain, tantôt il se réfère au droit coutumier français. Alors, c'est tout de même un certain flottement ou une marge de tolérance.

Franklin

There may be a way of reconciling Reulos' and Derathé's position, because I think it is one part of Bodin himself, in a way. At one passage

Bodin himself is aware, that his definition of «monarchie royale» is incompatible with the existence of feudal law. He says, although the king of France has the dominium directum, at least the individuals have the dominium utile. So I think that you are both right. because in the concept of «monarchie royale» Bodin attempted to reconcile the feudal relationship as much as he could to the Roman standard.

Villey

Le rapport de Euchner me paraît avoir touché un point extrêmement important en ce qui concerne toute l'histoire de la pensée juridique et politique, c'est l'opposition entre la sphère de l'économie, qui est la sphère du dominium, du droit privé, du droit du père de famille, et la sphère de la politique, qui est pour les romains la sphère de l'imperium. Cette opposition est fondamentale au droit romain et à la *Politique* d'Aristote, tandis que le féodalisme a tendance à tout réduire au dominium et à faire confusion de la souveraineté et du dominium, et aussi cette société bourgeoise dont parle Euchner qui soumet aussitôt à la propriété.

La position de Bodin me paraît ambiguë. D'un côté il y a ces éléments où Bodin paraît revenir à la discussion antique, par exemple le thèse de Sénèque, et puis la distinction de la monarchie seigneurale et de la monarchie royale. Et pourtant, toute cette analogie dans tout l'œuvre de Bodin entre la souveraineté du roi et la propriété du père de famille, du dominium montre que Bodin est loin d'avoir surmonté, au point d'Aristote, la confusion entre ces deux domaines.

Reulos

Concernant la distinction entre la propriété au domaine comme ressource de l'état et le pouvoir du monarque en tant que roi, c'est une interprétation donnée au Bodin que d'employer dans tous les cas le terme de propriété sans distinguer le propos au sujet. Il y a une imprécision dans les termes qui tient à la terminologie même de l'époque sur les mots proprietas, dominium, domaine direct ou utile, interprétation des textes romains à la situation faite au 16ᵉ siècle. C'est cette confusion qui me paraissait délicate à éclaircir.

Hinrichs

Il faut lire, pour comprendre les textes de Bodin sur le dominium directum et le dominium utile, les textes du droit privé ou du droit féodal de ce temps là. Il y a une grande discussion, dont notamment parle Dumoulin, où l'on commence pour la première fois à reconnaître que les vassaux ont une sorte de propriété sur le domaine utile, sauf les droits matériels, les droits naturels et les droits pécuniers qui doivent continuer. C'est là l'ambiguïté qui est aussi dans les textes de Bodin.

Schnur

refers to Otto Brunner's research about the transition from political systems based upon the idea of oikos to the market system. In the transitional period of the Renaissance, old feudal positions are interfering with the bourgeois idea of property. Bodin makes a distinction between public law and privat law, but it is difficult for him to locate the feudal rights. In the sphere of public law the prince is bound by contract, whereas in the domain of private law he is bound by natural law, that is a law binding equal subjects. But it is difficult for Bodin to use the modern notion of property and contract in relation to churches, monastries and so on. The ambiguities in Bodin stem from the legal situation at that time.

I think we should conclude by locating Bodin's political and legal Thinking in a broader context.

Greenleaf

Surveying the development of the history of political thought, one could treat it chronologically or in terms of the social and economic framework at the time, or in terms of different kinds of analytical concepts as sovereignty, property, consent or whatever it might be. But one could also categorize it in terms of certain fundamental paradigmas or models of thinking, in terms of which each individual writer may be seen to be an example or a case study. The most appropriate way is to categorize the whole history of Western political thought in terms of three ways of thinking: one is fundamentally critical and utilitarian, another is concerned with the notion of natural order and rational law, and the third is associated with the concept of rational will. Bodin is representing a particular manifestation of the way of thinking associated with the concepts of reason, nature, law and order. And this is a continual tradition from Plato to Saint-Thomas, Hooker and many of the writers of the period with which we have been dealing. The categories of hierarchy, order, reason, law, unity and therefore supreme political power and stress on monarchy, these are caracteristics of the writers in this tradition.

Schoeck

There may well be an affinity between the theory of Bodin and his generation and the reason why our generation finds him so fascinating. An immense amount of material was being rushed into print in the century before the *République*. And there was an enormous problem of digesting and relating this material. Just as the 13th century produced a world of summae reproducing each other, Bodin's generation faced the problem of comprehending and digesting and relating this enormous amount of material: christian, mediaeval, classical and contemporary (the number of titles printed on history, law and political science during the 16th century is simply immense) by an ambitious attempt at synthesis.

Franklin
comments on Greenleaf's scheme. It is very dangerous to set up a scheme and to try to induce what are the characteristics of a thinker within that scheme. For example, you can take the hierarchical sense of order, and you might get Bodin with his emphasis on personal will (the sovereign), or you might get Saint Thomas who surely emphasizes hierarchy of order; they are incomparable. So I think it is very suspect to jump from methodology or form to substance.

TEIL III: BODIN – BIBLIOGRAPHIE

Vorbemerkung

Es wurde eine möglichst vollständige Zusammenstellung aller Ausgaben von Bodins Werken und der Literatur über Bodin seit 1800 erstrebt, soweit dieses Ziel mit den einschlägigen bibliographischen Hilfsmitteln und dem Wissen der Teilnehmer der Bodin-Tagung erreichbar war. Bei einigen Ausgaben der *Six Livres de la Republique* konnte ihre Existenz nicht zweifelsfrei festgestellt werden.

Bei der Literatur über Bodin wurden auch solche Werke aufgenommen, die nicht zentral Bodin behandeln, ihm aber einen größeren Abschnitt widmen.

Die Darstellungen und Untersuchungen über Bodin wurden chronologisch geordnet, um die Entwicklung der Bodin-Forschung aufzuzeigen. Die alphabetische Auffindung der Autoren ist über das Personenregister möglich.

I. WERKE

1. 1549 'Οππιανου Κυνηγετικων βιβλια τεσσαρα,
   Ed. probabilis: Bodin, Paris 1549.

2. 1555 Oppiani De venatione libri IIII, Joanne Bodino interprete

   2.1 –, Paris (Vascosanus) 1555.
   2.2 –, Paris   1597.

3. 1559 Oratio de instituenda in Republica iuventute ad Senatum Populumque Tolosatem

   3.1 –, Tolosa (Petrus Puteus) 1559.
   3.2 –, Paris 1951 (Œuvres Philosophiques de Jean Bodin, I, Ed.
   P. Mesnard, pp. 7–30, franz. Übersetzung pp. 33–65).

4. 1566 Methodus ad facilem historiarum cognitionem

   4.1 J. Bodini Advocati –, Paris (M. Juvenis) 1566.
   4.2 –, ab ipso recognita et multo quam antea locupletior, Paris
   (M. Juvenis) 1572.
   4.3 Methodus Historica, duodecim eiusdem argumenti scriptorum
   tam veterum quam recentiorum commentariis adaucta a
   Johanne Wolfio, Basilea (Petrus Perna) 1576.
   4.4 Artis historicae penus, octodecim scriptorum tam veterum
   quam recentiorum monumentis, et inter eos Jo. praecipue Bodini methodi historicae sex, instructa (auctore J. Wolfio),
   Basilea (P. Perna) 1579.
   4.5 –, accurate denue recusus, Lugduni (Mareschallus) 1583.
   4.6 –, Heidelberg 1583.
   4.7 –, Lugduni (Mareschallus) 1591.
   4.8 –, Heidelberg 1591.
   4.9 –, Geneva 1591.
   4.10 –, accurate denua recusa, subiecto rerum indice, Geneva
   (J. Stoer) 1595.
   4.11 –, Argentorati (Lazarus Zetznerus) 1599.
   4.12 –, Argentorati (L. Zetznerus) 1607.
   4.13 –, Geneva (J. Stoer) 1610.
   4.14 –, Francoforti ad Moenum 1610.
   4.15 –, Geneva (J. Stoer) 1620.
   4.16 –, Francoforti ad Moenum (Dulseck) 1627.
   4.17 –, Argentorati (haeredes Lazari Zetzneri) 1627.
   4.18 –, Amstelaedami (J. Ravenstein) 1650.
   4.19 –, Paris (M. Juvenis) 1672.

4.20 –, Paris 1951 (=Œuvres Philosophiques de J. Bodin, I, Ed.
P. Mesnard, pp. 106–269).

Französisch: La méthode de l'histoire

4.21 –, traduite pour la première fois et presentée par P. Mesnard,
Paris 1941.
4.22 –, Paris 1951 (= Œuvres Philosophiques de Jean Bodin, I, Ed.
P. Mesnard, pp. 271–473).

Englisch: Method for the Easy Comprehension of History

4.23 –, translated by B. Reynolds, New York (Columbia Univ.
Press) 1945. Reprinted 1966 (Octagon), 1969 (Norton).
4.24 –, Ann Arbor, Mich. 1960.

5. 1568 Les paradoxes du seigneur de Malestroit... sur le fait des
monnoyes, presentez à sa Majesté, au mois de mars 1566, avec la
responce de M. Jean Bodin ausdicts paradoxes

5.1 –, Paris (Le Jeune) 1568.
5.2 Discours sur les causes de l'extrème cherté..., Paris 1574.
5.3 –, Paris (Le Jeune) 1578.
5.4 Les paradoxes.... monnoyes, et discours de J. Bodin sur le
moyens d'y remedier, Paris (Du Puys) 1578.
5.5 Discours de Jean Bodin sur le rehaussement et la diminution
des monnoyes, tant d'or que d'argent, et le moyen d'y remedier, et response aux paradoxes de Malestroict. Avec les Paradoxes sur le faict des monnoyes par F. Garrault, Paris (Du
Puys) 1578.
5.6 Les paradoxes... (wie 5.4), Paris (Du Puys) 1580.
5.7 Discours de J. Bodin... (wie 5.5) et Apologie de René Herpin, Lyon (Vincent) 1593.
5.8 Discours de J. Bodin... (wie 5.5), Genève (Cartier) 1608.
5.9 La vie chère au XVIe siècle. La response de Jean Bodin à M.
de Malestroit, 1568. Nouvelle édition publiée avec une introduction et des notes par H. Hauser, Paris 1932.
5.10 La response de maistre Jean Bodin, advocat en la cour, au
paradoxe de monsieur de Malestroit, touchant l'encherisse-
ment de toutes choses et le moyen d'y remedier. Neudruck v.
1568, besorgt v. J. Y. Le Branchu, Paris 1934.

Latein:

5.11 Tractatus de augmento et decremento auri et argenti... quo
respondetur Paradoxis Domini de Malestroict, in: R. Budelius,
De monetis et re numaria (zusammen mit anderen Traktaten),
1591.
5.12 Responsio ad Paradoxa Malestretti de caritate rerum eiusque
remediis (Zusammen mit den Kapiteln aus der *République* De

aerario et re numaria und Traktaten anderer Autoren, Kommentar von Hermann Conring), Helmstedt (Müller) 1671.

Englisch:

5.13 The Response of Jean Bodin to the Paradoxes of Malestroit, transl. from the French second edition 1578 by George Albert Moore, Chevy Chase, Maryland, and Washington, D. C. 1946/1947.

Deutsch:

5.14 Discours dess berühmten Johannis Bodini ... von den Ursachen der Theurung wie auch dem Auff- und Abschlag der Müntz, Hamburg 1624.

6. 1573 Harangue de Messire Charles des Cars ... prononcee aux magnifiques Ambassadeurs de Pologne, tournée du latin en françois par J. Bodin

   6.1 –, Paris 1573.
   6.2 –, Lyon (Rigaud) 1573.
   6.3 –, in: Memoires de l'estat de France sous Charles Neufiesme, Vol. II, pp. 500–518, Heidelberg 1578.

7. 1576 Les six Livres de la Republique

   7.1 –, Paris (Du Puys) 1576.
   7.2 –, Paris (Du Puys) 1577.
   7.3 –, Genève (Le Juge) 1577.
   7.4 –, Paris (Du Puys) 1577.
   7.5 –, Paris (Du Puys) 1578.
   7.6 –, Paris (Du Puys) 1579.
   7.7 –, Lyon (J. de Tournes) 1579
   7.8 –, Lyon (J. de Tournes) 1580.
   7.9 –, Paris (Du Puys) 1580.
   7.10 –, Paris (Verdier) 1582. – zweifelhaft –
   7.11 –, Paris (Du Puys) 1583.
   7.12 –, Lyon (Cartier) 1583. – zweifelhaft –
   7.13 –, Paris (Du Puys) 1587.
   7.14 –, Lyon (Cartier) 1587.
   7.15 –, Lyon (Cartier) 1588.
   7.16 –, Lyon (des Jontes) 1591.
   7.17 –, Lyon (Vincent) 1593.
   7.18 –, Lyon (Cartier) 1593.
   7.19 –, Lyon (Cartier) 1594.
   7.20 –, s. l. (Cartier) 1599.
   7.21 –, Genève 1600. – zweifelhaft –
   7.22 –, s. l. (Cartier) 1608.

7.23 –, Lyon (Cartier) 1610.

7.24 –, Paris (Du Puys) 1612.

7.25 –, Genève (Gamonet) 1629.

7.26 –, Aalen 1961 (Faksimile von 7. 11).

Latein: De Republica libri sex

7.27 –, Lugduni, Paris (Du Puys) 1586.

7.28 –, Lugduni, s. l. (Paris) (Du Puys) 1591.

7.29 –, Geneva 1588. – zweifelhaft –

7.30 –, Frankfurt (Wechel & Fischer) 1591.

7.31 –, Frankfurt (Wechel & Fischer) 1594.

7.32 –, Argentorati 1598. – zweifelhaft –

7.33 –, Ursellis (C. Sutorius) 1601.

7.34 –, Coloniae 1603. – zweifelhaft –

7.35 –, Frankfurt (Hoffmann & Fischer) 1609.

7.36 –, Paris, Frankfurt 1619.

7.37 –, Frankfurt (J. Rosa) 1622.

7.38 –, Frankfurt (J. Rosa) 1641.

Italienisch: I sei libri della republica

7.39 –, Tradotti da Lorenzo Conti, Genova 1588.

Spanisch: Los seis libros de la republica

7.40 –, Traducidos por Gaspar de Anastro Ysunza, Turin 1590.

Deutsch:

7.41 Respublica. Das ist: Gruendtliche und rechte Underweysung, oder eigentlicher Bericht, in welchem ausführlich vermeldet wirdt, wie nicht allein das Regiment wol zu bestellen, sonder auch in allerley Zustandt, so wol in Krieg und Widerwertigkeit, als Frieden und Wolstand zu erhalten sey. Übers. v. Johann Oswaldt, Mumpelgart (N. Bassaei) 1592.

7.42 Von Gemeinem Regiment der Welt. Ein Politische, gruendtliche und rechte Underweisung, auch herrlicher Bericht, in welchem ... (weiter wie 7.41), Frankfurt (Saur & Kopffen) 1611.

Englisch: The Six Bookes of a Commonweale

7.43 –, done into English by Richard Knolles, London (B. Bishop) 1606.

7.44 –, A Facsimile reprint of the English translation of 1606, Ed. with an Introduction, Notes and Indices by Kenneth D. McRae, Cambridge (Harvard U. P.) 1962.

Polnisch:

7.45 Übersetzung von R. Bierzanek, Z. Izdebski und J. Wroblewski, mit einer Einführung von Z. Izdebski, Warschau 1958.

Teilausgaben und gekürzte Ausgaben:

7.46 De speciebus rerum publicarum (Latein. Übersetzung des 2. Buches von J. Schröder, Inhaltsverzeichnis des Gesamtwerkes), Magdeburg (J. Frank) 1581.

7.47 Synopsis: sive medulla in sex libr. Johan. Bodini Andegavensis, De Republica (von J. A. v. Werdenhagen), Amsterdam 1635.

7.48 De republica librorum brevarium, Amsterdam (J. Jansson) 1645.

7.49 The Necessity of the Absolute Power of all Kings; and in particular of the King of England, London 1648 (extracts prepared by Sir Robert Filmer).

7.50 Abrégé de la République de Bodin (von J.-C. de Lavie) 2. Vols., London (J. Nourse) 1755.

7.51 De la République, traité de Jean Bodin, ou traité du gouvernement (von Ch.-A. L'Escalopier de Nourar) London, Paris 1756 (1. Buch).

7.52 Des Corps politiques et de leurs gouvernements, (von J.–Ch. de Lavie), 2 Vols., Lyon (P. Duplain) 1764.

7.53 (wie 7.52) Lyon 1766 – 2 Vols.

7.54 (wie 7.52), Lyon 1766 – 3 Vols.

7.55 (wie 7.52), Lyon 1767.

7.56 De la Législation; ou du gouvernement politique des Empires: extrait de Bodin (von Lavie), London, Paris 1768.

7.57 Des Etats Généraux, et autres assemblées nationales, Ed. Charles-Joseph Mayer, 18 Vols., La Haye, Paris (Buisson) 1788–1789, Vol. VI: Auszüge aus der République.

7.58 Abrégé de la République de Bodin (von Lavie), 2 Vols., Paris (Cailleau) 1793.

7.59 La Repubblica e suo governo (anonym), s.l. 1808.

7.60 De la République: Extraits (Paris) de Médicis 1949.

7.61 Six Books of the Commonwealth, Oxford (Blackwell) 1955. Translated and abridged by M. J. Tooley.

7.62 De la Soberania, «Seminario de Derecho Politico», Salamanca 1955, pp. 121–152.

7.63 I sei libri dello Stato (I–II), trad., intr. e comm. di M. Isnardi Parente, I, Torino 1964.

7.64 Six Books of the Republic, translated and abridged by M. J. Tooley, New York 1965.

7.65 Los seis libros de la Republica, gekürzt und hrsg. v. Pedro Bravo, Caracas 1966.

8. 1577 Recueil de tout ce qui s'est negotié en la compagnie du Tiers Estat de France en l'assemblée générale des trois estats, assignez par le roy en la ville de Blois, au novembre 1576.

8.1 –, s.l. 1577.

8.2 –, Paris (Gobert) 1614.

8.3 –, in: Recueil général des Estats de France, tenus en France sous les rois Charles VI, Charles VIII, Charles IX, Henri III, Louis XIII, Paris 1651.

8.4 –, in: C. J. Mayer (Ed.), Des Etats Généraux et autres assemblées nationales, Vol XIII, pp. 212–315, La Haye 1789.

Latein:

8.5 Commentarius de iis omnibus quae in Tertii ordinis conventu acta sunt, generali Trium Ordinum concilio Blesis a rege indicto ad 15 novembris diem 1576, Rignavia 1577.

9. 1578 Juris universi distributio

9.1 –, Lyon (J. de Tournes, J. du Puys) 1578.
9.2 –, Colonia (J. Gymnicus) 1580.
9.3 –, explicata a Joanne Cocino, Praga 1581.
9.4 –, in: Œuvres Philosophiques de Jean Bodin (Ed. P. Mesnard) I, pp. 67–80.

Französisch:

9.5 Tableau du droit universel, in: Œuvres philosophiques de Jean Bodin, Ed. P. Mesnard, I, pp. 81–97.

10. 1580 De la demonomanie des sorciers

10.1 –, Paris (du Puys) 1580.
10.2 –, Paris (du Puys) 1581.
10.3 –, Paris (du Puys) 1582.
10.4 –, Anvers (A. Coninx) 1586.
10.5 –, revue, corr. et augm. d'une grande parti, Paris (du Puys) 1587.
10.6 –, Lyon (Frellon et Cloquemin) 1593.
10.7 –, Anvers (Coninx) 1593.
10.8 –, revue diligemment et repurgée de plusieurs fautes qui s'estoyent glissees ès precedentes impressiones, Lyon (Frellon) 1598.
10.9 –, Lyon, ed. A. de Harsy, 1598.
10.10 –, Paris (A. Perier) 1598.
10.11 –, Paris (E. Prevosteau) 1598.
10.12 –, Rouen (R. du Petit Val) 1604.
10.13 –, Le Fléau des Démons et des sorciers, Nyort (du Terroir) 1616.
10.14 (wie 10.13), Anvers (Coninx) 1693.

Latein: De magorum daemonomania libri IV

10.15 –, übers. v. F. Junius, Basilea (T. Guarinus) 1581.
10.16 –, seu detestando lamiarum ac magorum cum satana commercio, Frankfurt (N. Bassaeus) 1590.

10.17 –, (wie 10.16) accessit eiusdem opinionum Joannis Wieri confutatio, Frankfurt (N. Basseus) 1603.

10.18 –, Frankfurt (N. Bassaeus) 1609.

Deutsch: De daemonomania magorum. Vom ausgelaszenen wütigen Teuffelsheer der besessenen unsinnigen Hexen und Hexenmeyster

10.19 –, durch Johann Fischart aus Frantzösischer Sprach ins Teutsche gebracht und an etlichen enden gemehret und erklaret, Strassburg (B. Jobin) 1581.

10.20 –, (wie 10.19), Strassburg (B. Jobin) 1586.

10.21 –, Strassburg (B. Jobin) 1591.

10.22 Daemonomania oder auszführliche Erzehlung des wütenden Teuffels in seinen damahligen rasenden Hexen und Hexenmeistern, Hamburg (T. von Wiering) 1698.

Italienisch: Demonomania degli stregoni, cioè furori et malie de' demoni, col mezo de gli huomini, tradotta dal Hercole Cato

10.23 –, Venetia (d'Aldo) 1587.

10.24 –, Venetia (d'Aldo) 1589.

10.25 –, Venetia (d'Aldo) 1592.

11. 1581 Apologie de Rene Herpin pour la Republique de J. Bodin

11.1 –, Paris (du Puys) 1581.

11.2 –, Lyon (B. Vincent) 1591.

11.3 –, Lyon (B. Vincent) 1593.

11.4 –, Lyon (Cartier) 1594.

11.5 –, Lyon ou Genève (Cartier) 1599.

11.6 –, Genève (Cartier) 1608.

11.7 –, Genève (E. Gamonet) 1629.

Latein: Renati Herpini ad verius illustrandum Johannis Bodini de Republica methodum ... apologia

11.8 –, recentissima interpretatione Johannis Friderici Salveld, Frankfurt (J. Rosa) 1615.

12. 1588 Sapientiae moralis epitome, quae bonorum gradus ab ultimo principio ad summum hominis extremumque bonum continua serie deducit, ab Helia Bodino Joannis filio collecta. Ad Laodunensem iuventutem (von Bodin selbst zusammengestellt)

12.1 –, Paris (du Puys) 1588.

13. 1596 Universae naturae theatrum

13.1 –, Lugduni (J. Roussin) 1596.

13.2 –, Paris (Du Val) 1596.

13.3 –, Frankfurt (Haeredes A. Wecheli) 1597.

13.4 –, Hanovia (Claudius Marnius) 1607.

Französisch: Le théatre de la nature universelle ... traduit par Fr. de Fougerolles

13.5 –, Lyon (J. Pillehotte) 1597.

Deutsch: Die Problemata Johannis Bodini. Von den Dingen, die sich an Himmel, auff Erden, und in der Erden sich begeben und zugetragen

13.6 –, übers. v. Lissart von Lindau, Magdeburg 1607.

13.7 –, in gewisse Frag und Antwort gestellt, Basel 1622.

14. 1596 Paradoxon, quod nec virtus ulla in mediocritate, nec summum hominis bonum in virtutis actione consistere possit

14.1 –, Paris (Du Val) 1596.

Französisch:

14.2 –, Le Paradoxe de J. Bodin ... qu'il n'y a pas une seule vertu en médiocrité, ny au milieu de deux vices, traduit du latin en françois et augmenté en plusieurs lieux, Paris (Du Val) 1598.

14.3 –, Paradoxe de M. J. Bodin, dictes et excellents discours de la vertu ... traduit du latin en françois par Claude de Magdaillan, Paris (Du Bray) 1604.

15. 1603 Consilia Johannis Bodini et Fausti Longiani de principe recte instituendo, latine reddita a Joh. Bornitio

15.1 –, Erfurt 1603.

16. 1841 Colloquium Heptaplomeres de aditis rerum sublimium arcanis

16.1 –, Ed. G. E. Guhrauer (deutsche Auszüge, 2/3 des 4. Buches und 5. Buch lateinischer Text).

16.2 –, ed. Ludwig Noack, Schwerin 1857.

16.3 –, Faksimile vom 16.2., Stuttgart 1966.

16.4 –, Colloque de Jean Bodin des secrets cachez des choses sublimes entre sept sçavans qui sont de differents sentiments, Ed. R. Chauviré, Paris 1914 (Auszüge aus einer ungedruckten frühen franz. Übersetzung).

16.5 –, De naturalismo cum aliorum tum maxime J. Bodini ex opere ejus manuscripto ... de abditis rerum sublimium arcanis schediasma J. Diecmanni Stadens, Lipsiae 1683 (Kritik des Heptaplomeres).

16.6 (wie 16.5), Lipsiae 1684.

16.7 (wie 16.5), Jena 1700.

17. Briefe von Bodin

17.1 Lettre à Jan Bautru des Matras, 1561 oder 1563 (?) in Comomiès, Gallia Orientalis, Hagae Comitis 1665, 76 ff. und Chauviré [65], 521–524.

17.2 Tumulte d'Anvers escrit par Bodin, copie d'une lettre de Bodin à Nic. Trouilliart, 20. 1. 1583, in: Chauviré [65], 524–529.

17.3 Brief Bodins an Schwiegervater aus Antwerpen v. 21. 1. 1583 über die Unteilbarkeit der Souveränität, in: *Compte rendu des séances de la Commission Royale d'Histoire de l'Académie Belgique* 12 (1859), 463; und teilweise in: G. Griffiths, Representative Government in Western Europe in the Sixteenth Century, Oxford 1968, 505.

17.4 Lettre de Bodin à Castelnau-Mauvissière, 30. 9. 1585, in: Chauviré [65], 529 f.

17.5 Lettre à Castelnau-Mauvissière, 9. 12. 1586, in: Chauviré [65], 530–532.

17.6 Epistre de Jean Bodin touchant l'institution de ses enfans a son nepueu, 9. 11. 1586, in: Guhrauer [21], 254 und Baudrillart [25].

17.7 Lettre de Monsieur Bodin ou il traicte des occasions qui l'ont faict rendre ligueur.

17.71 –, Paris (Chaudière) 1590.

17.72 –, Lyon (Pillehotte) 1590.

17.73 –, Troyes (Moreau) 1590.

17.8 Lettre à Monsieur Pierre Ayrault, 27. 3. 1595, in: Chauviré [65], 532–534 und Menage, Vita Petri Aerodii, Paris 1675.

17.9 Lettre à M. Roland Bignon, 1595, in: Devisme, Histoire de la ville de Laon, Laon 1822 und Chauviré [65], 534 f.

17.10 Weitere Briefe in Moreau-Reibel [106]; *Compte rendu des séances de la Commission Royale d'Histoire de l'Académie Belgique,* 12 (1859), 458–463; Calendars of State Papers Foreign, 1581/2, No. 584; 1583, No. 72.

II. DARSTELLUNGEN UND UNTERSUCHUNGEN SEIT 1800

18. Devisme, J. F. L., Notice historique et critique sur Bodin, *Magazin ency-clopédique de Millin* 4 (1801), 42–59.

19. Heeren, Arnold Hermann Ludwig, Über die Entstehung, die Ausbildung und den praktischen Einfluß der politischen Theorien in dem neueren Europa, in: Kleine historische Schriften, 2. Teil, Göttingen 1805, 146 ff., (über Bodin: 160 ff.).

20. Hallam, Henry, Introduction to the Literature of Europe in the 15th, 16th and 17th Centuries, London 1837–9, 4 Vol., ⁶1860, II, 148–166.

21. Puymaigre, Théodore de, Traité de la Demonomanie contre les sorciers par J. Bodin, Metz 1840.

22. Vogel, Ernst Gustav, Zur Geschichte des ungedrückten Werks Collo-quium Heptaplomeres, *Serapeum* 1 (1840), 113–116, 132–138, 152–155.

23. Guhrauer, Gottschalk Eduard, Das Heptaplomeres des Jean Bodin. Zur Geschichte der Kultur und Literatur im Jahrhundert der Reformation, Berlin 1841.

24. Löhn, Eduard Wilhelm, De Joannis Bodini colloquio Heptaplomere Dis-sertatio, Tübingen 1843.

25. Colombel, E., Jean Bodin, *Annales de la Société de Nantes* (1845), 326 bis 332.

26. Bonnière, Eug., Biographie des deux Bodins, Angers 1846.

27. Baudrillart, Henri, Jean Bodin et son temps. Tableau des théories politi-ques et des idées économiques au seizième siècle, Paris 1853, Neudruck Aalen 1964.

28. Feugère, Léon, Anciens écrivains français: Jean Bodin, Paris 1853.

29. Meaux, Vicomte de, Un publiciste du seizième siècle et la monarchie française, *Correspondant* 37 (1855/6), 840–860.

30. Planchenault, N., Etudes sur Jean Bodin, *Academie des sciences et bel-les lettres d'Angers, Memoires* II, 11–105, V, 155–201, VII, 124–135 (1858–1860).

31. Feugère, Léon, Caractères et portraits littéraires du XVI siècle, Paris 1859, Bodin: II, 423–451.

32. Vinet, Alexandre, Jean Bodin, in: Moralistes des seizième et dixseptième siècles, Paris 1859, 151–170.

33. Bertauld, Alfred, Biographie de Jean Bodin, in: Philosophie politique de l'histoire de France, Paris 1861.

34. Baudrillart, Henri, Jean Bodin et l'Heptaplomeres, in: Publicistes mo-dernes, Paris 1862, 229–240.

35. Franck, Adam, Jean Bodin, in: Reformateurs et publicistes de l'Europe: moyen âge, renaissance, Paris 1864, 395–506.

36. Molinier, Victor, Aperçus historiques et critiques sur la vie et les travaux de Jean Bodin, *Mémoires de l'Academie de Toulouse*, 4 (1866), 334–388.

37. DUVAL, A.-A., Barreau de Paris: Jean Bodin, Paris 1867.

38. RICHART, ANTOINE, Mémoires sur la Ligue dans le Laonnois, Laon 1869.

39. BARTHÉLEMY, EDOUARD DE, Étude sur Jean Bodin, *Société Académique de Saint Quentin, Mémoires*, 18 (1874/5), 130–197.

40. WHITE, HENRY, Jean Bodin and the History of Witchcraft, *The Student and Intellectual Observer* 4 (1878), 327–338.

41. HAAG, EMILE, Bodin sieur de Saint-Amand, in: La France Protestante, 1879.

42. BLOCH, JOSEPH SAMUEL, Jean Bodin, ein französischer Staatsmann und Rechtslehrer, ein Vorläufer Lessings aus dem 16. Jahrhundert, *Aus der Vergangenheit für die Gegenwart*, Wien 1886, 221–258.

43. JACQUET, A., De historiarum cognitione quid senserit J. Bodinus, Paris 1886.

44. JANET, PAUL-ALEXANDRE, Histoire de la science politique dans ses rapports avec la morale, Bd. 2, Paris ²1872, ³1887, 114 ff.

45. CASTONNET DES FOSSES, HENRI, Jean Bodin, sa vie et ses œuvres, *Revue de l'Anjou* 20 (1889), 1–19, 147–168.

46. POLLOCK, SIR FREDERICK, An Introduction to the History of the Science of Politics, London, 1890, ²1895, 46–53.

47. WEILL, GEORGES, Les théories sur le pouvoir royal en France pendant les guerres de religion, Paris 1892, 159–171.

48. HANCKE, ERNST, Bodin. Eine Studie über den Begriff der Souveränität, Breslau 1894.

49. ERRERA, PAUL, Un précurseur de Montesquieu: Jean Bodin, *Revue de Belgique*, 2 série 14 (1895), 36–62 und *Annales de l'Académie d'Archéologie de Belgique* 1896, 197–228.

50. DUNNING, W. A., Jean Bodin on Sovereignty, with some Reference to the Doctrine of Thomas Hobbes, *Political Science Quarterly* 11 (1896), 82–104.

51. FOURNOL, ETIENNE, Bodin, prédécesseur de Montesquieu, Paris 1896.

52. REHM, H., Bodin, in: Geschichte der Staatsrechtswissenschaft, Freiburg 1896, 218–231.

53. DOCK, KARL ADOLF, Der Souveränitätsbegriff von Bodinus bis zu Friedrich dem Großen, Diss. Straßburg 1897.

54. FOURNOL, ETIENNE, Sur quelques traités de droit public du XVIᵉ siècle, *Nouvelle revue historique de droit français et étranger* 21 (1897), 298–325.

55. HAUFFEN, ADOLF, Fischart-Studien. Der Malleus Maleficarum und Bodins Demonomanie, *Euphorion* 4 (1897), 1–15, 251–261.

56. REHM, H., Bodin, in: Allgemeine Staatslehre, Freiburg 1899, 43–46, 215.

57. JARRIN, ALB., Jean Bodin, un économiste liberal au XVI siècle, Chambéry 1904.

58. MEUTEN, ANTON, Bodins Theorie von der Beeinflussung des politischen Lebens der Staaten durch ihre geographische Lage, Bonn 1904.

59. GUTTMANN, J., Jean Bodin in seinen Beziehungen zum Judentum, *Monatsschrift für Geschichte und Wissenschaft des Judentums* 1905, 315–348, 459–489.

60. HAUSER, HENRI, La controverse sur les monnaies de 1566 à 1578, in: Congrès des Sociétés savantes, Alger 1905, 10–31.

61. Renz, Fritz, Jean Bodin. Ein Beitrag zur Geschichte der historischen Methode im 16. Jahrhundert (= Geschichtliche Untersuchungen III, 1), Gotha 1905.

62. Bodin de Saint-Laurent, Jean, Les idées monétaires et commerciales de Jean Bodin, Bordeaux 1907.

63. Brunetière, Ferdinand, Trois artisans de l'idéal classique au XVIᵉ siècle: Henri Estienne – Jacques Amyot – Jean Bodin, *Revue des deux mondes, 5ᵉ série* 38 (1907), 7–18.

64. Cornu, P., Jean Bodin de Montguichet, *Revue de l'Anjou* 54 (1907), 109–111.

65. Figgis, John N., Political Thought from Gerson to Grotius, Cambridge 1907, 143 ff.

66. Généalogie de la famille de Bodin, Tours 1907.

67. Lemaire, André, Les Lois fondamentales de la monarchie française d'après les théoriciens de l'ancien régime, Paris 1907.

68. Collinet, Paul, Jean Bodin dans les Ardennes (1572–1573), *Revue Ardenaise* 16 (1908/9), 106 ff.

69. Collinet, Paul, Bodin et la Saint-Barthélemy, *Nouvelle Revue de Droit* 1909, 752–758.

70. Bezold, Friedrich, Jean Bodin als Okkultist und seine Demonomanie, *Historische Zeitschrift* 105 (1910), 1–64

71. Chauviré, Roger, La physique de Bodin, *Revue de l'Anjou* 65 (1912), 145–177.

72. Menke-Glückert, Emil, Die Geschichtsschreibung der Reformation und Gegenreformation. Bodin und die Begründung der Geschichtsmethodologie durch Bartholomaeus Keckermann, Leipzig 1912.

73. Kvačala, Jan, Zu Bodin und Leibniz. Handschriftenstudien, *Zeitschrift für Kirchengeschichte* 34 (1913), 582–592.

74. Oberfohren, Ernst, Jean Bodin und seine Schule. Untersuchungen über die Frühzeit der Universalökonomik, *Weltwirtschaftliches Archiv, Zeitschrift für Allgemeine und Spezielle Weltwirtschaftslehre*, 1 (1913) 249 bis 285.

75. Bezold, Friedrich, Jean Bodins Colloquium Heptaplomeres und der Atheismus des 16. Jahrhunderts, *Historische Zeitschrift* 113 (1914), 260 bis 315, 114 (1915), 237–300; Rezension dazu: Walser, Ernst, *Giornale storico della Letteratura italiana* 72 (1918), 337–341.

76. Chauviré, Roger, Jean Bodin, auteur de la République, Paris 1914.

77. Dilthey, Wilhelm, Weltanschauung und Analyse des Menschen seit Renaissance und Reformation, in: Gesammelte Schriften II, Leipzig-Berlin 1914, ⁶Göttingen-Stuttgart 1960, 145 ff., 274 f.

78. Jellinek, Georg, Bodin, in: Allgemeine Staatslehre, Berlin ³1914, ⁴1922, 453–463.

79. Montfort, H. de, Un théoricien de la monarchie au XVIᵉ siècle: Jean Bodin, *La revue critique des idées et des livres* 25 (1914), 425–438.

80. Oberfohren, Ernst, Jean Bodin und seine Schule, Kiel 1914.

81. Oberfohren, Ernst, Die Idee der Universalökonomie in der französischen wirtschaftswissenschaftlichen Literatur bis auf Turgot, Jena 1915.

82. SERRURIER, C., Jean Bodin, Colloque des secrets cachez des choses sublimes, *Neophilologus* 1 (1915/6), 22–43.

83. BEZOLD, FRIEDRICH VON, Zur Entstehungsgeschichte der historischen Methodik, in: Mittelalter und Renaissance, München 1918.

84. CHIALVO, G., Dell'identità del bene nello stato e nell'individuo in G. Bodin, Rom 1918.

85. BURY, JOHN BAGNELL, The Idea of Progress, London 1920, ch. I. «Some Interpretations of Universal History: Bodin and Le Roy».

86. MORET, J., Jean Bodin et la vie chère, *Revue d'économie politique* 34 (1920), 739–750.

87. SCHMITT, CARL, Die Diktatur von den Anfängen des modernen Souveränitätsgedankens bis zum proletarischen Klassenkampf, München-Leipzig 1921, Berlin ³1964, 25–42.

88. BUSSON, HENRI, Les sources et le développement du rationalisme dans la littérature française de la renaissance (1533–1610), Paris 1922, 539–565 (Un «Achriste»: Jean Bodin).
²1957: «Le rationalisme dans la litt. franç. au XVIᵉ siècle».

89. FIGGIS, JOHN N., The Divine Rights of Kings, Cambridge ²1922, 126 ff.

90. DOWDALL, HAROLD C., The Word ‹State›, *Law Quarterly Review*, 39 (1923), 98–125.

91. Huguenots emprisonnés à la Conciergerie du Palais à Paris (documents), *Bulletin de la Société de l'histoire du Protestantisme français* 1923, 86 ff.

92. MEINECKE, FRIEDRICH, Die Idee der Staatsräson, München-Berlin 1924, ²1925, ³1929, 70–80, Neudrucke: München 1957, 1960, 1963. Ins Englische übersetzt von D. Scott, London 1957.

93. BREDVOLD, LOUIS IGNATIUS, Milton and Bodin's Heptaplomeres, *Studies in Philology* 21 (1924), 399–402.

94. HEARNSHAW, FOSSEY JOHN COBB, Bodin and the Genesis of the Doctrine of Sovereignty, in: R. W. Seton-Watson (ed.), Tudor Studies, London 1924.

95. MANTZ, HAROLD ELMER, Jean Bodin and the Sorcerers, *Romanic Review* 15 (1924), 153–178.

95a. MURRAY, R. H., The Political Consequences of the Reformation, New York 1925, Ch. V.

96. ALLEN, JOHN WILLIAM, Jean Bodin, in: F. J. C. Hearnshaw (ed.), The Social and Political Ideas of Some Great Thinkers of the Sixteenth and Seventeenth Centuries, London 1926, 42–61, reprinted New York 1949.

97. ALLEN, JOHN WILLIAM, A History of Political Thought in the Sixteenth Century, London 1928, 394–446, ³1951.

98. HARSIN PAUL, Bodin et la théorie monétaire au XVIème siècle, *Revue belge de philologie et d'histoire* 7 (1928), 1301–1304.

99. PONTHIEUX, A., Quelques documents inédits sur Jean Bodin, *Revue du seizième siècle* 15 (1928), 56–99.

100. BENOIST, G., Jean Bodin et Machiavel, *La Province d'Anjou* 4 (1929), 388–399.

101. CHAUVIRÉ, ROGER, La pensée religieuse de Jean Bodin d'après des documents nouveaux, *La Province d'Anjou* 4 (1929), 434–452.

102. GARDOT, ANDRÉ, Jean Bodin et la vie chère. La Réponse aux Paradoxes de Malestroit, *La Province d'Anjou* 4 (1929) 371–387.

103. LEFRANC, ABEL, La place de Jean Bodin dans la Renaissance et dans la science politique, *La Province d'Anjou* 4 (1929), 400–432.

104. MARCHAND, G., Bodin et les sorciers, *La Province d'Anjou* 4 (1929), 453 bis 464.

105. MESNARD, PIERRE, La pensée religieuse de Bodin, *Revue du seizième siècle* 16 (1929), 77–121.

106. MORANDI, C., Botero, Campanella, Scioppio e Bodin, *Nuova Rivista Storica* (1929), 3 ff.

107. SACHÉ, MARC, Bodin et Pocquet de Livonnière, *La Province d'Anjou* 4 (1929), 465–472.

108. FEIST, ELISABETH, Weltbild und Staatsidee bei Jean Bodin, Halle 1930.

109. RUGGIERO, GUIDO DE, Rinascimento, Riforma e Controriforma (= Storia della Filosofia, parte 3, vol. II), Bari 1930, 77–82.

110. SHEPARD, M. A., Sovereignty at the Crossroads: a Study of Bodin, *Political Science Quarterly* 45 (1930), 580–603.

111. HAUSER, HENRI, Quelques points de la bibliographie et de la chronologie de Jean Bodin, in: Saggi di storia e teoria economica in onore e ricordo di Guiseppe Prato, Turin 1931, I, 59–67.

112. HAUSER, HENRI, Un précurseur – Jean Bodin, Angevin (1529 ou 1530 – 1596), *Annales d'histoire économique et sociale* 3 (1931), 379–387.

113. REYNOLDS, BEATRICE, Proponents of Limited Monarchy in Sixteenth Century France: François Hotman and Jean Bodin, Columbia/New York 1931.

114. SABINE, GEORGE HOLLAND, The Colloquium Heptaplomeres of Jean Bodin, in: Persecution and Liberty. Essays in Honor of G. L. Burr, New York 1931.

115. COLE, CHARLES WOOLSLEY, French Mercantilist Doctrines before Colbert, New York 1931, 47–57 (Bodin).

116. MOREAU-REIBEL, JEAN, Jean Bodin et le droit public comparé dans ses rapports avec la philosophie de l'histoire, Paris 1933.

117. PASQUIER, EMILE, La famille de Jean Bodin, *Revue d'histoire de l'eglise de France* 19 (1933), 457–462.

118. BENZ, ERNST, Der Toleranzgedanke in der Religionswissenschaft. (Über den Heptaplomeres des J. Bodin), *Deutsche Vierteljahresschrift* 12 (1934) 540–571.

119. FÈBVRE, LUCIEN, L'universalisme de Jean Bodin, *Revue de synthèse* 54 (1934), 165–168.

120. FICKEL, GEORG, Der Staat bei Bodin, Leipzig Diss. 1934.

121. GARDOT, ANDRÉ, Jean Bodin. Sa place parmi les fondateurs du droit international. *Recueil des Cours de l'Académie de Droit International à la Haye* 50 (1934) 549–747.

122. GAROSCI, ALDO, Jean Bodin: Politica e Diritto nel Rinascimento Francese, Milano 1934.

123. CONDE, FRANCISCO JAVIER, El pensamiento politico de Bodin, *Anuario de historia del derecho espanol* 12 (1935), 5–96.

124. MOREAU-REIBEL, JEAN, Bodin et la Ligue d'après des lettres inédites, *Humanisme et Renaissance* 2 (1935), 422–440.

125. SÉE, HENRI, La philosophie de l'histoire de Jean Bodin, *Revue historique* 175 (1935), 497–505.

126. HO, YUNG-CHI, The Origin of Parliamentary Sovereignty or «Mixed» Monarchy, Shanghai 1935, 178–243 (Bodin on sovereignty), 244–304 (Bodin in England).

127. CARLYLE, R. W. and A. J., A History of Mediaeval Political Theory in the West, 6 Vol., London 1903–1936, VI: Political Theory from 1300 to 1600 (1936), 417–429.

128. HAUSER, HENRI, Recherches et documents sur l'histoire des prix en France de 1500 à 1800, Paris 1936.

129. MESNARD, PIERRE, L'essor de la philosophie politique au XVIe siècle, Paris 1936, ²1952, 473–546.

130. STRIESOW, HANS, Bodins Staatslehre, eine Exegese, Hamburg (Diss.) 1936.

131. WELIES, BERNARDUS VAN, Thomas van Aquinas en Joannes Bodinus, Nijmwegen 1936.

132. COOK, THOMAS I., History of Political Philosophy from Plato to Burke, New York 1936, 365–396 (Bodin, kingly sovereignty and the new middle class).

133. BUDDEBERG, KARL THEODOR, Gott und Souverän. Über die Führung des Staates im Zusammenhang rechtlichen und religiösen Denkens, *Archiv für öffentliches Recht* 28 (1937), 282 ff.

133a. LÉON, PAUL-L., L'Evolution de l'idée de la souveraineté avant Rousseau, *Archives de philosophie du droit et de sociologie juridique* 7 (1937), 169 ff.

134. SABINE, GEORGE H., A History of Political Theory, New York 1937, 399–414 (Jean Bodin); Revised eds. 1950, 1962.

135. CARDASCIA, GUILLAUME, Sur une édition genevoise de la République de Jean Bodin, *Humanisme et Renaissance* 4 (1937), 212–214.

136. BALDWIN, SUMMERFIELD, Jean Bodin and the League, *Catholic Historical Review* 23 (1937/8), 160–184.

137. CHIRIOTTI, EMILIO, La ‹Résponse› al Malestroit e il pensiero economico di Jean Bodin, *Annali di economia* 13 (1938), 281–325.

138. GIANTURCO, ELIO, Bodin's Conception of the Venetian Constitution and his Critical Rift with Fabio Albergati, *Revue de littérature comparée* 18 (1938), 684–695.

139. RADETTI, GIORGIO, Il problema della religione nel pensiero di Giovanni Bodin, *Giornale critico della filosofia italiana* 19 (1938), 265–294.

140. BROWN, JOHN L., The Methodus ad facilem historiarum cognitionem of Jean Bodin, a Critical Study, Washington 1939.

141. BROWN, JOHN L., Bodin and Ben Jonson, *Revue de littérature comparée* 20 (1940), 66–81.

142. CHAUVIRÉ, ROGER, Grandeur de Bodin, *Revue historique* 188/9 (1940), 378–397.

142a. DIÈS, A., Le nombre de Platon. Essai d'exégèse et d'histoire, *Mémoires de l'académie des Inscriptions et Belles-Lettres* 14:1 (1940), 54 ff.

143. Váczy, Peter, Jean Bodin sur le rapport des rois de Hongrie et du Saint-Siège, *Archivum philologicum* 64 (1940), 250 ff.

144. Buddeberg, Karl Theodor, Souveränität und Völkerrecht bei Jean Bodin, *Archiv für öffentliches Recht* N. F. 32 (1941), 193 ff.

145. Church, William Farr, Constitutional Thought in Sixteenth-Century France. A Study in the Evolution of Ideas (Harvard Historical Studies 47), Cambridge (Mass.) 1941.

146. Gilmore, M. P., Argument from Roman Law in Political Thought, 1200 to 1600, (Harvard) Cambridge (Mass.) 1941.

147. Buddeberg, Karl Theodor, Sovranità e diritto delle genti in G. Bodin, *Rivista internazionale di filosofia del diritto* 1942, 330–358.

148. Dean, Leonard Fellows, Bodin's Methodus in England before 1625, *Studies in Philology* 39 (1942), 160–166.

149. Nancey, Paul, Jean Bodin économiste, Bordeaux 1942.

150. Cardascia, Guillaume, Machiavel et Jean Bodin, *Bibliothèque d'humanisme et renaissance* 3 (1943), 129–167.

151. Rindfleisch, Edith, Studien zu den «Six Livres de la République» von Jean Bodin, Diss. Berlin 1943 (unveröffentlichtes Manuskript).

152. Basdevant, Jean, La contribution de Jean Bodin à la formation du droit international moderne, *Revue historique du droit Français et étranger* 23 (1944), 143–178.

152a. Maravall, José, Teoría española des Estado en el siglo XVII, Madrid 1944, 191 ff.

153. Naef, Henri, La jeunesse de Jean Bodin ou les conversions oubliées, *Bibliothèque d'humanisme et renaissance* 8 (1946), 137–155.

154. Göhring, Martin, Weg und Wieg der modernen Staatsidee in Frankreich (Vom Mittelalter bis 1789), Tübingen ²1947, 99 ff.

155. Groethuysen, Bernard, Mythes et portraits. Bodin, in: *Essais* 22 (1947), 57–69.

156. Ulph, Owen, Jean Bodin and the Estates General of 1576, *Journal of Modern History* 19 (1947), 289–296.

157. Dennewitz, Bodo, Machiavelli, Bodin, Hobbes, Hamburg 1948.

158. Droz Eugénie, Le carme Jean Bodin, hérétique, *Bibliothèque d'humanisme et renaissance* 10 (1948), 77–94.

159. Gianturco, Elio, Bodin et Vico, *Revue de littérature comparée* 22 (1948), 272–290.

160. Levron, Jacques, Jean Bodin, sieur de Saint-Amand ou Jean Bodin, originaire de Saint-Amand?, *Bibliothèque d'humanisme et renaissance* 10 (1948), 69–76.

161. Mosse, Georg Lachmann, The Influence of Jean Bodin's République on English Political Thought, *Medievalia et humanistica* 5 (1948), 73–83.

162. Shackleton, Robert M., Botero, Bodin and Robert Johnson, *Modern Language Review* 43 (1948), 405–409.

163. Picot, Gilbert, Cardin Le Bret (1558–1655) et la Doctrine de la Souveraineté, Nancy 1948, 125 ff.

164. Wagner, Robert L., Le vocabulaire magique de J. Bodin dans la Démonomanie des sorciers, *Biblioth. d'humanisme et renaissance* 10 (1948), 95–123.

165. KAMP, MATHIAS ERNST, Die Staatswirtschaftslehre Jean Bodins, Bonn 1949.

166. KRAUSE, O. W., Naturrechtler des 16. Jahrhunderts. Ihre Bedeutung für die Entwicklung eines natürlichen Privatrechts, Göttingen 1949.

167. SIBERT, MARCEL, Parallèle entre Francisco Suarez et Jean Bodin, Paris 1949.

168. MESNARD, PIERRE, Jean Bodin et la critique de la morale d'Aristote, Revue thomiste 57 (1949), 542–562.

169. ULLMANN, WALTER, The Development of the Medieval Idea of Sovereignty, English Historical Review 64 (1949), 1–33.

170. CHEVALLIER, JEAN-JACQUES, Les grandes oeuvres politiques de Machiavel à nos jours, Paris ²1950, 38–51 [Les Six Livres de la République de Jean Bodin (1576)].

171. LEVRON, JACQUES, Jean Bodin et sa famille, Textes et commentaires, Angers 1950.

172. MESNARD, PIERRE, Introduction à la méthode de l'histoire de Jean Bodin, Bibliothèque d'humanisme et renaissance 12 (1950), 318–323.

173. MESNARD, PIERRE, Un rival heureux de Cujas et de Bodin, Etienne Forcadel, Zeitschrift der Savigny-Stiftung für Rechtsgeschichte 67 (1950), 440–458; auch in: Umanesimo e scienza politica, Milano 1951, 309–322.

174. MESNARD, PIERRE, Jean Bodin à Toulouse, Bibliothèque d'humanisme et renaissance 12 (1950), 31–59.

175. MOSSE, GEORGE LACHMANN, The Struggle for Sovereignty in England, East Lansing, Michigan, 1950, ch. II.

176. ALBERTINI, RUDOLF VON, Das politische Denken in Frankreich zur Zeit Richelieus (Beihefte zum Archiv f. Kulturgeschichte, 1), Marburg 1951, 33 ff.

177. GALIZIA, MARIO, La Teoria della Sovranità dal Medioevo alla Rivolzione Francese, Mailand 1951, 125–154.

178. GALVAN, E. T., Los supuestos scotisticas en la teoria politica de Jean Bodin, Murcia 1951.

179. MESNARD, PIERRE, Jean Bodin et le problème de l'éternité du monde, Bulletin de l'Association G. Budé 1951, 117–131.

180. REULOS, MICHEL, L'édition de 1577 de la Republique, Bibliothèque d'humanisme et renaissance 13 (1951), 342–354.

181. ULPH OWEN, The Mandate System and Representation to the Estates General under the Old System, Journal of Modern History 23 (1951), 225–231.

182. EBENSTEIN, WILLIAM, Introduction to Political Philosophy, New York 1952, 117–121 (Bodin).

183. TOOLEY, MARIAN J., Bodin and the Mediaeval Theory of Climate, Speculum 28 (1953), 64–83.

184. MCRAE, KENNETH D., The Political Thought of Jean Bodin (unpublished Ph. D. thesis), Harvard University 1954.

185. MESNARD, PIERRE, Le platonisme de Jean Bodin, in: Congrès de Tours et Poitiers 1953, Paris 1954, 352–361.

185. ASHER, R. E., The Attitude of French Writers of the Renaissance to Early French History (unpublished Ph. D. thesis) University of London 1955.

187. ADDIO, MARIO D', «Les six livres de la Republique» e il pensiero cattolico del Cinquecento, in: Medioevo e Rinascimento, Studi in onore di Bruno Nardi, Florenz 1955, I, 127–144.

188. LECLER, JOSEPH, Histoire de la tolérance au siècle de la Réforme, Bd. 2, Paris 1955, 91 ff, 153 ff.

189. MCRAE, KENNETH D., Ramist Tendencies in the Thought of Jean Bodin, *Journal of the History of Ideas* 16 (1955), 306–323.

190. MARONGIU, AATONIO, Jean Bodin et les Assemblées d'états, *Schweizer Beiträge zur allgemeinen Geschichte* 15 (1957).

191. LACOUR, CHR.-M.-A., Les rencontres de pensées entre Bodin et Paul Valéry, d'après la «République», le «Methodus» et «Les Regards sur le monde actuel», Poitiers 1957.

192. KOSSMANN, ERNST, Bodin, Althusius en Parker, of over de modernitut van de Nederlandse opstand, in: Festschrift für F. H. K. Kossmann, Gravenhage 1958.

193. WALKER, DANIEL PICKERING, Spiritual and Demonic Magic from Ficino to Campanella, London 1958.

194. BURNS, JAMES HENDERSON, Sovereignty and Constitutional Law in Bodin, *Political Studies* 7 (1959), 174–177.

195. CAPRARIIS, VITTORIO DE, Propaganda e pensiero politico in Francia durante le guerre di religione, Napoli 1959, 318–371.

196. DICKMANN, FRITZ, Der Westfälische Frieden, Münster, 1959, ²1965, 127 bis 137.

197. GARANDERIE, PAUL DE LA, L'humanisme politique de Jean Bodin et son actualité, Mémoires de l'Academie d'Angers (1959), 93–144.

198. MESNARD, PIERRE, Jean Bodin devant le problème de l'éducation, *Revue des travaux de l'Academie des Sciences morales et politiques* 1959, 217–228.

199. MESNARD, PIERRE, Entre Bodin et Quevedo: l'humanisme politique de Juan Pablo Martin Rizo, in: Miscelanea de estudos a Joaquim de Carvalho, 1959, 184–194.

200. MESNARD, PIERRE, La conjuration contre la renommée de Jean Bodin: Antoine Teissier (1684), *Bulletin de l'Association Guillaume Budé. Lettres d'Humanité* 18 (1959), 535–559.

201. SALMON, J. H. M., The French Religious Wars in English Political Thought, Oxford 1959.

202. SECRET, FRANÇOIS, Notes sur G. Postel: G. Postel et J. Bodin, *Bibliothèque d'humanisme et renaissance* 21 (1959); Postel contre Bodin, *Bibliothèque d'humanisme et renaissance* 23 (1961).

203. TENTLER, T. W., The Meaning of Prudence in Bodin, *Traditio* 15 (1959), 365–384.

204. TOUCHARD, JEAN, Histoire des idées politiques, Paris 1959, I, 286–293.

205. KLEMPT, ADALBERT, Die Säkularisierung der universalhistorischen Auffassung. Zum Wandel des Geschichtsdenkens im 16. und 17. Jahrhundert, Göttingen 1960.

206. MATTEI, RODOLFO DE, Difese italiane del «governo misto» contro la critica negatrice del Bodin, in: Studi in onore di E. Crosa, Milano 1960, 739–758,

auch in: Temi e dibatti di storia del pensiero politico (ed. Ricerche), Rom 1967, 211–237.

207. MESNARD, PIERRE, État present des études bodiniennes, *Filosofia* 11 (1960), 687–696.

208. MESNARD, PIERRE, Jean Bodin à la recherche des secrets de la nature, in: Umanesimo ed esoterismo. V. Congresso Internazionale di studi umanistici, Padua 1960, 221–234.

209. MESNARD, PIERRE, Jean Bodin teoretico de la Republica, *Revista de estudios politicos* 113/4 (1960), 89–103.

210. MESNARD, PIERRE, Le nationalisme de Jean Bodin, *La Table Ronde* 147 (1960), 66–72.

211. GIESEY, RALPH E., The Juristic Basis of Dynastic Right to the French Throne (= Transactions of the American Philosophical Society, Vol. 51, 5), Philadelphia 1961.

212. GELDER, H. A. ENNO VON, The Two Reformations in the 16th Century, Den Haag 1961, 393 ff.

213. HORNICK, H., Jean Bodin and the Beginning of Voltaire's Struggle for Religious Tolerance, *Modern Language Notes* 76 (1961), 362–375.

214. KOGAN-BERNSTEIN, F. A., Jean Bodin et sa critique du christianisme, *Annuaire d'études françaises 1961*, Moskau 1962, 2–35 (russisch mit französischer Zusammenfassung).

215. Jean Bodin et Toulouse. Catalogue de l'Exposition présentée Ie 3 octobre 1960 à Toulouse; Introduction de Pierre Mesnard, Toulouse 1961.

216. MESNARD, PIERRE, A fisica de Jean Bodin, segundo o «Anfiteatro da natureza», *Revista Portugesa di Filosofia* 17 (1961), 164–200.

217. COTRONEO, GIROLAMO, La storia integrale nella Methodus di J. Bodin, *Historica* 15 (1962) 95–107.

218. ENTRÈVES, A. PASSERIN D', La dottrina dello stato. Elementi di analisi e di interpretazione, Turin 1962, 144–149, 167–169.

219. GROETHUYSEN, BERNARD, Bodin, *Tableau de la littérature française* 1 (1962), 400–407.

220. ISNARDI, MARGHERITA, Appunti per la storia di état, republique, stato, *Rivista Storica Italiana* (1962), 372–379.

221. ISNARDI, MARGHERITA, A proposito di un'interpretazione cinquecentesca del rapporto teoria-prassi in Aristotele e Platone, in: La Parola del Passato 1962, 436–447.

222. MESNARD, PIERRE, The Psychology and Pneumatology of Jean Bodin, *International philosophical Quarterly* 2 (1962), 244–264.

223. MESNARD, PIERRE, Jean Bodin en la historia del pensamiento (introducción por J. A. Maravall), Madrid 1962.

224. SCHNUR, ROMAN, Die französichen Juristen im konfessionellen Bürgerkrieg des 16. Jahrhunderts. Ein Beitrag zur Entstehungsgeschichte des modernen Staates, Berlin 1962.

225. BARBER, GILES, Haec a Joanne Bodin lecta, *Bibliothèque d'humanisme et renaissance* 25 (1963), 362–365.

226. FRANKLIN, JULIAN H., Jean Bodin and the Sixteenth-Century Revolution in the Methodology of Law and History, New York, London 1963.

227. IMBODEN, MAX, Johannes Bodinus und die Souveränitätslehre, Basel 1963.
228. MCRAE, KENNETH D., A Postscript on Bodin's Connections with Ramism, *Journal of the History of Ideas* 24 (1963), 569–571.
229. PLAMENATZ, JOHN P., Man and Society, 2 Vol., London 1963, Vol. I. Ch. 3., 89–115.
230. SCUPIN, HANS ULRICH, La notion de souveraineté dans les oeuvres de Jean Bodin et de Johannes Althusius, in: Annales de la Faculté de Droit de l'Université de Lille 1963, 7–27.
231. ROELLENBLECK, GEORG, Zum Schrifttum über Jean Bodin, *Der Staat* 2 (1963), 339–349 und 3 (1964), 227–246.
232. SMITH, CONSTANCE I., Filmer and the Knolles Translation of Bodin, *The Philosophical Quarterly* 13 (1963), 248–252.
233. TENENTI, A., Milieu XVIe siècle, début XVIIe siècle. Libertinisme et hérésie, *Annales* 18 (1963), 1–19.
234. ALLEN, DON CAMERON, Bodin, in: Doubt's boundless Sea, Baltimore 1964, 97–110.
235. COTRONEO, GIROLAMO, Il senso della storia nella «Methodus» di Jean Bodin, *Rivista di studi crociani* 1 (1964), 296–311.
236. COTRONEO, GIROLAMO, Introduzione allo studio della Methodus di J. Bodin, *Atti Accademia Pontaniana di Napoli* 12 (1964).
237. DENNERT, JÜRGEN, Ursprung und Begriff der Souveränität (= Sozialwissenschaftliche Studien, 7), Stuttgart 1964, 56–73.
238. GREENLEAF, WILLIAM HOWARD, Order, Empiricism, and Politics. Two Traditions of English Political Thought 1500–1700, London 1964, 126 ff.
239. ROELLENBLECK, GEORG, Offenbarung, Natur und jüdische Überlieferung bei Jean Bodin. Eine Interpretation des Heptaplomeres (= Studien zur Religion, Geschichte und Geisteswissenschaft, 2), Gütersloh 1964.
240. SMITH, CONSTANCE I., Jean Bodin and Comparative Law, *Journal of the History of Ideas* 25 (1964), 417–422.
241. COTRONEO, GIROLAMO, Un tentativo di storia della storiografia nella «Methodus» di Bodin, *Giornale critico della filosofia italiana* 44 (1965), 504–526.
242. IZDEBSKI, ZYGMUNT, Quelques observations sur les idées politiques de Jean Bodin (Lódzkie Towarzystwo Naukowe Nr 59) Lódź 1965.
243. LECLER, JOSEPH, Geschichte der Religionsfreiheit, Bd. 2, Stuttgart 1965, 136 ff., 221 ff.
244. MESNARD, PIERRE, La Démonomanie de Jean Bodin, in: L'opera e il pensiero di G. Pico della Mirandola, Florenz 1965, II, 333–356.
245. SCUPIN, HANS ULRICH, Der Begriff der Souveränität bei Johannes Althusius und bei Jean Bodin, *Der Staat* 4 (1965), 1–26.
246. COTRONEO, GIROLAMO, Bodin teorico della storia, Napoli 1966.
247. COTRONEO, GIROLAMO, Bodin e Vico, *Rivista di studi crociani* 3 (1966), 75–82.
248. GARANDERIE, PAUL DE LA, Note sur Jean Bodin et la géographie humaine, *Mémoires de l'Academie des Sciences, Belles-Lettres et Arts d'Angers* 10 (1966), 31–36.
249. HASSINGER, ERICH, Religiöse Toleranz im 16. Jahrhundert. Motive – Argu-

mente – Formen der Verwirklichung (= Vorträge des Aeneas-Silvius-Stiftung an der Universität Basel, 6), Basel, Stuttgart 1966.

250. HINSLEY, FRANCIS HARRY, Sovereignty, London 1966, 120 ff., 179 ff.

251. MARONGIU, ANTONIO, Jean Bodin e la polemica sulle «assemblee di stati», in: Gouvernés et gouvernants, 3e partie, Brüssel, 1966, I, 49–70.

252. MESNARD, PIERRE, Jean Bodin fait de l'histoire la base des sciences humaines, in: Organon d'Academie polonaise des sciences, Vol. 3., Warschau 1966, 181–184.

253. MÜLLER, CHRISTOPH, Das imperative und freie Mandat. Überlegungen zur Lehre von der Repräsentation des Volkes, Diss. Leiden 1966, 185 ff., 191 ff.

252. SCHUBERT, FRIEDRICH HERMANN, Die deutschen Reichstage in der Staatslehre der frühen Neuzeit, Göttingen 1966, 339–343, 360–382.

253. BAWCUTT, N. W., Nashe and Bodin, Notes and Queries 212 (1967), 91.

253a. CHANTEUR, JANINE, Jean Bodin et les critères de la légitimité dans «Les six livres de la République», in: L'idée de Légitimité, Annales de philosophie politique, Paris (PUF) 1967.

254. CORPACI, FRANCESCO, Intorno ad una ristampa della «Repubblica» del Bodin, Rivista internazionale di filosofia del diritto 44 (1967), 344–351.

255. HINTON, R. W. K., Husbands, fathers and conquerors (Sir Thomas Smith, Jean Bodin, Sir Robert Filmer), Political Studies 15 (1967), 291–300.

256. BAZZOLI, M., Il diritto naturale nella «République» di J. Bodin, Critica storica VII (1968), 586–593.

257. BENJAMIN, E. B., Donne and Bodin's Theatrum, Notes and Queries for Readers, Writers, Collectors and Librarians 15 (1968), 92–94.

258. DENZER, HORST, Bodin, in: Klassiker des politischen Denkens (ed. H. Maier, H. Rausch, H. Denzer), München 2 Vol., 1968, I, 321–350.

259. GARGALLO DI CASTEL LENTINI, G., Nota su Jean Bodin, Rivista di studi crociani 5 (1968), 96–101.

260. HOKE, RUDOLF, Die Reichsstaatsrechtslehre des Johannes Limnaeus (= Untersuchungen zur deutschen Staats- und Rechtsgeschichte N. F. 9), Aalen 1968, 54–64, 152–155.

261. LEWIS, J. U., Jean Bodin's «Logic of Sovereignty», Political Studies 16 (1968), 202–222.

262. MAGER, WOLFGANG, Zur Entstehung des modernen Staatsbegriffs (Akademie der Wissenschaften und Literatur Mainz), Abhandlungen 1968 Nr. 9, 396–498 (489).

263. MOMMSEN, KARL, Bodins Souveränitätslehre und die Exemption der Eidgenossenschaft, in: Festschrift für Edgar Bonjour, 2 Vol., Basel 1968, II, 433–448.

264. SCHUBERT, FRIEDRICH HERMANN, Französische Staatstheorie und deutsche Reichsverfassung im 16. und 17. Jahrhundert, in: Lutz-Schubert-Weber, Frankreich und das Reich im 16. und 17. Jahrhundert, Göttingen 1968, 20–35.

265. WOLFE, MARTIN, Jean Bodin on Taxes: The Sovereignty Taxes Paradox, Political Science Quarterly 83 (1968), 268–284.

266. HINRICHS, ERNST, Fürstenlehre und politisches Handeln im Frankreich

Heinrichs IV. (= Veröffentlichungen des Max-Planck-Instituts für Geschichte, 21), Göttingen 1969, 48 f., 73 f., 92 f.

267. MESNARD, PIERRE, Jean Bodin a-t-il établi la théorie de la Monocratie? Recueils de la Société Jean Bodin, Vol. 21, Bruxelles 1969, 637–656.

268. MONTER, E. WILLIAM, Inflation and Witchcraft: The Case of Jean Bodin, in: Action and Conviction in Early Modern Europe (Ed. T. K. Raab u. J. E. Seigel), Princeton 1969, 371–389.

269. DREITZEL, HORST, Protestantischer Aristotelismus und absoluter Staat, Wiesbaden 1970 (Veröffentlichungen des Instituts für Europäische Geschichte, Mainz Bd. 55), Wiesbaden 1970, 143/44, 242/44, 313/16.

270. HUPPERT, GEORGE, The Idea of Perfect History, Urbana, I., 1970.

271. LANGE, URSULA, Untersuchungen zu Bodins Demonomanie. Frankfurt/M., 1970.

272. MARTINO, V., Jean Bodin e la «Revolution des prix», *Annali Facoltà di Magistero dell'Università di Bari*, 9 (1970), 3–49.

273. REULOS, MICHEL, Une institution romaine vue par un auteur du XVIème siècle: la censure dans Jean Bodin, in: Etudes offertes à Jean Macqueron, Aix-en-Provence 1970, 585–590.

274. VAHLE, HERMANN, Bodins Polenbild. Zur französischen und polnischen Souveränitätslehre im 16. Jahrhundert, *Archiv für Kulturgeschichte* 52 (1970), 4–27.

275. VASOLI, CESARE, Il problema cinquecentesco della Methodus e la sua applicazione alla conoscenza storica, *Filosofia* 21 (1970), 137–172.

276. QUARITSCH, HELMUT, Staat und Souveränität, Bd. 1: Die Grundlagen, Frankfurt 1970, 39–43, 243–394.

277. TELLE, E. V., Thomas More dans la «République» de Jean Bodin, *Moreana* 7 (1970) No 27–28, 103 ff.

278. ISNARDI PARENTE, MARGHERITA, Il volontarismo di Jean Bodin: Maimonide o Duns Scoto? *Il pensiero politico* 4 (1971), 21–45.

DIE AUTOREN

Baxter, Christopher R.
Born in 1938, Lecturer in French, University of Sussex, England.
Publications: Chapters on The Poetry of Violence; Problems of the Religious
Wars; Montaigne, in J. Cruickshank (ed.) French Literature and its Background,
Vol. I, London 1968. Introductions to Jean Bodin, De la Démonomanie des
Sorciers, and to Johan Weyer, Histoires, Disputes et Discours in the reprint
series, Bibliotheca Diabolica, Theatrum Orbis Terrarum Ltd., Amsterdam
(forthcoming).

Chanteur, Janine, née Ganneron
Née en 1924. Agrégée de Philosophie, Maître-Assistant à l'Université de Paris-
Sorbonne.
Principales publications: Jean Bodin et les critères de la légitimité dans «Les
six livres de la République», dans: L'idée de Legitimité. Annales de philosophie
politique, P. U. F. 1967; Problèmes de l'interprétation de l'histoire, dans: Etudes
philosophiques 1965; Les notions de Peuple et de Multitude chez Hobbes, dans:
Hobbes – Forschungen, Berlin 1968; La violence dans l'œuvre politique de Platon, dans: Annales de Philosophie politique, P. U. F. (à paraître); Mort de
l'obligation politique, dans: Annales de Philosophie politique, P. U. F. (à
paraître).

Cotroneo, Girolamo
Geb. 1934 in Campo Calabro (Reggio Calabria, Italien). 1957 Dr. phil. an der
Universität Messina. An der Facoltà di Lettere e Filosofia der Universität Messina seit 1966 Assistente ordinario für theoretische Philosophie, seit 1968 Privatdozent für Geschichtsphilosophie, seit 1969 Professore incaricato für Philosophiegeschichte. Lehrt heute Philosophiegeschichte und ist Direktor des Instituts
für Philosophie an der Universität Messina.
Wichtigste Veröffentlichungen: Jean Bodin teorico della storia, Napoli 1966;
Croce e l'Illuminismo, Napoli 1970; I trattatisti dell'«Ars historica», Napoli
1971.

Dennert, Jürgen
Geb. 1935. 1958 bis 1962 Studium der Politik, Geschichte und des Öffentlichen
Rechts in Hamburg. 1964 Promotion zum Dr. phil. in Hamburg bei Siegfried
Landshut, ebenda 1968 Habilitation, venia legendi für Politische Wissenschaft.
Gestorben 1970.
Wichtigste Veröffentlichungen: Ursprung und Begriff der Souveränität, Stutt-
gart 1964; Beza, Brutus, Hotman, Calvinistische Monarchomachen, Köln-
Opladen 1968; Entwicklungshilfe geplant oder verwaltet?, Bielefeld 1968; Ver-

schwiegenes Zeitgeschehen, Wien-Düsseldorf 1970; Die ontologisch-aristotelische Politikwissenschaft, Berlin 1970.

Denzer, Horst

Geb. 1941. Studium der Politischen Wissenschaft, Geschichte, Philosophie und Germanistik in Freiburg, Berlin und München; 1971 Dr. phil.; wiss. Assistent am Geschwister-Scholl-Institut für Politische Wissenschaft der Universität München.

Veröffentlichungen: Mitherausgeber von Maier-Rausch-Denzer, Klassiker des politischen Denkens, 2 Bde., München 1968, ⁴1972; Moralphilosophie und Naturrecht bei Samuel Pufendorf, München 1972; Herausgeber und Übersetzer von Pufendorfs «De statu imperii Germanici», Stuttgart 1972; Aufsätze zur politischen Kybernetik, zum Rechtsradikalismus und zum deutschen Naturrecht des 17. Jahrhunderts; Mitarbeiter bei der Entwicklung eines Fernstudiums für Sozialkundelehrer.

Derathé, Robert

Né à Besançon (Doubs) le 20 décembre 1905. Agrégé de philosophie (1931), Docteur-ès-Lettres (1950). Professeur d'Histoire de la Philosophie à l'Université de Nancy depuis 1952. Secrétaire Général de l'Institut International de Philosophie Politique.

Principales publications: Le rationalisme de J.-J. Rousseau (thèse complémentaire), Paris 1948; Jean-Jacques Rousseau et la Science politique de son temps (thèse principale), Paris 1950 (2ème éd. 1970); Article «Jean-Jacques Rousseau» dans l'International Encyclopedia of the Social Sciences, New York 1968. Plusieurs études sur J.-J. Rousseau et la pensée politique, parmi lesquelles: «Les philosophes et le despotisme» (dans le Recueil Utopie et Institutions au XVIIIᵉ siècle, Paris-La Haye, 1963); «Le droit de punir chez Montesquieu, Beccaria et Voltaire» (Atti del convegno internazionale su Cesare Beccaria, Torino 1966). Edition du Contrat social, du Discours sur l'Economie politique, et des fragments politiques (Œuvres complètes de J.-J. Rousseau, Paris, Gallimard, Bibliothèque de la Pléiade, tome III, 1964). Edition de l'Esprit des lois (sous presse, Classiques Garnier).

Euchner, Walter

Dr. phil., geb. 1933 in Stuttgart. Studium der Rechtswissenschaften, Politikwissenschaft, Soziologie und Geschichte in Tübingen, München, Heidelberg und Frankfurt a. M., Wissenschaftlicher Assistent und Lehrbeauftragter für Politikwissenschaft am Fachbereich «Gesellschaftswissenschaften» der Universität Frankfurt a. M. Seit 1971 Professor für politische Wissenschaft an der Universität Göttingen.

Wichtigste Veröffentlichungen: Naturrecht und Politik bei John Locke. Frankfurt a. M. 1969; Demokratietheoretische Aspekte der politischen Ideengeschichte. In: Politikwissenschaft (ed. Kress, Senghaas). Frankfurt a. M. 1969; Freiheit, Eigentum und Herrschaft bei Hegel. In: PVS XI (1970), S. 531–555; Der Parlamentarismus der Bundesrepublik als Gegenstand politikwissenschaftlicher Untersuchungen. In: PVS X (1969), S. 388–414. Herausgabe der «Zwei

Abhandlungen über die Regierung» von John Locke und der «Bienenfabel» von Bernard Mandeville. Deutsche Übersetzung der englischen Version des «Leviathan» von Thomas Hobbes.

Franklin, Julian H.

Born in New York City on March 26, 1925; A. B. from Queens College, New York, in 1946; Ph. D. from Columbia University in 1960. Professor of Government at Columbia, specializing in the history of political thought.

Publications: «Bureaucracy and Freedom», Man in Contemporary Society, Vol I, Columbia University Press, New York, 1955. Jean Bodin and the Sixteenth Century Revolution in the Methodology of Law and History, Columbia University Press, New York 1963. «Jean Bodin», Encyclopedia of Social Sciences, 2nd ed. «Constitutionalism in the Sixteenth Century: The Protestant Monarchomachs», in David Spitz ed., Political Theory and Social Change, Atherton Press, New York, 1967. Constitutionalism and Resistance in the 16th Century, New York, Pegasus, 1969. Jean Bodin and the Rise of Absolutist Theory (forthcoming).

Freund, Julien

Né en 1921, Agrégé de philosophie, Professeur de Sociologie à l'Université des Sciences humaines de Strasbourg.

Principales publications: L'Essence du Politique, Paris 1965; La Sociologie de Max Weber, Paris 1966; Europa ohne Schminke, Goslar 1967; Max Weber, philosophe, Paris 1969; Le Nouvel Age, Paris 1970.

Giesey, Ralph E.

Born 1923. Professor of History, University of Iowa (since 1966). Previously at University of Washington and University of Minnesota. PhD from University of California (Berkeley) in 1954. Fellowships from Fulbright Commission (1951–1952), American Council of Learned Societies (1952–1953), Guggenheim Foundation (1970). Assistant at the Institute for Advanced Study (1953–1955) and member there (1964–1965).

Publications: The Royal Funeral Ceremony in Renaissance France (1960); The Juristic Basis of Dynastic Right to the French Throne (1961); If Not, Not: The Oath of the Aragonese and the Legendary Laws of Sobrarbe (1967); forthcoming, from Cambridge Univ. Press: The Francogallia of François Hotman (with J. H. M. Salmon).

Greenleaf, W. H.

Born 1927. B. Sc. (Econ.) 1951; Ph. D. 1954, University of London. Lecturer etc. in Political Studies, University of Hull, 1954–67. Professor of Political Theory and Government, University College, Swansea, 1967 to date.

Publications include Order, Empiricism and Politics (1964), Oakeshott's Philosophical Politics (1966), The World of Politics (inaugural lecture, 1968) and papers in various symposia and professional journals.

Hinrichs, Ernst

Geb. 1937 in Hamburg. Studium der Geschichte, Philosophie und Germanistik in Hamburg, Freiburg und Göttingen. 1966 Promotion in Göttingen, seit 1966 Wissenschaftlicher Referent am Max-Planck-Institut für Geschichte. Besondere Interessengebiete: Sozial- und Verfassungsgeschichte Frankreichs vom 16. bis zum frühen 19. Jahrhundert.

Veröffentlichungen: «Fürstenlehre und politisches Handeln im Frankreich Heinrichs IV.», Göttingen (Veröffentlichungen des MPI für Geschichte 21) 1969; «Produit net, propriétaire, cultivateur. Aspekte des sozialen Wandels bei den Physiokraten und Turgot», in: Festschrift Hermann Heimpel 1, Göttingen 1971, S. 473–510; in Vorbereitung zwei Aufsätze über Begriff und Problem des Feudalismus am Ende des 18. Jahrhunderts und eine größere Untersuchung über die französischen Parlamente im 18. Jahrhundert.

Hinton, R. W. K.

Born 1920. Ph. D. Cambridge. Fellow of Peterhouse and College Lecturer in History.

Publications: The Port Books of Boston 1601–1640, Lincoln Record Society, 1956; The Eastland Trade and the Common Weal in the Seventeenth Century, Cambridge 1959. On English political ideas e.g. ‹English Constitutional Theories from Sir John Fortescue to Sir John Eliot›, English Historical Review 75 (1960), 410–425, ‹Husbands, Fathers and Conquerors›, Political Studies 15 (1967), 291–300 und 16 (1968), 55–67.

Hoke, Rudolf

Geb. 1929 Duisburg. Dr. jur., Dr. rer. pol., o. Universitätsprofessor f. Deutsches Recht und Österreichische Verfassungs- und Verwaltungsgeschichte, Vorstand des Instituts für Österreichische und Deutsche Rechtsgeschichte und des Instituts für Europäische Rechtsgeschichte, Universität Wien. Privatdozent Universität Saarbrücken 1966, Dozent 1967, Apl. Univ. Prof. 1971, o. Univ. Prof. Wien 1971.

Veröffentlichungen: Die Reichsstaatslehre des Joh. Limnaeus 1968; Die Freigrafschaft Burgund, Savoyen und die Reichsstadt Besançon im Verbande des mittelalterlichen deutschen Reiches, Zs. d. Savigny-Stift. f. Rechtsgeschichte, German. Abt. 79 (1962); Die rechtliche Stellung der national gemischten Bevölkerung am Nordrand der Adria im mittelalterl. deutschen Reich, ebenda 86 (1969); L'Incorporation du Comté de Bourgogne à l'Empire Germanique, Soc. Hist. Droit et Inst. Dijon 23 (1962); Willensmängel beim Verwaltungsakt, Die Öffentl. Verwaltung 1962; Zur Ausbildung f. d. höheren Verwaltungsdienst, Deutsches Verwaltungsblatt 1962; Die rechtl. Stellung d. ökumenischen Konzils, Jurist. Schulung 1962.

Isnardi Parente, Margherita

Geb. 4. 10. 1928 in Catanzaro. Seit 1956 Lehrerin am Gymnasium; 1963 Privat-Dozent für Storia della Filosofia antica; seit 1965 Lehrauftrag in dieser Disziplin, seit 1970 Professore aggregato für Philosophiegeschichte, seit 1971 ao. Professor für die Geschichte der antiken Philosophie an der Universität Cagliari.

Wichtigste Veröffentlichungen: Studien über die pseudoplatonischen Dialoge und die platonische Alte Akademie; Techne, momenti del pensiero greco da Platone ad Epicure, Firenze (La Nuova Italia) 1966; Filosofia e Politica nelle lettere di Platone, Napoli (Guida ed.) 1970; Einleitung, Übersetzung und Kommentierung von Jean Bodins *République*, Bd. 1, Torino (UTET) 1964, die weiteren Bde. in Vorbereitung.

Kelley, Donald R.

Born 17 Feb. 1931, Elgin, Ill. Professor of History, State University of New York, Binghamton, N. Y., 13901. Educated Harvard College (B. A., 1953) and Columbia University (M. A., Ph. D., 1962). Fulbright fellow (Paris, 1958–59), American Council of Learned Societies fellow (France, Switzerland, Germany, Netherlands, England, 1967–1968), and member of Institute for Advanced Study (Princeton, 1969–1970).

Published: Foundations of Modern Historical Scholarship (New York 1970) and a number of articles on 16th century political, legal and historical thought, including studies of François Baudouin and La Popeliniere. Presently completing a biography of François Hotman and a study of Vico.

Maier, Hans

Geb. 1931 in Freiburg i. Br. Studium der Geschichte, neueren Sprachen und Sozialwissenschaft in Freiburg, München und Paris. 1957 Promotion zum Dr. phil., 1962 Privatdozent, seit 1963 o. Professor für politische Wissenschaft an der Universität München.

Hauptveröffentlichungen: Revolution und Kirche 1959, ³1973; Die ältere deutsche Staats- und Verwaltungslehre 1966; Politische Wissenschaft in Deutschland 1969; Kritik der politischen Theologie 1970; Kirche und Gesellschaft 1972; Zwischenrufe zur Bildungspolitik 1973.

McRae, Kenneth D.

Born 1925, studied at Toronto, Harvard and Oxford Universities, and is now Professor of Political Science at Carleton University, Ottawa.

Publications: After editing Bodin's Six Bookes of a Commonweale (1962), he wrote Switzerland: Example of Cultural Co-existence (1964), and collaborated with Louis Hartz and others on The Founding of New Societies (1964). He has been a supervisor of research for the Canadian Royal Commission on Bilingualism and Biculturalism and is currently working on a comparative study of several bilingual societies.

Polin, Raymond

Né 1910 à Briançon (Htes-Alpes), ancien élève de l'Ecole normale supérieure, Agrégé de philosophie, Docteur ès lettres. Assistant à l'Ecole normale supérieure (1935–1938), Professeur aux Lycées de Laon (1938–1939), Chartres (1939–1942) et Paris (1942–1945); Professeur à la faculté des lettres de Lille (1945–1961) et maintenant de l'Université de Paris-Sorbonne (debuis 1961). Visiting professor aux Universités Harvard, Yale, Columbia et New York State University.

Principales publications: La Création des Valeurs, Paris (PUF) 1944; La Compréhension des Valeurs, Paris (PUF) 1945; Du Laid, du Mal, du Faux, Paris (PUF) 1948; Politique et Philosophie chez Thomas Hobbes, Paris (PUF) 1953; La Politique Morale de John Locke, Paris (PUF) 1960; Le Bonheur considéré comme l'un des Beaux-Arts, Paris (PUF) 1965; Ethique et Politique, Paris (Sirey) 1968; La Politique de la Solitude: Essai sur la Philosophie politique de Jean Jacques Rousseau, Paris (Sirey) 1971; L'obligation politique, Paris (PUF) 1971; John Locke, Lettre sur la Tolérance, Introduction et traduction du latin, Casalini et PUF 1964.

Reulos, Michel

Né à Paris 20 déc. 1909. Etudes à Paris. Docteur en droit 1935. Licencié ès lettres (histoire). Chargé d'enseignement de droit romain et histoire du droit: Ecole de droit de Rouen, lycées Chaptal, Henri IV et Louis le Grand à Paris. Conseiller à la cour d'appel de Paris.

Travaux: Etude sur l'esprit, la méthode et les sources des Institutes coustumières d'Antoine Loisel et édition des Institutes coustumières 1935. Divers travaux sur l'humanisme juridique français, les collèges parisiens au XVIème siècle, leur organisation et leur enseignement, la Discipline des Eglises réformées françaises et les institutions ecclésiastiques. Comptes rendus nombreux dans le Bull. de la Soc. de l'histoire du Protest. franç.

Roellenbleck, Georg

Geb. 1932 in Darmstadt. Studium der romanischen Philologie an der Universität Frankfurt a. M., seit 1960 Assistent in Frankfurt, seit 1962 in München. Promotion 1960 mit einer Arbeit über Bodins «Heptaplomeres». Habilitation 1971 mit einer Arbeit über die epische Lehrdichtung Italiens im 15. und 16. Jahrhundert.

Salmon, J. H. M.

Born 2 Dec. 1925, Lit. D., F. R. H. S., Marjorie Walter Goodhart Professor of History, Bryn Mawr College (Pennsylvania). Former appointments include Foundation Professor of History, University of New South Wales (Sydney) and Dean of Humanities, University of Waikato (Hamilton).

Publications: The French Religious Wars in English Political Thought (Oxford 1959), Cardinal de Retz (London 1969: editor of The French Wars of Religion (Boston 1967) and co-editor (with R. E. Giesey) of Francogallia by François Hotman (Cambridge 1972): contributor to History and Theory, History, Today, Journal of Modern History, Journal of Religious History, Past and Present.

Scheuner, Ulrich

Geb. 24. 12. 03 in Düsseldorf. Studium der Rechtswissenschaft in München und Münster, Privatdozent in Berlin (1930), o. Professor in Jena, Göttingen, Bonn, Mitglied der Rheinisch-Westfälischen Akademie der Wissenschaften.

Veröffentlichungen zur Rechtsgeschichte: Die neuere Entwicklung des Rechtsstaats in Deutschland, Festschrift des Deutschen Juristentages 1960, Bd. 2, S. 229–262; Hegel in der deutschen Staatslehre des 19. Jahrhunderts, Studium

Berolinense 1960, S. 129–51; Das repräsentative Prinzip in der modernen Demokratie, Festschrift für Hans Huber, Bern 1961, S. 224–246; Das Amt des Bundespräsidenten als Auftrag verfassungsrechtlicher Gestaltung, Tübingen 1966; Die großen Friedensschlüsse und die europäische Staatenordnung zwischen 1648 und 1815, Festschrift f. M. Braubach 1964, S. 220–225.

Schoeck, Richard J.

Born 1920, Ph. D. Princeton University (1949). Has taught at Cornell University, University of Notre Dame, University of Toronto, and been Visiting Professor at Princeton; lectured at numerous universities in Canada and the U. S. Professor ordinarius in Pontifical Institute of Mediaeval Studies (Toronto). Now Director of Research Activities, Folger Shakespeare Library, Washington, and Director of the Folger Institute of Renaissance and 18th-century Studies.

Publications: Co-editor of Chaucer Criticism, editor of Editing 16th-century Texts, etc.; author of more than 100 articles and papers in medieval, Renaissance, and modern literature, history (including legal history). Fellow of the Royal Historical Society and the Royal Society of Canada. Member of several editions (including Yale Edition of Thomas More and Toronto Edition of Erasmus), advisory boards (Richard Hooker, American Journal of Jurisprudence, etc.).

Villey, Michel

Né le 6 avril 1914, professeur à l'Université de Droit et des Sciences Sociales Paris, anterieurement aux Facultés de Droit de Saigon et de Strasbourg.

Principales publications: Leçons d'histoire de la philosophie du droit, Dalloz 1962; La Formation de la pensée juridique moderne, Monchrestien 1968; Seize Essais de Philosophie du droit, Dalloz 1969. – Direction des Archives de philosophie du droit.

PERSONENREGISTER

Personen werden prinzipiell unter dem in ihrem Heimatland gebräuchlichen Namen aufgeführt. Bei mehreren gebräuchlichen Namen sind Querverweise eingeführt. Werden Personen nur in den Anmerkungen zitiert, ist die Seitenziffer kursiv gesetzt.

Meinecke, Friedrich 504
Melanchthon, Philippp 4, 116 f., 140
Ménage, Gilles 163, 500
Menander 16
Menke-Glückert, Emil 503
Menenius Agrippa 276
Mesnard, Pierre 1, 3, 19, 41, 53, 55, 60, 69, 105, 106, 108, 110, 112, 115, 125, 141, 151, 163, 179, 215, 187, 236 f., 243, 267, 269, 306, 334, 337, 345, 399, 400, 406, 412, 437, 444, 492 f., 497, 505 f., 508–513
Meuten, Anton 142, 502
Milieu, Christophe 140 f.
Millar, John 279
Milton, John 504
Mochi Onory, Sergio 134
Mohler, Ludwig 48
Molinier, Victor 501
Mommsen, Karl 512
Monro 173
Montaigne, Jean de 136, 157 f.
Montaigne, Michèle 7, 88, 100, 114
Monter, E. William 2, 7, 8, 399, 513
Montesquieu 113, 123, 147, 155, 234 f., 245, 259, 276, 285, 304, 444, 477, 502
Montfort, H. de 503
Moore, George Albert 494
Morandi, C. 505
Morazé, Ch. 287 f., 289, 292, 298
Moreau 500
Moreau-Reibel, Jean 18, 125, 145, 168, 246, 253, 267, 333, 364, 395, 441, 500, 505 f.
Moret, J. 504
Mornay ↗ Plessis-Mornay
Morus, Thomas 281 f., 286, 294, 301, 399–407, 409–412, 426, 513
Moses 13 f., 20, 45
Mosse, Georg Lachmann 507 f.
Mousnier, Roland 151 f.
Mügler, Ch. 81
Müller, Christoph 512
Müller 494
Munk, Salomon 45
Murray, R. H. 504

Mylaeus ↗ Milieu
Mystagogus 16, 24, 43, 57

Naef, Henri 507
Nancey, Paul 507
Nardi, Bruno 509
Nashe, Thomas 512
Nedham, Marchamont 455
Nimrod 310, 465
Nipperdey, Thomas 286
Noack, Ludwig 17, 40, 53, 55, 499
Nock, A. D. 9
Nourse, J. 496
Numa, Pompilius 306

Oberfohren, Ernst 215, 264, 503
Ockham, Guillelmus de (Occam, William) 47 f., 416
Octavius 65
Odowakar (Odovacer) 310
Oehler, Klaus 213
Oestreich, Gerhard 389, 392
Oldradus da Ponte 192 f.
Olivier-Martin, Fr. 251
Oppianos 492
Orosius, Paulus 101
Oswaldt, Johann 495

Palazzini Finetti, Luigi 137
Palinurus 407
Panaitios (Panétius) 42
Panormitanus (Nicholaus de Tudeschi) 174
Paolo Emilio, Lucio ↗ Aemilius Paulus, Lucius
Papinianus, Aemilius 339 f.
Papon, Jean 190
Parker, Matthew 455, 509
Pasquier, Emile 505
Pasquier, Etienne 126, 129, 132, 141, 217, 220, 372, 395, 434, 448
Patrizi, Francesco 401, 408, 411
Paul III., Papst 91
Paulus, Julius 192
Paulus, Apostel 178, 473
Paurmeister, Tobias 186
Pelopidas 100

SACHREGISTER

Damit das Sachregister dreisprachig (deutsch, englisch, französisch) gelesen werden kann, sind bei den zentralen Stichworten die englischen und französischen Begriffe, sofern sie erheblich vom deutschen Begriff differieren, gesondert aufgeführt und mit einem Verweis (↗) auf das jeweilige deutsche Stichwort bezogen.

BUCHANZEIGEN

Horst Denzer

Moralphilosophie und Naturrecht bei Samuel Pufendorf

Eine geistes- und wissenschaftsgeschichtliche Untersuchung zur Geburt
des Naturrechts aus der praktischen Philosophie

XV, 405 Seiten. Leinen DM 52,– (Band 22)

Das Buch ist die erste größere Monographie über Pufendorfs Werk in deutscher Sprache. Schwerpunkt der Untersuchung ist die Naturrechtslehre Pufendorfs, doch hat der Verfasser durch die Einordnung des Naturrechts in die Moralphilosophie den Schlüssel für die richtige Zuordnung der historischen, kirchen- und staatsrechtlichen und theologischen Schriften zum zentralen Naturrecht gefunden. Aus der genauen Kenntnis der Quellen gelingt dem Verfasser nicht nur eine klare Darstellung der Ideen Pufendorfs, sondern auch die Erforschung seiner Traditionsbezüge und die Bestimmung seiner wissenschaftsgeschichtlichen Stellung in der Lehre von der praktischen Philosophie und Politik seiner Zeit.

Rolf K. Hocévar

Stände und Repräsentation beim jungen Hegel

Ein Beitrag zu seiner Staats- und Gesellschaftslehre sowie zur Theorie
der Repräsentation

X, 225 Seiten. Leinen DM 35,– (Band 8)

Rolf Hocévars Untersuchungen über den Ursprung des Hegelschen Repräsentationsgedankens aus der Beschäftigung mit dem Frühkonziliarismus, die Quellenanalyse der Frühschriften Hegels und der Nachweis, daß der Philosoph – bereits vor Gentz – die den Verfassungsstreit des Vormärz beherrschende Alternative ‹landständisch› oder ‹repräsentativ› aufgestellt hat, führen über die bisherige Hegelforschung hinaus. Auf diesen neuerarbeiteten Grundlagen aufbauend, gelingt es dem Verfasser, erstmals alle Phasen der Genesis von Hegels früher Staats- und Gesellschaftslehre sowie sein Verhältnis zur Französischen Revolution nachzuzeichnen.

VERLAG C. H. BECK · MÜNCHEN

KLASSIKER DES POLITISCHEN DENKENS

Herausgegeben von Hans Maier, Heinz Rausch, Horst Denzer

Erster Band: Von Plato bis Hobbes

Dritte, durchgesehene Auflage. VIII, 433 Seiten. In Leinen DM 19,80

Zweiter Band: Von Locke bis Max Weber

Zweite, durchgesehene Auflage. VIII, 423 Seiten. In Leinen DM 19,80
(Reihe Beck'sche Sonderausgaben)

«Dieses zweibändige Werk hält eine glückliche Mitte zwischen einem Abriß politischer Ideengeschichte und einer Textauswahl klassischer Autoren der Staatsphilosophie. Die beiden Bände enthalten 28 Einzeldarstellungen politischer Theoretiker von der Antike bis zur unmittelbaren Vergangenheit. So ergibt sich das Gesamtbild einer Geschichte abendländischer Staatstheorie ... Man kann von einer bereits festgefügten Tradition, einem anerkannten Kanon sprechen: Der erste Band reicht von Plato über Aristoteles, Cicero, Augustin bis Grotius, Bodin, Hobbes, der zweite von Locke, Pufendorf, Montesquieu bis Marx, Nietzsche, Max Weber. Obgleich die Einzelmonographien in sich geschlossen sind und das Zeitbedingte der jeweiligen Persönlichkeit in ihrem historischen Standort gezeigt wird, ist die Kontinuität ideengeschichtlicher Entwicklung gewahrt. Bei aller Spezialisierung und trotz des politischen Engagements der einzelnen Autoren, das unverkennbar, aber nirgends aufdringlich ist oder die wissenschaftliche Qualität mindert, ist eine Gemeinschaftsleistung erbracht, die auf diesem Gebiet zur Zeit, jedenfalls in deutscher Sprache, kaum Gleichwertiges hat. Das Werk, in Universitätsübungen und in der Erwachsenenbildung bereits vielfach erprobt, eignet sich, da zudem mit weiterführender Bibliographie ausgestattet, vorzüglich zum Studium, zur allgemeinen und wissenschaftlichen Orientierung und nicht zuletzt auch für den politischen Unterricht in den Oberklassen der Gymnasien.»

Die Zeit

VERLAG C. H. BECK · MÜNCHEN